THE HOLY ROMAN EMPIRE, RECONSIDERED

SPEKTRUM: Publications of the German Studies Association
Series editor: David M. Luebke, University of Oregon

Published under the auspices of the German Studies Association, *Spektrum* offers current perspectives on culture, society, and political life in the German-speaking lands of central Europe—Austria, Switzerland, and the Federal Republic—from the late Middle Ages to the present day. Its titles and themes reflect the composition of the GSA and the work of its members within and across the disciplines to which they belong—literary criticism, history, cultural studies, political science, and anthropology.

Volume 1
The Holy Roman Empire, Reconsidered
Edited by Jason Philip Coy, Benjamin Marschke, and David Warren Sabean

Volume 2
Weimar Publics/Weimar Subjects
Rethinking the Political Culture of Germany in the 1920s
Edited by Kathleen Canning, Kerstin Barndt, and Kristin McGuire

Volume 3
Conversion and the Politics of Religion in Early Modern Germany
Edited by David M. Luebke, Jared Poley, Daniel C. Ryan, and David Warren Sabean

Volume 4
Walls, Borders, Boundaries: Spatial and Cultural Practices in Europe
Edited by Marc Silberman, Karen E. Till, and Janet Ward

Volume 5
After The History of Sexuality: German Genealogies With and Beyond Foucault
Edited by Scott Spector, Helmut Puff, and Dagmar Herzog

Volume 6
Becoming East German: Socialist Structures and Sensibilities after Hitler
Edited by Mary Fulbrook and Andrew I. Port

The Holy Roman Empire, Reconsidered

Edited by

JASON PHILIP COY, BENJAMIN MARSCHKE,
& DAVID WARREN SABEAN

First published in 2010 by
Berghahn Books
www.berghahnbooks.com

©2010, 2013 Jason Philip Coy, Benjamin Marschke, and David Warren Sabean
First paperback edition published in 2013

All rights reserved. Except for the quotation of short passages
for the purposes of criticism and review, no part of this book
may be reproduced in any form or by any means, electronic or
mechanical, including photocopying, recording, or any information
storage and retrieval system now known or to be invented,
without written permission of the publisher.

Library of Congress Cataloging-in-Publication Data

The Holy Roman Empire, Reconsidered / edited by Jason Philip Coy, Benjamin Marschke, and David Warren Sabean.
 p. cm. -- (Spektrum : publications of the German Studies Association ; . v . 1)
Includes bibliographical references and index.
ISBN 978-1-84545-759-4 (hardback) -- ISBN 978-1-84545-992-5 (institutional ebook)
ISBN 978-1-78238-089-4 (paperback) -- ISBN 978-1-78238-090-0 (retail ebook)
 1. Holy Roman Empire--History. 2. Germany--History--1517-1871. 3. Austria--History--1519-1740. I. Coy, Jason Philip, 1970- II. Marschke, Benjamin. III. Sabean, David Warren.
 DD89.H65 2010
 943'.02--dc22

2010023807

British Library Cataloguing in Publication Data
A catalogue record for this book is available from the British Library

Printed in the United States on acid-free paper.

ISBN: 978-1-78238-089-4 paperback   ISBN: 978-1-78238-090-0 retail ebook

For Amy, Marianne, and Ruth

CONTENTS

List of Illustrations	ix
Series Preface	x
Volume Preface	xi
List of Contributors	xii
Introduction: The Holy Roman Empire in History and Historiography *Jason Coy*	1

Section I. Presence, Performance, and Text

1. Discontinuities: Political Transformation, Media Change, and the City in the Holy Roman Empire from the Fifteenth to Seventeenth Centuries — 11
   Philip Hoffmann-Rehnitz

2. Overloaded Interaction: Effects of the Growing Use of Writing in German Imperial Cities, 1500–1800 — 35
   Alexander Schlaak

3. Princes' Power, Aristocratic Norms, and Personal Eccentricities: *Le Caractère Bizarre* of Frederick William I of Prussia (1713–1740) — 49
   Benjamin Marschke

Section II. Symbolic Meaning, Identity, and Memory

4. The Illuminated Reich: Memory, Crisis, and the Visibility of Monarchy in Late Medieval Germany — 71
   Len Scales

5. The Production of Knowledge about Confessions: Witnesses and their Testimonies about Normative Years in and after the Thirty Years' War — 93
   Ralf-Peter Fuchs

6. Staging Individual Rank and Corporate Identity: Pre-Modern Nobilities in Provincial Politics — 107
   Elizabeth Harding

7. The Importance of Being Seated: Ceremonial Conflict in
    Territorial Diets   125
    Tim Neu

Section III. Ceremony, Procedure, and Legitimation

8. Ceremony and Dissent: Religion, Procedural Conflicts, and the
   "Fiction of Consensus" in Seventeenth-Century Germany   145
   David M. Luebke

9. Contested Bodies: Schwäbisch Hall and its Neighbors in Conflicts
   Regarding High Jurisdiction (1550–1800)   163
   Patrick Oelze

10. Conflict and Consensus around German Princes' Unequal Marriages:
    Prince's Autonomy, Emperor's Intervention, and the Juridification
    of Dynastic Politics   177
    Michael Sikora

11. Power and Good Governance: The Removal of Ruling Princes in
    the Holy Roman Empire, 1680–1794   191
    Werner Trossbach

Section IV. Imperial Institutions, Confession, and Power Relations

12. Marital Affairs as a Public Matter within the Holy Roman Empire:
    The Case of Duke Ulrich and Duchess Sabine of Württemberg at
    the Beginning of the Sixteenth Century   213
    Michaela Hohkamp

13. The *Corpus Evangelicorum*: A Culturalist Perspective on its
    Procedure in the Eighteenth-Century Holy Roman Empire   229
    Andreas Kalipke

14. Gallican Longings: Church and Nation in Eighteenth-Century
    Germany   249
    Michael Printy

Conclusion: New Directions in the Study of the Holy Roman
    Empire—A Cultural Approach   265
    André Krischer

Glossary   271

Bibliography   273

Index   319

~: ILLUSTRATIONS :~

Figure 6.1. Official Seal of the Nobility in Münster.   111

Figure 6.2. Detail of the Prince-Bishop's Residence in Münster: The Nobility's Coat of Arms.   112

Figure 6.3. Ferdinand Karl von Galen (1750–1803), with an added Cathedral Chapter's Cross, 1774.   117

Figure 6.4. Colonel (Reiteroberst) Heinrich Johann von Droste-Hülshoff (1735–1798) in uniform, with an added Knight's Cross of the Teutonic Order, 1774.   118

Figure 8.1. Ernst of Bavaria (1554–1612), Bishop of Freising (1566), Hildesheim (1573), Liège (1581), and Münster (1585); Archbishop of Cologne (1583).   149

Figure 9.1. A Sketch on the Legal and Authoritative History of the Mettelmühle.   169

~: SERIES PREFACE :~

This volume is the first in a new book series entitled *Spektrum: Publications of the German Studies Association*. The series represents the culmination of four long-standing trends within the association. The first is the growing tendency among members of the GSA to organize their work around common topics and to present their collaborations in a series of panels at the association's annual conference. The second is an effort both to expand the GSA's sponsorship of scholarly work into a broader array of disciplines and historical periods and to strengthen thematic connections between them. The third is the increasing collaboration at the GSA among scholars from around the world who share interests in the society, politics, and culture of the German-speaking peoples, from the Middle Ages to the present day. The fourth is the GSA's burgeoning role as a venue for the introduction of state-of-the-art research and scholarship on the German-speaking peoples to an Anglophone audience.

Spektrum seeks to promote these trends by providing a venue for the publication of scholarly monographs and collections of papers originally presented at the association's annual conference. Our hope is that the volumes of *Spektrum*, taken as a whole, will reflect the dizzying variety of GSA members in terms of scholarly discipline—cultural anthropology, musicology, sociology, art, theology, film studies, philosophy, art history, literary criticism, history, and political science—as well as methodology, subject matter, and historical period.

PREFACE

The papers in this volume are a selection from ten panels on "The Holy Roman Empire Reconsidered" at the German Studies Association meeting in San Diego. When we approached the GSA Executive Director David Barclay about our plans to hold so many sessions, he enthusiastically encouraged us and suggested several themes. During the planning stage, we also corresponded with Barbara Stollberg-Rilinger, the Director of the Sonderforschungsbereich at the University of Münster, "Symbolic Communication and Social Value Systems from the Middle Ages to the French Revolution," and with Rudolf Schlögl, Director of the "Cluster of Excellence" at the University of Konstanz, "Cultural Foundations of Integration." As we always do, we talked over all of our plans with the wise and charming Mary Lindemann at the University of Miami.

We want to thank all of the participants in the sessions at the San Diego meeting. One of the highlights was an evening presentation of the wonderful pictures from the exhibition of the Holy Roman Empire of the German Nation at the Museum of Cultural History in Magdeburg by the Curator, Alexander Schubert.

Finally, we called upon the editorial skills of Daphne Rozenblatt and Carrie Sanders, who put together the bibliography and index, and we want to thank them for their careful and professional work.

~: CONTRIBUTORS :~

Jason Philip Coy is an Associate Professor of History at the College of Charleston, in Charleston, South Carolina. He earned his doctorate in History at the University of California, Los Angeles in 2001, studying under David Sabean. He has received a DAAD Research Grant and a Maria Sibylla Merian Fellowship for Postdoctoral Studies from the University of Erfurt, Germany. His publications include: "Our Diligent Watchers and Informers: Denunciation, False Accusation, and the Limits of Authority in Early Modern Ulm," in *Ways of Knowing: Ten Interdisciplinary Essays*, ed. Mary Lindemann (Boston, 2004) and *Strangers and Misfits: Banishment, Social Control, and Authority in Early Modern Germany* (Studies in Central European Histories, XLVII) (Leiden, 2008). His current research examines divination and demonology in Baroque Germany.

Ralf-Peter Fuchs, PD Dr. phil., is an Associate of the Institute of Modern History at Ludwig-Maximilians-Universität in Munich and currently substituting for the chair of Early Modern History in Duisburg-Essen. He studied under Winfried Schulze and participated in several research projects. His publications focus on the history of witchcraft, history of crime, history of honor, legal history, concepts of time, peacemaking after the Thirty Years' War, and the history of jazz. Publications include: *Ein Medium zum Frieden. Die Normaljahrsregel und die Beendigung des Dreißigjährigen Krieges* (Munich, 2010); *Hexerei und Zauberei vor dem Reichskammergericht* (Wetzlar, 1994); *Um die Ehre. Westfälische Beleidigungsprozesse vor dem Reichskammergericht (1525 - 1805)* (Paderborn, 1999).

Elizabeth Harding received her Ph.D. in History at the University of Münster in 2009. She has been a research fellow at the Research Training Group Gesellschaftliche Symbolik im Mittelalter, Münster, and at the Institute for European History, Mainz. Publications include: "Zeremoniell im Nebenland. Frühneuzeitliche Bischofseinsetzungen in Münster," in *Westfälische Forschungen* 57 (2007); "Von Vorgängern, Einzelgängern und Gliedern eines Körpers. Frühneuzeitliche Ritterschaften als Orte genealogischer Präsenz," in *Familie—Generation—Institution. Generationenkonzepte in der Vormoderne*, eds. Hartwin Brandt, Maximilian Schuh, and Ulrike Siewert (Bamberg, 2008). Forthcoming: *Landsässige Ritterschaften im Nordwesten des Alten Reiches, Organisation—*

Autorität—Repräsentation, 1650–1800. Harding is currently a postdoctoral research fellow at the Herzog August Bibliothek, Wolfenbüttel, researching professors' households in the early modern period.

Philip R. Hoffmann-Rehnitz was Academic Coordinator of the Collaborative Research Center, "Norm and Symbol" at the University of Konstanz from 2006 to 2010, where he also worked on the research project on "Political Culture and Social Order of the Early Modern City" under the direction of Rudolf Schlögl. He is now Research Assistant at the Universtity of Münster. His main research comprises political communication in pre-modern cities, early modern guilds, and the history of illicit work. Publications include: "Soziale Differenzierung und politische Integration. Zum Strukturwandel der politischen Ordnung in Lübeck (15.–17. Jahrhundert)," in *Stadtgemeinde und Ständegesellschaft. Formen der Integration und Distinktion in der frühneuzeitlichen Stadt*, eds. Patrick Schmidt and Horst Carl (Berlin and Münster, 2007); "In Defence of Corporate Liberties: Early Modern Guilds and the Problem of Illicit Work," in *Urban History* 34 (2007).

Michaela Hohkamp is Professor at the Free University Berlin and a graduate of the University of Göttingen. Her main interests are rural society, European court society, aristocratic power, kinship, issues of gender and power, and early modern historiography. Her writings include: "Do Sisters have Brothers? Or the Search for the 'rechte Schwester.' Brothers and Sisters in Aristocratic Society at the Turn of the Sixteenth Century," in *Sibling Relations and the Transformations of European Kinship*, eds. Christopher H. Johnson and David Warren Sabean (in preparation); "Eine Tante für alle Fälle: Tanten-Nichten-Beziehungen und ihre politische Bedeutung für die reichsfürstliche Gesellschaft der Frühen Neuzeit (16. bis 18. Jahrhundert)," in *Politiken der Verwandtschaft*, eds. Margareth Lanzinger and Edith Saurer (Vienna, 2007); and *Herrschaft in der Herrschaft. Die voderösterreichische Obervogtei Triberg von 1737 bis 1780* (Göttingen, 1998).

Andreas Kalipke graduated from the University of Bochum in 2004 in History, Catholic Theology, and Pedagogy. He is now a Research Associate in the Leibniz-Project "Vormoderne Verfahren" at the University of Münster. He has published on the characteristics of pre-modern procedures and decision-making, including "'Weitläufftigkeiten' und 'Bedencklichkeiten'—Die Behandlung konfessioneller Konflikte am Corpus Evangelicorum," in *Zeitschrift für historische Forschung* 35 (2008).

André Krischer is Junior-Professor for British Studies at the University of Münster. From 2005 until 2009, he was Research Group Leader of the Leibniz-Project of Barbara Stollberg-Rilinger. He has published extensively on court and urban history, the history of crime and media, political delinquency, and British history, including: *Reichsstädte in der Fürstgesellschaft. Politischer Zeichengebrauch in der Frühen Neuzeit* (Darmstadt, 2006); "Das diplomatische Zeremoniell der Reichsstädte, oder: Was heißt Stadtfreiheit in der Fürstengesellschaft," in *Historische Zeitschrift* 281 (2007); "Traditionsverlust: Die Krise der Todesstrafe in England 1750–1868," in *Strafzweck und Strafform zwischen religiöser und weltlicher Wertevermittlung*, ed. Reiner Schulze (Münster, 2008); "Politische Repräsentation und Rhetorik der Reichsstädte auf dem Reichstag nach 1648," in *Politische Redekultur in der Vormoderne. Die Oratorik europäischer Parlamente in Spätmittelalter und Früher Neuzeit*, eds. Jörg Feuchter and Johannes Helmrath (Frankfurt, 2008).

David M. Luebke received his Ph.D. from Yale in 1990 and is an Associate Professor of history at the University of Oregon. His publications include *His Majesty's Rebels: Communities, Factions, and Rural Revolt in the Black Forest, 1725–1745* (Cornell, 1997), *The Counter-Reformation: Essential Readings* (Blackwell, 1999), and numerous articles on the religious and political cultures of ordinary people the German-speaking lands. He is currently at work on a study of conflict and coexistence among the Christian religions in the late sixteenth and seventeenth centuries, based on an analysis of religious life in twelve "hometowns" in the Westphalian bishopric of Münster, between 1553 and 1650. It bears the provisional title *Hometown Religion: Conflict and Coexistence among the Christian Religions of Germany, 1553–1650*.

Benjamin Marschke is an Associate Professor of History at Humboldt State University, in Arcata, California. He holds a Ph.D. in History from UCLA (2003), where he studied under David Warren Sabean and Geoffrey Symcox. His publications include *Absolutely Pietist: Patronage, Factionalism, and State-Building in the Early Eighteenth-Century Prussian Army Chaplaincy* (Tübingen, 2005). He is currently working on a close study of the court and monarchical self-representation of King Frederick William I of Prussia (1713–1740), from which he has published tentative results: "'Von dem am Königl. Preußischen Hofe abgeschafften *Ceremoniel*:' Monarchical Representation and Court Ceremony in Frederick William I's Prussia," in *Orthodoxies and Diversity in Early Modern Germany*, ed. by Randolph C. Head and Daniel Christensen (Boston, 2007).

Tim Neu is currently Research Associate at the Chair of Early Modern History at the University of Münster. A graduate of the University of Münster, where he studied under Barbara Stollberg-Rilinger, Neu received his M.A. in History in 2005. He has published on the institutional and political culture of early modern Estates and Diets, including: "Zeremonielle Verfahren. Zur Funktionalität vormoderner politisch-administrativer Prozesse am Beispiel des Landtags im Fürstbistum Münster," in *Im Schatten der Macht*, eds. Stefan Haas and Mark Hengerer (Frankfurt a.M., 2008); and "Rhetoric and Representation: Reassessing Territorial Diets in Early Modern Germany," in *Central European History*, 43 (2010). He is co-editor, with Michael Sikora and Thomas Weller, of *Zelebrieren und Verhandeln. Zur Praxis ständischer Institutionen im frühneuzeitlichen Europa* (Münster, 2009). Currently, he is completing his doctoral dissertation on the institutional culture of the territorial estates in Hesse-Cassel.

Patrick Oelze received his Ph.D. in History at the University of Konstanz in 2009 and is currently an editor at Verlag Herder (Freiburg). He has published extensively on the history of late medieval and early modern cities, including: "Decision-Making and Civic Participation in the Imperial City: Guild Conventions and Open Councils in Constance," in *Elections and Decision-Making in Early Modern European Cities*, ed. Rudolf Schlögl (Cambridge, 2009); *Recht haben und Recht behalten. Konflikte um die Gerichtsbarkeit in Schwäbisch Hall und seiner Umgebung* (Konstanz, 2010); "Fraischpfänder: Ein frühneuzeitlicher Rechtsbrauch im Südwesten des Alten Reichs," in *Zeitschrift für Württembergische Landesgeschichte* 69 (2010). He is co-editor, with Rudolf Schlögl, of *Herrschaft und ihre Medien in der europäischen Stadt der Vormoderne* (Göttingen, forthcoming). His next book will be about charlatans, frauds, and impostors in Europe 1750–1950.

Michael Printy received his Ph.D. in History from the University of California, Berkeley. He has taught as a Visiting Assistant Professor at Wesleyan University, where he is currently a visiting scholar in History. He was awarded a Fulbright Fellowship for study in Germany in 1994, and a DAAD in 1999. His publications include *Enlightenment and the Creation of German Catholicism* (Cambridge, 2009), as well as articles in *German History*, *The Catholic Historical Review*, and *History and Theory*. He co-edited *Politics and Reformations* (Leiden, 2007), a two-volume Festschrift for Thomas A. Brady, Jr. With Ulrich L. Lehner, he edited *A Companion to the Catholic Enlightenment in Europe* (Leiden, 2010). His current research includes a study of ideas about Protestantism and freedom in eighteenth- and nineteenth-century Europe.

David Warren Sabean is Henry J. Bruman Professor of German History at the University of California at Los Angeles. A graduate of the University of Wisconsin where he studied under George Mosse, Sabean has taught at the University of East Anglia, University of Pittsburgh, and Cornell, and he has been a fellow at the Max Planck Institute for History in Göttingen, the Maison des Science de l'Homme, the Wissenschaftskolleg zu Berlin, the American Academy in Berlin, and the National Humanities Center. He is a fellow of the American Academy of Arts and Sciences. His publications include: *Power in the Blood: Popular Culture and Village Discourse in Early Modern Germany* (Cambridge, 1984); *Property, Production, and Family in Neckarhausen, 1700–1870* (Cambridge, 1990); *Kinship in Neckarhausen, 1700–1870* (Cambridge, 1998).

Len Scales teaches medieval European history at Durham University. He has written on medieval ethnic stereotypes (the "warrior" Germans), the relationship between identity and power in late medieval Germany, and the question of medieval German exceptionalism. He has also explored the history of medieval ideas about ethnicity and common identity more broadly, across the whole of the c.500–c.1500 period. His current work in the field examines medieval ideas about the destruction of peoples. His publications include *Power and the Nation in European History* (edited with Oliver Zimmer) (Cambridge, 2005). His study of German nationhood in the late Middle Ages, entitled *In a German Mirror: Authority, Crisis, and German Identity, 1245–1414*, will shortly be published by Cambridge University Press.

Alexander Schlaak studied History, Political Science, and English and American Literature in Konstanz and London and received his M.A. in Konstanz in 2004. He was Junior Research Fellow at the University of Konstanz from 2004 to 2007, and a Fellow at the Institute of European History in Mainz before resuming his position as Junior Research Fellow at the University of Münster until the end of 2008. Currently, he is Press Officer of the University of Regensburg in Bavaria.

Michael Sikora teaches early modern history at the Westfälische Wilhelms-Universität at Münster and has also taught at the Ruhr-Universität Bochum. He studied in Cologne and Munich and received his Ph.D. in Cologne. His publications include: *Disziplin und Desertion. Strukturprobleme militärischer Organisation im 18. Jahrhundert* (Berlin, 1996); *Armeen und ihre Deserteure. Vernachlässigte Kapitel einer Militärgeschichte der Neuzeit* (edited with Ulrich Bröckling) (Göttingen, 1998); *Der Adel in der Frühen Neuzeit* (Darmstadt, 2009); and *Zelebrieren und Verhandeln. Zur Praxis ständischer Institutionen im frühneuzeitlichen Europa* (edited with Tim Neu and Thomas Weller) (Münster, 2009). For several years, his main research focus has been on *mésalliances* among the German higher nobility. He wrote his habilitation, which is currently being prepared for print, on this subject.

Werner Trossbach is Professor of Agrarian History at the Faculty of Organic Agricultural Sciences at the University of Kassel. Trossbach has taught at the University of Bochum, the University of Rostock, the University of Gießen, and the University of Göttingen. His publications include: *Soziale Bewegung und politische Erfahrung. Bäuerlicher Protest in hessischen Territorien, 1648–1806* (Weingarten, 1987); *Der Schatten der Aufklärung. Bauern, Bürger und Illuminaten in der Grafschaft Wied-Neuwied* (Fulda, 1991); *Bauern 1648-1806* (München, 1993); and *Die Geschichte des Dorfes* (Stuttgart, 2006, together with Clemens Zimmermann). He is co-editor of *Zeitschrift für Agrargeschichte und Agrarsoziologie* and *Enzyklopädie der Neuzeit*. Currently, he is engaged in studies on the transition to modern agriculture in German territories.

INTRODUCTION

The Holy Roman Empire in History and Historiography

JASON COY

The Holy Roman Empire is increasingly presented in positive terms in historical scholarship. Recent studies contend that the empire provided a durable and dynamic political framework in central Europe from the Carolingian period until the Napoleonic era, one that protected the privileges and liberties of its constituents, while coordinating collective action. This reappraisal seeks to overturn a century of negative assessments of the empire and its institutions. During the Enlightenment, the *philosophe* Voltaire notoriously—and acerbically—quipped that it was neither Holy, nor Roman, nor an empire. Since the nineteenth century, scholars have followed his lead, presenting the empire as a weak state, a failed state, or a non-state, even a "monstrosity" thankfully put out of its misery by Napoleon.[1]

Goethe, on the other hand, in his work, *Faust*, released in 1806 as the empire crumbled, asked, "The dear old holy Roman realm, what holds it still together?" Goethe's question displays not only a perception of dysfunction and decline, but also of nostalgic sympathy, and suggests that some thinkers who had experienced the Holy Roman Empire had more positive attitudes about it than the French *philosophes* of the eighteenth century or the German nationalists of the nineteenth century.[2] Most early modern political philosophers considered the empire to be anomalous, given their concern with sovereignty and their misgivings about the contest for power between the emperors and the territorial princes, and they struggled to classify it. In the Wake of the Peace of Westphalia, some scholars argued that the empire was a sort of federation, with sovereignty shared between the emperor and the German princes, while others considered it to be a monarchy like other major European states, but hampered by the emperor's inability to exercise full sovereignty. Most seventeenth-century thinkers, however, considered imperial politics to be a sort of compromise, with the emperor as a sovereign who shared the exercise of his authority with his subjects. Despite these disagreements, early modern scholars generally viewed the empire as a *positive* force in European politics and as a model for peacefully reaching political consensus and compromise, while protecting individual rights and privileges.³ Concerns about the nature of the Holy Roman Empire, and its effects on German history, came to the fore again in the late nineteenth century, but, under the pressures of nationalism and unification, modern appraisals of the empire turned decidedly negative.

For German historians of the late nineteenth century, viewing their history through the prism of the ardent nationalism of the period, the Holy Roman Empire, a political entity with medieval origins, religious divisions, and decentralized administrative structures, not to mention ethnic and linguistic diversity and diffuse borders, was the cause of the German people's history of disunity and passivity. Admiring the centralized and militaristic Prussian state that had unified Germany between 1866 and 1871, the Prusso-centric attitudes of these historians set the agenda for a century of negative scholarly appraisals of the Holy Roman Empire.⁴ Indeed, after the turn of the twentieth century, scholars of the Berlin constitutional school, most prominently Otto Hintze, examined the empire's constitutional history, seeking to uncover why it had "failed" to develop into a modern nation-state.⁵ While the nationalistic impulses of these prominent early studies were discredited after 1945, scholars in divided, postwar Germany continued to focus on the constitutional stagnation and decline that hampered the empire after Westphalia, seeking to explain Germany's traumatic past. This reaction continued to shape scholarship on the Holy Roman Empire during the 1980s and 1990s, by prompting two divergent approaches that also explored questions related to the *Staatlichkeit* (statehood) of the Holy Roman Empire. Scholars interested in uncovering traces of democratic and communal activity in the German past, including Peter Blickle and Thomas A. Brady, investigated the prevalence of "communalism" in the early modern empire.⁶ Other scholars focused instead on demonstrating German particularism, exploring the notion that Germany's historical development deviated from that of other European states. Interestingly, this *Sonderweg* interpretation, that sought to chart Germany's particular historical path toward Nazism, supported the same negative picture of the Holy Roman Empire, interpreting it as the weak, failed state presented by the ardent Prussian nationalists of the nineteenth century.⁷

In the late 1960s, revisionist historians, beginning with Karl Otmar von Aretin, began to approach the Holy Roman Empire from a new perspective. Rather than treating the empire as a failed state, these revisionists began to consider it in its own right as a dynamic political system that served as a site for compromise and consensus.⁸ Continuing this revisionist project, historians such as Volker Press reinvigorated the study of the Holy Roman Empire by treating it as a viable legal and institutional framework for negotiating political and religious issues and by abandoning the earlier obsession with its obsolescence and inevitable decline.⁹ Indeed, with German reunification and the integration of Europe after 1990, some scholars have looked to the Holy Roman Empire as a pre-modern example of the kind of loose federation embodied by today's European Union, a flexible association that balanced coordinated action and regional autonomy.¹⁰ In a particularly dramatic reappraisal of the nature of the empire, Georg Schmidt contends that rather than representing an abortive nation-state, it was in fact a distinctive early modern *Reichs-Staat*. For Schmidt, this "Empire State" was defined by notions of "German Freedom" that emerged from the imperial reforms that began in 1495, that were institutionalized by the Peace of Augsburg and the Peace of Westphalia, and that fostered effective cooperation between the empire and its constituents.¹¹

Current scholarship on the Holy Roman Empire seeks less to provide assessments of the empire's *Staatlichkeit*, than to examine the empire and its institutions as a framework for political and intellectual interaction. These more recent studies emphasize the empire's stability and flexibility, examining the operation of imperial political and legal institutions and presenting them as a dynamic arena for shifting behavioral norms and intellectual currents. In Germanophone scholarship, the momentum for this shift can be found in the social systems theory of Niklas Luhmann, a model itself based upon the analysis of communication networks and processes.¹² Luhmann's emphasis on communication as the crucial element in the maintenance of social systems has provided a major impetus to recent scholarship on the Holy Roman Empire, with its emphasis on communication within the *Reich*: symbolic, procedural, and ceremonial, as well as oral and written communication. A pair of ongoing collaborative research projects in Germany, one on "Symbolic Communication and Social Value Systems" at the Westfälische Wilhelms-Universität Münster and another on "Norm and Symbol" at the Universität Konstanz, have advanced scholarship on the Holy Roman Empire as a communication system. At Münster, scholars associated with Barbara Stollberg-Rilinger focus on the role of symbolic communication and ceremonial procedure in imperial politics and consensus-formation. Influenced by Luhmann's theories, these scholars highlight the idea of "legitimation by procedure."¹³ The other major research project, at Konstanz, is directed by Rudolf Schlögl and works to explain political life in the empire through an analysis of the processes of communication that governed its political and social operation, both oral and written. Here, the functioning of media and communication within the pre-modern *Anwesenheitsgesellschaft*, a "community of presence" where communication was determined by physical proximity, has been crucial to understanding political decision-making in early modern German territories and towns.¹⁴

The first group of essays included in this volume follows this lead by examining the relationship during the early modern period between physical presence, political performance, and written communication in the Holy Roman Empire. In the first essay in this collection, Philip Hoffman-Rehnitz examines how chronicles written in Hanseatic cities during the early modern period maintained a myth of continuity amid the dramatic transformation of the urban political and social structure, demonstrating the role of texts not only in facilitating change in early modern cities, but also in shaping our understanding of the urban history of the empire. The next contribution, by Alexander Schlaak, also considers the role of written communication—here, petitions delivered to the magistrates of various imperial cities—in urban political life, arguing that the cities of the early modern empire were not stagnant, moribund entities, but rather remained vibrant political communities until well into the eighteenth century. Benjamin Marschke examines political performance through an examination of contemporary accounts of Frederick William I's often-erratic behavior, in order to uncover the boundaries of acceptable behavior for eighteenth-century rulers and the consequences of overstepping these bounds.

The second selection of essays included in this volume explores the symbolic construction of meaning, identity, and memory in the Holy Roman Empire, from the fall of the Staufer dynasty in the late Middle Ages to the eighteenth century. In the first essay in this section, Len Scales examines how the late medieval imperial monarchy, without a fixed capital, used physical presence and architectural symbols of an ancient imperial legacy to establish its identity and assert its legitimacy. Scales also shows how other German rulers and magistrates "illuminated the *Reich*" for their own purposes, quite apart from the dynastic goals of their emperors. Ralf-Peter Fuchs also deals with the issue of memory in his contribution, providing detailed analysis of the testimony delivered by witnesses in the aftermath of the Thirty Years' War. This testimony, delivered before commissions charged with restoring religious order in the empire in the wake of the conflict, shows the role of memory in attempts to establish confessional identity and to demarcate the unstable boundaries between confessions. Elizabeth Harding's contribution turns to the role of symbolic action and representation in constructing and demonstrating corporate identity among the nobility. Focusing on the lower nobility in eighteenth-century Westphalia, Harding analyzes the elaborate modes of symbolic presentation that served to balance individual status and group cohesion among these minor aristocrats. Tim Neu also examines the role of symbolic communication in imperial politics by analyzing a conflict over ceremonial procedure that erupted at the territorial diet in Hessen-Kassel in the early eighteenth century. This conflict over ceremony, a controversy about the right of urban magistrates to be seated during deliberations, demonstrates the importance of both presence and precedence in early modern politics.

The next group of essays presented here considers politics in the Holy Roman Empire, analyzing the role of ceremony, procedure, and legitimation in early modern governance. The first contribution in this section, by David

Luabke, provides detailed analysis of a specific conflict over ceremonial procedure, exploring the importance of procedural disputes in expressing and managing growing confessional tension in the territorial estates of the Prince-Bishopric of Münster in the early seventeenth century. Patrick Oelze offers a detailed examination of conflicts over jurisdiction between the imperial city of Schwäbisch Hall and its neighbors, including the principality of Brandenburg-Ansbach. Within these disputes, penal jurisdiction was crucial in establishing territorial boundaries and claims of legitimacy, and sometimes involved grisly struggles to gain control over the bodies of people who died in areas of overlapping jurisdictional claims, leading to long and tense disputes between urban magistrates and their princely neighbors. As Michael Sikora demonstrates in his contribution to the volume, within the Holy Roman Empire, the marriage strategies of princely dynasties played a crucial role for the maintenance and improvement of political and economic status. Thus, when princes sought to marry below their own station, they often sparked bitter conflicts with their own families that involved the institutional and legal mechanisms of the empire, with important implications for imperial politics. Werner Trossbach investigates the intrusion of the emperor into the dynastic affairs of the empire's princely houses, examining the effort during the eighteenth century to remove rulers of small German territories deemed unfit to rule. The scandalous cases that Trossbach explores demonstrate the dynamic interaction between territorial states and the imperial administration, interaction that during the eighteenth century often sparked vigorous public debate.

The final section of the collection concerns "Imperial Institutions, Confession, and Power Relations," exploring how imperial institutions regulated politics and religion in the Holy Roman Empire from the sixteenth to the eighteenth century. Michaela Hohkamp's contribution to this section explores a scandalous case of such princely misconduct. By examining the notorious marital discord between Duke Ulrich of Württemberg and his wife, Sabine, Hohkamp explores the centrality of dynastic marriages in imperial politics and in the fates of both male and female rulers and their families. Andreas Kalipke analyzes decision-making at the *Corpus Evangelicorum*, the Protestant group of estates at the imperial diet, approaching his subject from the perspective of symbolic communication and procedural legitimation. After a useful discussion of seminal works on these topics, Kalipke uncovers the ways in which the operation of the *Corpus* served to express Protestant parity and to manage confessional conflict with the empire during the eighteenth century. Turning to the other side of the confessional divide, Michael Printy rounds out the collection of essays with an examination of the efforts of German Catholics to gain ecclesiastical autonomy from Rome in the eighteenth century, using arguments at once rooted in late medieval notions of the liberty of the German Church and in Enlightenment concepts of rational reform.

Notes

1. Gerald Strauss questioned these negative portrayals of the Holy Roman Empire in an important review article in the late 1970s. See Gerald Strauss, "The Holy Roman Empire Revisited" in *Central European History* 11: 3 (September 1978): 290–301. For more recent appraisals of the historiography of the Holy Roman Empire chronicling the continuation of this positive reevaluation, see also James A. Vann, "New Directions for Study of the Old Reich," in *The Journal of Modern History* 58 (1986): 3–22; Michael Hughes, *Early Modern Germany, 1477–1806* (Philadelphia, 1992), ix–xii; T.C.W. Blanning, "Empire and State in Germany, 1648–1848," in *German History* 12:2 (1994): 220–236; Helmut Neuhaus, *Das Reich in der Frühen Neuzeit* (Munich, 1997); Peter H. Wilson, *The Holy Roman Empire, 1495–1806* (New York, 1999), and "Still a Monstrosity? Some Reflections on Early Modern German Statehood," in *The Historical Journal* 49: 2 (2006): 565–576.
2. See Strauss, "Holy Roman Empire Revised," 290.
3. See Peter H. Wilson, "Still a Monstrosity?," 566–567.
4. For concise treatment of these historiographical developments, see Wilson, *Holy Roman Empire*, 4-5.
5. See Otto Hintze, *The Historical Essays of Otto Hintze* (New York, 1975), for an introduction to Hintze's work in English.
6. See Peter Blickle, *The Communal Reformation: The People's Quest for Salvation in the Sixteenth Century* (Leiden, 1985), originally published as *Gemeindereformation: die Menschen des 16. Jahrhunderts auf dem Weg zum Heil* (Munich, 1985). See also Thomas A. Brady, *Turning Swiss: Cities and Empire, 1450–1550* (Cambridge and New York, 1985).
7. For useful discussions of the *Sonderweg* paradigm and its relevance for understanding German history, see Jürgen Kocka, "German History before Hitler: The Debate about the German *Sonderweg*," in *Journal of Contemporary History* 23 (1988): 3–16, and William W. Hagen, "Descent of the *Sonderweg*: Hans Rosenberg's History of Old-Regime Prussia," in *Central European History* 24:1 (1991): 24–50. See also Wilson, "Still a Monstrosity?," 565, 574.
8. Karl Otmar von Aretin, *Heiliges Römisches Reich, 1776-1806: Reichsverfassung und Staatssouveränität*, 2 vols. (Wiesbaden, 1967), and Aretin, *Das Alte Reich, 1648–1806*, 4 vols. (Stuttgart, 1993–2000). For discussion of the "decisive and almost wholly beneficial" historiographical influence of von Aretin's *Heiliges Römisches Reich*, see Blanning's "Empire and State in Germany, 1648–1848."
9. Volker Press, *Kriege und Krisen: Deutschland, 1600–1715* (Munich, 1991), and also Volker Press and Dieter Stievermann, eds., *Alternativen zur Reichsverfassung in der Frühen Neuzeit?* (Munich, 1995).
10. For this perspective of the Holy Roman Empire as a federal system, see Maiken Umbach, ed., *German Federalism: Past, Present, Future* (Houndmills and Basingstoke, 2002). See also Peter-Claus Hartmann, *Kulturgeschichte des Heiligen Römischen Reiches 1648 bis 1806* (Vienna, 2001).
11. See Georg Schmidt, *Geschichte des alten Reiches: Staat und Nation in der Frühen Neuzeit, 1495–1806* (Munich, 1999). Peter Wilson provides useful analyses of Schmidt's perspective: see "Still a Monstrosity?," 570–571.
12. Niklas Luhmann, *Social Systems* (Stanford, 1995), originally published in German as *Soziale Systeme. Grundriß einer allgemeinen Theorie* (Frankfurt a.M., 1984).

13. See Niklas Luhmann, *Legitimation durch Verfahren* (Neuwied am Rhein, 1969). See also Barbara Stollberg-Rilinger, "Symbolische Kommunikation in der Vormoderne. Begriffe—Forschungsperspektiven—Thesen," in *Zeitschrift für historische Forschung* 31 (2004): 489-527, and André Krischer, *Reichsstädte in der Fürstengesellschaft. Politischer Zeichengebrauch in der Frühen Neuzeit* (Darmstadt, 2006).
14. See Rudolf Schlögl, "Vergesellschaftung unter Anwesenden. Zur kommunikativen Form des Politischen in der vormodernen Stadt," in Rudolf Schlögl, ed., *Interaktion und Herrschaft. Die Politik der frühneuzeitlichen Stadt* (Konstanz, 2004), 9-60.

SECTION I

Presence, Performance, & Text

CHAPTER 1

Discontinuities
Political Transformation, Media Change, and the City in the Holy Roman Empire from the Fifteenth to Seventeenth Centuries

PHILIP R. HOFFMANN-REHNITZ

Introduction

In modern historiography on pre-modern cities in the Holy Roman Empire, medieval and early modern towns represent two very different and distinct types of historical development. Because it is designated as one of those historical places where revolutionary developments took place, the medieval city has been seen as a force of historical and cultural significance (*Kulturbedeutung*).[1] There, a genuinely urban, political culture was established that constituted an alternative to the dominant feudal and aristocratic order. On the basis of the *coniuratio* of the burghers, it was constituted on the civic values of liberty and equality, and characterized by communal and participatory political structures integrating the middle and—at least partially—the lower ranks of the population. The city's political culture, together with its growing wealth, was the basis for its rise as a powerful political player in the medieval Holy Roman Empire, particularly in the southern and western regions, as well as in parts of Northern Germany.

The grandeur of this depiction of the medieval city stands in sharp contrast to the traditional and still dominant view of its early modern successor. According to that view, the urban societies and especially the imperial cities lost their ability to transform or "modernize" their social and political structures after the Reformation (at the latest), which is commonly regarded as the last event in which the imperial towns played a significant and innovative historical role.[2]

According to the *communis opinio*, the cities underwent a steady decline in the early modern period; while it was the territorial state that took over their role as *the* historically determining force and also exerted a major influence on urban development.[3] Particularly, the decline of the imperial cities was explained by the dominant conservative mentality of the citizens, especially the guilds. As a result, innovations of the urban economic, social, and political structures were either inhibited or adopted from the outside, and it is particularly the constitutional order that has been ascribed a high degree of structural constancy until the end of the *ancien régime* by traditional historiography.[4]

In this chapter, an alternative interpretation of the political history of the pre-modern (imperial) cities will be developed. It connects historiographical and conceptual revisions in the study of the urban history of the *ancien régime*. First, this essay argues that urban political structures were transformed in a fundamental way between the fifteenth and seventeenth centuries. Although these structural changes correlate with overall developments, such as the transformation of the media system, they are seen as genuinely urban due to towns finding specific solutions to those general problems. Hence, the early modern town—and this includes imperial as well as territorial cities—represents a distinct type of political organization. Its patterns differ in central respects from those of the medieval city as well as from those of the early modern territorial state and court.[5] This shift in the description from continuity to transformation is connected with a reconceptualization of the study of pre-modern urban politics that does not focus on political institutions and their legal foundations as done in the traditional *Rechts- und Verfassungsgeschichte* that has dominated political historiography on pre-modern towns since the nineteenth century, but rather it focuses on political communication and the media system.[6] By focusing on forms of political communication and their media-related substructures, fundamental transformations of the urban political order between the late medieval and early modern periods become evident. In what follows, this general thesis will be explicated in more detail by concentrating on developments in Lübeck between the fifteenth and seventeenth centuries and by comparing them with the situation in other Hanseatic and imperial towns, particularly Cologne. Before that, however, we take a closer look at the traditional narrative of the political history of pre-modern (imperial) cities as well as at trends and approaches in recent historiographical research.

Continuity and Transformation: Trends in the Study of the German City and its Political Order between the Late Medieval and Early Modern Periods

The traditional political history of the pre-modern—and, to a large extent, the medieval—city in the Holy Roman Empire has been chiefly concentrated on the evolution of constitutional and juridical institutions and underlying social developments and conflicts. Two processes have been identified as being of central importance: first, the foundation in the eleventh and twelfth centuries of urban communalities (*Gemeinde* or *universitas civium*) as a new and "revolutionary" form of social and political organization based on a *coniuratio* of the citizens;[7] and second, the establishment in most German towns during the thirteenth century of the council as the central political and judicial institution (*Ratsverfassung*).[8] The dualism of council and communality, or in a more general sense between corporative (*genossenschaftlich*) and autocratic (*herrschaftlich*) principles, has been regarded as a central moving force for the political and constitutional history of the empire between the fourteenth and eighteenth centuries.[9] According to this dominant line of interpretation, this period was determined mainly by two conflicting developments. On the one hand, there was the so-called *Verobrigkeitlichung* of the social and political order, which circumscribed the concentration of power in the hands of the urban authorities and prescribed an extension of an exclusive, "sovereign" position of the council (*Ratsherrschaft*), thus leading to a disassociation of the urban government and the citizens.[10] The social-historical background of this process has commonly been identified in a hierarchization of the social order and an oligarchization of the political elites, especially in restricting access to the council to members of a few distinguished families.[11] On the other hand, the numerous civic movements that emerged in many late medieval cities in the fourteenth and fifteenth centuries have been seen as a reaction to these processes, as attempts to broaden civic participation and to implement new participatory institutions and forms of representation. In several cases, particularly in imperial towns in Southern and Western Germany (such as Cologne), these movements were successful in bringing about a reform of the political order and implementing new and typically corporate forms of political organizations (*Zunftverfassung*).[12] Nevertheless, according to the common opinion of historians, these attempts to enforce civic participation and to curb the power of the authorities were only temporarily successful, while the extension of autocratic rule and the trend toward more oligarchic structures prevailed in the long run.[13] Since the second half of the fifteenth century, at the latest, communal institutions were generally on the retreat.[14] Accordingly, the renaissance of civic participation as well as of communal ideas and institutions in the Reformation was no more than a short-lived matter. Instead, the Reformation is commonly seen to have ultimately strengthened the position of the (urban) authorities and reinforced the rule of the council in the end.[15] Thus, according to this dominant line of interpretation, most early modern towns and specifically the imperial cities "conserved" (as Volker Press has put it) their traditional oligarchic-autocratic constitutions.[16] In this sense, urban political and constitutional history after the Reformation was characterized by the absence of internal dynamic development and the declining ability to produce structural innovation from within.[17] If there was change, then it was initiated by external forces, particularly by the early modern state. German historiography has thus regarded the urban communities, and particularly the imperial cities since the middle of the sixteenth century, as mainly passive victims of external "modernizing" forces such as the territorial state.[18] Against these, they tried to defend their traditional, medieval order and political culture, in the end without success

This traditional and long-term image has been challenged and revised by recent research on the history of pre-modern towns and urban politics in the Holy Roman Empire. Several major shifts can be identified. First, there has been a new evaluation of the significance of communal institutions for the urban polity, at least in the Middle Ages. Highly influential in this respect is Peter Blickle's concept of *Kommunalismus*. It circumscribes a social and political system, in which the subjects and citizens have autonomous power (*Gewalt*) to decide over central aspects concerning their daily life and "good policy" (*gute Policey*). The communal assembly is thus assigned an essential role as the institutional core of the communalistic order (*verfasste Gemeinde*) where central decisions were made; it also had the right to appoint political representatives of the community.[19] While Peter Blickle's studies are concentrated mainly on Upper Germany, several recent publications, especially by Ernst Pitz and Robert Giel, have revised the traditional, authority-biased view on the late medieval urban constitutional order in Lower Germany, and specifically Hanseatic cities, in favor of an interpretation stressing the role of communality and of communally-based institutions, such as civic assemblies, commissions or corporations, in urban politics.[20]

While these communalistic interpretations—specifically the studies of Peter Blickle and Ernst Pitz—mainly follow a traditional model of political and legal history, there have recently been two interrelated tendencies for developing new conceptual approaches to pre-modern urban history. First, several publications have concentrated on the cultural dimension of urban politics and particularly on forms of symbolic communication and rituals, such as election ceremonies, the *Schwörtage* or processions.[21] Second, and of greater relevance for this chapter, are studies analyzing the social logic of political and public communication in pre-modern urban societies as well as the role of the media system and its transformations for urban politics.[22] These approaches are influenced by sociological concepts, such as Jürgen Habermas' *Strukturwandel der Öffentlichkeit*[23] or by Niklas Luhmann's systems theory. This is especially true with the conceptual and heuristic framework of *Anwesenheitsgesellschaft* or *Vergesellschaftung unter Anwesenden* ("presence" or "face-to-face" society) that Rudolf Schlögl and a research group at the Universität Konstanz have recently developed (not only) for the study of urban political history in pre-modern times.[24] The term *Anwesenheitsgesellschaft* describes a form of social association whose structures are determined by the communicative logic of physical presence and the primacy of forms of direct, face-to-face-interaction.[25] Its media system is therefore characterized by the primary role of orality and performance as well as by corporally bound media. Further, one central element of such social figurations is the significance of events in which those who are physically present experience themselves as members of one association and one political body. In addition, these events are of central importance for the representation and reproduction of basic social relations and central cultural norms, as accomplished by the "production of presence" (Gumbrecht), i.e., by how those present interact with each other, how they perform, and how their bodies are arranged. In this respect, such events are an important means of social and political integration and the constitution of social identity.[26]

Several case studies have demonstrated that, in many respects, the political order of pre-modern and particularly of medieval towns supports this concept. They have shown that forms of direct, face-to-face interaction and "media of presence" were dominant (particularly in the political and legal sphere) and that they determined the logic of political communication (for example, in council elections).[27] Besides offering a heuristic framework for analyzing the social and political structures of pre-modern towns, the concept of *Anwesenheitsgesellschaft* also allows identification of transformations in the fabric of urban political communication between medieval and early modern times. Although "media of presence" as well as orality still played an important role after the Reformation, the spread of written and printed media and their growing relevance for political and legal communication is of central importance. Although the diffusion of written media had already commenced in medieval times, this development took on (at least in German cities) a new quality since the end of the fifteenth century, as the use of written—and in some cases even print—media to publish and diffuse decisions of the authorities became more and more common.[28] There was also a significant increase in supplications and petitions as a means of communication between the citizens and the authorities, as can be observed especially since the middle of the sixteenth century.[29]

These processes and their contributions to the transformation of the communicative patterns of urban politics have yet to be studied in great detail.[30] While many historians tend to see the diffusion of written media as an important impetus in enlarging and centralizing the "sovereign" power of the authorities, there is also clear evidence that this could also result in the dispersion of power and public communication and the decentralization of the political system, inasmuch as a growing number of citizens and particularly urban corporations (such as the guilds) were becoming accustomed to the use of written media for their own purposes.[31] Of course, these changes in the media and communication system were not restricted to urban societies; they were rather one part of a general transformation of the pre-modern political culture that was of central importance for the evolution of modern political systems, in general, and of the modern state and—since the eighteenth century—a *bürgerliche Öffentlichkeit*, in particular.[32] On the one hand, the towns as centers of literacy and the production of written and printed texts played a decisive role in these processes—and not just during the Reformation.[33] On the other hand, early modern urban societies developed specific communicative structures combining the new written-based media with patterns of direct, face-to-face-interaction, thereby entangling their respective communicative logics. As a result, the political culture of early modern urban societies differed in a significant manner from that of medieval cities.

The structural discontinuity between the medieval and early modern city can be demonstrated in an exemplary way when taking a close look at civic assemblies.[34] In the late Middle Ages and also (but decreasingly) during the early modern period, these were of central importance for political life in many towns as a forum of political decision-making and public communication, where the citizens could experience and exert their political rights. In that sense, urban societies manifested themselves as a political entity (*res publica* or *Gemeinde*) immediately in civic assemblies. What the "city" in the sense of the *res publica* was and what structural patterns determined its social and political order could be directly perceived and experienced by everyone who participated in assemblies, and specifically was experienced on the occasion of the election of the council and the collective confirmation of the civic oath (*Schwörtage*).[35] However, with the Reformation, civic assemblies disappeared in several (imperial) cities, or at least they lost many of their former political functions.[36] In traditional historiography, this process was either neglected or seen as a by-product in the implementation of authoritarian political patterns and the strengthening of the sovereign position of the council.[37] When focusing on communicative structures, a different explanation seems obvious: the disappearance or vanishing relevance of the civic assemblies appears to be a subprocess of the aforementioned transformations of the urban media system and communicative structures. Thus, since the second half of the fifteenth century, central functions of civic assemblies in terms of direct and oral face-to-face interaction were substituted step-by-step by indirect and decentralized forms of political communication mainly based on written media.

In the following, this thesis will be explicated in greater detail by focusing on Lübeck (as the capital of the Hanseatic League), but also by drawing attention to Cologne and (in passing) other Hanseatic and imperial cities in the Holy Roman Empire.

Structural Transformations of the Political Order in Lübeck between the Fifteenth and Seventeenth Centuries: A Case Study

In the historiographical discourse on the medieval city, Lübeck has always played a prominent role. It was not only one of the most populous and prosperous cities in the Holy Roman Empire, but it was also the capital of the Hanseatic League, and as such a major political player in Northern Germany and the Baltic region, particularly between the fourteenth and sixteenth centuries. Lübeck has also been a prime example of the declining political significance of the (imperial) cities after the Reformation.

When looking at the dominant position in traditional historiography on the political and constitutional development of pre-modern Lübeck, which was proposed by Wilhelm Ebel, among others, and which primarily follows the general historiographical narratives outlined above, one can distinguish three main aspects.[38] First, the council emancipated itself to a relatively large extent from the community and attained a position as the leading political power already in the first decades of the thirteenth century. The political order of late medieval Lübeck was thus characterized by strong hierarchical and aristocratic structures.[39]

Second, communal elements and forms of civic participation have been seen as relatively insignificant for Lübeck, even in comparison to other Hanseatic cities.[40] In turn, the traditional historiography on Lübeck has chiefly been focused on the council as the nucleus of the political system and its development, while communal institutions have been widely neglected.[41] Although several forms of civic political participation have been mentioned by Ebel as consultations between the council and the distinguished citizens, especially the aldermen of the civic corporations (the so-called *discretiores* or *maiores*[42]) as well as civic conventions (the so-called *Bursprake*), like most other historians, he has not attached great significance to them, especially when regarding the *Bursprake* as an instrument of the council's regime that left the citizens in a mainly passive role.[43] One reason for the strong autocratic (*obrigkeitliche*) and aristocratic character of the government and the weak position of the citizens has been seen in the failure of attempts by the latter to challenge and limit the rule of the council and to establish forms of communal participation through civic protest and uprisings as was the case in many other imperial cities in southern and western Germany, such as Ulm or Cologne.[44]

In late medieval and early modern Lübeck, there were no major constitutional alterations caused by upheavals, which is the main reason (according to

Heinz Stoob among others) why—and this is point three—the constitution of pre-modern Lübeck (as in most other Hanseatic cities) had a highly enduring character.[45] From this perspective, the urban government mainly kept the shape it had acquired during the thirteenth century, experiencing only minor alterations up until the end of the early modern era.[46] Therefore, in traditional historiography on pre-modern Lübeck, the four centuries between 1400 and 1800 are seen as a time of great stability or "ossification"—not only of the political and constitutional structures. Not least of all, it was the prevailing conservative mentality among the citizens and particularly the urban elite that (allegedly) contributed to the inability to develop or introduce new elements or to reform the social, economic, and political structures.[47]

In his (aforementioned) seminal study, Ernst Pitz has undertaken a thorough revision of traditional views on the constitutional history of the medieval Hanseatic city in general, and of Lübeck in particular, by stressing the significance of communal principles and the role of civic assemblies.[48] According to Pitz, it was the civic assembly—and not the council—that was the core of the constitutional order in the late medieval Hanseatic city, and the basis for politics was the identity and consensus of council and communality.[49] The council had to ensure that its political actions and decisions complied with the will of the community, and if this was questionable, then it had to reassure itself of the intent of the citizenry either by corresponding with distinguished burghers and representatives of the civic corporations or by convening a *Bursprake*.[50] Such civic assemblies not only served as an opportunity for proclaiming the decisions of the authorities, but they were also the place where issues of general significance for the entire *res publica* were discussed and decided. Furthermore, these decisions were binding for the council. In contrast to Ebel, Pitz regards the role of the citizens in such *Bursprake* to be an active one; even when the citizens remained silent, this still has to be seen as an act of explicitly articulating consensus.[51]

Pitz's line of interpretation, limited to the Middle Ages, leads us to reevaluate the development of the political and constitutional order during and after the Reformation. When we compare the forms and institutions of political communication typical in the seventeenth century with those of the late medieval period, significant differences are apparent.[52] As a result, the traditional view, focused on structural continuity, has to be revised in favor of a perspective emphasizing transformation and structural discontinuity. In particular, the Reformation and associated political conflicts (the so-called *Wullenweversche Unruhen*), between 1528 and 1535, appear in a rather different light from in traditional historiography.[53] According to the latter, the Reformation as well as the *Wullenweversche Unruhen*, which were mainly brought about and reinforced by a civic-democratic movement, led to a "renaissance" of forms of civic participation, such as assemblies and committees.[54] This resulted in a political "revolution" by overthrowing the traditional aristocratic regime and by electing a new council dominated by representatives of the civic opposition and their leader, Jürgen Wullenwever.[55] When the old council, and with it the traditional *Ratsverfassung,* was restored in 1535, the position of the authorities and the domination of the council became even stronger than before due to the council's new ecclesiastical responsibilities.[56] The period of the Reformation was thus evaluated by traditional historiography as a temporary interruption and irritation in the (otherwise) continuous stream of Lübeck's political and constitutional history. It was not seen as an epoch that brought about the enduring transformation of political structures, other than the strengthening of the authorities and thereby the reinforcement of a general trend.

If we follow the approach of the communalistic interpretation put forward by Pitz, the events around 1530 lose much of their revolutionary character. Rather, they appear to be part of the late medieval political culture of the Hanseatic city. Hence, it is not the manner or form of political communication that was of extraordinary character, but rather the intensification of civic-participatory political communication. As far as we can observe, at least since the beginning of the fifteenth century, there had not been such an accumulation of civic assemblies making such far-reaching decisions, and never before had a civic committee accumulated as much formalized power as they had at the beginning of the 1530s.[57]

On the other hand, the Reformation also marks in certain respects an endpoint and a critical transitional moment for the development of political structures in Lübeck. This becomes obvious when comparing forms and structural settings of political communication and conflict regulation in the Reformation period with those during the so-called *Reisersche Unruhen* (1598–1605), along with political and constitutional conflicts in the 1660s.[58] Probably the most obvious difference is the disappearance of traditional forms of civic participation, especially the civic assembly, as a forum for political communication and the formation of public opinion. In the *Reisersche Unruhen,* civic assemblies were still present, but they played a much less significant role than in the Reformation period; there were very few civic assemblies, and their legitimacy was precarious and disputed.[59] Rather, the civic corporations elected representatives to negotiate with the council and issued a mandate to legitimize their actions. In the political conflicts of the 1660s, the citizens of Lübeck no longer convened in civic assemblies; moreover, no civic committee was elected, as had been the case in the *Reisersche Unruhen* or in the conflicts during the Reformation period.

The disappearance of the civic assembly as a forum for political interaction and an institution for making and legitimating decisions of vital significance was closely interrelated with the growing political relevance of civic corporations in the sixteenth and seventeenth centuries.[60] In conflicts around 1600 and in the 1660s, the civic corporations of merchants and artisans (*bürgerschaftliche*

Kollegien) were the main political players on the side of the citizenry, and they formed the organizational platform for civic opposition. While in the *Reisersche Unruhen*, the civic corporations had already played an important role, in the conflicts of the 1660s, their significance—represented by their aldermen as the only remaining institutional form of civic participation and opposition—was even more pronounced.[61] The growing significance of civic corporations is also reflected in the way in which accords (*Rezesse*) between council and citizenry were ratified. The *Rezess* of 26 August 1535, which finally settled the *Wullenweversche Unruhen* and legitimated the reintroduction of the "old" regime, was agreed to by a civic assembly. However, the corresponding agreement of 1605, which put an end to the conflicts occurring around 1600, was the result of negotiations between the council and representatives of the citizenry (who were, for the most part, leaders of civic corporations), and the accord was enacted by their consent and signature. The two accords of 1665 and 1669 were ratified in the same way.[62] In those cases, a convention of citizens in a civic assembly (as in 1535) was no longer necessary for ratifying and legitimating the accords, although they constituted significant reforms to the political order.

By the second half of the sixteenth century, then, the civic corporations had become the institutions through which citizens could exercise their political participatory rights. In this regard, they had replaced the civic assemblies (at least partially). Moreover, by functioning as an intermediary institution between individual citizens and the authorities, civic corporations included citizens in the political system. This led to a shift in the core mode of political inclusion—a shift from presence (in central political events) to membership (in corporative organizations). In both respects, the Reformation period had set the course for further development.

On the one hand, under the "regime of Wullenwever" (particularly in 1534 and 1535), the traditional forms of direct civic participation were reduced. In the accord between the council and the communality of 26 August 1535, which was ratified by a civic assembly, the citizens agreed no longer to organize conventions (*neine vorsammelinge hier bynnen edder anderswor anrichtenn*). Thus, after 1535, the council viewed any convention of citizens in political affairs held without authorization as illicit.[63] On the other hand, the growing significance of civic corporations was reflected in the fact that several of them, particularly the four *Große Ämter* that had leading positions among the artisan guilds, acquired their own buildings in and after the 1530s.[64] This contributed to a closing off of the internal communicative space of the corporations and further fixing the rules of inclusion and exclusion, thereby resulting in a (spatial) differentiation of political communication in Lübeck. In this fashion, the structure of Lübeck's political order (in general) and of the *Gemeinde* (in particular) was transformed in a fundamental way, because the formation of public opinion was increasingly taking place in and through a highly segmented communicative network constituted both by the civic corporations and the authorities. This also changed the mode of political integration: while the possibility of integrating the whole *res publica* via face-to-face interaction in one centralized event disappeared along with the civic assemblies, the integration of political space in early modern Lübeck was taking place through a complex and decentralized system of formal and informal communication between largely autonomous, corporative subsystems. In addition, the *Gemeinde* came to assume a different shape: it was no longer (or at least not primarily) something that manifested itself in a concrete and directly perceivable event. Rather, due to the decentralized structure of civic participation, it had largely become a legal abstraction as well as a symbol and central value of political communication.[65]

With the disappearance of the civic assembly and the transformation of the *Gemeinde*, the council had finally become the sole institutional center, heading the political system as the organ that represented the unity of the *res publica* and had (or at least should have had) the final say in political decision-making. Moreover, due to the processes of stratification and hierarchization of the social and political order taking place in the fifteenth and sixteenth centuries, it could strengthen its role as the highest and most distinguished political institution (and, in this sense, as *Obrigkeit*).

The political position of the council should not be overestimated, though, because the reorganization of civic participation on the basis of a decentralized network of corporative organizations counterbalanced the extension of the authorities' political power. Additionally, in the seventeenth and eighteenth centuries, the council had rather limited possibilities for steering political communication and public opinion. This was so not only because the authorities were (owing to their very modest executive opportunities) dependent on the support of the citizens and particularly on the civic corporations for putting political decisions and decrees into effect, but also because they could hardly influence—at least not directly—communication inside and between the civic corporations, which operated as largely autonomous parts of the political system.[66] Thus, because of its high degree of segmented differentiation and its decentralized structures, the political order of early modern Lübeck guaranteed the dispersion of political power. This in turn ensured that no one—and particularly not the government—could gain a controlling and dominating (and in this sense "sovereign") position. From this perspective, the traditional view on political development in urban societies between the late medieval and early modern periods, a view that focused primarily on processes of hierarchization and the centralization of power at the hands of the authorities (*Verobrigkeitlichung*), has to be revised in favor of a more complex concept that correlates them with interrelated and (partially) conflicting processes of segmentization and decentralization. This also renders a more dynamic image of how the political structures in Lübeck as well as in other (imperial) cities between the fifteenth and seventeenth centuries evolved.

These considerations open up many further questions. In the final section, two of them summarily shall be treated. First, to what extent are the findings on Lübeck representative for other cities in the Holy Roman Empire? In this regard, a short comparative view of Cologne shall provide some answers. Second (and with regard to the concepts explicated above), we shall pose the question: what role does the change of media play for structural transformations?

Further Perspectives: Political Transformation and Media Change in German Cities between the Late Medieval and Early Modern Periods

It can be demonstrated that the developments outlined in the previous section are not limited to Lübeck, but refer to general trends in the political history of the pre-modern (and especially the Hanseatic) city between the late medieval and the early modern eras. This is particularly the case when we take a comparative look at the situation in Cologne. Though it was also a Hanseatic city, with respect to its political order, Cologne has always served as a counterpoint to Lübeck. Since 1396, Cologne had a corporatively based constitution in which the *Gaffeln*, as the political corporations were called, had acquired a central role in electing the town council. These corporations were, together with the *Vierundvierziger* (an institutionalized civic commission), at least partially involved in political decision-making.[67] Although the constitutional order of late medieval and early modern Cologne was characterized by elements that cannot be found in Lübeck, the differences were less distinctive on the level of everyday politics. Following Robert Giel's analysis of public political communication in Cologne between 1450 and 1550, we can find structural transformations similar to those taking place in Lübeck. First and foremost, this was due to the *Morgensprache* (as the civic assembly was called in Cologne), around 1500, having lost most of its functions and relevance for everyday politics. In the late Middle Ages, the *Morgensprache* was used to mediate important information and to make political decisions public; in addition, it was an important forum of public communication and civic participation. However, by the early modern epoch, quite similar to the *Bursprake* in Lübeck, all that was left was the ceremonial form of *Morgensprache* for reminding the people of Cologne about central norms and orders. Moreover, it was integrated into the *Große Gottestracht* as the central socio-religious ritual of pre-modern Cologne, symbolically representing and visualizing the city as a social and religious community.[68] According to Giel, the declining political relevance of the *Morgensprache* did not necessarily have negative consequences for the political position of the citizens; nor did it extend the power of the council. Instead, many of the former functions of the *Morgensprache* were taken over by the corporations, especially the *Gaffeln*, thereby strengthening them as political actors. Thereafter, it became the *Gaffeln* that served primarily as the intermediary institutions through which citizens were informed about important events and decisions of the council and through which the council organized political consensus in the cases of difficult and far-reaching decisions.[69] As a result, according to Gerd Schwerhoff, the council could never really achieve its claim of being the "sovereign" center of political life and decision-making due to the high degree of corporative participation and the fragmentation of the public sphere.[70]

Furthermore, as Giel has shown, handwritten as well as printed texts had gained in importance since the end of the fifteenth century, which ran parallel to and in relation to the aforementioned transformation of the political order. On the one hand, these texts were an instrument of the authorities to diffuse politically important information and to publish decrees to the citizens.[71] On the other hand, they functioned as a medium used by citizens, and especially the corporations, as a way to communicate with the authorities. In Cologne as in other cities (Lübeck, for instance), there was not only a significant rise in the number of supplications, especially during the second half of the sixteenth century and the first half of the seventeenth century, but there was also standardization of how a supplication had to be written, submitted, and handled by the authorities.[72]

The example of Cologne reveals the close connection between the transformations of the political structures and changes in the urban media system occurring between the fifteenth and seventeenth centuries. Despite differences in the details, this model can also be basically applied to other cities, such as Lübeck.[73] First, the diffusion of written media in everyday politics primarily took place in the spaces of interaction between political subsystems, particularly between authorities and corporations. The logic of written communication stabilized and intensified a general tendency toward segmented differentiation and a decentralization of the political system owing to the increasing significance of corporatively organized subsystems. Written media increased the communicative distance between authorities and civic corporations, thereby securing their respective institutional autonomy. They also made it possible—despite the differentiated and decentralized political system—for the *same* information to be diffused at the *same* time among *all* of the relevant (albeit spatially dispersed) recipients, usually either single citizens or corporations. As a result, informational redundancy was produced before the existence of a modern public media system, without needing to purposefully organize public events involving face-to-face communication. Thus, the diffusion of written media can at least partially explain why civic assemblies, in their earlier role as a forum of urban politics and public communication, disappeared—or at least why they lost much of their old functions—after the end of the fifteenth century. In addition, the significance of physical presence in urban politics and public communication was generally limited, particularly with regard to exercising civic participation and including citizens in political systems. That is not to say that face-to-face-communication and "media of presence" lost their importance altogether in early modern urban political communication. Rather, forms of oral and face-to-face-interaction were significant not just for communication inside the political subsystems (and particularly the council), but also as a means of dealing with specific problems emerging with the diffusion of written media and (in general) the "media of distance" (*Distanzmedien*), as Niklas Luhmann refers to them.[74] In particular, it was difficult to control the consequences when communicating with others, because these "others" and their reactions could not be directly observed. As a result, producing trust was a crucial problem in the diffusion of written-based forms of communication and decentrally organized political systems. The aforementioned formalization and standardization, particularly of supplications, was one possible response; recourse to forms of face-to-face communication and their combination with written media (very typical for political communication in the early modern city) was another.[75]

In the processes of structural transformation, as have been portrayed in the period between the fifteenth and seventeenth centuries, a form of urban politics was constituted that remained relatively constant in its medial principles and social-communicative conditions up to the end of the *ancien régime*, and it only changed in the course of the "long nineteenth century."[76] The early modern city thus represents a genuine, independent model of political order under conditions of early modern sociality, a model that—for all of its continuities—was as structurally different from the medieval (and modern) city, as it was—for all of their linkages and influences—from the early modern territorial state. To the extent that the city in the early modern period found a quite durable solution to the general problems of the political order, it was no less "modern" than the latter.

Notes

1. See among others Max Weber, *Die Stadt* (Tübingen, 2000). On the idealization of the medieval city in the nineteenth century see Klaus Schreiner, "'Kommunebewegung' und 'Zunftrevolution.' Zur Gegenwart der mittelalterlichen Stadt im historisch-politischen Denken des 19. Jahrhunderts," in Franz Quarthal and Wilfried Setzler, eds., *Stadtverfassung, Verfassungsstaat, Pressepolitik. Festschrift für Eberhard Naujoks zum 65. Geburtstag* (Sigmaringen, 1980), 139–168. On the history of the medieval city in the Holy Roman Empire see among others Eberhard Isenmann, *Die deutsche Stadt im Spätmittelalter 1250–1500. Stadtgestalt, Recht, Stadtregiment, Kirche, Gesellschaft, Wirtschaft* (Stuttgart, 1988); and Felicitas Schmieder, *Die mittelalterliche Stadt* (Darmstadt, 2005).

2. This sharp break between the late medieval and the early modern town is stressed by Erich Maschke, among others. According to him, in the history of the pre-modern town, the period between the end of the fourteenth century and the middle of the sixteenth century was characterized by a multitude of political, economic, and cultural transformations and a general disposition of the citizens to innovation, while, after the Reformation, there was an all encompassing standstill in urban development: Erich Maschke, "Die Stadt am Ausgang des Mittelalters," in Erich Maschke, *Städte und Menschen. Beiträge zur Geschichte der Stadt, der Wirtschaft und Gesellschaft 1959–1977* (Wiesbaden, 1980), 56–99. On the notion of the time of Reformation as a watershed between the heyday of the cities during medieval times and their decline in the early modern period see Georg Ludwig von Maurer, *Geschichte der Städteverfassung in Deutschland*, 4 vols. (Erlangen, 1869–71; reprinted, Aalen, 1962); and Otto von Gierke, *Das deutsche Genossenschaftsrecht*, Vol. 1: *Rechtsgeschichte der deutschen Genossenschaft* (Berlin, 1868), 697ff.
3. "Die Stadt verliert ... die Führerschaft in der historischen Entwicklung (oder Geschichte der 'Modernisierung') an den Staat (In the historical development (or the history of "modernization"), the city loses leadership to the state)." Gerhard Dilcher, "Die Rechtsgeschichte der Stadt," in *Deutsche Rechtsgeschichte. Land und Stadt—Bürger und Bauer im alten Europa*, eds. Karl S. Bader and Gerhard Dilcher (Berlin, 1999), 251–827, here 257. See also Heinz Schilling, "Stadt und frühmoderner Territorialstaat: Stadtrepublikanismus versus Fürstensouveränität. Die politische Kultur des deutschen Stadtbürgertums in der Konfrontation mit dem frühmodernen Staatsprinzip," in *Recht, Verfassung und Verwaltung in der frühneuzeitlichen Stadt*, ed. Michael Stolleis (Cologne and Vienna, 1991), 19–39.
4. According to Gerhard Dilcher, what was characteristic for early modern urban history was "Bewahrung und Wandlung der im Mittelalter aufgebauten Rechts- und Verfassungsstrukturen (preservation and transformation of legal and constitutional structures constructed in the Middle Ages)." Therefore, the early modern city has to be understood "als ein Bestehendes, als Struktur gegenüber den Kräften der Veränderung (as a survival, as structure opposed to the forces of change)." Dilcher, "Rechtsgeschichte," 688, 690. The conservative character of the constitutional order and political culture of the early modern German "home towns" is also stressed by Mack Walker, *German Home Towns. Community, State and General Estate 1648–1871* (Ithaca, NY, 1971); Klaus Gerteis, *Die deutschen Städte in der Frühen Neuzeit. Zur Vorgeschichte der "bürgerlichen Welt"* (Darmstadt, 1986); Heinz Schilling, *Die Stadt in der frühen Neuzeit*, 2nd ed. (Munich, 2004); Christopher R. Friedrichs, *The Early Modern City, 1450–1750* (London and New York, 1995); and Ulrich Rosseaux, *Städte in der Frühen Neuzeit* (Darmstadt, 2006). Exemplary of this notion of strong structural continuities between late medieval and early modern cities have been the studies by Otto Brunner: see "Souveränitätsproblem und Sozialstruktur in den deutschen Reichsstädten der frühen Neuzeit," in Otto Brunner, *Neue Wege der Verfassungs- und Sozialgeschichte*, 2nd ed. (Göttingen, 1968), 294–321. Although there has been a growing interest in early modern urban history since the 1970s, the general opinion that the (imperial) towns are of only minor historical relevance for German history between the Reformation and the end of the eighteenth century has not changed significantly. See Volker Press, "Die Reichsstadt in der altständischen Gesellschaft," in *Neue Studien zur frühneuzeitlichen Reichsgeschichte*, ed. Johannes Kunisch (Berlin, 1987), 9–42.

5. On the early modern court see Rudolf Schlögl, "Der frühneuzeitliche Hof als Kommunikationsraum. Interaktionstheoretische Perspektiven auf die Forschung," in *Geschichte und Systemtheorie. Exemplarische Fallstudien*, ed. Frank Becker (Frankfurt/Main, 2004), 185–225; and Mark Hengerer, *Kaiserhof und Adel in der Mitte des 17. Jahrhunderts. Eine Kommunikationsgeschichte der Macht in der Vormoderne* (Konstanz, 2004).
6. See Rudolf Schlögl, "Vergesellschaftung unter Anwesenden. Zur kommunikativen Form des Politischen in der vormodernen Stadt," in Rudolf Schlögl, ed., *Interaktion und Herrschaft. Die Politik der frühneuzeitlichen Stadt* (Konstanz, 2004), 9–60; and Rudolf Schlögl, "Politik- und Verfassungsgeschichte," in *Kompass der Geschichtswissenschaft. Ein Handbuch*, eds. Joachim Eibach, Günther Lottes (Göttingen, 2002), 95–111. This shift goes along with recent trends in (German) historiography, which focuses on the history of the media system. See among others Fabio Crivellari and Marcus Sandl, "Die Medialität der Geschichte. Forschungsstand und Perspektiven einer interdisziplinären Zusammenarbeit von Geschichts- und Medienwissenschaften," in *Historische Zeitschrift* 277 (2003): 619–654; Fabio Crivellari et al., eds., *Die Medien der Geschichte. Historizität und Medialität in interdisziplinärer Perspektive* (Konstanz, 2004); and Johannes Burkhardt and Christine Werkstetter, eds., *Kommunikation und Medien in der Frühen Neuzeit* (Munich, 2005).
7. See among others Knut Schulz, *"Denn sie lieben die Freiheit so sehr ..." Kommunale Aufstände und Entstehung des europäischen Bürgertums im Hochmittelalter* (Darmstadt, 1992); Michael Borgolte, *Sozialgeschichte des Mittelalters. Eine Forschungsbilanz nach der deutschen Einheit* (Munich, 1996), 278ff; Dilcher, *Rechtsgeschichte*, 327ff; and Schmieder, *Die mittelalterliche Stadt*, 53ff.
8. See among others Isenmann, *Die deutsche Stadt*, 131ff.
9. See particularly Brunner, "Souveränitätsproblem," and Heinz Schilling, "Gab es im späten Mittelalter und zu Beginn der Neuzeit in Deutschland einen städtischen 'Republikanismus?' Zur politischen Kultur des alteuropäischen Stadtbürgertums," in *Republiken und Republikanismus im Europa der Frühen Neuzeit*, eds. Helmut G. Koenigsberger et al. (Munich, 1988), 101–143, here 108ff. and 137–138.
10. While authors like Eberhard Isenmann stress the autocratic character of the political order of late medieval towns, others, like Klaus Schreiner, place more emphasis on the role of the community and of civic consensus as the legitimizing basis of the urban government (*konsensgestützte Herrschaft*), Isenmann, *Die deutsche Stadt*, 131ff.; Eberhard Isenmann, "Ratsliteratur und städtische Ratsordnungen des späten Mittelalters und der frühen Neuzeit. Soziologie des Rats—Amt und Willensbildung—politische Kultur," in *Stadt und Recht im Mittelalter / La ville et le droit au Moyen Age*, eds. Pierre Monnet and Otto G. Oexle (Göttingen, 2003), 215–479; Klaus Schreiner, "Teilhabe, Konsens und Autonomie. Leitbegriffe kommunaler Ordnung in der politischen Theorie des späten Mittelalters und der frühen Neuzeit," in *Theorien kommunaler Ordnung in Europa*, ed. Peter Blickle (Munich, 1996), 35–61; and Ulrich Meier and Klaus Schreiner, "Regimen civitatis. Zum Spannungsverhältnis von Freiheit und Ordnung in alteuropäischen Stadtgesellschaften," in *Stadtregiment und Bürgerfreiheit. Handlungsspielräume in deutschen und italienischen Städten des Späten Mittelalters und der Frühen Neuzeit*, eds. Klaus Schreiner and Ulrich Meier (Göttingen, 1994), 11–34. On the evolution and implementation of the idea of the urban council as a God-given *Obrigkeit* see also Erich Maschke, "'Obrigkeit' im spätmittelalterlichen Speyer und in anderen Städten," in Maschke, *Städte und Menschen*, 121–137; and Eberhard Naujoks,

Obrigkeitsgedanke, Zunftverfassung und Reformation. Studien zur Verfassungsgeschichte von Ulm, Eßlingen und Schwäbisch Gmünd (Stuttgart, 1958).
11. See, among others, Press, "Reichsstadt." Both oligarchization as well as *Verobrigkeitlichung* are seen here as developments characterizing late medieval as well as early modern urban history.
12. On the study of late medieval conflicts, see Wilfried Ehbrecht, *Konsens und Konflikt. Skizzen und Überlegungen zur älteren Verfassungsgeschichte deutscher Städte*, ed. Peter Johanek (Cologne, 2001); Peter Johanek, "Bürgerkämpfe und Verfassung in den mittelalterlichen deutschen Städten," in *Einwohner und Bürger auf dem Weg zur Demokratie: Von den antiken Stadtrepubliken zur modernen Kommunalverfassung*, ed. Hans Eugen Specker (Stuttgart, 1997), 45–73; and Peter Blickle, *Unruhen in der ständischen Gesellschaft 1300–1800* (Munich, 1988), 7ff. and 52ff.
13. Dilcher, *Rechtsgeschichte*, 561ff; and Gudrun Gleba, *Die Gemeinde als alternatives Ordnungsmodell. Zur sozialen und politischen Differenzierung des Gemeindebegriffs in den innerstädtischen Auseinandersetzungen des 14. und 15. Jahrhunderts. Mainz, Magdeburg, München, Lübeck* (Cologne and Vienna, 1989).
14. On the decline of the communal principle after the fifteenth century see Gierke, *Genossenschaftsrecht*, 1: 296–300.
15. See, for example, Bernd Möller, *Reichsstadt und Reformation* (Gütersloh, 1962): "Die Einführung der Reformation vollzieht sich dann in sehr vielen, wenn nicht in allen Städten unter unmittelbarer Teilnahme der Gemeinde (the introduction of the Reformation took place in very many, if not all, cities directly with participation of the community)," either by conventions of the political guilds or in communal assemblies (29). However: "In dem Prozeß des Zerfalls der alten Stadtgenossenschaft ist die Reformation nur retardierendes Moment gewesen, hat ihn im ganzen aber nicht aufhalten können (In the process of the decline of the old city communal organization, the Reformation only slowed things down but could not stop the process)" (74). See also Rainer Postel, "'Van gehorsame der overicheyt.' Obrigkeitsdenken in Hamburg zur Zeit der Reformation," in *Studien zur Sozialgeschichte des Mittelalters und der Frühen Neuzeit*, eds. Franklin Kopitzsch, et al. (Hamburg, 1977), 155–185.
16. Press, *Reichsstadt*, 22–24.
17. See, besides the aforementioned publications by Press and Dilcher, Volker Press, "Der Merkantilismus und die Städte. Eine Einleitung," in *Städtewesen und Merkantilismus in Mitteleuropa*, ed. Volker Press (Cologne and Vienna, 1983), 1–14.
18. In Heinz Schilling's view, it is, when looking on early modern towns, "das Passiv die angemessene Sprachform, die mit der Staatsbildung verbundenen Vorgänge zu beschreiben (only with passive constructions of language can one describe the processes of state building)." Schilling, *Stadt in der frühen Neuzeit*, 38.
19. Peter Blickle, *Kommunalismus. Skizzen einer gesellschaftlichen Organisationsform*, 2 vols. (Munich, 2000), 1: 41ff., 67–69; Peter Blickle, *Das Alte Europa. Vom Hochmittelalter bis zur Moderne* (Munich, 2008), 66–71; and Urs Hafner, *Republik im Konflikt. Schwäbische Reichsstädte und bürgerliche Politik in der frühen Neuzeit* (Tübingen, 2001). On the pre-modern understanding of the (urban) communality in the sense of the *Gemeinde* see also Eberhard Isenmann, "Obrigkeit und Stadtgemeinde in der frühen Neuzeit," in Specker, *Einwohner*, 74–126, here 82–83, and Patrick Oelze, "Die Gemeinde als strukturierendes Leitsymbol: Konstanz im Konflikt mit dem Kaiser (1510/11)," in Schlögl, *Interaktion und Herrschaft*, 217–236.

20. Ernst Pitz, *Bürgereinung und Städteeinung. Studien zur Verfassungsgeschichte der Hansestädte und der deutschen Hanse* (Cologne and Weimar, 2001); and Robert Giel, *Politische Öffentlichkeit im spätmittelalterlich-frühneuzeitlichen Köln (1450–1550)* (Berlin, 1998). The communalistic interpretations accord with the approach to pre-modern politics in general and to urban politics in particular, which has been advanced in the last twenty years by Anglo-American and German historians, such as Christopher R. Friedrichs, Sheilagh Ogilvie or André Holenstein; it emphasizes consensus-based patterns of political communication and forms of politics "from below" instead of antagonistic and authority-based interpretations. Christopher R. Friedrichs, *Urban politics in Early Modern Europe* (London and New York, 2000). Sheilagh Ogilvie, "The State in Germany: A Non-Prussian View," in *Rethinking Leviathan. The Eighteenth-Century State in Britain and Germany*, eds. John Brewer and Eckhart Hellmuth (Oxford, 1999), 167–202; André Holenstein, *"Gute Policey" und lokale Gesellschaft im Staat des Ancien Régime. Das Fallbeispiel der Markgrafschaft Baden(-Durlach)* (Tübingen, 2003); Dagmar Freist, "Einleitung: Staatsbildung, lokale Herrschaftsprozesse und kultureller Wandel in der Frühen Neuzeit," in *Staatsbildung als kultureller Prozess. Strukturwandel und Legitimation von Herrschaft in der Frühen Neuzeit*, eds. Ronald G. Asch and Dagmar Freist (Cologne, 2005), 1–47; and Wim P. Blockmans, André Holenstein, and Jon Mathieu eds., *Empowering Interactions. Political Cultures and the Emergence of the State in Europe, 1300-1900* (Farnham, 2009).

21. On symbolic communication in pre-modern times generally, see Barbara Stollberg-Rilinger, "Symbolische Kommunikation in der Vormoderne. Begriffe—Forschungsperspektiven—Thesen," in *Zeitschrift für historische Forschung* 31 (2004): 489–527. On forms of symbolic communication in pre-modern cities see Schlögl, *Interaktion und Herrschaft*; Patrick Schmidt and Horst Carl, eds., *Stadtgemeinde und Ständegesellschaft. Formen der Integration und Distinktion in der frühneuzeitlichen Stadt* (Berlin, 2007); Thomas Weller, *Theatrum Praecedentiae. Zeremonieller Rang und gesellschaftliche Ordnung in der frühneuzeitlichen Stadt: Leipzig 1500–1800* (Darmstadt, 2006); André Krischer, *Reichsstädte in der Fürstengesellschaft. Politischer Zeichengebrauch in der Frühen Neuzeit* (Darmstadt, 2006); and Andrea Löther, *Prozessionen in spätmittelalterlichen Städten. Politische Partizipation, obrigkeitliche Inszenierung, städtische Einheit* (Cologne, 1999).

22. See Rudolf Schlögl, "Politik beobachten. Öffentlichkeit und Medien in der Frühen Neuzeit," in *Zeitschrift für historische Forschung* 25 (2008): 581-616; Schlögl, "Vergesellschaftung"; Rudolf Schlögl, "Interaktion und Herrschaft. Probleme der politischen Kommunikation in der Stadt," in *Was heißt Kulturgeschichte des Politischen?*, ed. Barbara Stollberg-Rilinger (Berlin, 2005), 115–128.

23. See, among others, Esther-Beate Körber, *Öffentlichkeiten der frühen Neuzeit. Teilnehmer, Formen, Institutionen und Entscheidungen öffentlicher Kommunikation im Herzogtum Preußen von 1525 bis 1618* (Berlin and New York, 1998); and Andreas Gestrich, *Absolutismus und Öffentlichkeit. Politische Kommunikation in Deutschland zu Beginn des 18. Jahrhunderts* (Göttingen, 1994). In recent times, research has focused also on urban public spaces, such as churches, town halls or taverns. See Gerd Schwerhoff, "öffentliche Räume und politische Kultur in der frühneuzeitlichen Stadt: Eine Skizze am Beispiel der Reichsstadt Köln," in Schlögl, *Interaktion und Herrschaft*, 113–136; Susanne Rau and Gerd Schwerhoff, eds., *Zwischen Gotteshaus und Taverne. Öffentliche Räume in Spätmittelalter und Früher Neuzeit* (Cologne, 2004); and Christian Hochmuth and Susanne Rau eds., *Machträume der frühneuzeitlichen Stadt* (Konstanz, 2006).

24. See Rudolf Schlögl, "Kommunikation und Vergesellschaftung unter Anwesenden. Formen des Sozialen und ihre Transformation in der Frühen Neuzeit," in *Geschichte und Gesellschaft* 34 (2008): 155–224; see also Patrick Oelze, "Politische Kultur und soziale Ordnung in der frühneuzeitlichen Stadt. Das Projekt B4 im Kulturwissenschaftlichen Forschungskolleg/SFB 485 an der Universität Konstanz," in *Jahrbuch der historischen Forschung 2004* (Munich, 2005), 77–87. For the underlying system-theoretical approach see particularly Niklas Luhmann, *Soziale Systeme. Grundriß einer allgemeinen Theorie*, 7th ed. (Frankfurt a.M., 1999) (English translation: *Social Systems* (Stanford, 1995); and André Kieserling, *Kommunikation unter Anwesenden. Studien über Interaktionssysteme* (Frankfurt a.M., 1999). In many respects, the concept of *Anwesenheitsgesellschaft* complies with Hans Ulrich Gumbrecht's considerations on the "production of presence," Gumbrecht, *Production of Presence: What Meaning Cannot Convey* (Stanford, 2004) (German: *Diesseits der Hermeneutik. Die Produktion von Präsenz* (Frankfurt a.M., 2004)).
25. According to Rudolf Schlögl, it is characteristic for associations based on face-to-face-interaction that "sozial relevant und strukturbildend ...hauptsächlich das wird, was in Interaktion, also in Kommunikation unter Anwesenden geschieht (what is socially relevant and contributes to structure takes place in interaction or communication among people who are present)." Schlögl, "Vergesellschaftung," 28.
26. According to Luhmann, interactions "use the presence of persons as a boundary-defining device." Niklas Luhmann, "The Evolutionary Differentiation between Society and Interaction," in *The Micro-Macro Link*, eds. Jeffrey C. Alexander et al. (Berkeley, 1987), 112–131, here 114.
27. Besides the aforementioned publications by Rudolf Schlögl, see also Gerd Schwerhoff, "Kommunikationsraum Dorf und Stadt. Einleitung," in Burkhardt and Werkstetter, *Kommunikation*, 137–146, here 138–39; and Uwe Goppold, *Politische Kommunikation in den Städten der Vormoderne. Zürich und Münster im Vergleich* (Cologne, 2007). On the election of the council see also Dietrich W. Poeck, *Rituale der Ratswahl. Zeichen und Zeremoniell der Ratssetzung in Europa (12.–18. Jahrhundert)* (Cologne, 2003).
28. On literacy and literate culture in the Middle Ages in general, see Hagen Keller and Christel Meier, eds., *Schriftlichkeit und Lebenspraxis im Mittelalter. Erfassen, Bewahren, Verändern* (Munich, 1999); Christel Meier, *Pragmatische Dimensionen mittelalterlicher Schriftkultur* (Munich, 2002); and especially regarding the late medieval urban legal system, see Franz-Josef Arlinghaus, *Inklusion/ Exklusion. Funktion und Formen des Rechts in der spätmittelalterlichen Stadt. Das Beispiel Köln* (Konstanz, forthcoming).
29. For everyday politics in early modern cities, it was, as Christopher R. Friedrichs remarks, not the printing press, "(i)t was ink that greased the wheels of government in the early modern city." Friedrichs, *The Early Modern City*, 259. The increasing use of (hand-)written media deployed by the authorities around 1500 to strengthen their position encountered resistance, for example, during the Peasants' War, when seigniorial archives were destroyed by insurgent subjects. Bob Scribner, "Mündliche Kommunikation und Strategien der Macht in Deutschland im 16. Jahrhundert," in *Kommunikation und Alltag im Spätmittelalter und Früher Neuzeit* (Vienna, 1992), 183–197. On supplications in early modern cities, see the article by Alexander Schlaak in this volume and Schlaak, "An den Grenzen des Machbaren. Zur Entwicklung von Schriftlichkeit in frühneuzeitlichen Reichsstädten am Beispiel des Esslinger Supplikenwesens," in *Esslinger Studien* 44 (2005): 63–83; Gerd Schwerhoff, "Das Kölner Supplikenwesen in der Frühen Neuzeit—Annäherungen an ein Kommunikationsmedium zwischen

Untertanen und Obrigkeit," in *Köln als Kommunikationszentrum. Studien zur frühneuzeitlichen Stadtgeschichte*, eds. Georg Mölich and Gerd Schwerhoff (Cologne, 2000), 473–496; and Cecilia Nubola and Andreas Würgler, eds., *Forme della communicazione politica in europa nei secoli XV-XVIII. Suppliche, gravamina, lettere / Formen der politischen Kommunikation in Europa vom 15. bis 18. Jahrhundert. Bitten, Beschwerden, Briefe* (Bologna and Berlin, 2004).
30. See Schlögl, "Vergesellschaftung," 54–57; Friedrichs, *Urban Politics*, 38–39.
31. This line of argument is stressed in Philip R. Hoffmann, "Soziale Differenzierung und politische Integration. Zum Strukturwandel der politischen Ordnung in Lübeck (15.–17. Jahrhundert)," in Schmidt and Carl, *Stadtgemeinde*, 166–197.
32. Besides the studies on the *Strukturwandel der Öffentlichkeit* mentioned above, see also David Zaret, *Origins of Democratic Culture. Printing, Petitions and the Public Sphere in Early-Modern England* (Princeton, 2000).
33. According to Christopher R. Friedrichs, the spread of literacy in early modern towns has to be seen as a "radical change." Friedrichs, *The Early Modern City*, 258ff. Because of the increasing role of written media, the ability to read and write—or at least to employ literately educated persons—became an important factor for political inclusion and exclusion, in particular.
34. See also Patrick Oelze, "Decision-Making and Civic Participation in the Imperial City (Fifteenth and Sixteeth Century): Guild Conventions and Open Councils in Constance," in *Urban Elections and Decision-Making in Early Modern Europe, 1500–1800*, ed. Rudolf Schlögl (Newcastle upon Tyne, 2009), 147-178; Oelze, "Gemeinde"; and Hoffmann, "Soziale Differenzierung." These studies try to reformulate the research on pre-modern communities and civic assemblies (see above) by concentrating on their communicative and medial logic.
35. Jörg Rogge, "Stadtverfassung, städtische Gesetzgebung und ihre Darstellung in Zeremoniell und Ritual in deutschen Städten während des 14. bis 16. Jahrhunderts," in *Aspekte und Bestandteile der städtischen "Identität" in Italien und Deutschland im 14.–16. Jahrhundert*, eds. Giorgio Chittolini and Peter Johanek (Berlin and Bologna, 2003), 193–226, here 209ff.; Jörg Rogge, "Kommunikation, Herrschaft und politische Kultur. Zur Praxis der öffentlichen Inszenierung und Darstellung von Ratsherrschaft in Städten des deutschen Reiches um 1500," in Schlögl, *Interaktion und Herrschaft*, 381–407, here 388ff.; and Blickle, *Kommunalismus*, 1: 41ff.
36. Oelze, "Decision-Making." Yet, in the case of the (imperial) cities of Upper Germany, in several towns at least, the yearly *Schwörtag* retained a certain, though limited, political significance beyond mere symbolic functions: see Hafner, *Republik im Konflikt*, 74ff.
37. See, for example, Alexander Cowan, *Urban Europe 1500–1700* (London and New York, 1998), 37.
38. See Wilhelm Ebel, *Lübisches Recht*, Vol. 1 (Lübeck, 1971). See also Bernhard Am Ende, *Studien zur Verfassungsgeschichte Lübecks im 12. und 13. Jahrhundert* (Lübeck, 1975); Erich Hoffmann, "Lübeck im Hoch- und Spätmittelalter," in *Lübeckische Geschichte*, Antjekathrin Graßmann, 3rd ed. (Lübeck, 1997), 79–339, here 216ff.; Rolf Hammel-Kiesow, "Stadtherrschaft und Herrschaft in der Stadt," in *Die Hanse. Lebenswirklichkeit und Mythos*, eds. Jörgen Bracker et al., 2nd ed. (Lübeck, 1998), 446–479; Heinz Stoob, *Die Hanse* (Graz, 1995), 83ff.; and Burchard Scheper, *Frühe bürgerliche Institutionen norddeutscher Hansestädte. Beiträge zu einer vergleichenden Verfassungsgeschichte Lübecks, Bremens, Lüneburgs und Hamburgs im Mittelalter* (Cologne and Vienna, 1975),

99ff. For an overview of the traditional constitutional historiography of Lübeck, see Pitz, *Bürgereinung*, 138ff.
39. This is why Lübeck (alongside towns such as Nuremberg or Frankfurt) is regularly mentioned in handbooks on medieval urban history as an important example of an imperial town characterized by strong authoritarian rule by the council and an aristocratic regime. On the autocratic position of Lübeck's council see Karl Friedrich Wehrmann, "Die obrigkeitliche Stellung des Raths in Lübeck," in *Hansische Geschichtsblätter* (1884): 53–73.
40. In this sense, Gudrun Gleba has characterized medieval Lübeck as a town without communality (*Stadt ohne Gemeinde*), at least before 1400. Gleba, *Gemeinde*, 193.
41. "Das Kernstück der lübischen Stadtverfassung war der Rat." Ebel, *Lübisches Recht*, 225.
42. Ebel, *Lübisches Recht*, 293–301; Pitz, *Bürgereinung*, 76.
43. In this sense, Wilhelm Ebel characterizes, according to Jörg Rogge, the *Bursprake* in Lübeck as an "ins Obrigkeitliche gewendeter Schwörtag." Rogge, *Kommunikation*, 391. Regarding the *Bursprake*, see Ebel, *Lübisches Recht*, 307ff.; Wilhelm Ebel, "Bursprake, Echteding und Eddach in den niederdeutschen Stadtrechten," in *Festschrift für Hans Niedermeyer zum 70. Geburtstag* (Göttingen, 1953), 53–76; and Jürgen Bolland, "Zur städtischen Bursprake im hansischen Raum," in *Zeitschrift des Vereins für Lübeckische Geschichte und Altertumskunde* 36 (1956): 96–118.
44. On the constitutional conflicts in late medieval Lübeck see (among others) Gleba, *Gemeinde*, 190ff.; Hoffmann, "Lübeck im Hoch- und Spätmittelalter," 248ff.
45. Stoob, *Hanse*, 346.
46. See, for example, Isenmann, *Die deutsche Stadt*, 137; and Wolf-Dieter Hauschild, "Frühe Neuzeit und Reformation: Das Ende der Großmachtstellung und die Neuorientierung der Stadtgemeinschaft," in Graßmann, *Lübeckische Geschichte*, 341–432, here 346–348, 411–412.
47. In this sense, the political conflicts of the 1660s have been seen as an affirmation of traditional, medieval structures, resulting in only a modest "modernization" of the constitutional order. Dilcher, "Rechtsgeschichte," 738–740; and Marie-Louise Pelus, "Lübeck au milieu du XVIIe siècle: conflits politiques et sociaux, conjoncture économique," in *Revue d' Histoire diplomatique* 92 (1978): 189–209, particularly 206–209. On the political and constitutional conflicts in early modern Lübeck, see Jürgen Asch, *Rat und Bürgerschaft in Lübeck 1598–1669. Die verfassungsrechtlichen Auseinandersetzungen im 17. Jahrhundert und ihre sozialen Hintergründe* (Lübeck, 1961); and Antjekathrin Graßmann, "Lübeck im 17. Jahrhundert: Wahrung des Erreichten," in Graßmann, *Lübeckische Geschichte*, 435–488, here 440–446, 454–461.
48. On the following see Pitz, *Bürgereinung*, particularly 30–33, 211ff.; and Rolf Hammel-Kiesow, "Neue Aspekte zur Geschichte Lübecks: von der Jahrtausendwende bis zum Ende der Hansezeit. Die Lübecker Stadtgeschichtsforschung der letzten zehn Jahre (1988–1997), Teil 2: Verfassungsgeschichte, Bürger, Rat und Kirche, Außenvertretungen und Weltwirtschaftspläne," in *Zeitschrift des Vereins für Lübeckische Geschichte und Altertumskunde* 80 (2000): 9–61, here 16ff.
49. For the similar concept of consensus-based rule (*konsensgestützte Herrschaft*), see above.
50. Yet, because of their oral character, negotiations between council and the *discretiores* are hardly perceptible in the sources. In Lübeck, this form of civic participation was—ex-

cept in times of political crises—never institutionalized in a formal way (such as in a permanent committee). Pitz, *Bürgereinung*, 76.
51. See Pitz, *Bürgereinung*, 220ff.; and Bolland, *Bursprake*. Here, Bolland criticizes Ebel's authority-biased opinion and refers to sources that suggest that in the late medieval period, the role of the *Bursprake* was more important than Ebel assumes.
52. On this, see for more detail Hoffmann, "Soziale Differenzierung."
53. Also Rolf Hammel-Kiesow suggests, as one consequence of Pitz's study, that we have to review the Reformation as well as the constitutional conflicts in early modern Lübeck. Hammel-Kiesow, "Neue Aspekte," 25–26.
54. On the Reformation in Lübeck see Hauschild, "Frühe Neuzeit," 377ff.; Wolf-Dieter Hauschild, *Kirchengeschichte Lübecks. Christentum und Bürgertum in neun Jahrhunderten* (Lübeck, 1981), 165ff.; and Wilhelm Jannasch, *Reformationsgeschichte Lübecks von Petersablaß bis zum Augsburger Reichstag 1515–1530* (Lübeck, 1958). On the consequences of the Reformation on the political culture in Lübeck, see Stefanie Rüther, *Prestige und Herrschaft. Zur Repräsentation der Lübecker Ratsherren in Mittelalter und Früher Neuzeit* (Cologne, 2003), 76ff. and 167ff.
55. Wullenwever became mayor in 1533, but had to resign two years later after the devastating defeat of Lübeck and its allies by Denmark. Regarding Wullenwever, see Hauschild, "Frühe Neuzeit," 391ff.; Georg Waitz, *Lübeck unter Jürgen Wullenwever und die europäische Politik*, 3 vols. (Berlin, 1855–1856); and Günther Korell, *Jürgen Wullenwever. Sein sozial-politisches Wirken in Lübeck und der Kampf mit den erstarkenden Mächten Nordeuropas* (Weimar, 1980).
56. After the Reformation, according to Rolf Hammel-Kiesow, the council as *Obrigkeit* had a "Machtvollkommenheit, wie er sie nie zuvor erreicht hatte." Hammel-Kiesow, "Stadtherrschaft," 477. In his voluminous work on Jürgen Wullenwever, Georg Waitz, in close analogy to the failed revolution of 1848/49, evaluated the *Wullenweverschen Unruhen* as a civic-democratic movement that led to a "political revolution," but that was finally terminated by the "restoration" and a strengthening of the old aristocratic regime. See particularly Waitz, *Wullenwever*, 3: 119–123. Even in more recent publications, interpretations are applied such as "new civic constitution," "constitutional democracy," "Wullenwever's revolutionary rule," or "restoration of the council's aristocracy," when describing the political events in Lübeck between 1530 and 1535. See, for example, Hauschild, "Frühe Neuzeit," 387–388, 398, 411.
57. Much of the power of the civic committees derived from their legitimation through a civic assembly and from the possibility of convening such assemblies when needed, which in turn was used as a powerful means in the conflicts with the council. In other Hanseatic towns, the introduction of the Reformation also brought about a temporary boom of forms of civic participation. See Heinz Schilling, *Konfessionskonflikt und Staatsbildung. Eine Fallstudie über das Verhältnis von religiösem und sozialem Wandel in der Frühneuzeit am Beispiel der Grafschaft Lippe* (Gütersloh, 1981), 73ff. and 138ff.; and Schilling, "Städtischen Republikanismus," 114–115, 137–142 (stressing the traditional character of the *Hansestadtreformation* at least as far as its social and political forms are concerned); Rainer Postel, "Bürgerausschüsse und Reformation in Hamburg," in *Städtische Führungsgruppen und Gemeinde in der werdenden Neuzeit*, ed. Wilfried Ehbrecht (Cologne and Vienna, 1980), 369–383; and Johannes Schildhauer, *Soziale, politische und religiöse Auseinandersetzungen in den Hansestädten Stralsund, Rostock und Wismar im ersten Drittel des 16. Jahrhunderts* (Weimar, 1959), 117ff.

58. On the *Reisersche Unruhen*, see particularly Asch, *Rat und Bürgerschaft*, 56ff.; and Graßmann, "Lübeck im 17. Jahrhundert," 440–446.
59. Asch, *Rat und Bürgerschaft*, 57ff.
60. At the latest, since the beginning of the fifteenth century, the civic corporations played a certain role in political communication, but they remained rather secondary political players for a long time. This also holds true for the Reformation era. Nevertheless, the boom of corporative associations, which in the fourteenth and fifteenth centuries comprised the upper social strata of traders as well as the artisans (the latter being forerunners because they had been organized in guilds since the thirteenth century), was a central precondition for their increasing political importance during early modernity. Hoffmann, "Soziale Differenzierung," 173–174.
61. See also Hoffmann, "Soziale Differenzierung," 196–197.
62. On the *Bürgerrezess* of 1669 see Asch, *Rat und Bürgerschaft*, 170–173; and Graßmann, "Lübeck im 17. Jahrhundert," 458–461.
63. Asch, *Rat und Bürgerschaft*, 51; and Waitz, *Wullenwever*, 3: 118 and 442. On the other hand, joint conventions of the civic corporations were still allowed. In the *Bürgerrezess* of 1669, citizens were only permitted to convene in their single corporations to debate urban affairs. Asch, *Rat und Bürgerschaft*, 171.
64. Most of the more distinguished und influential corporations (the "aristocratic" *Zirkelgesellschaft*, the *Kaufleutegesellschaft*, as well as several of the merchant corporations) had already had their own buildings since the fifteenth century. Particularly in the cases of the prestigious *Zirkel*- and *Kaufleutegesellschaften*, the purchase of their own buildings went along with them becoming more socially exclusive. Sonja Dünnebeil, "Die drei großen Kompanien als genossenschaftliche Verbindungen der Lübecker Oberschicht," in *Genossenschaftliche Strukturen in der Hanse*, eds. Nils Jörn et al. (Cologne, 1998), 205–222, here 216–217. In many other (imperial) cities, especially in Southern Germany, many structures were already built or bought by guilds in the fourteenth and fifteenth centuries. In those towns where the corporations were politically and constitutionally important, the control and regulation of their inner communicative space became a central political problem during the fifteenth century. Rainer S. Elkar, "Kommunikative Distanz: —berlegungen zum Verhältnis zwischen Handwerk und Obrigkeit in Süddeutschland während der frühen Neuzeit," in *Geschlechtergesellschaften, Zunft-Trinkstuben und Bruderschaften in spätmittelalterlichen und frühneuzeitlichen Städten*, eds. Gerhard Fouquet et al. (Ostfildern, 2003), 163–179, here 164ff.; and Patrick Oelze, "Die Austreibung der Geselligkeit. Der Wandel städtischer Politik im spätmittelalterlichen Konstanz," in *Kommunikation im Spätmittelalter. Spielarten—Wahrnehmungen—Deutungen*, eds. Romy Günthart and Michael Jucker (Zürich, 2005), 27–39.
65. In this sense, the *Gemeinde* can be termed, according to Patrick Oelze, a "strukturierendes Leitsymbol der politischen Kommunikation." Oelze, "Gemeinde." Certainly, during the Middle Ages, the *Gemeinde* already had a symbolic dimension, but this was closely linked to its performative dimension, which manifested itself particularly in civic assemblies as events of directly visible face-to-face-interaction. On the difference between the symbolic and performative dimensions of *Gemeinde* see also Isenmann, *Obrigkeit*, 82–83.
66. The limited possibilities of the council become especially obvious when studying the political conflicts of the 1660s. On this as well as other aspects treated in this essay, see the forthcoming publication of the Ph.D. dissertation of the author.

67. Gerd Schwerhoff, "Apud populum potestas? Ratsherrschaft und korporative Partizipation im spätmittelalterlichen und frühneuzeitlichen Köln," in Schreiner and Meier, *Stadtregiment und Bürgerfreiheit*, 188–243, here 200ff.; and Pitz, *Bürgereinung*, 108ff. According to Gerd Schwerhoff, the linking of the council to the will of the community has to be seen as a precondition for the extension of its power and the growing social and cultural distance between the political elite and the citizenry since the fifteenth century. Schwerhoff, "Apud populum potestas," 205–207.
68. On the *Große Gottestracht*, see Kathrin Enzel, "'Eins Raths Kirmiß...' Die 'Große Kölner Gottestracht' als Rahmen der politischen Selbstdarstellung städtischer Obrigkeiten," in Schlögl, *Interaktion und Herrschaft*, 471–497.
69. Yet in everyday politics, it was mainly the occupationally organized guilds (*Gewerbe*) through which common citizens represented their interests and exerted political influence, and thereby being included in the political system. Giel, *Öffentlichkeit*, 38 and 242ff.
70. Schwerhoff, "Öffentliche Räume," 126–127, 133. Yet, as Schwerhoff stresses, based on Hermann von Weinsberg's description of Cologne's political order in 1588, it was not the council, but the six mayors who had the decisive say in politics and, according to Weinsberg, a nearly absolute "*autoriteit*." Schwerhoff, "Apud populum potestas," 210–212.
71. Giel, *Öffentlichkeit*, 66ff. and 86ff. In the political conflicts of 1513, printed documents played a central role in Cologne's domestic politics for the first time. According to Giel, it was the breakthrough of print as a political medium. Ibid., 122ff., particularly 137–138.
72. For Cologne, see Schwerhoff, "Kölner Supplikenwesen." See also the article of Alexander Schlaak in this volume.
73. With respect to the implementation of the print medium, Cologne obviously played a special role among German and Hanseatic cities, because in other cases, like Lübeck, print was not used as early and as extensively as in Cologne. For example, the council of Lübeck preferred using handwritten texts to diffuse information among other Hanseatic cities (e.g., on meetings of the Hanseatic League), while the council of Cologne regularly used printed texts instead (and for a long time was the only one to do so). Giel, *Öffentlichkeit*, 96–101.
74. See Goppold, *Politische Kommunikation*.
75. Therefore, in the post-Reformation city, oral or face-to-face-communication had an ancillary function in respect to indirect, written-based communication. In contrast, writing in medieval urban politics was used primarily (and for a long time almost exclusively) as an auxiliary means for conserving important acts or the results of oral and face-to-face political or legal communication.
76. This process of change, beginning in the second half of the eighteenth century, was characterized by the growing significance of the modern media of distance, especially print media, for local everyday politics, the formation of a "new" urban bourgoisie and of a modern political public, alongside the bureaucratic takeover of urban policy by the national state. See, among others, Lothar Gall, ed., *Vom alten zum neuen Bürgertum. Die mitteleuropäische Stadt im Umbruch, 1780–1820* (Munich, 1991).

CHAPTER 2

Overloaded Interaction
Effects of the Growing Use of Writing in German Imperial Cities, 1500–1800

ALEXANDER SCHLAAK

Introduction

Numerous travelogues and chronicles from the early modern period have survived and present a picture of a steady decay of the German imperial cities, particularly in contrast to larger territorial entities within the Holy Roman Empire. Furthermore, various reports from imperial commissions that visited these urban communities, clustered especially in the south of the empire, tell a similar story.[1] According to these portrayals, the free imperial cities were marked by deficient civic administration, economic and military impotence, and dwindling political influence until the collapse of the imperial order at the beginning of the nineteenth century.

Many of the traditional approaches in the field of urban history accepted such judgments at face value.[2] In recent years, however, urban historians have challenged this rather negative image of the German imperial city. The ongoing debates over terms such as "Communalism" and "Republicanism" provide examples of this. Thus, Peter Blickle has drawn attention to the longevity of self-governing bodies in rural and urban communities,[3] while Heinz Schilling has highlighted the civic ideals that persisted in many imperial cities until the end of the empire.[4] Nonetheless, neither Blickle nor Schilling radically rejected assumptions about the inferiority of these autonomous municipalities in comparison with the emergent territorial state.

To be sure, it seems unquestionable that a large number of the free imperial cities faced a substantial economic crisis at the end of the eighteenth century.[5]

But the predominantly negative picture of the German imperial city has come to be seen in a new light as recent approaches, which have adopted concepts from modern communication and media theory, have helped to reevaluate the political culture of the municipalities.[6] These studies have introduced a new understanding of politics as a specific form of communication, and this has led to new modalities in historical research on the imperial cities. Recent research on political communication in imperial cities has accentuated stability and flexibility, rather than decay and decline, as historians have increasingly taken into account the complex media change that took place during the early modern period, namely, the growing use of writing in many domains of the urban social and political sphere.[7]

By focusing on the effects of the growing number of petitions to city councils on the structures and procedures of everyday decision-making within the communities, this essay will demonstrate that the autonomous cities of the empire experienced substantial stability and political vitality well into the eighteenth century. Most of the evidence presented here was drawn from the city archives of Esslingen am Neckar in Swabia, but this chapter will also offer occasional glances at other urban settlements, including Cologne, Ulm, Schwäbisch Hall, the autonomous Swiss city of Zurich, and—to provide a comparison with the observations from the autonomous cities—Dresden, the capital of Saxony. We will begin by taking a detailed look at the framing of early modern city council meetings, which will help us to understand the distinct nature of decision-making within urban magistracies. Subsequently, we will turn our attention to the development of pre-modern petitioning in the Holy Roman Empire in general, before then discussing in detail the specific situation in the imperial cities. The final section will sum up the foregoing arguments and raise questions and certain further speculations about a specific political culture of the German imperial city.

Council Meetings in Early Modern Imperial Cities: The Framing of Face-to-Face Interaction

Around 1500, early modern German towns still relied chiefly on oral communication for the reproduction of their political culture.[8] Within these "face-to-face societies," visuality, locality, specific arrangements of symbolic matters in space, as well as strictly observed norms for performances in political and social rituals, seem to have been of essential value for the stability of the urban community as a whole.[9] Examples of this "principle of presence" include elections to the city council, with their detailed scripts of all actions accompanying these civic events.[10] Writing was used in urban politics, but foremost it was used for its "memory function." Its purpose seems to have been the perpetuation of the city's collective memory, and it scarcely touched upon the execution of inner urban communication processes.

In this context, historians studying imperial cities have recently highlighted the durability of the norms and regulations that framed large-scale rituals of oral interaction, such as the *Schwörtag*, the annual gathering of the citizenry after city council elections in order to swear an oath of obedience and loyalty in front of the newly elected authorities.[11] Despite their waning importance through the eighteenth century, such rituals survived until the collapse of the empire. Moreover, historians such as Uwe Goppold have recently underlined the constancy of the modes of decision-making in the context of city council meetings.[12] His research supplies valuable insights into the structures and procedures of the periodic meetings of urban magistrates in the early modern period that may be valid for imperial cities in general.

Like other important acts of pre-modern political communication, everyday decision-making in the city council was standardized by detailed regulations, as shown by the normative sources we possess from the period. A prescription for the members of the city council in Esslingen from 17 September 1532 offers an initial example of this.[13] The council meetings were marked as discrete social areas, in which specific procedural standards were of immense importance. Some of the most obvious "communicative frames" for the face-to-face interaction during the sessions of the council were the regularity of the meetings at a fixed place (normally in the town hall), compulsory attendance with strict enforcement, and the rituals that began and ended the interaction.[14] Other planned gatherings among councilors outside of this highly standardized spatial-temporal framework, as well as accidental contacts between the council members before and after the sessions, were not considered to have constituted legitimate council meetings.[15] It was feared that such informal interactions would encourage the consideration of issues that were not pertinent or significant, and that they would jeopardize the obligatory confidentiality of the official proceedings.

Nevertheless, as was the case for almost all forms of social interaction in early modern times, considerations relating to status—an individual magistrate's honor or a councilman's seniority—also played their part in structuring the meetings. Consequently, it becomes clear that the sophisticated seating arrangements were not merely ceremonial, without any connection to the decision-making processes. In fact, the opposite was true. In keeping with this, the importance of seating arrangements was reflected in the nature of the decision-making process during the council meetings, as exemplified by normative records from the autonomous city of Zurich. In this Swiss municipality, a maximum of six agenda items was considered to be the limit for a one-day meeting of the magistrate, and each topic had to be consecutively discussed.[16] The discussion of an agenda item commenced with the mayor asking each councilor, one after the other, starting with the person next to him (thus normally according to the seniority of the councilors), for his opinion on the given topic. Subsequently, in the case of an important or controversial topic, another poll—normally with the same routine at first—could take place.[17]

However, a letter from a syndic (or chief lawyer) of the imperial city of Esslingen to the local magistrate from 14 July 1669 provides examples for the problems that could arise if the members of the councils did not follow these strict regulations.[18] The syndic lodged several grievances in connection with the meetings of the city council. Focusing on the discussion procedures at the meetings, he complained about the fact that younger councilmen frequently "offered their judgments prematurely, and before the question was put to them."[19] Another example can be taken from the imperial city of Ulm in Swabia. The underlying motivations for the passing of a statute dealing with some single aspects of the procedures of decision-making during the meetings in 1590 of the local city council reveal the problems associated with ensuring an orderly discussion during the magistracy's sittings. One of the most disruptive nuisances was the "constant going in and out or leaving" of the chamber by some of the members of the council.[20]

Given these observations, it is remarkable that large-scale attempts to reform the procedures of council meetings in imperial cities did not take place until the middle of the eighteenth century. This is even more astonishing when we take into account not only the often contentious social and political events in the early modern period, but also the (above-mentioned) growing use of writing—a shift to a new medium that intensively affected and overloaded the social system of the council meetings, and that was closely connected to the "constraints of oral communication."[21]

Writing and Petitioning in Early Modern Germany

From the sixteenth century onward, the increase in the number of written petitions in almost every part of the Holy Roman Empire is a major indicator of the growing importance of writing in everyday communication, in general, and in political communication, in particular.[22] Previously, most demands and complaints were apparently brought forward in oral communication, and accordingly in direct interaction with the rulers.

In seeking an explanation, it would be difficult to overestimate the impact of the Reformation and of the printing press for the development of written petitions in many social and political domains.[23] The invention of the printing press boosted the dissemination of books and documents in general, and of judicial and political literature in particular, and thus probably strengthened the notion of the written petition as an important tool in the framework of political and legal communication and decision-making.

Petitions became a key factor in stabilizing early modern rule.[24] Firstly, they functioned as an important information tool for the authorities.[25] Due to the lack of far-ranging statistical methods, petitions were the primary means of gathering information on existing grievances or conflicts among the population. Secondly, they also provided an opportunity for the common people to influence decision-making processes on a higher level. Many of the decrees issued by the authorities were initiated, modified, revised, or even suspended as a result of petitions. The growing number of regulations in the context of the *Policey-Gesetzgebung* and the development of petitioning in written form went hand-in-hand. Furthermore, the rising number of written pleas had an enormous effect on the structure of early modern legal proceedings, as the written petition offered a novel form of influencing the outcome of court decisions.

The attraction of the new media arose from the fact that virtually anybody was able to lodge a petition in such situations, which—from the viewpoint of the supplicants—required the intervention of the authorities. In addition, petitions provided a means by which a wide range of issues could be brought to the ears (or better, the eyes) of the rulers. Countless people chose the option of petitioning in written form in the most varied sort of matters. However, as David Zaret has pointed out, "the right to petition was far from absolute."[26] The act of writing a petition had to follow certain standards or norms, a point that distinguished petitions from other media that could also allow more or less direct communication with the sovereign.

The growing use of written petitions during the early modern period is obvious for the historian, and it did not go unnoticed by the local authorities within the empire. The heightened need to acquire information about existing grievances among the population in the context of the ongoing process of "territorialization" in early modern Germany was accompanied by the danger of not being able to adequately address the fast-growing communicative pressure "from below." One option for the authorities in dealing with the increasing number of written petitions was the stricter regulation of acts of petitioning by installing official intermediaries in order to filter the masses of requests and grievances. Thus, petitioning could cause the formation of new institutions.[27] Moreover, many princes in the Holy Roman Empire tried to regulate the increasing "flood" of petitions by prescribing stricter rules for how petitions should be formulated, or by limiting the number of persons allowed to write petitions in their own hand. Eventually, the writing and delivery of a petition by a lawyer became mandatory.

Documents from the city of Dresden reveal the treatment that might be meted out to those who ignored these regulations. Daniel Walber, a casual scribe without legal training and son-in-law of a burgher of the Saxon capital, found himself in a difficult situation in August 1585.²⁸ He was arrested by the urban authorities for writing petitions to the city council of Dresden on behalf of the municipal population. In prison, he eventually saw no other option than to remedy his situation by using the very media that appeared to be the cause of his incarceration: a petition to the city council. Walber's story was far from being an isolated case in the Saxon capital at the end of the sixteenth century.²⁹

Dresden was not alone in its attempts to standardize the procedures governing written petitions, and similar efforts can be found in territories such as Bavaria as early as the second half of the sixteenth century.³⁰ During the early modern period, the princely states tried to tighten their grips on "their cities," and aimed at further integrating the urban communities into the territory. In this context, the growing volume of written petitions could contribute to an expanding "distance" between the governed and the governing, and to the creation of a hierarchical administrative apparatus with clearer, more differentiated competencies for its various elements. However, if we turn our attention to the political culture of imperial cities in general, and to the structures of everyday petitioning and decision-making in the city councils of those municipalities in particular, we see a rather different picture.

Petitioning in Imperial Cities: Decision-Making between Stability and Overload

As in most other parts of the empire, the number of written petitions to local authorities in the Swabian imperial city of Esslingen am Neckar increased tremendously during the early modern period. This growth was not due to any major demographic change, as the population of the city remained at a relatively constant level between 1550 and 1802 of around 7,000 to 8,000 inhabitants.³¹ Nevertheless, dealing with the growing number of petitions was becoming a major part of the everyday work of the city council in Esslingen. Gerd Schwerhoff has made similar observations in the context of his research on the operation of the magistracy in the imperial city of Cologne.³²

As far as we know, during the early modern period, no inhabitant of Esslingen was excluded from the right to petition. The records give evidence of petitions from councilmen or higher officials, as well as of pleas from ordinary burghers. Even women and the poor were able to address a petition to the city's administration. The registered advocates were even obliged to write petitions for the latter free of charge.³³ Moreover, the mass of potential supplicants was matched by the wide range of issues that could be raised in a petition. The topics ranged from simple pleas for patronage or benefits to far-ranging proposals for the modification of a guild's fundamental laws.³⁴ In addition, petitions in Esslingen played an important part in the context of urban legal proceedings.

A first decision by the city's court did not have to be the final judgment. A petition often offered the possibility of altering or lessening its sentences. Likewise, the major role of petitions in the context of urban conflicts or revolts should not be underestimated. Petitions became an increasingly useful tool for the avoidance of physical violence.[35] The heterogeneous and ever growing mass of petitions certainly did not limit the number of conflicts in the urban sphere on their own, but petitions did support the emergence of a new culture of peacefully resolving conflicts. They seem to have been—also in Esslingen—a central element in a far-ranging development that Winfried Schulze has (by focusing mainly on the rural domains of the empire) identified as the "*Verrechtlichung sozialer Konflikte*," the gradual dilution of the violent character of early modern quarrels.[36]

Although we do not find any statutes in Esslingen that restricted the writing of a petition by the supplicant's own hand, the majority of the documents appear to have been composed by advocates in the city. Most of these petitions were addressed to the Small Council (*Kleiner Rat*), consisting of 21 aldermen who were normally drawn exclusively from a few influential families in the municipality.[37] The Privy Council (*Geheimer Rat*), which consisted of the five most powerful members of the Small Council, was the real center of power within the city, but it normally confined itself to discussing the "more important" aspects of politics, such as the foreign affairs of the city, and thus had little time for the workaday consideration of petitions.[38] As a result, written petitions to the Privy Council were rare. Dealing with petitions from the burghers of Esslingen appears to have been the business of the Small Council.[39] And, over the course of the early modern period, it became a more and more time consuming business.

Nonetheless, the history of Esslingen offers—for a considerable part of the early modern period—no evidence of calls for the creation of intermediary institutions to regulate the communication between the city council and the city population. Certainly, in Esslingen as in many other imperial cities, we find that institutions existed, such as the *Viermänner* or *Viertelsmeister* (district captains) and the *Handwerksverordnete* (craftsmen deputies) that were supposed to deal with minor issues among the townsfolk.[40] However, they apparently carried out their tasks through oral communication and were not intended to function as a filter in the context of the written communication between the urban magistrate and the inhabitants. In most cases, the city council in Esslingen reserved the right to decide all cases.[41] Even in cases where written demands, requests or grievances from the city's burghers were eventually delegated to secondary committees or institutions—which, at any rate, were normally headed by one of the councilmen —the final decision remained in the hands of the city council. In these deliberations, the presence of all 21 councilmen was deemed to be of essential importance for decision-making on everyday issues. Furthermore, written petitions were normally not circulated prior to a session but read out in their entirety during any given meeting.[42] Despite these demands, the city council of Esslingen succeeded in maintaining control over all aspects of the city's political culture until the first half of the eighteenth century, when the communicative pressures from below apparently overwhelmed it.

An indication that this overload had finally come can be found in a report from January 1736 by the two syndics of Esslingen, Eberhard Friedrich Eckher and Johann Frick.[43] With reference to the increasing workload of the council, they brought forward several proposals regarding the future structure of the council meetings. The syndics argued that the great increase in the volume of written petitions was one of the main reasons for the tremendous overload in the council's business. Consequently, they recommended that the lord mayor should carry out some pre-selection and classification of all petitions to the city council, in order to evaluate whether a petition should be dealt with directly by the council or first by a secondary institution. Additionally, they suggested that short summaries should be appended to the petitions by the writers of these documents and also suggested brevity in all written supplications. This seemed to be necessary to ensure the effective work of the council, since most of the petitions were read out in their entirety during the magistracy's sittings, as we saw earlier. Thus, the two syndics did not demand extraordinary meetings of the council, but rather a reorganization of the communication structures between the inhabitants and the center of power within the city. All of their suggestions were accepted by the city council on 21 January 1736. These measures represent a watershed, since we do not find similar statutes in the imperial city of Esslingen before the beginning of the eighteenth century. The reluctance of the magistrates of Esslingen to create intermediary institutions as a kind of filter for the growing written communication between urban inhabitants and the city council might be connected to the continuity of "face-to-face" political interaction. It seems that the Swabian imperial city was capable of withstanding, for a longer period than other cities, the "communicative pressure" of a far-ranging process of media change but had finally hit its limits in the middle of the eighteenth century.

The reluctance of Esslingen's magistrates to allow subordinates to address petitions may also have been rooted in the unique political nature of imperial cities. Addressing petitions often involved the granting of grace, a privilege of a sovereign possessing the right to rule by birth. In the territorial states of the empire, this was relatively unproblematic. However, the status of the magistrates in the German imperial cities as ruler over or representatives of the urban burghers never went unchallenged, and in this regard, the hesitant course of action by the magistrates in Esslingen might be more understandable. By deciding even less pressing issues, the councilmen of Esslingen could actually maintain or extend their symbolic capital. The observation that the city's burghers had to address the councilors with titles generally associated with nobility throughout the text of a petition points in this direction. However, since Esslingen was marked by a very radical form of oligarchic government, its circumstance may not be applicable throughout the empire.[44]

A Distinctive Political Culture of the German Imperial City? Questions and Hypotheses

There were, of course, numerous differences among the various imperial cities in the empire with regard to their social, political, economic, and cultural conditions.[45] Contemporaries such as Johann Jacob Moser, who highlighted some differences among the autonomous cities with regard to their political culture in the 1770s, had long noticed these dissimilarities.[46]

Although Moser mainly focused on a few aspects of the political constitution in general, like the composition of the city council or other central institutions, differences are also identifiable in the context of the communicative structures between city councils and urban populations. The reasons for these disparities were apparently not solely due to the mere size of a city. Gerd Schwerhoff has recently pointed out that no detailed regulations on the structures of inner-urban petitioning existed in early modern Cologne, although, over the course of the early modern period, it was one of the largest cities within the empire.[47] This reluctance to issue comprehensive regulations on urban petitioning could also have been linked to the council's fears that such norms might—in connection with the specific guild system in Cologne—have caused a weakening of its position as the sole arbiter within the city.

In other imperial cities, different factors might have influenced petitioning practices. Having a larger hinterland was apparently another factor: the imperial city of Schwäbisch Hall, with a relative large territory, began regulating urban communicative structures as early as the end of the sixteenth century.[48] The Swiss city of Zurich, as well as the Swabian imperial city of Ulm, a close neighbor of Esslingen that possessed a relatively large subject territory in the early modern period, are two other examples in this context. But for all that, even the magistrates of Schwäbisch Hall and Ulm in Swabia apparently managed to avoid a truly comprehensive and detailed regulation of urban petitioning until the eighteenth century. Instead, they limited their regulation of petitioning to some partial facets of written communication between a city's burghers and the center of power.

While formal petitioning was crucial to urban administration in the early modern period, the importance of informal and secretive networks should also not be underestimated. Several recent studies have examined these informal communications. Gerd Althoff, for example, has depicted traditional forms of neighborly, kin, or client relationships in the medieval period.[49] David Sabean has demonstrated their continued relevance for early modern cities.[50] Furthermore, Simon Teuscher, in his work on the political culture of late medieval Bern, has outlined the several "informal" steps a subject had to take before his personal requests were to be presented during a meeting of the city council.[51] The aforementioned letter from the syndic to the city council of Esslingen from 1669 points in this direction. The syndic mentioned another disturbance of the city council's work, which relates to informal processes of conflict resolution: councilmen who consistently acted as advocates or spokespersons for inhabitants of the city in the context of a magistracy's sitting.[52] It is possible that several elements of these customary, unofficial practices had survived in many German imperial cities until the eighteenth century and could relieve the work of the city councils by presenting alternative possibilities for solving everyday conflicts or exceptional emergencies, alongside the "novel" forms of petitioning in writing.

The act of writing petitions, which appears to be a right that is known to almost every citizen of our modern democracies, became common during the early modern period. A rapidly growing number of pleas and grievances addressed to the local authorities was the consequence of this development. However, the way authorities handled these petitions varied, as the aforementioned observations show. Within most of the princely states, the masses of petitions prompted the formation of new institutions and procedures. The installation of intermediaries in order to filter the communication from below or the imposition of strict standards for the writing of petitions can be observed in many territories of the empire. However, if we turn our attention to the political culture of imperial cities, we see a rather different picture. The magistrates within these cities succeeded in maintaining control over all aspects of the city's political culture until the communicative pressures from below apparently overwhelmed them in the first half of the eighteenth century.

The reasons for these disparities seem to be obvious. While the princely states needed to install a hierarchical structure within their administration apparatus in the context of their territorialization, the magistrates of the imperial cities tried to maintain or extend their symbolic capital by deciding even minor issues, since addressing petitions often involved the granting of grace, a privilege of a sovereign possessing the right to rule by birth. However, the reluctance of the urban magistrates to create intermediary institutions as a kind of filter for the growing written communication between urban inhabitants and the city council might also be connected to the continuity of "face-to-face" political interaction. The stability of central aspects of a "face-to-face" society in the early modern period, aspects demonstrated in this paper, certainly raises questions about a distinctive political culture of the German imperial city, which is an issue for further investigations.

Notes

1. On imperial commissions in the seventeenth century, see Eva Ortlieb, *Im Auftrag des Kaisers. Die kaiserlichen Kommissionen des Reichshofrats und die Regelung von Konflikten im Alten Reich* (1637–1657) (Cologne, Weimar, and Vienna, 2001). Some of the commissions during the eighteenth century resulted in slight modifications of the constitutional order of the imperial cities. One example is the city of Esslingen am Neckar in 1748–1752; see Ulrich Eberlein, "Die Esslinger Bürgerprozesse. Eine Untersuchung der innerstädtischen Auseinandersetzungen in den letzten Jahren der Reichsunmittelbarkeit unter besonderer Berücksichtigung rechtlicher, wirtschaftlicher und sozialer Hintergründe. Zugleich ein Beitrag zur Rechtsgeschichte der schwäbischen Reichsstädte im 18. Jahrhundert" (Ph.D. dissertation, University of Tübingen, 1987), 46ff.
2. Even works from the 1980s maintained this perspective on early modern imperial cities. See Volker Press, "Die Reichsstadt in der altständischen Gesellschaft," in Johannes Kunisch, ed., *Neue Studien zur frühneuzeitlichen Reichsgeschichte* (Berlin, 1987), 9–42.
3. See Peter Blickle, *Kommunalismus. Skizzen einer gesellschaftlichen Organisationsform*, 2 vols. (Munich, 2000).
4. Heinz Schilling, "Gab es im späten Mittelalter und zu Beginn der Neuzeit in Deutschland einen städtischen 'Republikanismus'? Zur politischen Kultur des alteuropäischen Stadtbürgertums," in *Republiken und Republikanismus im Europa der Frühen Neuzeit*, eds. Helmut G. Koenigsberger et al. (Munich, 1988), 101–143.
5. See Uwe Schmidt, *Südwestdeutschland im Zeichen der Französischen Revolution. Bürgeropposition in Ulm, Reutlingen und Esslingen* (Ulm, 1993), 20f.
6. With focus on the "foreign affairs" of German imperial cities, see André Krischer, *Reichsstädte in der Fürstengesellschaft. Zum politischen Zeichengebrauch in der Frühen Neuzeit* (Darmstadt, 2006).
7. The consequences of the growing use of writing for pre-modern societies are examined in Cornelia Bohn, *Schriftlichkeit und Gesellschaft. Kommunikation und Sozialität der Neuzeit* (Opladen, 1999).
8. See Rudolf Schlögl, "Vergesellschaftung unter Anwesenden. Zur kommunikativen Form des Politischen in der vormodernen Stadt," in *Interaktion und Herrschaft. Die Politik der frühneuzeitlichen Stadt*, ed. Rudolf Schlögl (Konstanz, 2004), 9–60.
9. Regarding an ideal type of a "face-to-face society," see Peter Laslett, "The Face to Face Society," in *Philosophy, Politics and Society*, ed. Peter Laslett (Oxford, 1956), 157–184.
10. The concept of a "principle of presence" became prominent after the publication of Hans Ulrich Gumbrecht, *Production of Presence: What Meaning Cannot Convey* (Stanford, 2004). See, in general, Uwe Goppold, *Politische Kommunikation in den Städten der Vormoderne. Zürich und Münster im Vergleich* (Cologne, 2007).
11. A detailed description of the *Schwörtag* in the imperial city of Esslingen am Neckar is provided by Rainer Jooß, "Schwörtage in Esslingen vor 1802," in *Esslinger Studien* 31 (1992): 1–14.
12. Uwe Goppold, "Stadtrichter, Rat und Landesherr. Die Ratskur in Münster während des 17. Jahrhunderts," in Schlögl, *Interaktion*, 93–112; and Goppold, *Kommunikation*, 197ff.
13. StAE (City Archives of Esslingen am Neckar), Bestand Reichsstadt, F. 11, Nr. 23a.
14. For these issues in the cities of Zurich and Münster, see Goppold, *Kommunikation*, 197ff.

15. Goppold, *Kommunikation*, 197ff.
16. StAZ (City Archives of Zurich), B III 13c ("Halbjährige Satzungen"), 248 (9 January 1668); see also StAZ, B III 34h ("Verhandlungen auf dem Rathaus 1780"), 184–195. In addition, see again Goppold, *Kommunikation*, 197ff.
17. StAZ (City Archives of Zurich), B III 13c ("Halbjährige Satzungen"), 248 (9 January 1668); StAZ, B III 34h ("Verhandlungen auf dem Rathaus 1780"), 84–195. Moreover, the above-mentioned regulations in Esslingen am Neckar from 1532 (StAE, Bestand Reichsstadt, F. 11, Nr. 23a) display similar normative standards.
18. See StAE, Bestand Reichsstadt, F. 21a.
19. StAE, Bestand Reichsstadt, F. 21a. According to the original source, "... *vor der zeit, und ehe die frag an sie kommen, Ihr weisheit vorbringen.*"
20. See StAU (City Archives of Ulm), Bestand A (Reichsstadt), A 3503. The original phrase in German is: "*steetig auß- und einlauffen oder abtretten.*"
21. With regard to these "constraints of oral communication," see André Kieserling, *Kommunikation unter Anwesenden. Studien über Interaktionssysteme* (Frankfurt a.M., 1999).
22. Werner Hülle, "Das Supplikenwesen in Rechtssachen. Anlageplan für eine Dissertation," in *Zeitschrift für Rechtsgeschichte, Germanistische Abteilung* 90 (1973): 194.
23. The impact of the Reformation on the development of writing has been emphasized by many historians over the last decades, for example, by Mark U. Edwards, *Printing, Propaganda and Martin Luther* (Berkeley, 1994).
24. See Peter Blickle, ed., *Gemeinde und Staat im Alten Europa* (Munich, 1998).
25. As Lex Heerma van Voss has argued: "Even the most autocratic of governments used petitions as a source of information about popular feeling." See Lex Heerma van Voss, "Introduction," in *Petitions in Social History*, ed. Lex Heerma van Voss (Cambridge, 2001), 4.
26. David Zaret, "Petitions and the 'Invention' of Public Opinion in the English Revolution," in *American Journal of Sociology* 101 (1996): 1513.
27. Andreas Würgler, "Bitten und Begehren. Suppliken und Gravamina in der deutschsprachigen Frühneuzeitforschung," in *Bittschriften und Gravamina. Politik, Verwaltung und Justiz in Europa (14.–18. Jahrhundert)*, eds. Cecilia Nubola and Andreas Würgler (Berlin, 2005), 17–52, here 37.
28. See the documents on the case of Daniel Walber in StAD (City Archives of Dresden), C.V.1.
29. Compare the other cases in StAD, C.V.1.
30. The development of petitioning in early modern Bavaria has been discussed in Renate Blickle, "Laufen gen Hof. Die Beschwerden der Untertanen und die Entstehung des Hofrats in Bayern. Ein Beitrag zu den Varianten rechtlicher Verfahren im späten Mittelalter und in der frühen Neuzeit," in Blickle, *Gemeinde und Staat*, 241–266.
31. On the population development in Esslingen am Neckar see Otto Borst, *Geschichte der Stadt Esslingen am Neckar* (Esslingen, 1977), 250.
32. Gerd Schwerhoff, "Das Kölner Supplikenwesen in der Frühen Neuzeit. Annäherungen an ein Kommunikationsmedium zwischen Untertanen und Obrigkeit," in *Köln als Kommunikationszentrum. Studien zur frühneuzeitlichen Stadtgeschichte*, eds. Georg Mölich and Gerd Schwerhoff (Cologne, 2000), 476.
33. See the official oath of the legal advocates in Esslingen am Neckar from the middle of the seventeenth century in StAE, F. 18, Nr. 3.

34. The bakers' guild, the butchers' guild, and the coopers' guild, in particular, are noteworthy in this context for the early modern period, see StAE, Bestand Reichsstadt, F. 7, F. 167, F. 181.
35. See Alexander Schlaak, "Social Space and Urban Conflict: Unrest in the German Imperial City of Esslingen am Neckar," in *Political Space in Pre-Industrial Europe*, ed. Beat Kümin (Aldershot, 2009) 135–150.
36. The term "*Verrechtlichung sozialer Konflikte*" was outlined most prominently in Winfried Schulze, *Bäuerlicher Widerstand und feudale Herrschaft in der frühen Neuzeit* (Stuttgart 1998).
37. Compare the regulations with regard to the manning of the small city council of Esslingen am Neckar in StAE, Bestand Reichsstadt, F. 4.
38. StAE, Bestand Reichsstadt, F. 4.
39. In order to avoid misunderstandings, the Small Council is generally referred to as the "city council" in the following text.
40. See the norms dealing with the responsibilities of the *Viermänner* and *Handwerksverordnete* in StAE, Bestand Reichsstadt, F. 4.
41. See Eberlein, *Bürgerprozesse*, 39.
42. Compare StAE, Bestand Reichsstadt, F. 21a.
43. StAE, Bestand Reichsstadt, F. 21a. All of the following references to the survey of Frick and Eckher have been taken from that file.
44. Compare, in general, Eberlein, *Bürgerprozesse*.
45. Karl Siegfried Bader, "Die oberdeutsche Reichsstadt im alten Reich," in *Esslinger Studien* 11 (1965): 25.
46. See Johann Jacob Moser, *Neues Teutsches Staatsrecht. Band 18: Von der Reichs-Stättischen Regiments-Verfassung* (Frankfurt a.M. and Leipzig, 1772).
47. Schwerhoff, "Supplikenwesen," 485ff.
48. See the specific regulations in StASH (City Archives of Schwäbisch Hall), 4/492, 17; and in StASH, HA B 158.
49. Gerd Althoff, *Spielregeln der Politik im Mittelalter. Kommunikation in Frieden und Fehde* (Darmstadt, 1997).
50. See, especially, David Warren Sabean, "Social Background to Vetterleswirtschaft: Kinship in Neckarshausen," in *Frühe Neuzeit—Frühe Moderne? Forschungen zur Vielschichtigkeit von Übergangsprozessen*, ed. Rudolf Vierhaus (Göttingen, 1992), 113–132.
51. Simon Teuscher, "Chains of Favor. Approaching the City Council in Late Medieval Bern," in *Forme delle comunicazione politica in Europa nei secoli XV–XVIII. Suppliche, gravamina, lettere / Formen der politischen Kommunikation in Europa vom 15. bis 18. Jahrhundert. Bitten, Beschwerden, Briefe*, eds. Cecilia Nubola and Andreas Würgler (Bologna and Berlin, 2004), 311–328.
52. StAE, Bestand Reichsstadt, F. 21a.

CHAPTER 3

Princes' Power, Aristocratic Norms, and Personal Eccentricities
Le Charactère Bizarre of Frederick William I of Prussia (1713–1740)

BENJAMIN MARSCHKE

Frederick William I of Prussia said, "*wir sind Herr und König und können tun, was wir wollen.*"[1] Perhaps more than any other prince in the Holy Roman Empire, Frederick William epitomized the tension between a ruler's dynastic responsibilities and interests and his/her exceptional opportunity to pursue his/her own personal inclinations and eccentricities.[2]

Frederick William's refusal to follow the contemporary standards of behavior that applied to his position led contemporaries (and modern scholars) to discuss his "bizarre character."[3] Johannes Kunisch states that Frederick William was "exceptionally headstrong and bizarre."[4] Gerhard Ritter called Frederick William not only "half-barbaric," but also "strange."[5] While acknowledging that Frederick William was a "*seltsamer Wildling,*" Fritz Hartung found it necessary to argue that Frederick William was *not* insane.[6] Others, like Gerhard Oestreich, have characterized Frederick William as an "*Ekel*" and a "psychopath."[7] Suffice to say that his contemporaries found, and scholars continue to find, Frederick William's behavior astounding, enigmatic, and often in any case objectionable.[8]

This article approaches Frederick William's willful and conspicuous rejection of contemporary aristocratic norms as a unique opportunity to explore the edges of acceptable eccentricity for princes and the effects of overstepping such boundaries in the eighteenth-century Holy Roman Empire. The aim of this is certainly *not* to rehabilitate or condemn Frederick William, but rather to consider him as an extreme case and to find and analyze the limits of normality and the consequences of going beyond these boundaries. This essay discusses several aspects of Frederick William and his rulership: first, his ascension to the throne and the various shocking things that he did when he became king; second, Frederick William's reign, his court, and his behavior in Potsdam and Berlin; and finally, his rejection of contemporary protocol norms when traveling abroad.

The Iconoclasm

Upon taking the throne, even King Frederick William I's name was a break with contemporary norms. It was customary for kings to use only one first name, but Frederick William immediately announced that he would use both.[9] While this significant break with tradition seems to have been a non-issue, the new king's refusal to undergo any ceremonial coronation was controversial. It is especially interesting that Frederick William, who disdained baroque ceremonies and court rituals, could not simply do as he wanted in this regard. Instead, he and his ministers found it necessary to explain why there would be no coronation.[10] Relying on theory—the coronation did not make the king, but was only a symbol and a means of making the people aware of the new monarch—and on precedent—many monarchies eschewed coronations by the early eighteenth century—the lack of a coronation was explained away.[11] The details of Frederick William's justification of his lack of a coronation are not so important as his clear understanding that such a justification was necessary, because he knew that he was pushing the envelope of acceptability.

Indeed, contemporary reports of Frederick William's ascension to the throne reveal open dissatisfaction. Periodicals such as the *Europäische Fama*, dedicated to "discovering the present state of the preeminent courts," wanted to see more pomp and ceremony.[12] It was disappointing enough that there was no coronation, but Frederick William did not even sit while his subjects paid homage to him.[13] Worse yet, much of the crowd departed immediately after the ceremony, because of the rain, and did not partake in the offered feast.[14] However, while this may have been noteworthy, this was certainly acceptable in the sense that it did not create any problem regarding foreign and domestic recognition of Frederick William as king. On the contrary, Frederick William's ascension to the throne was infinitely less problematic than his predecessor's new claim to royal status had been in 1701.[15]

Frederick William's ascension to the throne is typically described in modern scholarship as an "iconoclasm."[16] The infamously miserly and militaristic king spectacularly rejected and dismantled his father's typical baroque representative court. He flattened baroque gardens into parade grounds, he gave away the exotic animals from the royal menagerie, he sold or leased out most of the royal palaces, he sent the horses from the royal stables to the cavalry, he dismissed dozens of musicians, artists, and architects, and he drastically cut the salaries of the remaining courtiers and ministers.[17] Scholars have described Frederick William's iconoclastic austerity program as simply "unthinkable," but we should look at this more closely.[18]

The so-called iconoclasm at court was not only *not* unthinkable, but also quite passable within the empire. Though some courtiers were horrified, it was calmly reported in the press that Frederick William had leased out or even sold superfluous palaces, discharged *"unnötige"* servants, did away with the unnecessarily opulent dress code, imposed various other economical measures, and generally cared only for his soldiers. Contemporary reports recognized this as newsworthy, but actually looked on rather approvingly.[19]

When examined closely, the other seemingly radical steps taken by Frederick William in the first weeks of his reign also appear less excessive than scholars have supposed them to be. For example, the new king immediately up-ended the table of ranks of the Prussian court and gave high-ranking military officers precedence over ministers and other state officials and courtiers.[20] Contemporary sources published the new *Rangliste* without commentary.[21] Rather than viewing this as an extreme step, we might recognize that even though Frederick William drastically reordered the *Rangliste*, in doing so he also confirmed its relevance and importance, and he clearly recognized that ceremonial precedence and protocol would continue to matter at the Prussian court. Indeed, tables of rank and various address/title books (for properly addressing people at court) continued to be produced throughout Frederick William's reign.[22]

At Home with Frederick William

Contemporaries found Frederick William's behavior at his courts in Potsdam and Berlin somewhat strange. However, we should not think that Frederick William was free to do whatever he pleased. There seem to have been some bounds that the king knew (or should have known) not to cross.

While much of what happened at Frederick William's court was typical of other European courts, he took several elements of court culture to extremes. For example, visiting dignitaries were invited (and expected) to help Frederick William review his troops and to visit the arsenal in Berlin. Reviewing troops during state visits was normal at the time. It was already common practice under Frederick William's predecessor to provide visiting dignitaries with a tour of the newly constructed arsenal in Berlin.[23] Furthermore, Frederick William himself was often invited to review the troops of his hosts when he traveled abroad.

Nonetheless, Frederick William certainly took these military spectacles to an abnormal extreme. Whereas reviewing troops in other countries was one activity among many, in Prussia under Frederick William, the annual "general review" was *the* great spectacle in Berlin.[24] In any case, his guests do not seem to have protested, and this was reported as merely newsworthy. Indeed, Frederick William's militarily-themed spectacles seem to have inspired imitation—after attending the general review in Berlin in 1728, King August II ("the Strong") of Saxony-Poland presented a similar spectacle outside of Dresden in 1730.[25]

More problematic was Frederick William's obsession with collecting tall soldiers for his army and the Prussian army's aggressive recruiting abroad to support this. This was quite objectionable, but only as a matter of kidnapping and a violation of sovereignty, not because collecting tall soldiers was unfashionable or weird. Indeed, this was also imitated—after his aforementioned visit in 1728, August II began recruiting especially tall young men for his own army[26]—and other rulers were most outraged because they wanted tall young men for their own representative military units.[27] Regardless of whether Frederick William actually believed that God had granted him all tall men,[28] Frederick William's obsessive pursuit of tall young men was not only extremely expensive, but also caused him serious trouble on the international scene.[29] His contemporaries noted that Frederick William's (and Prussia's) diplomatic troubles stemmed primarily from the excesses of Prussian recruiters.[30]

In many other regards, the Prussian court was noteworthy, but hardly objectionable. Frederick William's inclination to reject various aspects of baroque ceremonial and precedence seems to have been readily accepted, even if it was notable. For example, assigning seats at the royal table (*Tafel*) by lot rather than by rank or precedence was reported but not commented upon by contemporaries.[31] The attire at Frederick William's court became more and more austere as his reign continued, and he ultimately stopped wearing a baroque wig and adapted the Prussian army officer's uniform as his daily attire.[32] Contemporaries found this abnormal enough to make a point of warning newcomers on the idiosyncratic dress code at Frederick William's court.[33] Those who presumed to continue to appear in baroque fashions at Frederick William's court were openly ridiculed—courtiers dressed the court fool and dishonorable people in absurdly exaggerated "fashions" to mock those wearing extravagant clothing and towering wigs.[34] Frederick William embarrassed the French ambassador and his entourage by having hangmen's assistants appear in exaggerated French fashions at the annual general review in Berlin in 1720:

> The King, this same year [1720], on Whitsun-Tuesday, reviewed nine Regiments of Infantry ... This Review was attended with a very comical Circumstance, which made it remarkable; the King designing to ridicule those extravagant Sticklers for Fashions, and hair-brained young Fellows, who think they undervalue themselves, if they are not *Petit Maitres*, ordered all the Provosts (a Sort of Servants to the Executioner) of these Regiments, to be dressed after the *French* Mode, with great Hats, Feathers, their Hair in Bags, and the Cuffs of their Coat-Sleeves

turned up with the same Stuff their Waistcoats were made of. Count *Rottenbourg*, the *French* Ambassador, who came in his Coach, with a Retinue of above thirty Persons, to this Review, was surprised to see the Provosts dressed so like himself and his servants; there being no other Difference, except that the Cuffs of their Sleeves were longer; their Hats larger; and as to their Bags, they seemed rather to be Sacks hanging at their backs, than Bags for their Hair.[35]

Indeed, the public within the empire and even throughout Europe tended to agree with Frederick William's derision of luxury and extravagance.[36] We should view Frederick William's conspicuous lack of consumption in the larger context of the "luxury debates" and the associated shift from "ceremonial representative" to "economic cameralist" monarchical legitimation, which marked eighteenth-century political culture.[37]

While the 1720 case involving the French ambassador shows that Frederick William could afford to humiliate his rivals, a few truly objectionable happenings at Frederick William's court did get him in trouble. Even as king he did not have the freedom to do whatever he wanted or to offend anyone he wanted with impunity. Of course, Frederick William's treatment of foreign envoys falls away into diplomatic/international political concerns. For example, dressing up hangmen's assistants to look like the French ambassador and his entourage to ridicule their appearance provoked a response—as it assuredly was intended to do.[38] Acts of violence against diplomats (or even their possessions), especially those from allied countries, was another matter. After the Dutch arrested and executed two Prussian recruiters operating illegally in the Netherlands in 1732–1733, Prussian soldiers beat up the driver and vandalized the carriage of the Dutch resident envoy in Berlin.[39] The Dutch diplomat threatened to leave Berlin because of the "insult" to his livery.[40] Under pressure from his prospective allies in the impending War of Polish Succession (1733–1738), Frederick William was ultimately forced to punish the soldiers involved and to apologize.[41]

Obviously, there were limits to what the King in Prussia was allowed to do to the representatives of foreign powers, but there were also limits to what Frederick William could do even when dealing with his own subjects. Frederick William was famously impatient and violent. He gained a reputation for spontaneously beating his subjects in the streets, and he imposed exemplary punishments on corrupt officials. His anecdotal threats to recalcitrant royal servants are legend; for example: "They must dance to my tune, or the devil take me: I will execute and burn like the tsar, and treat them as rebels."[42] Nonetheless, the outlandish threats seem less illustrative of the king's actual behavior than his frustration at his inability to do as he wanted.

Though Frederick William's court was exceptional in terms of its (lack of) formality, it was governed by certain rules of decorum problematic to violate. The misfortunes of Paul Jacob von Gundling, who was President of the Royal

Academy of Sciences, but better known as Frederick William's court fool, provides a useful example.[43] Gundling was famous then (and is still known) as the subject of David Faßmann's *Der gelehrte Narr* and Johann Michael von Loen's "unglückliche Gelehrte am Hof."[44] Frederick William and his rowdy courtiers ceaselessly tormented Gundling. They played practical jokes on him, forced him to wear ridiculous clothing and wigs, and insulted and denigrated him in various ways.[45] Gundling was named *Oberzeremonienmeister*, which did not mean much at a court that had abolished most ceremonies, but he was required to wear an absurdly gigantic gold-painted key around his neck.[46] It was apparently great fun to set Gundling's towering wig on fire, or at formal occasions, to seat Gundling next to a monkey dressed just like him. On his wedding night, the pranksters slipped Gundling a powerful laxative. Denigrating Gundling was not just a private entertainment for Frederick William and his inner circle, but the king also ensured that this behavior was publicized. Gundling was regularly trotted out in public to be mocked and humiliated, even during state visits.[47] Frederick William supported the publication of *Der gelehrte Narr* and made sure that the torments of Gundling made it into the Amsterdam newspapers.[48]

However, there were limits to what Frederick William could do with Gundling. Ennobling Gundling was not a problem, apparently, but making him a baron raised protests.[49] Perhaps worse, publicizing Gundling's torments was not just embarrassing for Gundling. Queen Sophie seems to have been mortified by the antics involving Gundling and the public reports of the same.[50] Worse, not everybody at the king's court in Potsdam wanted to play along with this. When Gundling died, Frederick William ordered the local clergy to take part in his funeral, which was an irreverent parody. Gundling's body, dressed ridiculously, was paraded through the streets of Potsdam in a wine cask-shaped casket, and various ribald songs mocking Gundling were composed. The local clergy flatly refused to take part in this, even though Frederick William insisted that they do so. At this point, Frederick William seems to have been rather powerless and was unable to force them to participate.[51] Indeed, in the commemorative literature, Gundling's burial was (falsely) portrayed as a suitably solemn affair, without further insult or irreverence.[52] The king seems to have recognized that he had gone too far, and he wanted to deny what had happened, but he soon found a new court jester and his court continued the same sort of public antics.

There were limits to what Frederick William was allowed to do to his subjects, but he seems to have been largely free to do what he wanted with his own children. For example, Frederick William married off four of his daughters as he pleased—all four were endogamous matches, and none of them very prestigious.[53] The king's harsh treatment of the crown prince, his son Frederick, is well known.[54] Frederick William does *not* seem to have been out of line in berating and beating his son in public, ordering him to lick his boots, etc., even though Frederick was certainly correct when he protested that it would have been totally unacceptable for the king to treat any other nobleman the same way.[55]

There was an international outcry only when 18-year-old Frederick was caught fleeing his father's jurisdiction in 1730 and it seemed possible that Frederick William might sentence him to death. However, it was moral pressure from outside of Prussia, not legal or political pressure, that constrained him. Conversely, Frederick William's attempt to use the Prussian state apparatus legally to punish Frederick and his accomplices was very problematic. The court martial recused itself from trying the crown prince for desertion, and Frederick William did not (or could not) force them to do so; ironically, the court martial recused itself on the grounds that they could not interfere in the affairs of a sovereign king and his son.[56] The repeated failure of the same military officers to sentence the crown prince's accomplices to death meant that Frederick William was forced to override their decision.[57] Especially significant is that the king not only failed to instrumentalize the court martial, but also found it necessary to explain why he overturned its judgment.[58] Frederick William may have been king and able to do what he wanted, but the Prussian officer corps would not allow him to use them to punish the *frondeurs*, and moreover, he was not free to act without justifying his actions to them. Despite the king's insistence that if they existed, he would execute 100,000 such accomplices, it seems clear that he understood that his actions were pushing at the limits of what was acceptable.[59]

Frederick William on Tour

Frederick William's rejection of contemporary aristocratic norms and his eccentric behavior was not only an issue at his own court, but also when he traveled abroad. A great deal has been made of the supposed importance of protocol, precedence, and symbolic communication in early modern Europe.[60] Frederick William's often-oblivious ignorance, casual dismissal, and obnoxious rejection of his contemporaries' expectations offer a unique counterpoint.

Frederick William traveled a great deal and met with many heads of state— he actually did much more of this than his predecessors or his successor.[61] Many of the seemingly odd things that Frederick William insisted upon doing were quite acceptable. The Prussian king's desire to work around the baroque court norms was not so uncommon in the early eighteenth century. For example, contemporary sources frequently noted that Frederick William traveled in foreign lands "incognito," which meant not so much "anonymous" as it did "without ceremony."[62] This was quite typical at the time, and usually quite acceptable.⁶³ Frederick William often traveled with an extraordinarily small entourage, or even no entourage at all.⁶⁴ This, too, was noteworthy, but does not seem to have been at all problematic.

Things did not always go smoothly, and sometimes Frederick William's refusal to cooperate with his hosts in ceremonial pomp posed problems. In 1721, Frederick William tried to visit Hamburg unannounced and incognito.⁶⁵ He was recognized his first day in the city, and the Hamburgers insisted on formally receiving him. Frederick William refused to receive a deputy of the *Stadt-Rath*, and refused to accept "even the least signs of honor."⁶⁶ Instead, he left Hamburg the day after he had arrived.⁶⁷

Indeed, Frederick William's failure or refusal to follow standard protocol comes up again and again in the sources on his life. The two great state visits of Frederick William's reign were his visit to August II of Saxony-Poland in Dresden in 1728, and his visit to Emperor Charles VI in Bohemia in 1732. Contemporary descriptions of both portray a litany of *faux pas* done by Frederick William.

Frederick William's visit to August II in Dresden in 1728 began with a series of mis-steps. The commemorative literature notes that the Prussian king announced his visit to Dresden for the winter carnival at the last minute—less than two weeks before his arrival—which left the Saxons scrambling to prepare to receive him.⁶⁸ In doing so, Frederick William interrupted the mourning period for the recently deceased queen of Saxony-Poland.⁶⁹ The 76-page pamphlet commemorating his visit claimed that Frederick William was greeted in the countryside and then escorted to Dresden. It admits that he entered Dresden incognito—he refused any ceremony, not even the customary firing of the city's artillery—and explains that, therefore, the Saxons fired their cannon as a welcome only that evening.⁷⁰ On the other hand, manuscript sources describe a debacle. Frederick William arrived much earlier than anticipated, and the streets were virtually empty when he entered Dresden. When he arrived at the house of the count with whom he would be staying, his host was not there, so instead he was received by his own resident envoy in Dresden. Frederick William, rather than being put off by the lack of a reception, seemed very pleased by the surprise.⁷¹

The pomp and ceremony surrounding Frederick William's visit was understated, presumably in keeping with his wishes.⁷² For his part, Frederick William seemed unamused by the amusements. Seemingly true to form, Frederick William reportedly observed the sleigh ride, which was led personally by August II and had been arranged only with great exertion (by hauling hundreds of wagon-loads of snow into the city), from an upstairs window.⁷³ However, he enthusiastically took part in the "hunt" that was staged in one of the palace courtyards, and he personally shot one bear six times.⁷⁴ Again, it was briefly noted that Frederick William only watched from a window as a giant carousel was staged at the Zwinger, the description of which took three pages, but he took special delight in the four-hour-long "*Sau Stechen*," in which 300 wild pigs were speared.[75]

After two weeks in Dresden, there was no end in sight for Frederick William's visit. Concrete plans had been laid ahead of time for events and entertainments in case the Prussians stayed for five days or eight days.[76] In the case that Frederick William and his entourage stayed for as long as fourteen days, then there was no real plan for the last six days, except "gatherings at the palace" and "comedies" on alternate evenings.[77] Though it did not seem to have occurred to anyone that he would stay longer than two weeks, "this controversial monarch," as the Saxon commemorative literature politely referred to Frederick William, actually stayed in Dresden for four weeks, until the end of carnival.[78]

Frederick William's visit to Emperor Charles VI and Empress Elisabeth Christine in Bohemia in 1732 was another opportunity to upset protocol. Problems arose as soon as Frederick William was underway. The commemorative literature noted that Frederick William's entourage counted only 10 people (plus 20 servants). Charles, despite the Prussian king's wish to travel incognito, had him received at every stop along his way.[79] Frederick William, in turn, refused the lodgings offered by the local notables and instead selected his own.[80] The commemorative literature explained that he consistently went to bed early every night instead of socializing (or even dining) with his presumptive hosts, because he was either tired from the day's journey or wanted to get an early start the next morning.[81] Ironically, it was noted that Frederick William, who wanted to avoid all ceremony and travel quickly, could not seem to pass by any of the emperor's troops without stopping his carriages, getting out, and drilling them thoroughly.[82]

Once Frederick William arrived at the planned rendezvous point, he messed things up further. The commemorative literature reported that, in keeping with the excruciatingly complicated and presumably critically important rules of precedence and ceremony, the imperial hosts had built a special pavilion for the first meeting of the Prussian king with the emperor and empress. To accommodate proper protocol, it was constructed with two portals, so that both parties could enter at the same time, from opposite directions.[83] Instead, as the emperor and empress approached in their carriage, Frederick William "spontaneously decided" to go out to meet them—he hurried through his door, through the pavilion where they were to meet, out the door through which the imperial couple was to enter, and then went to them and very affectionately embraced them as they exited their carriage.[84] Frederick William's bursting enthusiasm would seem to have totally ruined the carefully laid plans, but the commemorative literature pointed out that the Prussian king and the imperial couple then entered the pavilion together, simultaneously.[85]

As the visit continued, so did Frederick William's blunders. For example, it was reported that whereas Charles raised himself slightly from his seat to toast the Prussian king, Frederick William stood up completely to toast the emperor and empress. This was not a problem, except that he then refused to sit back down, until asked repeatedly to do so.[86]

Once Frederick William and Charles moved on to Prague, things did not improve. In keeping with his "expressly conditional" incognito status, Frederick William was welcomed with a special salute from the city's artillery (but no further ceremony).[87] His imperial hosts, clearly very concerned about protocol and precedence, followed Frederick William everywhere in Prague with a large armchair, and wherever he ate, they put the chair at the head of the table for him.[88] It is noted in the commemorative publications that Frederick William never sat in the special chair, and instead he sat himself wherever he liked, usually next to Eugene of Savoy.[89] Finally, as he had done in Dresden, Frederick William stayed longer in Prague than was planned. After two days in Prague, instead of departing as planned, Frederick William sent an apology for staying longer than anticipated—Charles graciously offered that Frederick William could stay as long as he wanted.[90] Moreover, Frederick William continued to ignore established protocol (and even the protests of the emperor) regarding how hosts and guests should approach each other. The commemorative literature reported that when the emperor unexpectedly visited the Prussian king in his quarters for what would be the last time, Frederick William rushed through two antechambers to greet Charles.[91] After their visit, despite the emperor's "completely earnest" insistence that Frederick William refrain from doing so, the king then insisted upon walking the emperor all the way back to his carriage and then waited until he drove away.[92]

Frederick William's freedom to ignore, dismiss, or reject contemporary standards of behavior was perhaps even greater when dealing with weaker powers. The best example of this is his repeated visits to Braunschweig-Bevern to arrange and carry out two of his children's marriages, as recorded in the *Hof-Journal* of a local courtier.[93]

Presumably, at this lesser court, Frederick William was much freer to insist upon doing whatever he pleased and to refuse to cooperate in anything he did not want to do. Predictably, Frederick William repeatedly declined to be received with any ceremony or formality. As he approached Wolfenbüttel, the crown prince of Braunschweig-Bevern, his future son-in-law, rode out with troops to meet him. However, Frederick William refused to have any escort.[94]

Despite the purportedly crucial importance of court ceremony at the table, the Beverners only got one chance to host a formal ceremonial meal—the Prussian king made it clear he did not want to eat *"en ceremonie"* thereafter.[95] Frederick William did not want to be served by people carrying the food around the table, but instead wanted the food set on the table. Frederick William did not want people seated and served according to rank, but insisted on assigning seats by drawing lots (as he did in Berlin).⁹⁶

As in Prague, the Beverners provided a satin armchair for Frederick William. As in Prague, Frederick William refused to sit in it, and he instead insisted on sitting on a normal wooden chair.⁹⁷ Even at the wedding celebration, when the Beverners again offered the satin armchair, Frederick William again refused (though on this occasion he did allow them to serve *en ceremonie*).⁹⁸ The Beverners had arranged to have a concert played while they ate, but once again, Frederick William countermanded the order.⁹⁹ After several visits and many rebuffs, the Braunschweig-Bevern source casually mentions Frederick William's preference to eat in his quarters with only a few people, without any ceremony, and that most of the Prussian entourage ate at what the Beverners referred to as "nach der Berlin manier sogenandt[en] ambassadeur-tafel"—at the Prussian court the best attended (and best prepared) table was typically that of one of the ambassadors, not that of the king.¹⁰⁰

Conclusion

Frederick William's position as sovereign allowed him a great deal of freedom to indulge his personal preferences and dispositions. It is virtually impossible to gauge just how outlandish contemporaries found Frederick William, but especially in matters of taste and conduct, Frederick William's "odd" behavior and his eccentricities were often simply deemed *merckwürdig*: "noteworthy."¹⁰¹ His repeated rejection of contemporary norms of court ceremonial, for example, was noteworthy. This usually seemed to be acceptable, even if it sometimes pushed against the limits so much so that Frederick William found it necessary to justify his actions. At his own court, this was never a significant issue, and he could generally impose his will at smaller courts as well.

Similarly, Frederick William's enthusiastic obliviousness toward protocol and precedence at foreign courts was noteworthy, as was the refusal of his hosts to accommodate his wishes, such as the emperor's denial of the Prussian king's desire to travel incognito. During visits to the King of Poland in Dresden or to the emperor in Bohemia, this kind of thing was noticed, but does not seem to have gotten in the way of diplomacy (as witnessed by August II's subsequent reciprocal visit to Berlin, or the sustained alliance between Charles VI and Frederick William). On the contrary, the commemorative literature seems to have found the Prussian king's overeager informality almost endearing, and as we have seen in the case of his visit to Dresden, the commemorative publications often papered over some of the embarrassments described in manuscript sources. We might assume that the published description of the king's visit to the emperor in Bohemia, even though it still describes many awkward moments, is a similarly sanitized version of events (or even an exercise in damage control).

Only in rather rare cases did Frederick William's eccentric and willful behavior actually prove problematic in the sense that it provoked a direct response or resistance. The outlandish mockery of Gundling continued for years and was only reined in after the *Der gelehrte Narr* was dead. For Frederick William and his court to insult the ambassador of an enemy power was allowed (even applauded), but acts of violence against the representatives of friendly powers were clearly off limits and necessitated apologies. Frederick William's public denigration of the crown prince was allowed, but he was unable to convince (or force) his officers to go along with trying Frederick and executing his accomplices (and the king found it necessary to explain his actions to his officers). In each of these cases, having passed the limits of acceptability, Frederick William yielded to contemporary expectations before the situation became a larger (or more public) controversy or scandal.

Moreover, Frederick William's position as the ruler of a relatively large and militarily powerful state meant that to the extent to which he was "bizarre," he enjoyed a certain immunity from intervention by the empire.[102] Contemporaries clearly noted that Frederick William's outlandish pursuit of his idiosyncrasies—for example, the kidnapping of tall young men—would not have been tolerated on the international stage without his value as a military ally and the danger that he presented as a potential enemy.[103] As he claimed, Frederick William was king, and he largely could do what he wanted.

Notes

1. Fritz Hartung, "Die politischen Testamente der Hohenzollern," in *Forschungen zur brandenburgischen-preussischen Geschichte* 25 (1913): 333–363, here 344.
2. This essay is part of a larger project on the court of Frederick William and his representation(s) of himself and the Prussian monarchy. See also Marschke, "'Von dem am Königl. Preußischen Hofe abgeschafften *Ceremoniel:*' Monarchical Representation and Court Ceremony in Frederick William I's Prussia," in *Orthodoxies and Diversity in Early Modern Germany*, eds. Randolph C. Head and Daniel Christensen (Boston, 2007), 227–252.
3. When Frederick William assumed the throne, the French envoy wrote home about the new king as *"le caractère bizarre."* Quoted by Klaus Malettke, "Die französisch-preußischen Beziehung unter Friedrich Wilhelm I. bis zum Frieden von Stockholm (1. Februar 1720)," in *Preußen, Europa, und das Reich*, ed. Oswald Hauser (Cologne, 1987), 123–150, here 123.
4. "Der Stil, in dem sich Friedrich Wilhelm I. der Fürstenwelt seiner Zeit präsentierte, [hat] als ausgesprochen eigenwillig und bizarr zu gelten." Johannes Kunisch, "Funktion und Ausbau der kurfürstlich-königlichen Residenzen in Brandenburg-Preußen im Zeitalter des Absolutismus," in *Forschungen zur brandenburgischen-preußischen Geschichte, Neue Folge (FBPrG)* 3 (1993): 167–192; reprinted in Peter-Michael Hahn,

ed., *Potsdam, Märkische Kleinstadt, europäische Residenz: Reminiszenzen einer eintausendjährigen Geschichte* (Berlin, 1995), 61–83, here 79.
5. Gerhard Ritter, *Frederick the Great: A Historical Profile*, trans. Peter Paret (Berkeley, 1974), 19.
6. Hartung, "König Friedrich Wilhelm I., Der Begründer des preussischen Staats," in *Preussischen Akademie der Wissenschaften Vorträge und Schriften* 11 (Berlin, 1942): 6, 10.
7. Gerhard Oestreich, *Friedrich Wilhelm I.: Preußischer Absolutismus, Merkantilismus, Militarismus* (Göttingen, 1977), 9. Scholars who adopt a psycho-historical approach have agreed with Oestreich's assessment. For example, Kurt R. Spillmann and Kati Spillmann credit deep-seated emotional problems for making him Prussia's *"größter innere König."* Spillmann and Spillmann, "Friedrich Wilhelm I. und die preußische Armee: Versuch einer psychohistorischen Deutung," in *Historische Zeitschrift* 246 (1988): 549–589, here 589. The aforementioned works refer to Frederick William's "normal" psyche, not the periodic bouts of dementia brought on by porphyria. See Claus A. Pierach and Erich Jennewein, "Friedrich Wilhelm I. und Porphyrie," in *Sudhoffs Archiv* 83:1 (1999): 50–66.
8. From a recent handbook: "Frederick William I is perhaps the least understood Hohenzollern ruler ... because of his puzzling and contradictory behaviour." Rodney Gothelf, "Frederick William I and the Beginnings of Prussian Absolutism, 1713–1740," in *The Rise of Prussia, 1700–1830*, ed. Philip G. Dwyer (Harlow, UK, 2000), 47–67, here 48. Peter Baumgart says of Frederick William: "Schon die Zeitgenossen und ganz besonders die Geschichtschreibung taten sich schwer, der komplizierten Persönlichkeit und der 27jährigen Regierung des zweiten preußischen Königs gerecht zu werden. Die Spannweite der Urteile über Friedrich Wilhelm I. war und ist denkbar weit und in ihren Extremen kaum miteinander vereinbar." ("Already contemporaries, and most especially the historical scholarship have had a hard time doing justice to the complicated personality and the 27-year reign of the second Prussian king. The range of judgements about Frederick William I was and is considerably wide and in their extremes hardly compatible with each other.") Baumgart, "Friedrich Wilhelm I.," in *Preußens Herrscher: Von den ersten Hohenzollern bis Wilhelm II.*, ed. Frank-Lothar Kroll (Munich, 2000), 134–159, here 134.
9. Carl Hinrichs, "Der Regierungsantritt Friedrich Wilhelms I.," in *Jahrbuch für die Geschichte Mittel- und Ostdeutschlands* 5 (1956): 183–225.
10. This argument is included in a handwritten description of Frederick William's reception of the homage of his subjects in Königsberg in 1714, in lieu of a coronation: *"Quaestio*: Ob ein Nachfolger im Reich ohne öffentliche Cröhnung ein König könne genennet und von demselben die Jura regalia exerciret werde?" ("Question: Whether a successor in the Empire can be named a king without a public coronation and whether he can exercise royal law?") Geheimes Staatsarchiv—Preußischer Kulturbesitz (GStA-PK), BPH, Rep. 46, E 7.
11. GStA-PK, BPH, Rep. 46, E 7.
12. *Die Europäische Fama, welche den gegenwärtigen Zustand der vornehmsten Höfe entdecket*, 1702–1733. *Die neue Europäische Fama, welche den gegenwärtigen Zustand der vornehmsten Höfe entdecket*, 1735–1756.
13. "Man hat durchgehends geglaubet, Se. Königl. Maj. von Preussen würden den 10. Sept. in Königsberg dero Crönung vollziehen lassen, weilen sie, in Gesellschafft des

Printzens von Anhalt=Dessau und anderer Grossen ihres Hofes dahin abgereiset. Allein es ist diese Preußische Crönung gäntzlich nachgeblieben, und den 11. Sept. die Huldigung der Preußischen Stände, ohne grossen Pomp, umb. 10 Uhr vor Mittage geschehen, bey welcher Ihro Maj. nur gestanden, und sich nicht niedergesetzet." ("One had thought all along, that His Royal Majesty of Prussia would have his coronation on 10 Sept. in Königsberg, because he traveled there in the company of the Prince of Anhalt-Dessau and other greats of his court. However, the Prussian coronation has been totally dropped, and on 11 Sept. at 10 o'clock the estates paid homage, without great pomp, and His Majesty only stood, and did not seat himself.") *Europäische Fama* 164 (1714): 711.
14. "Es hat sich aber kaum die Helffte mit dem Schmauß auf dem Königl. Schlosse regaliren lassen, sondern die meisten sind nach verrichtetem Actu, wegen eingefallenen Regen=Wetters nach Hause gegangen." ("Only about half let themselves be regaled with the feast in the royal palace, instead most went home after the performance of the act, because of the falling rain.") *Europäische Fama* 164 (1714): 711.
15. See Marschke, "Von dem am Königl. Preußischen Hofe abgeschafften *Ceremoniel*," 235–236; and Marschke, "The Crown Prince's Brothers and Sisters: Succession and Inheritance Problems and Solutions among the Hohenzollerns, From the Great Elector to Frederick the Great," in *Sibling Relationships and the Transformations of European Kinship, 1300-1900*, eds. Christopher H. Johnson and David Warren Sabean (forthcoming).
16. "Bildersturm," Baumgart, "Friedrich Wilhelm I.," 134. See also Hinrichs, "Regierungsantritt," 183–225; reprinted in Hinrichs, *Preussen als historisches Problem: Gesammelte Abandlungen* (*Veröffentlichungen der historischen Kommission zu Berlin*, 10), Gerhard Oestreich, ed. (Berlin, 1964), 91–137, here 91.
17. Contemporaries reported in 1713 that Frederick William had ordered the silver tableware and utensils collected, melted down, cast into ingots, stamped with the seal of the Prussian army, and cached away in the cellar of the royal city palace in Berlin (in a vault that lay directly under his bed chamber). Hinrichs, "Regierungsantritt," 113–114. Actually, Frederick William had the silver tableware and utensils collected in 1713 so that they would not be stolen during the interregnum, and it was Frederick II who liquidated the silver during the Seven Years War. See Peter-Michael Hahn, "Pracht und Selbstinszenierung. Die Hofhaltung Friedrich Wilhelms I. von Preußen," in *Der Soldatenkönig: Friedrich Wilhelm I. in seiner Zeit*, eds. Friedrich Beck and Julius H. Schoeps (Potsdam, 2003), 69–98, here 87–91.
18. Hinrichs, "Regierungsantritt," 115.
19. "Dieser glorieuse Printz, dessen Succession Gott auch schon durch einen Männlichen Erben einigermassen stabiliret, und dessen Frau Gemahlin sich wiederum gesegnetes Leibes befindet, hat zwar, was den Pracht des Hofes betrifft, unterschiedenes abgedanckt, auch so gar einige Lust– und Land–Schlößer inzwischen verpachtet, viel unnöthige Bedienten abgeschafft, und sorget am meisten vor seine Militz" ("This glorious Prince, whose sucession God has already somewhat stabilized with a masculine heir, and whose wife finds herself again blessed with child, has indeed, regarding the splendor of the court, given up various things, and meanwhile even leased some pleasure and country palaces, dismissed many unnecessary servants, and cares most for his military.") *Europäische Fama*, 142 (1713): 782. "An dem Königl Preußischen Hofe wird alle unnöthige Kleider–Pracht durch scharffe Edicta verboten, und die Oeconomie gantz anders, als vorhin, eingerichtet. Die Soldaten sind liebe Kinder des

neuen Königes; vor dieselben sorget er hauptsächlich" ("At the royal Prussian court all unnecessary splendor in dress is forbidden by strict edicts, and the economy is established totally differently from before. The soldiers are the dear children of the new king, and it is mainly for them that he cares.") *Europäische Fama* 145 (1713): 82.
20. Hinrichs, "Regierungsantritt," 109.
21. This was published in contemporary sources in the context of describing his predecessor's funeral. *Europäische Fama* 142 (1713): 958–960.
22. Not only was the *Adress-Calendar* published annually by the Royal Academy of Sciences in Berlin (and sold well enough to be the primary source of revenue for the academy), but publications, such as the directories of titles for the Berlin court appended to French textbooks, were also continuously revised, printed, and (presumably) sold. See, for example, the many editions of Robert Jean de Pepliers's *Verbesserter und viel vermehrter, Nöthiger Unterricht, Von denen Französischen Tituln* that were published in Berlin.
23. For example, when Eugene of Savoy visited Berlin in 1710, he was first received by a Prussian field marshal and then toured through the arsenal, *Europäische Fama* 100 (1710): 293–294. When Peter I of Russia visited Berlin in 1712, he was received similarly, *Europäische Fama* 135 (1712): 222. Regarding construction of the arsenal, see Regina Müller, *Das Berliner Zeughaus: Die Baugeschichte* (Berlin, 1994).
24. This took place at the end of May every year.
25. David Faßmann, *Das Glorwürdigste Leben und Thaten Friedrich Augusti, des Großen, Königs in Pohlen und Chur-Fürstens zu Sachsen...* (Hamburg und Frankfurt, 1733), 918.
26. Faßmann, *Das Glorwürdigste Leben*, 917–918.
27. "... und die Fürsten liessen sich dieß nun weniger gefallen, als ehemals, weil große Soldaten überall Mode zu werden anfiengen." ("... and the princes were even less pleased by this than before, because tall soldiers began to be the fashion everywhere.") Theresius von Seckendorff, *Versuch einer Lebensbeschreibung des Feldmarschalls Grafen von Seckendorf, meist aus ungedruckten Nachrichten bearbeitet*, 4 vols. (Leipzig, 1792–1794), 3: 178.
28. Samuel Morgenstern (1706, or 1708–1785) was at Frederick William's court from the mid 1730s until the king's death: "Wegen der Anwerbung großer Leute glaubte er in seinem Gewißen, daß ihm durch deren Verweigerung Unrecht geschehe, und die großen Männer ihm von Gott so gut als vermacht wären, da er solche zu schätzen und vorzuziehen wisse, und er pflegte sich zuweilen recht zu ereifern, wenn andere Grundherren Schwierigkeiten machten, da sie die großen Leute selbst nicht zu brauchen wüßten, noch auch so hoch bezahlen und unterhalten könnten." ("Regarding the recruiting of tall people, he earnestly believed that he was done an injustice when they refused and that the tall men were as good as granted to him by God, because he knew to treasure and favor such, and he sometimes tended to become really excited when other lords made difficulties, because they did not know to use the tall people themselves, and could not pay them or maintain them as well.") Morgenstern, *Über Friedrich Wilhelm I. Ein nachgelassenes Werk vom Hofrath und Professor Morgenstern, Mitglied des Tobaks–Kollegii Friedrich Wilhelm I.* (1793; reprinted Osnabrück, 1978), 203.
29. Regarding the extravagant costs of recruiting and maintaining Frederick William's tall soldiers, see Willard R. Fann, "Foreigners in the Prussian Army, 1713–1756: Some

Statistical and Interpretive Problems," in *Central European History* 123:1 (March 1990): 76–84, here 80.

30. Friedrich Heinrich, Graf von Seckendorff (1673–1763), who was one of Frederick William's favorites (and also an agent of the emperor) from 1727 to 1734, chalked up most of the Prussian king's diplomatic difficulties to the excesses of the Prussian recruiters. Von Seckendorff, *Lebensbeschreibung des Feldmarschalls Grafen von Seckendorf*, 3: 161–204.
31. *Europäische Fama* 266 (1723): 169.
32. Based on images of the king on Prussian coins, Frederick William ceased appearing in a wig in 1717. He appeared with only his own hair until the mid 1730s, when he began occasionally wearing a small pony-tailed wig again. See numismatic books, such as Bernd Jacob von Arnim, *Von Thalern des Chürfürstlich–Brandenburgischen und Königlich–Preussischen regierenden Hauses* (Berlin, 1788). Frederick William did not start wearing a uniform daily until the early 1720s. Hartung, "König Friedrich Wilhelm I.," 13.
33. One Pietist client at the court in Berlin ended a letter to August Hermann Francke: "PS: Für die erinnung [sic] weg[en] *peruque* und handschue dancke hertzlichst. Sie ist wohl beobachtet." ("PS: Hearty thanks for the reminder regarding wigs and gloves. It is well observed.") Johann Ulrich Christian Köppen, Berlin, letter to Francke, Halle, 12 May 1725. Staatsbibliothek zu Berlin - Preussischer Kulturbesitz (SBB-PK), Handschriftenabteilung, Nachlass Francke, Kasten 13,1, #30.
34. Regarding the preposterous attire of Paul Jakob Freiherr von Gundling, see below.
35. Éléazar de Mauvillon, *The Life of Frederick-William I: Late King of Prussia. Containing Many Authentick Letters and Pieces, very necessary for understanding the Affairs of Germany and the Northern Kingdoms*, trans. William Phelips (London, 1750), 229–230.
36. Johann Michael von Loen's oft-quoted statement that Frederick William's court had "nothing lustrous and nothing showy but its soldiers," has been misunderstood as implying that there was nothing splendid or magnificent in Prussia, when in reality, von Loen clearly endorsed Frederick William's transformation of the Prussian court: "Ich sehe hier einen königlichen Hof, der nichts glänzendes und nichts prächtiges als seine Soldaten hat. Es ist also möglich, daß man ein groser König seyn kan, ohne die Majestät in dem äusserlichen Pomp und in einem langen Schweiff bundfärbigter, mit Gold und Silber beschlagenen Creaturen zu suchen." ("I see here a royal court, which has nothing lustrous and nothing showy but its soldiers. It is possible, then, that one can be a great king without seeking majesty in superficial pomp and in a long train of colorful creatures encrusted with gold and silver.") Von Loen, "Der königlich Preußische Hof in Berlin, 1718," in *Des Herrn von Loen gesammelte Kleine Schrifften, Dritter Abschnitt*, ed. J.C. Schneider (Frankfurt a.M. and Leipzig, 1750; reprinted Frankfurt a.M., 1972), 22–39, here 22.
37. See Volker Bauer, *Hofökonomie: Der Diskurs über den Fürstenhof in Zeremonialwissenschaft, Hausväterliteratur und Kameralismus* (Vienna, 1997). Bauer portrays the "representative" and "economic" perspectives as mutually exclusive and diametrically opposed. I argue that in Frederick William's Prussia, the emphasis upon the "economic" was clearly "representative." See Marschke, "Von dem am Königl. Preußischen Hofe abgeschafften *Ceremoniel*," 243–245.
38. De Mauvillon, *The Life of Frederick-William I.*, 229–230. Prussia had been at war with France several years before, and France had backed Sweden, Prussia's enemy, in the Great Northern War (1700–1719), which had just ended. We can place Freder-

ick William's mockery of the French ambassador at the beginning of Roosen's spectrum of unfriendly options, ranging from disinterest, to insult, and, ultimately, to war. See William Roosen, "Early Modern Diplomatic Ceremonial: A Systems Approach," in *Journal of Modern History* 52 (1980): 452–476, here 470–471.
39. Von Seckendorff, *Lebensbeschreibung des Feldmarschalls Grafen von Seckendorf,* 3: 180–190.
40. "Seiner Livree angethanen Schmipf," von Seckendorff, *Lebensbeschreibung des Feldmarschalls Grafen von Seckendorf,* 3: 190.
41. Von Seckendorff, *Lebensbeschreibung des Feldmarschalls Grafen von Seckendorf,* 3: 193–194.
42. Ritter, *Frederick the Great,* 155. Frederick William's admiration and imitation of the other contemporary ruler famous for non-conformity, Peter I of Russia, has never been investigated. Suffice it to say here that Frederick William's frequent references to the brutality and immediacy with which Peter appeared able to rule are part of a larger pattern of the Prussian king modeling his own ruling style on that of the Russian tsar.
43. See especially Martin Sabrow, *Herr und Hanswurst: Das tragische Schicksal des Hofgelehrten Jacob Paul von Gundling* (Stuttgart, 2001). Space limitations preclude a thorough exploration of Frederick William's intellectualism and his anti-intellectualism in the context of the early eighteenth century. Much of the king's supposed anti-intellectualism was quite in tune with the early Enlightenment's criticisms of arrogant and ignorant "intellectuals" and a general skepticism of potential charlatans.
44. David Faßmann, a prominent satirist, was employed at Frederick William's court c. 1726–1731. Faßmann, *Der gelehrte Narr, Oder, Ganz natürliche Abbildung Solcher Gelehrten, Die da vermeynen all Gelehrsamkeit und Wissenschafften verschlucket zu haben, auch in dem Wahn stehen, daß ihres gleichen nicht auf Erden zu finden, wannenhero sie alle andere Menschen gegen sich verachten, einen unerträglichen Stoltz und Hochmuth von sich spüren lassen; in der That aber doch selber so, wie sie in ihrer Haut stecken, Ignoranten, Pedanten, ja Ertz=Fantasten und dumme Sympel sind, die von der wahren Gelehrsamkeit, womit die Weisheit verknüpffet seyn muß, weit entfernet...* (Freiburg, 1729). See also Johann Michael von Loen, "Der unglückliche Gelehrte am Hof. Oder: Einige Nachrichten von dem geheimen Rath und Ober=Ceremonienmeister, Freyherrn von Gundling" and "Abbildung des Professor G**," in Loen, *Des Herrn von Loen gesammlete* [sic] *Kleine Schrifften: Besorgt und herausgegeben von J.C. Schneider* (Frankfurt a.M. and Leipzig, 1749; reprinted Frankfurt a.M., 1972), 198–218, 218–221.
45. Sabrow, *Herr und Hanswurst.*
46. This was perhaps done not so much to mock Gundling as to mock former *Oberzeremonienmeister* Johann von Besser, who had left Berlin for Dresden upon Frederick William's ascension to the throne. Sabrow, *Herr und Hanswurst,* 94, 98–99.
47. Sabrow, *Herr und Hanswurst,* 95, 146.
48. Sabrow, *Herr und Hanswurst,* 140–141.
49. Sabrow, *Herr und Hanswurst,* 97. Frederick William, for his part, thought that naming someone a baron was a "Bagatelle." Von Seckendorff, *Lebensbeschreibung des Feldmarschalls Grafen von Seckendorf,* 3: 53.
50. Sabrow, *Herr und Hanswurst,* 68–69.
51. The letters of Heinrich Schubert, preacher at the Dreifaltigkeitskirche in Potsdam, illustrate this especially well. Schubert, Potsdam, letter to Gotthilf August Francke, Halle, 16 April 1731, AFSt, HA I, C 632:52.

52. Sabrow, *Herr und Hanswurst*, 159–162. As I have discussed elsewhere, the apparent self-contradiction of the earnest religiosity and piety (but *not* "Pietism") and the irreverent, drunken, ribald amusements at Frederick William's court is best explained by a close study of changes at the Prussian court over time. "Experiencing King Frederick William I. Pietist Experiences, Understandings, and Explanations of the Prussian Court, 1713–1740," in *Pietismus un Erfuhrung: Beiträge zum III. Internationalen Kongress für Pietismusforschung 2009*, ed. Christian Soboth (forthcoming).
53. Regarding monarchs' freedom in marrying, see Michael Sikora's contribution to this volume. For the marriages of Frederick William's children, see Marschke, "The Crown Prince's Brothers and Sisters."
54. Regarding the relationship between Frederick William and his crown prince—and the rest of the court's interest in currying favor with both—see Marschke, "The Crown Prince's Brothers and Sisters."
55. Detlef Merten, *Der Katte-Prozeß. Vortrag gehalten vor der Berliner Juristischen Gesellschaft am 14. Febrary 1979* (Berlin/New York, 1980), 37.
56. Merten, *Der Katte-Prozeß*, 36.
57. See Merten, *Der Katte-Prozeß*; Gerhard Simon, "Der Prozeß gegen den Thronfolger in Rußland (1718) and in Preußen (1730): Carevic Aleksej and Kronprinz Friedrich," in *Jahrbücher für Geschichte Osteuropas* 36:2 (1988): 218–247; Carl Hinrichs, *Der Kronprinzen Prozeß: Friedrich und Katte* (Hamburg, 1936), 5–20; reprinted as "Friedrich Wilhelm I. und Kronprinz Friedrich," in Hinrichs, *Preussen als historisches Problem: Gesammelte Abandlungen* (*Veröffentlichungen der historischen Kommission zu Berlin*, 10), 185–202; and Peter Baumgart, "Kronprinzenopposition: Friedrich und Friedrich Wilhelm I.," in *Friedrich der Große in seiner Zeit* (*Neue Forschungen zur Brandenburgisch-Preussischen Geschichte*, 8), ed. Oswald Hauser (Cologne, 1987), 1–16, here 2; reprint of Peter Baumgart, "Kronprinzenopposition: Zum Verhältnis Friedrichs zu seiner Vater Friedrich Wilhelm I.," in *Friedrich der Große, Franken und das Reich*, ed. Heinz Duchhardt (Cologne and Vienna, 1986), 5–23; reprint of Peter Baumgart, "Die Welt des Kronprinzen Friedrich und sein Konflikt mit dem Vater," in *Friedrich der Große. Herrscher zwischen Tradition und Fortschritt*, ed. Erhard Bethke (Gütersloh, 1985), 46–58.
58. This was not a public explanation—Frederick William wrote a memorandum to the court martial. Merten, *Der Katte-Prozeß*, 41.
59. Merten accepts this statement at face value, and concludes that Frederick William was dismissive of public opinion. Merten, *Der Katte-Prozeß*, 42. Perhaps it is significant that there seems to have been virtually nothing published at the time regarding crown prince Frederick's flight, arrest, and imprisonment. This incident seems to have been kept out of the public eye (or at least out of the print media) throughout the eighteenth century. In contrast, after the flight, arrest, imprisonment, torture, and killing of the Russian crown prince in 1718, there was a significant effort to "inform the public" and explain Peter I's actions and his son's misdeeds through the print media. See for example, "Manifest, Oder Umständliche Nachricht Von der in Moscau Den 3,14. Februar. 1718 geschehenen *Renunciation* und *Degradirung* Ihrer Hoheit Des *Czarowitzen* Alexii Petrowitz, Und Ihro Hoheit dem Jüngeren *Czarowitzen* Peter Petrowitzen, inwiedrum conferirten *Succession* Auf die *Monarchie* Von Groß-Rußland. Samt Der Endes-Leistung, Welche die Stände deßfals ablegen müssen" (1718); and "Manifest Wegen der Gerichtlichen *Inquisition* und Urtheils, so auf hohe *Ordre* Sr.

Zarischen Majestät Uber den Zarewitsch Alexium Petrowitsch Zu St. Petersburg gehalten, auch daselbst dem Publico zur Nachricht in Druck herausgegeben worden, den 25ten Junii st. v. 1718. Nach den Rußischen *Original* übersetzet" (Frankfurt a.M. and Leipzig [Berlin], 1719).

60. See, for example, the contributions of Tim Neu, Elisabeth Harding, and David M. Luebke in this volume.

61. Ironically, the insistence of Elector Frederick William (1640–1688) and Elector/King Frederick III/I (1688–1713) on being treated correctly regarding protocol, precedence, and ceremony often seems to have precluded them from directly interacting with other rulers, or even their representatives. See Barbara Stollberg-Rilinger, "Höfische Öffentlichkeit: Zur zeremoniellen Selbstdarstellung des brandenburgischen Hofes vor dem europäischen Publikum," in *Forschungen zur Brandenburgischen und Preußischen Geschichte, Neue Folge*, 7:2 (1997): 145–176. By contrast, Frederick William's ignorance or rejection of protocol, precedence, and ceremony actually made meeting other rulers possible. See Marschke, "Von dem am Königl. Preußischen Hofe abgeschafften *Ceremoniel*," 239–241.

62. The press casually reported that Frederick William visited The Hague in 1714 and Amsterdam and The Hague in 1720, both times traveling incognito. During both journeys, the king met with dignitaries and diplomats. *Europäische Fama* 160 (1714): 335; *Europäische Fama* 235 (1720): 646–647.

63. For example, it was newsworthy that in 1716, Peter I of Russia arrived in Königsberg unannounced, and that he refused to meet with anyone. *Europäische Fama* 183 (1716): 246. Again, it seems that much of Frederick William's disdain for contemporary norms was inspired by that of Peter.

64. For example, during his visit to The Hague in 1714, Frederick William made a day trip to Rotterdam *"ohne allen Gefolg"* ("without any entourage"). *Europäische Fama* 160 (1714): 335. When he visited the estates of Prince Leopold von Anhalt-Dessau ("Der alte Dessauer," 1676–1747) in 1728, the king traveled with only the crown prince and five military officers. *Europäische Fama* 315 (1728): 308. When he visited von Seckendorff's estates, Frederick William arrived with only the crown prince and *"einem kleinen Gefolg"* ("a small entourage"). Von Seckendorff, *Lebensbeschreibung des Feldmarschalls Grafen von Seckendorf*, 3: 232.
Even when making state visits, Frederick William's entourage was remarkably small. When he visited Dresden in 1728, his entire entourage was *"bey nahe auf 100 Personen"* ("nearly 100 persons"). *Das fröliche Dretzden, als daselbst zu Ehren Sr. Königl. Majestät in Preußen 2c.2c. und Dero Kron-Printzen Königl. Hoheit, bey Dero selben hohen Anwesenheit täglich Lustbarkeiten angestellet und vergnüglich vollbracht worden. Mit allen merckwürdigen Umständen ausführlich beschrieben* (Dresden, 1728), 6.
By contrast, when August II made a reciprocal visit to Berlin the following year, his entourage included 316 people, and a listing of it took six pages in the commemorative literature. *Das frolockende Berlin, Oder Historische Nachricht Dererjenigen öffentlichen Freudens-Bezeigungen und sinnreichen Illuminationen, Die bey hoher Anwesenheit Jhro Königl. Majestät in Pohlen, Und Dero Königl. Printzens Hoheit Daselbst angestellet worden, nebst einem Anhange aller auf diese fröhliche Begebenheit verfertigter Gedichte.* (Berlin, 1728), 12–18.
When Frederick William returned to Dresden again the following year, however, it was *"mit einer noch kleinern Suite als zuvor"* ("with an even smaller entourage than before"). Faßmann, *Das Glorwürdigste Leben*, 915. Even when meeting the emperor

in 1732, Frederick William was accompanied by a *"kleine Suite"* of only ten people, plus twenty pages and servants. *Wahrhafte Nachricht, von demjenigen, Was sich bey Ihro Königlichen Majestät in Preussen im Monat Julio und Augusto nach Böhmen unternommenen Reise Und daselbst mit beyderseits Kayserlichen Majest. Majestäten gehabten Zusammenkunfft zugetragen* (1732), 3–4.

65. This, again, was incognito in the sense of "without ceremony," not "anonymous"—Frederick William stayed with the Prussian resident envoy in Hamburg and used the pseudonym "Captain von Wusterhausen," (the small palace at Wusterhausen had been Frederick William's chief residence as crown prince and remained his summer retreat throughout his reign). *Europäische Fama* 243 (1721): 258.

66. "Der Rath schickte sodann Deputirten an Ihre Majestät, Sie wolten aber weder dieselben noch die geringsten Ehren-Bezeigungen annehmen" ("The council then sent deputies to His Majesty, but he wanted to accept neither them nor the least signs of honor"). *Europäische Fama* 243 (1721): 258.

67. *Europäische Fama* 243 (1721): 258.

68. Frederick William apparently announced his desire to visit Dresden with his New Year's greeting. He arrived in Dresden on 14 January 1728. *Das fröliche Dretzden*, 1.

69. Mourning was suspended for the duration of Frederick William's visit. *Das fröliche Dretzden*, 2.

70. *Das fröliche Dretzden*, 2.

71. This eight-page manuscript seems to be the travel journal of Privy Councilor Heinrich Rüdiger von Ilgen (1654–1728), one of Frederick William's favorites since before he took the throne. GStA-PK, BPH, Rep. 46, C 2, "Journal über den Besuch des Königs Friedrich Wilhelm I am Königlich Polnische Hofe zu Dresden (Mitte Januar–Mitte Februar 1728)."

72. For example, the commemorative literature notes that Frederick William rode with August II in a carriage drawn by only two horses: *"in einem nur mit 2 Pferden bespannten Wagen"* ("in a carriage pulled by only two horses"). *Das fröliche Dretzden*, 2. As royalty, they should have been in a carriage drawn by at least six horses.

73. *Das fröliche Dretzden*, 4.

74. *Das fröliche Dretzden*, 7.

75. *Das fröliche Dretzden*, 7–11.

76. GStA-PK, BPH, Rep. 46, C 2, "Besuch des Königs Friedrich Wilhelm I am Königlich Polnische Hofe zu Dresden."

77. GStA-PK, BPH, Rep. 46, C 2, "Besuch des Königs Friedrich Wilhelm I am Königlich Polnische Hofe zu Dresden."

78. "Diesem streitbaren Monarchen." *Das fröliche Dretzden*, 2.

79. *Wahrhafte Nachricht*, 4.

80. *Wahrhafte Nachricht*, 5–6.

81. *Wahrhafte Nachricht*, 6.

82. It was reported that in his first day of traveling in the Habsburg lands, Frederick William drilled all three of the units of troops that he encountered. Even before lunch on the second day, the Prussian king had been received by two more units of Habsburg soldiers, *"welche, wie allezeit, Ihro Majestät besahen und vor sich defiliren liessen"* ("which, like always, His Majesty viewed and had defile before him"). The same day, the plans to eat lunch in the open were cancelled due to rain (they moved to a nearby barn), but two companies of Habsburg troops were paraded before Frederick William regardless of the weather. *Wahrhafte Nachricht*, 6. On the way back from his rendevous with

the emperor to Prague (see below), it was noted that Frederick William was delayed because he stopped to drill the Habsburg troops he passed by. *Wahrhafte Nachricht*, 11. Even as he (finally) departed from Prague (see below), he only left once he viewed the detachment of troops who had been mustered for his departure, "Ihro Majestät stiegen aus dem Wagen, besahen die Trouppen und liessen solche vor sich defiliren." *Wahrhafte Nachricht*, 15.

83. *Wahrhafte Nachricht*, 7–8.
84. *Wahrhafte Nachricht*, 8.
85. *Wahrhafte Nachricht*, 8.
86. *Wahrhafte Nachricht*, 9–10.
87. "Unter einem ausdrücklich bedingenen incognito, folglich sonder Lösung der Canonen" ("under an expressly conditional incognito, following a special firing of the cannon"). *Wahrhafte Nachricht*, 9–10.
88. "Ihro Königliche Majestät war zwar allhier, und aller Orten, wo Sie in Praag gespeiset, ein grosser Lehn-Stuhl obenangesetzet" ("For His Royal Majesty here, and at all locations, where he dined in Prague, a large wing chair was set at the head"). *Wahrhafte Nachricht*, 12.
89. The above quote continues immediately: "Sie haben sich aber dessen niemahls bedienet, sondern einen Platz nach Gefallen erwählet, und ein vor allemahl des Printzen Eugenii Durchl. zum Nachbar sich ausgebethen" ("He never made use of this one, but instead chose a seat where he pleased, and once and for all asked to have His Highness Prince Eugene next to him"). *Wahrhafte Nachricht*, 12.
90. *Wahrhafte Nachricht*, 13.
91. "Der König, nachdem Er von Ihro Kayserl. Majestät Ankunfft verständidet [sic], kahme Ihro Majestät durch zwey Vorgemächer entgegen" ("The king, after he understood that His Imperial Majesty had arrived, came through two antechambers to meet His Majesty"). *Wahrhafte Nachricht*, 14.
92. "Die Beurlaubung geschahe mit hertzlicher Umarmung; des Königs Majestät begleiteten Ihro Kayserl. Majestät bis an die Treppen, allwo Ihro Kayserl. Majestät ganz ernstlich des Königs Majestät ersuchten, sich nicht weiter zu bemühen; allein, Ihro Königl. Majestät liessen sich nicht abhalten, Ihro Kayserl. Majestät die Treppe herab bis an die Kutsche zu führen und nicht ehender wieder davon zu weichen, bis Ihro Kayserliche Majestät würcklich abgefahrten waren" ("The farewell happened with a hearty embrace; His Majesty the King accompanied His Imperial Majesty as far as the steps, where His Imperial Majesty completely seriously implored His Majesty the King not to trouble himself further; however, His Royal Majesty did not allow himself to be held back from leading his Imperial Majesty down the steps to his coach, and did not let go again until His Royal Majesty had really driven away"). *Wahrhafte Nachricht*, 14.
93. Staatsarchiv (StA) Wolfenbüttel, 6 Hs 5 (Abt. VI, Gr. 5), #12 "G.S.A. v. Prauns Journal über die Ereignisse am Blanckenburgischen, bezw. Wolfenbüttler Hofe vom Jahr 1727 bis Aug. 1742." Georg Septimius Andreas von Praun (1701–1786) was a *Hof-Rath* in Wolfenbüttel at the time.
94. StA Wolfenbüttel, "v. Prauns Journal," 7 Feb. 1733, 148.
95. StA Wolfenbüttel, "v. Prauns Journal," 9 Feb. 1733, 150. Regarding table ceremony, see Barbara Stollberg-Rilinger, "Ordnungsleistung und Konfliktträchtigkeit der höfische Tafel," in *Zeichen und Raum. Ausstattung höfisches Zeremoniell in den deutschen*

Schlössern der Frühen Neuzeit, eds. Peter-Michael Hahn and Ulrich Schütte (Munich, 2006), 103–122; Uta Löwenstein, "Voraussetzungen und Grundlagen von Tafelzeremoniell und Zeremonientafel," in *Zeremoniell als höfische Ästhetik in Spätmittelalter und Früher Neuzeit*, eds. Jörg Jochen Berns and Thomas Rahn (Tübingen, 1995), 266–279; Ilsebill Barta-Fliedl, Andreas Gugler, and Peter Parenzan, eds., *Tafeln bei Hofe. Zur Geschichte der fürstlichen Tafelkultur. Sammlungsband 4.* (Hamburg, 1998); and Hans Ottomeyer and Michaela Völkel, eds., *Die öffentliche Tafel: Tafelzeremoniell in Europa 1300–1900* (Wolfratshausen, 2002).

96. StA Wolfenbüttel, "v. Prauns Journal," 9 Feb. 1733, 150–151.
97. StA Wolfenbüttel, "v. Prauns Journal," 9 Feb. 1733, 150–151.
98. StA Wolfenbüttel, "v. Prauns Journal," 10 June 1733, 162.
99. StA Wolfenbüttel, "v. Prauns Journal," 9 Feb. 1733, 151.
100. StA Wolfenbüttel, "v. Prauns Journal," 12 June 1733, 163.
101. The word seems to have been used literally in the eighteenth century, and seems to have been without the connotation of "strange" that it has in contemporary German.
102. Ronald G. Asch pointed this out in his comment on an earlier version of this paper at the German Studies Association. Regarding the possibility of outside intervention in the principalities of the empire, see especially Werner Troßbach's contribution to this volume.
103. On the excesses related to recruiting tall soldiers: "Des Königs Glück war es, daß ihn die protestantischen Fürsten für einen der standhaftesten Vertheidiger ihrer Religion ansahen, und daß die katholischen ihn fürchteten: sonst wären zuverläßig ernstlichere und allgemeinere Maasregeln gegen den immer mehr überhand nehmenden Unfug ergriffen worden" ("It was the king's good fortune that the Protestant princes viewed him as one of the most steadfast defenders of their religion and that the Catholics feared him: otherwise there would surely have been more serious and widespread measures taken against the ever more out-of-hand mischief"). Von Seckendorff, *Lebensbeschreibung des Feldmarschalls Grafen von Seckendorf*, 3: 180.

SECTION 2

Symbolic Meaning, Identity, & Memory

CHAPTER 4

The Illuminated *Reich*
Memory, Crisis, and the Visibility of Monarchy in Late Medieval Germany

LEN SCALES

Writing toward the close of the thirteenth century, the German polemicist Alexander von Roes returned a dismal judgment on his times. In the half century between Frederick II's imperial coronation and the Council of Lyon in 1274, the "Roman Empire" had so declined as to pass almost out of remembrance. In fact, it had reached a point from which it could "not decrease any further without being completely destroyed."[1] The image of an empire stunted and diminished after its ostensible heyday in the high-medieval *Kaiserzeit* remains an all-too-familiar one, nourished in the nineteenth and early twentieth centuries by the nationalist longings and anxieties of a German historiography morbidly preoccupied with false turnings. Yet it is a difficult image to banish altogether, and perhaps we should not try. A chronicler writing during von Roes' calamitous half-century observed that King Richard of Cornwall (1257–1272) "came nowhere in the German lands except to the Rhine, and was in fact impotent in the empire."[2] Richard's reign may have marked a particular low point, yet the chronicler's words point toward a theme which might be inscribed above the entire late medieval history of the imperial monarchy: the problem of *presence*.

Across much of Latin Europe, the late Middle Ages were a time of expanding royal administration and revenues and of multiplying points of institutionalized contact between rulers and the ruled.[3] Not so in Germany, where the growth of imperial institutions was never better than fitful and sluggish, while revenues from the empire plummeted between the thirteenth and the fifteenth centuries.[4] Largely lacking the means to assert their will in their absence, late medieval kings and emperors continued to rely heavily upon itinerant rule, even as the means of supporting the *iter* declined and its scope contracted.[5] The regions of Germany that Peter Moraw has termed *königsfern*—"remote" from the monarch and his government—grew steadily.⁶

The ruler's presence among his people was also, however, a reflection of the style and vision of monarchy that he was able to set before them. In part, this too was a factor of resources. When Rupert of the Palatinate (1400–1410) came back impoverished into Germany from his disastrous Italian expedition (1402), he was hardly in a position to impress. Contemporary versifiers were duly scathing:

> Oh, oh, the traveling trickster's here.
> He's brought along an empty purse,
> That much is all too clear.⁷

But ideological, no less than material, resources mattered here. German kings, raised to the throne by the election of the princes, had little of the powerful dynastic charisma that their western neighbors, the kings of France, were by this time able to command. No one celebrated the special holiness of the blood that flowed in the veins of an Adolf of Nassau or a Wenceslas of Luxemburg. The unfortunate Rupert would not be curing anyone's scrofula. Also lacking, it would seem, was much of the infrastructure of monarchy that we encounter elsewhere. Even in death, kings and emperors in the late Middle Ages were increasingly remote. While some continued until the start of the fourteenth century to be interred beside their Salian and Staufer forebears in the great imperial mausoleum in Speyer, thereafter, royal remains were scattered among a plethora of mainly dynastic sites, from Pisa to Prague, Bavaria to Hungary.⁸ Not only, then, did Germany lack a Paris; it also lacked—and with time, increasingly so—a Saint-Denis, a site of concentrated imperial memory, where the sacred continuity of monarchy might find appropriately monumental expression.⁹

This chapter does not seek directly to challenge this well-established view of an imperial monarchy weakened both materially and in the public's perception during the two centuries that lie between the fall of the Staufer and the consolidation of the Habsburgs on the throne. It will, however, suggest that the presence in Germany of the late medieval empire and its rulers—their public visibility and hold upon the minds of contemporaries—had a more multi-faceted and paradoxical character than may at first appear. As we will see, the very problems besetting the empire had a part in placing it before people's eyes. But the imperial monarchy also had some potently visible resources of its own, to which modern scholarship has not always paid sufficient regard. To approach these, we might begin with the words of a Milanese envoy, writing home in 1461 from the empire's western edge:

> Having viewed a large number of edifices in this region, ... I send ... to Your Excellency the sketch of a town gate in these parts, derived from a design of Julius Caesar, who has left in these territories numerous glorious memorials to himself. I have [also] taken the trouble of having another gate reproduced, which he himself constructed in a town in lower Germany, which is called Julius Caesar.[10]

The town named from Caesar is probably Jülich, near Aachen. The association is traceable back to Widukind, writing in the tenth century, and, in repeating it, the writer was reflecting a perception well established among later medieval Germans: that the towns and cities of western and southern Germany were of ancient, illustrious, and imperial ancestry.[11] Chroniclers counted off, with variable etymological accuracy, the cities boasting an origin in acts of imperial power: Augsburg from Augustus, Cologne (Colonia Agrippinensis) supposedly from Agrippa, and so on. Mighty rulers had once laid hold upon the landscape in ways that, literate observers insisted, remained significant many centuries later. Some of the marks of their greatness had, inevitably, passed from sight: the bridge that Caesar built across the Rhine at Mainz had long since yielded to the elements, in punishment, it was said, for the people's sins.[12] Not all vestiges of ancient imperial glory had disappeared, however. Most striking in the words of the Milanese envoy (a skeptical, culturally literate Italian) is the conviction that verbal tradition was authenticated by the physical vestiges of a remote imperial past, which still marked the landscape in the second half of the fifteenth century.[13]

The legendary peregrinations of the Roman Empire's reputed founder had taken root in the soil itself, in local memories and memorials. The Strasbourg chronicler Jakob Twinger, writing around the end of the fourteenth century, told how, after subduing all of the German lands, Caesar had come to the temple at nearby Ebersheimmünster, given thanks for his victory, and renewed the image there: "And from that self-same temple was afterwards built the magnificent monastery of Ebersheimmünster."[14] Elsewhere, the symbolism of temporal dominance asserted a more direct continuity. An inscription to be seen in the fifteenth century on the castle at Nijmegen (well off the paths traveled by most late medieval emperors) claimed Caesar as its first builder.[15] Nor was it only in Jülich that names and objects combined to inscribe his originating presence. One tradition had him making his way through the *königsfern* north, and happening by moonlight upon the site of Lüneburg. In remembrance of the fact, he had set up a golden moon (*luna*) on a pillar, which was worshipped by the local inhabitants.[16] The story is preserved in the *Saxon World Chronicle*, from the thirteenth century, and found visual embodiment in the roughly contemporary world map from nearby Ebstorf, where Caesar's golden moon still stands above the town.[17]

The empire's first rulers, it was clear, had dominated the German lands as their late medieval successors could not. And where they had not been in fact, imagination bore them nonetheless, fixing their presence in legends, inscriptions, artifacts, and ancient sites. The medieval western empire was actually a comparatively young historical formation, with its roots in the fragmentation of the Carolingian patrimony in the ninth and tenth centuries; but in the understanding of its German partisans, it was uniquely ancient, heir to the Romans as well as the Franks—and to the putative forebears of both, the Trojans.[18] And beneath the deposits of these illustrious lost realms lay, in some traditions, the strata of yet more remote pasts upon which they had been built. The very complexity of the empire's long imagined history, and the diverse regional perspectives in which it enfolded, by the late Middle Ages had made of the German lands a dense palimpsest of imagined sites and landscapes of political memory. Reading such ramified and numinous visual texts was an uncertain and subjective matter: monuments nourished myths. Late Roman Trier remained, through its surviving works, massively present to the observer; yet the Trier which fired the imagination of Jakob Twinger was a more ancient one, "the first and oldest town in the German lands," the pre-Roman imperial capital of the Assyrian Trebata—and only much later to be taken, by stealth rather than arms, by Caesar.[19]

To expect to find the landscape densely marked by past monarchies was only natural. To Germans of even modest education or experience, it would have been evident that the forebears to whom their late medieval kings looked back were numerous as well as illustrious. The imperial idea underscored remarkable continuities. The fourteenth-century Dominican Heinrich von Herford could register without a blink that Count Adolf of Nassau (1292–1298) was the empire's hundredth ruler since Caesar.[20] Such protracted lineages might take on visible form: carved or cast, or painted on walls or in windows, the ruler cycle was a characteristically (though not exclusively) German genre. An array of some thirty carved kings and emperors was to be seen, for example, on the façade of Aachen's *Rathaus*, following its renovation in the 1370s.[21] The perpetuation of the local memory of past rulers was also, however, a consequence of the empire's historic *discontinuities*, which had left sites and monuments scattered far and wide in its German territories, reflecting the different regional power bases of successive ruling dynasties. The Conciliarist Dietrich von Niem knew of Charlemagne's reputed birth at Ingelheim "on the River Rhine" close to Mainz, where still stood in the fifteenth century, recently renovated, "the palace in which he was born."[22] Nor was it everywhere different in the *königsfern* north. Henry III's great palace at Goslar had, by the mid thirteenth century, largely passed out of the monarchy's orbit; but that did not end its importance as a symbol of the empire for the town's burghers, who jealously guarded their right to receive justice there.[23] The *iter* of the king-emperors might shift its geographical focus and contract altogether with the passing centuries; but the artifacts left strewn across the German lands at its receding often proved to have a more tenacious presence and remembrance.

Not everywhere, of course. The great Salian and Staufer residences had mostly passed out of use, and some out of existence, by the later Middle Ages. The palace at Paderborn, for example, was not rebuilt following its destruction by fire in the twelfth century.[24] Occasionally, iconoclasm was intentional. Images of Ludwig the Bavarian (1314–1347)—to his opponents a heresiarch and persecutor of the Church—were defaced and erased;[25] more was doubtless lost in this way than we can know. Yet, while oblivion is a part of the picture, the durability of these resonant locations and objects looms larger. The burghers of fourteenth-century Aachen, who incorporated the crumbling Carolingian palace into their town hall, were not blind to the traditions upon which they built—as the monumental figure of Charlemagne that guarded their new portal attested.[26] Even destruction might mean the dissemination, not obliteration, of memory. Demolition work at Magdeburg seems to have resulted in the dispersal of some of the antique marble columns that, with their imperial resonances, Otto the Great (936–973) had reportedly brought to his metropolis, among a number of religious foundations in north-central Germany.[27] The later Middle Ages, moreover, saw the renovation of some earlier memorials, and the establishment of new sites in honor of long-dead rulers.[28]

Historically, the empire's several pasts had done more than merely overshadow the land: they radiated an active legitimacy that did not depend upon the presence of a reigning monarch. One source of this lay in the cults of imperial and crypto-imperial saints. Late medieval kings may seldom have come to Bamberg, but Henry II (1002–1024) and Kunigunde, canonized in the twelfth century, were permanently in residence, their skulls preserved in the cathedral treasury, while their representations in stone were multiplied around them.[29] Nor were the Three Kings of Cologne going anywhere—though late medieval tradition dictated that the newly crowned *rex Romanorum* should solemnly come to *them*, thus also reaffirming the Magi as historic pillars of the empire.[30] Charlemagne, a saint by imperial decree (1165), was by tradition much more besides that—wise judge, lawgiver, holy warrior, the empire's very translator to the Germans—and as such was to be met with in effigy in diverse media and locations, from tapestry to town gate.[31] The historicizing urge was well established in the empire's visual culture from an early date. Charlemagne's Aachen was modeled on late antique Ravenna; high medieval Speyer borrowed from Roman Trier; and Aachen and Speyer were in their turn reproduced and cited in the imperial architecture that came after them.[32] The unparalleled urge among German builders and patrons to cling onto and invoke the vestiges of times past must be understood in light of the special prestige to which that past seemed to hold a key.[33] Never had visible prestige seemed as needful as in the centuries that began with the fall of the Staufer. Even Heinrich Raspe, Thuringian landgrave and fleeting papal anti-king (1246–1247), boasted a golden bull with an inscription trumpeting in traditional manner the boundless dominion of *Roma caput mundi*.[34] Charles the Great's palace chapel was reproduced afresh, now in the mature gothic style, under his namesake Charles IV (1346–1378).[35] In Caroline Prague, imperial *mimesis* found expression in a whole new cityscape, making reference at once to Rome, Constantinople, and the heavenly Jerusalem.[36] Charles himself proved to be a living, breathing palimpsest of monarchy, repeatedly reproducible in words and rituals, stone, paint and goldsmith's work, in the guise of Charlemagne, Constantine, and Vespasian—to say nothing of St. Wenceslas, Balthazar, David, and Melchizedek.[37]

While the empire's wealth of legitimizing memory certainly favored its visual invocation, it was cultural, social, and economic changes afoot in Germany that accelerated and elaborated the process, setting imperial imagery before the eyes of a much broader public. In the late Middle Ages, the empire and its rulers attained a significantly heightened visibility for reasons that often had little to do with their own actions or potentialities. Chief among these new currents was the elaboration in Germany of a dense gothic visual culture, which gave a novel priority to image making and made available its own complex repertoire of imperial signs and symbols. Monumental statues of crowned and mounted monarchs, in Bamberg (c. 1235–1237) and Magdeburg (c. 1240–1245), were the dramatic harbingers of a style that entered Germany late, but then spread swiftly in the troubled decades after 1250.[38] From galleries of kings (of the Old or the New Law) in the windows of great churches, to pictured genealogies, individual images of past and living rulers, carved friezes of the seven electors or public fountains adorned with the chivalric "Nine Worthies" (two of them emperors), the gothic impulse to externalize, elaborate, attest, and make manifest embraced the imperial monarchy as well, heedless of its evident disabilities.[39] Or rather, in some ways it did heed them, so that the empire's perceived weakness became a further spur to image making.

With the gothic style came a new stress upon seeing—and believing. Images were ascribed an active power to work, through the eye, upon the beholder.[40] By seeing, people were to know and to accept. Apertures and crystal phials were now cut and inserted into reliquaries to render their contents incontestably real. Christ's body itself was held up to general view at the mass and borne in procession before the faithful in monstrances.[41] In the realm of government, in much of Latin Europe the task of inducing acceptance of that which could not be experienced directly fell increasingly to written documents.[42] It was above all through their mandates, writs, and decrees that rulers were present among their people in their absence. In Germany, however, the late medieval monarchy manifested itself only intermittently and geographically very unevenly through words on parchment.[43] In these circumstances, images and artifacts offered their own kind of symbolic proximity. They satisfied in-some-ways comparable demands, for authentication amid complexity and contestation, and for tangible and talismanic endurance in the face of change and disintegration.

Explaining the availability in this period of new, more readily reproducible, images of the empire in more widely accessible locations also means, however, looking beyond the imperial monarchy and its German territories. It was as part of a pan-European process, the elaboration of a ubiquitous elite visual language of heraldry, that, from around the start of the thirteenth century, the black eagle on gold became firmly established as an instantly recognizable code for the empire and its ruler.[44] A complex, and in some respects ambiguous, symbol, the eagle was depicted in both double- and (much more commonly) single-headed forms. Only in the fifteenth century did a firmer distinction emerge, between the by-then haloed *Doppeladler*, for the emperor, and its simpler cousin, for a mere Aachen-crowned *rex Romanorum*.[45] The unchecked multiplication of forms in the preceding decades points, however, to an urgent impulse to render the imperial monarchy visible in ways that allowed varied facets of its existence and authority to be given expression. Some imperial towns placed the eagle in their seals, the first as early as c. 1180.[46] The new dynasties on the throne took it up, not only for the reigning monarch himself, but also in variant forms for his sons and wider kin. Coupled with dynastic devices, like the double-tailed Bohemian lion, eagles proliferated about their glittering residential cities. Illustrious emperors from the pre-heraldic past were posthumously granted double-eagle shields, while their late medieval descendants introduced the empire's heraldry in an increasingly deliberate and flexible way into the paraphernalia of their rule.[47]

Economic change in late medieval Germany further speeded the proliferation of signs and symbols of the empire. The rise of urban markets and urban crafts made for an environment in which images were readily commissioned and produced—and widely viewed. A document from Strasbourg records how, on a visit to the city, Charles IV had borrowed a tent decorated with heraldic roses, which "Konrad the painter" was charged to repaint with the emperor's arms.[48] With the urbanization of much of the empire's visual culture therefore went, over time, what might almost be termed its commodification. By the fifteenth century, the imperial armorial was being applied to a wide range of portable, personal, and manufactured objects: clothing, banners, hats, brooches, horse-trappers, saddles, belt-fasteners, and caskets, to name but a few.[49] The coins for purchasing such objects might likewise bear the imperial eagle, or (such was the great variety of Germany's late medieval coinages) some other, more indirect, imperial reference, such as the devices of the electors.[50] In the fifteenth century, new media and manufacturing processes facilitated further the dissemination of visual invocations of the empire and its rulers—on ceramic tiles, on tableware, in woodcuts, or even via that ubiquitous, portable, and intrinsically political medium, the playing card.[51]

How much attention contemporaries may have paid to their political iconography these objects themselves cannot disclose. Here, however, some general guidance can be drawn from a variety of written texts, which indicate that at least among literate (though not necessarily highly educated) Germans, the symbolism of the empire was from early on the object of keen-eyed, sometimes sharply ironic, comment. A vernacular political singer of the late thirteenth century, the "Schoolmaster of Eßlingen," glossed the imperial escutcheon—"an eagle rampant on gold"—as a visible reproach to the contemporary monarch, the Habsburg Rudolf I (1273–1291).[52] The eagle's "grim" black hue did not, he thought, suit its under-mighty bearer. A "woodpecker on a rotten tree" instead, the king inspired as much fear as an outstretched scarecrow in a barley field —an allusion, perhaps, to Rudolf's notoriously gaunt and lanky frame.[53] The towns increasingly functioned as venues for a political public capable of forming, and acting upon, a view of such matters. When Charles IV came to Passau in 1348, the house in which he stayed was adorned with *signa imperialia aquilarum*—which, however, were quickly smeared with filth by partisans of his Wittelsbach rivals, unwilling to recognize Charles as their rightful bearer.[54]

In Germany, the downfall of the Staufer, the troubled times that followed, *and* the reception of the gothic style had all coincided with an era of spectacular urban growth.[55] The towns now provided the audience for the kind of spectacle of late medieval monarchy that kings and emperors of the high-medieval *Kaiserzeit* had largely lacked. One chronicler believed that when the Habsburg Frederick the Fair handed over the imperial regalia to Ludwig the Bavarian at Nuremberg in 1324, "many thousands of people" assembled to view them.[56] The ruler's *adventus*, his public entrance into a town, became, in the late Middle Ages, a central element in imperial ceremonial and, particularly when a monarch came for the first time, was accompanied by spectacular symbolic display.[57] When Sigismund entered Bern in 1414, he was greeted in the suburbs by five hundred liveried boys, bearing flags and banners of the empire and town and wearing garlands adorned with imperial armorials made from paper.[58] Such scenes were designed to live on in the minds of those townspeople who lined the streets, and they were often recollected in some detail by town chroniclers.[59] That such interest was not always merely parochial is indicated by a report in the German vernacular of Charles IV's funeral in Prague (December 1378), which was incorporated into a chronicle in far-off Augsburg. The eyewitness account, which may have circulated as a newsletter, is remarkable for its identification of the numerous artifacts, banners, and armorials that were shown during the protracted solemnities.[60] It points to the fluency with which at least some in the towns were able to read the symbolism of the empire. Some Germans, indeed, were quite capable not only of interpreting, but also judging the constitutional spectacles enacted in their rulers' names. Heinrich von Herford observed of Charles IV that not only was he elected and crowned in constitutionally incorrect locations, but also that his Bonn coronation (1346) was conducted "as if in secret, without due pomp."[61] The crises afflicting the late medieval monarchy made appropriate forms of public visibility more, not less, necessary.

The constitutional and political peculiarities of the late medieval empire—its elective crown and polycentric character—lent their own encouragement to the proliferation of sites and symbols in its German territories. The monarchy's contracting public scope and power, for which these elements are often blamed, itself stimulated various forms of image making. Much has traditionally been made of the lack of an imperial capital. Yet, whatever may have been its wider contributions to the course of German history, it should not be assumed that this necessarily rendered the empire's rulers less visible than their counterparts in neighboring realms. Indeed, it is possible to argue an opposite case. In the famously centralized late medieval kingdom of England, for example, the visual culture of monarchy was disproportionately focused on (often quasi-private) locations around Westminster, where the kings spent much of their time.[62] This same centralization goes far to explain the heavy concentration of English royal imagery upon reflecting back to the monarchs themselves a glorious but introverted vision of divinely favored, dynastic kingship.[63] The constitutional acts of the empire's rulers in Germany, by contrast, were shared among a number of historically significant sites, mostly major towns, each enjoying some of a capital's representative qualities. Merely attaining the throne entailed a succession of public progresses and state occasions: election, normally in Frankfurt, followed by coronation, rightfully in Aachen, and then on, via the Magi's shrine at Cologne, to Nuremberg for the king's first great court.[64] Attaining these several destinations involved, whenever circumstances allowed, a stately and magnificent progress through some of the most populous, urbanized, and culturally advanced landscapes of German-speaking Europe. The solemn assemblies that the monarch held with the princes and other members of the empire, and which by the fifteenth century were also convening in his absence, were likewise shared among a plurality of locations.[65] In the late Middle Ages, these meetings were invariably held north of the Alps—most commonly, but by no means invariably, in those southern and western German regions where imperial properties survived longest and that stood, in Moraw's typology, "close" to the king. They attracted considerable contemporary notice.[66]

If the era of dynastic *Hausmacht* in the fourteenth and fifteenth centuries meant the periodic withdrawal of the ruler from some of these established landscapes of monarchy, it also nurtured new sites of imperial iconography and display: Prague, Munich, Vienna, Wiener Neustadt, Heidelberg, to say nothing of other, lesser, and related sites.[67] In some of these centers, pre-eminently

Prague, the symbolism of the empire, now interwoven with that of the ruling house, gained visual articulation of quite unprecedented scope and magnificence. Once again, such locations, and their visible traces in the landscape, tended naturally to multiply over time. As one symptom of this harnessing of the empire to the cause of dynastic glory, the imperial regalia, which for much of the high Middle Ages had been locked away in strongholds in the German countryside, were given a new visibility in the *Hausmacht* capitals. Ludwig the Bavarian was the first to furnish them with an urban home, in Munich.[68] Under the Luxemburger, their public display became an annual event, first in Prague and later in the imperial town of Nuremberg, where they were thereafter destined to remain.[69] Fortified by papal indulgences, boasting their own feast day, they drew substantial crowds.

Beneath the impulse of the new ruling dynasties—Habsburg, Luxemburg, Wittelsbach—visibly to draw down upon themselves the empire's prestige, lay another, more pressing one, bound up with the elective character of the crown: to establish their right to wear that crown at all. Between the thirteenth and fifteenth centuries, split elections, anti-kingships, and the deposition of reigning monarchs repeatedly placed in doubt the identity of the empire's rightful head.[70] It is no coincidence that the regalia, with their sacred relics, were first put on show by Frederick of Habsburg, in 1315 in Basel, as part of his efforts to lend legitimacy to his contested kingship.[71] The profusion, and confusion, of physical manifestations of monarchy in post-Staufer Germany found startling expression in the periodic counterfeiting of the ruler's own person. The late thirteenth century saw the appearance of a succession of obscure figures claiming to be the by-then thoroughly mythologized emperor Frederick II (d. 1250).[72] One such self-made monarch was able to "rule" in considerable style for several months in the mid 1280s, holding court at Neuß by the Rhine and at Wetzlar, and even issuing documents authenticated with a seal apparently based on Frederick's own.[73]

It is against this backdrop of contending personifications of the empire, and the consequent difficulty of taking even the monarch himself at face value, that we should probably understand the growing emphasis that came to be placed upon the ruler's own physiognomy as an authenticating code. The portrayal of living kings and emperors became more common and attained an increased variety in forms and locations.[74] Of Charles IV, who was in this respect exceptional, over seventy different depictions are known.[75] While many of these were to be found in and around Prague, others were set up in more remote locations—occasionally, in an apparently deliberate attempt by the emperor to propagate his presence in effigy in his lands.[76] They also, however, propagated increasingly stable and characteristic representations of his appearance. Charles' big eyes and high forehead and cheekbones became familiar, readily reproducible motifs, whether on his great seal or in crypto-portraits within devotional images. His son Sigismund developed a similarly recognizable profile, marked by abundant hair and a long, often two-pronged beard and topped with a hooped crown or fur hat.[77] A visual language distinct to each ruler therefore evolved, at once personalized and stereotypical. That there existed in some quarters a lively interest in the monarch's physiognomy is attested by repeated reference in written sources.[78] It was probably the aim of those close to the Luxemburg emperors (and thereafter their Habsburg successors) to satisfy or stimulate such interest by propagating their caricatured likeness, and thereby to identify them more firmly with the imperial title. No less remarkable, however, are the widespread and varied ways in which the communicative resources at their disposal enabled them to achieve this.

The territories of late medieval Germany, particularly the towns, were home to a riotous proliferation of diverse signs and symbols of power, within which that minority that invoked the empire had to compete for attention. Yet representations of the empire were also in some respects in contention with one another. Images that portrayed or made allusion to the seven electors struck a note quite different from, and potentially in conflict with, those linking the empire with its ruling dynasties. Even among the electors themselves there was competition, which might be given enduring and visible form. It was in this way that the cathedral church at Mainz came, in the late Middle Ages, to be thronged with monumental representations not only of the archbishop-electors themselves, but also of the kings whom they claimed, with varying accuracy, to have crowned.[79] One purpose of these effigies was clearly to keep alive Mainz's fading claim to a right of coronation. (Significantly, Cologne, which had the stronger title, took no comparable steps to commemorate it visually.) Late medieval contests for the throne, which divided the electors against one another, meanwhile added further sites of king-making: Bonn, Cologne, and Rhens, with its open-air throne beside the Rhine by Koblenz.[80]

For some late medieval commentators, the electors were the true repository of the Roman Empire's historic translation to the German people. The exclusive college of seven princes that emerged over the course of the thirteenth century quickly attained a central place in the political theology and constitutional life of the empire, as reaffirmed and defined in detail in the Golden Bull of 1356.[81] Already during the thirteenth century, this new centrality was receiving visible expression in public artifacts.[82] In the decades that followed, monumental depictions of the electors or their devices—often, though not invariably, accompanied by the empire's ruler or armorial—were set up on the façades of town halls and other civic buildings, and on urban fountains, mainly but not only in towns directly under the empire.[83] The extent to which they came, along with the ruler, to symbolize imperial authority as such is illustrated in the foundation of a chapel in Sluis to commemorate sixty Germans killed in 1436 in fighting in the town. The chapel, in coastal Flanders, remote from the empire's German heartlands, was nevertheless to have windows showing not only the imperial armorial, but also those of the electors.[84] The electors visibly partook of a more abstract form of that sacrality that elsewhere in Europe was vested in holy dynasties and wonder-working kings. On the fourteenth-century bronze door-pull from Lübeck's *Rathaus*, they surround a figure of the emperor in a manner that deliberately recalls Christ with his apostles or prophets.[85]

Yet the mere fact of visual representation did not secure hegemonic acceptance for the electors' view of the empire's order, any more than for the pretensions of the would-be imperial dynasts such as the Luxemburger. By the fifteenth century, other, more broadly inclusive figurations of the empire were coming to the fore, reflecting social and political changes afoot in Germany and challenging the electors' privileged symbolic isolation. The complex heraldic assemblage known as the *Quaternionen*, representing the empire as the sum of its various estates, received its earliest known depiction in Sigismund's reign.[86] The location is significant: the great chamber of the "Römer," Frankfurt-am-Main's new *Rathaus*—a space within which, in the imperial towns, the doctrines of the empire and perspectives of the burgher communities under its rule characteristically met and merged.

In the imperial towns, the king-emperor was summoned in effigy to the defense of his loyal burghers. In the great chamber of Nuremberg's newly rebuilt town hall was set up (c. 1340) a monumental stone relief of Ludwig the Bavarian. Seated on an eagle throne and flanked by angels, the powerfully majestic figure of the emperor appears to have been paired with a representation of Nuremberg's imperial privileges.[87] A comparable cycle of figures was established around the same time in Cologne—not yet an imperial city, but one that looked to the empire to guarantee its extensive autonomies against its lords, the archbishops. There, in the stately *Hansasaal* in the town hall, carvings show a crowned ruler holding a sealed charter, accompanied by figures bearing a water jug and a city gate: personifications of the Rhine staple and right of fortification, grants upon which Cologne's prosperity and independence particularly rested.[88] If the emperor's proxies in wood and stone were called on to guarantee the status of rich and powerful communities, they might also, however, come to the aid of more remote and imperiled ones. Such was the situation of the imperial town of Mühlhausen in Thuringia, where larger-than-life figures of Charles IV and his consort still incline their heads to the spectator from above the south portal of the *Marienkirche*.[89] Where the ruler and his court seldom or never came, image making might ensure an enduring, prophylactic presence. The empire's symbolic protection had especially striking, if abstract, invocation in those towns in the *königsfern* north, which set up or renovated monumental statues of the paladin Roland, the strong right arm of that pre-eminent safeguard of imperial rights and justice, Charles the Great.[90]

The functioning of such artifacts within the political culture of the towns was often unstable, reflecting the ambivalent and shifting nature of their relations both with the empire and with other masters. Just as some Roland statues came to be infused with new meaning in the late Middle Ages, as champions of burgher autonomy, so other images also were reinterpreted. The mounted emperor in the market place at Magdeburg, which at first had probably represented the archbishops' lordship over the town, was subsequently made into the townspeople's ally against him.[91] How far the urban iconography of the empire was intended to exalt its ruler, and how far to constrain him, was not in every case clear. The gate through which Charles IV entered Dortmund in 1377 bore an inscription warning against selling the remote imperial town for gold.[92] It was in the nature both of the late medieval empire and of the towns' place within it that its portrayal tended both to trumpet the empire's special prestige *and* tacitly confess its weakness, to affirm the allegiance of its burghers *and* symbolically declare their independence.

The empire was visibly present among the populations of late medieval Germany in a range of ways and to a surprising degree. This was partly in spite of the limited and faltering scope of its material power, and partly as a consequence of it. The direct role of the empire's rulers in its propagation was on the whole rather small. What is sometimes seen as an age of burgeoning royal image making—indeed, "propaganda"—in western Europe as a whole was scarcely that in Germany. Kings and emperors made only intermittent, often half-hearted, attempts at crafting their own visual representation and that of the empire.[93] Charles IV went the farthest, but even his achievements were mostly confined to a handful of regions and locations. Many more memorials to the empire and its rulers were established by other political actors, such as urban elites, the electors and other princes. Entire genres of image came into being largely as a consequence of processes of social, economic, and cultural change, which provided venues, means, and motivations for their making. Many sites and artifacts already existed by the thirteenth century; but their persistence, reinterpretation, and, in certain instances, renovation reflected the imperializing eye with which some Germans in the late Middle Ages read their native landscapes.

The remarkable extent to which vestiges of the empire were in this period perceived on the ground, renewed, and put in place reflects in part the prestige of an institution that commanded for its partisans unequalled status, antiquity, and legitimizing potential. But it reflects also the need felt by Germans in the late Middle Ages to conjure up the talismanic benefits of that prestige—which, in its turn, directs attention toward the imperial monarchy's limitations. Image making, one might say, was called upon to fill the gap that yawned between authority and material power, aspiration and daily experience. In the late Middle Ages, the gothic style became a language of visible proof for an age of anxieties and growing doubts—of which there were many surrounding the *Reich* and its rulers. This was, in Germany, an age of multiple and conflicting perspectives and messages, of disputed claims, uncertain titles, impostors, and, as some maintained, "traveling tricksters" in imperial guise. Such circumstances naturally encouraged a proliferation of images. The gothic style had originated in western Europe as an urban form, and it made its late entry into Germany in the great age of urban growth, beginning in the thirteenth century. Henceforth, the towns were to be nodal points of representation, and the venues for the contest of images and symbols. They also supplied an audience, and textual sources provide evidence that the signs were indeed noticed and read—although how widely and reflectively is mostly much harder to assess. Nevertheless, it is the number and diversity of those with a stake in the image making process, along with the comparative absence of direction from above, which commands attention. Illuminating the late medieval empire was to a large extent the work of the populations that stood under its rule.

Notes

1. Alexander von Roes, *Noticia seculi*, cap. 8, in *Alexander von Roes: Schriften*, eds. Herbert Grundmann and Hermann Heimpel (*Monumenta Germaniae Historica* [henceforth *MGH*] Staatsschriften des späteren Mittelalters, 1.i, Stuttgart, 1958), 154.
2. Ludwig Weiland, ed., *Sächsische Weltchronik: Sächsische Fortsetzung* (*MGH Deutsche Chroniken* [henceforth *MGH DC*] 2, Hannover, 1877), 284.
3. For an overview see Bernard Guenée, *States and Rulers in Later Medieval Europe*, trans. J. Vale (Oxford, 1985).
4. Karl-Friedrich Krieger, *König, Reich und Reichsreform im Spätmittelalter* (Munich, 1992). For estimated revenues, see 34.
5. See, generally, Peter Moraw, "Die Reichsregierung reist: Die deutschen Kaiser von den Ottonen bis zu den Staufern ohne festen Regierungssitz," in *Die Hauptstädte der Deutschen: Von der Kaiserpfalz in Aachen zum Regierungssitz Berlin*, ed. Uwe Schultz (Munich, 1993), 22–32, here 24, 32.
6. For his influential scheme for classifying the regions of late medieval Germany in terms of their relationship with the monarchy, see Peter Moraw, *Von offener Verfassung zu gestalteter Verdichtung: Das Reich im späten Mittelalter* (Berlin, 1985), 175.
7. "O o der goeckelman ist kumen / hat ein lere taschen praht, / das hab wir wol vernumen." Quoted in Ernst Schubert, "Probleme der Königsherrschaft im spätmittelalterlichen Reich: Das Beispiel Ruprechts von der Pfalz (1400–10)," in *Das spätmittelalterliche Königtum im europäischen Vergleich*, ed. Reinhard Schneider (Sigmaringen, 1987), 178.
8. See generally: Rudolf J. Meyer, *Königs- und Kaiserbegräbnisse im Spätmittelalter: Von Rudolf von Habsburg bis zu Friedrich III.* (Cologne, Weimer, and Vienna, 2000); Olaf B. Rader, "Erinnern für die Ewigkeit: Die Grablegen der Herrscher des Heiligen Römischen Reiches," in Matthias Puhle and Claus-Peter Hasse, eds., *Heiliges Römisches Reich Deutscher Nation 962 bis 1806: Von Otto dem Großen bis zum Ausgang des Mittelalters: Essays* (Dresden, 2006), 173–184.

9. For the image of kingship in France see, J.R. Strayer, "France: the Holy Land, the Chosen People, and the Most Christian King," in *Action and Conviction in Early Modern Europe: Essays in Memory of E.H. Harbison*, eds. Theodore K. Rabb and Jerold E. Seigel (Princeton, NJ, 1969), 3–16; and Colette Beaune, *The Birth of an Ideology: Myths and Symbols of Nation in Late-Medieval France*, trans. S.R. Huston and ed. Frederic L. Cheyette (Berkeley, CA, 1991).
10. Paul M. Kendall and Vincent Ilardi, ed., *Dispatches with Related Documents of Milanese Ambassadors in France and Burgundy, 1450–1483*, 3 vols. (Athens, OH, 1970–1981), II: 118 (2 March 1461).
11. See František Graus, *Lebendige Vergangenheit: Überlieferung im Mittelalter und in den Vorstellungen vom Mittelalter* (Cologne and Vienna, 1975), especially 222; and more generally H. Wesemann, *Die Cäsarfabeln des Mittelalters* (Löwenberg, 1879). The legendary foundation of Jülich by Caesar was repeated in the fifteenth century by the publicist Gobelinus Persona: see Frank L. Borchardt, *German Antiquity in Renaissance Myth* (Baltimore, 1971), 32.
12. For the bridge (and a long list of Caesar's alleged town foundations), see Edward Schröder, ed., *Kaiserchronik eines Regensburger Geistlichen* (*MGH DC* 1, Berlin, 1892), 87.
13. For the anchoring of memory in locality and landscape in the Middle Ages, see, generally, Patrick J. Geary, *Phantoms of Remembrance: Memory and Oblivion at the end of the First Millennium* (Princeton NJ, 1994), especially 124.
14. C. Hegel, ed., *Chronik des Jacob Twinger von Königshofen* (*Chroniken der deutschen Städte* [henceforth *CdS*] 9, Leipzig, 1870), 702.
15. Gerard Nijsten, *In the Shadow of Burgundy: The Court of Guelders in the Late Middle Ages*, trans. T. Guest (Cambridge, 2004), 324.
16. *Sächsische Weltchronik*, 86.
17. Illustrated in P.D.A. Harvey, *Medieval Maps* (London, 1991), 30.
18. Graus, *Lebendige Vergangenheit*, ch. 3.
19. *Twinger*, 700.
20. Augustus Potthast, ed., *Liber de rebus memorabilioribus sive Chronicon Henrici de Hervordia* (Göttingen, 1859), 213.
21. Ernst Günther Grimme, "Das gotische Rathaus der Stadt Aachen," in *Krönungen: Könige in Aachen—Geschichte und Mythos*, ed. Mario Kramp, 2 vols. (Mainz, 1999), II: 509–515, here 512.
22. Dietrich von Nieheim, *Viridarium Imperatorum et Regum Romanorum*, ed. Alphons Lhotsky and Karl Pivec (*MGH Staatsschriften des späteren Mittelalters* 5, Stuttgart, 1956), 1–2.
23. Bernd Schneidmüller, "Reichsnähe—Königsferne: Goslar, Braunschweig und das Reich im späten Mittelalter," in *Niedersächsisches Jahrbuch für Landesgeschichte* 64 (1992): 1–52, here 12.
24. Ulrich Großmann, "Burgen und Pfalzen des Reiches," in Puhle and Hasse, *Heiliges Römisches Reich: Essays*, 223–235, here 232–233.
25. For examples see Mattias Puhle and Claus-Peter Hasse, eds., *Heiliges Römisches Reich Deutscher Nation 962 bis 1806: Von Otto dem Großen bis zum Ausgang des Mittelalters: Katalog* (Dresden, 2006), nos. V.6, V.10, 375–376, 379–380.
26. Grimme, "Rathaus," in Kramp, *Krönungen*, II: 512.
27. Puhle and Hasse, *Heiliges Römisches Reich: Katalog*, no. II.10, 56–57.

28. Gabriele Köster, "Zwischen Grabmal und Denkmal: Das Kaiserdenkmal für Speyer und andere Grabmonumente für mittelalterliche Könige und Kaiser im 15. und 16. Jahrhundert," in Puhle and Hasse, *Heiliges Römisches Reich: Essays*, 399–409, here 400–401.
29. Rader, "Erinnern," 177. In the early fifteenth century, the well-traveled Dietrich von Niem was able to cite Henry II's Bamberg tomb inscription: Hermann Heimpel, *Dietrich von Niem (c.1340–1418)* (Münster, 1932), 226.
30. See Klaus Militzer, "Der Erzbischof von Köln und die Krönungen der deutschen Könige (936-1531)," in Kramp, *Krönungen*, I: 105–111, here 107.
31. See generally Robert Folz, *Le Souvenir et la Légende de Charlemagne dans l'Empire germanique médiévale* (Paris, 1950); for Charlemagne's representation on Frankfurt's fourteenth-century Galgentor, see Lieselotte E. Saurma-Jeltsch, "Das mittelalterliche Reich in der Reichsstadt," in *Heilig—Römisch—Deutsch: Das Reich im mittelalterlichen Europa*, eds. Bernd Schneidmüller and Stefan Weinfurter (Dresden, 2006), 403–411; for a Charlemagne tapestry, see Puhle and Hasse, *Heiliges Römisches Reich: Katalog*, no. IV.41, 233–235.
32. See, generally, Klaus Niehr, "Herrscherliche Architektur," in Puhle and Hasse, *Heiliges Römisches Reich: Essays*, 159–171.
33. See Wolfgang Schenkluhn, "Monumentale Repräsentation des Königtums in Frankreich und Deutschland," in Kramp, *Krönungen*, I: 369–378, here 374–376; and Klaus Niehr, "Zeichen des mittelalterlichen Reichs? Speyer—Königslutter—Prag," in Schneidmüller and Weinfurter, *Heilig—Römisch—Deutsch*, 372–398, here 389–390.
34. Puhle and Hasse, *Heiliges Römisches Reich: Katalog*, no. IV.123, 354–355.
35. For gothic imitations of Charlemagne's minster in Nuremberg and Prague, see František Kavka, "Karl IV. (1349–1378) und Aachen," in Kramp, *Krönungen*, II: 477–84, here 478–479.
36. Franz Machilek, "Privatfrömmigkeit und Staatsfrömmigkeit," in *Kaiser Karl IV.: Staatsmann und Mäzen*, ed. Ferdinand Seibt (Munich, 1978), 87–101, here 91–92; and Rudolf Chadraba, "Der 'zweite Konstantin': Zum Verhältnis von Staat und Kirche in der karolingischen Kunst Böhmens," *Umeni* 26 (1978): 505–520, here 508. On Prague's role in the projection of Charles' rulership see generally Paul Crossley, "The politics of presentation: the architecture of Charles IV of Bohemia," in *Courts and Regions in Medieval Europe*, eds. S. Rees Jones et al. (Woodbridge, 2000), 99–172.
37. Lieselotte E. Saurma-Jeltsch, "Zeichen des Reiches im 14. und frühen 15. Jahrhundert," in Puhle and Hasse, *Heiliges Römisches Reich: Essays*, 337–347, here 346.
38. For the entry of French gothic into Germany see Willibald Sauerländer, "Two glances from the north: the presence and absence of Frederick II in the art of the empire; the court art of Frederick II and the opus francigenum," in *Intellectual Life at the Court of Frederick II Hohenstaufen*, ed. W. Tronzo (Washington, 1994), 188–209, here 192–194; and Paul Williamson, *Gothic Sculpture 1140–1300* (New Haven and London, 1995), especially 174–177.
39. See, generally, Schenkluhn, "Monumentale Repräsentation"; and regarding the "Nine Worthies," see Thomas H. von der Dunk, *Das Deutsche Denkmal: Eine Geschichte in Bronze und Stein vom Hochmittelalter bis zum Barock* (Cologne, Weimar, and Vienna, 1999), 45–48.
40. Michael Camille, *Gothic Art* (London, 1996), 18, 22–25.
41. For late medieval reliquaries see Susanne Wittekind, "Heiligen- und Reliquienverehrung in staufische Zeit," in Puhle and Hasse, *Heiliges Römisches Reich: Essays*, 211–221,

here 216–218, 221; for the eucharist, Miri Rubin, *Corpus Christi: The Eucharist in Late Medieval Culture* (Cambridge, 1991). The relationship of the visual to problems of doubt and proof is discussed in Caroline Walker Bynum, *Wonderful Blood: Theology and Practice in Late Medieval Northern Germany and Beyond* (Philadelphia, 2007), "Introduction."

42. For England, one of the kingdoms that led the document revolution, see M.T. Clanchy, *From Memory to Written Record: England 1066–1307* (London, 1979).
43. For the empire, there are figures for numbers of documents in Moraw, *Von offener Verfassung,* 172, and for their relative distribution in Moraw,"Vom Raumgefüge einer spätmittelalterlichen Königsherrschaft: Karl IV. im nordalpinen Reich," in *Kaiser, Reich und Region: Studien und Texte aus der Arbeit an den Constitutiones des 14. Jahrhunderts und zur Geschichte der Monumenta Germaniae Historica,* eds. Michael Lindner et al. (Berlin, 1997), 61–81, here 70, 73. The c. 10,000 imperial documents known from the long and busy reign of Charles IV might be contrasted with the 3,646 documents that the papal chancery was issuing on average *each year* under John XXII (1316–1324), see R.W. Southern, *Western Society and the Church in the Middle Ages* (Harmondsworth, 1970), 109.
44. Ernst Schubert, *König und Reich: Studien zur spätmittelalterlichen deutschen Verfassungsgeschichte* (Göttingen, 1979), 358–366; Bettina Pferschy-Maleczek,"Der Nimbus des Doppeladlers: Mystik und Allegorie im Siegelbild Kaiser Sigmunds," in *Zeitschrift für historische Forschung* 28 (1996): 433–471; and Claus D. Bleisteiner,"Der Doppeladler von Kaiser und Reich im Mittelalter: Imagination und Realität," *Mitteilungen des Instituts für österreichischen Geschichtsforschung* 109 (2001): 4–52.
45. Pferschy-Maleczek,"Nimbus," 447.
46. Bleisteiner,"Der Doppeladler," 42.
47. For an example of Charles IV's pairing of the imperial eagle with the Bohemian lion on his seals, see the plates in Seibt, *Kaiser Karl IV,* 327–328; for the double eagle's ascription to earlier emperors, see Bleisteiner,"Der Doppeladler," 46.
48. Hegel, *Twinger,* Beilagen, 11: 1042. For a magnificent tent adorned with the emblems of King Wenceslas, the black-on-gold eagle prominent among them, see Barbara Drake Boehm and Jiří Fajt, eds., *Prague: The Crown of Bohemia 1347–1437* (New Haven and London, 2005), 234.
49. Saurma-Jeltsch,"Zeichen des Reiches," 338, 343.
50. Bernd Kluge, "Das Münzwesen des Mittelalters im Römisch-deutschen Reich," in Puhle and Hasse, *Heiliges Römisches Reich: Essays,* 373–382; François Reinert, "Die Reichsprägung unter Sigismund von Luxemburg (1410–1437)," in *Sigismundus Rex et Imperator: Kunst und Kultur zur Zeit Sigismunds von Luxemburg 1387–1437: Ausstellungskatalog,* ed. Imre Takács (Mainz, 2006), 173–179.
51. Puhle and Hasse, *Heiliges Römisches Reich: Katalog,* no. VI.2, 492–495, though the cards shown are of atypically high quality.
52. Ulrich Müller, ed., *Politische Lyrik des deutschen Mittelalters: Texte I* (Göppingen, 1972), 89.
53. For Rudolf as "mager und lank" see the poet "Boppe" in ibid., 90.
54. Adolf Hofmeister, ed., *Die Chronik des Mathias von Neuenburg* (*MGH Scriptores rerum Germanicarum in usum scholarum* [henceforth SrG], Nova series, 4, Berlin, 1924), 260; and, for the often-violent contest of signs and symbols in late medieval German towns more generally, see Valentin Groebner, *Defaced: The Visual Culture of Violence in the Late Middle Ages,* trans. P. Selwyn (New York, 2004), ch. 2.

55. For this period in German urban history see Eberhard Isenmann, *Die deutsche Stadt im Spätmittelalter 1250–1500* (Stuttgart, 1988), especially ch. 1.
56. Georg Leidinger, ed., *Chronica de gestis principum*, in *Bayerische Chroniken des XIV. Jahrhunderts* (*MGH SrG*, 19, Hannover and Leipzig, 1918), 98–98.
57. See especially Gerrit Jasper Schenk, *Zeremoniell und Politik: Herrschereinzüge im spätmittelalterlichen Reich* (Cologne, Weimar, and Vienna, 2003); and Anna M. Drabek, *Reisen und Reisezeremoniell der römisch-deutschen Herrscher im Spätmittelalter* (Vienna, 1964).
58. Drabek, *Reisen*, 15.
59. On these accounts, see Schenk, *Zeremoniell*, 192–193.
60. F. Frensdorff, ed., *Chronik von 1368 bis 1406 mit Fortsetzung bis 1447*, in *CdS* 4 (Leipzig, 1865), 59–63. For a full discussion of the evidence for Charles' funeral, see Meyer, *Königs- und Kaiserbegräbnisse*, 100–118.
61. Potthast, *Liber de rebus memorabilioribus*, 275.
62. John L. Watts, "Looking for the state in later medieval England," in *Heraldry, Pageantry and Social Display*, eds. P. Coss and M. Keen (Woodbridge, 2002), 243–267.
63. Ibid., 251.
64. See Wolfgang D. Fritz, ed., *Die goldene Bulle Kaiser Karls IV. vom Jahre 1356*, MGH Fontes iuris Germanici antiqui in usum scholarum, 11, (Weimar, 1972), 87.
65. For full details of locations and attendance, see Gabrielle Annas, *Hoftag—Gemeiner Tag—Reichstag: Studien zur strukturellen Entwicklung deutscher Reichsversammlungen des späten Mittelalters (1349–1471)*, 2 vols. (Göttingen, 2004).
66. As an example see Frensdorff, *Chronik von 1368 bis 1406*, 74, for those attending the assembly held by Wenceslas at Heidelberg in 1384. For the typology, see Moraw, *Von offener Verfassung*, 175.
67. For Prague see Drake Boehm and Fajt, *Prague*; for Munich, see Richard Bauer, "München als Landeshauptstadt," *Zeitschrift für bayerische Landesgeschichte* 60 (1997): 115–121, here 120; for Habsburg Vienna, see von der Dunk, *Das Deutsche Denkmal*, 30–33; for Wiener Neustadt, see Heinrich Koller, *Kaiser Friedrich III.* (Darmstadt, 2005), 23–24; for Heidelberg, see Schubert, "Probleme," 142–143.
68. Robert Suckale, *Die Hofkunst Kaiser Ludwigs des Bayern* (Munich, 1993), 22–25.
69. Dankwart Leistikow, "Die Aufbewahrungsorte der Reichskleinodien—vom Trifels bis Nürnberg," in *Die Reichskleinodien: Herrschaftszeichen des Heiligen Römischen Reiches* (Göppingen, 1997), 184–213; for Munich, see Alexander Markschies, "Ludwig IV., der Bayer (1314–1347): Krone und Krönungen," in Kramp, *Krönungen*, II: 467–476, here 474; for Prague, see Crossley, "The politics," 131; for the display of the imperial regalia in Nuremberg, see also Puhle and Hasse, *Heiliges Römisches Reich: Katalog*, nos. V.77-81, 483–490.
70. For a convenient narrative history, see Heinz Thomas, *Deutsche Geschichte des Spätmittelalters 1250–1500* (Stuttgart, 1983).
71. Hermann Fillitz, "Die Reichskleinodien: Entstehung und Geschichte," in Puhle and Hasse, *Heiliges Römisches Reich: Essays*, 61–72, here 66.
72. Rainer Christoph Schwinges, "Verfassung und kollektives Verhalten: Zur Mentalität des Erfolges falscher Herrscher im Reich des 13. und 14. Jahrhunderts," in *Mentalitäten im Mittelalter: Methodische und inhaltliche Probleme*, ed. František Graus (*Vorträge und Forschungen*, 35, Sigmaringen, 1987), 177–202.
73. Schwinges, "Verfassung," 180–181; Tilman Struve, "Die falschen Friedriche und die Friedenssehnsucht des Volkes im späten Mittelalter," in *Fälschungen im Mittelalter: In-*

ternationaler Kongress der Monumenta Germaniae Historica, München, 16.–19. September 1986 (MGH Schriften 33.i, Hannover, 1988), 317–337, here 319–320.
74. In this, Germany also shared in a broader European trend of the period. See, e.g., Claire Richter Sherman, *The Portraits of Charles V of France (1338–1380)* (New York, 1969).
75. Iva Rosario, *Art and Propaganda: Charles IV of Bohemia, 1346–1378* (Woodbridge, 2000), 13; and see also Helga Wammetsberger, "Individuum und Typ in den Porträts Kaiser Karls IV.," *Wissenschaftliche Zeitschrift der Friedrich-Schiller-Universität Jena, Gesellschafts- und Sprachwissenschaftliche Reihe* 16 (1967): 79–93; Johanna von Herzogenberg, "Die Bildnisse Kaiser Karls IV.," in Seibt, *Kaiser Karl IV.*, 324–334.
76. Thus, the carved busts of Charles and his queen, Elizabeth of Pomerania, set up on the rebuilt church of St Nicholas at Luckau in Lusatia, to which the emperor had donated a valuable relic: Michael Lindner, "Kaiser Karl IV. und Mitteldeutschland," in Lindner et al., *Kaiser, Reich und Region*, 83–180, here 134–135.
77. Saurma-Jeltsch, "Zeichen des Reiches," 346–347; János Végh, "Die Bildnisse Kaiser Sigismunds von Luxemburg: Typus und Individuum in den Herrscherdarstellungen am Ende des Mittelalters," in *Künstlerischer Austausch / Artistic Exchange: Akten des XXVIII. Internationalen Kongresses für Kunstgeschichte, Berlin, 15–20 July 1992*, ed. Thomas W. Gaehtgens (Berlin, 1993), II: 127–138.
78. For the supposedly wrinkles-and-all veracity of Rudolf I's tomb effigy in Speyer Cathedral, see Joseph Seemüller, ed., *Ottokars östereichische Reimchronik (MGH DC*, 5.i, Hannover, 1890), 508–509. For tomb and anecdote, see also Robert Suckale, "Die Hofkunst im 14. Jahrhundert," in Puhle and Hasse, *Heiliges Römisches Reich: Essays*, 323–335, here 323–324.
79. Ernst-Dieter Hehl, "Die Erzbischöfe von Mainz bei Erhebung, Salbung und Krönung des Königs (10. bis 14. Jahrhundert)," in Kramp, *Krönungen*, I: 97–104, here 101–102.
80. Otto Volk, "Von Grenzen ungestört—auf dem Weg nach Aachen: Die Krönungsfahrten der deutschen Könige im späten Mittelalter," in *Grenzen erkennen—Begrenzungen überwinden: Festschrift für Reinhard Schneider zur Vollendung seines 65. Lebensjahres*, eds. Wolfgang Haubrichs et al. (Sigmaringen, 1999), 263–297, here 268, 270, 291–292.
81. See generally Ernst Schubert, "Königswahl und Königtum im spätmittelalterlichen Reich," *Zeitschrift für historische Forschung*, 4 (1977): 257–338; Armin Wolf, *Die Entstehung des Kurfürstenkollegs 1198–1298: Zur 700-jährigen Wiederkehr der ersten Vereinigung der sieben Kurfürsten* (Idstein, 1998).
82. Thus, in the civic meeting hall on the Fish Market in Aachen, which in the second half of the thirteenth century appears to have acquired its frieze showing a ruler with six electors: Saurma-Jeltsch, "Reichsstadt," 411–413; and Grimme, "Rathaus," in Kramp, *Krönungen*, II.512.
83. See Henry J. Cohn, "The electors and imperial rule at the end of the fifteenth century," in *Representations of Power in Medieval Germany 800–1500*, eds. Björn Weiler and Simon MacLean (Turnhout, 2006), 295–318, here 296–297; and Armin Wolf, "Von den Königswählern zum Kurfürstenkolleg: Bilddenkmale als unerkannte Dokumente der Verfassungsgeschichte," in *Wahlen und Wählen im Mittelalter*, eds. Reinhard Schneider and Harald Zimmermann (Vorträge und Forschungen, 37, Sigmaringen, 1990), 15–78. For the celebrated Nuremberg *Schöne Brunnen* see von der Dunk, *Das deutsche Denkmal*, 45–46, and (for the representative role of fountains more generally), 50–51;

for an example from a princely town in the *königsfern* north—Braunschweig—see Schneidmüller, "Reichsnähe—Königsferne," 48–49.

84. See Werner Paravicini, "Schuld und Sühne: der Hansenmord zu Sluis in Flandern, anno 1436," in *Wirtschaft, Gesellschaft, Mentalitäten im Mittelalter: Festschrift zum 75. Geburtstag von Rolf Sprandel*, eds. Hans-Peter Baum et al. (Stuttgart, 2006), 401–451, here 425. I am indebted to Erik Spindler for this reference.
85. Saurma-Jeltsch, "Reichsstadt," 412–418; and Puhle and Hasse, *Heiliges Römisches Reich: Katalog*, no. V.37, 422–424.
86. Cohn, "The electors," 295–296; and Puhle and Hasse, *Heiliges Römisches Reich: Katalog*, no. VI.55, 572–574.
87. Suckale, *Die Hofkunst*, 257–259; and Saurma-Jeltsch, "Zeichen des Reiches," 340–342.
88. Saurma-Jeltsch, "Reichsstadt," 419–422.
89. Von der Dunk, *Das deutsche Denkmal*, 52.
90. W. Trusen, "Rolandsäulen," in *Handwörterbuch zur deutschen Rechtsgeschichte*, eds. A. Erler and E. Kaufmann, vol. 4 (Berlin, 1990), cols. 1102–1106; and von der Dunk, *Das deutsche Denkmal*, 54–56.
91. Puhle and Hasse, *Heiliges Römisches Reich: Katalog*, vol. IV.95, 314–316. For the reinterpretation of Roland-statues see von der Dunk, *Das deutsche Denkmal*, 56.
92. Schenk, *Zeremoniell*, 316 n354. Whether the inscription was set up specifically for Charles' visit is not known. On the mixed messages in royal receptions in towns see also Michail A. Bojcov, "Ephemerität und Permanenz bei Herrschereinzügen im spätmittelalterlichen Deutschland," in *Marburger Jahrbuch für Kunstwissenschaft* 24 (1997): 87–107, here 90.
93. For the modest image projected by the early post-Staufer kings see Suckale, *Die Hofkunst*, 323–325; for Frederick III's largely ineffectual attempts in this regard, see Koller, *Kaiser Friedrich III.*, 250.

CHAPTER 5

The Production of Knowledge about Confessions
Witnesses and their Testimonies about Normative Years In and After the Thirty Years' War

RALF-PETER FUCHS

Introduction

No doubt about it, Christoph Wippermann, an eighty-year-old Lutheran witness from Wiedenbrück, said things the interrogators were glad to hear. Yes, Holy Communion had been administered in both kinds before the Jesuits' appearance. No, he had never been taught that the Pope should be the head of Christendom, nor had he ever been instructed that the Holy Scripture should be interpreted in the manner of the Roman Catholic Church, and not a single word had been spoken about purgatory.[1] Thus, his testimony gave evidence that the church of Wiedenbrück had been a Lutheran church in the year 1624—the Peace of Westphalia's normative year.

Nevertheless, on the whole, his testimony must have been rather disappointing for the members of the Lutheran consistory of Osnabrück, who had commissioned this interrogation in 1649. Christoph Wippermann declared that he did not know much about the Lutheran catechism and he remembered that he had bought the catechism of Petrus Canisius and given it to his son many years ago. He further explained that several catechisms had been allowed and used at Wiedenbrück's school at that time.[2] Similar to other witnesses, he also attested that requiem liturgies were celebrated in the church.[3]

Some years before, in 1642, quite similar hearings had taken place in the County (*Grafschaft*) of Mark in Westphalia, and the results there had sometimes been somewhat confusing as well.[4] Heinrich Bonnemann, a witness living in Bochum, a former linen weaver of the Roman Catholic confession, had attested that he had participated in funeral services where evangelical songs had been sung.[5] Another witness, the preacher Arnold Tack, had declared himself a Catholic who administered Holy Communion in both kinds, sang psalms in German, and did not believe in purgatory.[6] Tack's additional statements give reason to suppose that he was a Protestant claiming the term "Catholic" for the evangelical cause. Nevertheless, his testimony shows that there existed an uncertainty in clearly marking the boundaries between confessions, an uncertainty that made it possible to play with words. Often the interrogators' records indicate the witnesses' awareness of the power of language.[7]

In this chapter, I will present some more detailed information about the testimonies of witnesses—peasants, linen weavers, sometimes preachers—who had to unfold their knowledge about confessions shortly before and after the end of the Thirty Years' War. The historical background of these hearings was the need to restore religious order in the Holy Roman Empire after a long war, a war supposedly caused by religious conflicts. This order was to be based on normative years, the dates negotiated in order to fix the possessions and rights of confessional groups in territories and localities.

The idea to fix confessional possessions had its origins in the Catholics' claim to restitution of the so-called *Kirchengüter*—chapters, churches, and even territories—as ecclesiastical properties that had been secularized by princes and bishops, who had converted to Protestantism in the sixteenth century. In 1555, the Catholic estates had tried to prevent further losses of territory within the empire by means of the "ecclesiastical reservation" (*Geistlicher Vorbehalt*), a clause within the Treaty of Augsburg.[8] Its aim had been to secure the Catholics' possession of *Kirchengüter* even after further conversions of princes and other clericals. But after 1555, the Protestants adjudicating the ecclesiastical reservation had gained more possessions. Finally, the experiences of the Thirty Years' War and the desire on both sides to avoid further hostilities had stimulated the willingness to compromise.[9] One of the most important results of the negotiations in Münster and Osnabrück was the decision to return to the status quo of the year 1624.[10]

Generally speaking, all Catholic possessions of the year 1624 were to be made Catholic, while Protestant claims were to have adequate legitimation. However, there existed exceptions in many regions and sometimes even other normative years.[11] The aforementioned interrogations in the County of Mark had been arranged to gain knowledge about the confessional situation in 1609, the year of the last Duke of Cleve's death, which was to be the normative year.[12] The main purpose of these hearings in 1642, as well as the interrogations in the Bishopric of Osnabrück in 1648–1649, was to restore the past in the towns and villages where subjects of different confessions lived together as neighbors.

In neither instance were these attempts to establish a new order of peace free from conflicts. The confessional groups challenged to give proof of their rights and possessions tried to mobilize their members, calling on them to support their churches. Giving depositions that could consolidate claims was regarded as an important form of assistance.

I would like to reflect on the records of hearings as sources of a history of communication. First, I shall outline some of the specific problems of this kind of historical source and deal with the conditions of the normative years' interrogations to describe the situation of communication at the moment of the hearings.[13] Based on the witnesses' depositions, I shall further examine the strategies and mediums rulers used to construct confessions as a pattern of social order remembered by the interrogated persons.[14] In this context, I also would like to discuss what kind and what degree of success the rulers had in producing social reality and memory. An important domain of early modern rulership should thereby appear as a matter of communication—communication, as we will see, which was not free of contingency.

To act as a witness was a duty that could be a burden as well as an opportunity: a burden because one could get into trouble answering questions about matters better kept in one's own mind; an opportunity because sometimes the chance arose to do something useful for oneself. The behavior of witnesses—keeping silent or speaking—often was a result of either of these possibilities. Many records include the depositions of subjects who carefully declared themselves unable to answer. Frequently, the term *nescit* suggests that they tried to hide their knowledge. On the other hand, we can find witnesses who freely gave detailed information and sometimes told whole stories, experiences, and adventures.[15]

However, the witnesses' ability to react flexibly to safeguard their interests was limited, because they regularly were admonished to tell the truth and testified under oath. Within an ordinary proceeding, a *commissarius* regularly illustrated the dramatic consequences of perjury—fingers cut off and eternal punishment in Hell—so that only shameless characters would remain unimpressed and tell bald lies.[16] Transcripts of interrogations, therefore, should be considered the results of interactions between interrogators and interrogated subjects. Though we usually are not informed about the exact words spoken, we may conclude that this interaction was essentially influenced by rules of legal procedure, as well as by structures of conflicts, and not least by the roles of the witnesses taking part.[17]

The witnesses testifying in the hearings about the normative years were not always obliged to take an oath. In the Bishopric of Osnabrück, the hearings were organized by the Lutheran consistory and sometimes by the leading members of the parishes themselves.[18] Only seldom did they require oaths.[19] The desire to elicit information useful for their own cause was paramount and strongly determined the selection of the men who were ordered to testify. On the other hand, notaries were involved. They signed with their own hands that the proceedings were correct and generally were interested in upholding juridical standards. The district officials (*Drosten*) who surveyed the hearings in the County of Mark were accompanied by jurists who wrote down the testimonies.[20] On the whole, we may conclude that the duty to tell the truth was present even without oaths. Furthermore, the witnesses had to take into account that officials and jurists could put them under oath after the hearings.

Through exhortations and juridical procedures, the witnesses were induced to caution and seriousness. They were ordered to tell the truth entirely and exactly. Nevertheless, most of them may have felt under pressure from two sides, because they knew that their parishes were in danger. Two different kinds of expectations formed a dilemma: one appealing to them as witnessing subjects and the other one appealing to their social role as pious parish members and good neighbors.

No matter what kind of dilemma existed, the principle aim of the hearings was to get conclusive information. From the legal point of view, this lack of ambiguity should have led to justice. However, the witnesses sometimes responded rather creatively when conclusive answers were demanded, as was mentioned above. Very often they followed a strategy of alluding to the complexity of the world: to be illiterate and inerudite, or to be incapable of providing knowledge of the world's secrets could be a safe refuge. Not even jurists could deny the fact that the world, especially the social world and the world of religion, was complex.

When jurists, nevertheless, demanded unambiguity, they proceeded on the assumption that such unambiguity had been communicated before. The officials and jurists as interrogators and surveyors of the normative years' hearings were aware that the relevant elements of religious knowledge were based on previous communications between rulers and preachers on the one side, and the subjects, on the other side. Besides, we have to bear in mind that such witnesses' depositions depended heavily on collective memories—memories the subjects had communicated before amongst themselves and that had become stocks of "social knowledge."[21] Jan Assman has coined the term "communicative memory" (*kommunikatives Gedächtnis*) to describe this phenomenon.[22] It was not the witnesses' piety or their religious experiences as individual characters that stood in the center of the interrogations, but rather religious doctrine and practice experienced in companionship with their neighbors. A further focal point was how religious or confessional changes had been communicated during the war as rulers had alternated. Basically, the hearings focused on the temporal specification of changes. It was in this specific context that the witnesses had to meditate on the question of how their own confession differed from another one.

Last, it has to be noted that the records are comprised of words originally spoken and thereafter brought to paper in several steps.[23] The notaries surely took certain liberties in shortening sentences and making changes to produce a manuscript that would satisfy the general expectations and customs of jurists. Latin words, such as *nescit, negat, affirmat,* and *ad praedeposita,* are manifestations of the notaries' professionalism.[24] We may assume that many of the spoken words were deleted to produce comprehensible and clear documents, but it was strictly forbidden to falsify depositions. Rather, it was the writers' task to produce texts that correlated closely with the witnesses' spoken words.[25] Comparing the different depositions of the interrogations in the County of Mark and the Bishopric of Osnabrück, we can discern the notaries' attempt to create texts reflecting the depositions of different individuals.

Confessional Identity

On closer inspection, we can see that—for perspicuous reason—names of confessional groups were used to gain knowledge about the confessional situation in the towns and villages in both territories. Terms such as "evangelical" (*evangelisch*) or "Lutheran" (*lutherisch*) and "Catholic" (*catholisch*) were common. However, we have already seen that Lutherans could denominate themselves as "Catholics"—if only in order to provoke members of the other confession. A more clear designation could therefore be "popish" (*päpstisch*), a word, however, that could sound somewhat pejorative.[26] As we can see in the records, Catholic witnesses mostly used the term "Catholic" to name their own belief, while they called their neighbors practicing the other religion "Lutherans." We have to point out, though, that there were only seven Catholics among the 81 witnesses whose testimonies are the basis of this paper.[27] In sum, the Lutherans mostly said "evangelical Lutheran" (*evangelisch-lutherisch*) to denominate themselves or their confession. Obviously, the term "evangelical," sometimes also used as a noun, served better than "Lutheran" to declare their identification with their religion. However, they also sporadically used the term "Lutheran" as a noun.[28]

Furthermore, the interrogated persons were ordered to answer questions concerning special signs and actions that could be characterized as indicators of confessions. The following criteria were considered sure signs indicating the Lutheran confession: the administration of Holy Communion in both kinds; the singing of German church songs (sometimes even called Lutheran songs); the celebration of baptism in German; an admonishment spoken out by the preacher before the Holy Communion (*Vermahnung*); and the matrimony of preachers.

Analogous to this, the Lutheran witnesses were expected to confirm that their communities had not practiced specific Catholic rituals, such as: worshipping saints; worshipping pictures; requiems (*Seelmessen*); and church processions (*Processionen*). Further indicators of Catholicism included: the belief in the supremacy of the Pope; the doctrine concerning purgatory; the doctrine defining seven sacraments (in opposition to two sacraments, characterizing the Lutheran teaching); liturgical features such as the use of chrism-oil (*Krisamöl*) and the elevation of the chalice (*elevatio*); and the clerics wearing costly tunics.

The inquiry roster certainly had been constructed by theologians, who were not mentioned in the writs. This framework was, as we have already seen, not effective in every case. Nevertheless, it was generally suitable for portraying homogenous confessions and confessional groups. However, one reason for this was that the framework was communicated through the interrogation itself. The questions posed to the witnesses from Bochum were formulated in such a suggestive way: the witnesses were asked whether it was not true that evangelical Lutheran songs had always been sung at funeral services.[29] They were asked further, whether it was not true that the parish of Bochum had been deprived of God's chalice in the war and that many people had been furious about this and refused to go to church or to Holy Communion.[30] So, the witnesses were informed by the interrogation and their answers confirmed the interrogators' statements.

Comparing the presumed indicators of confession, we may recognize the administration of the Holy Communion in both kinds as the clearest symbol delineating the confessions. However, we have to note that in the County of Mark, it had become a clear indicator only after 1622–1623, when Spanish troops had occupied the country and abolished it. Before that time, even Catholics—or at least people who thought that they were Catholics—had apparently participated in it. The peasant Johann Bußdreisch revealed that Holy Communion had always been distributed in both kinds before the Spaniards arrived, and that he had converted to the Lutherans afterward.[31] Evert Anhalt, baker and brewer, declared himself "Roman-popish-Catholic" (*römisch-papstcatholisch*) and noted that everybody had received it without any distinction from 1617 until the "Spanish times."[32] The close proximity of different confessions seems to have produced several forms of crossover. However, we have to remember that Arno Herzig has discovered the Holy Communion *sub utraque specie* even in Austrian Catholic churches of the sixteenth century.[33] Regardless, the experience of changes during the war forced subjects to come to a decision. From that moment on, communion in both kinds was a characteristic emblem of the evangelical-Lutheran confession in the County of Mark.

For many witnesses, the singing of church songs in German had a similar meaning. The Lutherans in the Bishopric of Osnabrück named a lot of songs, and unquestionably regarded them as their own.[34] Such songs—even "Erhalt uns Herr bei deinem Wort," a song that named the pope as a murderous enemy—doubtless had a strong influence on the Lutherans' identity.[35] On the other hand, some Catholics testified that they had sung Latin songs and German songs, too. This testimony implied that they were fascinated by the German songs: Evert Anhalt from Bochum testified that he knew all of the Lutheran songs and did not scorn them.[36]

As already mentioned, the interrogators must have been astonished that many of their presumed indicators failed to produce certainty concerning the confessional status in 1624. The questions about the preachers' wives also had very dubious results, because many witnesses declared that they did not know whether the women living together with their preachers had been married to them. Testimonies such as, "They had concubines and begot children with them," were scarcely helpful.[37] None of the Osnabrück witnesses were able to assert that the preachers and their women had lived in wedlock.

Other kinds of answers were indefinite as well. Many of the Lutheran witnesses from Osnabrück did not remember a priest's admonition before Holy Communion. Others confused requiems with ordinary church services.[38] Even the declaration that a community had not been taught that the Pope was the head of Christendom was not significant. It would be interesting to see how the Catholic witnesses from Bochum would have answered this question, had they been asked.[39] Ultimately, the interrogators in both territories received a lot of vague answers. Moreover, they could see more and more clearly that liturgy in the villages and towns had had Catholic as well as Lutheran elements in the early seventeenth century. The realization of this enraged the members of the Lutheran communities in Osnabrück, who feared that the religion that they practiced in the past could be regarded as a "crazy religion" (*Wahnreligion*).[40]

Confession Building

How can it be explained, then, that confessional identities were doubtlessly strong in both territories, even though it often proved difficult to ascertain where the differences between confessions lay? The reason may be that confession building (*Konfessionsbildung*) was a complex process of communication and that the character of this communication as well as its structure resulted in lapses.[41]

The records of the hearings shed light on the fact that the question of the confessions' difference had become very important in situations marked by changes. In 1622, at the beginning of the great war, when Spanish troops had been quartered on communities in the County of Mark, they imposed Catholicism by force. Afterward, the Duke of Pfalz-Neuburg's officials had continued to enforce the Catholic confession. Signs of a change in religion were remembered as "alterations" (*neuerungen*). Old priests had been removed; new priests had been appointed. Furthermore, Holy Communion *sub utraque specie* had been abolished. The witnesses from Osnabrück remembered similar "alterations" imposed in 1624 by Bishop Eitelfriedrich von Hohenzollern, who had enforced the Counter-Reformation. In both cases, confession had been marked through power and the ability to replace priests and change Holy Communion, which had become the peoples' central collective experience in church. Arndt Grolmann, a cloth-maker from Bochum, also remembered that books belonging to his former priest had been confiscated and some burned.[42] Taking into account the communicative aspect of early modern confession, it becomes evident that the disenfranchisement and humiliation of the Lutheran confession's former representatives and the destruction of its literature were strategic actions and surely not senseless cruelties.

Instead, those acts of destruction and disenfranchisement were measures of signification. The actions of the new rulers signified changes of eminent importance concerning power, rulership, and religion. I would like to recall a term coined by Marco Bellabarba, which perhaps resembles Rudolf Schlögl's conception of communication:[43] *retorica dell'azione*, meaning "rhetoric of action," or perhaps "communication through action."[44] The records from the County of Mark's hearings illustrated that the new rulers tried to inscribe new structures into society as well as attempted to change the inhabitants' patterns of behavior through this kind of communication. The records and the further course of events show that this "rhetoric of action" attained some success. The witnesses spoke about the new "Spanish rulers" (*spanische herren*) of that time, a time called the "Spanish time."

However, in many respects, success in the area of religion failed to appear. The witnesses reported that some of the inhabitants had adjusted to the new conditions. Others, however, had gone to visit other church communities in the area. We may conclude that the new rulers had failed to make their power omnipresent in a society that was generally still a "presence society," where face-to-face interactions dominated communication.[45] They also had failed to communicate that their rulership would prove lasting, since after 1624, fighting continued in the County of Mark.[46] Dutch and Brandenburg troops captured some villages, so that the Lutherans could nourish hope that the political and religious conditions would change once again.

The Lutherans' key concept under those circumstances was to hold on to tradition.[47] Those forms of religion practiced before aggression and war were regarded as legitimate forms. As we have seen, the soldiers' and their successors' demonstrations of power were understood as unjust alterations. The same was true of some of their Catholic neighbors' religious actions. In the "Spanish times," the Catholic inhabitants had demonstrated their power, too. They had introduced loud and colorful church processions to show that the Catholic confession had acquired possession of the towns and villages. The witnesses remembered them firing volleys and using flags.[48]

The Lutherans in the County of Mark who suffered such things under the Catholics and perhaps ground their teeth while waiting for better times affirmed themselves by drawing on stocks of knowledge acquired in the past. A similar base of legitimation existed in the Bishopric of Osnabrück, where the Lutheran subjects, confronted with their Prince's unfavorable orders, later had the chance to recover when Swedish troops occupied the country.[49] While undergoing bad times, the Lutherans had insisted on the legitimacy once communicated by former rulers and their officials. They insisted on the legitimacy of their own practices of the past. The Lutheran witnesses fashioned themselves as active believers and congregants resisting an illegitimate rulership, violence, and the attempt to establish a new belief. The norms remembered to have existed before "alterations" were brought to mind as their own confession.

Catholics had lived in many villages in Mark before the war, but obviously a very important difference between confessions in the villages was the decision either to insist on tradition or to follow the new rulers and their priests. This decision fixed the inhabitants into groups. However, we can see that some Lutheran inhabitants had gone to church in spite of the "alterations" and avoided expressing their disagreement. Some of them even had participated in the church processions, and later tried to assure their questioners that they only had carried some paltry flags and pictures and were not really aware of the significance.[50] They obviously had tried to keep traditions in mind, but as we know from Jack Goody, this kind of tradition is not a very solid one.[51] Loss of memory was significant for early modern societies in towns and villages, where scripture was overshadowed by spoken words and practices as resources for conservation. Worshipping together with the other confessions' congregants had doubtlessly resulted in a drift toward smoothing differences between old and new or "Catholic" and "Lutheran." But a sharp contrast becomes evident through the records of the hearings: for some inhabitants, confession had been strengthened as identity at the same time. Especially those diehard subjects who decided to receive Holy Communion in both kinds during the "bad times" drew the line.[52]

Conclusions

Generally, the witnesses' concept of confession seems to have rested less on liturgical details and more on group mentality, on appreciation of legitimacy, and on political and personal aspects. Though some church practices were of great importance and truly significant, rather few of them were remembered as practices defining differences. The predominant failure of illiterate communication to freeze knowledge may be considered one reason for this. The fact that rulers and preachers generally were afraid to spread more detailed knowledge about the other confession was surely another one. Uncertainties concerning the others' rites may have been an additional reason for an incapability to define one's own confession as an authorized and regularized sample of religious exercises.

The interrogators therefore received a great deal of information that was incongruent and did not correspond with their expectations. Allowing the witnesses to speak meant accepting that different contents and degrees of knowledge would come to light.[53] Those kinds of results put the interrogators' aim of definitively fixing confessions at risk. Similar kinds of experiences may have caused the decision in some Osnabrück parishes (such as Quakenbrück, Engter, and Bramsche) to forego individual hearings and to produce interrogation records that included mass depositions of large groups of witnesses or the Lutheran parishes as a whole.[54] Analysis of these collective interrogation records indicates that "a hearing was also a silencing," although attempts to control the witnesses' answers were also present in individual interrogations.[55] After the Thirty Years' War, there was an increasing general trend toward shortening interrogation records through the abridgement of texts as well as the reduction in the number of witnesses.[56] The modern state's requirements of unambiguous and useful information for building rational forms of rulership led to the depositions of witnesses becoming less important in political and confessional matters. Even the normative years' interrogation records examined here were ultimately ignored in the process of modernization and peacemaking that followed the war.[57]

In view of the parish members as witnesses, we have to conclude that visiting different churches and behaving differently in times of change were generally sufficient to establish identities and to mark confessional affinities. Many aspects of doctrine and liturgy, however, were not accurately defined and were not fixed within the subjects' memories.[58] This kind of confession, which rulers and clerics tried to communicate with mixed success, was still a rather open category after the Thirty Years' War in the Bishopric of Osnabrück and the County of Mark. On the other hand, confessional identity often caused weighty conflicts when the rights and possessions of parishes were to be determined by normative years.

Notes

1. This study results from a research project called "Normaljahre, Kalenderreform. Verarbeitung konfessioneller Pluralität im frühneuzeitlichen Alltag" funded by the DFG (Deutsche Forschungsgemeinschaft) located in the SFB (Sonderforschungsbereich) "Pluralisierung und Autorität in der Frühen Neuzeit" at the LMU in Munich.
   The interrogation records of Wiedenbrück are transcribed and edited, see Franz Flaskamp, "Das Wiedenbrücker Verhör. Ein Beitrag zur Geschichte der Gegenreformation," in *Jahrbuch für westfälische Kirchengeschichte*, 45/46 (1952/53): 151–192, here 178f.

2. "Er wisse davon nichts gewisses. Er hätte seinem Sohn den Cathechismum Canisii gekauffet. Wer sonst einen andern Cathechismum gehabt, der wäre auch in der schule geduldet worden." Flaskamp, "Das Wiedenbrücker Verhör," 179.
3. "Ob Messe gehalten unnd, da daß vielleicht geschehen, ob auch die Elevation unnd Seelmessen üblich gewesen?"—"Affirmat." Flaskamp, "Das Wiedenbrücker Verhör," 179.
4. "Die amtlichen Erkundigungen aus den Jahren 1664–1667," Part 4, ed. Hugo Rothert, in *Jahrbuch für westfälische Kirchengeschichte* 11/12 (1909/10): 183–303.
5. Rothert, "Die amtlichen Erkundigungen," 201.
6. "Sey zwar catholisch allein administrire das Sacrament in beider Gestalt und singe teutsche psalmen, glaube an kein fegfeuer." Rothert, "Die amtlichen Erkundigungen," 203.
7. See also my studies of these and other normative years' interrogations in Ralf-Peter Fuchs, "Die Autorität von 'Normaljahren' bei der kirchlichen Neuordnung nach dem Dreißigjährigen Krieg—Das Fürstbistum Osnabrück und die Grafschaft Mark im Vergleich," in *Die Autorität der Zeit in der Frühen Neuzeit*, eds. Arndt Brendecke, Ralf-Peter Fuchs, and Edith Koller (Berlin, 2007), 353–374.
8. On the ecclesiastical reservation, see Axel Gotthard, *Der Augsburger Religionsfrieden* (Münster, 2004), 143ff.
9. I have recently conducted extensive research on the generation and implementation of normative years. See Ralf-Peter Fuchs, *Ein 'Medium zum Frieden.' Die Normaljahrsregel und die Beendigung des Dreißigjährigen Krieges* (Munich, 2009). Robert Bireley's research on confession and politics in the Thirty Years' War has been very instructive. See Bireley, *Religion and Politics in the Age of the Counterreformation. Emperor Ferdinand II, William Lamormaini, S.J., and the Formation of Imperial Policy* (Chapel Hill, NC, 1981); Bireley, "The Thirty Years' War as Germany's Religious War," in *Krieg und Politik 1618–1648. Europäische Probleme und Perspektiven*, ed. Konrad Repgen (Munich, 1988), 85–106; and Bireley, *The Jesuits and the Thirty Years War: Kings, Courts and Confessors* (Cambridge, 2003).
10. See Ronald G. Asch, *The Thirty Years War: The Holy Roman Empire and Europe, 1618–48* (London, 1997), 144ff.
11. The year 1618 was selected as a normative year for confessional possessions in the Electoral Count-Palatine (Kurpfalz) and in Baden-Durlach. See the Treaty of Osnabrück: Antje Oschmann, ed., *Die Friedensverträge mit Frankreich und Schweden. Bd. 1: Urkunden* (Münster, 1998) (Acta Pacis Westphalicae. Serie III. Abt. B), here Nr. 18, Art. IV, p. 6, 26.
12. The County of Mark had been part of the possessions of the Dukes of Cleve, Jülich, Berg, etc., until 1609. Before the Peace of Westphalia, the Elector of Brandenburg and the Count-Palatine of Neuburg, who were both pretending to the hereditary title, had already tried to find their own settlement based on 1609 and 1612 as fixed dates. See Klaus Jaitner, *Die Konfessionspolitik des Pfalzgrafen Philipp Wilhelm von Neuburg in Jülich-Berg von 1647–1679* (Münster, 1973). After the stipulation of the general normative year, 1624, the question about the proper normative year arose and led to war in 1651, see Fuchs, "Medium zum Frieden."
13. See Winfried Schulze, "Zur Ergiebigkeit von Zeugenbefragungen und Verhören," in *Ego-Dokumente. Annäherung an den Menschen in der Geschichte*, ed. W. Schulze (Berlin, 1996), 319–325; Werner Troßbach, "'Mercks Baur.' Annäherung an die Struktur

von Erinnerung und Überlieferung in den ländlichen Gesellschaften (vorwiegend zweite Hälfte des 16. Jahrhunderts)," in *Kommunikation in der ländlichen Gesellschaft*, ed. Werner Rösener (Göttingen, 2000), 209–240; and Ralf-Peter Fuchs and Winfried Schulze, "Zeugenverhöre als historische Quellen—einige Vorüberlegungen," in *Wahrheit, Wissen, Erinnerung. Zeugenverhörprotokolle als Quelle für soziale Wissensbestände der Frühen Neuzeit*, eds. Fuchs and Schulze (Münster, 2002), 7–40.

14. On concepts of communicating social order developed in early modern towns, see Rudolf Schlögl, "Vergesellschaftung unter Anwesenden. Zur kommunikativen Form des Politischen in der vormodernen Stadt," in *Interaktion und Herrschaft. Die Politik der frühneuzeitlichen Stadt*, ed. Rudolf Schlögl (Konstanz, 2004), 9–60, here 46ff.
15. See Winfried Schulze's reflections on the concept of ego-documents: Schulze, "Zeugenbefragungen."
16. Ralf-Peter Fuchs, "'Gott läßt sich nicht verspotten.' Zeugen im Parteienkampf vor frühneuzeitlichen Gerichten," in *Kriminalitätsgeschichte. Beiträge zur Sozial- und Kulturgeschichte der Vormoderne*, eds. Andreas Blauert and Gerd Schwerhoff (Konstanz, 2000), 315–335.
17. Fuchs, "Gott läßt sich nicht verspotten."
18. Regarding motives and procedures, see StAOsn, Erw. F 100 Akz. 35/97, Nr. 16: Akten des braunschweigisch-lüneburgischen Kammerrats Heinrich Langenbeck betr. die konfessionellen Verhältnisse im Hochstift Osnabrück seit 1624 (1648/49).
19. More records have been found in StAOsn, Rep. 100, Abschnitt 367: Von Religionssachen überhaupt, von den Fasten, Jubilais, Buß- und Bettagen, Nr. 11: Normaljahr.
20. See the documents edited in addition to the interrogation records: Rothert, "Die amtlichen Erkundigungen," 176ff. and 204.
21. See also Troßbach, "Mercks Baur." On "social knowledge," see Alfred Schütz and Thomas Luckmann, *Strukturen der Lebenswelt. Bd. 1* (Frankfurt a.M., 1994), 311.
22. See his distinction between "communicative memory" and "cultural memory" in Assmann, *Das kulturelle Gedächtnis-Schrift, Erinnerung und politische Identität in frühen Hochkulturen* (Munich, 1997), 50ff.
23. About the methods of producing records for courts of law with regard to penal law, see Elvira Topalović, *Sprachwahl—Textsorte—Dialogstruktur. Zu Verhörprotokollen aus Hexenprozessen des 17. Jahrhunderts* (Trier, 2003).
24. See also the reflections on this topic by David W. Sabean: "we will never encounter the 'authentic' voices of the various villagers." Sabean, *Property, Production, and Family in Neckarhausen, 1700–1870* (Cambridge, 1990), 76.
25. Ralf-Peter Fuchs, "Soziales Wissen nach Reichskammergerichts-Zeugenverhören," in *Zeitenblicke* 1 (2002), http://www.zeitenblicke.de/2002/02/fuchs/index.html (accessed 12 June 2008).
26. See the article "päpstisch," in Heino Speer, ed., *Deutsches Rechtswörterbuch. Wörterbuch der älteren deutschen Rechtssprache. Bd. 10, Notsache-Ræswa* (Weimar, 2001).
27. In Bochum, 14 witnesses had been interrogated in total: Rothert, "Die amtlichen Erkundigungen," 181–204. With regard to the Bishopric of Osnabrück, the records of the Wiedenbrück interrogations have been included for this study with interrogation records concerning the Osnabrück parishes of Holte, Borgloh, Dissen, Neuenkirchen, Hilter, Buer, Badbergen, Schwagsdorf, Voltlage, Ueffeln, Bippen, and Merzen, included in StAOsn, Rep. 100, Abschnitt 367: Von Religionssachen überhaupt, von den Fasten, Jubilais, Buß und Bettagen, Nr. 11: Normaljahr. The depositions from Engter, Bramsche, and Quakenbrück are not taken into account because they were collective.

28. Johann Bußdreisch, a tailor from Bochum, declared that he had converted to the Lutherans (*Lutherische*) because he had felt angry after the abolishment of the Holy Communion's administration in both kinds. Perhaps he spoke of "Lutherans" because in his memory, he still viewed the situation from the Catholic perspective. Rothert, "Die amtlichen Erkundigungen," 186.
29. "Ob nicht bei allen Begrebnußen und Leichbegleitungen in und außerhalb der Kirchen die evangelische-lutherische Begrebnußgesänge jedeßmahls gepraucht ... sein?" Rothert, "Die amtlichen Erkundigungen," 182.
30. "Ob nicht viel daruber, besonderlich daß der Gemeine der kelch des Herren voriger Observantz zuwieder entzogen und geweigert und das Abendmahll des Herren nur unter einer Gestalt gereichet werden wollen, scandaliciret sein und sich betrubet, darumb ein theill zu der lutherischen-evangelischen Confession und deßen exercitio sich von den Pabstischen gescheiden und anderwertlich begeben, theilß bei den Priestern, wiewoll nach alter gewonheit zu der Pfarrkirche in Bochumb sich gehalten, dannoch in vielen Jahren nicht communiciren wollen?" (Rothert, "Die amtlichen Erkundigungen," 183)
31. Rothert, "Die amtlichen Erkundigungen," 186.
32. Ibid., 188.
33. Arno Herzig, "Die Rekatholisierung in deutschen Territorien im 16. und 17. Jahrhundert," in *Geschichte und Gesellschaft* 26 (2000): 76–104, here 95.
34. "O Lamb Gottes," "Mein Seel o Herr mueß loben dich," "Lobet den Herren," "Allein Gott in der Höhe sei Ehr," "Vatter unser im Himmelreich," and "Wir glauben all an einen Gott," a song that some Lutheran witnesses simply called "der Glauben" ("the belief").
35. Martin Luther's song "Erhalt uns Herr bey deinem Wort, und steur des Babsts und Türcken Mord" was constitutive for Lutheran conscience in moments of danger. See Thomas Kaufmann, "Apokalyptische Deutung und politisches Denken im lutherischen Protestantismus in der Mitte des 16. Jahrhunderts," in *Die Autorität der Zeit in der Frühen Neuzeit*, eds. Arndt Brendecke, Ralf-Peter Fuchs, and Edith Koller (Berlin, 2007), 411–453.
36. "er könne die lutherische Gesänge alle und verachte sie nicht." Rothert, "Die amtlichen Erkundigungen," 188.
37. See the deposition of Magnus Schwichtenhövel from Wiedenbrück: "Sie hätten Concubinen gehabt und damit kinder gezeuget." Flaskamp, "Das Wiedenbrücker Verhör," 175.
38. "Es wären Misse gehalten von den Chorpfaffen." Deposition of Carsten zum Bechsel, Flaskamp, "Das Wiedenbrücker Verhör," 167.
39. This question was only posed to the Lutheran witnesses from the Osnabrück communities.
40. StA Osnabrück, Erw. F 100 Akz. 35/97, Nr. 16, fol. 54.
41. See Ernst Walter Zeeden, *Die Entstehung der Konfessionen. Grundlagen und Formen der Konfessionsbildung im Zeitalter der Glaubenskämpfe* (Munich, 1965).
42. "haben die Spanischen Herren Melchiorn [the preacher] seine Bucher theils genommen, theilß verbrandt." Rothert, "Die amtlichen Erkundigungen," 195.
43. On his concept of replacing "action" with "communication" see: "Perspektiven kommunikationsgeschichtlicher Forschung. Ein E-Mail-Interview mit Prof. Dr. Rudolf Schlögl, Constance," in *Sehepunkte* 4, Nr. 9 (2004), http://www.sehepunkte.de/2004/09/interview.html (accessed 17 June 2008).

44. See Marco Bellabarba, "Zeugen der Macht: Adelige und tridentinische Bauerngemeinden vor den Richtern (16.–18. Jahrhundert)," in Fuchs and Schulze, *Wahrheit, Wissen, Erinnerung,* 201–224, here 205.
45. We discussed Schlögl's concept of "presence society" and Schlögl and Mark Hengerer's paper "Social Transformation by Processing Information: Early Modern Towns and Courts in Comparison" at the German Studies Association conference in San Diego in 2007.
46. See Manfred Wolf, "Das 17. Jahrhundert," in *Westfälische Geschichte, Bd. 1: Von den Anfängen bis zum Ende des Alten Reiches,* ed. Wilhem Kohl (Düsseldorf, 1983), 537–604, here 542.
47. Fuchs, "Die Autorität von 'Normaljahren,'" 360ff.
48. See the deposition of Hermann Mars: "daß von Richtern Daniell solches erst eingefuhret." Rothert, "Die amtlichen Erkundigungen," 196.
49. The last Lutheran priest before the "Swedish time" in Dissen had been expelled on 25 December 1624. See StAOsn, Rep. 100, Abschnitt 367, Nr. 11, fol. 18, Deposition of Jacob Veltmann.
50. "habe bei den Processionen nur eine Fahne und einige Bildercken getragen." Deposition of Hermann Mars, Rothert, "Die amtlichen Erkundigungen," 195f.
51. On the lack of written materials and the consequences for memory in ancient societies, see Jack Goody and Ian Watt, "Konsequenzen der Literalität," in *Entstehung und Folgen der Schriftkultur,* eds. Jack Goody, Ian Watt, and Kathleen Gough (Frankfurt a.M., 1986), 63–122, here 73.
52. "Sey derozeit etzliche Lutherische catholisch und etzliche Catholische lutherisch worden, die ursach wisse nicht." Deposition of Evert Anhalt, Rothert, "Die amtlichen Erkundigungen," 188.
53. On different kinds of memory depending on different parties within the local communities, see David W. Sabean, "Gute Haushaltung und schlechtes Gewissen," in Sabean, *Das zweischneidige Schwert. Herrschaft und Widerspruch im Württemberg der frühen Neuzeit* (Berlin, 1986), 169–202, here 188ff.
54. StAOsn, Rep. 100, Abschnitt 367, fol. 27ff, fol. 58f, fol. 60f.
55. I refer to William Clark's paper, discussed at the German Studies Association conference in San Diego: "A Hearing Is Always Also A Silencing: On the Repressed in Early Modern Ministerial Interventions in Academia."
56. Hearings including large numbers of witnesses and conducted by commissions were mostly displaced by notaries' interrogations in the second half of the seventeenth century. See Ralf-Peter Fuchs, "Erinnerungsschichten: Zur Bedeutung der Vergangenheit für den 'Gemeinen Mann,'" in Fuchs and Schulze *Wahrheit, Wissen, Erinnerung,* 89–154, here 143f.
57. See Fuchs, "Medium zum Frieden."
58. See also and compare Michelle Zalinsky Hanson, *Religious Identity in an Early Reformation Community: Augsburg, 1517 to 1555* (Leiden, Boston, 2009).

CHAPTER 6

Staging Individual Rank and Corporate Identity
Pre-Modern Nobilities in Provincial Politics

ELIZABETH HARDING

Modern historiography continues to emphasize the significance of pre-modern provincial estates for early modern society. Research therefore focuses mainly on conflicts that the estates had to face while trying to participate in the ruler's political decision-making.[1] In recent years, historical interest has shifted from an analysis of the growth of central power to the question of how political participation and social order were demonstrated and renewed by the estates.[2] However, these corporations were not alone in using the provincial diets as a platform to communicate their claims. Individual participants also demonstrated both their political influence and rank at a diet. While on the one hand, corporate unity was an ideal that had to be demonstrated outside of the various curiae, individuals, on the other hand, sought to demonstrate rank and title inside the meetings.[3]

Members of noble corporations (*Ritterschaften*) were particularly concerned with displaying rank, since they gathered only on the day of a diet. Noblemen, who spent a vast amount of their time holding commissions, appearing at court, or administering lands and goods, saw the assemblies as a stage on which they could network and reinforce status. Up until now, however, research on noble corporations mainly dealt with cathedral chapters and noble families' efforts to maintain exclusiveness. Scholars have viewed these gatherings of early modern nobles primarily as an opportunity to secure economic resources,[4] and have largely neglected the communicative dimensions of these noble corporations.[5]

An analysis of the assembly room of the lower Westphalian nobility[6] in the eighteenth century demonstrates how corporate identity and individual rank were staged both at provincial diets and in everyday life. The aim is to show how noble corporations developed various strategies in order to integrate their members' different interests, and how, despite conflicting values within the corporation, they continuously attracted the lower nobility, thereby ensuring the knighthood's collective role in political decision-making. My intention is not to trace the emotional aspects of the knights' relationship to political assemblies; rather than applying sociological concepts of (modern) group theory to early modern societies—which in itself is problematic and has been subject to academic controversy[7]—this essay focuses on processes by which something was made identifiable for an outside community.[8] Used in this context, the term "identity" denotes the visual display of a body of knights, which made it possible for others to address them as a corporation.

By presenting three examples, this essay uncovers how the lower nobility symbolically demonstrated corporate unity. In a second step, it takes a closer look at a nobleman's desire to represent his rank and status by focusing on forms of decision-making in the assembly room. It will reveal that while the procedures of negotiation prevented the knights from demonstrating their individual titles, they soon found symbolic alternatives. The various examples are taken from the geographical area of Westphalia. The main focus will be on the ecclesiastical territories of Münster and Osnabrück, though the results do not apply exclusively to these states and their pre-modern constitution (*ständische Verfassung*). These territories have been chosen because the noble clergy who assembled in the cathedral chapters dominated these territories' diets.[9] The knightly nobles were second in prominence at the provincial diets and had to cope with the dominating influence of a first curia. An analysis of the *Ritterschaften* is therefore an ideal way to illustrate conflicting interests of corporate identity and individual title.

Nobility in Westphalia—An Introduction

Westphalian diets were held once or twice a year and lasted for a few weeks, mostly in the capital city of a territory. The debates over the state's and prince's matters, public affairs, and taxes usually took place in designated assembly rooms. If there was, as in Münster and Osnabrück, no special conference hall, the meetings were either situated in the outbuildings of the cathedral (Osnabrück) or in the government building (Münster). There, the cathedral chapter (first estate), the *Ritterschaften* (second estate), and the delegates of the cities (third estate) met to negotiate, network, and display their claims for political participation.[10]

At the beginning of the seventeenth century, the corporations of knights were—in comparison to the other estates—less defined. While membership in the cathedral chapter depended on being granted a benefice, and the civic councils elected representatives of the cities, the criteria for attending the assembly of knights still were subject to discussion. On first entering the knights' room, members had to prove their noble pedigree and also attest that they occupied a manor, which for decades had been owned by a noble person. These regulations aimed at defining membership. Yet, neither the government nor the knights themselves were able to keep track of who had to be invited to a diet. Often, it seems, belated invitations had to be sent out to knights who had been overlooked.[11]

The criteria of membership in the corporations of knights were not only ill defined compared to those of the other corporations, but the knights' meetings were also less well organized. Whereas the cathedral chapters met on a regular basis and considered themselves relatively independent from the regent, and, on the basis of this self-image, had developed a corporate bond, the *Ritterschaften* were less institutionalized.[12] In seventeenth-century Münster, the knights met in the same assembly room as the cathedral chapter,[13] whereas in Osnabrück, they "rented" a room in the cathedral's outbuildings from the chapter without gaining independent access to the hall.[14] In times of conflict with the chapter, this meant that the *Ritterschaft* was denied access to its assembly room, which explains why it partly transferred its meetings to the private residences of its members in the eighteenth century. Besides lacking membership rules and an independent assembly room, the *Ritterschaften* also had, to a lesser extent, reliable corporate memories. In fact, they only slowly introduced the idea of keeping written minutes. They first did this in Münster in the 1650s; however, this was only a short episode and it took another 30 years until the corporation commissioned its secretary to take minutes on a regular basis. In Osnabrück, early written minutes date back to the sixteenth century, but as in Münster, the knights in Osnabrück at first recorded only the corporation's conclusions. Discussions and differing opinions were not recorded before the end of the seventeenth century. Given the brevity of the written minutes from both Münster and Osnabrück after 1700, the knights obviously still hesitated to record their consultations, and the meetings of *Ritterschaften* can be characterized as an early modern oral culture.[15]

While the institutionalization of the provincial estates was gradual, the corporations also had the immediate task of integrating various noble groups with conflicting loyalties. Previous historians have pointed out that the powerful cathedral chapters prevented a unity within the *Ritterschaften*, because they monopolized benefices and were related to the knights.[16] To some extent, this might account for the struggle the *Ritterschaften* faced when trying to express an independent political claim and corporate identity. However, this explanation is only one side of the coin. In fact, even directly related knights pursued individual interests that did not always coincide with the dominating, self-confident political strategies of the chapters. Consequently, whether or not a corporation staged a corporate identity did not depend exclusively upon family ties. A lack of corporate unity was also caused by internal conflicts over matters such as religious confessions.

Corporate Symbols

In the course of the seventeenth and eighteenth centuries, the corporations developed various strategies to demonstrate claims of corporate identity and political power through assorted rituals and symbols. These symbolic expressions were relevant both for noble members as well as for the non-members, because they were a visual expression of the group, not just when the provincial diet was assembled, but also throughout the year. The following examples will uncover how corporate identity was presented, on the basis of two symbols and one ritual.

The first symbol that pre-modern contemporaries would have encountered in their bureaucratic interaction with the noble curia was the corporation's official seal. Seals and their iconographical structure give an insight into the corporation's self-perception. The nobles' corporation of Osnabrück, for example, extended its motto in the seventeenth century from *Sigillum Ministerialium Ecclesiae Osnabrugensis* to *S. Ministerialium Equestris Ordinis Ecclesiae Osnabrugensis*, after having fought and won a battle with the cathedral chapter for political independence. The extended motto now demonstrated explicitly the knightly status of its members.[17]

Other noble corporations not only changed the writing on the seal, but also looked for emblems that represented their noble background. In many cases, the nobility referred to knightly virtues by choosing St. George slaying the dragon as a symbol.[18] The seal of the *Ritterschaft* of Münster, for example, featured this iconography (see Figure 6.1). By using these seals in their day-to-day business, they tried to communicate their prestige and aristocratic values, such as military valor and, to some extent, education. These official seals were mainly used to certify noble ancestry. In northwest Germany, noble corporations were able to maintain their social exclusivity by evaluating the pedigree of those seeking to join them. Noble corporations were closed both to the non-noble and to the newly ennobled families. Due to their strict regulations, these *Ritterschaften* were regarded as authorities in defining noble status and sat in judgment over questions of noble lineage.[19] Thus, by certifying coats of arms and noble status, these corporations successfully secured the right to define noble status.

These kinds of emblems were not used exclusively in correspondence, but can also be found in architecture. In Münster, for example, the nobility had its coat of arms installed at the front of the princely court, which was built in the late eighteenth century (see Figure 6.2). By publicly presenting its coat of arms at the two side wings of the hall, the nobility demonstrated at the same time its

Figure 6.1. Official Seal of the Nobility in Münster.

Photo: Nordrhein-Westfälisches Landesarchiv-Staatsarchiv Münster.

"corporate identity" and its political claims.[20] The princely residence played an important role in ceremonial acts, such as the bishop's solemn inauguration and the festive reception of embassies, which meant that the knight's seal was nicely on display at public events for the regent and subjects to see.[21]

A second sort of symbol that noble corporations used to distinguish members of their assembly from those who were not entitled to political participation was aristocratic clothing.

In the late eighteenth century, many noble corporations decided to introduce a ceremonial uniform, which only knights who had proven their noble status and had become official members of the assembly were allowed to wear.[22] In Osnabrück, it is recorded that the corporation wanted, at the very least, to appear in uniform at the diet's inaugural ceremony: the first day of the diet's meeting.[23]

Figure 6.2. Detail of the Prince-Bishop's Residence in Münster: The Nobility's Coat of Arms.

Photo: Elizabeth Harding.

Modern historiography has argued that these uniforms were a symbol for change in political thought, which led noblemen to concentrate more on their role as functionaries in civil service than on their privileged lineage.[24] Supposedly, uniforms were worn in order to demonstrate a new form of civil service mentality that had replaced the original noble independence from central power. From the comments that can be found in the diet's records, however, it is clear that these uniforms also resulted from a need to demonstrate rank and status. The corporation in Osnabrück, for example, chose its pattern from the military order of St John.[25] Its intention was not only to demonstrate a genuine interest in its political welfare, but also, by using the same patterns as military orders, to indicate noble splendor and history. Therefore, the uniform also expressed traditional noble values alongside any new civil service ethos.

In order to guarantee that people on the streets would recognize the uniforms and the exclusiveness they were supposed to symbolize, it was requested that newspapers and other media publish the patterns. A description can therefore be found not only in the *Hof- und Adresskalender*, intended for a broad audience, but also in enlightened magazines, such as Weddigen's *Westphälisches Magazin zur Geographie, Historie und Statistik*, which was read by a mainly bourgeois audience.[26]

The final example that shows how the nobility displayed its unity is the so-called *Adelsprobe*, or the proof of noble ancestry. As has already been pointed out, noble corporations tried to exclude social climbers from their ranks by enforcing strict requirements on candidates for admission. Candidates applying for membership in the corporation of the knighthood had to present a genealogical table with thirty-one coats of arms and prove that all sixteen of their great-great-grandparents had been noble.[27] Satisfying the criteria did not mean going through a mere bureaucratic procedure. In fact, the procedure, whereby noble filiations had to be proven, was flexible and open to discussion.[28] Regardless of the conflicts the nobility had to face when assessing an application, the corporations used this procedure to demonstrate their social exclusivity. After having accepted an application, two (or as was the case in Osnabrück, four) noblemen affirmed under oath that the candidate and his ancestors were clearly noble and therefore met the requirements. By swearing an oath in front of the assembled corporation, these knights ritually expressed the corporation's social exclusiveness and its homogenous noble pedigree. Afterward, the new candidate was introduced to the assembly and had to take the oath of membership. He vowed to uphold the corporation's values and thus was united with the other members by sharing the same ideals of conduct. Reinforced through these oaths, this ritual played an important role in constituting the corporation's stability.[29]

While the official seal and uniform were used in public and therefore helped to make the nobility identifiable as a corporation, these oath rituals took place in the assembly room and were not open to a wider public. Nevertheless, to ensure that noble status and the group's ritual were visualized, corporations used various means to display their genealogy for the public to see. In Paderborn, for example, the clergy publicly processed around the cathedral, a ceremony that made for a great public attraction.[30] The knights in Münster and Osnabrück did not demonstratively stage their ritual, but their genealogical tables were displayed in the assembly room, and were accessible and viewable by a wider public.[31]

The official seal, uniform, and genealogical table were essential means by which the nobility demonstrated its claims for both social exclusiveness and political participation. Previous research has only focused on how the ruling prince demonstrated his power through symbols, ignoring the symbols representing the different chambers of provincial diets.[32] However, the symbols employed by the estates were also of great importance to the overall structure of order, guaranteeing that not only the prince, but also the other estates and the wider public perceived the chamber's claims.

Knightly Symbols

Signs and symbols shaped the pre-modern perception of the *Ritterschaften*. However, the provincial diets also served as a platform upon which individual rank and status were staged. Even though corporate unity had to be demonstrated, the *Ritterschaften's* knights also displayed their own claims for rank. On the one hand, the *Ritterschaften* had to demonstrate corporate identity to maintain their claim for political participation as the second estate. Conflicting interests with the self-confident cathedral chapters or the prince-bishops, who both to some extent strove to reduce the *Ritterschaften's* influence, represented an especially imminent danger in this respect. Displaying individual rank, on the other hand, was necessary in order to maintain one's place in the pre-modern social order, which was subject to instability. Demonstrating individual rank and title meant protecting them against offences from other nobles or lower contemporaries. In a pre-modern face-to-face community, which lacked a written constitution and was open to some social mobility, demonstrating rank meant securing it.[33]

Public display also increased the knights' chances of gaining new titles and honors. Access to princely circles and commissions, which were recruited through patronage networks, depended on the public display of political influence and rank. It was also essential to display status when establishing a clientele or when making plans for a future match. Even highly influential knights had to demonstrate their various titles in order for others to recognize the political power they possessed or claimed.

Thus, attending diets and demonstrating rank and title were not only necessary with respect to political participation, but also were important for social acceptance within the lesser nobility. Although knights had the option of staying away from a diet, as long as they did not move their residence to another territory or larger court and enter a new social context, they needed to attend the provincial diets to convince and reassure their equals that they still shared the same social background.[34] Thus, the assemblies served to keep both the social and political hierarchies stable.

Among the nobility, we find knights who were not only members of the corporation, but also had been appointed to external offices or had acquired titles through membership in other corporations or chapters. Some of them were officeholders at court or in the princely administration. Others belonged to military orders, such as the Bavarian Order of St Michael, the Imperial Order of St Josef, or the Maltese Order of St John, to name but a few.[35] However, it seems that the *Ritterschaften* managed to establish largely functioning and egalitarian corporations where conflicts over precedence, notorious in other political assemblies, did not dominate the proceedings.[36] In order to achieve this goal, some knights had to be excluded from the corporation, apparently when they either became too influential or rose too high in rank, leaving a gap between the majority of noblemen and the individual.[37] This was, for example, the case in Osnabrück, where the *Ritterschaft* excluded its corporate chairman, the so-called *Erblanddrost*, from the assembly. Members of the family von Bar had held this title until 1710, when the *Ritterschaft* denied the son and heir access to the corporation, or at least made it more complicated for him to enter by demanding that he had to prove his noble pedigree. Seemingly because the family von Bar had orientated itself toward the courts of Vienna and Hanover, and was also gaining various new titles, the knights of Osnabrück claimed that their directorate was not a hereditary title, but rather subject to the corporation's disposal.[38]

Another example as to how the corporations developed a functioning order is how they treated members of the cathedral chapter. In the eighteenth century, the clergymen, who owned matriculated manors and therefore were registered both as knights and as members of the cathedral chapter, were excluded from the noble corporations. On the one hand, this meant that the knights' negotiations were more confidential than before and thus the corporation was more independent. On the other hand, excluding the clergy ensured that the cathedral chapter did not undermine the order of rank. In various conflicts over rank, the cathedral chapter had claimed precedence. By closing up against the cathedral chapter, the nobility therefore guaranteed that henceforth the knights would never have to discuss matters of rank concerning the role of the clergy in the assembly.[39]

In order to balance the competing demands of cohesion within the corporation and the desire of their members to express their status, the corporations developed modes of interaction and forms of negotiation that tried to level individual rank. In many corporations of the lower nobility, rank was predetermined by the date of admission. This meant, that, as in Osnabrück, a knight took his seat according to his "length of service." The procedure of voting, therefore, was not determined by external claims of rank, but rather by an order of seniority that resulted from within the corporations.[40] On the day of the diet, the assembled knights would take their seats, and on order of the syndic, vote successively according to their seniority.

Even in those corporations, like Münster, where there was no fixed order of voting and a knight could give his vote almost at any point of the proceedings, disputes over questions of rank were not accepted. Homogenous rank was, it seems, a corporate ideal that was regularly upheld. The fact that the knights repeatedly stressed that they proceeded according to majorities documents this. The ideal of equality was aimed at preventing external claims of rank from being demonstrated. But did this mean that individual rank or family honor could not be demonstrated at provincial diets at all?

To answer this question, the focus must return once again to one of the symbolic expressions of membership in the nobles' corporation: the uniform. As is generally the case with uniforms, they were introduced in the corporations in order to even out differences in rank, influence, and wealth. Although this could have led to a visual conformity, implementation was a problem. In Osnabrück, for example, a contemporary stated that some nobles did not appear "in state," but only in "common," clothing.[41] It is difficult to ascertain what contemporaries meant by calling something "common" when referring to noble clothing, but this quote shows that the corporations obviously had difficulties in persuading their members to attend the corporation in their ceremonial uniform. Moreover, even those nobles who wore the uniform sought just a few years later to give their wardrobe an update by making various alterations to the uniform.[42] The nobility's minutes in Osnabrück demonstrate that a resolution to change parts of the uniform was rejected by various knights for financial reasons. As a compromise, the corporation agreed that modifications could be made, but only as a voluntary act. In the knight's self-perception, every chamber was a "free" corporation that had no power to regulate how its members dressed.[43]

In spite of the fact that sartorial regulations were not binding, the uniforms were still accepted by many noblemen. They even integrated such ceremonial dress into their representation and thus made it what it was intended to be, a symbolic expression of identity. By wearing the uniform, they ensured that the nobility was an identifiable group. Although the uniform was intended to help level rank within the corporations, some knights created a new system to express individual rank. A closer look at pictures of noblemen in ceremonial uniform shows that they had added other symbols to their clothing. On top of their uniform, they wore badges and emblems that symbolized their membership in other noble societies, like military orders or cathedral chapters (see Figures 6.3 and 6.4).[44]

Figure 6.3. Ferdinand Karl von Galen (1750–1803), with an added Cathedral Chapter's Cross, 1774.

Source: LWL-Landemuseum für Kunst und Kunstgeschichte, Westfälische Landesmuseum, Inv. Nr. KdZ 4933 LM. Photo: Sabine Ahlbrand-Doruseif.

Figure 6.4. Colonel (*Reiteroberst*) Heinrich Johann von Droste-Hülshoff (1735–1798) in uniform, with an added Knight's Cross of the Teutonic Order, 1774.

Source: LWL-Landemuseum für Kunst und Kunstgeschichte, Westfälische Landesmuseum, Inv. Nr. KdZ 4942 LM. Photo: Sabine Ahlbrand-Doruseif.

Appearing in ceremonial uniform, therefore, meant demonstrating not only corporate identity, but also individual rank and claims to both political and social status.

Conclusion

In line with modern research on provincial estates, this analysis set out to emphasize the significance of symbolic communication for early modern societies. By not focusing exclusively on economic-functionalistic aspects of political participation, but rather by also highlighting the communicative interaction of a diet's members, this chapter has explored how the *Ritterschaften* demonstrated their claims for political participation through signs and symbols. The official seals, uniforms, and genealogical tables displayed by noble corporations ensured that they were perceptible by the prince, other estates, and society at large, not only when a diet was assembled, but also throughout the year. Thus, their claim for political participation was not just demonstrated at the provincial diets, but also repeatedly renewed by its public demonstration. Demonstrating corporate identity involved being able to express unity; however, this meant that individual ranks had to be leveled. Taking part in the assembly required knights to submit to the corporation's internal hierarchy and to accept its restrictions on demonstrating individual rank. Outside of the assembly room, noblemen could display their individual claims of rank and family honor by means of architecture[45] or by competing for precedence at court.[46]

On entering the assembly, however, nobles had—at least to some extent—to accept the corporation's inner social structure and modes of voting and negotiating. In the assembly room, ideally, no external rank was of any importance, and procedures within the corporations supported corporate identity and unity. Provincial diets therefore attracted different sorts of noble families. For example, those who were not officeholders at court or in the princely administration could demonstrate equality with influential noblemen in the corporations. Thanks to the ideal of homogeneity within the corporations, they were of the same rank as all of the other families when negotiating and voting. Likewise, those who had an arsenal of titles could not alter the internal hierarchy by their claims to rank, but they also could, in a very adept way, still use the provincial diet as a platform to present individual rank. As we have seen, even when wearing the uniform, which should have eliminated disparities in rank, symbolic alternatives were open to them.

While modern historiography has mainly focused on the relationship between the ruling prince and his estates, the aim of this chapter was to point out the need of research that takes a closer look into the assembly room of the various corporations. In the case of *Ritterschaften*, this means looking at the two poles: pre-modern noble assemblies successfully demonstrated their claims for political participation by displaying unity, while at the same time permitting their members to demonstrate individual claims for rank. Thanks to their quality of being highly integrative, the corporations were a platform where noblemen, when attending provincial diets, could demonstrate both corporate identity and individual rank, making a visit to the provincial diet an important occasion in the life of early modern nobles.

Notes

1. See among others for a summary of research Kersten Krüger, *Die landständische Verfassung* (Munich, 2003). A more recent overview is offered by Raingard Eßer, "Landstände im Alten Reich. Ein Forschungsüberblick," in *Zeitschrift für Neuere Rechtsgeschichte* 25 (2005): 254–271.
2. For Westphalia, see Barbara Stollberg-Rilinger, ed., *Politisch-soziale Praxis und symbolische Kultur der landständischen Verfassungen im westfälischen Raum*, in *Westfälische Forschungen* 53 (2003): 1–240, particularly the articles by Stefan Brakensiek, David Luebke, and Michael Kaiser. See also Ulf Brüning, "Wege landständischer Entscheidungsfindung. Das Verfahren auf den Landtagen des rheinischen Erzstifts zur Zeit Clemens Augusts," in *Im Wechselspiel der Kräfte. Politische Entwicklungen des 17. und 18. Jahrhunderts in Kurköln*, ed. Frank Günter Zehnder (Cologne, 1999), 161–184; Tim Neu, "Inszenieren und Beschließen. Symbolisierungs- und Entscheidungsleistungen der Landtage in Münster," in *Westfälische Forschungen* 57 (2007): 257–284; and, referring to further research, Elizabeth Harding, "'concludiret per majora' oder 'ausgemachet durch das los'—Entscheidungsverfahren landsässiger Ritterschaftskurien im 17. und 18. Jahrhundert," in *Zelebrieren und Verhandeln. Zur Praxis ständischer Institutionen im frühneuzeitlichen Europa*, eds. Tim Neu, Michael Sikora, and Thomas Weller (Münster, 2008) 195–211.
3. For a detailed introduction to early modern society and the significance of signs and symbols, see Barbara Stollberg-Rilinger, "Symbolische Kommunikation in der Vormoderne. Begriffe—Thesen—Forschungsperspektiven," in *Zeitschrift für Historische Forschung* 21 (2004): 489–527; Rudolf Schlögl, "Symbole in der Kommunikation. Zur Einführung," in *Die Wirklichkeit der Symbole. Grundlagen der Kommunikation in historischen und gegenwärtigen Gesellschaften*, eds. Rudolf Schlögl, Bernhard Giesen, and Jürgen Osterhammel (Konstanz, 2004), 9–38; and Marian Füssel and Thomas Weller, "Einleitung," in *Ordnung und Distinktion. Praktiken sozialer Repräsentation in der ständischen Gesellschaft*, eds. Marian Füssel and Thomas Weller (Münster, 2005), 9–22.
4. Following Heinz Reif's influential masterwork, various regions and states of the Holy Roman Empire have been treated by scholars with respect to noble strategies of procuring ecclesiastical benefices and private wealth, giving insights into kinship relations and ways of redefining elite status. See Heinz Reif, *Westfälischer Adel 1770–1860. Vom Herrschaftsstand zur regionalen Elite* (Göttingen, 1979); Christophe Duhamelle, "The Making of Stability: Kinship, Church and Power among the Rhenish Imperial Knighthood," in *Kinship in Europe: Approaches to Long-Term Developments (1300–1900)*, eds. David Warren Sabean, Simon Teuscher, and Jon Mathieu (New York, 2007), 125–144;

and William D. Godsey, *Nobles and Nation in Central Europe: Free Imperial Knights in the Age of Revolution, 1750–1850* (Cambridge, 2004).
5. An important exception is Ronald G. Asch, "Noble Corporations and Provincial Diets in Ecclesiastical Principalities of the Holy Roman Empire ca. 1648–1802," in *Realties of Representation: State Building in Early Modern Europe and European America*, ed. Maija Jansson (New York, 2007), 93–111.
6. With a few exceptions, the Westphalian *Ritterschaften* consisted only of families of the lesser nobility.
7. See Peter Stachel, "Identität. Genese, Inflation und Probleme eines für die zeitgenössischen Sozial- und Kulturwissenschaften zentralen Begriffs," in *Archiv für Kulturgeschichte* 87 (2005): 395–425.
8. On concepts of "identity" see also Christoph Dartmann and Carla Meyer, eds., *Identität und Krise. Zur Deutung vormoderner Selbst-, Welt- und Fremderfahrungen* (Münster, 2007).
9. On the cathedral chapter in Osnabrück, see Johannes Freiherr von Boeselager, *Die Osnabrücker Domherren des 18. Jahrhunderts* (Osnabrück, 1990). For Münster, Wilhelm Kohl, *Das Domstift St. Paulus zu Münster* (Berlin and New York, 1987).
10. On concepts of "identity" see also Dartmann and Meyer, *Identität und Krise*.
11. For a general overview on Münster, see Marcus Weidner, *Landadel in Münster 1600–1760*, 2 vols. (Münster, 2000); and on Osnabrück, Reinhard Renger, *Landesherr und Landstände im Hochstift Osnabrück in der Mitte des 18. Jahrhunderts* (Göttingen, 1968).
12. See, on cathedral chapters, Günter Christ, "Selbstverständnis und Rolle der Domkapitel in den geistlichen Territorien des alten deutschen Reiches in der Frühneuzeit," in *Zeitschrift für Historische Forschung* 16 (1989): 257–328.
13. In the course of the eighteenth century, this *Ritterschaft* was given a more exclusive assembly room, though it is not quite clear where exactly the knights met. See Max Geisberg, *Die Stadt Münster*, vol. 1 (Münster, 1932), 283–310.
14. Höfing, [no first name], *Nutzung eines Versammlungslokals im Domportikus seitens der Osnabrückischen adeligen Ritterschaft* (Osnabrück, 1897).
15. Christian Hoffmann, "Das Archiv der Osnabrücker Ritterschaft. Zur Geschichte eines ständischen Verwaltungsinstrumentes im 17. und 18. Jahrhundert," in: *Osnabrücker Mitteilungen* 102 (1997): 195-208; and Weidner, "Landadel".
16. By focusing on the dominating influence of the clergy, who monopolized benefices, social historians dealing particularly with Münster point out that members of these families can also be found in the *Ritterschaften*, arguing that there were homogenous interests in both estates, see Reif, "*Westfälischer Adel*"; and Rudolfine Freiin von Oer, "Landständische Verfassungen in den geistlichen Fürstentümern Nordwestdeutschlands," in *Ständische Vertretungen in Europa im 17. und 18. Jahrhundert*, ed. Dietrich Gerhard (Göttingen, 1969), 94–119.
17. Niedersächsisches Landesarchiv - Staatsarchiv Osnabrück (hereafter StA Os) Rep 100, Abschn. 28, 7 ("Alterations to the nobility's official seal", 1613). The new seal was used as a frontispiece to the nobility's nineteenth-century bylaws, StA Os, Dep. 1b, 736. See Renger, "Landesherr", 73.
18. For example, *Ritterschaften* in Minden, Münster, Saxony, or Ravensberg. For a discussion on official seals, see Landesarchiv Nordrhein-Westfälen, Staatsarchiv Münster (hereafter StA Ms), Grafschaft Ravensberg, Landstände, 410.
19. On pre-modern nobility in Germany, see also Asch, "Noble Corporations," 101.

20. See Geisberg, "Münster," 414.
21. See Elizabeth Harding, "Zeremoniell im Nebenland. Frühneuzeitliche Bischofseinsetzungen in Münster," in *Westfälische Forschungen* 57 (2007): 229–256.
22. On uniforms, see Alheidis von Rohr, "Zur Wahrung des Standes—Die Uniformen der deutschen Ritterschaften," in *Nach Rang und Stand. Deutsche Ziviluniformen im 19. Jahrhundert*, ed. Elisabeth Hackspiel-Mikosch (Krefeld, 2002), 144–149. On the importance of clothing for early modern society, see also Martin Dinges, "Der 'feine Unterschied'. Die soziale Funktion der Kleidung in der höfischen Gesellschaft," in *Zeitschrift für Historische Forschung* 19 (1992): 49–76; and Elisabeth Hackspiel-Mikosch and Stefan Haas, eds., *Die zivile Uniform als symbolische Kommunikation: Kleidung zwischen Repräsentation, Imagination und Konsumption vom 18. bis zum 21. Jahrhundert* (Munich, 2006).
23. StA Os, Dep. 1b, Nr. 496 (Record of 1775). A full-length painting of a uniform is published in Hildegard Westhoff-Krummacher, ed., *Johann Christoph Rincklake: Ein westfälischer Bildnismaler um 1800* (Munich, 1984), 325.
24. See among others Josef Mazerath, *Adelsprobe an der Moderne. Sächsischer Adel 1763 bis 1866. Entkonkretisierung einer Sozialformation* (Stuttgart, 2006). See also von Rohr, "Wahrung."
25. StA Os, Dep. 1b, 498, p. 389.
26. Friedrich Wilhelm Coppenrath, ed., *Hof- und Adreß-Calender des Hochstifts Münster* (Münster, 1785; reprinted Vreden, 1988); and Peter Florens Weddigen, ed., *Westphälisches Magazin zur Geographie, Historie und Statistik*, vol. IX (Minden, 1787), 415–416.
27. See Asch, "Noble Corporations," 101.
28. See, for example, the discussion in Münster on the noble quality of the urban patriciate (*Erbmänner*), StA Ms, Münstersche Ritterschaft, 11.
29. On social groups and rituals of initiation, see Pierre Bourdieu, "Initiationsriten," in *Was heißt sprechen? Die Ökonomie des sprachlichen Tauschs*, ed. Pierre Bourdieu (Vienna, 1990), 84–93.
30. Wilhelm Tack, "Aufnahme, Ahnenprobe und Kappengang der Paderborner Domherren im 17. und 18. Jahrhundert," in *Westfälische Zeitschrift. Zeitschrift für vaterländische Geschichte und Altertumskunde* 96 (1940): 3–51.
31. See Reif, "Westfälischer Adel," 36.
32. For the Reichstag, see Barbara Stollberg-Rilinger "Zeremoniell als politisches Verfahren. Ranordnung und Rangstreit als Strukturmerkmale des frühneuzeitlichen Reichstages," in *Neue Studien zur frühneuzeitlichen Reichsgeschichte*, ed. Johannes Kunisch (Berlin, 1997), 91–132; and Albrecht P. Luttenberger, "Pracht und Ehre. Gesellschaftliche Repräsentation und Zeremoniell auf dem Reichstag," in *Alltag im 16. Jahrhundert. Studien zu Lebensformen in mitteleuropäischen Städten*, ed. Alfred Kohler (Munich, 1987), 290–326. Various princely signs and symbols (such as clothing, coats of arms, and architecture) have been treated with respect to their role in stabilizing social order.
33. For examples on pre-modern mobility in the lesser nobility, see Günther Schulz, ed., *Sozialer Aufstieg. Funktionseliten im Spätmittelalter und in der frühen Neuzeit* (Munich, 2002); Lieselott Enders, "Standeswechsel in der Stille. Vom Lehnbürger zum Landadligen, untersucht am Beispiel der Altmark," in *Jahrbuch für Brandenburgische Landesgeschichte* 57 (2006): 9–31; and Claus Fackler, *Stiftsadel und geistliche Territorien*

1670–1803. *Untersuchungen zur Amtstätigkeit und Entwicklung des Stiftsadels, besonders in den Territorien Salzburg, Bamberg und Ellwangen* (St. Ottilien, 2006).
34. Most families who tried their luck outside of Westphalia were not fully integrated in other courtly societies.
35. For Münster, see the prosopographic analysis by Weidner in "Landadel." For Osnabrück, see Renger, "Landesherr"; and also Christine van den Heuvel, *Beamtenschaft und Territorialstaat. Behördenentwicklung und Sozialstruktur der Beamtenschaft im Hochstift Osnabrück 1550–1800* (Osnabrück, 1984).
36. For conflicts at the Reichtag, see Stollberg-Rilinger, "Zeremoniell"; and Luttenberger, "Pracht."
37. To a much greater extent, this phenomenon can be found in corporations such as the Free Imperial Reichsburg Friedberg, where princes and counts were excluded after a raise in rank. Albrecht Eckhardt, "Die Burgmannenaufschwörungen und Ahnenproben der Reichsburg Friedberg in der Wetterau 1473–1805," in *Wetterauer Geschichtsblätter* 19 (1970): 133–167.
38. Seen also Asch, "Noble corporations."
39. In Münster, this led to a court suit at the Imperial Chamber Court: see StA Ms, Reichskammergericht, M 1669/ 4457.
40. See Stollberg-Rilinger, "Zeremoniell."
41. See Christine van den Heuvel, "Osnabrück am Ende des Alten Reichs und in hannoverscher Zeit," in *Geschichte der Stadt Osnabrück*, ed. Gerd Steinwascher (Osnabrück, 2006), 313–444, 913–923, 916.
42. For example, in Münster, where the knights discussed introducing a *porte-épée*. See StA Ms, Münstersche Ritterschaft Nr. 146, Bd. 27 (1791). At the same time, the knights in Osnabrück were arguing about how to change the uniform: StA Os, Dep. 1b, 315 (1792).
43. StA Ms, Münstersche Ritterschaft 146, vol. 27, fol. 82.
44. For Osnabrück, for example, see Ernst Idel Jobst Vincke (1738-1813), StA Ms, ed., *Ludwig Freiherr Vincke (1774–1844)* (Münster, 1994), 15.
45. See the examples in Weidner, "Landadel."
46. StA Ms, Fürstbistum Münster, Kabinettsregistratur, 2440.

CHAPTER 7

The Importance of Being Seated
Ceremonial Conflict in Territorial Diets

TIM NEU

"In German, the word 'parliament' means 'talking-shop.'"[1] In suggesting this "translation," Houston Stewart Chamberlain—racial ideologist and anti-Semite—joined a notorious group of men who despised elected representative assemblies. Later on, not only Hitler, but also Lenin defamed parliaments literally as talking-shops.[2] However intolerable such invectives sound today, they do contain a grain of etymological truth.

The German loanword *Parlament* and its cognates in the other European languages stem from the Old French verb *parler*, which literally means "to talk." In etymological terms, then, parliaments are primarily places of oratory and discourse. In pre-modern times, the word was used to denote two specific institutions, the English Parliament and the French *parlements*. Only since the late eighteenth century has the term been generalized to denote political representation. Accordingly, "parliament" became synonymous with "representation of the people."[3] Following this example, Anglophone researchers often refer to early modern representative assemblies as parliaments—notwithstanding the fundamental differences between pre-modern und present-day concepts of representation.[4] The implicitly modernist connotations of "parliament," moreover, tend to focus research on the instrumental aspects of "talk," namely deliberation and voting.[5]

While it is legitimate to analyze the diets of the Holy Roman Empire in this way, we must not overlook a constitutive element of diets at both the imperial and territorial level: their ceremonial shaping. Solemnities gave rise to incessant conflicts, especially at the *Reichstag*.[6] Ceremony also formed the framework of the deliberations at most territorial assemblies (*Landtagen*).[7] From a strictly "modernist" perspective, these ceremonial aspects always appear as unimportant or even detrimental to the "real" purpose of the assemblies. And yet early modern contemporaries understood that territorial diets were not constituted by parliamentary debate alone. In 1768, a legal dissertation argued that, "the territorial estates are landowners holding vote and session in territorial diets."[8] In the legal formula *votum ac sessio*, the term *sessio* described a certain position in the ceremonial order. This "place," in the literal sense, was the necessary condition for participating in deliberations and for casting a vote. If this ceremonial dimension is reincorporated into parliamentary history, we regain a topic of great importance to the estates and can extend our understanding of early modern diets.[9]

The Institutional Moment: Corporations as Actors in the Empire and its Territories

Why, one might ask, should one concentrate on the institutional culture of the territorial diets if one is interested in reassessing the political culture of the empire? The first answer is that perhaps no other territorial institution was more literally "part" of the empire than the estates—except, of course, the prince himself, who was by definition a member of the imperial diet. By the seventeenth century, if not before, these territorial corporations had been integrated into imperial law. With this development, princes pushed to codify the territorial estates' duties and obligations, in order to raise imperial taxes more effectively and to fund military forces under princely control.[10] Initially, therefore, the incorporation of territorial estates into imperial law was favorable to princes and their interests. In the longer term, however, incorporation functioned as an extraterritorial legal guarantee for the estates' continued existence—an argument that the estates' lawyers quickly learned to make.[11] In addition, the territorial estates were also subjects playing an active role in the empire and its institutions. For example, territorial estates frequently sued their princes at the imperial courts of law.[12] Analyzing the territorial estates, then, can contribute to a better understanding of how the empire actually functioned.

A second answer is that an examination of provincial diets and their ceremonial order can expose the empire's underlying institutional architecture. A cornerstone of any polity's structure is formed—in analytical terms—by the existence and significance of "corporate actors."[13] At all levels of the empire, certain key concepts governed relationships among the various elements of the polity and the whole. One of these distinguished between personal and corporate embodiments of the polity, a distinction captured in the ubiquitous terminological pair "*Kaiser und Reich.*"[14] But what went for the empire also held for the principalities, most of which were structured likewise around a dualism between the territorial prince (*Landesherr*) and the provincial estates (*Landstände*), which gathered in assembly at the territorial diet.[15] And, in fact, this parallelism was no accident, because the imperial diet that acquired institutional form in the decades after 1495 could serve as a model for the concurrent institutional development of representative bodies at the territorial level.[16] Later on, the territorial estates were conceptualized in terms of their imperial counterparts.[17] Because of these analogies, the actions taken by the estates in any particular principality can tell us a great deal about the possibilities and limitations that corporate actors faced in the empire in general.

Turning to ceremony: after two decades of renewed interest in the subject, there can be no doubt that rituals and ceremonies were vital to the early modern commonwealths as means to constitute and express the socio-political order.[18] And the same holds for concrete decision-making: most institutions relied on a ceremonial order to get things done. We know a great deal about how and through what symbolic means individuals could make their rank visible *within* the diet.[19] But what if the assembly itself and its status as a corporate actor were dragged into a serious conflict over ceremony?[20]

The following essay examines one such conflict, which emerged in the Landgraviate of Hessen-Kassel in 1704.[21] The Hessian diet's two *curiae* seriously disagreed on whether or not the second chamber's director had the right to sit while present in the first chamber. In this case, the "importance of being seated" can be explained through the most obvious function of ceremony—that of expressing rank. When the right to sit was claimed for all members of the second *curia* in 1709, the conflict intensified and produced additional sources, revealing the different functions of ceremony in relation to the specific conditions of corporate action. Examination of this conflict will demonstrate that ceremony not only expressed socio-political hierarchy, but also structured the decision-making process and constituted the chambers as autonomous corporations.

Conventus publicus: the Institutional Structure of the Diet in Hessen-Kassel

As in most of the empire's territories, the estates of Hessen-Kassel were thought to represent the land and all of the people who lived in it.[22] In a dissertation published in 1752, the jurist Johann Wilhelm Fech asserted that, "the territorial estates represent the people, when they come together for considering the common weal."[23] To be sure, this was hardly an impartial definition. Fech's dissertation had been supervised by Johann Georg Estor, who had participated at several territorial diets as a delegate on behalf of the University of Marburg. But it is also true that ever since Wilhelm VI concluded a fundamental treaty with the territorial nobility in 1655, the Landgraves of Hessen-Kassel had pledged to communicate with the estates "in matters concerning land and people."[24]

What were the specific corporate actors that constituted the diet?[25] Originally, there were diets for the whole of Hessen, but these came to an end in the early seventeenth century with the final division of the Landgraviate into two principalities, one centered in Kassel and the other in Darmstadt.[26] In their place, the diets that had been particular to each of the two halves of the Landgraviate, called *Landkommunikationstage*, evolved into general diets for the two Hessian territories.[27] The diet of Hessen-Kassel consisted of two *curiae*. The first chamber was for the "prelates and knights" (*Prälaten und Ritterschaft*). The only real prelate was the commander of the Teutonic Order's Hessian Province. The remaining "prelates" were delegates from three worldly institutions that were the legal successors of secularized monasteries and had inherited their right to sit in the first chamber. These were, in descending order of rank, the chief directors of the noble convents Kaufungen and Wetter, the chief director of the four Hessian Hospitals, and the representatives of the University of Marburg. With the noteworthy exception of the university delegates, all of these "prelates" were nobles and the vast majority of them also belonged to the class of knights, the other part of the first chamber. The titular president of the knights, the hereditary marshal (*Erbmarschall*) of Hessen, presided over both the noble *curia* and the diet as a whole. Under normal circumstances, his counterpart in the second chamber was the mayor of Kassel, whose city held the directorship by customary right. This *curia*, called the *Landschaft*, comprised the forty privileged territorial cities.[28]

Günter Hollenberg distinguished three types of assemblies. Originally, all prelates, nobles, and two delegates from each town were summoned, but "full" diets such as this were not held after 1666. The second type was much smaller in size: in a "narrow diet," representation was based on the division of the territory into five districts (*Strombezirke*).[29] Under this system, the nobility of each district elected two delegates and the towns another two. In contrast, all of the prelates were still summoned to this so-called "narrow" diet. A third form emerged in the eighteenth century, when attendance was reduced again to a maximum of three prelates, one noble, and one communal delegate for every district.[30] In addition to the full-fledged diets summoned by the prince, the estates had the right to hold so called *Deputationstage*. Organized by the hereditary marshal with permission of the Landgrave, these meetings discussed the "private" matters of the estates.[31] Through all of these varieties and changes, however, two essential structures remained unaffected. First, each of the two *curiae* saw itself as an autonomous *corpus*, an independent legal person. Second, the noble chamber insisted on its own superior rank and precedence.[32] This preeminence would come under serious challenge in the early eighteenth century.

"Custom" or "Innovation"? Ceremony and Symbolizing Rank

It all began with the diet of 1704.[33] The inaugural ceremonies started on 3 April. That morning, all of the delegates assembled at the landgrave's palace in Kassel and took up position in two rows separating nobles and commoners. There, they awaited the prince, who, accompanied by his court and officials, finally appeared and sat down on his throne. The princely proposition was read out and the hereditary marshal of Hessen responded in the name of the estates with a short address.[34] Afterward, all of the delegates were permitted to kiss the prince's hand. With that, the inaugural solemnities were at an end.[35]

The next day, the first chamber was told that the monthly contribution had to be raised by 12,000 *Reichsthaler* to meet the unspecified financial requests that were contained in the *Proposition*. Afterward, the knights sent for the municipal delegates, who appeared and were told about the demanded amount. Up to this point, everything conformed—from the knights' perspective—to the traditional procedure. But then a rupture occurred. Instead of commenting on the financial matters at stake, several communal delegates "turned up ... and claimed on behalf of all cities that whenever something should be proposed to them by the hereditary marshal, a chair should be provided for Mayor [Henrich Christoph] Ehinger, as was customary in the past, because he held the directorship among them."[36]

The commoners, in short, demanded a seat for the mayor of Kassel. Two reasons were given for this ceremonial change: the mayor's status as director of the second chamber and the precedent of custom. But the knights rejected the claim and told the cities "that such was not found in any protocol."[37] This explanation is typical of the prevailing customary law that made legal claims conditional upon their constant exercise.[38] The nobles acknowledged that the director's status justified some sort of priority over the other commoners. But the manner in which this abstract priority could be visualized in ceremonial practice should, they argued, be determined by custom.

But the cities insisted. In the afternoon, they demanded the seating once more, but this time only "*honoris gratia*," i.e., honorary and not thanks to a legal title.[39] In addition, they presented an extract from the protocol of a diet held in 1700 to prove that it was customary for the director to sit in the nobles' presence. Again the knights refused the request. They considered the protocol insufficient because its date was wrong. It is noteworthy that the first chamber did not refuse the claim itself, but only the evidence the urban delegates submitted, while offering not to dispute the mayor's privilege if the custom could be proven. Accordingly, the delegates of the cities appeared for a third time and produced a calendar of 1700 trying to support their protocol's dating, again without success.

Meanwhile, the deliberation about the financial matters was pushed completely into the background. From the beginning of the ceremonial conflict, the knights had demanded to return to this "main issue," as they called it.[40] But the second chamber was only willing to discuss the prince's financial requests if the knights consented to further investigations into the ceremonial case. Before the diet was finished, the cities delivered a humble petition to the landgrave, Karl. This move bore fruit: Karl decided in favor of the cities and instructed the hereditary marshal to provide a seat for the mayor of Kassel every time he was called into the nobles' room.[41]

Before turning to the role ceremony played in this conflict, it has to be explained why the prince decided the case the way he did. Perhaps he intended to use the conflict as a means to achieve purposes having nothing to do with ceremony at all. But the sources provide no evidence for such an assumption; quite to the contrary, the landgrave seems to have resolved the conflict without respect to any possible advantage to his own position. Karl granted the contested seat "because ... the petitioning mayor and council, by virtue of the enclosed testimony, have the custom on their side."[42] It is important to note that all three political forces, the prince as well as the two chambers, completely agreed on *what* was decisive in a ceremonial conflict, and that was custom.[43] What was controversial was the means by which the nature of customary usage should be ascertained. Initially, the cities presented evidence that was discredited by the knights on good grounds. In their petition to the landgrave, however, they tried another type of evidence—the attestation mentioned in the resolution. In it, Councilor Justin Motz testified that in 1688—when he was executive mayor of Kassel—he "was provided a chair at meetings and talks with prelates and knights every time."[44] It was this eyewitness account that eventually won the case for the cities.

The whole affair illustrates the centrality of custom to the manner in which early modern political actors—individual and corporate alike—framed situations and conceptualized conflicts. And because this category seemed so "natural" and self-sufficient, it was far less likely to be deployed strategically. That is not to say that princes could not use arguments referring to custom as pretext. In this particular case, however, it is plausible to conclude that the prince impartially resolved the conflict.[45] That returns us to the diet of 1704 and to what the two chambers tried to achieve through ceremonial change.

At the beginning of the diet, the conflict over the ceremonial session had blocked deliberation of the prince's request for taxes. As a matter of fact, ceremonial acts played an important role in early modern societies.[46] In a polity based on face-to-face-interaction and customary law, one's position in the socio-political order had to be constantly expressed in visible signs. By means of such symbolizations, rank became perceptible and effective. Under such conditions, neither imperial nor territorial diets could suspend the imperative of expressing rank. As Ronald Asch pointed out recently, territorial diets functioned as "places where the overall structure of order and authority found its symbolic expression."[47] Both aspects are precisely summarized in the phrase *votum ac sessio*. The delegates of the cities wanted a visible sign: to sit in the presence of the also-sitting nobles would symbolize the institutional dignity and preeminence of their director and their chamber. To gain this, the cities were willing to block the entire decision-making process—despite "His Serene Highness's extreme disapproval," as the first chamber had admonished them.[48] To be sure, this maneuver was in no sense dysfunctional or detrimental because the expression of hierarchy was one of the diet's vital purposes.[49] But the symbolization of rank was not the only function of ceremony.

The Knights' Tale, or Three Functions of Ceremony

The next assembly took place five years later. It was a *Deputationstag* and, accordingly, the cities' minutes referred to it as a "private conference" between the two *curiae*.[50] The occasion for this meeting was the upcoming marriage between a Hessian princess and a prince of Orange. To meet the extraordinary expense that the proper nuptial festivities would entail, the landgrave had asked the estates to grant a subsidy of 40,000 *Gulden*.[51]

In January 1709, the two *curiae* convened in Treysa, halfway between the Hessian capitals, Kassel and Marburg. A few days before, the landgrave had repeated his decision to grant the mayor of Kassel the contested seat whenever the civic delegates were to be called into the first chamber.[52] And because the *Proposition* was always read aloud in the presence of all of the delegates, the issue had to be addressed right at the beginning. A servant was sent to the commoners, who told them in the name of the knights, "that they would end the dispute that had arisen previously over the seating and if the civic delegates would like to appear before them the mayor of Kassel will receive a chair."[53] The response was nothing less than shocking for the knights, as their protocol tells: "The delegates of the cities thereupon gave the answer that this would not be necessary at the moment, because at such 'narrow' conferences all of them had the right to sit at the prelates and knights' table."[54] The minutes of the cities are even more plainspoken, noting that the urban delegation had the right to be seated "at this private conference as a fellow estate (*Mitstand*)."[55] In the view of the nobles, these were "irresponsible new pretensions."[56] Not only did *all* civic delegates now demand to be seated, they also claimed a right to sit *together with the knights* at one and the same table. What happened next resembled the sequence of events at the preceding diet in 1704. First, the cities reduced their claim and proposed that they should all be seated, but at a separate table. Again, the knights rejected this as "nonsense."[57] Protestations from both sides followed, but in the end, the *Proposition* was delivered in the form favored by the knights—with the mayor of Kassel sitting on a separate chair and the other municipal delegates standing. As in 1704, however, the cities did not let the matter rest. Hoping to duplicate the success of their earlier strategy, the cities again delivered a petition to the landgrave, in which they once more put forward the customary usage as the sole argument to support their claims.[58] This time, however, the prelates and knights delivered their own letter of complaint to the Privy Council.

In contrast to the cities' petition, the knights' petition contains arguments that are full of information about the functions of ceremonial acts. So far in this essay, I have described the most obvious function of ceremony—that of expressing and constituting rank. This symbolic function can be separated analytically from the instrumental function of reaching a decision. In 1704, the cities had deployed the symbolic function to block deliberation of a request for tax monies.[59] The knights referred to the socially expressive aspects of ceremony when they complained that the cities' "never-customary wishes infer a parity and confusion among the chambers against the privileges and liberties."[60] In this case, the knights insisted on the symbolic difference between standing and sitting, because they perceived that there was a challenge to the hierarchy of rank between the two chambers. In this instance, *sessio* and *votum* served different purposes: *sessio* expressed rank-order, while *votum* pertained to decision-making.

But ceremony had more functions than this. In particular, the nobles suspected that, in addition to the parity of rank, the cities were demanding ceremonial changes in order to obtain the *"jus suffragandi simultaneum"*—the right to vote simultaneously, in plenary session, with the knights.[61] In the end, the right to sit would give the second chamber a means to introduce simultaneous and joint voting. In the knights' view, that would have changed the traditional procedure dramatically, "because it is well-known that at all territorial diets and public congresses the cities took their votes separately."[62] In this line of argumentation, *sessio* and *votum* were closely intertwined because the cities tried to influence the voting procedure through ceremonial change—or so the knights insinuated. As Barbara Stollberg-Rilinger has shown, this was possible because "the order of seating that was a ceremonial, visible, and symbolic procedure can be considered as a functional equivalent to an abstract technical procedure."[63] To put it briefly: ceremony functioned as a sort of standing, procedural order for the diet. Deliberating and voting were possible only because the diet was structured by solemnities.[64] This can be called the instrumental function of ceremony. From the knights' point of view, the cities were striving for a procedural advantage and tried to realize it through ceremonial change.[65]

Ultimately, though, the nobles' anxieties about sitting with commoners at one and the same table were prompted neither by parity of rank nor by procedural advantage. Serious though they were, the nobles thought of these threats as "mere" consequences resulting from a more fundamental change. Specifically, the nobles charged that what really motivated the civic delegates was their desire "to form one corpus with prelates and knights."[66] The first chamber feared nothing less than the loss of its status as an independent corporation. This function of ceremony is different from its symbolic and instrumental ones. The status of the noble *curia* was based almost entirely on custom; maintaining its preeminence required the constant and visible reiteration of that aristocratic superiority through ceremonial acts. Ceremony therefore functioned not only as the standing procedural order, but also as the very "embodiment" of the diet as a whole and of both chambers, respectively. For this reason, I would like to call this the constitutive function of ceremony. This label is not meant to connote "constitutions" in the conventional sense; rather, it stresses the idea that ceremony made the chamber present as a *corpus* in the literal sense. For individual actors, there is normally no need to be made present *as* bodies, because they obviously *have* bodies. But corporate actors lack "real," physical bodies and, for that reason, must be embodied through acts of representation. Not without reason was it said that corporate actors came into existence by a *fictio iuris*.[67] But in the Hessian case, neither the diet nor its two chambers possessed a common purse, staff, seal, or archive, and they therefore had virtually no material symbol of their status as a corporation.[68] Nevertheless, they could be powerful institutions because their institutional "being" found its constitutive expression in the ceremonial arrangements.[69]

These three functions of ceremony help explain why the conflict broke out when it did. Why did it erupt in 1704 and not in the decades before or after? As we have seen, one and the same issue—the seating of the second chamber's director—was interpreted as a matter of customary right by the cities and as an "innovation" by the knights. Although they deployed it differently, both corporate actors relied on the same categorical distinction between "custom" and "innovation" to frame the situation: both chambers claimed that, before 1704, a clear and customary ceremonial order had existed; each chamber claimed that the other had attempted to alter unlawfully an old practice. If one adopts the view that there had indeed been an undisputed ceremonial order before 1704, then the institutional structure of the diet cannot have been the source of conflict. Instead, this view would compel us to search for factors beyond the diet—factors such as general political animosities or conflicting economic interests. The problem with this approach is that there are no signs of external conflicts that originated, intensified, or culminated in the years before 1704; even the principal conflict over the exemption of the knights from the monthly contribution was only latent at that time.[70]

Factors arising *within* the diet, by contrast, offer a more satisfactory explanation. To see how, it is important to bear in mind that a full-fledged ceremonial system that fulfilled all three functions was not an inherent feature of representative institutions, but the product of a long-term process of institutionalization. In that process, according to Arnold Gehlen, more and more elements of a given institutional arrangement acquire "autonomous value" (*Selbstwert*); that is, they transform from simple expedients valuable for their utility into procedural norms.[71] The role of ceremony in territorial diets is a perfect example of increasing institutionalization: in the sixteenth century, for instance, the Hessian diets were typically brief affairs—normally just one or two days. No one objected if the prince summoned only one of the estates; and we hear of virtually no solemnities apart from the inauguration.[72] As in many other principalities, these were ad hoc assemblies without a developed ceremonial order.[73] Over the course of the seventeenth century, however, the diet's ceremonial order became institutionalized. A territorial settlement in 1655, for example, codified the diet's bicameral structure.[74] As institutionalization accelerated, more and more instrumental arrangements were "ceremonialized" and became charged with meaning and value. Until then, questions of ceremonial order had been settled ad hoc, according to each diet's specific circumstances. It is therefore unlikely that a uniform practice developed before the mid seventeenth century. Later on, when seating arrangements started to fulfill ceremonial functions, the very *disorder* of earlier practices created potential for conflict. Both *curiae* could find advantageous "precedents" in the past and attempt to redefine them as procedural norms that carried the legal weight of "ancient custom."

By 1700, the "importance of being seated" was paramount: fifty years of institutionalization (since 1655) had produced so much tension that it was only a question of time until an actual conflict erupted. There are other signs supporting this interpretation: in 1722, the estates of Hessen-Darmstadt became embroiled in an almost identical quarrel.[75] The estates were a tinderbox, but as yet there was no spark—until Mayor Henrich Christoph Ehinger asked to be seated. The new delegate from Kassel had already caused a stir by attempting to address the landgrave directly—an undisputed privilege of the hereditary marshal.[76] Ehinger's demand for a seat one day later added fuel to the fire. Thus, an utterly contingent factor—the personal impetuosity of the capital's mayor—was enough to release tensions that had been welling up for decades.

Conclusion: Diets as *lieux de mémoire* for Modern Parliamentary Government?

As polities, the empire and its territories were characterized by the presence of corporate actors—the imperial and the provincial estates, respectively—whose predominant sites of activity were the diets. Between the Peace of Westphalia and the empire's end, most diets developed or adopted elaborate systems of ceremony. Because of this connection, the analysis of conflicts over ceremony can shed light on its political functions and on the changing conditions of corporate action.

Early modern diets should be understood as institutions characterized both by ceremonial shaping and by decision-making in ways that closely intertwined *sessio* and *votum*.[77] For the diet of the Landgraviate of Hessen-Kassel, it is possible to distinguish three functions of ceremony: it constituted the diet and the chambers as independent institutions; it symbolized the socio-political rank order; and it structured the instrumental procedures of deliberation and voting. Ceremony was no trivial matter, but rather one of the diet's fundamental, structuring principles.

For corporate actors, the constitutive function was of utmost importance, because they were compelled to represent their fictious, "mystical" bodies with visible signs and symbols. Ceremony was an appropriate means to this end and in Hessen-Kassel, the diet's two *curiae* heavily relied on ceremonial arrangements to symbolize their status as corporations. Of course, this function could also be fulfilled by other means, such as buildings, written constitutions, or signatures.[78] But solemnities remained the primary mode of corporate representation. The estates' insistence on adhering to proper ceremonial forms, and their readiness to do battle over perceived violations of custom, was therefore rational and necessary.

On the other hand, such full-fledged systems of ceremony were also the product of long-lasting institutionalization processes. Originally, questions of seating and procedure were resolved ad hoc, according to the circumstances. Later, as seating arrangements became charged with meaning, the earlier disorganization inevitably led to conflicts over which procedure had *really* been customary.

Paradoxically, the end of this story brings us back to the perspective of critics of parliamentary institutions, such as Houston Stewart Chamberlain. Ultimately, it took the intervention of a prince, Elector Wilhelm I (the former Landgrave Wilhelm IX),[79] to change the institutional structure of the diet fundamentally: in 1815, he ordered "that at meetings of all chambers the members of the diet should take their seats at one table."[80] Wilhelm's leveling intervention banished forever "the importance of being seated." In his memoirs, this same Wilhelm referred to the estates' delegates as "troublemakers," and his absolutistic decision obviously did not aim at strengthening the "parliamentary" aspects of the assembly.[81] Left to their own devices, the estates would in all likelihood have clung to their "customary" ways. In their reliance on ceremony, the majority of territorial diets remained pre-modern in character. The procedural hallmark of modern representative bodies is that they transfer the constituting and instrumental functions to non-ceremonial constitutions and written standing orders. The fact that in most cases, early modern estates were not able to break away from the imperatives of symbolizing rank should raise some doubts about claiming these territorial diets for the history of modern parliamentary government.[82]

Notes

1. Houston Stewart Chamberlain, *Demokratie und Freiheit* (Munich, 1917), 74; on Chamberlain, see Geoffrey G. Field, *Evangelist of Race. The Germanic Vision of Houston Stewart Chamberlain* (New York, 1981).
2. Adolf Hitler, *Mein Kampf. Zwei Bände in einem Band* (Munich, 1934), 57. Vladimir I. Lenin, *Staat und Revolution. Die Lehre des Marxismus vom Staat und die Aufgaben des Proletariats in der Revolution*, in Lenin, *Ausgewählte Werke*, vol. 2 (Berlin, 1951), 158–253, here 192.
3. See Hans Boldt, "Parlament, parlamentarische Regierung, Parlamentarismus," in *Geschichtliche Grundbegriffe. Historisches Lexikon zur politisch-sozialen Sprache in Deutschland*, eds. Otto Brunner, Werner Conze, and Reinhart Koselleck, vol. 4 (Stuttgart, 1978), 649–676.
4. See Francis L. Carsten, *Princes and Parliaments in Germany. From the 15th to the 18th Century* (Oxford and London, 1959), and recently Michael A.R. Graves, *The Parliaments of Early Modern Europe* (Harlow, 2001); see Barbara Stollberg-Rilinger, "Ständische Repräsentation—Kontinuität oder Kontinuitätsfiktion?" in *Zeitschrift für Neuere Rechtsgeschichte* 28 (2006): 279–298.
5. See Peter Blickle, "Politische Landschaften in Oberschwaben. Bäuerliche und bürgerliche Repräsentation im Rahmen des frühen europäischen Parlamentarismus," in *Landschaften und Landstände in Oberschwaben. Bäuerliche und bürgerliche Repräsentation im Rahmen des frühen europäischen Parlamentarismus*, ed. P. Blickle (Tübingen, 2000), 11–32. See also Kersten Krüger, *Die landständische Verfassung* (Munich, 2003), 1.
6. See Albrecht P. Luttenberger, "Pracht und Ehre. Gesellschaftliche Repräsentation und Zeremoniell auf dem Reichstag," in *Alltag im 16. Jahrhundert. Studien zu Lebensformen in mitteleuropäischen Städten*, ed. Alfred Kohler (Munich, 1987), 290–326; Barbara Stollberg-Rilinger, "Zeremoniell als politisches Verfahren. Rangordnung und Rangstreit als Strukturmerkmale des frühneuzeitlichen Reichstags," in *Neue Studien zur frühneuzeitlichen Reichsgeschichte*, ed. Johannes Kunisch (Berlin, 1997), 91–132.
7. See Ulf Brünning, "Wege landständischer Entscheidungsfindung. Das Verfahren auf den Landtagen des rheinischen Erzstifts zur Zeit Clemens Augusts," in *Im Wechselspiel der Kräfte. Politische Entwicklungen des 17. und 18. Jahrhunderts in Kurköln*, ed. Frank G. Zehnder (Cologne, 1999), 161–184; and Tim Neu, "Zeremonielle Verfahren. Zur Funktionalität vormoderner politisch-administrativer Prozesse am Beispiel des Landtags im Fürstbistum Münster," in *Im Schatten der Macht. Kommunikationskulturen in Politik und Verwaltung 1600–1950*, eds. Stefan Haas and Mark Hengerer (Frankfurt a.M., 2007), 23–50.
8. Johann August Reichardt and Michael de Huttern, *De statibus provincialibus eorumque variis iuribus*, vol. 1 (Jena, 1768), 4. See also Johann Jacob Moser, *Von der Teutschen Reichs-Stände Landen, deren Landständen, Unterthanen, Landes-Freyheiten, Beschwerden, Schulden und Zusammenkünfften* (Frankfurt a.M. and Leipzig, 1769), 322.

9. For territorial diets see the contributions in the special issue "Politisch-soziale Praxis und symbolische Kultur der landständischen Verfassungen im westfälischen Raum," in *Westfälische Forschungen* 53 (2003): 1–240, especially the ones by Stollberg-Rilinger, Luebke, and Brakensiek. Regarding the imperial diet see Barbara Stollberg-Rilinger, "Die Symbolik der Reichstage. Überlegungen zu einer Perspektivenumkehr," in *Der Reichstag 1486–1613. Kommunikation, Wahrnehmung, Öffentlichkeit,* eds. Maximilian Lanzinner and Arno Strohmeyer (Göttingen, 2006), 77–93.

10. See Ronald G. Asch, "Estates and Princes after 1648: The Consequences of the Thirty Years' War," in *German History* 6 (1988): 113–132, here 125–127.

11. See, for instance, [Georg Adolf Caroc], *Begründete Deduction von Land-Ständen, derselben Befugnissen, Pflichten und Nutzen, absonderlich in denen Landen des Reichs Teutscher Nation* (n.p., 1718).

12. See, for instance, Gabriele Haug-Moritz, "Die Behandlung des württembergischen Ständekonflikts unter Herzog Carl Eugen durch den Reichshofrat (1763/64–1768/70)," in *Die politische Funktion des Reichskammergerichts,* ed. Bernhard Diestelkamp (Cologne, 1993), 105–133.

13. See James S. Coleman, *Foundations of Social Theory* (Cambridge, MA, 1990), 325–530.

14. See Friedrich Hermann Schubert, *Die deutschen Reichstage in der Staatslehre der frühen Neuzeit* (Göttingen, 1960); and Peter Moraw, "Versuch über die Entstehung des Reichstags," in *Politische Ordnungen und soziale Kräfte im Alten Reich,* ed. Hermann Weber (Wiesbaden, 1980), 1–36.

15. For a list of principalities with territorial estates see Krüger, *Die Landständische Verfassung,* 18–26. For greater detail, see Moser, *Von der Teutschen Reichs-Stände Landen,* 346–485.

16. See Volker Press, "Formen des Ständewesens in den deutschen Territorialstaaten des 16. und 17. Jahrhunderts," in *Ständetum und Staatsbildung in Brandenburg-Preussen. Ergebnisse einer internationalen Fachtagung,* ed. Peter Baumgart (Berlin and New York, 1983), 280–318, here 295.

17. See Heinrich Binn and Ludolf Hugo, *De Statu Regionum Germaniae, Et Regimine Principum Summae Imperii Reip. Aemulo, Nec Non De Usu Autoritate Iuris Civilis Privati, Quam In Hac Parte Iuris Publici Obtinet, Disputatio Inauguralis* (Helmstedt, 1661), ch. 4, § 12. See also Barbara Stollberg-Rilinger, *Vormünder des Volkes? Konzepte landständischer Repräsentation in der Spätphase des Alten Reiches* (Berlin, 1999), 28–45 and 56–76.

18. See the seminal contributions: Robert Darnton, "A Bourgeois Puts His World in Order: The City as a Text," in Darnton, *The Great Cat-Massacre and Other Episodes in French Cultural History* (New York, 1984), 107–143; Hedda Ragotzky and Horst Wenzel, eds., *Höfische Repräsentation. Das Zeremoniell und die Zeichen* (Tübingen, 1990); Jörg J. Berns and Thomas Rahn, eds., *Zeremoniell als höfische Ästhetik in Spätmittelalter und früher Neuzeit* (Tübingen, 1995); and Edward Muir, *Ritual in Early Modern Europe,* 2nd ed. (Cambridge, 1997), 252–293.

19. See Stollberg-Rilinger, "Zeremoniell als politisches Verfahren"; and Luttenberger, "Pracht und Ehre."

20. See, for instance, André Krischer, who analyzes the imperial cities' struggle for ceremonial equality at the imperial diet. Krischer, *Reichsstädte in der Fürstengesellschaft. Politischer Zeichengebrauch in der frühen Neuzeit* (Darmstadt, 2006), 44–80.

21. On Hessen-Kassel in general, see Charles W. Ingrao, *The Hessian Mercenary State: Ideas, Institutions, and Reform under Frederick II. 1760–1785* (Cambridge, 1987); and Hans Philippi, *Die Landgrafschaft Hessen-Kassel 1648–1806* (Marburg, 2007).
22. See the classical account in Otto Brunner, *Land and Lordship: Structures of Governance in Medieval Austria*, trans. and intro. by H. Kaminsky and J. Van Horn Melton (Philadelphia, 1992); and Hasso Hofmann, *Repräsentation. Studien zur Wort- und Begriffsgeschichte von der Antike bis ins 19. Jahrhundert*, 4th ed. (Berlin, 2003). For Hessen-Kassel see Günter Hollenberg, "Die Repräsentation von Land und Leuten in Hessen," in *Reformation und Landesherrschaft*, ed. Inge Auerbach (Marburg, 2005), 31–38.
23. Johann Georg Estor and Johann Wilhelm Fech, *De Comitiis et Ordinibus Hassiae praesertim Cassellanae provincialibus opusculum* (Frankfurt/Main, 1752), 4.
24. "Vergleich Landgraf Wilhelms VI. mit der Ritterschaft, Kassel 1655 Okt. 2," in *Hessen-Kasselische Landtagsabschiede 1649–1798*, ed. Günter Hollenberg (Marburg, 1989), 56–66, here 59. See Armand Maruhn, "Duale Staatsbildung contra ständisches Landesbewusstsein. 1655 als Epochenjahr der hessischen Landesgeschichte," in *Zeitschrift des Vereins für Hessische Geschichte und Landeskunde* 109 (2004): 71–94.
25. On the Hessian *landständische Verfassung* in general see Hollenberg, "Einleitung," in Hollenberg, *Hessen-Kasselische Landtagsabschiede*, xiii–lxix; Conrad Wilhelm Ledderhose, *Von der landschaftlichen Verfassung der Hessen-Casselischen Lande*, in Ledderhose, *Kleine Schriften*, vol. 1 (Marburg, 1787), 1–176. The institutional sketches in Carsten, *Princes and Parliaments*, 149–190, and Ingrao, *Mercenary State*, 37–43, contain some mistakes. See Hollenberg, "Einleitung," xxi.
26. See Ledderhose, *Von der landschaftlichen Verfassung*, 66–68; and Hollenberg, "Einleitung," xxii.
27. On the estates of Hessen-Kassel in the second half of the seventeenth and in the eighteenth century, see Andreas Würgler, "Desideria und Landesordnungen. Kommunaler und landständischer Einfluß auf die fürstliche Gesetzgebung in Hessen-Kassel 1650–1800," in *Gemeinde und Staat im alten Europa*, ed. Peter Blickle (Munich, 1998), 149–207; Günter Hollenberg, "Die hessen-kasselischen Landstände im 18. Jahrhundert," in *Hessisches Jahrbuch für Landesgeschichte* 38 (1988): 1–22; Karl E. Demandt, "Die Hessischen Landstände nach dem 30jährigen Krieg," in *Ständische Vertretungen in Europa im 17. und 18. Jahrhundert*, ed. Dietrich Gerhard (Göttingen, 1974), 162–182.
28. After the cession of Treffurt to Electoral Saxony in 1736, thirty-nine corporate members remained.
29. See Gunter Thies, *Territorialstaat und Landesverteidigung. Das Landesdefensionswerk in Hessen-Kassel unter Landgraf Moritz (1592–1627)* (Darmstadt, 1973).
30. The reality was far more complex than this general overview. For details, see Hollenberg, "Einleitung," xxix–xxx; and Ledderhose, *Von der landschaftlichen Verfassung*, 19–47.
31. See Hollenberg, "Einleitung," xlviii; Ledderhose, *Von der landschaftlichen Verfassung*, 111–114.
32. This corporate identity had developed since the 1620s; see Robert von Friedeburg, "Widerstandsrecht und Landespatriotismus. Territorialstaatsbildung und Patriotenpflichten in den Auseinandersetzungen der niederhessischen Stände mit Landgräfin Amelie Elisabeth und Landgraf Wilhelm VI. von Hessen-Kassel 1647–1653," in *Wissen, Gewissen und Wissenschaft im Widerstandsrecht (16.–18. Jh.)*, eds. Angela De Benedictis and Karl-Heinz Lingens (Frankfurt a.M., 2003), 267–327, here 319–324.

33. See Hollenberg, *Hessen-Kasselische Landtagsabschiede*, 203–211.
34. For the functions of parliamentary oratory see Jörg Feuchter and Johannes Helmrath, eds., *Politische Redekultur in der Vormoderne. Die Oratorik europäischer Parlamente in Spätmittelalter und Früher Neuzeit* (Frankfurt a.M., 2008); and Peter Mack, *Elizabethan Rhetoric. Theory and Practice* (Cambridge, 2002), 215–252.
35. Hessisches Staatsarchiv Marburg (hereafter HStAM), 304 Stift Kaufungen, no. 541, fols. 19r–29v, "Ritterschaftl. Protocollum beym Landt-Communications tage ao 1704" (hereafter "Ritterschaftl. Protocollum"), the inauguration ceremony fol. 19r, 3 April 1704.
36. HStAM, "Ritterschaftl. Protocollum," fol. 21v, 4 April 1704.
37. HStAM, "Ritterschaftl. Protocollum," fol. 22r, 4 April 1704.
38. See Thomas Simon, "Geltung. Der Weg von der Gewohnheit zur Positivität des Rechts," in *Rechtsgeschichte* 7 (2005): 100–137.
39. HStAM, "Ritterschaftl. Protocollum," fol. 22r, 4 April 1704. See Milos Vec, "Juristische Normen des Anstands. Zur Ausdifferenzierung und Konvergenz von Recht und Sitte bei Christian Thomasius," in *Rechtssymbolik und Wertevermittlung*, ed. Reiner Schulze (Berlin, 2004), 69–100.
40. HStAM, "Ritterschaftl. Protocollum," fol. 23r, 4 April 1704.
41. HStAM, "Ritterschaftl. Protocollum," fol. 29v, 12 April 1704. See Andreas Würgler, "Voices From Among the 'Silent Masses.' Humble Petitions and Social Conflicts in Early Modern Central Europe," in *International Review of Social History* 46: 9 (2001): 11–34.
42. HStAM, 73 Hessische Landstände, no. 222, fols. 9r-9v, "Cop[ia] fürstl[ich] g[nädig]ster resolution vor die Statt Cassell wegen Stuhlsetzens undt Session bey denen Landtagen" (hereafter "Resolution"), 31 December 1708. In the archive of the Privy Council, one also finds a file regarding the conflict, but it contains only two copies of the cited resolution and the cities' plea for it. See HStAM, 5 Geheimer Rat, no. 14674 "Anspruch der Stadt Kassel auf Stuhlsetzung an den Landtagen."
43. See, in general, Hermann Krause, "Gewohnheitsrecht," in *Handwörterbuch zur deutschen Rechtsgeschichte*, eds. Adalbert Erler and Ekkehard Kaufmann, vol. 1 (Berlin, 1971), 1675–1684. On custom as the vital argument in conflicts regarding ceremony and rank, see Maren Bleckmann, "Suppliken zu Rangkonflikten an den Herzog von Braunschweig-Wolfenbüttel im 17. und 18. Jahrhundert," in *Formen der politischen Kommunikation in Europa vom 15. bis 18. Jahrhundert. Bitten, Beschwerden, Briefe*, eds. Cecilia Nubola and Andreas Würgler (Berlin, 2004), 95–115, here 114; and Barbara Stollberg-Rilinger, "Rang vor Gericht. Zur Verrechtlichung sozialer Rangkonflikte in der frühen Neuzeit," in *Zeitschrift für historische Forschung* 28 (2001): 385–418, here 413.
44. HStAM, 73 Hessische Landstände, no. 304, fols. 9r-10v, "Attestatum vom H[err]n Rath Mootzen wegen des stuhl setzens," 10 April 1704, here fol. 9r.
45. The same conclusion concerning another territory in Bleckmann, "Suppliken," 111.
46. See Karl-Siegbert Rehberg, "Institutionen als symbolische Ordnungen. Leitfragen und Grundkategorien zur Theorie und Analyse institutioneller Mechanismen," in *Die Eigenart der Institutionen. Zum Profil politischer Institutionentheorie*, ed. Gerhard Göhler (Baden-Baden, 1994), 47–84; Barbara Stollberg-Rilinger, "Symbolische Kommunikation in der Vormoderne. Begriffe—Thesen—Forschungsperspektiven," in *Zeitschrift für Historische Forschung* 31 (2004): 489–527.

47. Ronald G. Asch, "Noble Corporations and Provincial Diets in the Ecclesiastical Principalities of the Holy Roman Empire ca. 1648–1802," in *Realities of Representation: State Building in Early Modern Europe and European America*, ed. Maija Jansson (New York, 2007), 93–111, here 94.
48. HStAM, "Ritterschaftl. Protocollum," fol. 23r, 4 April 1704.
49. See Barbara Stollberg-Rilinger, "Herstellung und Darstellung politischer Einheit: Instrumentelle und symbolische Dimensionen politischer Repräsentation im 18. Jahrhundert," in *Die Sinnlichkeit der Macht. Herrschaft und Repräsentation seit der Frühen Neuzeit*, eds. Jan Andres, Alexa Geisthövel, and Matthias Schwengelbeck (Frankfurt/Main, 2005), 73–92, here 90; and Axel Gotthard, *Das Alte Reich. 1495–1806* (Darmstadt, 2003), 23. For the Middle Ages see Thomas N. Bisson, "Celebration and Persuasion: Reflections on the Cultural Evolution of Medieval Consultation," in *Legislative Studies Quarterly* 7 (1982): 181–204; 183.
50. HStAM, 73 Hessische Landstände, no. 222, fols. 1r–5r, "Protocollum bey der den 9 t: Jan: gehaltenen Conferentz zu Treysa" (hereafter "Protocollum"), here fol. 1v and passim, 9 January 1709.
51. See Hollenberg, *Hessen-Kasselische Landtagsabschiede 1649–1798*, 211–216.
52. HStAM, "Resolution." The mayor and council of Kassel requested the repetition: see their letter to the landgrave in HStAM, 5 Geheimer Rat, no. 14674, fol. 2r/v and fol. 7 r/v.
53. HStAM, "Protocollum," fols. 1r–1v, 9 January 1709.
54. HStAM, 73 Hessische Landstände, no. 76, fols. 65r–73r, "Actum Treysa in der Stadt Rath Stube" (hereafter "Actum"), here fol. 65r, 9 January 1709.
55. HStAM, "Protocollum," fols. 1v, 9 January 1709.
56. HStAM, "Actum," fol. 66r, 9 January 1709.
57. HStAM, "Actum," fol. 67r, 9 January 1709.
58. HStAM, 73 Hessische Landstände, no. 222, fols. 19r–20v, "Memorial und Relation," 14 January 1709.
59. A similar case from the Prince-Bishopric of Münster is in Neu, "Zeremonielle Verfahren," 44–49.
60. HStAM, 73 Hessische Landstände, no. 76, fols. 143r–145v, "Copia Schreibens ahn die hochfürstl[ichen] H[erren] geheimbde Räthe zu Caßell von dem H[errn] Erb-Marschall per Staffetta de dato Treiß d 11. t Jan: 1709 abgeschickt" (hereafter "Copia Schreibens"), here fol. 144r.
61. HStAM, "Copia Schreibens," fol. 144r.
62. HStAM, "Copia Schreibens," fol. 144r.
63. Stollberg-Rilinger, "Zeremoniell als politisches Verfahren," 117.
64. The jurists writing on the territorial estates and their diets in many cases identified the ceremonial and the procedural order. For instance, the chapter dealing—from a modern perspective—with the standing orders in Johann Theodoretus von Fliessenhaussen, *De Comitiis Provincialibus. Das ist gründlicher Bericht von Land-Tägen* (n.p., 1692), 14–22, is entitled "On the territorial diets in particular and their solemnities."
65. Another means of using the ceremonial/procedural order instrumentally is demonstrated by David M. Luebke in "Ceremony and Dissent: Religion, Procedural Conflicts, and the 'Fiction of Consensus' in Seventeenth-Century Germany," included in this volume. Luebke convincingly shows that procedural conflict could function as a code to discuss very delicate matters in an indirect way.

66. HStAM, "Copia Schreibens," fol. 143v.
67. On the close connection between the concepts "representation" and "fiction" see Edmund S. Morgan, "Government by Fiction: The Idea of Representation," in *The Yale Review* 72 (1983): 321–339.
68. See Ledderhose, *Von der landschaftlichen Verfassung*, 114; Hollenberg, "Einleitung," xlvii.
69. The reliance on visible, normative solemnities and procedures is typical of the so-called "corpus" representation. See Hasso Hofmann, "Der spätmittelalterliche Rechtsbegriff der Repräsentation in Reich und Kirche," in Ragotzky and Wenzel, *Höfische Repräsentation*, 17–42, here 27. See also Christoph Besold, *De Jure Universitatum*, in idem, *Iuridico-Politicae Dissertationes. De Iure Rerum, (2) Familiarum, (3) Collegiorum, (4) Academiarum (5) aliarumque Universitatum, (6) ac item Territoriorum* (Strasbourg, 1624), 224–264, here 242.
70. See Hollenberg, "Einleitung," xxxii.
71. See Arnold Gehlen, *Urmensch und Spätkultur. Philosophische Ergebnisse und Aussagen*, 6th edn. (Frankfurt a.M., 2004), 15, and also Karl-Siegbert Rehberg, "Eine Grundlagentheorie der Institutionen: Arnold Gehlen. Mit systematischen Schlußfolgerungen für eine kritische Institutionentheorie," in *Die Rationalität politischer Institutionen. Interdisziplinäre Perspektiven*, eds. Gerhard Göhler, Kurt Lenk, and Rainer Schmalz-Bruns (Baden-Baden, 1990), 115–144; Peter L. Berger and Thomas Luckmann, *The Social Construction of Reality: A Treatise in the Sociology of Knowledge* (Garden City, NY, 1967).
72. See the table in Günter Hollenberg, ed., *Hessische Landtagsabschiede 1526–1603* (Marburg, 1994), 401–402; and Hans Siebeck, *Die landständische Verfassung Hessens im sechzehnten Jahrhundert* (Kassel, 1914), 61–84.
73. See Günter Hollenberg, "Einleitung," in Hollenberg, *Hessische Landtagsabschiede 1526–1603*, 1–59, here 37, describing very different procedures of voting. See also Gabriele Haug-Moritz, "Reichstag, schmalkaldische Bundestage, ernestinische Land- und Ausschußtage der 1530er Jahre als ständische Institutionen. Eine vergleichende Betrachtung," in *Zelebrieren und Verhandeln. Zur Praxis ständischer Institutionen im frühneuzeitlichen Europa*, eds. Tim Neu, Michael Sikora, and Thomas Weller (Münster, 2009) 37–60.
74. See Armand Maruhn, *Necessitäres Regiment und fundamentalgesetzlicher Ausgleich. Der hessische Ständekonflikt 1646–1655* (Darmstadt, 2004), 86–96.
75. See Hessisches Staatsarchiv Darmstadt, F 27 Herrschaft Riedesel zu Eisenbach, A Samtarchiv, no. 64/53: "Korrespondenz mit Landgraf Ernst Ludwig von Hessen-Darmstadt über die Forderung der Landschaft auf Sitzen in der Ritterstube und Berufung durch einen Kavalier bei Abhaltung von Landtagen."
76. See HStAM, "Ritterschaftl. Protocollum," fols. 21v, 4 April 1704, and Hollenberg, *Hessen-Kasselische Landtagsabschiede*, 212.
77. See Stollberg-Rilinger, "Herstellung und Darstellung politischer Einheit," 90; and Tim Neu, "Landtag," in *Enzyklopädie der Neuzeit*, ed. Friedrich Jaeger, vol. 7 (Stuttgart and Weimar, 2008), 564–566.
78. See David M. Luebke, "Signatures and Political Culture in Eighteenth-Century Germany," in *The Journal of Modern History* 76 (2004): 497–530.
79. See Ludolf Pelizaeus, *Der Aufstieg Württembergs und Hessens zur Kurwürde 1692–1803* (Frankfurt a.M., 2000), 301–494.

80. HStAM, 7 a Oberhofmarschallsamt 1 Gef. 212, no. 2, "Oberhofmarschallamts-Protokoll das Ceremoniel bei dem engeren Landtag im Jahr 1815 betreffend," 26 February 1815. The emphasis is on "fundamentally," because one minor change was introduced in 1764: during long plenary conferences between the two chambers, all civic delegates were allowed to sit. But the ceremonial separation was maintained, because they had to sit behind the seats of the nobles. See Ledderhose, *Von der landschaftlichen Verfassung*, 95–96; and Hollenberg, "Einleitung," 212–213.
81. Rainer von Hessen, ed., *"Wir Wilhelm von Gottes Gnaden." Die Lebenserinnerungen Kurfürst Wilhelms I. von Hessen. 1743–1821* (Frankfurt/Main, 1996), 415.
82. Also stressing the aspect of discontinuity are Barbara Stollberg-Rilinger, "Ständische Repräsentation," 293, and Mathias Mesenhöller, "Entwicklungspotentiale und –grenzen des Adelsparlamentarismus am Beispiel des polnischen Lehnsherzogtums / russischen Gouvernements Kurland," in *Aufbrüche in die Moderne. Frühparlamentarismus zwischen altständischer Ordnung und monarchischem Konstitutionalismus 1750–1850. Schlesien—Deutschland—Mitteleuropa*, ed. Roland Gehrke (Cologne, 2005), 317–332.

SECTION 3

Ceremony, Procedure, & Legitimation

CHAPTER 8

Ceremony and Dissent
Religion, Procedural Conflicts, and the "Fiction of Consensus" in Seventeenth-Century Germany

DAVID M. LUEBKE

Thumbing one's way through the protocols of territorial assemblies, one is easily lulled into an impression of serene harmony among the members of the *corpus mysticum*, in which all things necessary for the common good are provided with dutiful alacrity. The inaugural solemnities having been performed, the prince or his representative makes his formal *Proposition*. The *curiae* then separate from one another to consult and to offer emendations. After the proposals and counterproposals have been considered and reconciled, the chambers cast their corporate ballots on the final *Recess*, and with its sealing, the well-being of the body politic is assured for another year. This impression of harmonious interaction was, of course, fully intended and, strictly speaking, fictitious. Behind the scenes, bickering over credentials, precedence, and rank order often consumed a great deal of any diet's business.[1] And, of course, the material interests of princes, nobility, clergy, and civic corporations diverged as often as they coincided. But the dramaturges and stenographers of these proceedings avoided explicit reference to any such tensions. The dominant metaphors of political life, after all, were organic; territorial estates could no more afford the appearance of discord than a human body could tolerate warfare among its vital organs. Therefore, the estates' solemnities theatricalized social order with a communicative ambiguity that both obscured conflict and reinforced the fiction of consensus and concord among all of the members of the polity.[2]

If anything could tear the mask of tranquility from the face of politics, surely it was a conflict over religion. In sixteenth- and seventeenth-century Germany, every territorial assembly (*Landtag*) containing more than one religion among its members was forced to confront the inherent tension between confessional pluralism and the fiction of consensus—a tension that only sharpened when princes began requiring demonstrations of orthodoxy, even from corporations that claimed a privilege to determine their own confession. Sometimes these tensions drove a wedge between Protestant and Catholic estates; in ecclesiastical territories of the empire, they often pitted reforming princes against conservative coalitions united by a common interest in preserving the ability of privileged estates to determine their own religion.[3] Sometimes territorial assemblies dealt with these tensions straightforwardly, by holding tax grants hostage to concessions in matters of religion. Conversely, a *Landtag* might deal with confessional tensions obliquely, through the manipulation of ceremony and procedure.

This essay is about an assembly—the territorial estates of the Prince-Bishopric of Münster—that in November 1608 attempted to establish a regime of de facto religious toleration by using the oblique methods of ceremonial and procedural manipulation. In the history of European religion, this territory is best known for the spectacular upheavals of 1534 and 1535, when Melchiorite Anabaptists tried to remake the capital city in anticipation of the Apocalypse.[4] Less well understood is the pluriconfessional culture that gradually took shape in the aftermath of that trauma; virtually unknown is the manner in which the territorial diet strove to preserve that regime when it came under attack from a reforming prince-bishop.[5] This is because the question of religious toleration never became the object of explicit bargaining between the prince and the diet. Rather than confronting them head on, the estates treated confessional matters through procedural maneuvers, but in ways that both expressed precise ecclesio-political aims and instrumentalized a collective need to uphold the appearance of concord.

To read procedural conflicts this way, indeed to attribute *any* instrumentality to the "merely" ceremonial or procedural aspects of parliamentary deliberation, is to buck a venerable historiographical tradition. The tendency to distinguish sharply between decision-making and "external and symbolic demonstrations" is at least as old as Denis Diderot, who defined "ceremonies" in these terms for the *Encyclopédie* he co-edited.[6] During the French Revolution, of course, this polarity between political essence and affect would be mobilized to demolish the system of political representation by metaphorical embodiment—in which the mystical body politic was incarnated through the solemn convening of its constituent organs—and to replace it with a system of general, liberal delegation. In nineteenth-century Germany, historians of the Prussian school disparaged early modern conflicts over ceremony as inconsequential squabbles. Instead, they painted territorial politics in the stark tones of dualistic confrontation, narrating the slow eclipse of estates before the ever-expanding power of the sovereign *Fürsten-Staat*. From their statist perspective, the growing preoccupation of territorial diets with matters of rank and precedence were symptomatic of institutional decay: the more estates were excluded from any *real* influence over matters of political importance, the more they filled their aimless time with petty quarrels over ritual and procedure.

The interpretation offered here could hardly differ more. First and foremost, I argue that to dismiss procedural conflicts as inconsequential trivia is to project modernist assumptions about the nature and function of political representation onto institutions that were structured around notions of embodiment and the *corpus mysticum*.[7] To understand the formalities of pre-modern estates in their proper cultural context means recognizing that there was more to their deliberations than decision-making. Indeed, as G.R. Elton, Peter Moraw, Barbara Stollberg-Rilinger, and others have argued, the purpose of pre-modern representation was not always, or even primarily, about reaching a decision, but equally about demonstrating social, political, and confessional relationships through ceremony and procedure.[8] Pre-modern assemblies, in other words, had socially expressive functions that transcended their narrowly legislative purposes.[9] Interpreting them as performances also means recognizing that these expressive functions did not necessarily require a "public" in the conventional modern sense—an autonomous, self-aware, and critical audience that was external to the assembly itself. This chapter argues instead that in the increasingly juridified world of early modern Europe, every ceremonial instantiation of social relationships had the potential to set precedents for litigation in the future. Whether or not anyone was watching, the eye of the law saw all that transpired.[10]

Territorial Estates, Noble Power, and Confession

Let us begin with the bishopric and its power structures. The prince-bishops of Münster presided over the largest ecclesiastical territory in the Holy Roman Empire.[11] But this wealth of lands was not always matched by political dominance inside the diocese. Since the thirteenth century, that position had most often been occupied by the territory's landed aristocracy, which kept a tight grip on membership in its own ranks.[12] Since 1392, moreover, membership in the cathedral chapter had been restricted to candidates of noble blood, which subsequently came to mean only those who could prove sixteen noble ancestors.[13] As a result, the territory's noble families supplied over eighty-five percent of the chapter's canons.[14] Thus, the interests of the cathedral chapter and the noble *curia*, though not identical, were densely interwoven by ties of kinship and status-group solidarity. In order to hold the bishop's power in check, the nobility and cathedral chapter occasionally formed pacts of mutual aid and defense with the cities and towns; these pacts laid the institutional foundation for the territorial estates.[15] Noble power peaked in the sixteenth century and was reflected, among other things, in the fact that for a century after 1522, bishops assumed office not by papal appointment, but as the result of election by the cathedral chapter.[16]

It was also reflected in a generally latitudinarian policy toward religion. Although the diocese never departed formally from the Roman fold, the chapter elected a series of bishops who were either Lutheran (Franz von Waldeck, 1532–1553; Wilhelm Ketteler, 1553–1557) or Erasmian by inclination (Bernhard von Raesfeld, 1557–1566; Johann von Hoya, 1566–1574).[17] Two of them, Ketteler and Raesfeld, were elected from within the ranks of the territorial nobility—yet another indication of its preeminence. All four were generally ill disposed toward forcible catholicization, least of all where the beliefs of their fellow nobles were concerned. As a result, noble families were usually left to worship as they pleased, a freedom that they believed was protected under imperial law by the *Declaratio Ferdinandea*, that much-contested codicil to the Peace of Augsburg, which extended toleration to privileged "nobles, cities, and communes" situated within ecclesiastical territories that "for a long time" (*lange Zeit und Jahr*) had adhered to the "Augsburg Confession."[18] By the late sixteenth century, a large percentage of the nobility—probably the great majority, although it is difficult to say precisely—had converted to some form of Protestantism.[19] It therefore comes as no surprise that the cathedral chapter never published the decrees of the Council of Trent in full, or that in 1575, it endorsed a Protestant candidate for the episcopal throne by a vote of seventeen to eleven.[20]

This regime began to change with the election of Ernst of Bavaria in 1585 (see Figure 8.1).[21] Here was a different sort of bishop: a Wittelsbach prince favored by King Philip II of Spain, Ernst already occupied the sees of Freising, Hildesheim, Liège, and Cologne by the time he acquired Münster. Unconstrained by local bonds of kinship, the *totus romanizatus et catholicissimus* Ernst was less deferential to the religious sensibilities of the Westphalian nobility than his predecessors had been; on the contrary, Ernst's familial and political ties placed him at the forefront of Tridentine reform in the empire.[22] Ernst was not as energetic a reformer as his two successors, his nephew Ferdinand I of Bavaria (1612–1650) and Christoph Bernhard von Galen (1651–1678), but his impact on confessional relations within the diocese was profound. One of his first acts upon taking office was to promulgate a thorough-going *Reformatio Religionis*.[23] To that end, Ernst established, in 1601, an Ecclesiastical Council to enforce Catholic orthodoxy among the parish clergy—a move that elicited an allergic response from the cathedral chapter, whose members, as diocesan archdeacons, exercised ecclesiastical jurisdiction within the diocese.[24] As a result, new lines of confrontation formed between forces of Tridentine reform and the defenders of a moderate status quo that tolerated Protestant religious observance on the part of nobles and the inhabitants of privileged towns.

Figure 8.1. Ernst of Bavaria (1554–1612), Bishop of Freising (1566), Hildesheim (1573), Liège (1581), and Münster (1585); Archbishop of Cologne (1583).

G *Ermanos inter Proceres, qui iura creandi*
Cæsaris antiquo more parata tenent;
Vox Moguntini princeps est Præsulis; HVIVS
Vnctio delecti Cæsaris esse solet.
AGRIPPINA; tuus nunc hunc ANTISTES honorem
Prisca Ducum soboles, non sine laude gerit.

M

Source: Image courtesy Mannheimer Texte Online (MATEO), http://www.uni-mannheim.de/mateo.

The *Landtag* of November 1608

These relationships framed the territorial diet of November 1608. On 14 November, the first day of proceedings, a delegation from the nobility met with the Vice-Chancellor, Antonius Weidenfeld, and representatives of the cathedral chapter to convey their desire for an alteration in the diet's decision-making procedure. The official protocol of the assembly records that in view of recent but unspecified "*difficulteten*," the nobles were unwilling to deliberate the *Proposition* unless certain grievances, which they shared with the privileged cities and towns that were represented in the diet, were first heard and "brought into" the estates' final resolution. The nobles' wording let slip that they had already discussed their grievances with the townsmen before the regular process of deliberation had begun—a mode of deliberation that the diet's existing procedures forbade. The cathedral chapter objected to the nobles' proposal, insisting that the diet's only business was to deliberate the items that were already contained in the prince's *Proposition*. From the canons' point of view, the matter turned on a question of princely authority: only the prince-bishop could decide what went into the *Proposition*. Negotiations over the procedural change dragged on another day. In the end, however, neither side was prepared to compromise. The cathedral chapter rejected any alteration of the diet's rules of procedure. As a result, the nobles' grievances received no formal airing, nor were they "brought into" the final resolution. But the chapter's intransigence came at a price to Bishop Ernst, who did not get the money he had requested that year for the "work of defense" (*Defensionswerk*). From a narrowly legislative perspective, therefore, the *Landtag* was a failure.[25]

Nowhere in the diet's protocols is it spelled out just what the nobles' grievances were. To find out, we must enter the chambers of the secular governing council (*weltlicher Rat*) and the cathedral chapter, where the dust-up was discussed in secret.[26] From the transcripts of these meetings, we learn that the nobles' intervention had been triggered by a "Mandate on Communion and Burial" that Ernst had been urging on the governing council since the spring of 1606. This decree forbade laypeople to receive the Eucharist "in both kinds"; it also forbade the laity from claiming the communion chalice by right of some special privilege granted by Ernst's predecessors in office. Even more upsetting, the mandate outlawed the burial *in loco sacro* of any person who had not received communion according "to the Catholic rite."[27] Nobles considered it a mark of their prestige to maintain domestic ministers (*Hauspriester*), from whom they might receive the sacraments in whatever manner they desired, in both kinds, or perhaps with the *fractio panis*.[28] Moreover, nobles of all religious inclinations claimed the right to an honorable burial. As recently as 1607, the noble *curia* had protested against an attempt by the cathedral chapter to prevent the burial of a Protestant noblewoman in her parish churchyard.[29] Likewise, in

September 1608, the family of a "known heretic" noblewoman demanded that her remains be buried honorably, inside the parish church in Vreden.[30] Let us be clear about this: Protestant nobles *wanted* to be buried in the consecrated grounds of formally Catholic parish churches.[31]

If implemented with any consistency, therefore, Ernst's edict would have deprived Protestant nobles of their *Hauspriester* as well as the right to an honorable burial in the parish churchyard. It therefore struck at the heart of noble privilege. For certain nobles, the scope of religious freedom had already become the stuff of contention. Among the nobles in attendance at the 1608 diet was Johann von der Recke zu Drensteinfurt, who by then was already embroiled in a noisy fight with Bishop Ernst over the status of his *Hauspriester*, Johann Eyeringhoff, whom the Ecclesiastical Council had removed from office on account of his "admitted heresy."[32] Ernst's edict likewise challenged the right claimed by civic communities to regulate their internal religious affairs. To be sure, this privilege was by no means secure. Members of the prince-bishopric's governing councils groused that the arrogant towns "want to be master … in religion and other ecclesiastical matters."[33] But the townsmen saw things very differently. They believed that the Peace of Augsburg entitled them, as privileged corporations subject to the authority of a prince-bishop, to allow the practice of either religion "permitted under imperial law."[34]

The diet of November 1608 brought all of these tensions to a head. The "Mandate on Communion and Burial" had been published a few weeks before the assembly, but only within the walls of Münster; Bishop Ernst had traveled from Cologne to attend the diet, in part to press for publishing his edict throughout the diocese.[35] If that happened, nobles and townsmen could no longer claim that the mandate applied only to the capital city. For both of the secular estates, therefore, the diet was an occasion to thwart confessional pressure. But unless Ernst agreed to put his own edict on the diet's agenda—a highly unlikely prospect, to say the least—there was no procedural means for the nobility to intervene collectively, as a privileged corporation, against it. At a minimum, then, the nobles' intervention threatened to broaden the *Landtag*'s deliberative competence and to undermine the bishop's monopoly on setting its agenda.

Rank Order and the Expressive Functions of Procedure

As I have described them so far, these transactions are perfectly consistent with the dualist narrative of early modern territorial politics. However, to grasp the full significance of the nobles' intervention, we have to think about procedure in symbolic terms as well. Inaugural ceremonies, the order in which the *curiae* deliberated, the manner and sequence in which they cast their collective votes:

all of these gestures and transactions described hierarchies of rank and precedence among the various estates, relations that every delegate implicitly ratified by participating in them. The purpose of territorial estates was therefore not simply to legislate or to generate cash for the "work of defense." It was also to theatricalize social order itself. To effect a change in the rules of procedure of the kind proposed by the nobles in November 1608 would also have been to *enact*—in both the legislative-instrumental and the symbolic-expressive sense—an important shift in the order of society and politics.

To see how and why this was so, it is useful to recall what it was, precisely, that the nobles proposed to alter. As in most ecclesiastical territories, the *Landtag* was composed of three chambers: the cathedral chapter, representing the clergy; the matriculated nobility, whose members attended in their own right; and delegates from thirteen towns, led by the city of Münster, that were entitled by custom and privilege to attend. However, these three *corpora* were not equal in status and dignity; rather, hierarchies of rank and precedence among them informed the *Landtag's* every transaction. The inaugural ceremonies, for example, had, since the mid 1570s, taken place in the prince-bishop's palace, located on the cathedral plaza in the center of Münster. Bishop Ernst, if he was present for the occasion, sat at the head of the assembly, enthroned under a baldachin. Arrayed before him were the two "anterior estates"—*Vorderstände*—the cathedral chapter and the nobility. The common townsmen were consigned to the rear of the hall.[36]

This spatial ordering of hierarchy among the *corpora* was carefully reproduced in the temporal sequence of the diet's deliberations. There was no formal vote, as such, on the bishop's *Proposition*. Rather, as in most ecclesiastical territories, each of the diet's three chambers deliberated the *Proposition* in descending order of rank. That placed the cathedral chapter first in line to consider the bishop's proposal. Once the chapter had formulated its response, it conveyed its decision in writing to the noble chamber, which then proceeded to deliberate separately from the other two *curiae*. If the nobles had any disagreements with the cathedral chapter, the two anterior estates hammered out a *conclusum* acceptable to both chambers. Only then did the two anterior estates approach the towns, with the request that they review their resolution and convey either their approval or relate "the thoughts, reasons, and motivations why [they] cannot give their acclamation."[37] In sum, the existing procedure fused the anterior estates into a single, decisive voting bloc and relegated the towns to a passive, acclamatory role.

This is what the nobles proposed to alter in 1608. In symbolic-expressive terms, the nobles' proposal was significant in two ways. First, it threatened to dissolve the principle of aristocratic solidarity that underlay the diet's entire *modus operandi*. This principle was woven into the very structure of communication at the diet. Until they had arrived at a common *conclusum*, the two anterior estates were forbidden to have any substantive interactions with the townsmen, whether written or otherwise.[38] If the nobles had made good on their threat, all of this would have changed. The shroud of communicative silence that enveloped the "anterior estates" during the initial phase of the diet's deliberations would have been torn asunder.

Second and more importantly, the nobles' intervention augured a recalibration of rank among the three *corpora*. By communicating directly with the towns during the initial phase of the diet's deliberations, the anterior estates would confer upon the Third Estate a procedural parity of rank that the old rules had deliberately excluded. In effect, the cities' role would no longer be merely acclamatory. To be sure, the nobles were *not* proposing that the towns be treated as social equals with the two aristocratic estates—no noble could allow so grave an affront to the principle of status-group solidarity. However, they *were* threatening the cathedral chapter with the prospect of a new system, in which matters of religion would be decided outside the normal, rank-ordered sequence of deliberations. In such cases, the temporal ordering of hierarchy would dissolve in a moment of procedural parity among three autonomous *corpora* and the issues would be resolved by majority vote.

Expressive Functions and *Ius Reformandi*

In addition to these social-symbolic functions, the nobles' procedural intervention also expressed precise ecclesio-political objectives. As we have seen, their changes would have exposed the prince-bishop's decisions in matters of religion to the scrutiny of a diet composed, in large measure, of Protestant nobles and townsmen. This by itself would have been no small achievement. And yet here, too, we must also examine the symbolic-expressive aspects of these procedural quarrels in order to grasp their full range of implications for confessional politics in the diocese. For reasons that are not at all apparent from the protocol of the diet's proceedings, the nobles' threat to recalibrate the order of rank among the three *corpora* signified a great deal about the prince-bishop's *ius reformandi*.

Specifically, it gestured toward an ongoing debate over the legal implications of the Peace of Augsburg for the practice of religion within ecclesiastical territories, such as the prince-bishopric of Münster. Unlike most of his predecessors since 1555, Bishop Ernst understood the Peace of Augsburg as a mandate to extirpate heresy and to reform religion in the mold of the Council of Trent. Civic elites, however, typically understood the Peace of Augsburg to mean that the members of privileged civic corporations could legally practice either of the two recognized religions and that no estate should attempt to impose its beliefs by violence on any other. Thus, in a suit before the *Reichskammergericht*, the town of Warendorf argued that its citizens were entitled to practice either of the two religions "permitted in the Holy Roman Empire" (*alß im heyligen römischen reich zugelassen*), and that any attempt to limit this right was an impermissible "innovation" (*newerung*).[39] In a separate case, the town of Ahlen argued that "conflicts over religion should all be resolved ... by Christian and peaceful means."[40] The towns applied these precepts in two ways. The more cautious towns acknowledged the bishop's obligation to uphold Catholicism as the only permissible form of *public* religious observance, but also asserted the right of Protestants to practice their religion in private.[41] More venturesome towns argued that both religions "permitted in the Holy Roman Empire" could be practiced openly.[42] These positions were very much in accord with the views of the nobles, who likewise claimed that the right as privileged estates to choose between Catholicism and the Augsburg Confession.[43]

Obviously, these arguments were related to a question of rank and status—whether the towns constituted a privileged estate deserving of religious toleration. In fact, for many years, the towns had been claiming a corporate status equal to that of the "anterior estates." Back in 1593, the towns had filed suit before the *Reichskammergericht*, demanding an equal vote with the nobility and cathedral chapter in deliberations of the territorial diet. Had the towns won their lawsuit, only decisions that enjoyed the *unanimous* endorsement of all three *corpora* could enter into the diet's final resolution. This procedural change would have handed the towns an effective veto over the two anterior estates. In relation to confessional politics, the change would have enabled the towns to hold territorial finances hostage to religious toleration; the diocesan finances depended heavily on excise taxes that fell almost entirely on the towns, which the two anterior estates had enacted repeatedly, despite the towns' vehement objections, throughout the late 1580s and 1590s.[44] More broadly, the towns' lawsuit would have placed them on an equal footing with the other two *curiae* as an "undoubted fellow estate" (*ungezweifelter Mitstandt*).[45] The case was still pending in 1608.

All of this returns us to the specific theatricality of pre-modern territorial assemblies. Unlike most the public spectacles of political life—coronations, enthronements, *entrées*, ceremonies of homage and election—the solemnities and deliberations of territorial estates transpired behind closed doors.[46] Information about what transpired in early modern government was, to be sure, more widely available than most historians since have realized.[47] Still, one might well ask: if the symbolic-expressive functions of territorial assemblies were as important as legislation, who was the audience? To whom, in other words, was symbolic action addressed?

One answer is simply that the question itself is predicated on ahistorical assumptions about the relationship between pre-modern assemblies and the populations they represented. In the early seventeenth century, the actions of territorial estates were not yet subject to the judgment of a collective, political spectator—"public opinion"—that was conceived to be external to the assembly itself.[48] All of that would change, of course, in the eighteenth century. However, in 1608, an assembly that was thought to incarnate the body politic performed only for itself. There was nothing particularly mysterious about this. All delegates to the territorial diet, including the townsmen, understood the system of signs and gestures that defined relations of rank and hierarchy among them; all understood that to participate in that system was, implicitly, to endorse it; and all understood that any alteration implied a shift in relations among the political actors. The theatricality of pre-modern estates acknowledged no barrier between actors and audiences. They were one.[49]

But the estates had another, less tangible "audience"—the law. One can measure the importance of symbols and gestures by the precedent-setting weight they bore, and in the early seventeenth centuries, political ceremonies, such as homage, were still thought to animate relationships of hierarchy and the negotiated agreements on which they were based. This, too, would eventually change.[50] But in 1608, members of the governing council were aware that if the nobility were allowed to communicate directly with the Third Estate, the towns' suit before the *Reichskammergericht* might be reinforced.[51] In view of that lawsuit, moreover, *any* elevation of the towns' status, no matter how circumscribed, implicitly reinforced their pluralistic interpretation of the Peace of Augsburg. Perhaps to underscore the point, the city of Münster refused Bishop Ernst the honor of a ceremonial *entrée* on opening day of the November *Landtag*. The council gave as its reason the fear that Ernst's horsemen might use the occasion to stage a coup against the city and its privileges.[52] Whatever the reason, there was no mistaking the symbolism: all was not right between Ernst and the townsmen, and normal relations would remain in suspense until conflicts were resolved.

Procedural Conflict and the Fiction of Consensus

What, finally, about the fiction of consensus? Embedded in the nobles' intervention was a warning: "leave us to practice our religion as we please, or we will explode the myth of concord." Without saying so explicitly, the nobles were threatening to shatter the image of serene and harmonious hierarchy that the diet's managers labored so hard to maintain. Their intervention, in other words, instrumentalized the collective need of a face-to-face society to uphold the appearances of concord within the body politic. Had the nobles carried through on their threat, the structure of representation would have been altered profoundly. What, then, were the consequences of their intervention?

In the short run, the effects were not many. The *Landtag* of November 1608 ended in stalemate, as we have seen. The diet's procedures were not altered and in subsequent years, the cathedral chapter succeeded in keeping religion off of the diet's agenda and out of territorial law. Bishop Ernst and his successor, Ferdinand, kept up the pressure to conform in doctrine and practice. A crucial passage came in 1623, when Ferdinand deployed soldiers of the Catholic League to besiege all of the towns, except for Münster itself, that were represented in the territorial diet. The towns' defenses crumbled under the onslaught, and their lawsuits before the *Reichskammergericht* went down with them in defeat. From 1623 on, Protestant nobles were left to fend for themselves. Their cause never fully recovered.

Certain lessons of November 1608 did, however, endure over the long term. To be sure, the principle of aristocratic solidarity was never again challenged as it had been in 1608: in the later seventeenth and eighteenth centuries, the nobility and cathedral chapter were, if anything, *more* preoccupied with upholding symbolic distinctions between themselves and the commoners. As Tim Neu has shown, their ever-more elaborate fixation on the symbolics of hierarchy was coupled with an almost obsessive concern, especially among members of the cathedral chapter, to ensure that every resolution received the unanimous approval of all three *corpora*.[53] It was a delicate balance—getting consensus with a procedure designed to exclude townsmen from any active procedural role—and it required careful tending to the towns' grievances. In a sense, this outcome achieved what the towns had demanded in their lawsuit of 1593—unanimity, not decision-making *pro maiora vota*. Either way, the fiction of consensus grew stronger than it had been before 1608, and was less easily contested or instrumentalized.

More broadly, the episode shows how misleading it is to dismiss procedural squabbles as mere trivia—let alone to correlate their increase with the rise of early modern state power. To do so is to forfeit a wide range of interpretive possibilities. By analyzing the symbolic as well as the technical-instrumental dimensions of procedural conflicts, we are able to perceive *all* of their social implications, not just the narrowly legislative ones. In 1608, the nobles' intervention was about far more than the *Landtag*'s competence to deliberate matters of religion; in its symbolic-expressive dimension, the intervention augured a recalibration of hierarchy among the three *corpora*, which all three would affirm by their continued participation in the diet's proceedings.

By analyzing procedural conflicts in symbolic terms, we also gain a fuller understanding of their political function. In the present case, conflicts over procedure supplied a kind of code for discussing ecclesio-political conflicts indirectly, themes that could not be addressed head on without provoking a fundamental conflict between prince and diet. Through ceremony and procedure, the problem of religious plurality could be addressed without disrupting the fiction of consensus. In addition, the form and structure of the nobles' intervention expressed ideas about the proper relationship between secular and ecclesiastical authority and about the place of corporate privilege in the regulation of religious life. Under the existing rules, nobles were unable to register grievances prompted by the bishop's manner of implementing the Peace of Augsburg. However, through the symbolics of procedural conflict, they could get the point across by indirect means.

Common to all of these perspectives is the idea that territorial diets had the important societal function of demonstrating hierarchy and of making representation visible.[54] Far from signifying decay, conflicts over rank-order and precedence continually reanimated the formal hierarchies whose ceremonial expression had given rise to conflict in the first instance.[55] In this way, even *conflictual* symbolic action could have a legitimating effect on the institutions within which they unfolded.[56] Conflicts over procedure and ceremony, therefore, were not always dysfunctional, but often were *integral* to the production of institutional durability. In the present case, parties to a conflict over procedure shrank from carrying it to its full range of conclusions. Perhaps they recognized that an elevation of the towns' status necessarily diluted aristocratic prestige; perhaps they feared that if they made religion an *explicit* object of the diet's dealings, the result would be uncontainable violence. Whatever the motivation, the fiction of consensus won out in the end.

Notes

1. On rank-order conflicts see Barbara Stollberg-Rilinger, "Zeremoniell als politisches Verfahren: Rangordnung und Rangstreit als Strukturmerkmale des frühneuzeitlichen Reichstags," in *Neue Studien zur frühneuzeitlichen Reichsgeschichte*, ed. Johannes Kunisch (Berlin, 1997), 91–132; and Stollberg-Rilinger, "Rang vor Gericht: Zur Verrechtlichung sozialer Rangkonflikte in der Frühen Neuzeit," in *Zeitschrift für historische Forschung* 28 (2001): 385–418.
2. See Karl-Siegbert Rehberg, "Weltrepräsentanz und Verkörperung: Institutionelle Analyse und Symboltheorien—Eine Einführung in systematischer Absicht," in *Institutionalität und Symbolisierung: Verstetigung kultureller Ordnungsmuster in Vergangenheit und Gegenwart*, ed. Gert Melville (Cologne, 2001), 3–49; and Barbara Stollberg-Rilinger, "Symbolische Kommunikation in der Vormoderne: Begriffe—Thesen—Forschungsperspektiven," in *Zeitschrift für historische Forschung* 31 (2004): 489–527, here 506–509.
3. See Marc Forster, *The Counter-Reformation in the Villages: Religion and Reform in the Bishopric of Speyer, 1560–1720* (Ithaca, 1992), 49–57, 124–129, 149–154.
4. The literature on the Anabaptist interlude is vast; see most recently Ralf Klötzer, *Die Täuferherrschaft von Münster: Stadtreformation und Welterneuerung* (Münster, 1992); and Sigrun Haude, *In the Shadow of 'Savage Wolves': Anabaptist Münster and the German Reformation during the 1530s* (Atlantic Highlands, 2000).
5. The great exception is R. Po-Chia Hsia's *Society and Religion in Munster, 1535–1618* (New Haven, 1984).

6. "Les *cerémonies* sont en général des démonstrations extérieures & symboliques, qui sont partie des usages de la police & du culte d'une société"; "Cérémonies," in *Encyclopédie ou Dictionnaire raisonné des sciences, des arts et des métiers*, vol. 2 (Paris, 1752), pp. 838–839.
7. See Michael Sikora, "Der Sinn des Verfahrens: Soziologische Deutungsangebote," in *Vormoderne politische Verfahren*, ed. Barbara Stollberg-Rilinger (Berlin, 2001), 25–52.
8. G.R. Elton, "Parliament in the Sixteenth Century: Functions and Fortunes," in *English Historical Review* 22 (1979), 255–278; Peter Moraw, "Versuch über die Entstehung des Reichstags," in *Politische Ordnungen und soziale Kräfte im Alten Reich*, ed. Hermann Weber (Wiesbaden, 1980), 1–36; and Barbara Stollberg-Rilinger, "Die Symbolik der Reichstage: Überlegungen zu einer Perspektivenumkehr," in *Der Reichstag 1486–1613: Kommunikation—Wahrnehmung—Öffentlichkeit*, eds. Maximilian Lanzinner and Arno Strohmeyer (Göttingen 2006), 77–93.
9. See among others Johannes Kunisch, ed., *Neue Studien zur frühneuzeitlichen Reichsgeschichte* (Berlin, 1997); Heinz Duchhardt and Gert Melville, eds., *Im Spannungsfeld von Recht und Ritual: Soziale Kommunikation in Mittelalter und Früher Neuzeit* (Cologne, 1997); Melville, ed., *Institutionalität und Symbolisierung*; Barbara Stollberg-Rilinger, ed., *Vormoderne politische Verfahren* (Berlin, 2001); and Stollberg-Rilinger, ed., *Was heißt Kulturgeschichte des Politischen?* (Berlin, 2005).
10. Stollberg-Rilinger, "Rang vor Gericht," 385–418.
11. Rudolfine von Oer, "Münster," in *Die Territorien des Reichs im Zeitalter der Reformation und Konfessionalisierung: Land und Konfession 1500–1650*, vol. 3: *Der Nordwesten*, eds. Anton Schindling and Walter Ziegler, (Münster, 1995), 108–129, here 109.
12. On *Aufschwörung*—the formal mechanism for controlling entrance to the territorial nobility—see the contribution of Elizabeth Harding to this volume. On the Westphalian nobility in general see Heinz Reif, *Westfälischer Adel, 1770–1860: Vom Herrschaftsstand zur regionalen Elite* (Göttingen, 1979); and Marcus Weidner, *Landadel in Münster 1600–1760: Stadtverfassung, Standesbehauptung und Fürstenhof*, 2 vols. (Münster, 2000).
13. Reif, *Westfälischer Adel*, 34–36.
14. See Peter Hersche, *Die deutschen Domkapitel im 17. und 18. Jahrhundert* (Bern, 1984), 1: 133–139; 2: 75–76, 122–123, and 186–187; and 3: 198.
15. On the origins of territorial estates see Ludwig Schmitz-Kallenberg, "Die Landstände des Fürstbistums Münster bis zum 16. Jahrhundert," in *Westfälische Forschungen* 92 (1936): 1–88; Karl-Heinz Kirchhoff, "Ständeversammlungen und erste Landtage im Stift Münster, 1212–1278, und der Landtagsplatz auf dem Laerbrock," in *Westfälische Forschungen* 30 (1988): 207–234, 397–406; and Weidner, *Landadel in Münster*, 1: 141–162.
16. Wilhelm Kohl, *Das Bistum Münster*, vol. 1, *Die Diözese* (Berlin, 1999), 326–332 and 397–399.
17. Kohl, *Bistum Münster*, 1: 224–242. On the Lutheran inclinations of Franz von Waldeck and Wilhelm Ketteler, see Bishop Ernst von Bayern to Pope Clemens VIII, July 1599, in Alois Schröer, ed., *Vatikanische Dokumente zur Geschichte der Reformation und der Katholischen Erneuerung in Westfalen* (Münster, 1993), no. 151: 236–246, here 237.
18. Alois Schröer, *Die Kirche in Westfalen im Zeichen der Erneuerung* (Münster, 1986-1987), 1: 300, 303, 311–312. For the text of the *Declaratio Ferdinandea*, see Karl Brandi, *Der Augsburger Religionsfriede vom 25. September 1555: Kritische Ausgabe des Textes mit den Entwürfen und der königlichen Deklaration* (Göttingen, 1927), 52–54.

19. Bastian Gillner, "Landständischer Adel im Fürstbistum Münster im 16./17. Jahrhundert: Strategien adeliger Politik im konfessionellen Zeitalter." Ph.D. diss., Universität Münster, 2009.
20. Kohl, *Bistum Münster*, 1: 233–236, 249, 251; Schröer, *Kirche in Westfalen*, 2: 233.
21. On the politics surrounding Ernst's election, see Kohl, *Bistum Münster*, 1: 240–242; Schröer, *Kirche in Westfalen*, 1: 344–438 and 2: 222–229; and Ludwig Keller, *Die Gegenreformation in Westfalen und am Niederrhein: Actenstücke und Erläuterungen* (Leipzig, 1881–1895), 1: 334–342.
22. The appellation is reported by Schröer, *Kirche in Westfalen*, 1: 366.
23. "Abschied des Churfürsten Ernst in Angelegenheiten des Stifts Münster," 6 March 1590, in Keller, *Gegenreformation*, vol. 2, no. 281: 325–327. Ernst had not been permitted to assume his office until November 1589.
24. See Herbert Immenkötter, "Die Auseinandersetzung des Domkapitels in Münster mit dem Geistlichen Rat," in *Von Konstanz nach Trient: Beiträge zur Geschichte der Kirche von den Reformkonzilien bis zum Tridentinum*, ed. Remigius Bäumer (Munich, 1972), 713–727; and Schröer, *Kirche in Westfalen*, 2: 234–238.
25. Landesarchiv Nordrhein-Westfalen, Staatsarchiv Münster (hereafter StA Ms), Fürstentum Münster (hereafter FM), Landtagsprotokolle 25, fols. 375r–389v.
26. StA Ms FM, Regierungsprotokolle 12, fols. 158v–165v, 21 November 1608; StA Ms FM, Domkapitel A 4844, fols. 250r–v, 22 January 1609.
27. A draft of Bishop Ernst's edict may be found in Bischöfliches Archiv Münster (hereafter BAM) Domarchiv VI 4, *Mandatum in p[unct]o communionis & sepulturae*, November 1606.
28. BAM Generalvikariat (hereafter GV) Drensteinfurt A 10, no. 55–10, "Johan von der Recke zu Drensteinfurt laßet appellation insinuiren auf abgangenes mandat wegen abschaffungh des daselbst priuirten pastors" [May–June 1607].
29. "Bittschrift der Ritterschaft des Stiftes Münster an den Churfürsten Ernst," 23 October 1607, in Keller, *Gegenreformation*, 2: 398–399.
30. BAM GV Vreden St. Georg A 7, Pastor Lambertus Furböter to Dr. Johannes Hartmann, September 1608.
31. See David M. Luebke, "Churchyard and Confession: Grave Desecration, Burial Practices, and Social Order during the Confessional Age—The Case of Warendorf," in *Leben bei den Toten: Kirchhöfe in der ländlichen Gesellschaft der Vormoderne*, eds. Jan Brademann and Werner Freitag (Münster, 2007), 193–213.
32. See BAM GV Drensteinfurt A 10, 55–3, Ecclesiastical Council to Governing Council, 13 November 1606.
33. "woll[en] gleichfals in religion und andern geistlichen sachen exempt und meister sein;" StA Ms FM, Domkapitel A 4844 (1607) 14v–17r, 19 March 1607.
34. BAM GV Bocholt A 5, "Bericht unnd Ercleruüg mein Arndten von Büren Dhomdechandts uber zugestellte Articulum" [1597].
35. StA Ms FM, Regierungsprotokolle 12, fols. 158r–165v, 21 November 1608.
36. Tim Neu, "Inszenieren und Beschließen: Symbolierungs- und Entscheidungsleistungen der Landtage im Fürstbistum Münster," in *Westfälische Forschungen* 57 (2007): 257–284, here 263–271.
37. This description is based on a report contained in StA Ms Reichskammergericht M 1697, fols. 1r–10v, *Mandatum cum clausula*, Speyer, 28 August 1593.
38. Neu, "Inszenieren," 27.

39. StA Ms Reichskammergericht W 276, "*Libellus articulatus* in Sachen Warendorff contra Münster," 6 July 1608.
40. BAM Domarchiv XVIII A 1, *Communio seu administratio sacramenti Eucharistiae sub utraque specie in Ahaus et Ahlen, querelae ex parte magistratu ibidem super denegationem circa annum 1602.*
41. Unlike Catholics and doctrinaire Lutherans, Reformed Protestants in the Westphalian towns understood the "Augsburg Confession" to include themselves. On the contested meanings of the Augsburg Confession, see most recently Irene Dingel, "Augsburger Religionsfrieden und 'Augsburger Konfessionsverwandtschaft'—konfessionelle Lesearten," in *Der Augsburger Religionsfrieden 1555*, eds. Heinz Schilling and Heribert Smolinsky (Münster: 2007), 157–176.
42. See David M. Luebke, "Customs of Confession: Managing Religious Diversity in Late Sixteenth- and Early Seventeenth-Century Westphalia," in *Religion and Authority in Central Europe from the Reformation to the Enlightenment*, ed. Howard Louthan (New York, forthcoming).
43. BAM GV Drensteinfurt A 10, no. 55–10, "Johann von der Reck zu Drensteinfurt laßet appellation insinuiren."
44. At issue was an excise tax ordinance passed by the territorial diet on 17 January 1589, and promulgated as territorial law by episcopal decree dated 8 June 1590; see Johann Josef Scotti, *Sammlung der Gesetze und Ordnungen, welche in dem Königlich Preußischen Erbfürstenthume Münster…über Gegenstände der Landeshoheit, Verfassung, Verwaltung und Rechtspflege…ergangen sind* (Münster, 1849), nr. 59, 1: 178–182.
45. See StA Ms Reichskammergericht M 1697, fol. 58r, 23 March 1594.
46. See Esther-Beate Körber, *Öffentlichkeiten der frühen Neuzeit: Teilnehmer, Formen, Institutionen und Entscheidungen öffentlicher Kommunikation im Herzogtum Preussen von 1525 bis 1618* (Berlin, 1998).
47. Andreas Gestrich, *Absolutismus und Öffentlichkeit: Politische Kommunikation in Deutschland zu Beginn des 18. Jahrhunderts* (Göttingen, 1994); Gestrich, "Politik im Alltag: Zur Funktion politischer Information im deutschen Absolutismus des frühen 18. Jahrhunderts," in *Aufklärung*, 5 (1990): 9–27; and Andreas Würgler, *Unruhen und Öffentlichkeit: Städtische und ländliche Protestbewegungen im 18. Jahrhundert* (Tübingen, 1995).
48. I paraphrase here Anthony La Vopa, "Conceiving a Public: Ideas and Society in Eighteenth-Century Europe," in *Journal of Modern History* 64 (1992): 79–116.
49. Compare Paul Friedland, *Political Actors: Representative Bodies and Theatricality in the Age of the French Revolution* (Ithaca, 2002), 29–51.
50. André Holenstein, *Die Huldigung der Untertanen: Rechtskultur und Herrschaftsordnung (800–1800)* (Stuttgart, 1991).
51. StA Ms Fürstentum Münster, Regierungsprotokolle 12, fols. 92r–95r, 2 August 1608.
52. StA Ms Fürstentum Münster, Regierungsprotokolle 12, fols. 150r–154r, 14 November 1608, "Wegen fürst[licher] D[urchlau]cht Ankunft;" and StA Ms Fürstentum Münster, Domkapitel A 4844, 229v, 13 November 1608.
53. Neu, "Zeremonielle Verfahren," here 35–44.
54. See, for example, Ulf Brüning, "Wege landständischer Entscheidungsfindung: Das Verfahren auf den Landtagen des rheinischen Erzstifts zur Zeit Clemens Augusts," in *Der Riß im Himmel: Clemens August und seine Epoche*, ed. Frank Günter Zehnder (Cologne, 1999), 160–184.

55. Johannes Helmrath, "Rangstreite auf Generalkonzilien des 15. Jahrhunderts als Verfahren," in Stollberg-Rilinger, *Vormoderne politische Verfahren*, 139–173; Helmut Neuhaus, "Der Streit um den richtigen Platz: Ein Beitrag zu reichsständischen Verfahrensformen in der Frühen Neuzeit," ibid., 281–302; Stollberg-Rilinger, "Zeremoniel als politisches Verfahren"; and Stollberg-Rilinger, "Rang vor Gericht."
56. See Rehberg, "Weltrepräsentanz und Verkörperung," 13–17.

CHAPTER 9

Contested Bodies
Schwäbisch Hall and its Neighbors in the Conflicts Regarding High Jurisdiction (1550–1800)

PATRICK OELZE

Authority in the Schwäbisch Hall Region

In February 1661, Hans Ulrich Welck, a subject of the imperial town of Schwäbisch Hall, fell from his horse on the way from Gründelhart to his place of residence in nearby Hellmannshofen. In the process, he injured himself so badly that people thought he was near death. At the accident site, both Schwäbisch Hall and the margrave of Brandenburg-Ansbach claimed the *Fraisch* (or *Hochgerichtsbarkeit*)—the high jurisdiction—and thereby the competence for investigating major violent crimes as well as fatal accidents. Gründelhart and Hellmannshofen were part of the *Herrschaft Vellberg* that Schwäbisch Hall had acquired in 1595. The town of Vellberg and its surrounding villages was Schwäbisch Hall's last large acquisition. However, certain territories in the *Herrschaft Vellberg* had also reverted to Brandenburg-Ansbach. In particular, Hall and Brandenburg had to share authority over Gründelhart.[1]

Like Schwäbisch Hall, Brandenburg-Ansbach lacked a firmly defined territory, but it had the status of a *territorium non clausum*. Along with customs, safe conduct (*Geleit*), and hunting rights (*Wildbann*)—all of which were symbols of royal office—the high jurisdiction formed a substantial element of the so-called *hohe Obrigkeit* (high authority).[2] According to this concept of high authority, primacy of rule could be maintained in a clearly defined space, independent of power over persons or ownership of property. This authority can be seen as an early form of territorial rule.[3] Sometimes high authority was used by itself as a synonym for high jurisdiction. In realizing or practicing high jurisdiction, a variety of other rights could be claimed within a so-called *Fraischbezirk* (district of high jurisdiction).⁴ Given their overlapping claims of jurisdiction, the practice of high judicial activities caused numerous conflicts between Hall and Brandenburg.

The question of which rights were specifically connected with the high authority was continually disputed by Schwäbisch Hall and its neighbors. In the Schwäbisch Hall region, various rulers claimed or held rights to minor courts (*Niedergerichtsbarkeit*), hunting, taxation, customs, and church patronage.⁵ This complicated mix resulted in daily conflicts of demarcation, both for officeholders and subjects. It hardly needs to be stressed that in conditions where governance was so completely partitioned, high jurisdiction had special significance and was also contested with particular intensity.

Against this backdrop, the death of Hans Ulrich Welck became a political issue. The Hallian mayor from neighboring Honhardt and the Brandenburg mayor from Gründelhart met in Welck's tavern in Hellmannshofen. After discussing Welck's accident, they agreed to see it not "as a case of *Fraisch*." But the listening Welck "was deeply worried that his body would be dragged back and forth after his death. ... So startled was he that ... he allegedly lost his voice and was unable to utter another word until his death."⁶ Even though the local officeholders agreed this time not to investigate the incident or to interpret such an investigation as proof of high judicial competence, none of this would have stopped Welck from worrying. Welck's fear of dishonorable wrangling over his body had (quite literally) taken his breath away. Welck had seen or heard too often of such wrangling over bodies when a person was killed or died in an accident.

As recently as 1656, the body of a child killed in an accident in the neighboring town of Waldbuch had been forcibly moved by Brandenburg soldiers.⁷ In 1632, a man was killed in Hellmannshofen. His corpse was then removed from his home by Brandenburg subjects and brought to a church in Gründelhart. From there, however, it was taken away by Hallian subjects and buried in Untersontheim. When a short time later there were rumors that people from the margrave were planning to attack Untersontheim to exhume the corpse (something that actually happened often), the town council had the corpse carefully disinterred. It was then buried secretly in Unterlimpurg, very close to the city wall of Schwäbisch Hall.⁸ Welck's fear was thus anything but irrational. At places in which the high judicial authority was disputed—and there were many between Schwäbisch Hall and Brandenburg-Ansbach in the Vellberg district—such grisly competitions were not uncommon in the seventeenth and eighteenth centuries. It was not unusual for armed arguments to take place about a corpse, especially if someone had a fatal accident, committed suicide, or was killed.⁹ The disposition of a corpse was the presupposition for the exercise of high judicial rights. These rights could be claimed by taking possession of a so-called *Fraischpfand*, an object from the personal belongings of the victim, frequently an article of clothing. Another possibility, "taking the *Fraisch*" (as this procedure was also called) implied cutting off pieces of wood either from the victim's front door or from an object at the crime (or accident) scene. This was often done if the opposing authority had already taken possession of the body. This legal custom, usually seen as medieval, was typical practice in the surroundings of Schwäbisch Hall until at least the end of the eighteenth century.[10]

A few years after Welck's death, Schwäbisch Hall and Brandenburg resumed negotiations to settle the complex situation resulting from conflicts that had smoldered since Schwäbisch Hall acquired the *Herrschaft Vellberg* (in 1595). As already noted, they not only disputed high jurisdiction, but also the demarcation of church rights with respect to the parish of Gründelhart. Territorial rule was closely linked with the episcopal office on both sides. In 1651, for instance, "the margravian governor [*Vogt*] of Crailsheim, along with a few musketeers, entered the inn in Hall by means of force." They disturbed the annual fair (*Kirchweih*) and the protection of it exercised by a Hallian official there, whom they then took with them to Crailsheim.[11] Many similar conflicts over the protection of the annual fair or the jurisdiction of morals (*Sittengerichtsbarkeit*) took place in these years in the villages around Gründelhart. Starting in the mid 1650s, Schwäbisch Hall and Brandenburg-Ansbach sought a solution to these conflicts. The foreign policy of Schwäbisch Hall in the years following the Peace of Westphalia was characterized by conferences and almost simultaneous negotiations with other neighbors: the *Ritterstift* Comburg (and its lord, the bishop of Würzburg), the counts of Hohenlohe, and the *Schenken* of Limpurg.[12] In 1666, a treaty was concluded for the first time in order to address points of contention between Schwäbisch Hall and Brandenburg, "mainly over the parish of Gründelhart, both over a certain hunting district as well as over high authority and other jurisdictions."[13] The negotiations were obviously very difficult, since the treaty stated at the beginning that "various hearings and conferences" already had taken place that had "nevertheless been unfruitful."[14] After "many exchanged letters and communications," the parties finally agreed to "a complete remedying of the neighborly differences floating around to this point," resulting in the Gründelhart Treaty of 1678.[15] Schwäbisch Hall received exclusive high jurisdiction in a set area around Vellberg. For most of the areas under contention, the contracting parties agreed to complicated individual regulations. In most places, the urban high and minor jurisdiction was limited to the properties of Hallian subjects within the village fences, which was thus limited *de facto* to their usual and associated farm buildings. Everywhere else, however, Brandenburg-Ansbach had sole jurisdiction. Schwäbisch Hall also had to do without large sections of the hunting grounds. The fixed borders for hunting and high jurisdiction were marked with boundary stones.[16] Through the Gründelhart Treaty, an important preliminary decision had been made on the formation of territorial rule in the contested areas, one that favored Brandenburg-Ansbach. In the long disputed question of jurisdiction outside of the village boundaries, the issue that had caused several earlier conferences to fail, the town had had to give way. In the long run, Schwäbisch Hall could only really assert itself in the area directly around Vellberg, where it actually had retained high authority and where the margrave had almost no authority over rights or subjects. The councilmen concurred with the treaty primarily because the large number of disputes with Brandenburg-Ansbach made a compromise appear to be the lesser of two evils. The margrave was an opponent whose power made it possible for him to gradually cut off Schwäbisch Hall from its rights to authority—and particularly high authority—by constantly creating *Präjudizien* (predeterminations), i.e., individual cases out of which a continuous legal claim might arise having the character of a precedent.[17] The Gründelhart Treaty hence relieved the town, which had been put on the defensive, of this pressure.

It was routine for Schwäbisch Hall to hold conferences and sign agreements with neighboring authorities in order to regulate and demarcate various rights. For instance, the town concluded 22 treaties, between 1490 and 1661, with the different lines of the House of Hohenlohe. In the same period, 19 treaties were completed with the *Ritterstift* Comburg. There were also 14 such treaties with Württemberg.[18] The multiplicity of treaties and agreements is an impressive illustration of the extraordinary potential for conflict in the region surrounding Schwäbisch Hall. In addition, these mechanisms were very important as a way to work out conflicts and to compose the regional regime of authority in the Holy Roman Empire. In such respects, Schwäbisch Hall was no exception. Johann Jacob Moser speaks of the "extremely large quantity" of "agreements and treaties that have been concluded between the various imperial classes in all kinds of disputes and on many hundred subjects, in older and more recent times."[19] Similarly, Brandenburg-Ansbach signed many such agreements with its neighbors, and, in the eighteenth century alone, it successfully negotiated about 60 such treaties, "all of which dealt in some form with territorial rights, property, and subjects."[20]

Concluding a treaty was never the "final word" in a conflict, since the wording of individual passages often left leeway for interpretation. Quite often, the opposing party did not adhere so precisely to the treaty, making it possible to question its validity altogether. Many treaties were little more than snapshots of the current balance of power. Therefore, Schwäbisch Hall frequently negotiated with its neighbors on similar matters over often-protracted periods.[21] The detail and complexity, for instance, of the regime of authority in the Gründelhart Treaty elicited differing interpretations of individual clauses as well as a high level of misunderstanding. This is why the concrete realization of the treaty was spelled out so pedantically in the actual treaty itself. Since its individual parts could not "be understood immediately or explained by someone who did not have special knowledge of the country or could not understand the agreement or aspects of it from the outset," the treaty document was immediately followed by an extensive, fifty-page listing of the legal conditions that resulted tangibly from the Gründelhart Treaty, including the names of individual "villages, hamlets, spots, and yards."[22] Contracts provided a certain legal security. Their validity, however, depended on the continued practice of the rights laid out in the text. And when the injury of such rights went uncontested, it might then develop into a predetermination (*Präjudiz*).

Against the backdrop of these conditions, the consolidation of territorial authority in the early modern Holy Roman Empire, at least in the Southwest, was not merely—and not even primarily—an inner-directed process of administrative infiltration or social discipline.[23] Rather, such consolidation took place as a demarcation rapidly moving in an outward direction. Since complex conditions made it impossible to separate out spheres of influence in terms of place, authority in the region surrounding Schwäbisch Hall was primarily manifested in the ability to prevent or create *Präjudizien*. The legal significance of such cases prompted rulers to react to each alleged injury of authoritative right, in order to cancel out the actions of the opposite side and to ensure that the incident was remembered by the local subjects and officeholders for a long time thereafter or was recorded in written form in the archives. Direct access to the corpse of a subject thereby carried great symbolic weight, as the case of Hans Ulrich Welck suggests. This symbolic weight was fully developed in the conflicts to follow.

The Case of the *Mettelmühle*, 1758

As in the described case of Hans Ulrich Welck, the *Mettelmühle* conflict also took place in the framework of a long term, fundamental disagreement between two authorities. After Brandenburg-Ansbach had taken over Limpurg properties and rights in 1746, there were various renewed disagreements between Schwäbisch Hall and Brandenburg-Ansbach about the practice of high judicial or (general) sovereign rights, particularly in the village of Untersontheim and its local district.[24] The conflicts that resulted could not be (even temporarily) resolved, for example, in the form of a new treaty. Again, the conflicts were by no means limited to the issue of high jurisdiction.[25]

The *Mettelmühle* incident almost paradigmatically combines all of the elements of a dispute between neighboring polities. The Bühler River formed the border between the high jurisdiction of the town and the margrave. It was only on account of a mill (the *Mettelmühle*), which was actually on the Brandenburg-Ansbach side of the river (not far from Untersontheim), that the town had been granted high authority within the fenced mill property. In Obersontheim in July 1758, Leonhart Ritter fell into the floodwaters of the Bühler and was carried away.[26] While it was still dark, a Brandenburg administrator in nearby Markertshofen gathered together subjects under his authority from the surrounding villages. Using them and a few soldiers, he searched the riverbank for several days, albeit unsuccessfully, throughout the local district of Ummenhofen and Untersontheim. Referring to a treaty that had been concluded in 1670 with Limpurg, the legal predecessor of Brandenburg-Ansbach, Schwäbisch Hall issued a protest against the procedure inasmuch as the high jurisdiction for Ummenhofen and Untersontheim rested solely with the town.

It was not until 27 July that Ritter's corpse washed up near the *Mettelmühle*, specifically on the bank of a small island formed by the river and the mill ditch branching off from it. It was unclear whether this island was still part of the mill area, thereby falling under the high jurisdiction of the town, or whether it was part of the Brandenburg court district. The Hallian mayor in Untersontheim had the corpse brought immediately to his barn and from there it was rushed to Hallian Vellberg. Yet the news arrived that a margravian unit was advancing with the goal of seizing the deceased Ritter. In actuality, the margravian administrator arrived with "10 musketeers" at the site where the corpse had been discovered. There, in the name of the margravian count, he issued a protest against the Hallian procedure. He then allowed his soldiers to fire three salvos and pick up a piece of wood from the site as a *Fraischpfand*. From the other side of the Bühler, the Hallian mayor observed these actions with a hastily organized group of subjects from Untersontheim and Hausen. The Brandenburg administrator challenged him several times to come across the river and finally marched toward him over a bridge. Thus, the ensuing controversy clearly took place on Hallian territory. Following an intensive exchange of words, there was a wild brawl and one Hallian subject was critically wounded by a shot in the face. Two other subjects of the town were carried off to Crailsheim. The corpse of Ritter, in the meantime, had been brought to Vellberg, where it was carefully guarded. There, the body was buried as quickly as possible. Immediately after the news had been received of an incident near the *Mettelmühle*, the town council delegated a deputation of councilmen and doctors. They examined the corpse in Vellberg and inspected the discovery site near the mill. In addition, they were supposed to cross-examine eyewitnesses and write a detailed report on the incidents. Since no one was certain about the exact course of the *Fraisch* boundary, some Hallian subjects in Untersontheim who could provide very precise information about it were questioned. People in the village still remembered a case in 1699, nearly 60 years earlier, in which a corpse had washed up at the same location.[27]

Schwäbisch Hall and its Neighbors in the Conflicts Regarding High Jurisdiction ◦: 169

Figure 9.1. A Sketch on the Legal and Authoritative History of the *Mettelmühle* ("Beilage zum Bericht der städtischen Deputation über die Geschehnisse 1758").

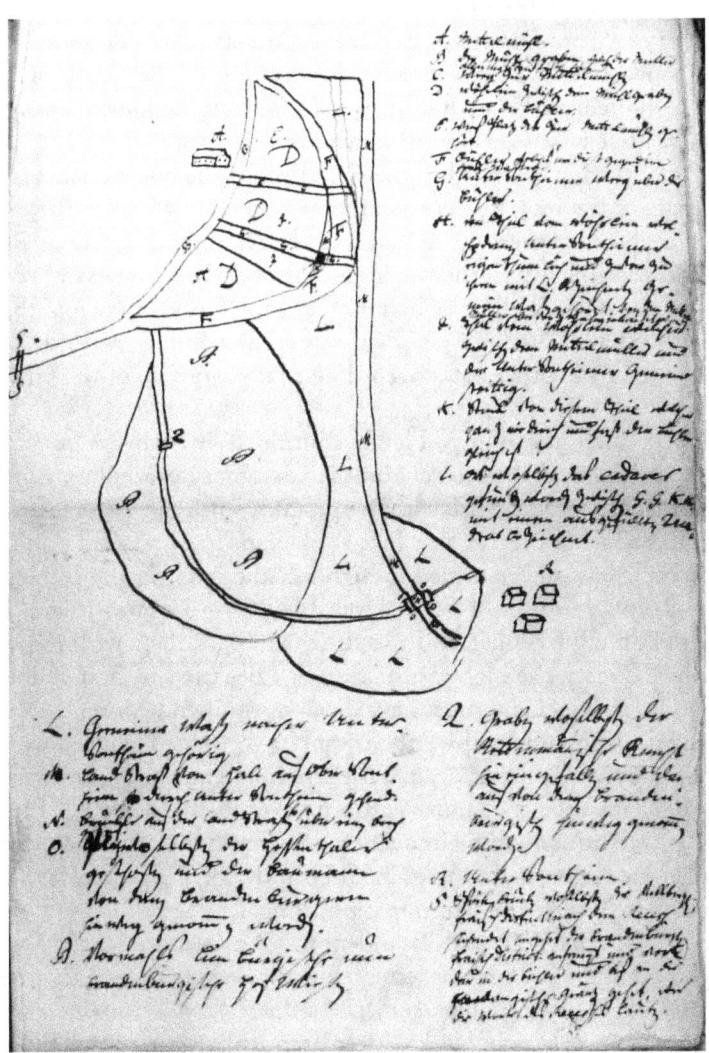

Source: Stadtarchiv Schwäbisch Hall StA SH 5/110.
Note: To orient the reader: the mill (Mettelmühle) is drawn in at the upper left (A) and Untersontheim is on the lower right (R). The site where the corpse was discovered is next to 1 (between GG und KK); the exchange of gunfire occurred at N, directly in front of Untersontheim.

The town's advisor (*Konsulent*), Hetzel, assigned to give an expert appraisal of the case, provided the following written *cri de coeur*. In view of the complex legal relations of the Mettelmühle: "one could only wish the drowned person had either remained lying in the Obersontheim local district or had been moved (much) further downstream so that this case of dispute had never taken place, though the exact boundaries of the *Fraisch* are still quite doubtful."[28] Hetzel was confirmed in this assumption by his reading of the treaty of 1678. To him, the Gründelhart Treaty had awarded the town high jurisdiction over the *Mettelmühle*, but it was questionable whether the place where Ritter's corpse had washed up truly belonged to the mill. Even if the questionable island was actually part of the mill, it was still an open question whether Ritter's corpse had truly been found there or instead had been found in the river.[29] Ritter had been found with his feet in the water and his body lying on a sand bar. Therefore, it was not clear whether he had been already found "in" or "on" the Bühler. On the other hand, the high jurisdiction over the Bühler was not clearly assigned to one or the other party according to the wording of the Gründelhart Treaty.

In view of such uncertainty, Hetzel continued, it is always best to rely on "past observance," and thus to rely on the customary procedure, which spoke in favor of Brandenburg-Ansbach. The practice since the Gründelhart Treaty showed, according to Hetzel, that (even) Hallians had assumed that Brandenburg-Ansbach was solely entitled to high jurisdiction over the Bühler. For example, in 1699, a subject of Schwäbisch Hall from Untersontheim fell from near the mill into the Bühler, and also drowned. Back then, with respect to the Gründelhart Treaty, the high jurisdiction had been left in Brandenburg-Ansbach's hands. This incident must have "been dutifully noted" on the margrave's side. The best thing under the circumstances, continued Hetzel, would be to ignore the margrave's protest "against the attempted raising of the drowned Ritter and not to mention the *Fraisch* authority over the Bühler at all." Hetzel's advice here was to do something frequently done amid the complex jurisdictional situation in the region: leave things in limbo and wait, if possible, for a favorable opportunity to create a predetermination (*Präjudiz*).

In the weeks that followed, Brandenburg-Ansbach and Schwäbisch Hall exchanged a number of protest letters, but these did not lead to a resolution of the conflict. The two Hallian subjects abducted to Crailsheim were held in prison there for nearly eight weeks. After Brandenburg permitted the two to be released, a controversy erupted over the expenses resulting from the imprisonment. The council feared that by assuming the expenses, it would be taken as an admission that the Hallian claims had been illegitimate, thereby creating an unfavorable precedent. Thus, the burden was ultimately placed on the imprisoned subject, Leonhard Baumann, who, in contrast to his fellow victim, enjoyed a modest prosperity. His two oxen were seized by Brandenburg-Ansbach as a deposit for covering the expenses. The ensuing protest from Schwäbisch Hall did not change anything.

As mentioned previously, this case is prototypical of the conflict over jurisdictional authority in the region. After being informed by their subjects of the incident, the local officeholders on both sides tried immediately to exercise their rights, either by seizing the corpse or by claiming their competence through symbolic actions, such as taking a *Fraischpfand*. In turn, there were frequently violent disagreements, and subjects were sometimes injured or even taken hostage. Deputations employed detailed hearings of witnesses and inspections of sites, and older cases and documents were collected in archives to support one's own claims. The authorities simultaneously exchanged a number of protest letters, which in the end only sought to maintain their own claims. In such conflicts, the subjects were to be impressed with belonging to a certain authority, so impressed that the knowledge of these things was embodied in the collective memory of a village for decades, indeed for half a century. The questioning of the oldest inhabitants and local officeholders frequently provided more reliable (and faster) information on the legal circumstances in one or the other village than the written chronicles found in archives.

On Political Culture in the Holy Roman Empire

The controversies described in this chapter, which I term micro-conflicts, were one of the central bases for territorialization processes in the Holy Roman Empire, alongside the construction of administrative structures and (to whatever extent it was successful) the implementation of a firm catalog of norms.[30] In their strict and contested demarcations, such conflicts rendered meaningful territorial authority as well as one's own subjection to this principle (both for subjects and local officeholders). These conflicts provided an incentive to undertake a systematic collection and questioning, and thus also to order comprehensively all of the cases and documents involving conditions of authority and law. In the case of political decision-makers and their legal advisers, micro-conflicts resulted in finding connections with a scholarly discourse on the general nature and qualities of a territory or a state.[31]

The micro-conflicts portrayed here functioned according to a restitutive logic. The reactions of both sides often were a direct reflection of a previous real or alleged encroachment by the other side. Since such restitution actions themselves often caused further reactions, they almost inevitably resulted in escalation. At the same time, however, in principle, the conflicts were not to be resolved violently. As in the case of the late medieval feud, we can say that these micro-conflicts (which are recognizably related) were focused on achieving an amicable agreement through arbitration, or, as was increasingly the case, through bilateral negotiations.[32] The best possibility was to forestall an encroachment by taking action oneself; the second best was to preempt an intrusion by means of force. Other possible ways to react to encroachments that had already taken place were: to arrest and punish the officeholders or opposing subjects involved;[33] to investigate and decide on the facts of the case again, by punishing a delinquent who had already been asked to take responsibility by the opposite side (the competence of which, however, was questionable);[34] to take from the crime or accident site a *Fraischpfand*; to lodge a written protest against the opposing party documenting the contradiction (as a sort of declaration of disagreement) and thereby one's own claim for the future; as well as (last of all) to file a suit at one of the imperial courts.

In these micro-conflicts in the Holy Roman Empire, towns had a special role to play. The territory of imperial towns interpenetrated those under princely authority, which in turn were increasingly pressuring for either demarcation or appropriation. At the start of the early modern period, even country towns had a high measure of self-awareness and numerous privileges and freedoms. When they could, they resisted the efforts at integration made by their lords. We will only refer to one case in the north of the Holy Roman Empire. In 1595, the messenger Lorenz Puttenheim was on his way from Stralsund to Greifswald when he fell from his carriage, breaking his neck. The council of Stralsund had the corpse claimed, examined, and buried. According to the Duke of Pomerania, Bogislav XIII, this infringed upon his jurisdiction over the roads. This was thus a central moment in Bogislav's attempt to spread his authority throughout his duchy. These charges resulted in a fierce dispute between Stralsund and its lord that went on for years.[35] Yet, this was only one example of many other micro-conflicts between the town and the duke.[36]

While towns such as Schwäbisch Hall seemed to have situated themselves well amidst this complex maelstrom of authority, the sovereign princes became increasingly reluctant to continue these disputes. Thus, Margrave Alexander von Brandenburg-Ansbach tried to end his conflicts with Nuremberg, which were basically the same as his conflicts with Schwäbisch Hall. Writing to the Nuremberg council, he remarked that, "contentious matters often do not interest us one way or the other at the level of the territory, yet they do concern the hunter, his fellow, or the servant." What is being fought over is "who should have jurisdiction on a barren strip of land" or "enjoy the grandeur of collecting the body of a murdered person at a great expense or having a criminal punished and executed." The outcome of such conflicts did not measure up to the "paper used or the harm caused," and the ones who suffer had always been the subjects on both sides.[37] However, it cannot be concluded from this that the margrave, for his part, meant to give up the disputed "deserted strip of land." His arguments, which were intended to make him appear more humane, were strategically justified. They were supposed to disavow the centuries-old policy in Brandenburg-Ansbach of preventing or creating predeterminations (*Präjudizien*) and thus to denounce the towns as hypersensitive and self-righteous troublemakers in their over-attentiveness in this particular dispute.

The municipal policy in Nuremberg, as in Schwäbisch Hall, was revealed to be less open to such pseudo-rational justifications. The imperial towns were often limited in their instruments of power. Therefore, they were able to preserve a comparatively large range of political options precisely by taking advantage of the frequently unsettled conditions of authority that had to be asserted in regularly recurring micro-conflicts. If rights and boundaries were determined in writing, they had to fear—as the Gründelhart Treaty of 1678 shows—that their influence would be restricted or even lost. Yet, the history of most of these treaties also reveals that they did not produce clear or definitive conditions of authority and law. On the contrary, from a contemporary perspective, they were subject to interpretation or were "questionable," as the Hallian adviser Hetzel wrote in 1758. The frequently violent practice or defense of legal authority created (at least for a moment) clear conditions and complete legal validity in the case of further conflicts or even suits and trials before the courts of the realm. Whenever possible, the Hallian council continued to act in a way characteristic of the political culture of the Holy Roman Empire, in general, and copied by other imperial towns, in particular: the territorial policies of Hall were designed to prevent or produce events that might function as precedents.[38]

Under these conditions, town policy toward neighbors was closely infused with sequential processes of negotiation and compromise. Individual documentation of the practice of jurisdiction in the surrounding region remained closely linked with the underlying conditions of authority or law, which were frequently unclear or disputed. The high degree of flexibility in the conditions of authority and law created a high degree of susceptibility in everyday political and legal life to reflection upon its (own) normative bases. In this sense, Schwäbisch Hall was still a "society of presence" at the end of the eighteenth century.[39] Against the backdrop of the conditions of authority in the region surrounding Schwäbisch Hall, it would not have been advantageous for the town, equipped as it was with only weak instruments of power, to attempt stronger consolidations or written codifications. The town could have continued making policy by means of selective interventions. This disposition toward the fundamental, even in the smallest of matters, as well as favoring of the exemplary over the abstract, decisively shaped the political culture of Schwäbisch Hall and perhaps of the Holy Roman Empire in general.[40]

Notes

1. Raimund Weber, "Die Vellberger Handlungen der Reichsstadt Schwäbisch Hall. Der Übergang einer fränkischen reichsritterschaftlichen Herrschaft an eine Reichsstadt des Schwäbischen Kreises zwischen 1592 und 1611, seine Vorgeschichte und seiner verfassungsrechtlichen Probleme," in *Vellberg in Geschichte und Gegenwart*, Vol. 1: *Darstellungen*, ed. Hansmartin Decker-Hauff (Sigmaringen, 1984), 225–271.
2. On the term *hohe Obrigkeit*, see Robert Schuh, "Anspruch und Inhalt des Prädikats 'hoch' in der politischen und Verwaltungssprache des Absolutismus," in *Landeshoheit. Beiträge zur Entstehung, Ausformung und Typologie des römisch-deutschen Reiches*, ed. Erwin Riedenauer (Stuttgart, 1994), 11–38, here 18f.
3. On the significance of customs and safe conduct as instruments in constructing a territorial state in Württemberg, see Dieter Mertens, "Württemberg" in *Handbuch der Baden-Württembergischen Geschichte*, Vol. 2: *Die Territorien im Alten Reich*, eds. Meinrad Schaab and Hansmartin Schwarzmaier (Stuttgart, 1995), 1–163, here 86f; and Meinrad Schaab, "Geleit und Territorium in Südwestdeutschland," in *Zeitschrift für Württembergische Landesgeschichte* 40 (1981): 398–417.
4. See Hanns Hubert Hofmann, *Adelige Herrschaft und souveräner Staat. Studien über Staat und Gesellschaft in Franken und Bayern im 18. und 19. Jahrhundert* (Munich, 1962); Dietmar Willoweit, *Rechtsgrundlagen der Territorialgewalt. Landesobrigkeit, Herrschaftsrechte und Territorium in der Rechtswissenschaft der Neuzeit* (Cologne and Vienna, 1975).
5. See Gerd Wunder, "Reichsstädte als Landesherren (Nürnberg, Ulm, Rothenburg und Hall)," in *Bauer, Bürger, Edelmann. Ausgewählte Aufsätze zur Sozialgeschichte von Gerd Wunder. Festgabe zu seinem 75. Geburtstag*, ed. Kuno Ulshöfer (Sigmaringen, 1984), 231–234.
6. Archives of the city of Schwäbisch Hall (hereafter StA SH) 5/1532.
7. StA SH HV HS 50, 257; StA SH 4/79, 131.
8. StA SH HV HS 50, 80, 111, 152, 155f., 250, 254; StA SH 4/435, 213; StA SH 4/79; 128; StA SH 4/84, 16; StA SH 4/88, 54.
9. On this, see Patrick Oelze, "Recht haben und Recht behalten. Konflikte um die städtische Gerichtsbarkeit im Umland von Schwäbisch Hall (1500–1800)" (Ph.D. diss., Konstanz, 2008), 320ff.
10. Patrick Oelze, "Fraischpfänder—Ein frühneuzeitlicher Rechtsbrauch im Südwesten des Alten Reichs," in *Zeitschrift für Württembergische Landesgeschichte* 69 (2010) (forthcoming).
11. StA SH HV HS 50, 71; StA SH 4/79, 72f.
12. Oelze, "Recht haben," 275. The Peace of Westphalia apparently affected the local conditions of authority in the Holy Roman Empire in two ways: on the one hand, it secured the imperial-free status of many smaller and midsize imperial classes, making them into sovereign partners in negotiations. On the other hand, the Peace of Westphalia and the ensuing peace conference provided them with a model for resolving conflicts on local levels.
13. StA SH 4/106, 1.
14. StA SH 4/106, 1. Copy of the treaty of 1666: StA SH 4/106, 1–27.
15. Copy of the treaty of 1678: StA SH 4/106, 29–43, here 30.
16. See Weber, "Vellberger Handlungen," 261, and the related card catalog (entitled "Herrschaft und Amt Vellberg").

17. On the meaning of "Präjudiz" in the period, see Johann Heinrich Zedler, *Grosses vollständiges Universal-Lexicon Aller Wissenschafften und Künste* (Leipzig and Halle, 1741), vol. 29, col. 59.
18. StA SH 4/105.
19. Johann Jacob Moser, *Neues Teutsches Staatsrecht*, Vol. 19: *Teutsches Nachbarliches Staatsrecht* (1773; reprinted, Osnabrück, 1967), 186f.
20. Robert Schuh, "Das vertraglich geregelte Herrschaftsgemenge. Die territorialstaatlichen Verhältnisse in Franken im 18. Jahrhundert im Lichte von Verträgen des Fürstentums Brandenburg-Ansbach mit Benachbarten," in *Jahrbuch für Fränkische Landesforschung* 55 (1995): 137–170.
21. See here the example of the treaties between Schwäbisch Hall and the Count von Hohenlohe: Oelze, "Recht haben," 172ff.
22. StA SH 47106, 57–107.
23. Newer research approaches can be found in Ronald G. Asch and Dagmar Freist, eds., *Staatsbildung als kultureller Prozess. Strukturwandel und Legitimation von Herrschaft in der Frühen Neuzeit* (Cologne, Weimar, and Vienna, 2005).
24. Gerd Wunder, Max Schefold, and Herta Beutter, *Die Schenken von Limpurg und ihr Land* (Sigmaringen, 1982), 51, 54; Heinrich Prescher, *Geschichte und Beschreibung der ... Reichsgraffschaft Limpurg ... 2nd part* (Stuttgart, 1790), 26–50. See the listing of properties and estates ceded in 1746 from Limpurg to Brandenburg-Ansbach in the same work, 414–420. At issue here are especially estates and rights in Bibersfeld, Hausen, Untersontheim, Ummenhofen, and Markertshofen.
25. Oelze, "Recht haben," 286ff.
26. Reference to the case can be found in StA SH 4/79, 188; the Hallian files on this dispute are transmitted in StA SH 5/110.
27. On this case, see as well StA SH 4/84, 21.
28. StA SH 5/110.
29. The question was often asked as to which part of a body would legally substantiate its circumstances in the case of a corpse washed ashore. In 1622, for instance, a subject of the *Ritterstift* Comburg from Tullau was drowned in the river Kocher near his home village. The town then asserted its jurisdiction over the entire river versus Limpurg-Sontheim. Even though the body had washed up on the Limburg bank of the river, Schwäbisch Hall declared itself competent in the case since the head of the drowned man was still in the water; StA SH 4/79, 56.
30. Micro-conflicts are here understood as disagreements between local power holders, which were mostly confined in terms of place and were carried out or solved locally. Violence was often used in such micro-conflicts, but it rarely turned into military action (in the narrow sense). For the most part, violence appears to have been spontaneous and uncontrolled.
31. On this, see as well Patrick Oelze, "Am Rande der Stadt—Grenzkonflikte und herrschaftliche Integration im Umland von Schwäbisch Hall," in *Stadtgemeinde und Städtegesellschaft. Formen der Integration und Distinktion in der frühneuzeitlichen Stadt*, eds. Patrick Schmidt and Horst Carl (Berlin, 2007), 140–165.
32. On how a feud "under customary law was referred to arbitration," see Klaus Graf, *Gewalt und Adel in Südwestdeutschland. Überlegungen zur spätmittelalterlichen Fehde*. http://projekte.geschichte.uni-freiburg.de/mertens/graf/gewalt.htm (last accessed on 25 June 2008).
33. StA SH 4/435, 214.

34. StA SH 4/79, 71.
35. Archives of the city of Stralsund, 3/560.
36. The incident portrayed above took place in the context of a small war, fought over decades by judicial as well as violent means, between the town and the Pomeranian counts. In this conflict, the town's jurisdiction, and its scope, played a central role. Herbert Langer, "Innere Kämpfe und Bündnis mit Schweden. Ende des 16. Jahrhunderts bis 1630," in *Geschichte der Stadt Stralsund*, ed. Herbert Ewe (Weimar, 1984), 137–167.
37. Quoted in Günther Schuhmann, *Die Markgrafen von Brandenburg-Ansbach. Eine Bilddokumentation zur Geschichte der Hohenzollern in Franken* (Ansbach, 1980), 255.
38. This central idea comes from Rudolf Schlögl.
39. On the town as a "society of presence" (*Anwesenheitsgesellschaft*) and on the specific composition of town politics, see Rudolf Schlögl, "Vergesellschaftung unter Anwesenden. Zur kommunikativen Form des Politischen in der vormodernen Stadt," in *Interaktion und Herrschaft. Die Politik der frühneuzeitlichen Stadt*, ed. Rudolf Schlögl (Konstanz, 2004), 9–60, here 30ff.
40. On this aspect, see also André Krischer, "Grenzen Setzen. Macht, Raum und Ehre der Reichsstädte," in *Machträume der frühneuzeitlichen Stadt*, eds. Christian Hochmuth and Susanne Rau (Konstanz, 2006), 135–154.

CHAPTER 10

Conflict and Consensus Around German Princes' Unequal Marriages
Prince's Autonomy, Emperor's Intervention, and the Juridification of Dynastic Politics

MICHAEL SIKORA

From a modern point of view, the marriages of the early modern higher nobility seem to be the result of relatively basic strategic interests. But we should remember two things. First, these interests were nothing less than the pillar upon which the privileged status of the noble families rested and, in a certain sense, they were fundamental principles of the society of orders as a whole. So, marrying within one's own rank or even into a higher rank was an indispensable precondition to maintaining one's own status, and advancing the political and economic interests and connections of the noble house was no less important to maintaining the family's standing. Secondly, one should not underestimate the fact that the members of the early modern nobility were also completely aware of the importance of striving for at least some basic harmony between the partners in order to prevent serious trouble, which could then actually jeopardize the reputation of the families.[1] As we know from other times and social orders, conflict between personal sympathy and the choice of a partner according to the similarity of rank and wealth was not inevitable; in fact, it seems that a marriage within the same social setting made a successful marriage that much more likely.[2]

However, there is no doubt that in the case of conflict between these factors, personal sentiments most likely had to take a backseat to the interests of the noble house. It was difficult enough merely to fulfill the strategic plans made for the match, as the still unwritten history of failed matrimonial projects would reveal, so the common result was the well-known one: many couples living with a courteous distance between them, at best. It is also well known that throughout the centuries, many early modern princes allowed themselves to fulfill their personal desires through extramarital relationships, whether in the form of short affairs or quasi-official mistresses.[3] In spite of these common practices, a small minority of princes did not content themselves with such relationships, and they sought official marriages, even with women from lower ranks. Such matches usually caused serious problems.

At first sight, one may assume that this subject is primarily about heart-warming stories of romance and public scandals. It cannot and must not be denied that the subject reveals some astonishing activities and attitudes, like every other study dealing with deviant behavior— deviant, to be sure, from the dominant values of the majority of the peers. To put it less superficially, there are indeed some details that may contribute to the often discussed history of emotions and gender relations, although, to be honest, the sources provide less evidence in this regard than one would expect. However, these conflicts bring up many questions, touching on a variety of other profound problems. They are centered around the question of how the families and the noble orders as a whole were really able to compel their individual members to adhere to principles of familial "strategy" and to prevent offenses. This was a central concern within noble culture as a whole.

The activities of nobles became increasingly entangled in the institutional framework of the Holy Roman Empire. Therefore, investigating the marital mismatches of German princes provides deep insight into the norms, rules, and practices of the empire, and we need to begin with how unequal relationships were viewed within its political and moral culture. There were, of course, aspects of the conflicts that will concern us that could not be determined by accepted rules. The second part of the chapter will concern the interests and options of the mismatched princes and those who opposed their unions. And finally, we will examine the intervention of the highest authorities in the empire, the emperor himself and the most powerful judicial instance, the *Reichshofrat* (Imperial Aulic Council).

As in other countries, the German nobility was divided into several ranks.[4] According to conventional wisdom, as reflected in noble practice and judicial theory, two distinctions were of major importance in regard to marriages: those between nobles and non-nobles, and those between members of the higher and lower nobilities. The higher nobility included the princely houses as well as the houses of the so-called imperial counts (*Reichsgrafen*): rulers of territories who were independent from other princes, and directly subordinated to the emperor (*reichsunmittelbar*).[5] While a marriage between a prince and an imperial countess was obviously unequal, it was nonetheless a fitting match in terms of social rank. Only marriages across the line between the higher and the lower nobility were considered mismatches in the narrow sense. Without any question, this was the case when a member of the higher nobility married a non-noble partner, but also when the partner stemmed from the lower nobility, especially because in this case, the partner may have been a subject of the territorial dominion.[6]

There were some discussions about the positions of ranks that were not as precisely defined as these simple rules may suggest. For example, the imperial knights, nobles of lower origin who did not rule territories, but were nevertheless subordinate only to the emperor, sought to blur the difference between themselves and the imperial counts.[7] The status of nobles who had gained their rank recently through an elevation by the emperor was also somewhat ambiguous, because under the stringent rules of the German nobility, "recently" could mean within several decades.[8] However, such disputed ranks usually did not figure in conflicts regarding unequal marriages, since the controversial nature of these relationships was more or less undisputed.

Most unequal relationships, of course, caused no serious troubles, because they were non-marital, whether short affairs or longer lasting partnerships. So many male members of the higher nobility took the liberty of such practices that even Martin Luther considered them a widespread custom, if not an unobjectionable one.[9] Some of those relationships gained a more binding character through gifts and written agreements assuring material support for the woman. However, in the cases to be discussed here, the couples officially entered the state of matrimony, where according to ecclesiastical law, there was no difference from any other legal marriage.[10]

A marriage with a wife from a lower rank raised the momentous question of whether she would accrue the rights and status of her new husband. According to the rules of Roman civil law, a wife from lower rank would indeed follow her husband's rank and status, allowing her all of the—gendered—rights to title, arms, and ceremonial precedence.[11] This also would have meant that she could claim material support to allow her a lifestyle representative of her high noble rank—including corresponding claims as a widow to a fitting standard of living. The most far-reaching consequence, however, would have been that the children of such a couple would enjoy the same rank of nobility and be fully entitled heirs and successors.

Toward the end of the sixteenth century, nobles and legal scholars in the Holy Roman Empire introduced an additional option, offering a very specific solution to the general problem. They adopted a special form of legal marriage, the roots of which went back to thirteenth-century Italian feudal law, the so-called "morganatic" marriage. This form allowed the validity of the marriage according to ecclesiastical law to be separated from the legal consequences in secular law.[12] In practice, this involved a marriage contract, promising the bride suitable gifts and a regular income, but less than normally accorded to a partner of equal rank. Usually, the bride was given a new name, derived from a virtual or real local manor, and a higher rank, not equal to that of the husband. In return, the bride renounced any further claims, including rights for their children, who could only succeed to the name and rank of the mother and inherit specified portions of their father's properties and incomes under certain conditions. They could not have the same succession or inheritance rights as the offspring of equal ranked couples. Above all, they were excluded from succession to the territorial throne. The point of this solution was not to limit rights, more easily done through a non-marital relationship, but to enable a nobleman to follow ecclesiastical norms without severe consequences for his noble house.

This leads to the question of why members of the higher nobility risked going against the rules of their houses through such marriages, although it must be said that morganatic marriages did not necessarily conflict with the interests of a noble family. Even in its origins in Italy, this juridical construction was expressly intended for *widowed* noblemen, who already had heirs, to marry again. In this case, a morganatic marriage with a bride from the lower ranks was, so to say, a cheaper option that saved the family the costs of marrying another partner from the higher nobility and the potential partition of the possession with even more fully legitimated heirs. In the case of a bride from a wealthy merchant family, such a marriage would have been a special chance to gain economic capital through a substantial dowry in return for the privileges of an hypergamous alliance. Even though such considerations have a compelling logic, I have found very few traces of such considerations.

Additionally, unequal partnerships could also arise in the context of particular familial situations.[13] Younger princes of less wealthy dynasties, who had little chance to succeed to a throne because of primogeniture, were less attractive for women of the higher nobility and therefore more likely inclined to choose partners of lower ranks. In other cases, elder princes, mostly widowed and already suffering from physical affliction, claimed for themselves, at least as arguments for their justification, the desire for a companion to care for them. However, such a role might not have been appealing for princesses of rank and reputation.

Certainly, affection played a role in many cases, or at least expressions of love made their way into the documents. Love could be described as an inescapable mandate from heaven, an argument suggesting the inevitability of marriage.[14] But these couples should not be considered forerunners of a new concept of partnership in keeping with the *bürgerliche Liebesideal*. The circle of mismatched princes includes rather different personalities, but one of the best known of them, Prince Leopold von Anhalt-Dessau, did not hesitate to take on a mistress, even while living in an unequal, but legal marriage. He behaved as a prince, so to say, but as a prince just a bit more eccentric than others.

Given that non-marital affairs were common practice, one may ask why some princes bothered to legitimize their unequal relationships at all. Nevertheless, one should not underestimate the impact of ecclesiastical norms on at least some of the princes and counts, whether from education or from the exhortations of court chaplains. Therefore, some nobles tried to avoid the impression of immoral concubinage, at least for their favorites.[15] And one has to look not only at the male partners: some evidence indicates that a marriage could also have been a precondition demanded by the selected women and their families, especially if they were of noble origin, and had to take care of their reputations even in such an unequal relationship.

In all such cases, a morganatic marriage was supposed to preclude any conflicts over the status of the wife and any heirs, though such a relationship hardly enhanced the reputation, rank, and prestige of the higher ranked house. However, not everyone accepted these compromise solutions, especially if the rights of children could become open to dispute: sometimes a prince attempted to change the conditions of an agreement to improve the status of his family.[16] Thus, the fate of a morganatic partnership was not fixed once and for all, but was subject to a dynamic process driven by the wish to bring it more and more in line with the husband's rank.

By far the most serious conflicts arose when a prince or count insisted on an unrestricted, fully valid marriage with an unequal partner. Of course, these cases were rather seldom. A few took place in the sixteenth century when morganatic marriage was not yet practiced in the empire, but some also occurred later. An example of this would be the marriage of Prince Karl Friedrich of Anhalt-Bernburg with the daughter of a non-noble civil servant. It was his second marriage and, already having a son from his first wife, who stemmed from the higher nobility, he should have been a perfect candidate for a morganatic marriage. However, he rejected this option and had more sons, which caused a great deal of trouble for about three decades.[17] Another example is Duke Anton Ulrich of Sachsen-Meiningen, the youngest of three brothers, who also married a non-noble wife. However, circumstances led him to the throne of Sachsen-Meiningen and therefore provoked serious conflicts about whether his sons would have the right to succeed him.[18] The best-known example, earlier than these two and perhaps their model, was Prince Leopold of Anhalt-Dessau, who married a druggist's daughter. As he noted himself, he had known her since childhood, and he managed to transfer his territory to his son with no problems (or almost no problems, as we shall see below).[19]

The particular motivations of individual princes are difficult to ascertain, beyond the general considerations we have outlined. One cannot ignore the importance of idiosyncratic personalities. In several cases, not only the marriage but also their policies and behaviors in other regards seem to demonstrate the principal dispositions of those princes toward making decisions without regard to opposition or conflict. Familial rivalry might have encouraged a prince's resolve to override collective norms. However, these men were no revolutionaries, but expressed their sense of sovereignty and power by attempting to determine their own lives. In this sense, they were well aware that they were princes.

The aforementioned Prince Leopold proved this in a very surprising way. He transferred his power not to his eldest, but to his second son. The eldest son, like his brother a son of the druggist's daughter, in turn married a spouse of unequal rank. His father, in this case, was in no way willing to accept this, and he ignored his daughter-in-law completely and excluded his son from the succession.[20] Unfortunately, there are no records to allow historians to grasp his motivations.

The opponents of unequal marriages—fathers, brothers, or other agnates—commonly claimed to be defending the reputation of their houses, often called their *lustre*. Without elaborate arguments, they referred to the usual items of noble dignity, defining themselves as descendents of a long line of noble ancestors, each of them, princes and counts as well as princesses and countesses, of impeccable noble origin. They were worried that the inclusion of even one person of less valuable lineage would spoil their exclusive treasure of symbolic capital, which could only be collected and augmented through time. Sometimes princes stressed the very distinct dignity of their rank, which reflected their status as quasi-sovereign monarchs and their claims of pre-eminence over the higher nobles of the other realms. The counts, for themselves, took special care of their reputations in order to reinforce their efforts to gain acceptance by the princes.

However, all of the claims of very distinct status for the higher nobles obviously could not prevent such unequal marriages, which typically took place in secret. What they could do was to question the wife's material support and ceremonial status and any son's legitimate succession. In fact, the opponents of unequal couples argued and acted as if every such marriage should be considered morganatic. This perception has also been widely adopted by later historians. In many cases, the status of unequal marriages was therefore rather doubtful, and only strong evidence of an agreement to restrict their effects should be regarded as a proof of their morganatic character.

It is even more difficult to determine what sort of damage to its reputation a noble house really had to fear from an unequal marriage. An indicator of crucial importance was whether the offspring of the couple would find partners of higher noble rank for themselves. This was probably the reason why Prince Leopold refused his son what he had allowed himself to do. Some of his children married princes and princesses, but perhaps it was feared that even the heir of the territory would have problems after two generations of non-noble mothers. The exclusion of the children, however, limited the threat to the house's reputation to the marriage itself and prevented the blemish from being transferred to the following generations. In this sense, perhaps the most important advantage of a morganatic marriage was that the children of the couple did not become members of the family in the strict sense, so that the pedigree remained unaffected. Typical for the treaties accompanying a morganatic marriage—and generally accepted by the agnates—was the right of a descendant to succeed in the absence of any other legitimate heir. Such offspring were considered a dynastic reserve meant to prevent the extinction of the house—when even an immaculate family tree would lose its importance.

Defending venerable values and principles was probably not the only motive the opponents of unequal couples had in mind. Such conflicts cannot be separated from the configurations within the families, and wherever the rights of potential successors were disputed, their opponents were stepbrothers, uncles, and cousins—in other words, direct or indirect rivals for the legacy and the succession.[21] In some cases, the frictions were even aggravated through longer lasting conflicts and personal animosities within the family. Moreover, the situation could change every time a protagonist died, which could cause new considerations of options and interests.[22] Conversely, unequal partnerships could much more easily be arranged where such rivalries were absent. This was true for younger brothers, but a strong ruler such as Leopold also benefited from the fact that he had no brothers.

Personal interests did not outweigh the general principles of rank and status, whose importance for the self-conception of the nobility and for the society of orders as a whole were beyond question. However, one should more precisely understand their impact. As Duke Anton Ulrich of Sachsen-Meiningen stated, there were no laws forbidding unequal marriages.[23] The unwritten customs of the nobility did not have a juridical quality in the sense that they would have defined the validity of such a marriage per se. When these rules were broken, the offender faced only a potential lack of acceptance from agnates and peers. As we have seen, whether this would cause disputes and would therefore be transformed into a lack of legitimacy largely depended on the family's configuration. This flexibility reflects the fact that dynastic policy was not a matter of simple principles, but was a process negotiated between hierarchical roles and conflicting values.[24] The highest priority was pragmatic rather than dogmatic, namely, to ensure the family's status.

When a conflict arose around an unequal marriage, there were two major facts that neither side could ignore. From the side of the opponents, there was a legal marriage, and from the side of the couple, an inequality of rank. It seems that the course of the sixteenth century sharpened these issues. During the 1500s, ecclesiastical reforms in both confessions specified the criteria for legal marriage and marginalized other forms of partnership. At the same time, the development of territorial rule (*Landesherrschaft*) deepened the distinction between the higher nobility and the lower territorial nobility, and even between the princely houses and the count's houses, whose minor status became apparent through the struggles of territorial dominance and through their insignificant role in the imperial diet.

During the sixteenth century, the way to deal with these problems also went through an important change. The establishment of both the *Reichskammergericht* and the *Reichshofrat*, along with the ongoing institutionalization of the empire, gave both sides the opportunity to seek juridical backing. Procedures on such matters did not appear before the turn of the seventeenth century and usually did not directly deal with the marriage itself, but with special claims and appeals deriving from different interests. From case to case, the legally relevant facts were different, and every lawsuit had its own characteristics. From a general perspective, however, they gave the problem a new shape.[25]

The most obvious consequence was the influence from outside on a matter which, from the perspective of the higher nobility, should have been negotiated within a noble house, all the more as the higher nobility claimed legal autonomy on topics concerning dynastic strategies, especially rules of succession. In fact, it was a major challenge for a noble house to maintain a collective consensus regarding common interests and to direct the behavior of its members. While this was the dominant practice during the early modern period, one has to admit that especially the problems of inheritance and succession made conflicts a relatively common occurrence. Going to court may have threatened the autonomy of the noble house, but it seems to have become more and more common from the middle of the seventeenth century, and not only in regard to unequal marriages.[26] Still, lawsuits on this special subject, while rather long-lasting and contentious, were few in number.

One may ask whether the juridification of these conflicts indicates a decline of the willingness to submit oneself to one's family's principles. Indeed, earlier generations seem to have managed these problems on their own. The tragic example of Agnes Bernauer makes clear that conflicts could not be completely avoided. In 1435, she was executed by order of Duke Ernst of Bavaria, her father-in-law, which was, to be sure, an outstanding exception.[27] One also has to consider that, except for a few cases, before the fifteenth century, mentions of unequal marriages were quite rare. For comparisons to the Middle Ages, more evidence is necessary, including quantitative data on births and deaths. However, it seems that the aforementioned normative, political, and institutional changes reduced the scope of options and therefore contributed, at least to some extent, in provoking offenses or even in creating their perception as such. From this point of view, the perception and treatment of unequal marriages took a specific early modern shape, as an interplay of traditional values and attitudes and modernizing practices.

The effects of juridical influence point in the same direction. At first it was sons from unequal couples who went to the courts to strengthen their rights and claims. At the end of the seventeenth century, juridical discourse usually underlined the rights of unequal couples.[28] Their noble opponents had no juridical basis to argue against the formal logic of civil law according to Roman tradition. This deficiency became even more threatening at the turn of the eighteenth century, when the number of unequal marriages rose. The nobles had to look for ways to transform their unwritten customs into legally valid instruments. Thus, they increasingly relied on testaments and family contracts, which included more and more interdictions against such mismatches.

In a more general sense, the princes profited from changes in legal theory, which, by emphasizing the special traditions specific to the German higher nobility, stressed the relevance of usage and historical argumentation against the rules of Roman law. In the end, non-noble jurists, above all Johann Stephan Pütter, became specialized experts in defending the integrity of the higher nobility.[29] In combining noble autonomy, collective integrity, and strategic flexibility, the core of Pütter's argument was that the legitimacy of every aberration in regard to partnership selection should depend on the consent of the agnates.

The debate was even more complicated because of another strong factor from outside the noble houses, a factor that had the power to impose change: the emperors, the heads of the social order. Although much of the emperors' authority depended on the consent of the imperial diet, especially in political matters such as assessing taxes or declaring war, they did have an important prerogative that they could administer on their own: the ability to raise people to higher ranks. This was a universal competence and included, for example, investing scholars as doctors, a change in rank perceived as entering a new social order. It also included the right to raise nobles to higher ranks. For example, during the Thirty Years' War, Ferdinand II raised several Catholic nobles from Austria and Bohemia to princely ranks to reward them for their loyalty. This caused disputes with the old princely houses of the empire about whether the newly raised princes could enter the imperial diet (and thereby strengthen the imperial-Catholic influence).[30]

A widely accepted practice for wives in unequal marriages—and even for concubines—was to give the woman a new name, sometimes combined with the transfer of a manor to which this name was linked, so that she could be considered as noble. In some cases, princes appear to have done this on their own authority, with more or less general acceptance, but sometimes they requested a formal confirmation or elevation from the emperor. This was definitely necessary if the partner were to be elevated in an undisputable manner into a rank of the higher nobility. This also seemed to be a way to overcome the inequality of rank and to confirm the unrestricted legitimacy and equality of the offspring.

The emperors raised the rank of several female partners of unequal couples. During the seventeenth century, the first examples established the practice of elevation to the rank of an imperial countess. Routinely, the documents declared that they should be treated as if they were descended from a family of counts equal to the others. Therefore, they formally entered the higher nobility and, if not of equal rank to the princes, nevertheless attained sufficient status for their husbands. The diplomas, however, did not always follow the same pattern and introduced variations with regards to offspring. This was a critical point, because the mismatched princes were interested in regarding their children as princes and princesses born of a princely couple.[31] An elevation to the rank of count still left a disparity in rank to the princely house, but there could be a way around even this. The aforementioned Prince Leopold of Anhalt-Dessau effected the elevation of his wife, the daughter of the druggist, to the rank of a princess of Anhalt-Dessau, a matchless example of social mobility in the society of orders, but he did not have to fear serious opposition. Some years later, Duke Anton Ulrich of Sachsen-Meiningen followed this example and also achieved the elevation of his wife of non-noble origin to princess. This act, however, provoked harsh objections from the agnates.[32]

There is no evidence that the policies of the emperors toward the problem of elevation pursued a particular strategy. They certainly did not intend systematically to muddle the social order. Nonetheless, one has to admit that the customs of the imperial court, where newly raised families exerted the most important influence, significantly differed from the practices of the older princely families of the empire. One has also to keep in mind that their limited options to wield power, always in competition with the powerful princes of the empire, led the emperors to favor minor princes, counts, and even the imperial knights, some of whom filled influential functions as high-ranking officials, generals, and even members of the high courts. Thus, on the one hand, maintaining the reputation and autonomy of the princes was not a major concern of imperial policy; on the other hand, debating the internal conflicts of the princely families at the *Reichshofrat* served to strengthen the emperors' dignity and influence.

Raising people in rank, moreover, was an instrument likely employed by the emperors to award proven military allies or to gain supporters within the higher nobility. Leopold of Anhalt-Dessau is a good example for this practice. While he, of course, could not be raised to an even higher rank, the elevation of his wife must be seen as a reward for Leopold's services to the emperor, which is explicitly underlined in the diploma.[33] It was a different situation for Anton Ulrich of Sachsen-Meiningen, who was not that important in his own right, but who seems to have profited from the fact that he was a relative of the empress. Even with all of these considerations, one should not underestimate the fiscal dimension of these acts, for, after all, an elevation to the rank of imperial count brought considerable fees to the imperial treasury. Finally, such acts of grace were most appropriate to demonstrate the emperors' dignity. Disposing over the social order, as the emperors' only undisputed prerogative, represented them as much like monarchs as possible. Emperors had to watch out for princes, who, on their own authority, treated their spouses as princesses, and defend themselves against those agnates who intended to exclude the option of an elevation.

These risks were explicitly discussed during the quarrels concerning Anton Ulrich of Sachsen-Meiningen and his wife.[34] Her elevation was not least of all a symbolic act to demonstrate the emperor's right in this regard, which he intentionally decreed against the remonstrances of the agnates. However, their resistance turned out to be rather persistent. Despite strong protests, they could not achieve a renunciation from Charles VI. After his death, 15 years after the elevation, a coalition of concerned princes profited from the dynastic crisis of the Hapsburgs. The newly elected Charles VII, the poorly backed prince elector of Bavaria, had to accept a new article in the *Wahlkapitulation* that prohibited the emperor from raising the rank of unequal spouses without the consent of the agnates.[35] So, the controversies around unequal marriages resulted in damaging the emperor's only important *ius reservata*.

Conclusion

This struggle neither put an end to unequal marriages nor shook the emperor's position to its foundations. No doubt, it strengthened the means of the nobles to restrict the risks of unequal marriages. From a more general point of view, it reveals a heretofore-overlooked phenomenon in the empire. It shows the princes not only as protagonists of modern state-building, but also underlines the importance of their identity as part of a privileged order by birth. It shows how closely the options of the emperors were linked not only to their political power, but also to their traditional role as head of a traditional concept of order. Altogether, these phenomena stress a perception of the empire that takes its traditional elements seriously and that not only considers it in light of its connection to modernity, but also tries to understand it on its own terms as a pre-modern socio-political system.

Notes

1. See, for example, Evelin Oberhammer, "Gesegnet sei dies Band. Eheprojekte, Heiratspakten und Hochzeit im fürstlichen Haus," in *Der ganzen Welt ein Lob und Spiegel. Das Fürstenhaus Liechtenstein in der frühen Neuzeit*, ed. Evelin Oberhammer (Vienna and Munich, 1990), 182–203.
2. For some principal reflections see Hans Medick and David Sabean, eds., *Emotionen und materielle Interessen. Sozialanthropologische und historische Beiträge zur Familienforschung* (Göttingen, 1984).
3. Stories of unconventional courtly love have stimulated much popular literature. Good examples for a serious discussion are, amongst others, Andrea Weisbrod, *Von Macht*

und Mythos der Pompadour. Die Mätressen im politischen gefüge des französischen Absolutismus (Königstein, 2000); Sybille Oßwald-Bargende, *Die Mätresse, der Fürst und die Macht. Christina Wilhelmina von Grävenitz und die höfische Gesellschaft* (Frankfurt a.M. and New York, 2000); especially regarding the later middle ages and the sixteenth century, see Andreas Tacke, ed.,"... *wir wollen der Liebe Raum geben." Konkubinate geistlicher und weltlicher Fürsten um 1500* (Göttingen, 2006); and Paul-Joachim Heinig, "'Omnia vincit amor'—Das fürstliche Konkubinat im 15./16. Jahrhundert," in *Principes. Dynastien und Höfe im späten Mittelalter*, eds. Cordula Nolte, Karl-Heinz Spiess, and Ralf-Gunnar Werlich (Stuttgart, 2002), 277–314.

4. For basic information covering the whole of Europe, see the excellent surveys by Ronald G. Asch, *Nobilities in Transition 1550–1700. Courtiers and Rebels in Britain and Europe* (London, 2003); and extended into the eighteenth century, Asch, *Europäischer Adel in der Frühen Neuzeit* (Cologne, Weimar, and Vienna, 2008). Regarding the nobility of the Holy Roman Empire, see Rudolf Endres, *Adel in der frühen Neuzeit*, (Munich, 1993); and Michael Sikora, *Der Adel in der frühen Neuzeit* (Darmstadt, 2009).

5. Recent studies on the status of the so-called *Reichsgrafen* are Stephanie Marra, *Allianzen des Adels. Dynastisches Handeln im Grafenhaus Bentheim im 16. und 17. Jahrhundert* (Cologne, Weimar, and Vienna, 2007); Thomas Mutschler, *Haus, Ordnung, Familie. Wetterauer Hochadel im 17. Jahrhundert am Beispiel des Hauses Ysenburg-Büdingen* (Darmstadt and Marburg, 2004); Vinzenz Czech, *Legitimation und Repräsentation. Zum Selbstverständnis thüringisch-sächsischer Reichsgrafen in der frühen Neuzeit* (Berlin, 2003); Barbara Stollberg-Rilinger, "Der Grafenstand in der Reichspublizistik," in *Dynastie und Herrschaftssicherung in der Frühen Neuzeit*, ed. Heide Wunder (Berlin, 2002), 29–53; and Johannes Arndt, "Zwischen kollegialer Solidarität und persönlichem Aufstiegsstreben. Die Reichsgrafen im 17. und 18. Jahrhundert," in *Der europäische Adel im Ancien Régime*, ed. Ronald G. Asch (Cologne, Weimar, and Vienna, 2001), 105–128.

6. For a general overview and reflections on partnerships in the higher nobility beyond princely marriages, see Michael Sikora, "Ungleiche Verbindlichkeiten. Gestaltungsspielräume standesverschiedener Partnerschaften im deutschen Hochadel der Frühen Neuzeit," in *zeitenblicke*, 4:3 (2005). http://www.zeitenblicke.de/2005/3/Sikora/index_html (accessed 12 December 2005).

7. See Christophe Duhamelle, *L'Héritage collectif: La noblesse d'Église rhénane, 17e 18e siècles* (Paris, 1998), 177–183; and Johannes Arndt, *Das niederrheinisch-westfälische Reichsgrafenkollegium und seine Mitglieder (1653–1806)* (Mainz, 1991), 238–243.

8. From the perspective of social climbers, see Hans Jürgen Jüngling, "Die Heiraten des Hauses Liechtenstein im 17. und 18. Jahrhundert," in *Liechtenstein—Fürstliches Haus und staatliche Ordnung*, eds. Volker Press and Dietmar Willoweit (Munich and Vienna, 1987), 329–345; from the defending perspective, see Ute Küppers-Braun, *Frauen des hohen Adels im kaiserlich-freiweltlichen Damenstift Essen (1605–1803)* (Münster, 1997), 52–59, 275–301. The author discusses the fact that Catholic cathedral and collegiate chapters, where nobles profited from benefices, asked new candidates to prove their noble parentage. This so-called *Adelsprobe* was the major instrument used to distance the nobility from social climbers, so that the ecclesiastical chapters functioned as a watchdog for the old nobility.

9. According to the so-called "Wittenberger Ratschlag," dated 10 December 1539, quoted from *Corpus Reformatorum*, Vol. III, by Karl Gottlieb Bretschneider, ed., *Philippi Melanthonis Opera quae supersunt omnia*, Vol. III (Halle, 1836; reprint, New York and London, 1963), 856–863, here 862. The "Ratschlag" was part of the discussion around

Landgrave Philipp's of Hesse bigamous marriage. Suffice it to say that Philipp's second spouse was of lower rank, in this case from the territorial nobility. For further information on this subject see also Stephan Buchholz, "Rechtsgeschichte und Literatur: Die Doppelehe Philipps des Großmütigen," in *Landgraf Philipp der Großmütige von Hessen und seine Residenz Kassel*, eds. Heide Wunder, Christina Vanja, and Berthold Hinz (Marburg, 2004), 57–73.

10. See Sikora, "Ungleiche Verbindlichkeiten," sections 8–13.
11. See Dietmar Willoweit, *Standesungleiche Ehen des regierenden hohen Adels in der neuzeitlichen deutschen Rechtsgeschichte* (Munich, 2004), 104–106.
12. See Sikora, "Ungleiche Verbindlichkeiten," sections 17–25, with further readings.
13. I have discussed such problems in Michael Sikora, "Über den Umgang mit Ungleichheit. Bewältigungsstrategien für Mesalliancen im deutschen Hochadel der Frühen Neuzeit—das Haus Anhalt als Beispiel," in *Zwischen Schande und Ehre. Erinnerungsbrüche und die Kontinuität des Hauses. Legitimationsmuster und Traditionsverständnis des frühneuzeitlichen Adels in Umbruch und Krise*, eds. Martin Wrede and Horst Carl (Mainz, 2007), 97–124.
14. See Sylvia Schraut, "'Die Ehen werden in dem Himmel gemacht'. Ehe- und Liebeskonzepte der katholischen Reichsritterschaft im 17. und 18. Jahrhundert," in *Tugend, Vernunft und Gefühl. Geschlechterdiskurse der Aufklärung und weibliche Lebenswelten*, ed. Claudia Opitz (Münster, 2000), 15–32.
15. One indication for this are the attempts of higher nobles to diffuse the character of their non-marital partnerships, see Sikora, "Ungleiche Verbindlichkeiten," sections 12–13, 22, 37–40. Even Landgrave Philipp of Hesse argued in this way, see ibid., section 26, with reference to Bretschneider, *Philippi*, 851–856; in this case, there is also evidence of the influence of the female partner's family, see William Walker Rockwell, *Die Doppelehe des Landgrafen Philipp von Hessen* (Marburg, 1904; reprint, Münster, 1985), 316–317.
16. For examples see Sikora, "Ungleiche Verbindlichkeiten," sections 33–36, Sikora, "Umgang," 102–107.
17. For details see Michael Sikora, "Eine Missheirat im Hause Anhalt. Zur sozialen Praxis der ständischen Gesellschaft in der ersten Hälfte des 18. Jahrhundert," in *Die Fürsten von Anhalt. Herrschaftssymbolik, dynastische Vernunft und politische Konzepte in Spätmittelalter und Früher Neuzeit*, eds. Werner Freitag and Michael Hecht (Halle, 2003), 248–265. With more emphasis on individual motives Carolin Doller, "Bürgerliche Gattinnen. Standesungleiche Verbindungen im Hause Anhalt-Bernburg," in *Adel in Sachsen-Anhalt*, ed. Eva Labouvie (Cologne, Weimar, and Vienna, 2007), 17–48.
18. For details see Michael Sikora, "Ein kleiner Erbfolgekrieg. Die sachsen-meiningische Sukzessionskrise 1763 und das Problem der Ebenbürtigkeit," in *Menschen und Strukturen in der Geschichte Alteuropas. Festschrift für Johannes Kunisch zur Vollendung seines 65. Lebensjahres*, eds. Helmut Neuhaus and Barbara Stollberg-Rilinger (Berlin, 2002), 319–339. As the title of this article indicates, this conflict even provoked military violence.
19. See Sikora, "Umgang," 112–116.
20. See Paul Herre, *Die geheime Ehe des Erbprinzen Wilhelm Gustav von Anhalt-Dessau und die Reichsgrafen von Anhalt* (Zerbst, 1933; reprint, Dessau, 2006).
21. For thorough insights into the different roles of siblings see Sophie Ruppel, *Verbündete Rivalen. Geschwisterbeziehungen im Hochadel des 17. Jahrhunderts* (Cologne, Weimar, and Vienna, 2006). The importance of the female family members cannot be discussed

here; there are examples that they took their own positions toward sisters-in-law from lower ranks. In regard to Duke Anton Ulrich, see Stefanie Walther, "Zwischen Emotionen und Interessen—Elisabeth Ernestine Antonie von Sachsen-Meiningen als Schwester, Schwägerin und Tante," in *WerkstattGeschichte* 46 (2007): 25–40.
22. A good example for changing constellations are the quarrels around Prince Karl Friedrich of Anhalt-Bernburg's marriage, see Sikora, "Missheirat."
23. See Sikora, "Erbfolgekrieg," 326.
24. Inspiring a less dogmatic point of view is Pierre Bourdieu, "Marriage Strategies as Strategies of Social Reproduction," in *Family and Society. Selections from the Annales*, eds. Robert Forster and Orest Ranum (London, 1976), 117–144.
25. For short case studies and an overview regarding aspects of legal history see Willoweit, *Standesungleiche Ehen*.
26. See Siegrid Westphal, *Kaiserliche Rechtsprechung und herrschaftliche Stabilisierung* (Cologne, Weimar, and Vienna, 2002).
27. Alfons Huber, *Agnes Bernauer. Ein Quellen- und Lesebuch* (Straubing, 1999). This is a useful reader with excerpts from sources and literature and a lot of further reading, but without critical depiction and discussion.
28. See, for example, Gerhard Feltmann, *De impari matrimonio* (Bremen, 1691).
29. Johann Stephan Pütter, *Ueber Mißheirathen Teutscher Fürsten und Grafen* (Göttingen, 1796).
30. For substantial studies on the emperors' creations of new princes, see Thomas Klein, "Die Erhebungen in den weltlichen Reichsfürstenstand 1550–1806," in *Blätter für deutsche Landesgeschichte* 122 (1986): 137–192; Harry Schlip, "Die neuen Fürsten," in Press and Willoweit, *Liechtenstein*, 249–292; and from a general point of view, Ronald G. Asch, "Das monarchische Nobilitierungsrecht und die soziale Identität des Adels im 17. und 18. Jahrhundert," in *Die frühneuzeitliche Monarchie in Europa und ihr Erbe. Festschrift für Heinz Duchhardt zum 60. Geburtstag*, eds. Ronald G. Asch, Johannes Arndt, and Matthias Schnettger (Münster, 2003), 91–107.
31. In one instance, opponents not only requested that the sons from an unequal couple be raised to the rank of imperial counts, but also requested that they be given names different from their own house and explicitly excluded from the succession, see Sikora, "Missheirat," 257.
32. See Sikora, "Erbfolgekrieg," 331.
33. See Sikora, "Umgang," 112–114. The diploma is published among others in Johann Christian Lünig, *Teutsches Reichs-Archiv*, Vol. 2: Partis specialis Continuatio II, 3, Supplementa Ulteriora 11. Band 2. Absatz (Leipzig, 1712), 93–95.
34. See Sikora, "Erbfolgekrieg," 328–332.
35. See Sikora, "Erbfolgekrieg," 332–333; the Wahlkapitulation is published in Johann Jacob Moser, *Ihro Römisch-Kayserlichen Majestät Carls des Siebenden Wahl-Capitulation ... Erster Theil* (Frankfurt a.M., 1742), no. XXII, 4. See also Fritz Georg Iwand, *Die Wahlkapitulationen des 17. und 18. Jahrhunderts und ihr Einfluß auf die Entwicklung des Ebenbürtigkeits- und Prädikatsrechts des deutschen hohen Adels* (Biberach, 1919), 18–20.

CHAPTER 11

Power and Good Governance
The Removal of Ruling Princes in the Holy Roman Empire, 1680–1794

WERNER TROSSBACH

By 1680, witch trials were still far from unusual in the Holy Roman Empire. What was unusual in the principality of Vaduz and Schellenberg was the high number of convictions. In these relatively small areas, with a population of no more than 1,600 adults, 122 cases were opened and fifty-four people lost their lives between 1678 and 1680.[1] Count Ferdinand Carl Franz saw no reason to interfere with these verdicts, as the property of the accused fell to him upon their executions.[2] Part of these gains helped to ameliorate the burden of the county's ruinous tax system, explaining the initial cooperation of the peasants' representatives, who strongly defended the rights given to them under an agreement on taxes in 1613.[3]

The case of the Count of Vaduz was set in motion by the flight of six people from the Vaduz area, who, on 17 December 1680, informed the local officials of the neighboring Habsburg county of Feldkirch about the witchcraft prosecutions. The petition was then passed on to the *Reichshofrat*, which, on 12 May 1681, prohibited the continuation of any further witchcraft proceedings and confiscations in Vaduz.[4] In August 1681, Rupert von Bodman, abbot of the imperial abbey in Kempten, received instructions to safeguard all of the documents of the proceedings so that they could be sent to a university for a ruling on their legality.[5] The abbot, who was known to be a good administrator and to be loyal to the emperor, immediately carried out these instructions. In October 1682, he received a complete dossier of 567 pages from the Benedictine University in Salzburg, which determined that all of 122 of the trials were null and void due to irregularities in the proceedings.[6] As a result, the *Reichshofrat* started public prosecutions against the count. On 22 June 1684, on the recommendation of the imperial fiscal prosecutor (*Reichshoffiskal*), the

Reichshofrat summoned the count to justify himself within the usual time limit of two months. He was made aware that he would be deprived of his criminal jurisdiction if he failed to disprove the charge. As a provisional measure, the criminal jurisdiction was immediately placed in the hands of the abbot of Kempten.[7]

By the 1680s, the judicial precedent for such spectacular actions was at least a hundred years old. The quote, "*Quod domini propter nimiam saevitiam in subditos iurisdictionem amittant aliisque poenis coerci possint*" (Those lords who treat their subjects with utmost fury can be punished and even lose their jurisdiction), was the essence of the legal basis in the Vaduz case, presented by Franz Karl Satorius von Schwanenfeld, the public prosecutor at the *Reichshofrat*.[8] It was a quotation from an authoritative legal handbook drawn up in 1578 by the influential jurist, Andreas Gail, who had referred to the Upper Italian jurist Baldus de Ubaldis, a classic medieval author on Roman law.[9]

For a time after the Thirty Years' War, however, this principle of law was difficult to reconcile with Article VIII, §1 of the Treaty of Osnabrück, which ensured that "no one should at any time or under any pretext be allowed to interfere with the imperial estates' right and possession of territorial sovereignty."[10] In addition, Ferdinand IV had already stated upon his election as king of the Romans in 1653 that he did not wish "any of the imperial estates' subjects to be exempted from their legitimate liabilities, neither from taxes nor tithes nor other public burdens."[11] And, in 1658, in his capitulation of election (*Wahlkapitulation*), Leopold I agreed that, even under "the pretext of feudal law" (*Lehensrecht*), no such restrictions should be made. He stated further that he would "not suspend or exclude any imperial estate from its session and vote at the imperial diet without the consent of the electors, princes, and estates."[12]

Despite these legal arguments, Count Ferdinand Carl Franz could not effectively defend himself, because by June 1684 he was already a prisoner of the abbot of Kempten. The sources reveal that the latter appointed the count's defense lawyer, whose weak written defense was put together in the Kempten chancellery.[13] The imprisonment, however, had nothing to do with the invalidated witch trials. Instead, his eventual removal from office resulted from two supplementary proceedings that had begun the previous year. At the beginning of 1683, the count's siblings had complained to the *Reichshofrat* that the "bad husbandry" of their ruling brother deprived them of their material well-being. He was said to have personally assaulted some of his honorable subjects, while having emptied the wine cellar, along with companions of the lowest sort. The bishop of Chur, as ecclesiastical lord, supported the complaint, adding that even clergy were exposed to violent attacks by the count. The latter was also accused of interrupting religious services with "obscenities and indecent acts."[14]

Consequently, on 11 June 1683, the abbot received a further commission. He should not only investigate the complaints, but also "reorganize" the count's household and government. Additionally, the *Reichshofrat* enabled him to arrest the count "in case of necessity."[15] On 10 January 1684, the commission was extended after the peasant communities raised complaints about the count regarding excess labor services and irregularities with the elections of their representatives.[16] When the count threatened one of his subjects, Rupert von Bodman made use of his authorization to arrest him. On 24 March 1684, the commission informed the subjects that, by order of the emperor, the count had "left the country." Three days later, the abbot took over the government.[17] On 20 September 1684, the *Reichshofrat* started a further public prosecution against the prisoner, this time for blasphemy.[18] When the count died in custody in Kempten in February 1686, the two proceedings were still pending. From the count's noble house, not a single word of protest was to be heard.

The neighboring imperial estates raised no objections either. In general, after 1648, adjacent princes mostly tolerated interventions by the emperor in the affairs of the small states in southwest Germany, although most of these interventions were relatively minor.[19] In the case of Vaduz, the neighborhood was evidently prepared to accept even stronger measures from a strengthened emperor, since such measures were seen to stabilize an area of traditional geopolitical insecurity.[20]

In territories outside of the Habsburg's immediate sphere of influence, especially where competing parties vied to increase their regional influence, the removal of ruling princes often turned out to be more complicated. One such affair in the territory of Nassau-Siegen seemed to resemble the Vaduz case at first, but soon became more difficult. Similar to the Count of Vaduz, Prince Wilhelm Hyacinth of Nassau-Siegen (of the Catholic line) maneuvered himself into political isolation. Bearing in mind the debts he assumed when taking office, he saw the estate of the English king, William of Orange, who died in 1702, as his lifeline.[21] Legally, his claims were fairly sound, but in practice they could not be realized. Eventually, William's estate was divided between the other claimants, the kings of France and Prussia as well as the line of Nassau-Diez.[22]

Hyacinth made himself unpopular with the House of Nassau (particularly with his Calvinist cousin, with whom he jointly ruled the city of Siegen), other imperial estates, and the emperor's court by his arrogant use of nomenclature, calling himself "the sovereign Prince of Orange" and insisting on being called "Your Royal Highness."[23] He also sought the counsel of dubious advisers while arbitrarily imprisoning long established officials.

Hyacinth also pursued policies that angered his subjects. He continued efforts to suppress Calvinism begun by his father, which affected the large number of Calvinists in the territory. Additionally, all citizens, regardless of confession, were forced to pay exorbitant sums so that the count could pay for his numerous legal proceedings and his extravagant lifestyle, while taxes due to the emperor and the *Reichskreis* went unpaid.[24] After the subjects' pleas for leniency were brutally dismissed, former chancellor Jung, who from 1702 onward had been repeatedly imprisoned by Hyacinth, at the subjects' request, petitioned the *Reichshofrat* on 30 August 1706 to "protect" the land by appointing an imperial commission. In answer to the petition, Hyacinth started to imprison prominent village heads, who he supposed to be the "ringleaders" of an emerging peasant movement, and to confiscate their property.[25] On 5 November, the peasants' attempt to rescue the village head of Weidenau, Johann Thomas Flender, ended in a hail of bullets fired from the "upper palace" at Siegen. Three people were injured, one of whom later died as a result.[26]

Initially, the *Reichshofrat* accepted Hyacinth's version of the event—that the skirmish was a rebellion—and instructed the Cologne cathedral chapter to investigate the incident.[27] Hyacinth responded by intensifying his confiscations, which in January led to several deaths in a charcoal-burning hamlet near Weidenau.[28] Only when a separate letter from the Calvinist prince of Siegen supported the peasants' version of the recent turmoil did the *Reichshofrat* reverse itself and instruct the commission to investigate the prince's arbitrary actions and to free the prisoners.[29] However, this did not prevent Hyacinth from publicly beheading without trial Friedrich Flender, a member of a prominent Weidenau Protestant iron forger family, on 29 March 1707.[30]

Shocked by this deliberate act, the Cologne cathedral chapter seems to have taken to heart the investigatory commission it had been given.[31] On 11 April 1707, they moved into the territory with approximately 2,000 armed men, while Hyacinth hastily fled the jurisdiction. In its report to the *Reichshofrat*, the commission stressed that his subjects were "in fear of life and limb" if the prince's "unrestricted domination was not abrogated and if the officials he had appointed remained in their posts."[32] In its report to the emperor, the *Reichshofrat* suggested that "until the prince changed his mind," an "ad interim government" should be installed, which would govern the land under the "highest Authority of His Imperial Majesty."[33]

In the actual decree, however, the words "administration" (*Administration*) or "ad interim government" (*Interims-Regierung*) were avoided. After all, the commissioners were called upon to "mobilize everything" to protect the citizens and to "reorganize the government."[34] The expression "administration" first appeared officially on 5 October 1708, when the *Reichshofrat* confirmed the powers of the Cologne cathedral chapter over Hyacinth's part of the city of Siegen.[35]

Regardless, Hyacinth was aware that there were good reasons to protest against the Cologne commission. He chose as the appropriate venue to pose a legal protest the imperial diet, which in the case of Vaduz had not been involved.[36] The question was presented as to how far the convening princes of the relevant *Reichskreis* should be favored as commissioners, particularly when it had to do with executive tasks.³⁷ It should be remembered, however, that in the case of Nassau-Siegen, the involvement of Cologne was initiated not as a commission of execution, but of inquiry. Furthermore, the appointment of the Cologne cathedral chapter had originally occurred at Hyacinth's own request. He had wanted to avoid involving the directorate of the *Reichskreis*, because these territories—Prussia in 1705 and the Palatinate in 1706—had already employed troops against him in earlier disputes.³⁸

On 22 June 1709, the three councils of the imperial diet gave Hyacinth permission to resume his rule. However, a new commission was to be established to care for the "subjects' safety and for lenient government." Indirectly, the emperor was blamed for his previous appointment, as the new commission was to be established in strict "accordance with the empire's constitution."³⁹ After the death of Joseph I, the elector of the Palatine, in his capacity as interim ruler of the western part of the empire (*Reichsvikar für die Länder des rheinischen, schwäbischen und fränkischen Rechtes*), ratified the decision and appointed the directorate of the imperial circle (consisting of the Duke of Cleve [i.e., the King of Brandenburg-Prussia] and the Bishop of Münster, alternating with the Duke of Jülich) as the new commissioners.⁴⁰

While Hyacinth had left his country to lead an expensive life in Madrid and Paris, his council took their responsibilities seriously.⁴¹ The directorate of the *Reichskreis* did the same. In Siegen, a type of dual government resulted. Initially, the delegates of the imperial circle set to work in harmony and in earnest. In their first decree, the country's officials were called upon to treat the subjects with moderation and to open a legal way for complaints.⁴² The emperor and *Reichshofrat* formed a kind of third party. They steadfastly refused to accept the administration of the former interim ruler (*Reichsvikar*), the elector of the Palatine, who had done nothing other than appoint himself (in his capacity as a Duke of Jülich) head of the commission, which did not go unnoticed in Vienna. In a decision of the *Reichshofrat* of 13 May 1713, the directorate of the imperial circle was completely ignored, and surprisingly Hyacinth was informed that "for the moment His Majesty would permit him to continue his government," on the condition that he govern in a manner the Cologne commission indicated.⁴³

The directorate of the *Reichskreis* had no intention of withdrawing—quite the opposite. The commission increased its activities, but unfortunately soon disintegrated along denominational lines—Pfalz-Jülich for the Catholics and Brandenburg-Cleve for the Protestants—further stoking the conflict. The upshot was several fatalities: in 1712, during the Corpus Christi procession in Siegen, when the participants entered the Calvinist part of the city;⁴⁴ and in 1716, when troops from Münster and the Palatinate confiscated the property of villagers in Weidenau who had refused to provide for a Catholic teacher.⁴⁵ The inhabitants tried to call in the *Corpus Evangelicorum*, which helped little.⁴⁶

Increasingly, the Siegen territory became a focus of the inter-confessional conflict that threatened the whole empire between 1715 and 1725. Only when these tensions lessened did the controversial commission begin to lose interest in the Siegen affair.[47]

In 1722, the *Reichshofrat* took up the reins again and this time appointed the elector of Cologne as administrator, after he had been reinstated at the end of the War of the Spanish Succession. Hyacinth, in spite of the wording of the 1713 ruling, received word that he could not "yet" be allowed to return to power, which was a courteous way of proclaiming his actual suspension.[48] Not until 1740, two years before his death, did the administration fall back to Hyacinth. Reinstatement took place after he had eventually signed a bill stating that in all his ruling activities, he would follow the course once set by the commission of the Cologne cathedral. In 1739, he had ceded his country to the prince of Nassau-Diez and, in exchange, acquired the small town of Hadamar.[49]

As the proceedings against William Hyacinth of Nassau became entangled in larger confessional and regional rivalries, so those against Carl Leopold of Mecklenburg-Schwerin (1679–1747) became entangled in European politics. This case, which had occupied the *Reichshofrat* since immediately after the Thirty Years' War, arose from a conflict between the duke and the Mecklenburg estates, in particular the territory's nobility.[50] The endemic conflict escalated when Duke Carl Leopold, who ascended the throne in 1713, revealed his intention to introduce absolute rule by creating a standing army with the support of Russian soldiers.[51]

In 1719, the *Reichshofrat* appointed the elector of Hanover as protector of the Mecklenburg nobility. When Carl Leopold continued to disregard the rulings of the *Reichshofrat*, Hanover was authorized to send troops to Mecklenburg and to occupy the country. Only a small part around the town of Dömitz was left to Carl Leopold. Among the imperial estates, the duke finally lost any remaining reputation when, on 5 and 6 April 1719, he raised arms against the Hanoverian occupants.[52]

However, when in 1728 the emperor ordered the duke's formal suspension, this was less due to his actual behavior than to the fact that the Hanover-England domination of Mecklenburg no longer appeared favorable to the emperor's diplomats. The relationship between Austria and England had meanwhile deteriorated,[53] and Vienna suspected that London would annex at least parts of Mecklenburg, possibly under the pretext that the costs for the occupation were still unpaid.[54] Consequently, on 11 May 1728, the emperor ordered Duke Christian Ludwig, the brother and heir apparent of Carl Leopold, to take over the administration of the duchy in "the all highest name of the Emperor's Majesty." Like the administrator of Siegen, he was obliged to submit all of the important decisions to be made to the emperor for his approval. Hanover did, however, retain its patronage over the Mecklenburg nobility, but it was, from that time on, retained jointly with Brandenburg-Prussia.[55]

Fueled by a Hanoverian pamphlet campaign, a storm of indignation arose among the imperial estates.[56] Moser reported that initially, "the emperor could not dare introduce this matter to the imperial diet."[57] However, similarly to the prince of Siegen, Carl Leopold continued to issue arrogant letters, which were considered to be an offence to the imperial institutions and the emperor himself.[58] This obstinate behavior gave Vienna the chance to regain the initiative and to inform the imperial diet about the cause of the action taken on 11 May 1728. In his report (*Kaiserliches Kommissionsdekret*), the emperor referred to a number of arbitrary executions between 1721 and 1723 for which Carl Leopold had been responsible.[59] Above all, the emperor emphasized, in keeping with his capitulation of election (1711), he had left the duke's rights of session and vote at the imperial diet untouched.[60]

Only in 1732, when the conflicts between London and Vienna were settled, did it come to a final legal revision of the matter in Mecklenburg.[61] On 30 October 1732, the emperor ordered Christian Ludwig to govern no longer in "His Majesty's name" as imperial commissioner, but instead to govern in the name of his suspended brother.[62] However, when, in 1733, Carl Leopold organized an armed rebellion against his brother, Brandenburg-Prussia—since 1728 formally Hanover's partner in the imperial commission to protect the Mecklenburg nobility—took the chance to send troops to Mecklenburg. With the tacit permission of the emperor, the Prussians stayed in southern Mecklenburg, putting an end to the Hanoverian supremacy in the country and restoring the regional balance of power in Germany's north.[63]

As a result, and in contrast to the Siegen case, after the death of the emperor, not even the interim regency (*Reichsvikariat*) used the "opportunity to restore the imperial estate's privileges, should they really have been violated."[64] In 1741 and 1745, the elector of Saxony, as vicar of the empire's eastern part, confirmed the decisions of the late emperors. When, in 1742, Karl Albrecht of Bavaria succeeded Charles VI, as a Prussian ally, he did not raise the issue either.

While in the Mecklenburg case the leading imperial powers agreed that it was impossible to reverse the decisions that already had been made, they could not ignore a clear sense among the smaller imperial estates that such steps should be avoided in the future. Both the acts of dispossession—in Siegen as well as in Mecklenburg—were described by Charles VI as "provisional." His successor from the House of Wittelsbach, in his electoral declaration of 1742, undertook not to "dispossess any imperial estate of its government, even if provisional and even if for contumacious behavior."[65] In the future, any removal of a ruling prince seemed to be subject to the endorsement of the imperial diet. This constitutional amendment went back to the claims raised at an assembly in Offenbach near Frankfurt, where, in 1741, delegates of the so-called "ancient princes" had met on the occasion of the emperor's coronation.⁶⁶

Nevertheless, under the rule of Joseph II, the depositions of ruling princes continued. To bypass the restricted impeachment procedures of 1742, the *Reichshofrat* under Joseph II resorted to criminal law. Undisputedly, the criminal jurisdiction over the immediate subjects of the empire was vested exclusively in the emperor and, through him, in the *Reichshofrat*.⁶⁷ Accordingly, the Rhinegrave Carl Magnus of Rheingrafenstein and the Lord High Steward Xavier Gebhard of Wolfegg-Waldsee lost "their governmental powers and the use of their votes in the imperial diet and in the assemblies of the imperial circle … as a punishment" for their "crimes committed."⁶⁸ Criminal proceedings were also started against Count Friedrich Ludwig of Leiningen-Guntersblum.⁶⁹

There was no general indignation throughout the empire, as there had been in the case of Carl Leopold of Mecklenburg, because the rulers involved came from the lower ranks of the imperial nobility. Their offenses were also not of the sort to arouse feelings of solidarity among their peers.⁷⁰ Wolfegg-Waldsee was an ordinary thief, who, among other things, had stolen a gold figurine from the prince of Koenigsegg-Aulendorf. He had also extorted money from individual subjects and sexually harassed the female kitchen staff.⁷¹ The Rhinegrave Carl Magnus had financed his grotesquely extravagant court by extorting guarantees from the village councils in this small land.⁷² Leiningen-Guntersblum, for his part, was a sort of newer version of the count of Vaduz. He was charged with bigamy and blasphemy, and his reign in the small country was characterized by sexual assaults, excessive beatings, arbitrary arrests, and expulsions of not only members of the general population, but also of priests, churchwardens, and prominent members of the Jewish community.⁷³

Only the act of sentencing the rhinegrave of Grehweiler to ten years imprisonment in the Mainz castle Koenigstein produced a written petition from some neighboring estates pleading for a reduction in his sentence.⁷⁴ In the other cases, the *Reichshofrat*'s use of criminal law made the imperial princes uncertain as to how far their constitutional rights were really being impinged. Bearing in mind the bizarre offenses being prosecuted, however, nobody felt himself to be in a position to take on the combined solidarity of the higher-ranking estates at the imperial diet; still less could they challenge the emperor, who guaranteed the very existence of the smaller estates.⁷⁵

Meanwhile, the *Reichshofrat* succeeded in optimizing the legal basis for removing unsuitable princes.⁷⁶ First, it was important to keep the trials legally separated from the rising number of bankruptcy proceedings. In the latter, ruling princes had to renounce their fiscal competences—more or less voluntarily. Accordingly, in these proceedings, the terminology of suspending a ruling prince "*in cameralibus*" had been adopted, while the prince's jurisdictional competences remained unaffected.⁷⁷ As a distinction, "total" removals were called "*in cameralibus et in jurisdictionalibus*" where the word "*jurisdictionalibus*" was to include ecclesiastical authority.⁷⁸

In practice, the distinction was not always easy. In the cases of Grehweiler and Wolfegg-Waldsee, a bankruptcy proceeding was already under way when the counts' crimes were uncovered. The counts had already been deposed "*in cameralibus*" and two trustees in insolvency—in the Grehweiler case, the prince of Nassau-Usingen, and in the Wolfegg case, the prince of Fürstenberg—had already been nominated.⁷⁹ When the two counts were convicted and consequently deposed not only "*in cameralibus*" but also "*in jurisdictionalibus*," the former trustees in insolvency took over the entire administration.

The Leiningen-Guntersblum case, however, was managed in a different way. Not unlike the count of Vaduz, Leiningen-Guntersblum was publicly accused and put under "personal arrest." This time, the inquiry was to be led by the directorate of the Upper Rhenish *Kreis*, consisting of the elector of the Palatinate and the elector of Mainz. Following the precedents of Siegen and Mecklenburg, the provisional administration of his small country was given to the next male heir, the prince of Leiningen-Hartenburg. However, as in the Mecklenburg example, the administration was to be carried out under the emperor's ultimate control and in the name of the suspended count.⁸⁰

This led to a considerable uncertainty among the imperial counts. Was this action still within the bounds of the capitulation of election?⁸¹ The Guntersblum count's subjects were also uncertain, although for different reasons. While it was true that the count of Guntersblum was imprisoned in his Heidenheim castle, decrees were still issued in his name. Consequently, scarcely any inhabitant felt safe testifying before the commission of inquiry about the count's manner of government.⁸² This guardedness only increased when the *Reichshofrat* allowed the count to confer from jail directly with the local government officials of his Alsatian territory of Dagsburg, which stood under French sovereignty and was not under the *Reichshofrat*'s jurisdiction.⁸³ However, as in the case of the count of Vaduz, the count of Guntersblum died in captivity before the proceedings reached their end. Strictly speaking, only the trials involving the rhinegrave and Wolfegg-Waldsee led to a final dispossession of a ruling prince. In the four other cases hitherto analyzed, the suspension in one way or another remained provisional.⁸⁴

This was also true of both suspensions pronounced by the *Reichskammergericht*, which was trying to follow the precedents of Joseph II.⁸⁵ In both instances, the *Reichskammergericht* was asked by influential members of the prince's noble houses to ratify modifications of the respective dynastic and territorial agreements. In the case of Lippe-Detmold, on 4 December 1790, the chamber court had confirmed a custody arrangement, according to which the territory would be governed by the estates until Count Leopold recovered from his mental illness.⁸⁶

The next case, Prince Friedrich Carl of Wied-Neuwied, was in some ways the opposite of the count of Guntersblum. He had settled century-long litigation between the Neuwied princes and the country's population by ceding a good part of the forests to the peasant communities. This agreement, however, was contested by his next of kin, the prince of Wied-Runkel, who claimed it contradicted a testament that Friedrich Carl had had to sign during his father's lifetime, according to which he was bound not to dispose of any parts of the forests. The prince of Wied-Runkel and Friedrich Carl's father-in-law, the prince of Wittgenstein, had also signed the testament as guarantors. In addition, the testament also contained a provision prohibiting the creation of any new debts. An additional clause also allowed the future prince a mistress, provided that he treated his wife with respect. This testament was a reaction to the prince's earlier abnormal conduct, which could be traced to his being a manic depressive, a condition that, it was said at the beginning of his reign, he had overcome.[87]

After the prince succeeded his father, he did not keep to the testament and failed in his execution of governmental duties due to his mental illness (called "scrupulosity" [*Skrupulosität*] by contemporaries), which he had apparently not overcome. The guarantors appealed to the chamber court not only for an annulment of the agreement with the peasant population, but also for confirmation of the testament. On 29 November 1792, the Second Senate, which already had prior experience with the case of Lippe-Detmold, delivered a judgment that not only granted the petition regarding the testament, but also went further. It stated that: "in accordance with the sense and meaning of the testament, not only governmental, budgetary, financial, dynastic, imperial, regional and foreign affairs, but also all other matters should only be carried out under the supervision of the guarantors."[88] In the case of any dispute between the prince and the guarantors a simple majority would decide; however, the decrees should be issued in the prince's name.

The prince of Neuwied refused to cooperate. Indeed, one of the guarantors, the count of Wied-Runkel, feared for his life when entering the Neuwied government buildings in December 1792. The chamber court reacted on 23 February 1793. It is revealing that the judgment stated that the court had decided that, "because of the mental illness of the prince, he was incapable of ruling alone, at least for the time being."[89] In addition, "all his legal courts and officers" were authorized to issue provisional decrees "in urgent matters and to avoid delay," to which the prince took extreme exception as an insult to feudal lordship as a whole.

In an atmosphere that was increasingly dominated by the fear that the French Revolution would spread to Germany, the prince tried to arouse public sympathy by describing the ruling of the Second Senate as the result of a plot by members of the Illuminati or the Jacobins. Actually, his opponents in Neuwied, as in the *Reichskammergericht*, were not Jacobins at all. However, his allegations regarding the Illuminati order were not completely untrue. Indeed, some leading members of the Second Senate were (former) Illuminati, but they did not use their power to spread the revolution—on the contrary. In the prince's case, they wanted to demonstrate that Germany did not need a revolution, as the existing courts were able to control any "despotic" excesses.[90]

At the imperial diet, the majority of the imperial estates shared the prince's "misunderstanding" and saw a revolutionary act in what was really designed to ward off the revolution. The emperor, however, did not totally adopt the proposal of the imperial diet. The chamber court rulings were suspended and the prince was reinstated, but the emperor avoided publicly blaming the *Reichskammergericht*, which instead he enabled to supervise the fulfillment of the testament.[91]

Conclusions

In the second half of the sixteenth century, a prominent chamber court member referred to provisions of Roman law to allow a higher authority to remove a tyrannical ruler. This became the basis for the deposing of several ruling princes between 1648 and 1792. Until 1790, the proceedings were exclusively conducted by the *Reichshofrat*. Under Joseph II, it became necessary to differentiate these depositions from the rising number of insolvency trials, which was accomplished by using the phrase *"in cameralibus et in jurisdictionalibus"* rather than only *"in cameralibus."* Additionally, the constitutional obstacles created in 1742 forced the *Reichshofrat* to use criminal law to carry out three new suspensions.

The suspension of a ruling prince could be de facto accomplished by merely appointing a commission of protection and administration.[92] Therefore, the official removal of a prince was a last resort. Under Charles VI, it was accomplished when—as in the cases of Siegen and Mecklenburg—the conduct of the candidate was considered to be an offence to the dignity of the imperial institutions and to the emperor himself. Under Joseph II—above all, in the rhinegrave's case—the proceedings were aimed much more at protecting the reputation of feudal lordship as a whole.

Secondary motives also played a role. Leopold I used the "scandal" over the rule of the count of Vaduz to remove any uncertainties in the geo-politically sensitive region of the upper Rhine.[93] Outside the areas of immediate Habsburg influence, however, as the examples of Siegen and Mecklenburg show, the emperors failed to exploit the suspensions for political gain. Under Joseph II, the symbolic, educational elements of the depositions came to the fore. Nevertheless, depositions were still limited to rulers of tiny territories.[94] The *Reichskammergericht* proceedings against Friedrich Carl of Neuwied were conducted in the same "Josephinian" sense. Their failure was due to the changes in the political atmosphere brought on by the fear that the French Revolution would spread to Germany.

Contrary to the suggestion of ex-Jacobin Friedrich Christian Laukhard in his popular account of the rhinegrave's case, published in 1798, the emperor did need powerful local partners to successfully suspend ruling princes.[95] Some cases even originated from complaints supported by the immediate neighbors of the wayward prince. In the eyes of the Feldkirch officials, for instance, the "scandalous" conduct of the count of Vaduz damaged the territory's good relationship with its neighbors.[96] In the Siegen case, in spite of all the controversial actions against him, the representatives of the directorate of the imperial circle agreed with the *Reichshofrat* that Wilhelm Hyacinth's conduct was "outrageous" and "dangerous."[97] The Guntersblum case was initiated by local officials of the neighboring town of Oppenheim.[98] In the course of the trial, the count's peers feared for the reputation of the less powerful estates in the empire, while the convening princes of the imperial circle saw the reputation of feudal lordship in general as damaged.[99] The same wording had already been used in 1684 by the Abbot Rupert of Bodman regarding the affair of the count of Vaduz.[100]

In all of the cases analyzed here, Vienna's first step was to transform local protest into a legal process. Only in the Vaduz case and—perhaps—initially in the Siegen case, did the emperors try—more or less successfully—to instrumentalize local powers for their purposes. The results were disastrous, and in the further course of the Siegen case and in the Mecklenburg affair, Vienna lost control and the cases became entangled with regional rivalries. In the "Josephinian" cases, however, the *Reichshofrat* had learned that a basic harmony of "central" and "local" authorities was crucial.

The excesses of the various princes concerned were not only noticed in the offices and chancelleries, but were closely observed by "the common people" in the surrounding countries. The inhabitants of Vaduz were forced to hear "in Swabia and other neighboring lands" that they came from "the land of witches," while the outrages of the Guntersblum count were a popular subject of conversation at the dinner tables in Worms and the surrounding areas.[101] Any trial before one of the imperial courts almost automatically brought with it wide-reaching publicity among learned people, particularly after the start of Johann Jakob Moser publications, which, in 1746, described William Hyacinth of Nassau-Siegen as a "peculiar ruler."[102] A person petitioning for an intervention of the imperial diet could be sure of enhanced publicity even in the imperial territorial states, because the envoys' reports from Regensburg potentially informed all of the home chancelleries of the territories represented at the imperial diet.[103]

If there was an accompanying leaflet campaign, as first occurred in the Mecklenburg case, then it practically ensured that the case became known in increasingly wide social circles.[104] In the Neuwied case, the numerous "public pamphlets" from both sides eventually turned the matter into a subject for public entertainment. Enriched with details of the count's sexual preferences, the reports had become "scarce" and had to be "paid for dearly."[105]

After 1770, the feeling of outrage among the imperial estates was increasingly accompanied by the growing sense of amusement in a developing civil society. Public disapproval was facilitated by the fact that the candidates detached themselves from their various networks. Prior to their suspensions, the candidates had isolated themselves within their noble houses. Their marriages, apart from the rhinegrave's, had failed, in some cases repeatedly.[106] The regional associations of counts and the imperial circle authorities remained remarkably silent, even when they found that the imperial courts were acting on questionable constitutional grounds.[107]

Assemblies of imperial circles, regional associations of princes, dynastic ties, and marriages were not solely the bases for networking. They also served as at least rudimentary systems of restraint, which sought to reproduce desired modes of behavior. In the case of ruling princes, this meant earnest attempts to ensure what can be called good governance.[108] This objective was widely shared by the ecclesiastical authorities, with whom the majority of the princes involved were also at odds. Indeed, they seemed to have preferred voluntary isolation, removing themselves from all of these systems of restraint. In one of his more sane moments, the count of Guntersblum gave a graphic description of this attitude. He was said to have stated that, "he was a Protestant and therefore protested against everything."[109]

Dedicated to Winfried Schulze on his 65th Birthday

Notes

1. Bernd Marquardt, "Über jedem Fürsten und Grafen ein höherer Richter: Frühneuzeitliche Reichsexekutionen am Alpenrhein," in *Montfort* 54 (2002): 216–235, here 219.
2. Manfred Tschaikner, "'Der Teufel und die Hexen müssen aus dem Land.' Frühneuzeitliche Hexenverfolgungen in Liechtenstein," in *Jahrbuch des Historischen Vereins für das Fürstentum Liechtenstein* 96 (1998): 1–197, here 38.
3. Felix Roth, "Das 'Fürststift Kempten Archiv' im Staatsarchiv Augsburg," in *Veröffentlichungen des Liechtensteinischen Landesarchivs* 2 (2003): 21–40, here 22f.; Tschaikner, "Teufel," 24, 38; Peter Kaiser, *Geschichte des Fürstenthums Liechtenstein* (1847; reprinted, Vaduz, 1989), 1: 404f.
4. Bernd Marquardt, "Zur reichsgerichtlichen Aberkennung der Herrschergewalt wegen Missbrauchs: Tyrannenprozesse vor dem Reichshofrat am Beispiel des südöstlichen schwäbischen Reichskreises," in *Prozesspraxis im Alten Reich*, eds. Anette Baumann, et al (Cologne, 2005), 53–89, here 68.
5. Tschaikner, "Teufel," 30–32.

6. Marquardt, "Richter," 222.
7. Staatsarchiv Augsburg, Fürststift Kempten, A 2972, fol. 6–8.
8. Haus-, Hof- und Staatsarchiv Wien, Reichshofrat, Decisa 2025, # 9; Schwanenfeld is mentioned by Gernot Peter Obersteiner, "Das Reichshoffiskalat 1596 bis 1806. Bausteine zu seiner Geschichte aus Wiener Archiven," in *Reichspersonal. Funktionsträger für Kaiser und Reich*, eds. Anette Baumann, et al (Cologne, Weimar, and Vienna, 2003), 89–164, 111. General information concerning the public prosecutor: Wolfgang Sellert, *Über die Zuständigkeitsabgrenzung von Reichshofrat und Reichskammergericht insbesondere in Strafsachen und Angelegenheiten der freiwilligen Gerichtsbarkeit* (Aalen, 1965), 82–83.
9. Winfried Schulze, *Bäuerlicher Widerstand und feudale Herrschaft in der frühen Neuzeit* (Stuttgart, 1998), 201. For Gail's biographical data see Karin Nehlsen-von Stryk, "Andreas Gail," in *Rheinische Justiz: Geschichte und Gegenwart, 175 Jahre Oberlandesgericht Köln*, ed. Dieter Laum (Cologne, 1994), 701–715. For additional sources from late medieval Roman law, see Ernst Schubert, *Königsabsetzung im deutschen Mittelalter* (Göttingen, 2005), 76. Schubert, however, deals with an elective monarchy, which is a different topic. See also Wim Blockmans, "Limitations to Monarchial Power," in *Murder and Monarchy. Regicide in European History, 1300–1800*, ed. Robert von Friedeburg (Basingstoke, 2004), 136–145, here 140.
10. Konrad Müller, ed., *Instrumenta Pacis Westphalicae. Die Westfälischen Friedensverträge 1648* (Bern, 1949), 47–48.
11. Christoph Ziegler, *Wahl-Capitulationes, welche mit denen Römischen Kaeysern und Königen, dann des H. Röm. Reichs Churfürsten, ... seit Carolo V. her, biß auff Ferdinandum IV. vor sich und folglich biß auff Josephum I. auffgerichtet ...* (Frankfurt a.M., 1711), 161.
12. Ibid., 205–206.
13. Staatsarchiv Augsburg, Fürststift Kempten, A 2972, fol. 20–24, 46, 16 May 1685.
14. Staatsarchiv Augsburg, Fürststift Kempten, A 2972, fol. 49–58, commissioners' report, sent on 4 July 1684 (See Staatsarchiv Augsburg, Fürststift Kempten, A 3014, aulic council decision of 9 September 1684, draft copy).
15. Staatsarchiv Augsburg, Fürststift Kempten, A 2972, fol. 49.
16. Albert Schädler, "Regesten zu den Urkunden der liechtensteinschen Gemeindearchive und Alpgenossenschaften," in *Jahrbuch des Historischen Vereins für das Fürstentum Liechtenstein* 8 (1908): 105–170, here 137–138.
17. Schädler, "Regesten," 138; Staatsarchiv Augsburg, Fürststift Kempten, A 2934, fol. 1–3, proclamation of 27 March 1684, draft copy. Later, the abbot used the terms "sequestration" (*Sequestration*) and "administration" (*Administration*), not contained in the *Reichshofrat*'s decision.
18. Staatsarchiv Augsburg, Fürststift Kempten, A 3014, fol. 13–15.
19. Eva Ortlieb, *Im Auftrag des Kaisers. Die kaiserlichen Kommissionen des Reichshofrats und die Regelung von Konflikten im Alten Reich (1637–1657)* (Cologne, Weimar, and Vienna, 2001), 243.
20. Volker Press, "Die Entstehung des Fürstentums Liechtenstein," in *Das Fürstentum Liechtenstein. Ein landeskundliches Porträt*, ed. Wolfgang Müller (Bühl, 1981), 63–91, here 66.
21. Carlo de Clerq, "Die katholischen Fürsten von Nassau-Siegen," in *Nassauische Annalen* 73 (1962): 129–152, here 142f.

22. de Clerq, "Fürsten," 146; Karl E. Demandt, *Geschichte des Landes Hessen* (Wiesbaden, 1972), 423.
23. Alfred Lück, *Siegerland und Nederland* (Siegen, 1981), 140.
24. Hans-Joachim Behr, "'Zu rettung deren hart getruckten Nassaw-Siegischen Unterthanen.' Der Niederrheinisch-Westfälische Kreis und Siegen im 18. Jahrhundert," in *Jahrbuch für westfälische Kirchengeschichte* 85 (1991): 159–184, here 160.
25. Wilhelm Weyer, *Geschichte der Familie Flender*, vol. 2 (Bocholt, 1961), 19; Haus-, Hof- und Staatsarchiv Wien, Reichshofrat, Vota 41.
26. Hermann Böttger, *Friedrich Flender vor der Hardt. Ein Kämpfer für Recht und Freiheit des Siegerländer Volkes* (Siegen, 1957), 21.
27. See the reports in: Staatarchiv Münster, Fürstentum Siegen, Landesarchiv Amtsakten (7), 6, Bd. 1, fol. 6–10 (subjects' perspective), fol. 15–20 (prince's perspective).
28. Böttger, *Flender*, 26; and Weyer, *Flender*, 22.
29. Haus-, Hof- und Staatsarchiv Wien, Reichshofrat, Vota 41; Hauptstaatsarchiv Düsseldorf, Niederrheinisch-Westfälischer Kreis I, N 15—Siegen, Nr. 46, fol. 18f.
30. Böttger, *Flender*, 22f., 27f.; and Weyer, *Flender*, 23–25.
31. On 10 November 1707, however, the delegate Solemacher wrote that the emperor had "ordered" the cathedral chapter to occupy "the prince's palace with their own armed force" (Hauptstaatsarchiv Düsseldorf, Niederrheinisch-Westfälischer Kreis I, N 15—Siegen, Nr. 46, fol. 26).
32. Böttger, *Flender*, 23.
33. Böttger, *Flender*, 23; Haus-, Hof- und Staatsarchiv Wien, Reichshofrat, Vota 41.
34. Haus-, Hof- und Staatsarchiv Wien, Reichshofrat, Vota 41; Hauptstaatsarchiv Düsseldorf, Niederrheinisch-Westfälischer Kreis I, N 15—Siegen, Nr. 46, fol. 39. "To reorganize the government": this was the same wording, which had been used in the Vaduz case on 11 June 1683.
35. Hauptstaatsarchiv Düsseldorf, Niederrheinisch-Westfälischer Kreis I, N 15—Siegen, Nr. 47, fol. 224–225.
36. Marquardt, "Richter," 71.
37. Raimund J. Weber, *Reichspolitik und reichsgerichtliche Exekution. Vom Markgrafenkrieg (1552–1554) bis zum Lütticher Fall* (Wetzlar, 2000), 14.
38. Behr, "Zu rettung," 161, 163. This was the reason why the circle administration initially did not object against the aulic council's decision to appoint the Cologne cathedral chapter: Hauptstaatsarchiv Düsseldorf, Niederrheinisch-Westfälischer Kreis I, N 15—Siegen, Nr., 46, fol. 13, 26; Nr. 47, fol. 81. Initially, the subjects' petition was to charge the elector of the Palatine with their protection (Böttger, *Flender*, 20).
39. Johann Jacob Moser, *Teutsches Staatsrecht*, Teil 24, (Nuremberg, 1746; reprinted, Osnabrück, 1968), 243; Hauptstaatsarchiv Düsseldorf, Niederrheinisch-Westfälischer Kreis I, N 15—Siegen, Nr. 47, fol. 264.
40. Hauptstaatsarchiv Düsseldorf, Niederrheinisch-Westfälischer Kreis I, N 15 - Siegen, Nr. 47, fol. 60. Generally, Mainz and Vienna contested the interim ruler's right to continue the imperial diet: Gerhard Granier, "Der deutsche Reichstag während des Spanischen Erbfolgekriegs (1700–1714)," (Ph.d. diss., Bonn, 1954), 235–236.
41. Lück, *Siegerland*, 144–147.
42. Hauptstaatsarchiv Düsseldorf, Niederrheinisch-Westfälischer Kreis I, N 15—Siegen, Nr. 48, fol. 59–64.
43. Haus-, Hof- und Staatsarchiv Wien, Reichshofrat, Vota 41, 13 May 1713.

44. Behr, "Zu rettung," 180.
45. Böttger, *Flender*, 13f.
46. Apparently, Hyacinth, the former Catholic zealot, was trying to improve his relationships with Brandenburg-Prussia. His half-brother Alexis Anton (de Clerq, "Fürsten," 140) was spreading rumors about Hyacinth's intention to sell his country to the King of Prussia: Hauptstaatsarchiv Düsseldorf, Niederrheinisch-Westfälischer Kreis I, N 15–Siegen, Nr. 47, fol. 95; see Lück, *Siegerland*, 144. Behr, "Zu rettung," 175f.
47. Karl Otmar Freiherr von Aretin, *Das Alte Reich, 1648–1806*, 4 vols. (Stuttgart, 1993–2000), 2: 293.
48. The decision: Haus-, Hof- und Staatsarchiv Wien, Reichshofrat, Vota 41.
49. Demandt, *Hessen*, 424.
50. Hans-Joachim Ballschmieter, *Andreas Gottlieb von Bernstorff und der mecklenburgische Ständekampf (1680–1720)* (Cologne and Graz, 1962), 1–112.
51. The alliance was sealed in 1716 by his marriage to one of the czar's nieces. Peter Wick, *Versuche zur Errichtung des Absolutismus in Mecklenburg in der ersten Hälfte des 18. Jahrhunderts* (Berlin, 1964), 44–49; and Walther Mediger, *Mecklenburg, Rußland und England-Hannover 1706–1721*, vol. 1 (Hildesheim, 1967), 205, 217.
52. Michael Hughes, *Law and Politics in Eighteenth Century Germany. The Imperial Aulic Council in the Reign of Charles VI* (Woodbridge, 1988), 176; Aretin, *Reich*, 2: 259f.; Ballschmieter, *Bernstorff*, 143; and Wick, *Absolutismus*, 136f.
53. Hughes, *Law*, 206–207; and Wick, *Absolutismus*, 172–175.
54. Aretin, *Reich*, 2: 324; and Hughes, *Law*, 227.
55. Johann Jacob Moser, *Neues teutsches Staatsrecht*, vol. 11.1 (Frankfurt a.M. and Leipzig, 1774; reprinted, Osnabrück, 1967), 657.
56. Aretin, *Reich*, 2: 323; and Hughes, *Law*, 214, 229.
57. Moser, *Neues teutsches Staatsrecht*, vol. 11.1: 660.
58. Hughes, *Law*, 99–100, 110; and Wick, *Absolutismus*, 244.
59. Hughes, *Law*, 179; and Wick, *Absolutismus*, 157.
60. Wick, *Absolutismus*, 173, 179. The duke still maintained an envoy at the imperial diet: Wick, *Absolutismus*, 241.
61. Aretin, *Reich*, 2: 326f.; and Hughes, *Law*, 230f.
62. Moser, *Neues teutsches Staatsrecht*, vol. 11.1: 660; Hughes, *Law*, 239; and Wick, *Absolutismus*, 208.
63. Wick, *Absolutismus*, 235–236, 251.
64. Moser, *Neues teutsches Staatsrecht*, vol. 11.1: 661.
65. Johann Jacob Moser, *Ihro Römisch-Kayserlichen Majestät Carls des Siebenden Wahl-Capitulation*, Teil 1 (Frankfurt a.M., 1742), 3.
66. Johann Jacob Moser, *Ihro Römisch-Kayserlichen Majestät Carls des Siebenden Wahl-Capitulation*, Teil 1 (Frankfurt a.M., 1742), 40. The group of the "ancient princes" consisted of imperial estates whose ancestors had been members of the imperial princes' council (*Reichsfürstenrat*) before 1582.
67. Sellert, *Zuständigkeitsabgrenzung*, 92f.
68. Carl Friedrich Häberlin, *Pragmatische Geschichte der neuesten kaiserlichen Wahlcapitulation und der an kaiserliche Majestät erlassenen kurfürstlichen Collegialschreiben* (Leipzig, 1792), 35.
69. Haus-, Hof- und Staatsarchiv Wien, Reichshofrat, Vota 29. The contents are summed up by Peter Leyers, "Reichshofratsgutachten an Kaiser Joseph II." (Ph.D. diss. Bonn, 1976), 189–191.

70. Staatsarchiv Detmold, L 41a, 1405, fol. 15, 53–4.
71. Haus-, Hof- und Staatsarchiv Wien, Reichshofrat, Vota 61/19.
72. The sources (the Rhinegrave's trial: Haus-, Hof- und Staatsarchiv Wien, Reichshofrat, Obere Registratur 1890; lawsuits of various creditors at the *Reichskammergericht*: Staatsarchiv Speyer, RKG 2923) basically confirm Friedrich Christian Laukhard's account, published in 1798 (*Leben und Thaten des Rheingrafen Carl Magnus ... zur Warnung für alle winzige Despoten, Leichtgläubige und Geschäftsmänner* [Leipzig, 1798]), which has been questioned, especially by Ernst Klug, "Friedrich Christian Laukhard und das Finanzwesen der Rheingrafen zu Gaugrehweiler," in *Mitteilungsblatt zur rheinhessischen Landeskunde* 17 (1968): 405–412.
73. Haus-, Hof- und Staatsarchiv Wien, Reichshofrat, Vota 29; Reichshofrat, Denegata Recentiora 523. Further trials of blasphemy mentioned by Sellert, *Zuständigkeitsabgrenzung*, 84f. For the previous centuries see Gerd Schwerhoff, *Zungen wie Schwerter. Blasphemie in alteuropäischen Gesellschaften 1200–1650* (Konstanz, 2005).
74. Haus-, Hof- und Staatsarchiv Wien, Kleinere Reichsstände 538.
75. See the correspondence in: Staatsarchiv Detmold, L 41a, Nr. 1405 und 1406.
76. Considerations in the Guntersblum case (Haus-, Hof- und Staatsarchiv Wien, Reichshofrat, Vota 29-9, 13. Aug. 1770).
77. See Jürgen Ackermann, *Verschuldung, Reichsdebitverwaltung, Mediatisierung. Eine Studie zu den Finanzproblemen der mindermächtigen Stände im Alten Reich. Das Beispiel der Grafschaft Ysenburg-Büdingen 1687–1806* (Marburg, 2002); Susanne Herrmann, "Die Durchführung von Schuldenverfahren im Rahmen kaiserlicher Debitkommissionen im 18. Jahrhundert am Beispiel des Debitwesens der Grafen Montfort," in *Reichshofrat und Reichskammergericht—ein Konkurrenzverhältnis*, ed. Wolfgang Sellert (Cologne, 1999), 111–128; and Siegrid Westphal, *Kaiserliche Rechtsprechung und herrschaftliche Stabilisierung. Reichsgerichtsbarkeit in den thüringischen Territorialstaaten 1648–1806* (Cologne, Weimar, and Vienna, 2002).
78. Staatsarchiv Detmold, L 41a, Nr, 1405, fol. 10f., 20 July 1770 (Rhinegrave); Haus-, Hof- und Staatsarchiv Wien, Reichshofrat, Vota 29, 13 Aug. 1770 (Guntersblum). Haus-, Hof- und Staatsarchiv Wien, Kleinere Reichsstände 538, aulic council opinion, 20 December 1770. In Mecklenburg, the *Reichshofrat* had omitted to clarify the ecclesiastical competences. Accordingly, the majority of the clergy supported Duke Carl Leopold—in spite of his temporary promises (motivated by his prosecution) to convert to Catholicism: Wick, *Absolutismus*, 183, 196.
79. Haus-, Hof- und Staatsarchiv Wien, Reichshofrat, Obere Registratur 1890; Haus-, Hof- und Staatsarchiv Wien, Reichshofrat, Vota, 61/25.
80. Häberlin, *Geschichte*, 35; Haus-, Hof- und Staatsarchiv Wien, Reichshofrat, Vota 29-9.
81. Staatsarchiv Detmold, L41a, Nr. 1405, fol. 17, 5. Dez. 1770, Count of Solms-Rödelheim to the counts' envoy at the imperial diet.
82. Haus-, Hof- und Staatsarchiv Wien, Reichshofrat, Denegata Recentiora 523, Kommissionsbericht, Beilagen: Verhöre vom Oktober 1770.
83. Moser, *Neues teutsches Staatsrecht*, Zusätze, vol. 2.1 (Frankfurt a.M., Nürnberg, 1782, reprinted, Osnabrück, 1968), 454; and Eva Kell, *Das Fürstentum Leiningen. Umbruchserfahrungen einer Adelsherrschaft zur Zeit der Französischen Revolution* (Kaiserslautern, 1993), 17f.
84. Reflections on the terminology: Moser, *Neues teutsches Staatsrecht*, vol. 11.1: 656f.

85. Joseph II was idolized at the chamber court, especially by the members of the Illuminati order: Monika Neugebauer-Wölk, "Reichskammergericht, Reichsstadt und Aufklärung. Wetzlar im späten 18. Jahrhundert," in *Recht—Idee—Geschichte. Beiträge zur Rechts- und Ideengeschichte für Rolf Lieberwirth*, eds. Heiner Lück and Bernd Schildt (Cologne, Weimar, and Vienna, 2000), 89–114, here 100–102.
86. Johannes Arndt, "Kabale und Liebe in Detmold. Zur Geschichte einer Hofintrige und einer Fürstenabsetzung in Lippe während des ausgehenden 18. Jahrhunderts," in *Lippische Mitteilungen* 60 (1991): 27–74, here 60–62. In the middle of the century, the *Reichshofrat* had rejected the agnates' pleas to remove Karl Thomas of Löwenstein-Wertheim from office because of an alleged "mental weakness." Harald Stockert, *Adel im Übergang. Die Fürsten und Grafen von Löwenstein-Wertheim zwischen Landesherrschaft und Standesherrschaft 1780–1850* (Stuttgart, 2000), 19. Regarding mental illness in the previous period, see H.C. Erik Midelfort, *Mad Princes of Renaissance Germany* (Charlottesville, VA, 1994).
87. Werner Troßbach, *Der Schatten der Aufklärung. Bauern, Bürger und Illuminaten in der Grafschaft Wied-Neuwied* (Fulda, 1991), 266–413.
88. Troßbach, *Schatten*, 290–291.
89. Troßbach, *Schatten*, 291.
90. Troßbach, *Schatten*, 383–397. A concise account of the controversial scholarly debate about the Illuminati influence at the chamber court: Sigrid Jahns, *Das Reichskammergericht und seine Richter*, Teil II, Biographien, Bd. 2, (Cologne, Weimar, and Vienna, 2003), 1396–1405.
91. Karl Härter, "Der Rekurs des Fürsten Friedrich Karl von Wied-Neuwied. Zum Verhältnis von Reichskammergericht und Reichstag am Ende des Alten Reiches," in *Vorträge zur Justizforschung* 2 (1993): 245–284, here 279–280.
92. See Moser's brief account of the consequences of the constitutional amendment of 1742: "Der Kayser kann den Landesherrn auch durch Executions- oder Mantenenz-Commißionen, Conservatoria u. d. ausser Stand sezen, die Unterthanen zu beschweren, nur solle Er ihn nicht in contumaciam der ganzen Regierung entsezen." Moser's *Neues teutsches Staatsrecht*, vol. 11.1: 663. This was the method initially applied in the Siegen and the Mecklenburg cases.
93. Tschaikner, "Teufel," 31.
94. Carl Eugen von Württemberg, for instance, who for the young Swabian intellectuals was the real image of "German despotism," was politically untouchable, because of his political importance in the Swabian *Kreis* and because of foreign guarantees. See Gerhard Storz, "Herzog Carl Eugen (1737–1793)," in *900 Jahre Haus Württemberg*, ed. Robert Uhland (Stuttgart, 1984), 237–266.
95. See Hans-Werner Engels, "Friedrich Christian Laukhards Rechtfertigung der revolutionären Jakobinerdiktatur," in *Die demokratische Bewegung in Mitteleuropa im ausgehenden 18. und frühen 19. Jahrhundert*, eds. Otto Büsch and Walter Grab (Berlin, 1980), 56–72.
96. Tschaikner, "Teufel," 30f.
97. Hauptstaatsarchiv Düsseldorf, Niederrheinisch-Westfälischer Kreis I, N 15–Siegen, Nr. 47, fol. 81.
98. Haus-, Hof- und Staatsarchiv Wien, Reichshofrat, Denegata Recentiora 523, Kommissionsbericht, Beil. Lit B, Oberamtmann Wüst und Landschreiber Baumann, 19 July 1768.

99. Staatsarchiv Detmold, L 41a, Nr. 1405, fol. 30, 42, 51. Haus-, Hof- und Staatsarchiv Wien, Reichshofrat, Vota 29-9, Vortrag vom 22. Juni 1770.
100. Staatsarchiv Augsburg, Fürststift Kempten, A 2972, Kommissionsbericht, draft copy.
101. Tschaikner, "Teufel," 22. Haus-, Hof- und Staatsarchiv Wien, Reichshofrat, Denegata Recentiora 523, Kommissionsbericht, Beilage Nr. 93, Ratskonsulent Donauer, Speyer.
102. Moser, *Teutsches Staatsrecht*, 24: 242. See Michael Stolleis, "Johann Jacob Moser oder: Der Erzpublizist des Alten Reiches," in *Johann Jacob Moser. Politiker—Pietist—Publizist*, eds. Andreas Gestrich and Rainer Lächele (Karlsruhe, 2002), 57–70.
103. The appropriate term would be "*reichsständische Öffentlichkeit,*" according to Andreas Gestrich. Gestrich describes the imperial diet as an information exchange. Gestrich, *Absolutismus und Öffentlichkeit. Politische Kommunikation in Deutschland zu Beginn des 18. Jahrhunderts* (Göttingen, 1994), 78, 98f., 201.
104. Hughes, *Law*, 214, 229. The role of leaflets in public debates is discussed by Gestrich, *Absolutismus*, 194–200; and Andreas Würgler, *Unruhen und Öffentlichkeit. Städtische und ländliche Protestbewegungen im 18. Jahrhundert* (Tübingen, 1995), 134–142.
105. Johann Nicolaus Becker, *Beschreibung meiner Reise in den Departementern vom Donnersberge, vom Rhein und von der Mosel im sechsten Jahr der Französischen Republik in Briefen an einen Freund in Paris* (Berlin, 1799), 27.
106. Vaduz: Haus-, Hof- und Staatsarchiv Wien, Reichshofrat, Denegata recentiora 261/9; Siegen: Lück, *Siegerland*, 136, 143, 146; Mecklenburg: Wick, *Absolutismus*, 35, 197, and Hughes, *Law*, 103, 179; Neuwied: Troßbach, *Schatten*, 271f., 284, 380.
107. Staatsarchiv Detmold, L 41a, 1405, fol. 15, 51–53. Without his peers' support, a count's intervention at the imperial diet did not have the slightest chance.
108. James Allen Vann, "New directions for the study of the Old Reich," in *The Journal of Modern History* 58, Supplement: Politics and Society in the Holy Roman Empire (1986): 3–22, identified in the influence of "the empire" a "concept of restraint" (12)—in the sense that, especially among the small estates, "the empire established the acceptable limits of maneuver for those forces jockeying for power within the individual territorial units" (11). To follow this important idea, it is crucial not to restrict the concept of "the empire" to its institutions in the closest sense (imperial diet, aulic council, chamber court), but to observe its interplay with a large variety of local self-organized associations, even at the grassroots level—some of them (like the dynastic treaties of noble families as well as the constitutions of some peasant communities) formally guaranteed by imperial privileges.
109. Haus-, Hof- und Staatsarchiv Wien, Reichshofrat, Denegata Recentiora 523, Kommissionsverhör, 4. Oktober 1770, Aussage Hofrat Michaelis, Heidesheim.

SECTION 4

Imperial Institutions, Confession, & Power Relations

CHAPTER 12

Marital Affairs as a Public Matter within the Holy Roman Empire
The Case of Duke Ulrich and Duchess Sabine of Württemberg at the Beginning of the Sixteenth Century

MICHAELA HOHKAMP

The instrumental character of marriage among the ruling classes during the late Middle Ages and early modern era is undisputed in historical research. Yet, the view that "emotional and material interests"[1] need not preclude one another has done nothing to change this general insight, nor has it deeply influenced the trend, particularly evident in cultural studies, to devote more attention to feelings.[2] Although the bourgeois concept of love-marriage, increasingly propagated since the eighteenth century, may not be viewed as a guarantee of a successful bond, it is at least viewed as its prerequisite. Indeed, in Western-oriented societies, marriages arranged for political or material reasons are considered to constitute an emotionally problematic and therefore potentially fragile form of union. Due to this cultural preconception, it is almost a truism in historical research that ruling couples in the late Middle Ages and early modern era were best able to cope with one another through the preservation of a polite and courtly distance, as a deficiency in affection, love, or respect—were this deficiency to be experienced on a daily basis—could easily lead to the decay or even total failure of a marriage that had been concluded for political or economic reasons.[3]

There is a widespread tendency in historical scholarship to direct attention to emotional facets of marriages between ruling couples. Yet at the same time, the relationships maintained by these couples with family members and friends are typically ignored or receive only rudimentary treatment. But recent academic work that incorporates perspectives from the field of gender history has begun to shift the focus of study from the affective internals of individual marriages toward the larger context of ruling couples' political and familial relations.⁴ This work has shown that in many cases, the absence of a legitimate successor and/or conflicts over property and compensation are not infrequently the cause of marital problems. That which can be applied to noble couples in general was particularly valid for princely ruling couples in the late Middle Ages and early modern era. These ruling couples maintained a dense network of familial ties, and family members not only met frequently at weddings and other celebrations, but also due to their elevated political status, for instance, they would meet at the diets of the Holy Roman Empire.⁵ This is one reason why marital strife in princely houses could easily develop into scandals. Another reason for the publicity of princely marital affairs in the late Middle Ages and the early modern period in the Holy Roman Empire is because they were seen as both institutional issues and as matters of kinship. In fact, politics in the Holy Roman Empire need to be understood as a complex dynamic in which marital affairs were strongly connected with gaining, keeping, or losing legitimate power: not only for the single prince and his house or his kin, but also for the married princess and her kin.⁶ Familiar with the very dense kin-network of noble families in the Middle Ages and the early modern period, Peter Moraw has recently argued that the history of the Holy Roman Empire should be characterized as an issue of just a few powerful families, houses or dynasties. In doing so, he adopts the traditional view of princesses as links (*bewegliche Elemente*) between two houses or dynasties. According to Karl-Heinz Spiess, on the other hand, these women were pulled out of their families and thrown into new ones, leaving their kin behind them.⁷ In her recent work, Heide Wunder challenged those points of view, arguing that one should analyze the noble or princely houses and dynasties as a kind of gendered formation (*Geschlechterverband*) that was constituted by men *and* women. This position seeks to understand houses and dynasties not as a construct of male agnates and houses of their own, but as a complex and powerful network of coexisting male and female agnates and cognates.⁸ Starting with this premise, the history of the Holy Roman Empire will be reconsidered by analyzing the marital spectacle of Duke Ulrich of Württemberg (1487–1550) and his wife, Duchess Sabine (1492–1564), a member of the Wittelsbach family.

The difficult marital relationship between Ulrich and Sabine was already considered a scandal by contemporaries and therefore has been an object of continuous interest, and not just to scholars of regional historiography. Ulrich married Sabine, the daughter of Duke Albrecht IV of Bavaria-Munich, in 1511. Sabine's mother, Kunigunde, was the sister of Emperor Maximilian I. The marriage between Sabine and Ulrich was short-lived. Sabine fled the duke's court in the fall of 1515 under the cover of darkness, returning to her brothers in Bavaria. In this act, she was assisted by her uncle, Emperor Maximilian I, and her aunt Elisabeth (1451–1524), who was the daughter of Albrecht Achilles (1414–1486), prince-elector of Brandenburg. This incident is anything but unknown. Yet, despite the amount of scholarship devoted to it, a fresh look is merited, and not solely because Sabine was one of the few duchesses in the Holy Roman Empire who managed to separate from her husband without forfeiting her status, her rights, and, above all, the claims of her offspring.[9] The incident is also interesting within the context of a reexamination of the history of the empire, because Sabine's accomplishment stands at the intersection of kinship and the power politics of the emperor and imperial princes and princesses at the level of the Holy Roman Empire and its territories. More specifically, the episode helps to illuminate the "interface" of the public sphere, political institutions, kinship networks, and above all, questions of the legitimacy of male and female princely power within the Holy Roman Empire.

The planning and arrangement of the marriage between Sabine and Ulrich should be understood within the framework of the political aspirations of the Habsburg family and its expansionist tendencies in the direction of Württemberg during the fifteenth and sixteenth centuries. Both the arrangement of the marriage and its final dissolution were events of political significance within the empire. The couple's separation was also closely linked with the complete, public, and empire-wide political removal of the duke of Württemberg. Duke Ulrich was removed from power in the context of the marital crisis (and vice versa), enabling the Habsburgs to bring the Duchy of Württemberg under their control in the early 1520s and maintain it as a vassal state (*Afterlehen*) until the end of the sixteenth century. The marital strife became evident when the duke of Württemberg fatally stabbed the husband of his mistress, Ursula Thumb, while on a hunt in May of 1515. Sabine fled the court of Württemberg in the fall of the same year.[10] The affair quickly grew into a scandal that lasted many years and preoccupied not only the Württemberg Estates and neighboring imperial princes—particularly Sabine's brothers—but also the emperor, the diet, and the wider erudite public political sphere.[11] The subsequent events came to involve the emperor and numerous relatives of the couple, both immediate and distant, and attracted the attention of the entire Holy Roman Empire.

Let us begin the following story of the princely marital affair as a public matter of power within the Holy Roman Empire by turning first to the history and historiographical writings of their separation. It is said that Ulrich fell in love with Ursula Thumb von Neuburg because of the obstinate disposition of his wife, Sabine. A short letter without an addressee or sender (and without a date, but which can be traced to 1516) is the earliest piece of evidence corroborating this explanation of Ulrich's romantic involvement with Ursula.[12] This view of events has remained the standard interpretation up to the present day. The historian Otto Borst, for instance, describes Duchess Sabine as a violent grumbler, who was bigger than a man, mannish, full of pride, obstinate, unable to withdraw, explosive, and sharp-tongued, even with men.[13] Volker Press, an early authority on southwestern German history, offers a similar characterization of Sabine, when he says that this Bavarian princess was a masculine, harsh, and aggressive person who did not want to cooperate in any way.[14] The eighteenth-century conception, that Ulrich's wife was an attractive princess in the eyes of political authorities because she was the niece of the emperor and not because she was a lovely and nice person, has also been kept.[15] Descriptions like this of Duchess Sabine can be found in most of the historical writings concerning either political, biographical or local history of the German lands and their dynasties. Ursula Thumb, on the other hand, is described as being comely, having a nice figure, and having helped Ulrich endure the curt and overbearing nature of his wife.

Yet Ursula Thumb was not only supposed to have been an attractive and appealing woman. She was also the daughter of Konrad Thumb von Neuburg, a long-standing confidant of Emperor Maximilian. She was also the wife of Hans von Hutten, who was Duke Ulrich's equerry and a close relative of Ulrich von Hutten, a member of the *res publica literaria*, who would later, after Sabine had left her husband, play a prominent role in the marital dispute as a talented pamphleteer.

Politically, Sabine's departure from Württemberg in November 1515 was unprecedented. To abandon one's dominion in a time of crisis—such as war— was already an almost treasonous act for a male ruler. Even a duchess was only permitted to leave her duchy for a limited time, and then only to visit relatives or for some similar purpose. If Sabine's flight were to remain without consequences in respect to her princely power, her actions would have to be portrayed in public as justified and legitimate. This was certainly the main reason why she explained her departure from Württemberg was not hasty and clandestine, but rather planned and carried out with the full knowledge of her uncle, Emperor Maximilian, a position she maintained from the beginning. This is apparent in a letter she wrote to her aunt Elisabeth, widow of the former duke of Württemberg (the so-called "Eberhard the younger") and sister of the ruling Margrave of Brandenburg-Ansbach.[16] This is also evident in the printed letters that she and her brothers publicized.

Ulrich quickly found himself in a politically precarious position. Yet, however difficult the situation was, it initially appeared that Ulrich would be able to assert his authority. When Ulrich attacked the free imperial city of Reutlingen in 1519, however, he provided Sabine's brothers in Munich—who had acted with hesitation up to this point—with a legally sound justification for moving against him. Covered by Ulrich's violation of imperial treaties, Sabine's brothers were able to launch a military action against Württemberg, which can be seen as a de facto annexation of the duchy. Simultaneously, they appealed to the inhabitants of the land by disseminating a printed letter addressed to the entire political public of the Holy Roman Empire.[17] At the same time, the Württemberg estates were also mobilized against the duke, whom they accused, as they had in previous years, of spending recklessly and damaging the duchy. The campaign against the duke was supported by his own brother-in-law, Duke Heinrich of Braunschweig-Wolfenbüttel, who had attempted in a letter in 1517 to encourage the Württemberg estates to dissuade Ulrich from his excess before he saw it necessary to refer the matter to the imperial diet.[18]

Ulrich was removed from power in 1519 in a relatively peaceable manner. He departed the duchy and first sought protection from Ludwig V, the Prince-Elector and Regent of the Palatinate. In Württemberg, the Bavarian judge (*Hofrichter*), Christoph von Schwarzenberg, assumed the reigns of power. At the subsequent meeting of the regional diet in Nördlingen, the duchess of Württemberg appeared with her brother, William, the reigning duke of Munich, and demanded that the rule of Württemberg be transferred to her son Christoph.[19] The members of the Swabian League (*Schwäbischer Bund*), who were well disposed toward the Emperor, declared their readiness to support this claim. Ulrich, however, had already returned to Württemberg in force. The transfer of rule to his son could therefore not be realized without difficulties.[20] Instead, the newly elected King Charles V, the grandson of Maximilian I, brought the duchy under his rulership with a formal treaty, paying the Swabian League a sum of "two times one hundred and twenty two florins,"[21] and appointing his brother Ferdinand as the "ruler" (*Regierer*) of the Habsburg lands in the south and southwest of the empire.[22] Thus, according to the Göttingen historian Timotheus Spittler, writing in the late eighteenth century, the young Emperor Charles V gained those German lands, which allowed him to ensure his power over the southwest of the Holy Roman Empire.[23] In 1530, Emperor Charles V enfeoffed his brother Ferdinand with the Duchy of Württemberg, but, in 1534, Ulrich returned to his former territory.

Duke Ulrich returned to power in Württemberg, which had become a vassal state (*Afterlehen*) of the Habsburgs. Yet his many years of exile cast a long shadow, an exile that was not least rooted in the murder of his mistress's husband. This crime had been publicly portrayed in the worst possible terms by Ulrich von Hutten, a relative of the duke's victim. In von Hutten's writings, the duke had been depicted as a sexually perverted tyrant whose brutish behavior transgressed all acceptable bounds. Therefore, at the end of the eighteenth century, a Württemberg historian was able to clearly characterize the murder as Ulrich's great misfortune. For, he argued, twenty feuding knights (*zwanzig befehdende Ritter*) would have caused less harm to the duke than one pen (*Feder*). According to this historian, Ulrich von Hutten, known for his biting sense of humor and poisonous satire, described the murder so vividly, and he also had such a tremendous audience ("... er hatte bey seiner trefflichen Schreibart und meisterhaften Darstellungskunst ein so großes Publicum"), that Ulrich would have lost power for this reason alone ("selbst wenn der Herzog keine weitere Veranlassung zu seinem Unglück gegeben hätte, der Schlag, der ihn treffen sollte, vielleicht doch nicht abzuwenden gewesen ware").[24]

In 1517, following Ulrich von Hutten's propaganda campaign against the duke, Maximilian named von Hutten *Poeta Laureatus*. This open commendation of von Hutten's work shows that Maximilian knew how skillfully to exploit the affair to advance his political interests in the Duchy of Württemberg and to distance himself from the husband of his niece Sabine, a man who had previously enjoyed his support.[25] In the same year, after separating himself symbolically from the duke, Maximilian used the imperial diet as a forum to dissociate himself politically from his former beneficiary. He accused the duke of breaching treaties, contended that Ulrich had allied himself with enemies of the Holy Roman Empire, and even pressed for the Swabian League to take military action against him.[26] Yet Maximilian had not taken such a stark position directly after the murder of Hans von Hutten. Ulrich, in fact, had been received by the emperor and had also been invited to the wedding of Maximilian's grandchildren in Vienna. Directly after Sabine's flight from Württemberg in 1515 and into the following year (Treaty of Blaubeuren, 1516), it even seemed like it might be possible to find a moderate solution. By the end of 1518, however, after Ulrich's denunciation in the diet, the change in Maximilian's political handling of the issue was clearly irreversible. Maximilian (who died in 1519) placed the duke of Württemberg under an imperial ban and allowed the accusations that had been raised against him to go public (e.g., that Ulrich had tormented, abused, and struck Duchess Sabine; that he had forced her to sleep in a pig sty; that he had gone to her bed with an unsheathed sword, etc.).[27]

These charges were underlined by the accusations made by Sabine's brothers, who, in an attempt to justify their sister's flight and preserve Sabine and her son Christoph's claim to the reigns of power in Württemberg, printed an open letter to the Württemberg estates. In this letter, the Wittelsbach brothers despaired of the indecency that Ulrich had shown toward their sister. To explain Sabine's departure from the duchy, the brothers cited the acts of violence that she had been forced to endure and also stressed her unimpeachable efforts to win Ulrich's love by being a very loyal, virtuous, and handsome princess.[28] They stated that, in order to rectify Ulrich's emotional and political distance and reluctance, Sabine had tried to correct her husband's inappropriate actions. Sabine, they argued, had endured all of her sufferings with patience and by exhausting her body. Yet this had failed to improve the situation, which had in fact worsened daily without any just cause. The permanent hostility of her husband had not been humanly tolerable. The Wittelsbach brothers wrote that Ulrich had been treating their sister with such horrible brutality that she could no longer be secure in her body or life. The agony had ultimately been so extreme that it would have broken a steadfast man, let alone a female.[29] As their sister had found herself in the highest distress, they had advised her solely for the given reasons, and for no others, to leave Württemberg and return to Munich under the protection of her brothers and mother. But she was to remain in Württemberg for the time being—or at least until the Württemberg estates had attended to the matter. Together with the people of Württemberg, her two brothers were anxious (*"begierig"*) to help in a way that neither the goods of the land (i.e., the goods of the estates), nor Sabine's goods, nor those of her children or of her brothers would be destroyed, they said.[30] The two brothers—having previously accounted for the tardiness of their statement with the explanation that their sister had been late in informing them of the true state of affairs at the court of Württemberg—concluded their printed appeal to the Württemberg estates by expressing their hope that no lies or disparagements published by Ulrich or anyone else would be given any credence.

In addition to her brothers, Sabine also made a direct address to the Württemberg estates. In her defense, she first emphasized that she had married Ulrich in spite of warnings she had received prior to the marriage. Over the course of the marriage, she had always comported herself as a well behaved princess. She had never given the duke reason for complaint or dissatisfaction. In fact, the opposite was the case. She had always cared for him and had prayed that God would grant her a good marriage. All of her aspirations were directed to living in a loving and friendly manner and in steady unity as befit a spouse. Sabine wrote also that she never treated Ulrich only as a husband, but had showed herself as a servant to her love, which Ulrich, however, only found to be detestable. Sabine added she had never given a moment's thought to insulting Ulrich, and she had always made efforts to stand by her husband's side and to understand his position in all things. Yet nothing, she concluded, could overcome their poor understanding of one another. Further, she wrote, the more she responded to his wishes, the crueler and angrier he became, so that she was never able to talk about it. In the end, Sabine reported, their marital relationship had reached a state that was unheard of between spouses, and especially among ruling persons. For this reason, she was finally forced to contemplate leaving the duchy (*sich dem Fürstentum "zu entreissen"*). She soon gave up on the idea, however, in the interest of protecting her small children and her duty to the people of the duchy. After trustworthy persons, familiar with the duke's violent dealings, warned her that her life was in danger, she was forced, under great personal anguish, to leave Württemberg. The decision had been an extremely difficult one, and she had, in fact, wished for nothing more than to spend her entire life in the duchy with her husband, her children, and the people. Because she expected, as she concluded in her appeal, that Ulrich would slander her after she had left the country in order to hide his own inappropriate actions, she asked the people not to lend a shred of credence to the disparaging remarks that he would surely make, and to view her departure from the duchy as an act of necessity.[31]

Sabine's explanations show that she was not only complaining in this public forum as a wife about the excessively violent behavior of her husband, but that she also was a duchess, and she wanted to remain one. For this reason, when justifying her actions to the estates, she did not restrict herself to a description of the sufferings she had endured during the marriage. She also attempted to establish a link between her status as wife, on the one hand, and her position as duchess, on the other. She stressed the fact that the circumstances of her marriage and particularly those between the princely spouses were unheard of and that she had always conducted herself well and virtuously, and she underlined that she has been born as a princess. In this way, she made it clear that she had measured up to her duties not only as a wife, but also as a duchess—indeed, almost to the point of self-abandonment. In her open letter to the Württemberg estates, Sabine marked a limit to hold out. As applicable law viewed the endangerment of life or limb as a legitimate reason for the dissolution of a marriage, Sabine's return to the brotherly court had to be portrayed not as an act of free will, but as a forced reaction to illegitimate, i.e., cruel and disempowering, violence against her as a wife and a mother of a future duke. But the voice we can hear talking through the printed letter here was not only a voice of a mother or a wife. We also can listen to a voice of a duchess in the full sense of the word, for Sabine argued together with her reigning brothers.[32]

The formulation of the letter to the estates gives a clear indication that the authors were aware of this. When Sabine raised the point in her address to the estates that her sufferings should have compelled her to think sooner about leaving the duchy, she employed the term "tear away" (*entreissen*), an expression that refers to the contemporary understanding of a dominion as a metaphorical "body." This metaphor was widespread in juridical documents from the premodern era. The written promotion of the former county of Württemberg to a duchy, the so-called "*Herzogsbrief*" from 1495, states, for instance, that the new duchy should not be divided or broken up, but should stay together and should remain undivided in the future.[33] In the early modern era, the Duchy of Württemberg and other similar territorial units were understood as political and legal bodies, whose ability to function depended on the smooth interplay of their contingent parts. In the sixteenth century, the duke and duchess were naturally two integral parts of the political "body."[34] Therefore, a permanent departure of a duke or duchess was nothing less than a form of dismemberment. The dominion had effectively lost one of its limbs, an injury that could potentially damage the entire body. If this missing part were to be replaced by the next male—in this case, Sabine's son, Christoph—then efforts would have to be made to ensure this son did not lose his rightful claim to succession. Due to the unique state of affairs in Württemberg, however, Christoph's claim to succeed could only be assured if his mother and her brothers were able to assert her authority as a duchess. To this end, it was absolutely necessary that the duchess portray her departure as a plausible act of necessity. This requirement was fulfilled by justifying her departure from Ulrich in terms of her need to escape his violent abuse, which, according to her, had overstepped all tolerable bounds and had become life threatening. To make sure that the wife's flight had no consequences for the duchess's power, Sabine described Ulrich's treatment as dishonorable. Regardless of the actual contours of the relationship between Sabine and Ulrich and of Sabine's true reasons for leaving Württemberg, from a legal perspective, the claim that Ulrich was intent on killing her not only physically, but socially and politically, was the only possible way to justify her departure and to assure her son Christoph's claim to the succession against the declared will of his father.

In the letter to the estates, Sabine clearly expressed her awareness of the problems associated with power and succession. She asserted that she had not wanted to leave the duchy because of their children. Perhaps these were the words of a concerned mother. In any event, they were first and foremost the words of the reigning duchess of Württemberg, speaking on behalf of the future duke. When Duke Ulrich responded to the accusations that he sought to kill his wife, by insisting that he had only struck her once, and not with excessive force, and that there were no grounds for her to leave the duchy, he was also speaking as duke and as husband at the same time. In order to preserve his power, Ulrich had to disclaim all charges of marital violence and dishonoring and even to launch his own counteraccusations.[35] Therefore, in his open letter, Ulrich announced that he had treated his wife, i.e., the sister of the Wittelsbach brothers, in such a fine way that he himself had the right to complain about the ungrateful, mannish, and barbarous conduct of Sabine, and not vice versa.[36] We do not know whether any of these statements of the duke and duchess of Württemberg and of her uncle and her brothers were accurate. What we see here, above all, are highly formalized, legalistic methods of argumentation engaged in by both parties, which hardly allow for the formulation of plausible pronouncements about the quality of Sabine's marriage.

This is a point that should be emphasized, because interest in the case of Sabine and Ulrich among historians of the late Middle Ages and early modern era has not waned, due to the dramatic events surrounding the couple's separation. Yet despite the scholarly interest in this historical episode, the portrayals in the numerous writings have failed to produce a multi-faceted view. As is shown above, the duchess has been mainly described in terms marked by gender-specific stereotypes. The operative stereotype here—in contrast to that of the highly emotionalized bourgeois woman—is the conception of the female prince as an obstinate figure incapable of love due to a haughty sense of pride, a cold woman who rejects her husband or—in the worst case—even plots to murder him.[37] It is entirely plausible that Sabine and some of the other princesses who were denounced, imprisoned, suspected of witchcraft, or rebuked for their obstinacy or haughtiness were in actual fact as abhorrent, traitorous, and criminal as they are portrayed by contemporary sources or in later historical writings. It is certainly possible that Anna von Württemberg (1408–1471) attempted to bewitch her husband, Duke Philipp von Katzenelnbogen, with a sweat-soaked bread roll.[38] We can, of course, imagine that Princess Katharina (1468–1524), of the Wettin dynasty, was set on killing her husband, the Tyrolean Archduke Sigismund (1427–1496). It is also plausible that Sidonie (1518–1575)[39]—another Wettin, married to Duke Erich II and, by the way, the niece of the aforementioned Princess Katharina—sought to poison her husband, as he claimed. It is also imaginable that the Palatinate Electoral-Princess Charlotte possessed such a capricious temperament, that she would constantly get herself into conflicts with everyone around her, as is recounted in historical texts of the eighteenth, nineteenth, and twentieth centuries.[40] Yet, from the perspectives offered by the field of gender history, it should be taken into consideration that the historical portrayals of Duchess Sabine and other princesses in this time period are colored by cultural preconceptions.

The goal of the present chapter is certainly not to conduct a fundamental analysis of European historiography's treatment of princely women in the late Middle Ages and early modern era. With a view to our object of study, it must be emphasized, however, that the evaluations of historical figures contained in scholarly works with a biographical focus—evaluations of moral character and personality, whether positive or negative—have in some cases remained unchanged for centuries. Some years ago, Karin Hausen drew attention to the problems that result when one reads historical writings from a perspective of gender history.[41] Her arguments were based on her own work with historiographical texts from the nineteenth century. She argued that these kinds of writings should be seen as part of the history of gender constructions. Her diagnosis can be extended to these kinds of historiographical writings that—until today—are rooted in nineteenth-century historicism. Such texts and their gender-specific descriptions of princes and princesses in the late Middle Ages and early modern era sometimes are based on background stories that have been transmitted over centuries. Even when these historical writings can be recognized as historiographical discourses about power and gender, all of these long lasting histories about male and female princes that were written between the sixteenth and the twentieth century can nevertheless provide insight into gendered writings of cultures of power, as we have seen in the case of Sabine and Ulrich.

Conclusion

This case study of Sabine and Ulrich's marital crisis interpreted written sources through close reading. In contrast to standard political, biographical, or historical treatments of the couple's tumultuous relationship, the reconstruction of any kind of reality of Sabine and Ulrich's marriage was not a primary aim. Rather, the goal of the present study has been to understand as gendered the juridical, historical, and literary writings in the context of legitimation and delegitimation of power. As discussed, the questions traditionally posed about this historical episode can and must remain unanswered for historiographic and methodical-theoretical reasons. We can neither know whether Sabine was truly an unattractive and obstinate duchess who forced her husband into the arms of a mistress, nor can we judge if the opposite was true, that Ulrich was a violent and perverted individual who constantly insulted and threatened to kill his wife. But it can be noted that Sabine and her kin prevailed politically; Sabine retained her rights as the duchess of Württemberg and her son assumed the reins of power, despite Ulrich's attempts to position his half-brother Georg as the rightful successor.[42] It should be expressly stated here that the activation of the complex machine of the public sphere was certainly a factor in hindering Ulrich's retention of power and also was certainly a key factor in establishing the rule that a direct male heir would succeed, a tendency that can be witnessed from the beginning of the sixteenth century onward by observing genealogical and dynastic customs. It remains to be noted that the reappraisal undertaken in this study of the Württemberg marital crises from the beginning of the sixteenth century has permitted a deeper insight into the complex structure of the Holy Roman Empire's public and political sphere and its interaction with other political forces, such as familial networks, while also illuminating new facets of the history of the Holy Roman Empire from the perspectives offered by the investigation of gender and kinship networking.

Notes

1. See Hans Medick and David Warren Sabean, eds., *Emotionen und materielle Interessen. Sozialanthropologische und historische Beiträge zur Familienforschung* (Göttingen, 1984).
2. Ingrid Kasten, "Einleitung: Lucien Febvre und die Folgen: zu einer Geschichte der Gefühle und ihrer Erforschung," in *Kulturen der Gefühle im Mittelalter und Früher Neuzeit*, eds. Ingrid Kasten et al. (Stuttgart, 2002), 9–21; and Helga Mitterbauer and Katharina Scherke, eds., *Themenschwerpunkt: Gefühle* (Kulturwissenschaftliches Jahrbuch, 3) (Innsbruck, 2007).
3. In the historiography on European nobility, there are countless examples of unhappy marriages. See the bibliography in the recent case study by Stephanie Marra, *Allianzen des Adels. Dynastisches Handeln im Grafenhaus Bentheim im 16. und 17. Jahrhundert* (Cologne, Weimar, and Vienna, 2007).

4. Sophie Ruppel, *Verbündete Rivalen. Geschwisterbeziehungen im Hochadel des 17. Jahrhunderts* (Cologne, Weimar, and Vienna, 2007); Ruppel, "Geschwisterbeziehungen im Adel und Norbert Elias' Figurationssoziologie," in *Höfische Gesellschaft und Zivilisationsprozeß. Norbert Elias' Werk in kulturwissenschaftlicher Perspektive*, ed. Claudia Opitz (Cologne, 2005), 207–224; Michaela Hohkamp, "Sisters, Aunts and Cousins: Familial Architectures and the Political Field in Early Modern Europe," in *Kinship in Europe: Approaches to Long-Term Developments (1300–1900)*, eds. Jon Mathieu, Simon Teuscher, and David Sabean (Oxford and New York, 2007), 128–145; and Ebba Severidt, *Familie, Verwandtschaft und Karriere bei den Gonzaga. Struktur und Funktion von Familie und Verwandtschaft bei den Gonzagaund und ihren deutschen Verwandten (1444–1519)* (Leinfelden-Echterdingen, 2002).
5. Regarding kinship networks in the early modern period, see Michaela Hohkamp, "Eine Tante für alle Fälle: Tanten-Nichten-Beziehungen und Holy Roman Empire politische Bedeutung für die reichsfürstliche Gesellschaft der Frühen Neuzeit (16. bis 18. Jahrhundert)," in *Politiken der Verwandtschaft*, eds. Margareth Lanzinger and Edith Saurer (Vienna, 2007), 149–171.
6. See Barbara Stollberg-Rilinger, "Was heißt Kulturgeschichte des Politischen? Einleitung," in *Was heißt Kulturgeschichte des Politischen?*, ed. Stollberg-Rilinger (Zeitschrift für Historische Forschung Beiheft, 35) (Berlin, 2004), 9–24; and Barbara Stollberg-Rilinger, "Symbolische Kommunikation in der Vormoderne. Begriffe—Thesen—Forschungsperspektiven," in *Zeitschrift für Historische Forschung* 31 (2004): 489–527.
7. Severidt, *Familie*, 69; and Karl-Heinz Spiess, *Familie und Verwandtschaft im deutschen Hochadel des Spätmittelalters. 13. bis Anfang des 16. Jahrhunderts* (Stuttgart 1993), 128.
8. Heide Wunder, "Dynastie, Geschlecht, Herrschaft. Frauen des hohen Adels in der Frühen Neuzeit," in *Frau und Bildnis 1600–1750. Barocke Repräsentationsfigur an europäischen Fürstenhöfen*, eds. Gabriele Baumbach and Cordula Bischoff (Kassel, 2001), 15–37, here 21.
9. Franz Brendle, *Dynastie, Reich und Reformation. Die württembergischen Herzöge Ulrich und Christoph, die Habsburger und Frankreich* (Stuttgart, 1998), 33. See also Frida Sauter, "Herzogin Sabine von Wirtenberg," in *Zeitschrift für württembergische Landesgeschichte (ZWLG)* 8 (1944–1948): 298–355; and Jörg Rogge, "Gefängnis, Flucht und Liebeszauber. Ursachen und Verlaufsformen von Geschlechterkonflikten im hohen Adel des deutschen Reiches im späten Mittelalter," in *Zeitschrift für Historische Forschung* 28 (2001): 487–511. Siegrid Westphal, "Der Kaiserliche Reichshofrat als protestantisches 'scheidungsgericht'" in *Österreichische Zeitschrift für Geschichte* 20:3 (2009): 31–58.
10. Brendle, *Dynastie*, 43.
11. Gerhard Raff, *Hie gut Wirtemberg allewege. Das Haus Württemberg von Graf Ulrich dem Stifter bis Herzog Ludwig*, 3 vols. (Stuttgart, 1988), 1: 480; and Dieter Mertens, "Württemberg," in *Handbuch der baden-württembergischen Geschichte*, vol. 2: *Die Territorien im Alten Reich*, eds. Meinrad Schaab and Hansmartin Schwarzmaier (Stuttgart, 1995), 1–163, here 72f.
12. Hauptstaatsarchiv Stuttgart (HStAS), HA 41, Bü. 2, Herzog Ulrich von Württemberg, 1516; see also Sauter, "Herzogin Sabine," 311.

13. "wahre Wuchtbrumme," "körperlich größer als ein Mann," "unweiblich, stolz und zu eigensinnig, um nachgeben zu können, aufbrausend und scharf mit der Rede, auch gegen Männer." Quoted by Raff, *Hie gut Wirtenberg allewege*, 1: 477.
14. "die Bayerin war eine maskuline, herbe, streitlustige Person, nicht gewillt klein beizugeben." Quoted by Raff, *Hie gut Wirtenberg allewege*, 1: 477.
15. "für die alte[n] Herrn Vormundschaftsräthe [war Sabine], als Schwestertochter des Kaisers[,] ein sehr angenehmes Mädchen ..., aber nicht für den jungen Naturmenschen Ulrich, dem schon das vornehmspröde und störrige Wesen der Jungfer Sabine abgeschreckt haben würde, wenn je sein Aug bey dem ersten Anblick derselben Liebe gefaßt hätte." Quoted by Ludwig Timotheus Spittler, *Geschichte Wirtembergs unter der Regierung der Grafen und Herzoge* (Göttingen, 1783), 93f.
16. See Ignaz von Streber, *Andenken an Herzog Ludwig von Bayern, Wilhelm des IV. Bruder. Ein Beytrag zur vaterländischen Münzkunde* (Munich, 1819), 15.
17. "Churfürsten/ Fürsten/ Geistlichen und Weltlichen Ptrelaten/ Graffen/ Freyen/ Heren / Ritter und Knechten/ Hauptleuten/ Schultheissen/ Bürgermeistern/ Richtern/ Räthen/ Bürgern/ Gemeinden vnnd sonst allen andern des H. Röm. Reichs/ vnd sonderlich des Schwäbischen Bunds Verwandten und Unterthanen/ in was Würden/ Stands/ oder Wesens die seynd/ denen diese Schrift fürkompt oder verlesen wird." These so-called *Ausschreiben* (public letters) were printed comments, published in the context of political differences and sent to the members of political institutions, like the diets. Quoted by Friedrich Hortleder, *Von den Ursachen des Teutschen Krieges* (Frankfurt a.M., 1617), vol. 1, third book, Cap. 2, 815 (23 March 1519).
18. HStAS, G 43, Bü. 3, Nr. 27–33 (10 September 1517), Nr. 34 (1 September 1517), Nr. 35 (1 September 1517), Nr. 36–38 (10 September 1517), Nr. 23 (11 September 1517). Regarding the claims of Herzog Heinrich, see Rainer Täubrich, *Herzog Heinrich der Jüngere von Braunschweig-Wolfenbüttel (1489–1568). Leben und Politik bis zum Primogeniturvertrag von 1535* (Braunschweig, 1991), 32.
19. On the kinship matters of the Wittelsbach and Habsburg princes who were involved in the problems of the succession of Christoph of Württemberg, see Heinrich Lutz and Walter Ziegler, "Das konfessionelle Zeitalter. First part: Die Herzöge Wilhelm IV. und Albrecht V.," in *Handbuch der bayerischen Geschichte, vol. 2: Das alte Bayern. Der Territorialstaat vom Ausgang des 12. Jahrhunderts bis zum Ausgang des 18. Jahrhunderts*, ed. Andreas Kraus (Munich, 1988), 324–392, here 334ff.
20. Mertens, "Württemberg," 74f. After Ulrich returned to Württemberg, it was clear that a military confrontation with the Swabian League could not be won. Eight weeks after his return, Ulrich left the country again.
21. Spittler, *Geschichte Wirtembergs*, 116.
22. Mertens, "Württemberg," p. 74f.
23. "[S]o hatte also der junge Kaiser noch eh er einmal Teutschland betretten eines der beträchtlichsten Länder erworben, das in Verbindung mit den übrigen Staaten, welche ihm und seinem Bruder vom Großvater Maximilian angefallen waren, seiner Macht in Oberdeutschland das Uebergewicht versicherte." Spittler, *Geschichte Wirtemberg*, 116. After the return of Ulrich, it was proposed that young Christoph, and with him the whole duchy of Württemberg, be given to King Charles V. If the king were unwilling to pay 300,000 fl., the Swabian League planned to make Württemberg a member of Switzerland ("*Eidgenossenschaf*").

24. "er hatte bey seiner trefflichen Schreibart und meisterhaften Darstellungskunst ein so großes Publicum ... selbst wenn der Herzog keine weitere Veranlassung zu seinem Unglück gegeben hätte, der Schlag, der ihn treffen sollte, vielleicht doch nicht abzuwenden gewesen wäre." Spittler, *Geschichte Wirtemberg*. Regarding media publicity see Martin Gierl, "Zeitschriften—Stadt—Information—London—Göttingen—Aufklärung," in *Jenseits der Diskurse. Aufklärungspraxis und Institutionenwelt in europäisch komparatistischer Perspektive*, eds. Gierl et al. (Göttingen, 2007), 243–264.
25. Ulrich von Hutten was very aware of the meaning of such a distinction. See Jan-Dirk Müller, *Gedechtnus. Literatur und Hofgesellschaft um Maximilian I.* (Munich, 1982), 52. For the distinction, see Brendle, *Dynastie*, 37ff. Ulrich von Hutten clearly supported the party of the Habsburgs in the context of the election in 1519. See also Paul Kalkoff, *Huttens Vagantenzeit und Untergang. Der geschichtliche Ulrich von Hutten und seine Umwelt* (Weimar, 1925), 271ff.
26. Mertens, "Württemberg," 73; and Hermann Wiesflecker, *Kaiser Maximilian I. Das Reich, Österreich und Europa an der Wende zur Neuzeit*, vol. V: *Der Kaiser und seine Umwelt. Hof, Staat, Wirtschaft, Gesellschaft und Kultur* (Munich, 1986), 18.
27. Sabine had declared that Ulrich raped her. Karl August Barack, ed., *Zimmerische Chronik*, vol. 1–4, (Freiburg i. Br., 1881–1882), 252f.
28. "mit sonder angeborner fürstlicher und frewlicher Tugent/ zucht/ eere/ lieb und gestallt/...ine [Duke Ulrich] dahin zubewegen/das Er sy alls sein Gemahl pillich lieben [werde]." HStAS, G 43, Bü. 2, open printed letter of the brothers Wilhelm and Ludwig to the Württemberg Estates.
29. HStAS, G 43, Bü. 2, fol. 21–25, fol. 22f.
30. "[so dass] unnser lieben Schwester/Irer Kinder/ auch des Lannds Wirttemberg wolfart/Eere/Nutz, und notturfft betracht/ und das unere/abfal unnd zerstörung verhuet werde." HStAS, G 43, Bü. 2, fol. 23.
31. HStAS, G 43, Bü. 2, fol. 24.
32. Ute Daniel, "Zwischen Zentrum und Peripherie der Hofgesellschaft: Zur biographischen Struktur eines Fürstenlebens der Frühen Neuzeit am Beispiel der Kurfürstin Sophie von Hannover," in *L'Homme. Zeitschrift für feministische Geschichtswissenschaft* 8:2 (1997): 208–217; Martin Kintzinger, "Die zwei Frauen des Königs, Zum politischen Handlungsspielraum von Fürstinnen im europäischen Spätmittelalter," in *Das Frauenzimmer. Die Frau bei Hofe in Spätmittelalter und früher Neuzeit. 6. Symposium der Residenzen-Kommission der Akademie der Wissenschaften in Göttingen*, eds. Jan Hirschbiegel and Werner Paravicini (Stuttgart, 2000), 377–398, here 380ff; and Michaela Hohkamp,"Do Sisters have Brothers? – Or the Search for the 'rechte Schwester.' Brothers and Sisters in Aristocratic Society at the Turn of the Sixteenth Century," in *Sibling Relations and the Transformations of European Kinship, 1300–1900*, eds. Christopher Johnson and David W. Sabean (forthcoming).
33. Klaus Graf, "Eberhard im Bart und die Herzogserhebung, 1495," in *Württemberg wird Herzogtum. Dokumente aus dem Hauptstaatsarchiv Stuttgart zu einem epochalen Ereignis* (Stuttgart, 1995), 9–43, here 16. The Golden Bull of 1356 had addressed the question of succession, stipulating that dominions should be preserved "*in sua integritate*" and should not be "dismembered" without plausible reason. Hansmartin Schwarzmaier, "Von der fürsten tailung," in *Blätter für deutsche Landesgeschichte* 126 (1990): 161–183, here 171.

34. Karl-Heinz Spiess, "Erbteilung, dynastische Räson und transpersonale Herrschaftsvorstellungen. Die Pfalzgrafen bei Rhein und die Pfalz im späten Mittelalter," in *Die Pfalz. Probleme einer Begriffsgeschichte vom Kaiserpalast auf dem Palatin bis zum heutigen Regierungsbezirk*, ed. Franz Staab (Speyer, 1990), 159–181, here 181. Still in the eighteenth century, Christoph Friderich Sattler wrote that Württemberg should remain an *"unzertrennlicher Körper."* Sattler, *Geschichte des Herzogthums Würtenberg unter der Regierung der Herzogen, mit 86 Urkunden und einigen Kupfern bestärket, Dritter Teil* (Ulm, 1771), 94. Regarding this idea, one can find formulations like *"Einverleibung"* (incorporation) in combination with agreements between houses in matters of heritage (*"Erbeinung"*) in political and historical texts until the nineteenth century. Christoph Rommel, *Geschichte von Hessen. Dritter Theil. Von der Theilung unter den Söhnen Ludwigs des Friedsamen bis zur Theilung unter den Söhnen Philipps des Großmüthigen oder bis zum Anfang der jetzigen Haupt-Linien, Erste Abteilung* (Kassel, 1827), 146.
35. See Sattler, *Würtenberg unter der Regierung*, 263–272. He provides an *Ausschreiben* from Maximilian, which is not transmitted in the archives. Ulrich's answer dates from 8 January 1519.
36. "daß es vns auff ihr vndanckbarlich unweiblich/ üppig/ und wol zu sagen/ unmenschlich Haltung und Fürmehmen gegen uns [den Herzog] leid ist." Quoted by Hortleder, *Von den Ursachen des Teutschen Krieges*, 815. Hortleder reproduces this *Ausschreiben* of Sabine's brothers.
37. Elisabeth Koch, "Die Frau im Recht der Frühen Neuzeit. Juristische Lehren und Begründungen," in *Frauen in der Geschichte des Rechts. Von der Frühen Neuzeit bis zur Gegenwart*, ed. Ute Gerhard (Munich, 1997), 73–93, here 80.
38. Johannes Merkel, "Die Irrungen zwischen Herzog Erich II. und seiner Gemahlin Sidonie (1545–1575)," in *Zeitschrift des Historischen Vereins für Niedersachsen* (1899), 11–101.
39. Andrea Lilienthal, *Die Fürstin und die Macht. Welfische Herzoginnen im 16. Jahrhundert: Elisabeth, Sidonia, Sophia* (Hannover, 2007); and Helga-Maria Kühn, "'... es gefellett mir reychtt woll hyr ...' Die letzten Lebensjahre der Herzogin Sidonie 1573–1575 in Weißenfels," in *Das Weißenfelser St. Klaren-Kloster. Zum 700-jährigen Bestehen*, ed. Astrid Fick (Weißenfels, 2001), 39–41.
40. "der Mensch mit sich selbst und mit anderen in einen unaufhörlichen Zwist verwickelt wird." Johann Friedrich August Kazner, *Louise, Raugräfin zu Pfalz: eine wahre Geschichte von dem Verfasser des Lebens Friedrichs von Schomberg* (Leipzig, 1798), 1: 20. In the age of historicism, this opinion was adopted. See Adolf Köcher, *Memoiren der Herzogin Sophie nachmals Kurfürstin von Hannover* (Publicationen aus den k. preussischen Staatsarchiven, 4) (Leipzig, 1879).
41. Karin Hausen, "Die Nicht-Einheit der Geschichte als historiographische Herausforderung. Zur historischen Relevanz und Anstößigkeit der Geschlechtergeschichte," in *Geschlechtergeschichte als Allgemeine Geschichte. Herausforderungen und Perspektiven*, eds. Hans Medick and Anne Charlott Trepp (Göttingen, 1998), 15–55; and Angelika Epple, *Empfindsame Geschichtsschreibung. Eine Geschlechtergeschichte der Historiographie zwischen Aufklärung und Historismus* (Bielefeld, 2003).
42. Regarding the opinions of the Strasbourg scholar Franz Frosch, HStAS, G 41 Bü.10.

CHAPTER 13

The *Corpus Evangelicorum*
A Culturalist Perspective on its Procedure in the Eighteenth-Century Holy Roman Empire

ANDREAS KALIPKE

Introduction

The *Corpus Evangelicorum*, the Protestant group at the imperial diet, is prominent in the historiography of both the Holy Roman Empire and its legal traditions. Scholars have stressed the *Corpus*'s role in the confessional quarrels of the empire, and have offered subtle reflections about its role during different phases of the eighteenth century as well as interpretations of the religious constitution of the empire. However, they have not examined how the association of the Protestant *Reichsstände* made its decisions.[1] Nor have they analyzed what mechanisms determined the outcome of its internal consultations. While the religious policies of single members have been examined, how these individual *Reichsstände* came to common conclusions has not been analyzed.[2] This essay will consider these neglected aspects of the *Corpus Evangelicorum*'s operation.

In order to provide a context for this examination, this chapter shall, first, very roughly outline the relevant framework of the empire's religious constitution. The second part will give an account of the theoretical foundations of these issues. The third part of the essay will focus on the internal procedures of the *Corpus* in dealing with confessional conflicts, using the approaches put forward in the second part. Finally, a conclusion will present the summary findings of this analysis.

The *Corpus Evangelicorum* in the Framework of the Religious Constitution of the Holy Roman Empire

The Peace of Westphalia prohibited majority votes in religious affairs and provided for direct negotiation between the two confessional groups at the imperial diet: the *Corpus Evangelicorum*, comprising the *Reichsstände* of both Lutheran and Reformed faith, and the *Corpus Catholicorum*, the association of the Catholic *Reichsstände*.[3] This procedure of separating Catholics and Protestants at the diet, the *itio in partes* (the act of going into parties),[4] was intended to replace the usual procedure of "relation and correlation" between the electoral and princely colleges, followed by the *votum* of the cities, in order to compensate for the Protestants' disadvantage of being in the minority in both the princely and electoral colleges of the diet.[5] The *itio in partes* was, in theory, a rule conducive to peace and order; de facto, it was founded upon the basic distinction between political and religious spheres.

Despite these considerations, the Peace of Westphalia was imprecise and ambiguous about when an *itio in partes* was allowed.[6] The two confessional parties disagreed on what precisely constituted a religious matter: for example, what about the reduction of taxes for a Catholic imperial city?[7] Furthermore, the Catholic side wanted to restrict the *itio* within narrow limits as an *exceptio odiosa*,[8] whereas the Protestants claimed that the mere fact of proclaiming the *itio* was sufficient for it to take effect, even in wholly political issues.[9] They claimed this in order to maintain their procedural autonomy against the Catholics, because if the consent of the Catholics had been required for an *itio*, the procedure would have been of no use to the Protestants.[10] Consequently, the Protestants developed their own interpretation of the *Reichsverfassung*, the *Principia Evangelicorum*, which, by 1720, became a coherent alternative to the Catholic interpretation.[11]

Nevertheless, the institutionalization of the *Corpus Evangelicorum* at the beginning of the eighteenth century cannot solely be explained by the *itio*. Rather, it crystallized around the concept of the *ius intercedendi*. This right to intercede in favor of confessionally oppressed individuals, municipalities, or estates was claimed by the *Corpus*, but denied by the Catholics, who stressed the competence of the imperial courts and the emperor.[12] Gabriele Haug-Moritz has shown that the emperor's last political prerogative of major importance was his judicial competence and that the *Reichshofrat* in Vienna functioned as "the emperor's right arm."[13] From that point of view, it is understandable that the emperor and the Catholic party had to reject the Protestants' interpretation of the constitution of the empire.[14] The Catholics did not even acknowledge the internal consultations of the Protestants, united in the *Corpus Evangelicorum*. By then, these consultations had become more and more frequent, because the religious troubles at the end of the seventeenth and the beginning of the eighteenth centuries—above all the dispute about the famous clause of the Peace of Ryswick that favored the Catholics in the Palatinate, but also several local conflicts of minor importance—made the meetings of Protestant envoys at the diet more and more indispensable.[15] The Catholics, on the other hand, rejected the *Corpus* as a state within the state.[16] This, among other reasons, is why they did not meet regularly and avoided using the terms *Corpus Catholicorum*[17] or *Corpus Evangelicorum*.[18]

The corporate *ius intercedendi* turned out to be quite attractive for Protestant subjects and municipalities that felt suppressed by their Catholic rulers. They addressed their grievances to the *Corpus Evangelicorum* in order to obtain help from their co-religionists against repressive Catholic authorities. In order to have these grievances resolved, the *Corpus* first interceded with the accused Catholic authority and demanded the reestablishment of the 1648 conditions. If the accused was not willing to comply, the *Corpus* appealed to the emperor's highest representative at the diet, the *Prinzipalkommissar*. If this did not lead to the resolution of the grievances, then it appealed directly to the emperor, who was supposed to appoint local imperial commissions to judge the case. From the Protestant point of view, the commissioners were to be confessionally proportional. Reprisals were threatened, if at all, only in the later phases of such conflicts. The most famous example of this is the measures taken by the "Soldier King," Frederick William I of Prussia, against his Catholic subjects in the course of the Palatine quarrels.[19] In extreme cases, the Protestants claimed the right of *Selbsthilfe*, that is, self-authorization to use force against an oppressor.[20] Such *Selbsthilfe* was put into practice only once. In 1750, at the dawn of the Seven Years' War, the *Corpus* charged the Margrave of Ansbach with an administrative and military intervention against the Catholic princes of Hohenlohe-Waldenburg to coerce them to reinstall the Protestant consistory and to address grievances in the principality.[21] It is important to note that in this specific context, the Protestants acted in explicit accordance with the *Reichshofrat*, which had issued several decrees against the Hohenlohe princes in 1744. It should also be noted that the Margrave of Ansbach was charged in the context of his function as co-director of the Franconian *Reichskreis*.[22] This shows that the *Corpus Evangelicorum* did not want to confront the emperor directly, but wanted to stay, at least formally, within the bounds of a common understanding of the imperial constitution.[23]

All in all, the *Corpus Evangelicorum* was active in a wide range of confessional affairs, affairs that included everything from dealing with small local conflicts resulting from Catholic processions to giving important confessional guarantees to the dissenting subjects of Catholic rulers.[24] In the second half of the seventeenth century and the first half of the eighteenth century, many of these cases arose as a result of the conversion of princes to Roman Catholicism or Catholic successions in Protestant territories. Disputes between subjects and authorities entailed extensive correspondence in the *Corpus* and frequent conferences, and often these disputes continued for decades.[25] The regulations of 1648 were, of course, the legal basis for the grievances, above all the *annus normalis*, the normative year of 1624, which was supposed to freeze confessional status in the territories of the empire.[26] In the course of the famous confessional troubles at the end of the seventeenth and beginning of the eighteenth centuries, the *Corpus* began to meet on a regular basis. With these more frequent meetings, its proceedings became standardized, and the course of business was fixed.[27] Confessional disputes continued until the end of the Holy Roman Empire, and even in the 1780s there were still harsh confrontations.[28]

Methodologically, it is thus necessary to distinguish between two different functions fulfilled by the *Corpus*. On the one hand, it constituted a kind of confessional committee at the diet, taking part in making collectively binding decisions. These decisions encompassed major issues such as the war constitution of the empire and the peace treaty with the French Crown, as well as several affairs that led to an *itio in partes*. On the other hand, the *Corpus* became an institution that acted independently of the diet, helping Protestants all over the empire to preserve their rights. Ideally, one could distinguish a political sphere—making collectively binding decisions—from a judicial sphere—judging what was right and wrong.

It is important to emphasize that the *Corpus* was not very successful in its intercessions. On the basis of several cases, it is possible to say that the Catholic authorities generally did not desist from their oppressive actions.[29] Nor did the emperor come to the Protestants' help. The Protestants themselves hardly ever made use of *Selbsthilfe*. The ineffectiveness of the *Corpus* in many cases is obvious.

The directorship of the Protestant *Corpus* was in the hands of the Elector of Saxony. Although Frederick Augustus I converted to Roman Catholicism in 1697 in order to become king of Poland (as Augustus II, "the Strong"), he managed to retain the directorship by delegating it to the duke of Sachsen-Weißenfels, who was placed in charge of Protestant affairs at the imperial level.[30] Research has shown that this was purely formal and illusory and that the real authority rested with Frederick Augustus.[31] Once his son officially embraced the Catholic faith in 1717 and a Catholic dynasty seemed to be established, Prussia and Hanover tried to take over the directorate. In 1720, at the end of this conflict over the directorate, Prussia and Hanover had failed to take over the directorate either together or alternately (which they also envisaged as a possibility), and Saxony succeeded in holding onto it.[32]

Throughout this period, Saxony's representative at the imperial diet received the *Gravamina* and ensured that they were dictated to the secretaries. He also invited participants to the sessions, which took place in the Regensburg town hall every two weeks, and sometimes more frequently than that. He presided over the sessions and formulated the official writings.[33] His correspondence and the attached documents—for instance, the minutes and petitions—are quite instructive about the constitution of the *Corpus*.[34]

Theoretical Approaches: Legitimation by Procedure and Symbolic Communication

The following remarks will not repeat the findings of recent research on the confessional conflicts themselves, on their causes, the parties' motives, and so on, although these cases might benefit from further analysis.[35] Rather, this chapter's focus is on the internal procedures at the *Corpus Evangelicorum*. The approach is based on Niklas Luhmann's theory of "legitimation by procedure."[36]

The sociologist Luhmann has maintained that, in modern societies, decisions are no longer legitimized by extra-procedural sources, for example, religion, tradition, or even consensus. According to Luhmann, one does not accept—and acceptance, in Luhmann's sense, is legitimacy—decisions because one believes that they are true, rational, or in accordance with the will of God, but because they are produced in a formally regulated manner. Luhmann makes this clear in describing the paradigm of modern judicial procedure. At the beginning of the proceedings, all participants assume their respective roles: judge, plaintiff, accused, and so on. In the course of the procedure, the participants bind themselves by making statements that afterward can hardly be retracted without losing face and appearing irrational. Little by little, the procedure develops its own history, which everybody has to take into account. Contingency is gradually reduced, and the decision seems to result undoubtedly from what has been said and done.[37] It is not necessary to the legitimacy of the procedure for the sentenced person to concur with the judgment; it is the specific function of these procedures to make the production of decisions independent of the consent of the parties concerned.[38] By assuming their roles, the participants affirm the procedure in an expressive and symbolic dimension. It is not *what* they say or do that legitimates the procedure, but the fact *that* they say or do something as a part of the procedure. Once they accept their role and once they act according to it, they cannot retract their engagement without losing face as rational people. Those on the losing side have ceremonially legitimized the procedure in the eyes of third parties (spectators, the public). As one can see, the expressive dimension is vital to the legitimacy of a procedure.

But what initially makes the parties take part in the procedure? It is absolutely necessary that at the beginning the outcome is open, because the prospective participants must have the hope of being able to achieve their own aims. Counterexamples are show trials where the judgment is fixed before the proceedings start. To a certain degree, participants must be willing to accept the sentences against them. Luhmann thus defines legitimacy as the generalized willingness to accept uncertain decisions in advance, within specific limits.[39]

As stated above, "legitimation by procedure" is characteristic of complex and differentiated societies. In contrast, the legitimacy of pre-modern procedure, especially political procedures, mostly depended on their outcome; "wrong" decisions could be rejected by the parties concerned. Of course, pre-modern procedures had to cope with or could even be overwhelmed by considerations of status and rank. Luhmann's theory helps in the analysis and description of early modern procedures, often through their contrast with modern ones. Concepts such as procedural autonomy and the assumption of roles are very useful here. Above all, the methodological differentiation between an instrumental and an expressive or symbolic dimension of interaction systems is very important.[40] Legitimacy is produced on the level of expressive symbolism and by means of it. This raises the question of symbolic communication, which will also be a major theme in what follows. [41]

Historical research has not yet made use of the possibilities offered by the theory of "legitimation by procedure." This is perhaps due to the fact that historians have long been skeptical about sociological approaches, especially about Luhmann's systems theory. When historians did become more receptive to the stimuli of different disciplines, systems theory had already become quite complex and quite abstract, which made its acceptance difficult. It should also be noted that there is no English translation of Luhmann's book *Legitimation durch Verfahren* and that systems theory is much better known in its Parsonian version in the English and US context. The argument here is that integrating systems theory into our analysis of the *Corpus* reveals new insights into its operation.

The concept of symbolic communication questions the ways in which social values and conceptions are visualized, stabilized, and are put into practice.[42] It asserts that symbolic forms, such as metaphors and gestures, and also more complex sequences such as rituals and ceremonies, have a vital function in this context.[43] It is important to stress that these symbolic forms are not just a façade hiding the "real" social or political agenda, but that they themselves constitute the form in which conceptions of values or order are embodied. In a sense, these forms produce the order they represent. Significantly, the way in which a corporation such as the *Corpus Evangelicorum* makes its decisions, i.e., *how* it reaches these decisions, has an influence on *what* it decides.

Symbolic communication and legitimation by procedure are not unrelated concepts. As has been mentioned, the legitimizing function of a procedure lies in its expressive, symbolic, non-explicit dimension. One can call this the performativity of the decision.[44] Procedures, even if they are presented as being purely rational and object-centered as they are today, always have a specific symbolism. *How* (not just *what*) the United States Senate or the German *Bundestag* decides indicates a specific horizon of social and political values. In addition, it strongly influences the outcome of the legislative procedure. Barbara Stollberg-Rilinger has coined the phrase: "ceremony as political procedure."[45] These two aspects should be kept in mind in the following analysis.

The Internal Procedure of the *Corpus Evangelicorum*

The internal procedure of the Protestant *Corpus* differed clearly from the rest of the political affairs at the *Reichstag*. Gradually, particular rules for how and what should be discussed at the *Corpus* and a particular basic law, the *Principia Evangelicorum*, developed.[46] Thus, as an interaction system, each individual case was pre-structured: the way in which a decision was reached (the procedure) and the material foundation (the law) were specified. The participants—the members of the *Corpus*, the plaintiffs, and, to a lesser extent, their Catholic adversaries—assumed their respective roles, became increasingly involved in the proceedings, and by their statements and actions bound themselves to a certain degree. Accordingly, they could not retract their declarations and acts without losing face. Thus, gradually over time, the participants became bound by the history of the case, which reduced complexity and itself became a determining factor of the procedure. Niklas Luhmann, who described these mechanisms in *Legitimation durch Verfahren*, refers to this phenomenon as "*Verstrickung*," or entanglement, which is a telling term for a highly complex issue.[47]

The *Corpus*, in accordance with the norms established by the Peace of Westphalia, rejected the majority vote in religious affairs at the *Reichstag* as a whole; however, it did postulate the majority vote for its internal decision-making in order to ensure its autonomy against the Catholics, who demanded Protestant unanimity for an *itio in partes*.[48] This would have meant that one single dissenting Protestant *Reichsstand* could have prevented the *itio*, which would have rendered it inefficacious; this, of course, was the goal of the Catholic argumentation.

However, for various reasons, the Protestants almost never practiced the internal majority vote. Majority rule requires, at least in principle, the voters' equality, and thus in a society of status and rank, it provides legitimacy only within very narrow limits.[49] This was true for the *Corpus*, especially because it did not have the leveling structure of a college. The huge discrepancy in power between Prussia and the imperial city of Ulm or the count of Wied-Runkel, for instance, is obvious. In addition, there was the problem that some *Reichsstände* combined several *vota*. Prussia, for example, spoke not only for Kurbrandenburg, but also for Magdeburg, Halberstadt, Eastern Pomerania, Minden, Kammin, and East Frisia.[50] Sachsen-Gotha also had several votes, while other polities did not.[51] So the rule of "one territory, one vote" would not have been useful in the *Corpus*. Moreover, it is clear that single, powerful states, such as the big three, Brandenburg-Prussia, Hanover-England, and Saxony-Poland, would not have yielded to majorities against their self-estimation as quasi sovereign powers.

In practice, the *Corpus* adopted the rule of the *Reichsräte* and used the *Umfrage* procedure, which meant that the director asked for the members' votes.[52] The order of the votes was based on status and rank. First, Saxony introduced the proposition, and then electoral Brandenburg and Brunswick-Hanover gave their opinion. Afterward came Sachsen-Gotha, Ansbach-Bayreuth, and so on. And so the *Umfrage* demonstrated *in actu* the hierarchy of the empire, at least its Protestant part, because the Catholic *Reichsstände*, who would have had their turn in the three colleges of the diet, were simply left out.[53] Altering the order of the votes arbitrarily was not allowed; and, making one's statement before one's turn would have been deemed inappropriate.[54]

In the end, the director summed up the discussion, which generally meant finding some common ground on which to base the decision. This was because the *Umfrage*, in contrast to modern parliamentary procedures, did not distinguish between deliberation and decision. Giving one's opinion meant voting; there was no clear-cut question that could be answered simply with yes or no. The director briefly introduced the topic and then asked the other envoys to give their superiors' opinion about it and to make suggestions of how the *Corpus* should act in the case.[55] The director had to find a consensus, which meant bringing the matter to a common resolution that took into account the divergent interests and considerations of the various members of the *Corpus*.[56]

A director's job was not always easy, as the famous *Reichspublizist* Johann Jakob Moser points out for the regular colleges of the diet. He relates how some of the envoys had complained that their votes had been misunderstood.[57] This raised the question of whether the envoys' own interpretation or the director's interpretation should be the basis of the decision, illustrating the director's difficult position.[58]

The need to produce consensus sometimes necessitated a second or third *Umfrage* during the same session, if the votes were too ambiguous or divergent or if the later *vota* might introduce new aspects or arguments, which, in the director's eyes, should be taken into consideration.[59] For many reasons, the pressure for consensus was quite strong. First, as Georg Simmel has pointed out, a minority opinion was considered immoral and unjust, a view that harked back to archaic times.[60] Second, the legitimacy of the *Corpus*, to a certain degree, lay in its internal cohesion. As we have seen, the Catholics demanded that the *vota communia* of the Protestants be unanimous. And most crucially, dissenting opinions made it obvious that decisions were contingent and could be made differently.[61] Thus, in this context it was advantageous to speak with one voice. Furthermore, because the *Corpus* had no proper means of executing its decisions beyond what the members were willing to provide, it would not have been clever to overrule a state whose assistance afterward would be necessary or at least helpful in its execution.

For these reasons, the votes were not counted, but weighed.[62] Before the director summed up the conclusion, he tried to generate consensus by asking the envoys a second or a third time. Sometimes this decision was delayed. The ideal of unanimity implied that, when a consensus could not be achieved, the minority aligned itself to the majority. This can be referred to as an "obscured majority vote," in the words of Heinrich Mitteis.[63] Once the decision was reached, a *Reichsstand*, whose opinion had not prevailed, could refuse to take part in the *Conclusum Corporis* when it considered certain limits to have been transgressed. In its role as an individual *Reichsstand*, for instance, Saxony abstained from the Protestant *votum commune* that was to hinder the ban against Frederick the Great in 1758, but drew up the conclusions in its role as *director corporis*.[64] Thus, on the one hand, there was the principle of consensus, and, on the other hand, the theory—but hardly ever the practice—of majority rule, a principle that indicates autonomy of procedure.

The consensus-seeking *Umfrage* and the fact that the representatives in Regensburg had to wait for instructions from their superiors rendered the procedure lengthy and cumbersome. Decisions frequently had to be delayed because an envoy, especially when he belonged to the *potentiores*, had not been instructed. To some degree, it was always possible to protract the whole process under the pretext of lacking instructions.[65]

In addition to these impediments to collective decision-making, the *Corpus*'s means of enforcing its decisions were weak. Conflicts remained unresolved for decades, and in the end, there was often only scant progress for the oppressed municipalities—if any. We certainly can note some success in the Palatinate crisis or in the case of Hohenlohe in 1750, but dozens of intercessions with the emperor, each of which reiterated dozens of *Gravamina* that had remained in suspension for years, illustrate the *Corpus*'s ineffectiveness.[66]

The merely instrumental dimension does not suffice to explain this inefficacy. Certainly, the Protestants were afraid of a new religious war, but we also should take a look at the strategies of the different Protestant *Reichsstände*. Very often, the *Corpus* was afraid of offending the emperor. The elector of Saxony and king of Poland, for example, certainly was very cautious not to ruin his good relationship with Vienna, but he also had to keep an eye on his reputation among his Protestant coreligionists, and therefore tried to play down the disputes. In the Saxon sources, we often find present the fear of "complications" (*Weitläufftigkeiten*) and "scruples about dangers and risks" (*Bedencklichkeiten*).[67] For this reason, the Saxon envoy very often sought to avoid or at least delay decisions. Altogether, confessional solidarity, the dualism of Habsburg versus Hohenzollern, antagonism between the estates and the monarchy, and conflicts of minor importance reinforced each other in various combinations.[68] Too many interests had to be taken into consideration and thus could not be consistently integrated.

The plaintiffs' chances of influencing the procedure were limited. Their strategy usually consisted of issuing incessant supplications for the envoys to deal with their case, keeping the procedure alive, or reanimating it. In their argumentation, we can find a strategy of adulation, submissiveness, and the search for compassion, which were all adequate for dealing with an *Obrigkeit*. In addition, unequivocal rights were stressed and the Peace of Westphalia was invoked. There was thus, on the one hand, a rhetoric consistent with a hierarchical society of status and rank, but, on the other, a desire to argue on a legal basis to which the *Corpus* felt bound.[69]

Often the underlying conflict involved economic, political, dynastic, or even personal interests, which were camouflaged in the petitions by religious matters. Sometimes this was a highly idealistic abstraction. Moreover, the underlying judicial norms themselves were not always unequivocal. First, the Westphalian rules frequently interfered with accords within a princely house or with hereditary pacts that themselves were not always exact. Second, the status of the normative year was questionable. Did the Catholic service in 1624 take place in the church or only in the private chapel of the castle? Who could answer that question with certainty a hundred years later? We must recognize that the petitions that were composed by lawyers or clerics provided a façade of rationality, reducing complex issues to the simple formula of the *annus normalis*.[70]

As shown above, in order to generate a motivation to participate, a procedure has to be—or at least must appear to be—initially open. This was the case with the *Corpus Evangelicorum*. The hope of realizing their goals with the help of the *Corpus* was, in the plaintiffs' eyes, sufficient motivation to engage in the procedure. This did not entail any significant risk because the *Corpus* was their last chance anyway: petitions to or negotiations with the Catholic ruler had already led to nothing; sometimes the imperial courts had already decided against them as well. Nevertheless, there are examples of municipalities that were deeply dissatisfied with the outcome of the procedure, but they became isolated and without other avenues to obtain their requests.[71] When it could not succeed in convincing its coreligionists to accept the result of the procedure, the *Corpus* refused any further assistance to those municipalities.[72] Although the decision was not in their favor, the concerned municipalities performed a vital function in the procedure as a whole. By playing their part in the game, they not only acknowledged the procedure as legitimate despite the disappointing result, but also represented it as legitimate in the public forum by participating in the ceremony.

In its public representation, the *Corpus* erected a façade of rationality by publishing its official writings in formal collections.[73] The genesis of the corporate conclusions—the informal discussions among the envoys, the formal statements in the sessions, the communication with the courts, and so forth—was rendered invisible, which facilitated their acceptance.

Finally, what should we make of the fact that the intercessions of the Protestant group were, as a rule, unsuccessful, but that it nevertheless continued unremittingly to address new (and old!) grievances to the Catholic *Reichsstände* and the emperor? Was it the particularly bureaucratic delight in producing endless files that was crucial here?[74]

Here, it is useful to consider the distinction between the instrumental and the expressive dimensions of social interactions. From an instrumental perspective, the aims of the *Corpus* were not realized. However, we can assume that the prime function of these interactions was the symbolic dimension. The *telos* of the official intercessions was not primarily their success—the *Corpus* knew that this would hardly be the case—but a direct, satisfying, and ostentatious self-assertion. In this context, the central point was to underline the *Corpus*'s interpretation of the religious constitution of the empire. The aim was less the attainment of the specific goal than expressing its own perception of what was just and unjust and what should or should not be.

This leads to a final hypothesis. Leaving aside the effective instrumentalization of the *Corpus* by Brandenburg-Prussia on several occasions, for example, in the Palatine crisis or in the run-up to the Seven Years' War, we have to say that, in terms of its instrumental effect, the procedure turned out to be relatively ineffective. It thus appears that one (of course not the only) reason for the existence of the *Corpus Evangelicorum* was to symbolically communicate Protestant parity in the empire. The *Corpus* in itself was a symbol of Protestant equality with the Catholic party.

Conclusion

With the help of the sociological theory of "legitimation by procedure," it is possible to re-approach the *Corpus Evangelicorum* and to analyze how decisions in the *Corpus* were made and how the different strategies of the Protestant *Reichsstände* fit into this procedure. Whereas Saxony generally tried to play down the disputes and attempted to avoid or at least delay decisions leading to intercessions and thus to *Weitläufftigkeiten* with the emperor and the Catholic party, Prussia often wanted to accelerate the procedure in order to gain support from the other Protestant *Reichsstände*. The pressure for consensus usually prevented the feared escalation and reduced the interests to their lowest common denominator.

The approach of "legitimation by procedure" also helps to explain why the Catholic side avoided interacting formally with the *Corpus*. The Catholics avoided any official contact with the *Corpus Evangelicorum*, whose Catholic counterpart became visible almost only during an *itio in partes*. The Catholic side, along with the emperor, did not want to become engaged in a procedure that it did not acknowledge. It avoided participating in the procedure and consequently avoided legitimating the *Corpus* and its procedure.

We probably have to see the procedure of the *Corpus Evangelicorum* as transitional. In many ways, it adhered to the social rationality of a pre-modern society of status and rank. Every *Umfrage* reasserted the hierarchy of the empire, because the order of the votes mirrored that of the *Reichstag*, except that the *Corpus* did not have three colleges or any Catholic votes. By following the common order of the votes, the *Corpus* referred to the empire as a whole and confirmed it. On the other hand, with the assertion, although rarely enforced, of majority rule and some traces of an autonomous procedure, a few characteristics of a Luhmannian procedure are visible.

This essay has also tried to bring together "legitimation by procedure" and "symbolic communication." The symbolic dimension of social interactions, whose fundamental function for a legitimate procedure has been stressed, is also the keystone of the latter. In this regard, the *Corpus* should be seen as an expressive symbol of Protestant parity in the Holy Roman Empire of the German Nation.

Notes

1. The term *Reichsstand* (plural: *Reichsstände*) signifies an individual territorial authority as member of the empire and of the imperial diet.
2. See Andrew C. Thompson, *Britain, Hanover and the Protestant Interest, 1688–1756* (Studies in Early Modern Cultural, Political and Social History, 3) (Woodbridge, 2006).
3. Johann Jacob Moser, *Von der Teutschen Religionsverfassung* (*Neues teutsches Staatsrecht*, 7) (Frankfurt and Leipzig, 1774; reprint, Osnabrück, 1967), 341–342: "Die versammlete samtliche Evangelische Stände des Reichs von beeden Parthien machen ein einiges und gewohnlicher, das *Corpus* derer Reichs-Stände aus, welches das *Corpus* Evangelicum, oder besser und gewohnlicher, das *Corpus* Evangelicorum, genannt wird."
4. IPO Art. V, § 1, in Karl Zeumer, ed., *Quellensammlung zur Geschichte der deutschen Reichsverfassung in Mittelalter und Neuzeit, Von Maximilian I. bis 1806* (Tübingen, 2nd ed., 1913), 403.
5. Martin Heckel, "Itio in partes. Zur Religionsverfassung des Heiligen Römischen Reichs Deutscher Nation," in *Zeitschrift der Savigny-Stiftung für Rechtsgeschichte, Kanonistische Abteilung* 64 (1978): 180–308.
6. IPO Art V § 52.
7. See Ulrich Belstler, *Die Stellung des Corpus Evangelicorum in der Reichsverfassung* (Bamberg, 1968), 114, 143.
8. Johann Adam Ickstatt, quoted in Heckel, "Itio in partes," 273.

9. See for example the "Votum commune Evangelicorum, 27 October 1727," in Eberhard Christian Wilhelm von Schauroth, *Vollständige Sammlung aller Conclusorum, Schreiben und anderer übrigen Verhandlungen des hochpreißlichen Corporis Evangelicorum von Anfang des jetzt fürwährenden hochansehnlichen Reichs-Convents bis auf die gegenwärtigen Zeiten. Nach Ordnung der Materien zusammengetragen*, 3 vols. (Regensburg, 1751–1752), here III: 879–889, esp. 880.
10. The confessionally divergent interpretations of the religious constitution of the empire, which are much more complex and cannot be described in detail here, have been lucidly examined, for example, by Martin Heckel, Klaus Schlaich, Gabriele Haug-Moritz, and others. Heckel, "Itio in partes"; Klaus Schlaich, "Maioritas—protestatio—itio in partes—Corpus Evangelicorum. Das Verfahren im Reichstag des Hl. Römischen Reiches Deutscher Nation nach der Reformation," in *Zeitschrift der Savigny-Stiftung für Rechtsgeschichte, Kanonistische Abteilung*, 63 (1977): 264–299, and 64 (1978): 139–179; Lothar Weber, *Die Parität der Konfessionen in der Reichsverfassung von den Anfängen der Reformation bis zum Untergang des alten Reiches im Jahre 1806* (Bonn, 1961). Regarding the *Corpus Evangelicorum*, see Fritz Wolff, *Corpus Evangelicorum und Corpus Catholicorum auf dem Westfälischen Friedenskongreß. Die Einfügung der konfessionellen Ständeverbindungen in die Reichsverfassung* (Schriftenreihe der Vereinigung zur Erforschung der neueren Geschichte e.V., 2) (Münster, 1966); Belstler, *Corpus Evangelicorum*; Gabriele Haug-Moritz, *Württembergischer Ständekonflikt und deutscher Dualismus. Ein Beitrag zur Geschichte des Reichsverbands in der Mitte des 18. Jahrhunderts* (Veröffentlichungen der Kommission für geschichtliche Landeskunde in Baden-Württemberg, Reihe B, Forschungen, vol. 122) (Stuttgart, 1992); Haug-Moritz, "Kaisertum und Parität. Reichspolitik und Konfessionen nach dem Westfälischen Frieden," in *Zeitschrift für historische Forschung* 19 (1992): 445–482; and Haug-Moritz, "*Corpus* Evangelicorum und deutscher Dualismus," in *Alternativen zur Reichsverfassung in der Frühen Neuzeit?*, ed. Volker Press (Schriftenreihe des Historischen Kollegs, Kolloquien, 23) (Munich, 1995), 189–207.
11. Haug-Moritz, "Kaisertum und Parität," 474.
12. "Vorstellungsschreiben an den Kaiser, 16 November 1720," in Schauroth, *Vollständige Sammlung II*, 759–808, here 788; "Kommissionsdekret, 12 April 1720," in Schauroth, *Vollständige Sammlung II*, 641–655; "Kommissionsdekret, 21 January 1752," in Schauroth, *Vollständige Sammlung III*, 965–971.
13. Gabriele Haug-Moritz, "Des 'Kaysers rechter Arm': Der Reichshofrat und die Reichspolitik des Kaisers," in *Das Reich und seine Territorialstaaten im 17. und 18. Jahrhundert. Aspekte des Mit-, Neben- und Gegeneinander* (Historia profana et ecclesiastica, 10), ed. Harm Klueting and Wolfgang Schmale (Münster, 2004), 23–42.
14. Haug-Moritz, "Kaisertum und Parität," 445–482.
15. The Peace of Ryswick (1697) between France and the empire, which ended the Nine Years' War (1688–1697), settled the succession in the Palatinate. The fourth clause of the treaty provided that the churches re-Catholicized by the French during the war had to remain so (in parts of the Palatinate west of the Rhine and in parts of the Duchy of Zweibrücken). The Protestants protested against this clause and wanted it to be abolished because it was a contravention of the normative year. The emperor and the Catholics, who were secretly pleased with the clause, blamed French pressure. In their eyes, an abolition of the clause was not achievable or desirable. See Karl Otmar von Aretin, *Das Alte Reich 1648–1806. II., Kaisertradition und österreichische Großmachtpolitik: 1684–1745* (Stuttgart, 1997), 41–51. It is not accidental that a separate hold-

ing of the *Corpus*'s files in the Hauptstaatsarchiv in Dresden commences in 1697, when the Ryswick treaty was concluded.

16. "Kaiserliches Kommissionsdekret, 12 April 1720," in Schauroth, *Vollständige Sammlung II*, 641–655, here 643; It was unheard of that: "erstlich unter sich, hernach unter dem Namen eines Corporis von einem Theil des Reichs zusammen gegangen und unter sich beständige, bis zu verbothenen unzeitigen Unionen oder Bündnüssen, gegen ihre Mit-Stände eingegangen würden, die nichtige Conclusa unter sich gemachet." The *Corpus* can be counted among the "in denen Reichs-Satzungen nicht gebilligte[n] Uniones," ibid., 649.
17. Moser, *Von der Teutschen Religionsverfassung*, 341–351, shows that the term *Corpus* was commonly used, even by the Catholics, before 1720.
18. "Kommissionsdekret, 12 April 1720," in Schauroth, *Vollständige Sammlung II*, 644–655, here 645.
19. Aretin, *Alte Reich II*, 263–295.
20. Belstler, *Corpus Evangelicorum*, 227–235.
21. Jürgen Luh, *Unheiliges Römisches Reich. Der konfessionelle Gegensatz 1648 bis 1806* (Quellen und Studien zur Geschichte und Kultur Brandenburg-Preußens, 1) (Potsdam, 1995), 62–63.
22. The *Kreisausschreibende* were considered to have authority in cases regarding the maintenance of the Peace of Westphalia. Belstler, *Corpus Evangelicorum*, 231.
23. Belstler, *Corpus Evangelicorum*, 231.
24. Moser tries in vain to define the *Corpus*'s portfolio. Moser, *Von der Teutschen Religionsverfassung*, 386–387:
Die Materie, wovon bey offtgemeldeten Conferentien gehandelt wird, seynd alle Sachen, welche das Evangelische Religions-Wesen in dem Reich, oder auch sonst das gemeinsame Interesse derer Evangelischen Reichs-Stände, oder auch übrigen Evangelischen im Reich, mittelbar oder unmittelbar betreffen, und entweder von ein oder anderem Stand oder Glid des Reichs selbsten bey dem Corpore anhängig gemacht, oder welche von dem Directorio, oder anderen Ständen, dafür angesehen werden, daß es die Nothdurfft erfordere, sich derselbigen ex officio und unersucht anzunehmen.
Moser's pseudo-precision cannot conceal the fact that this definition was empty and that the competence of the *Corpus* was highly arbitrary.
25. For example, the confessional conflict in the principality of Nassau-Siegen was pending at the *Corpus* from 1707 to 1725. See Andreas Kalipke, "'Weitläufftigkeiten' und 'Bedencklichkeiten'—die Behandlung konfessioneller Konflikte am *Corpus* Evangelicorum," in *Zeitschrift für historische Forschung* 35 (2008): 405–447; and Luh, *Unheiliges Römisches Reich*, 28–29.
26. Karl Otmar von Aretin, *Das Alte Reich 1648–1806. I.: Föderalistische oder hierarchische Ordnung*, (Stuttgart, 1993), 44–48.
27. Wolff, *Corpus Evangelicorum und Corpus Catholicorum*, 191–198.
28. Luh, *Unheiliges Römisches Reich*, 28–29.
29. Moser, *Von denen Teutschen Reichstagsgeschäfften, I* (*Neues Teutsches Staatsrecht*, 4, 1) (Frankfurt a.M., 1768; reprinted, Osnabrück, 1967), 442, deplores the situation in 1768: "Die alte Beschwerden werden nicht abgethan, die neue lässet man alt werden, und machet beständig neue. Alle Klagen und Vorstellungen, alle Tractaten haben nichts gefruchtet, und werden besorglich auch künfftig nichts fruchten."
30. Religious affairs inside the Electorate of Saxony were to be treated by the *Geheime Rat*, his privy council.

31. Jochen Vötsch, *Kursachsen, das Reich und der mitteldeutsche Raum zu Beginn des 18. Jahrhunderts* (Frankfurt a.M., 2003), 78–108, here 79: "Der Übertragung des Direktoriums des C.E. auf den Herzog von Sachsen-Weißenfels kommt damit lediglich formaler Charakter zu – in Verbindung mit der geheimen Nebeninstruktion für das Geheime Ratskollegium vom 21.12.1697 lag die Entscheidungsbefugnis letztlich weiterhin bei dem nunmehr katholischen Kurfürsten von Sachsen." Concerning the directorship, see also the earlier work of Adolf Frantz, *Das Katholische Directorium des Corpus Evangelicorum. Nach handschriftlichen Quellen dargestellt* (Marburg, 1880), 51: The Weißenfelsian expedient was "ziemlich illusorischer Natur, da Alles in Dresden ausgearbeitet und expedirt wurde."
32. Frantz, *Das katholische Directorium*, 137–168; and Vötsch, *Kursachsen*, 119–147.
33. Moser, *Von der Teutschen Religionsverfassung*, 370–376.
34. The term "petition" is used here and hereafter in a very general meaning, as Lex Heerma van Voss put it in his Introduction to Voss, ed., *Petitions in Social History* (Cambridge, New York and Melbourne, 2001), 1–10, here 1: "Petitions are demands for a favour, or for the redressing of an injustice, directed to some established authority." "Petition" is used to cover the terms used in the sources such as "Memorial," "Beschwerde," "Imploration," "Supplices," "Gravamina," "Vorstellung," and others.
35. Luh, *Unheiliges Römisches Reich*; and Frank Kleinehagenbrock, "Die Erhaltung des Religionsfriedens. Konfessionelle Konflikte und ihre Beilegung im Alten Reich nach 1648," in *Historisches Jahrbuch* 126 (2006): 135–156.
36. Niklas Luhmann, *Legitimation durch Verfahren* (Neuwied am Rhine, Berlin, 1969); see also the relevant passages in Luhmann, *Rechtssoziologie*, 2 vols. (Hamburg, 1972), esp. 1: 141–145 and 2: 263–266; Luhmann, *Das Recht der Gesellschaft* (Frankfurt a.M., 1995), esp. 207–211, 260–264, 332–333. See also the research concept of the Leibniz-Project "Vormoderne Verfahren" of Barbara Stollberg-Rilinger: http://www.uni-muenster.de/Geschichte/hist-sem/NZ-G/L1/leibniz_projekt.html (accessed 21 May 2008); and Uwe Goppold, *Politische Kommunikation in den Städten der Vormoderne. Zürich und Münster im Vergleich* (Cologne, Weimar, and Vienna, 2007), 31–34.
37. It can be shown that the main problem in the trial against Charles I of England was that he refused to take on the role of the accused. In his behavior, he showed that he was not at all willing to be part of the trial but still regarded himself as the legitimate king. See André Krischer, *State Trials. Die Genese des modernen Strafverfahrens* (forthcoming).
38. In contrast to procedure, negotiation is a way of making decisions based on consent. See Matthias Köhler, "Formalität—Repräsentation—Kalkül. Verhandlungen auf dem Kongress von Nimwegen, 1676–1679," in *Herstellung und Darstellung verbindlicher Entscheidungen. Legitimation in vormodernen und modernen Gesellschaften*, eds. Barbara Stollberg-Rilinger and André Krischer (Berlin, 2010).
39. Luhmann, *Legitimation durch Verfahren*, 28.
40. Luhmann, *Legitimation durch Verfahren*, 223–232.
41. Programmatic for the early modern period is Barbara Stollberg-Rilinger's "Die zeremonielle Inszenierung des Reiches, oder: Was leistet der kulturalistische Ansatz für die Reichsverfassungsgeschichte?" in *Imperium Romanum—irregulare Corpus—Teutscher Reichs-Staat. Das Alte Reich im Verständnis seiner Zeitgenossen und der Historiographie*. (Veröffentlichungen des Instituts für europäische Geschichte Mainz, Abt. Universalgeschichte, Beiheft, 57), ed. Matthias Schnettger (Mainz, 2002), 233–246. Important as well is Rudolf Schlögl, "Symbole in der Komunikation. Zur Einführung," in *Die*

Wirklichkeit der Symbole. Grundlagen der Kommunikation in historischen und gegenwärtigen Gesellschaften, eds. Rudolf Schlögl, Bernhard Giesen, and Jürgen Osterhammel. Historische Kulturwissenschaft, vol. 1 (Konstanz, 2004), 9–38.

42. The research theme of symbolic communication has been significantly developed by the collaborative research centers "Symbolic Communication and Social Value Systems from the Middle Ages to the French Revolution" in Münster and "Norm and Symbol" in Konstanz: http://www.unimuenster.de/SFB496/forschungsprogramm.html (accessed 21 May 2008); http://www.uni-konstanz.de/FuF/sfb485/Forschungsprogramm.htm (accessed 21 May 2008).

43. Barbara Stollberg-Rilinger, "Zeremoniell als politisches Verfahren. Rangordnung und Rangstreit als Strukturmerkmale des früneuzeitlichen Reichstags," in *Neue Studien zur frühneuzeitlichen Reichsgeschichte,* ed. Johannes Kunisch (Berlin, 1997), 91–132.

44. See André Krischer, "Inszenierung und Verfahren auf den Reichstagen der Frühen Neuzeit. Das Beispiel der Städtekurie und ihres politischen Verfahrens," in Gerald Schwedler, Jörg Peltzer, and Paul Többelmann, eds., *Versammlungen. Ritualisierungen politischer Willensbildung im Vergleich,* (Sigmaringen, 2010, forthcoming).

45. Stollberg-Rilinger, "Zeremoniell als politisches Verfahren."

46. Haug-Moritz, "Kaisertum und Parität," 474, shows how the Protestants developed a coherent alternative to the status quo during the confessional quarrels regarding the Palatinate. Regarding these *Principia Evangelicorum,* see "Vorstellungsschreiben an den Kaiser, 16 November 1720," in Schauroth, *Vollständige Sammlung II,* 759–808.

47. Luhmann, *Legitimation durch Verfahren,* 87, "Vermutlich ist dies die heimliche Theorie des Verfahrens: daß man durch Verstrickung in ein Rollenspiel die Persönlichkeit einfangen, umbilden und zur Hinnahme von Entscheidungen motivieren könne."

48. Schlaich, "Maioritas" II, 155. The Protestant *Reichspublizistik* also postulated the majority vote for the *Corpus.* See Belstler, *Corpus Evangelicorum,* 62.

49. Schlaich, "Maioritas," 283–285.

50. "Chur-Brandenburg vertritt Magdeburg, Halberstadt, Hinter-Pommern, Minden, Camin und Ostfrießland," HStADD, Geheimes Konsilium, Loc. 5143, Acta die Dierdorffer Religions Beschwerden betr., Anno 1755seqq., vol. I, fol. 32r.

51. Ibid.

52. For the *Umfrage* procedure at the *Corpus Evangelicorum* see Andreas Kalipke, "Verfahren—Macht—Entscheidung. Die Behandlung konfessioneller Streitigkeiten durch das *Corpus* Evangelicorum im 18. Jahrhundert aus verfahrensgeschichtlicher Perspektive," in Stollberg-Rilinger and Krischer, *Herstellung und Darstellung*; and Tim Neu, "Inszenieren und Beschließen. Symbolisierungs- und Entscheidungsleistungen der Landtage im Fürstbistum Münster," in *Westfälische Forschungen* 57 (2007): 257–284.

53. Stollberg-Rilinger, "Die zeremonielle Inszenierung des Reiches," 244; Moser, *Von der Teutschen Religionsverfassung,* 384: "In disen Conferentien der Evangelischen wird ferner in dem Sizen und Umfragen kein Rang beobachtet." Although the *Corpus* did not have the college structure, the Saxon minutes demonstrate that the order of the votes corresponded to the one at the diet. That is also why the Saxon records initially have hints, such as "*Inter Alternantes Stropha prima*" or "*Inter Altenantes Stropha secunda,*" etc.

54. Moser writes about the *Umfrage* at the imperial diet: "Ferner darff und solle niemand votiren, biß die Reyhe an ihn kommt, und er aufgeruffen wird, wann man nemlich nach einer ordentlichen Umfrage votirt." Moser, *Von Teutschen Reichs-Tägen (Neues*

Teutsches Staatsrecht, 6.2) (Frankfurt, Leipzig 1774) (reprinted, Osnabrück, 1967), 34.
55. Stollberg-Rilinger, "Zeremoniell als politisches Verfahren," 109. The director would ask, for example: "stellete hierauf die Sache selbst in Proposition, um zu vernehmen, was etwa hierbey ex parte Corporis vorzukehren für räthlich gefunden werden möchte?" "Evangelisches Konferenzprotokoll, 23 April 1755," HStADD, Geheimes Konsilium, Loc. 5143, Acta die Dierdroffer Religions-Beschwerden betr., 1755seqq., vol. I, fols. 32r–38v, here fol. 33r.
56. Consensus was the aim of the procedure. Stollberg-Rilinger, "Zeremoniell als politisches Verfahren," 110; see also Johannes Ludwig Schipmann, *Politische Kommunikation in der Hanse (1550–1621). Hansetage und westfälische Städte* (Quellen und Darstellungen zur hansischen Geschichte, N.F., 55) (Cologne, Weimar, and Vienna, 2004), 18–31; and Georg Schmidt, *Der Städtetag in der Reichsverfassung. Eine Untersuchung zur korporativen Politik der freien und Reichsstädte in der ersten Hälfte des 16. Jahrhunderts* (Veröffentlichungen des Instituts für europäische Geschichte Mainz, Abt. Universalgeschichte, 113/ Beiträge zur Sozial- und Verfassungsgeschichte des Alten Reiches, 5) (Stuttgart, 1984), 105–109.
57. Moser, *Von Teutschen Reichs-Tägen,* 86. These obvious misunderstandings could much more easily be revealed in the three colleges of the diet than in the *Corpus Evangelicorum,* because in the former, the votes could be compared with the official minutes. The *Corpus* did not have any official record.
58. Moser, *Von Teutschen Reichs-Tägen,* 87.
59. Moser, *Von Teutschen Reichs-Tägen,* 98. An example from the *Corpus Evangelicorum*: "Konferenzprotokoll, 23 April 1755," HStADD, Geheimes Konsilium, Loc. 5143, Acta die Dierdorfer Religions Beschwerden betr., Anno 1755 seqq., Vol. I, fols. 32r–38v.
60. Georg Simmel, "Exkurs über die Überstimmung," in Simmel, *Soziologie. Untersuchngen über die Formen der Vergesellschaftung,* ed. Otthein Rammstedt (Berlin, 1992) (Georg Simmel, Gesamtausgabe, 11), 218–228. Regarding the history of the majority vote, see Otto von Gierke, "Über die Geschichte des Majoritätsprinzipes," in *Schmollers Jahrbuch für Gesetzgebung, Verwaltung und Volkswirtschaft im Deutschen Reiche* 39 (1915): 7–29.
61. Similar problems can be cited for the diet of the imperial cities, the *Städtetag,* whose constitutional position was precarious as well. Schmidt, *Städtetag,* 105–109; and Niklaus Bütikofer, "Konfliktregulierung auf den Eidgenössischen Tagsatzungen des 15. und 16. Jahrhunderts," in *Parliaments, Estates and Representation* 11 (1991): 103–115.
62. Stollberg-Rilinger, "Zeremoniell als politisches Verfahren," 111.
63. "*verdeckter Mehrheitsentscheid.*" Heinrich Mitteis, *Die deutsche Königswahl. Ihre Rechtsgrundlagen bis zur Goldenen Bulle* (Vienna, 2nd ed., 1944; reprinted, Darmstadt, 1987), 169; and Kalipke, "Verfahren—Macht—Entscheidung."
64. Arthur Brabant, *Das Heilige Römische Reich teutscher Nation im Kampf mit Friedrich dem Großen.* Vol. 2: *Die Reichspolitik und der Feldzug in Kursachsen* (Berlin, 1911), 334–346, here 343; and Johann Jacob Moser, *Von der Evangelischen Reichsstände Collegial-Rechten, Besonders in Ansehung ihrer inneren Verfaßung. Zur Prüfung derer Riefelischen Betrachtungen darüber* (Regensburg, 1772), 26.
65. The Saxon envoy, von Ponickau, made sure that "sie [the chur-braunschweigian legation], um die bevorstehende Conferenz auf schickliche Art annoch zu hintertreiben, alles mögliche selbst versuchen wird, falls aber solches zu bewürcken ohnmöglich fallen sollte, die Sache durch den ihres Orths vorzuschüzenden Instructions-Mangel, unter

dem dißeitigen Beytritt und Zustimmung, in salvo zu erhalten gedenket.'"'Evangelische Relation, 11 August 1755," HStADD, Geheimes Konsilium, Acta die Dierdorfer Religions Beschwerden betr., Anno 1755 seqq., Vol. I, Loc. 5143, fols. 130r–135v, here fol. 135r.

66. Examples: "Schreiben an Ihro Röm. Kayserl. Majestät vom Corpore Evangelicorum sub dato 3. Aug. 1746. Die Religions-Gravamina im Reiche überhaupt betreffend," in Schauroth, *Vollständige Sammlung II*, 180–189; "Schreiben an Se. Römisch-Kaiserl. Majestät vom Corpore Evangelicorum d.d. 18. März 1767. sämtlicher im Reich fürwaltender Religions-Bedruckungen halber abgelassen, nebst einem summarischen Verzeichnisse der seit dem 17. May 1752. weiter neu eingelauffenen Religions-Beschwerden," in Nikolaus August Herrich, ed., *Sammlung aller Conclusorum, Schreiben und anderer Verhandlungen des hochpreißlichen Corporis Evangelicorum vom Jahre 1753 bis 1786. Als eine Fortsetzung des Schaurothischen Werks, nach Ordnung der Materien zusammengetragen* (Regensburg, 1786), 547–571.

67. "Evangelische Gesandtschaftsrelation, 17 January 1765," HStADD, Geheimes Konsilium, Loc. 5144, Acta der Evangelischen Gemeinde zu Cronenberg Religions- Beschwerden betr., Anno 1764seqq., Vol. I, , fols. 17r–19v, here fol. 18r ("Weitläufftigkeiten"); "Evangelische Gesandtschaftsrelation, 19 December 1765," HStADD, Geheimes Konsilium, Loc. 5144, Acta der Evangelischen Gemeinde zu Cronenberg Religions-Beschwerden betr., Anno 1764seqq., Vol. I, fols. 64r–71r, here fol. 67r ("Bedencklichkeiten"); and Kalipke, "Weitläufftigkeiten."

68. Haug-Moritz, "Kaisertum und Parität," 448, stresses the "hochgradige Atomisierung der Politik, die die Reichsstände, je nach anstehender Sachfrage in ständig wechselnden Parteiungen zusammenführte."

69. Very instructive is "Schreiben der evangelischen Bürgerschaft zu Cronenberg an das *Corpus* Evangelicorum, 27 October 1765," HStADD, Geheimes Consilium, Acta Der Evangelischen Gemeinde zu Cronenberg Religions-Beschwerden betr., Anno 1764seqq., Loc. 5144, Vol. I, , fols. 62r–63v passim.

70. The façade of rationality is a way of presenting petitions and decisions as just and not contingent upon anything. In the argumentation, some facts are stressed and others are overshadowed or left out. The scholarship has taken a closer look at this phenomenon, especially the research on organizations, which focuses on the social functions of hypocrisy and sense-making in retrospect in this context. See, for example, Günther Ortmann, "Katzensilber. Organisationsrituale und nachträgliche Sinnstiftung," in *Paragrana* 12 (2003): 539–556; Nils Brunsson, *The Organization of Hypocrisy. Talk, Decisions and Actions in Organizations* (Chichester, 1989).

71. It is important to stress that the *Corpus* did not investigate whether or not the petitions were substantiated before the procedure began. Only a few petitions that obviously were not qualified were rejected by the directorium in the very beginning. Moser, *Von der Teutschen Religionsverfassung*, 370–372. A discussion about the foundations of the grievances could take place during the procedure.

72. The municipality of Cronenberg, for instance, was dissatisfied with the result of the procedure, opposed it, and became isolated as a troublemaker. HStADD, Geheimes Konsilium, Loc. 5144: Acta Der Evangelischen Gemeinde zu Cronenberg Religions-Beschwerden betr., Anno 1764seqq.,Vol. I; and HStADD, Geheimes Konsilium, Lo. 5141: Acta Der Evangelischen Gemeinde zu Cronenberg Religions-Beschwerden betr., Anno 1771. Vol. II.

73. Schauroth, *Vollständige Sammlung* I-III; Herrich, *Sammlung aller Conclusorum*; Christian Gottfried Oertel, *Vollständiges Corpus Gravaminum Evangelicorum*, 8 Abtheilungen (Regensburg, 1771–1775); and Oertel, *Repertorium der gesammten Evangelischen Religions-Beschwerden, welche bey dem Hochpreißlichen Corpore Evangelicorum von 1720. bis 1770. theils fortgesetzt theils neuerlich angebracht worden sind, aus Archival-Acten gefertiget* (Regensburg, 1770).
74. As Jürgen Schlumbohm discusses for early modern legislation. Schlumbohm, "Gesetze, die nicht durchgesetzt werden—ein Strukturmerkmal des frühneuzeitlichen Staates?" in *Geschichte und Gesellschaft* 23 (1997): 647–663.

CHAPTER 14

Gallican Longings
Church and Nation in Eighteenth-Century Germany

MICHAEL PRINTY

Church and Nation in the Old Regime

In 1763, a canon law treatise by the suffragan bishop of Trier, Niklaus von Hontheim, took aim at the papal "monarchy" and accused the papacy and the curia of illegitimately accruing power and jurisdiction. Hontheim, writing under the pseudonym Febronius, argued that the pope should be granted only honorary primacy among bishops, and that the papacy had falsely acquired jurisdictional supremacy over the church through centuries of mistaken legal assumptions and even forgery. Hontheim asserted that the pope's "legitimate power" should be limited to a largely honorary primacy in the church. Much of the book dealt with the structures and laws of the church, while two chapters outlined a program for "recovering" the original "liberties" of the church.[1] "Scholars," Hontheim proclaimed, "ought to be considered the natural defenders of both the church and state."[2] This sentiment underpinned a broad German Catholic rethinking of the church in the eighteenth century.[3] From the outset, the Catholic reform program combined pious concern for religious renewal with intellectual engagement. Educated German Catholics did not see religion and reason as opposed—they sought instead to strengthen the bonds between them by rethinking and adapting the church to new times. As part of a broader Enlightenment in the Catholic world, eighteenth-century German Catholic intellectuals rethought the church in all of its aspects. In a series of efforts at practical reform, they imagined a church independent of, though still in communion with, Rome. This imagined church would be led by educated, "Enlightened" German Catholics in partnership with the state, and would solidify the links between religion, civilization, and morality.

The overarching argument motivating this essay is that confessional identities in the late eighteenth century grew out of the religious establishments of the later Holy Roman Empire and that, more importantly, these identities survived the collapse of the legal and institutional underpinnings that had been worked out in the Reformation settlements of the sixteenth century. Moreover, it can be argued that the Enlightenment was the agent of this transformation: in rethinking the relationship of Christianity to the state, civil society, notions of progress and human nature, and history, Germany's religious Enlightenment enabled the transition from what Christopher Ocker has called the "Holy Roman Empire of the two Churches" to the modern dilemma of competing Protestant and Catholic ideas of what it meant to be German, resulting in the creation of overlapping ideas of the nation that would play off one another for the next 150 years.[4] For Catholics, canon law and jurisprudence lay at the core of this process. I have labeled these reformist aspirations "Gallican" because the imagined reforms were predicated on a vision of legal autonomy for the German church that resembled an idealized version of the rights and privileges of the French Catholic church.

As is well known, German Protestantism in the eighteenth century underwent a radical rethinking, as the Lutheran orthodox establishment witnessed a decline in its prestige and power, as "neologians" reconceived core Christian doctrines in an effort to render Christianity more rational and "moral," and as religion itself had to contend for primacy with the rise of critical and then idealist philosophy for intellectual and cultural pre-eminence.[5] This was the intellectual context in which the idea of a German nation was actively rethought, and while scholars have been paying welcome attention to the importance of Protestant theology and philosophy to the evolution of German ideas of the nation, very little attention has been paid to the ferment within German Catholicism and its possible relation to the recasting of German ideas of the nation. But there was indeed a Catholic rethinking, and this essay will focus on German Catholicism in order to illuminate a different aspect of the religious role in the formation of national identity in Germany. Moreover, it will show how the empire and imperial structures were of intellectual significance to the very end of the empire, because it provided Catholics a structure around which they could imagine a new order for the church and its role for the nation. To do so, they looked especially to an idealized version of Gallican France and the legal privileges the French church enjoyed. Examining the Catholic reform movement, therefore, allows us to reconsider the way the empire could structure the political and religious imagination.

In order to best explain the nature and significance of this transformation, four principle points should be made up front. First, we may characterize this process as the emergence of an especially "German" Catholicism from a more diffuse "Baroque" Catholic culture present in early modern Europe. It is helpful to bear in mind that the "church" was conceived of as a totality. In Peter Hersche's words,

> Too often it is not sufficiently noticed that "church" in the early modern period cannot be reduced to apply only to "religion" and its ministers. "Church" was more: it served to demonstrate status, relationships and sociability. It was the major pillar of welfare, credit and education. Moreover, it was the only institution through which the culture of the upper classes also reached the common people. In the eyes of the laity, these profane functions were perhaps even more important than the strictly religious.[6]

Rethinking the church, therefore, meant much more than tinkering with the order of liturgy, training of the clergy, or devotion to a particular saint or cult. Rather, the church was a concept that could be both narrowly and legally defined, but which also made claims on the totality of social life. Catholic reformers and *Aufklärer* thereby grew out of and confronted a confessionally based culture that was woven throughout everything, from national economic and political life all the way down to the village and household level. This does not mean that everyone at the time perceived their relationships to confessional culture in such black and white terms. But such an overarching interpretation helps us conceptualize and synthesize a broad spectrum of changes and, at times, contradictory ideas and programs.

The second factor bearing on an explanation of the German Gallican program is its place in the chronology of the Catholic reform movement. Perceptible over the course of the century is a shift from a more harmonious, church-driven reform program at the head of which stood clergymen and theologians working in conjunction with secular authorities, to a sharper, more confrontational reform program after the middle to the end of the century. This was accompanied by a turn from Latin to the vernacular, a move that in itself showed, on the one hand, a turn toward the Protestant-dominated German public sphere—and therefore an appeal to membership in this notion of Germany—as well as a later, self-conscious assertion of specific German Catholic interests, on the other. Key to this change was the act of definition in public. We are dealing, in other words, with the specific form of the Enlightenment as public debate and discussion.[7]

Third, at the crux of this shift—from open-ended, harmonious reform, to more antagonistic and institutional definition—was law and jurisprudence. But just as there were two major categories of jurisprudence in early modern continental Europe (canon and civil law), so too could the jurisprudential thrust of reform writing situate itself in canon law or *Staats-* and *Reichsrecht*. The main part of this article will focus on the canonical aspect, because at play was the attempt of German churchmen to carve out autonomy for the German church from Rome, even though it will be indicated how the Gallican legal idea morphed into a broader conception of the nation. However, given the nature of the church as a social totality, it is important to keep in mind that civil and canon law—while separate in theory—occupied much overlapping and contested terrain. After all, many lawyers (including Hontheim) were educated in "both laws," and thus styled themselves *"iuris utriusque doctor."*

Finally, having unearthed this subterranean Gallicanism, it will be asked how this German Catholic story relates to the role of religion and religious establishments in old regime Europe in the formation of confessional and national identities that survived into the nineteenth century and beyond. What emerges is a tempered view of secularization that sees it not as a "subtraction story," in Charles Taylor's terms, but of creative re-imagining.[8] In contrast with earlier views, the formation of national identity is now seen as tied to (or at least compatible with) religion—both popular and institutional/ecclesiastical—and to have firmed up and taken shape in the period from 1648 to 1800. The assumption that the idea of the nation simply slid into or displaced an existing religious sense of belonging has been significantly qualified, if not completely overturned. Likewise, the idea that the end of the confessional wars witnessed a complete turnabout toward absolutism and rational state-building has been seriously revised.[9]

While this chapter is not about nationalism per se, it emerges from a general reconsideration of early modern ideas about the nation and their connection to later nationalist movements as such.[10] Modernist theories of nationalism, according to Philip Gorski, held that the phenomenon was a replacement for religion. These theories harbored modernizing and functionalist attitudes. Likewise, these older ideas also reflected uncritically the view that modernization and economic progress displaced religion, and that the Enlightenment could be so narrowly defined as to stand in for this practice, though to be sure these two tendencies have not always been explicitly linked.[11] A prominent statement reflecting the renewed emphasis on the importance of eighteenth-century religious establishments has been J.C.D. Clark's case for the centrality of the church to England's national identity during its "old regime" from 1660 to 1832.[12] In his view, "the Henrician union of church and state provide[d] a matrix with which a sense of normative ethical identity might ideally coincide with a political unit. It was the church, not the sects, which possessed both an institutional, legal expression and a clear sense of national identity."[13] But, if it is the case that older views downplaying religion have now been tempered, as Clark has done for England, what about the Holy Roman Empire?[14]

Of course, Germany has long held pride of place in discussions about the origins of modern nationalism, and no serious treatment of ideas of the nation can avoid the thought of Johann Gottfried Herder. As Helmut Walser Smith has recently noted, however, the sense of Germany as a nation was much older than the eighteenth century. Herder stood at the beginning of a new epistemology of the "discovery" of the nation, one tied to language and interiority. Preceding Herder, Smith argues, was the discovery of Germany as a "nation among other nations, as they are on maps," stretching back to the cartographical imagination of the sixteenth century.[15] By emphasizing how the linguistic turn in early modern German ideas of the nation displaced an already present sense of the nation, Smith enables us to ask what other possible models were at hand for the national imagination in eighteenth-century Germany. Reflecting the assertion of later German nationalism itself, most older scholarly treatments of the subject have operated under the assumption that Germany was a Protestant nation, and that the peculiarities of German Protestantism and its lack of a single state was also at the core of Germany's problematic nationalism. Germany lacked a national or state church, and was held together only by the empire. There were, of course, individual territorial churches, but without some type of national church, there would be no bones on to which to hang the flesh of confessional identity, leaving only Luther's bible and catechisms—the obvious bridge between religion and a language-based nationalism.[16]

But a reconsideration of German Catholicism and its Enlightenment in this period can show how Germany experienced developments similar to those in western Europe, where established churches formed the backbone of the national imagination. The problem can be formulated with reference to Christopher Ocker's aforementioned insight that the Reformation settlement resulted in the "Holy Roman Empire of the two Churches." If the church was seen in many European societies in the old regime as the foundation of the nation, what does it mean for subsequent German national identity that there were in fact two attempts—Protestant and Catholic—to define the nation in such a way that encompassed its religious underpinnings? Given the imbalance in the scholarly literature, the present chapter will consider the Catholic attempt, and will look at the problems of the Gallican idea of the nation. It should be borne in mind as well that this act of definition took place as German Protestants were constructing their own narrative, one that claimed that the Reformation resurrected German freedom.

German Gallicans: Canon Law and the Ancient Constitution of the Church

Hontheim's treatise—published the same year that the Seven Years' War came to an end—is often cited as the first salvo in the German Catholic Enlightenment, and was in many ways its most significant literary product. There was, however, no *direct* connection between the program of the pseudonymous Febronius for episcopalian autonomy from Rome and the later, practical reform programs of the Catholic Enlightenment in the 1780s and 1790s in such areas as liturgical reform or restraints on certain popular practices. On the other hand, the underlying concepts of *De statue ecclesiae*—the liberties of the German church and the papacy as an obstacle to German religious reunification—formed the basis upon which the German Catholic reform program would build.

If measured against the ambitions outlined by Hontheim's program, the Catholic Enlightenment in Germany was a failure, and that is usually how the movement is portrayed. Napoleon's destruction of the empire rendered obsolete any effort to strengthen the autonomy of the *Reichskirche*, while the rise of populist ultramontane Catholicism threatened the moderate sober religiosity of educated German Catholics. Nevertheless, in rethinking the church in the eighteenth century, German Catholics entered a new century of revolution and upheaval with a greater sense of identity and cohesion than they had possessed at the close of the seventeenth century. In recognizing that the church *could* be rethought in the eighteenth century, German Catholics were well prepared for the *task* of rebuilding it in the nineteenth century. An enduring legacy of the German Catholic Enlightenment, therefore, was the formulation of an entity that could survive the collapse of its own legal underpinnings—which was especially important given that most German Catholics were a political minority in the nineteenth century.

Hontheim's *De Statu* was not a wholly original work, in the sense that its major premises could be easily traced to other works in canon law and church history.[17] Although it precipitated a European-wide discussion, *De Statu* was in many ways a culmination of a series of historical and jurisprudential moves that soon grew into something larger than the author perhaps intended, rather than being a fundamentally new argument. Nor should we forget that its essential target was the papacy and its role in the universal church. "Febronianism," though growing out of intellectual and jurisdictional concerns of the German episcopate, applied just as well in theory to the Catholic episcopate in general. However, given that it called for increased authority for bishops, it was little suited to Gallican France or regalist Spain, where the monarchy already held significant control over the church. Nevertheless, denouncing and refuting Febronianism became a key act in any assertion of papal authority. Indeed, in 1799, Mauro Cappellari (the future Gregory XVI) wrote that the election of Pius VII—in spite of the death of Pius VI in Napoleonic captivity—represented a veritable "triumph of the Holy See" against the "assaults of the innovators."[18] For Cappellari, the continued succession of popes represented a divine retort to the Enlightenment, to revolutionary anti-clericalism, and especially to those Catholics who had called for autonomy from Rome throughout the eighteenth century.

Hontheim's work built on the German school of canon law, pioneered by Johann Kaspar Barthel (1697–1771).[19] Barthel emphasized the need for cooperation between secular and worldly authorities, and between the episcopate and the curia. In his 1762 *Historical-Canonical-Pragmatic Treatise...On the Concordat of the German Nation*, he noted that "the scope of this work is to defend the rights of the German nation while preserving the rights and authorities of the Roman pontiffs."[20] His collection served as a supplement for canonists who needed to know specifics about the canon law as applied to German conditions. Barthel and many of his generation wrote and acted in an age where compromise and accommodation between Rome and the national churches seemed possible.[21]

Barthel grafted German legal sensibility and conservatism onto the historical approach to Catholic church law. His method was not inherently anti-Roman: Barthel had studied under the greatest of the papal canonists (Benedict XIV), and he consciously sought the middle ground on disputed questions. However, as a practical matter, legal historicism in Germany had become linked to episcopalian politics. The sponsors of the historical and legal world were bishops and churchmen intent on establishing their legitimate independence from Roman influence. Much of their theology was inspired by Gallican legal theories of Pierre de Marca and Pierre Dupuy, who had elaborated and justified the rights and privileges enjoyed by the French church vis-à-vis Rome. There was, of course, a fundamental difference: the French episcopate was constituted as part of a unified French church, with the monarch at its head. The clergy made up one of the three estates in France, and the only one that was allowed to meet on a regular basis (though not in the form of a national synod). For all of that external glory, however, church and state were intertwined to such an extent in France that it can be plausibly asserted that the discrediting of that alliance over the course of the eighteenth century was a fundamental aspect in the ultimate fall of the monarchy.[22]

Soon after its publication, translations of Hontheim's book appeared in several languages (including German, French, and Italian). Subsequent editions were published with additions. The first edition was placed on the Index, and many notable Catholic theologians wrote refutations. Several prominent German theologians, notably Eusebius Amort and Martin Gerbert, were suspected of being the author of *De Statu*, based on their earlier works, though both quickly repudiated the arguments of *De Statu*.[23] Under intense pressure, Hontheim recanted in 1778, though he later issued an "explanation" of his recantation that, in fact, reconfirmed his original arguments. Febronianism as an ideology took on a scope far broader that the actual issues raised by Hontheim's book, galvanizing a cohort of German Catholics and laying the groundwork for the flowering of reform ideas and programs.[24]

The most notable outcome of Febronian ideas in the empire was the conference in 1786 of the four German metropolitans—the archbishop-electors of Trier, Cologne, and Mainz and the prince-archbishop of Salzburg—held at the German spa town of Ems. They hoped to form a coalition against the exercise of jurisdictional authority by papal nuncios in the empire. The political ambitions of each archbishop precluded any meaningful common action, especially since they did not have support of the other bishops of the empire, who saw little benefit in having papal "usurpations" replaced with increased control by their metropolitans. Papal diplomats skillfully exploited differences among German sovereigns and prelates, and did not hesitate to turn to Prussia for help. Like the empire itself, the constitution of the *Reichskirche* was eminently suited for factional politics and the dispersion of power; it did not aid in the creation of grand coalitions.

More important than the actual legal and constitutional changes wrought by Febronianism was the way in which the dispute shaped the consciousness of a generation of German Catholics. For them, the struggle for control was nothing less that a struggle over the organizing principles of culture and society, of church and nation. Hontheim had addressed the "doctors of theology and canon law," telling these teachers: "The state of the government of the church, as well as its vicissitudes, is due to you more than one thinks."[25] The canon lawyers and theologians were responsible for propagating a vision of the Catholic Church as a monarchy, a vision set forth in the classical collection of papal decrees that became the basis of canon law.[26] Hontheim laid the blame not only on the Curia and the partisans of the pope, but also on the learned men of Europe, because they came to study papal jurisprudence at Bologna, and then subsequently assumed positions of influence in civil and ecclesiastical institutions all over Europe.[27] This was a message that educated German Catholics were ready to hear. And while it was first through jurisprudence that the German Catholic reformers made their claims on the church, their reform program would soon become much more ambitious in scope. In 1773, following a wave of expulsions across Europe, the Jesuit order was suppressed worldwide by order of the pope, providing educated German Catholics with a perceived opening to remake the church.

From the *Reichskirche* to German Catholicism

In his recent grand survey of early modern Catholic culture and society, Peter Hersche makes a compelling case for using the baroque as an overarching conceptualization of Catholic culture, indeed, using it as a master category into which politics, religious practice, and style can be arranged. He thus appropriates the old charge that Catholicism fostered "leisure and waste" (*Muße und Verschwendung*), affirms it, and then proceeds to offer up that culture as a detailed counterpoint to European Protestant culture. An ambitious work, Hersche's survey represents an attempt to revisit and uproot the Weberian assumptions woven into the entire historiographical endeavor of confessional history. While such an ambitious argument will doubtless have its critics, Hersche's central insight—that Protestant and Catholic Europe in the early modern period formed two quite distinct confessional cultures—throws the concerns of the present article into sharp relief. Hersche concludes that the Catholic Enlightenment was a self-conscious rejection of the baroque (broadly construed), and that it was also confronted with a rival reforming movement originating within the church—a "reprise" of Trent.

Hersche's insight can be brought to bear specifically on the issues facing German Catholics in the last third of the eighteenth century. The suppression of the Jesuits gave Catholic intellectuals, now supported by either large dynastic states or independent ecclesiastical territories, an opportunity to redefine Catholicism. They mobilized ideas that were first formed in legal discourse, but also cast about more broadly for a definition of German Catholicism that differentiated it from a baroque culture that they increasingly associated with Italy and the Iberian peninsula. The Jesuits, having historically pioneered the introduction of many such baroque practices, served as ideological placeholders for a much wider assault on the baroque legacy in German Catholicism. At the heart of this attempt to refashion Catholicism in Germany on the part of educated German Catholics therefore lay a rejection of certain features of their religious heritage. If there were a unifying feature of the Catholic Enlightenment, not only in Germany, but also throughout Europe, it was in its anti-Jesuit impulse. In its turn away from the Jesuits, the *katholische Aufklärung* mirrored—albeit in less dramatic fashion—the assault on the Jesuits that was common to the European Enlightenment.

The Jesuits had played an important role in the formation of Catholic identity ever since the founding of the first colleges in Germany in the sixteenth century.[28] The society's activities in Germany ranged from rural missions to school theater, and eventually led to control of the education system. By the eighteenth century, every German Catholic university except Salzburg was run by the Society.[29] The Jesuits also established sodalities and Marian congregations that encouraged particular forms of devotion and communal religious practices. These congregations at first were intended for students at the colleges, but then grew to include large numbers of citizens and even rulers.[30] Finally, the Jesuits ran the German College in Rome, which was established in 1552 as a seminary for German priests.[31] As a Jesuit seminary, its goal was to educate pious, disciplined men, through rigorous spiritual practices.

In his four-volume *General History of the Jesuits*, Peter Philip Wolf asserted that the Jesuits "drove out the use of sound reason through their sensual religiosity, and implanted in the sensibilities of all Catholics an irresistible tendency toward enthusiasm and superstition [*unwiderstehlichen Hang zu Schwärmerey und Aberglauben*]."[32] Wolf was hardly unique in his strongly negative opinion of the Society of Jesus. In his account, the Jesuits exerted influence on all levels of society, from princely courts down to the common people. In Bavaria, the Fathers found a particularly potent tool in "the practically pagan and idolatrous" Marian devotion, which they initiated under Elector Maximilian I. Jesuit success only augmented their standing among German Catholics, who were led even further into superstition by the Fathers:

> One sees how the Catholics step-by-step were carried away by an extremely bigoted and superstitious devotionalism [*bigott- abergläubischen Andächtteley*] and how, during the Jesuit epoch, their religious practices became ever more tasteless and extravagant [*abgeschmackter und abentheuerlicher*]. It is therefore hardly surprising how, through such institutions, people were eventually led astray, forgot the simplicity of their religion, and slowly sank into the shadows of superstition. The enlightened Catholic, who had the misfortune to have been educated in Jesuit schools, will now shudder to look back on that path down which they led him during his schooling.[33]

Only recently, Wolf implies, has Catholicism escaped this dangerous path. The individual "enlightened Catholic" whom Wolf addresses stands for all German Catholics—or at least, so Wolf would desire. In this passage, Wolf expresses the hope that German Catholics will soon look back at their own religious and devotional history and shake their heads in shame.

Central to Wolf's story is the denial of the importance of Jesuits to Catholic survival. He argues that the old orders (such as the Benedictines) could just as well have served as a bulwark of Catholicism if their wealth and property had not been transferred to Jesuit colleges.[34] It is significant that he mentions the Benedectines because the Order of Saint Benedict was very active in the Catholic Enlightenment and represented an alternative vision of the German church—one that was stable and locally bound. While the Catholic Enlightenment in its more radical expressions was highly critical of monasticism, Wolf here argues that the enlightened Catholic: "will ... be convinced that, by far and wide, the monks were nowhere nearly as harmful to the religion of the people as the Jesuits were. Just as the monks could not affect every class [*Stände*] in the same way as the Jesuits, so, too, were the monks not as experienced in the art of ... forcing their superstitious rubbish on people [*ihren abergläubischen Kram aufzudringen*]."[35]

Once educational reformers met resistance on the part of an entrenched Society of Jesus, their antipathy grew. The imagined alternative to Jesuit education, however, was not lay teachers but the involvement of the other major religious orders.[36] In addition to differences in educational philosophies, there were also structural differences between the Jesuits and the pre-Reformation orders. For example, a Benedictine monk was bound to his house and his abbot. He could serve elsewhere, but needed permission from his superior. In Bavaria, the heads of these houses were part of the territorial estates (*Landstand*)—and while there was little real power left in that body by the eighteenth century, there was an important psychological and cultural sense in which the monasteries of the nation could be seen as part of the national treasury of wealth and intellect. The monastic settlements were part of the *Germania Sacra*, some having their origins as far back as Carolingian times. The great Benedictine abbeys that were being rebuilt in baroque splendor had served for centuries as centers of culture and devotion. Significantly, their contributions to Christianity long-preceded the Reformation. Defenders of monastic wealth argued that ecclesiastical foundations and lands could serve as financial reserves for the state, thus constituting a bulwark of the national wealth.[37]

If there was to be a restored German Catholicism—that is, a Catholicism that had lost its way with the onset of the Counter-Reformation—then it would need to find its roots in the era before the Reformation. Hontheim and, before him, Barthel, had suggested that the *Reichskirche* needed to recover the legal footing it had lost after the fifteenth century. Likewise, the intellectual resources for the reform program drew largely from religious orders that predated the arrival of the Jesuits in Germany. Although the appeal—and in many ways the driving force—of the Catholic reform program was rooted in the lay piety of educated, urban Catholics, monastic institutions remained vital centers of learning and education.

While Wolf's attacks on Jesuits framed German Catholicism negatively— as a rejection of an imposition—there existed as well positive steps to define a specifically *German* Catholicism that could stand up to Protestant culture. In 1775, Placidius Sprenger (1735–1806), a Benedictine monk of Banz in Franconia, began publishing a new journal entitled *Literature from Catholic Germany. For its Honor and Use. Published by Catholic Patriots*.[38] The editor writes that this new journal is proud to look beyond the borders of its Franconian home and serve as a "general library of Catholic Germany" (*allgemeine Bibliothek des katholischen Deutschlands*),[39] thereby alluding to Friedrich Nicolai's *Allgemeine deutsche Bibliothek*, the most important source of reviews and a major organ of the Berlin *Aufklärung*.[40] Sprenger complains that while "on one side, Protestant Germany is almost suffocated by the number of its learned journals and newspapers, we, on the other side," have almost nothing.[41] Sprenger announces that his journal will contain reviews of books by German Catholics, news from Catholic universities and academies and from Catholic states outside of Germany, and excerpts from recent Protestant journals as well as refutations of errors in Protestant journals concerning Catholic literature.[42] The intention of the Banz journal was to strengthen an awareness of German Catholicism, and it did so through an appeal to the public. In this, the Catholic reform program partook the particular idiom of the European Enlightenment—debate—to restate and redefine the church to the public at large. In rethinking the church, educated German Catholics imagined a Catholicism that would do away with worn out accretion and would be suited to the world in which they lived. The educated German Catholics who participated in this forum considered the church to be subject to public discussion and debate.

The effort to rethink and adapt the church to new times was carried out by the same class of people—educated, self-consciously "Enlightened" Germans—who were also confronting the question of what it meant to be German, and the lack of a firm resolution to this dilemma would tear at German Catholics for the century and a half following Napoleon's destruction of the empire. Educated German Catholics not only needed to situate themselves within—and make claims on—an international and socially diverse Catholic community, they also confronted competing notions of "German" that had taken on particular sharpness with the rise of Prussia and the solidification of a vernacular literary culture that was increasingly associated with Protestantism.

As mentioned above, Hontheim's treatise was published as the Seven Years' War came to a close. Coincidence though it may have been, the years following the war witnessed a surge of interest in defining the nation.[43] This debate was pushed further along by Friedrich Carl von Moser's pamphlet on the "German National Spirit," published in 1765, which argued that Germans needed to cultivate a sense of nationhood to overcome their weaknesses and divisions.[44] Moser stated that:

> We live under a single constitution that determines our respective rights and duties under the law. We are bound together in a common freedom and united by a national assembly directed toward this goal. In terms of inner power and strength, we are the first state [Reich] in Europe.... And yet, despite all this, we have for centuries been a political enigma.... We are a people at once great and despised. We have the possibility to be happy, but are in fact to be pitied.[45]

Moser chastised Germans for their disunity while exhorting them to place their hopes for the nation in the empire.[46] Despite its lofty appeals, the tract was not without partisan implications, given that Moser was on Joseph II's payroll. Nevertheless, it encapsulates the way in which the nation was a category of thought into which eighteenth-century Germans could pour their aspirations for political and social change, even if ideas about the nature of the nation widely varied. For Catholics, it provided a template for rethinking the church as well. This does not mean, however, that the Catholic reform debate was merely an add-on to a larger discussion, because Protestants, too, rethought their churches and the meaning of the Reformation in response to shifting notions of authority, the self, and society.[47] Seeking a balance between Germany and Rome, Catholic reformers desired a national church that would enjoy a large measure of autonomy, but would still be in communion with the universal church. In trying to reform the church, educated Catholics in the Holy Roman

Empire questioned not only what it meant to be Catholic, but also what it meant to be German.

How, then, does reconsidering the Holy Roman Empire—and specifically the emergence of German Catholicism from 1648 to 1806—open up a wider lens on the complex of religion, nation, and Enlightenment? It would appear that the church remained the backbone of a national idea, one that was inspired in the first place by the liberties of the Gallican church in neighboring France. Because the legal autonomy of the French church was long a settled issue—albeit with significant flare-ups—and because the monarchy had so successfully asserted its position, the legal redefinition of the French church was not as important as it was for German Catholics. Because the German church had not succeeded in securing the rights and liberties that its French counterpart had (as early as the fifteenth century), German Catholics could pin their hopes for moral and intellectual leadership of the church on an imagined future legal autonomy in ways that French Catholics did not. Nonetheless, as Clark has argued for England, an established church—even one only desperately longed for—could serve as the basis for a newly discovered national consciousness. In the transformation of confessional identity, Germany may indeed have taken a special path, but for all that, one not entirely unique either.

Notes

1. Niklaus von Hontheim, *Justini Febronii JCti de Statu Ecclesiae et Legitima Potestate Romani Pontificis Liber Singularis, ad Reuniendos Dissidentes in Religione Christianos Compositus* (1763). Hereafter: *De Statu*. Many versions were printed in several languages, including Niklaus Hontheim, *Buch von dem Zustand der Kirche und der rechtmäßigen Gewalt des römischen Papsts die in der Religion widriggesinnten Christen zu vereinigen.* (Wardigen, 1764). Hontheim's two main works (*De Statu* and his commentary on his subsequent "retraction") have been reissued, with a helpful introduction by Ulrich L. Lehner. See Niklaus Hontheim, *Commentarius in suam retractationem*, ed. Ulrich L. Lehner (Nordhausen, 2008 [1781]); and Niklaus Hontheim, *Febronius abbreviatus et emendatus*, ed. Ulrich L. Lehner (Nordhausen, 2008 [1777]).
2. Hontheim, *De Statu*, IX, §2, 2, 562. "Eruditi debebunt censeri *nati defensores* Sacerdotii & Imperii."
3. For a full account of this movement, as well as a detailed discussion of Hontheim and the German school of canon law, see Michael Printy, *Enlightenment and the Creation of German Catholicism* (New York, 2009). Portions of this essay are drawn from this book.
4. Christopher Ocker, *Church Robbers and Reformers in Germany, 1525–1547: Confiscation and Religious Purpose in the Holy Roman Empire* (Leiden, 2006). In particular, Ocker is referring to the settlements about the confiscation (or rededication) of church property by 1555.
5. On the rise of "German" philosophy in the later eighteenth century see Terry Pinkard, *German Philosophy 1760–1860. The Legacy of Idealism* (New York, 2002), 1–15.

6. Peter Hersche, *Muße und Verschwendung. Europäische Gesellschaft und Kultur im Barockzeitalter*, 2 vols. (Freiburg, 2006), 1: 384.
7. James Van Horn Melton, *The Rise of the Public in Enlightenment Europe* (Cambridge, 2001).
8. Charles Taylor, *Modern Social Imaginaries* (Durham, NC, 2004), 64.
9. The classic statement of this shift is Reinhart Koselleck, *Critique and Crisis: Enlightenment and the Parthogenesis of Modern Society* (Cambridge, MA, 1988).
10. For a recent overview see Len Scales and Oliver Zimmer, eds., *Power and the Nation in European History* (Cambridge, 2005).
11. Philip Gorski, "The Mosaic Moment: An Early Modernist Critique of Modernist Theories of Nationalism," in *American Journal of Sociology* 105, no. 5 (2000): 1428–1468.
12. J.C.D. Clark, *English Society, 1660–1832. Religion, Ideology, and Politics during the Ancien Regime*, 2nd ed. (Cambridge, 2000). For a concise version, with a pointed critique of other historians (especially Colley), see J.C.D. Clark, "Protestantism, Nationalism, and National Identity, 1660–1832," in *The Historical Journal* 43, no. 1 (2000): 249–276. His main target is Linda Colley, *Britons. Forging the Nation 1707–1837* (New Haven, 1992).
13. Clark, "Protestantism," 274. This particular passage is directed against Colley's argument that "Protestantism" was key to forging a *British* national identity after 1707. Clark, on the contrary, emphasizes the deep divisions within Protestantism, pointing instead to the vitality of the sense of the English nation structured around the Anglican Church.
14. Two important works that make room for religion (albeit in very different ways) are Colley, *Britons*; and David Avrom Bell, *The Cult of the Nation in France: Inventing Nationalism, 1680–1800* (Cambridge MA, 2001). An account of the place of a stable national church as the background for a modern state is Michael Roberts, "The Swedish Church," in *Sweden's Age of Greatness, 1632–1718*, ed. M. Roberts (New York, 1973).
15. Helmut Walser Smith, *The Continuities of German History: Nation, Religion and Race across the long Nineteenth Century* (New York, 2008), 73.
16. On the openness and variety of ideas about Germany up to 1848, see Brian E. Vick, *Defining Germany. The 1848 Frankfurt Parliamentarians and National Identity* (Cambridge, MA, 2002).
17. This was indeed part of Hontheim's strategy: he tried to make his points by citing approved authors in order to avoid condemnation.
18. *Il trionfo della santa sede e della chiesa contro gli assalti dei novatori combattuti e respinti colle stesse loro armi* (Venice, 1799). The work was reprinted many times, especially after Cappellari's election as Pope Gregory XVI in 1832.
19. Karl Otmar Freiherr von Aretin, *Das alte Reich, 1648–1806*, Vol. 2: *Kaisertradition und österreichische Großmachtpolitik, 1684–1745*, 4 vols. (Stuttgart, 1993–2000), 2: 396. On German canon law in this period see Herbert Raab, *Die Concordata Nationis Germanicae in der kanonistischen Diskussion des 17. bis 19. Jahrhunderts. Ein Beitrag zur Geschichte der episkopalischen Theorie in Deutschland* (Wiesbaden, 1956).
20. Full title: *Tractatus Historico-Canonico-Pragmaticus Loco Dissertationis Tertiae de Concordatis Germaniae Specialis Exhibens Commentarium Hermeneuticum ad Eorundem Textum et Literam* (Würzburg, 1762). In *Opsculorum Recentiorum*, Part I: 1f.
21. Barthel's epigoni included a wide range of canonists, some more radical than others. Georg Chrisoph Neller was perhaps his most significant pupil, for he brought Barthel's

ideas from Würzburg to Trier, where they most likely influenced Hontheim. Regional differences are apparent in the work of other canonists. For instance, Gregor Zallwein, a Benedictine monk from the Bavarian abbey of Wessobrun, taught canon law at the Benedictine University of Salzburg. Zallwein's *Principia juris ecclesiastici universalis, et particularis Germaniae*, published like Hontheim's *De Statu* in 1763, was a particularly elegant—and moderate—statement of the principles of the German canonists. Toward the end of the century, the Austrian canonists transformed the ideas of the moderate German canonists into a full-scale assault on papal supremacy in the Austrian lands. The most famous of these was Johann Nepomuk Pehem. While he borrowed much from his predecessor Riegger, Pehem's *Praelectionum in Jus Ecclesiasticum* (Vienna, 1789–1791) became the mandated teaching text in Joseph II's Austria and was still used into the nineteenth century.

22. See for example Dale K. Van Kley, *The Religious Origins of the French Revolution: from Calvin to the Civil Constitution, 1560–1791* (New Haven, 1996); and John McManners, *Church and Society in Eighteenth-Century France*, 2 vols. (Oxford, 1998).
23. In 1761, Gerbert had published *De communione potestatis ecclesiasticae inter summos ecclesiae principes pontificem, & episcopos*, a work that was hardly an attack on papal privileges, but did emphasize the sharing of power within the church.
24. Pitzer, "Febronius/Febronianismus," in *Theologische Realenzyklopädie* 11 (1983), 67-69.
25. Hontheim, *De Statu*, n.p. [Author's dedication].
26. Hontheim, *De Statu*, n.p.
27. See James A. Brundage, *Medieval Canon Law* (New York, 1995), 44.
28. John O'Malley, *The First Jesuits* (Cambridge, MA, 1993), 123f. For a comprehensive history of the role of the Society of Jesus in Germany see Bernhard Duhr, *Geschichte der Jesuiten in den Ländern deutscher Zunge* (Freiburg, 1907).
29. Although given their later dominance in education, the Jesuits did not at first intend to become a teaching order. For a good account of the development of Jesuit educational institutions, see O'Malley, *The First Jesuits*, 200–242.
30. On the role of the Marian congregations, see Louis Châtellier, *The Europe of the Devout: The Catholic Reformation and the Formation of a New Society*, trans. Jean Birrell (New York, 1989).
31. Peter Schmidt, *Das Collegium Germanicum in Rom und die Germaniker. Zur Funktion eines römischen Ausländerseminars (1552–1914)* (Tubingen, 1984).
32. Peter Philip Wolf, *Allgemeine Geschichte der Jesuiten. Von dem Ursprung ihres Ordens bis auf gegenwärtige Zeiten*, 4 vols. (Zürich, 1789), 2: 173.
33. Wolf, *Jesuiten*, 2: 178–179.
34. Wolf, *Jesuiten*, 2: 145.
35. Wolf, *Jesuiten*, 2: 178. When the society was suppressed in 1773, reformers were jubilant and hopeful that victory was now assured against what they saw as the curialism and obscurantism represented by the Jesuits. Yet, as the prelate Franziskus Töpsl, an anti-Jesuit leader in the reformation of Bavarian education, feared, once the Jesuits were out of the way, monastic culture itself came under attack. See Richard van Dülmen, *Propst Franziskus Töpsl (1711–1796) und das Augustiner-Chorherrenstift Polling* (Kallmünz, 1967), 208.
36. Van Dülmen, *Polling*, 201.

37. Anselm Desing, *Staatsfrage: Sind die Güter und Einkünfte der Geistlichkeit dem Staate schädlich oder nicht? Beantwortet und Lochstein und Neubergern entgegen gesetzt* (Munich, 1768).
38. Placidius Sprenger, *Literatur des katholischen Deutschlands, zu dessen Ehre und Nutzen, herausgegeben von katholischen Patrioten* (Coburg, 1775–). The journal was offered as a continuation of the short-lived *Fränkische Zuschauer*. For a history of the journal in the context of the intellectual life of the abbey, see Wilhelm Forster, "Die kirchliche Aufklärung bei den Benediktinern der Abtei Banz," *Studien und Mitteilungen zur Geschichte des Benediktinerordens und seiner Zweige* 63 (1951): 172–233, and 64 (1952): 110–233.
39. Sprenger, *Litteratur des katholischen Deutschlands*, "Vorrede," n.p.
40. On Nicolai, see Pamela Eve Selwyn, *Everyday life in the German Book Trade: Friedrich Nicolai as Bookseller and Publisher in the Age of Enlightenment, 1750–1810* (University Park, PA, 2000); Horst Möller, *Aufklärung in Preussen: der Verleger, Publizist und Geschichtsschreiber Friedrich Nicolai* (Berlin, 1974). On German periodicals in this period, see Joachim Kirchner, *Das Deutsche Zeitschriftenwesen. Seine Geschichte und seine Probleme. Teil 1. Von den Anfängen bis zum Zeitalter der Romantik. 2. neubearbeitete und erweiterte Auflage* (Wiesbaden, 1958). For Catholic periodicals, see especially 121f.
41. Sprenger, *Litteratur des katholischen Deutschlands*, I, 1, 1775, "Vorrede," n.p. [p. 5].
42. In a later issue, the editors rescind this request by giving a nod to the growing volume of Catholic writings: "Die Herrn Mitarbeiter weden ersucht, künftighin keine Recensionen von protestantischen Schriften mehr einzusenden, indem der Raum für die täglich mehr anwachsenden katholischen Schriftsteller zu enge werden will," Sprenger, *Litteratur des katholischen Deutschlands*, III, iv, 1780, 598.
43. Hans-Martin Blitz, *Aus Liebe zum Vaterland. Die deutsche Nation im 18. Jahrhundert* (Hamburg, 2000). Because the reversal of alliances had joined Catholic Austria and France against England and Prussia, some Protestant propagandists attempted to portray the war as a confessional war, although the Catholics did not reciprocate this effort.
44. See Nicholas Vazsonyi, "Montesquieu, Friedrich Carl von Moser, and the 'National Spirit Debate' in Germany, 1765–67," in *German Studies Review* 22, no. 2 (1999): 225–246.
45. Carl Friedrich von Moser, *Von dem Deutschen Nationalgeist* (1766; reprinted, 1976), 5.
46. Moser soon after became a (not-so) secret propagandist for Joseph II. See Derek Beales, *Joseph II: In the Shadow of Maria Theresa, 1741–1780* (Cambridge and New York, 1987), 130.
47. For a brief account of the ways in which Protestants redefined the Reformation in this period see Michael Printy, "The Reformation of the Enlightenment: German Histories in the Eighteenth Century," in *Politics and Reformations: Studies in Honor of Thomas A. Brady, Jr.*, eds. Christopher Ocker et al. (Leiden, 2007), 135–153.

CONCLUSION

New Directions in the Study of the Holy Roman Empire— A Cultural Approach

ANDRÉ KRISCHER

The Holy Roman Empire has received much attention from historians in the past twenty years. Historians' interest in the topic has not only resulted in the numerous brilliant case studies on the actors, institutions, and politics of the Holy Roman Empire,[1] but has also led to a fundamental discussion about what the empire actually was. There are two major approaches to the question. The first, put forward by Georg Schmidt, stresses the statehood of the empire, although in terms characteristic of the early modern state. Schmidt discusses the *Reichs-Staat* (a term used since the seventeenth century) as a "composite state" (*komplementärer Staat*), with relatively circumscribed state power, as compared with modern states. But he nevertheless insists on this composite *Reichs-Staat* as the political framework of a German nation, which ostensibly has existed since the late Middle Ages.[2] According to Schmidt, such a perspective on state- and nationhood would open up the *Heilige Römische Reich Deutscher Nation* for comparative analysis within European history. The self-confident use of terms such as "nation" and "state" in the analysis of early modern German history would not only lead away from the traditional *Sonderweg* approach, but it would also help modern Germans see the Holy Roman Empire as an integral part of their own history, and worthy of being dealt with in public discourse and, more importantly, in the schools.

The other major approach, represented most prominently by Barbara Stollberg-Rilinger, vehemently rejects this identification of early modern political structures with modern terms. In her interpretation, the use of the term "state" in relation to the Holy Roman Empire is not only incrementally, but also principally, misleading. Stollberg-Rilinger instead emphasizes the "otherness" of the empire not only in terms of its medieval origins and traditions, but also because it lacked a constitution in the modern sense of the word, producing a situation in which there were no political norms, fixed procedures, or regulations for the enforcement of binding decisions. The best way to understand this unique configuration, she suggests, is to set aside all of our normal associations and images of modern politics and to treat the Holy Roman Empire, its institutions, and structures as "strange" and in need of an "inductive" interpretation. As historians, she argues, we must start with the narration of the sources and not with the political and constitutional concepts of the modern world. Such an ethnological view (which is actually nothing but the hermeneutical view in the strictest sense of the word) brings the historian back to his or her proper starting point for historical research: reading something in a source and then looking for ways properly to understand it.

For Stollberg-Rilinger, the Holy Roman Empire was not constituted as a German nation, but was determined by a group of princes, dukes, counts, abbots, and abbesses as well as dozens of imperial cities that tried to become part of this exclusive society. As far as we know, imperial princes primarily considered themselves as part of the European nobility and not as prominent members of a German nation. In her latest book, Stollberg-Rilinger demonstrates at length that the central political spheres of the Holy Roman Empire, the imperial diets of the early modern era, were not structured by formal procedures, abstract regulations for decision-making, and administrative writing, but by face-to-face interaction, rituals, and ceremonies. In order to understand these methods of symbolic political communication within the empire, she believes historians should consult cultural and sociological theory.[3] Instead of treating the Holy Roman Empire as a would-be state lacking precise constitutional rules, Stollberg-Rilinger describes it as a symbolical order, a collectively shared fiction that had to be performed ritually in order to become a political reality. Rather than being founded on accurate and compelling norms, the empire rested on accurate and compelling ceremonies.[4]

The advantage of Stollberg-Rilinger's approach is not only the "scientific alienation" of the Holy Roman Empire as a genuine pre-modern (not just "early" modern!) structure, but also her interpretation of rituals and ceremonies as politics themselves, not simply events that also took place in the political sphere of decision-making. Anyone who has ever consulted the editions of the *Reichstagsakten* knows how important ceremonies were for the actors, as indicated by how many lines they wrote about that subject in their dispatches and descriptions. Therefore, the question cannot be: why did the princes and their representatives not care more about "real" politics? Rather, since rituals were such a prominent object of documentation, we should ask: what functions did they fulfill? In this volume, four articles focus directly on the political meaning of rituals in pre-modern decision-making. In his study on procedure and symbolism of the *Corpus Evangelicourm*, Andreas Kalipke considers the issue with respect to the imperial level, and David Luebke, Tim Neu, and Elizabeth Harding approach it in terms of the territorial diets. In many ways, the *Landtage* mirrored the problems of the imperial diet; for instance, this mirroring appears in questions of inclusion and exclusion, the interaction and treatment of the estates, deliberation and decision-making, as well as the communication of consensus and handling of dissent. All of these problems had to be solved ritually and symbolically, by the correct placing of the actors in the social space of the diets or through the use of rhetoric. The methods employed to handle these issues are striking evidence for the non-parliamentarian interpretation of imperial or territorial diets. They were in no way forerunners of modern institutions of democratic representation, but rather served the purposes of a noble society that was based on values such as rank, honor, and distinction.

The contributions by Len Scales and Ralf-Peter Fuchs offer excellent evidence for the thesis that the character of the Holy Roman Empire was essentially fictive. To understand the empire as fictive is not to see it as a mysterious construction of cultural historians, but rather to recognize that it existed as such in the perceptions and the actions of its contemporaries. For the non-noble subjects of the empire, the *Reich* was an object of communication and a protective power to whose institutions they appealed, but it was not an authority present in their daily world like the territorial state was in which they lived. The Holy Roman Empire was indeed represented symbolically by iconography and heraldry everywhere between the Alps and the North Sea, yet these symbols were not national emblems of authority as in modern states. They were rather open for various interpretations—and this makes further studies in imperial iconography and heraldry absolutely worthwhile. If the Holy Roman Empire was primarily a society of princes and nobles, dynastic strategies were not just "private," but were genuinely political matters. Michaela Hohkamp and Michael Sikora have both demonstrated this using the example of princely marriages, symbolical acts of great significance. The issue of who married whom was crucial for the social structure of and the subtle hierarchical differences within the empire.

However, the analysis of the political functions of symbolical communication is just one level of the cultural approach. The Konstanz-school, represented by Philipp Hoffman-Rehnitz, Alexander Schlaak, and Patrick Oelze, offers a new direction in the study of imperial cities by looking at the uses of writing as a political medium and the creation of territorial boundaries as a by-product of legal conflicts between princes and cities. In so doing, they extract the *expressive symbolism of functional acts*, not *the functions of symbolical acts*. This approach demonstrates just how flexible actually is the cultural approach: all politics can be considered either under a functional or symbolic aspect. Yet, this does not mean that political actions can be separated into symbolic and "real" politics. Even the most instrumental and rational action, like the deposition of ruling princes, fulfilled symbolic purposes; these acts represented the power of the empire as opposed to minor estates, thereby bringing the imperial fiction to life.

Despite the numerous "classic" works on the Holy Roman Empire and later cultural studies on the topic, we are still far away from a full understanding of this simultaneously strange and familiar construction, a situation that calls for further research. In my remarks on the possibilities for this research, I will concentrate on the subjects that deal directly with imperial institutions and their politics, rather than on those that address specific historical topics within the empire without being concerned with its particular structure. In the *Auerbachs Keller* scene in Goethe's *Faust*, the student Frosch raises a notorious question in song that has still not been answered sufficiently: what actually kept the empire together?[5] For example, who were the actors, beyond the level of the emperor and the princes, who represented the empire in its daily routine? The proposal to study such functionaries under the concept of *Reichspersonal*, as "imperial officials," has been rejected as misleading because it creates associations with modern bureaucratic administration.[6] The Holy Roman Empire was not a state, and it was not administered by a staff of professional executives, but by noble and civil persons who had very different motives for their services.[7] An imperial office was often prestigious, but seldom lucrative. Future studies of premodern imperial administration can profit greatly from the cultural approach, taking into consideration the costs and the symbolic profits of office-holding as well as the underlying structures of patronage and networking. The actors of the *Reichskammergericht* and the *Reichshofrat* or the diplomatic representatives of the imperial estates at the imperial diet are useful subjects for research from such a perspective.[8] We need to learn more about their habitus and their self-perception, for example.[9] After 1663 and as the *Reichstag* developed into a kind of diplomatic congress, structured by diplomatic communication and ceremonies, the interaction between the imperial estates became something like foreign relations.[10] Although they were not sovereign states, they used foreign policy and diplomatic protocol to demonstrate their political status. This manner of negotiating politics did not necessarily damage the corporate identity of the empire. Instead, it helped combine the self-definition of the imperial princes as (more or less) independent actors with their status as members of the *Reich*. The exploration of such inter-imperial forms of foreign policy is still a *desideratum*, especially in terms of the early modern scholar's concept of *nachbarliches Staatsrecht*. For instance, the imperial princes who cooperated with France during the reign of Louis XIV have been defamed as traitors, not only by contemporaries, but also by modern historians.

This leads to another issue that strongly needs to be revisited using a cultural approach, namely, concepts of enemies and patriotism. There were indeed contemporary discourses on patriotism and enemies, but whether they can provide information about a national consciousness is questionable.[11] What does it mean that the eighteenth-century princes who talked the most about patriotism also entered into coalitions with France? The older the Holy Roman Empire got, the more complex, even paradoxical, became the expectations of a "good" member of the empire.[12] Princes had to vow their "deepest affection," their "never ending faith," and their "patriotic diligence" to *Kaiser und Reich*, but foreign relations, even with the *Reichsfeind*, were often inevitable. We have to learn to understand such paradoxes, the separation of talk and action, not as hypocrisy in the moral sense of the word, but rather as organized hypocrisy, a typical occurrence within conflicts of values.[13] The eighteenth century is full of examples of such organized hypocrisy, because despite the fact that the traditional, and even quaint (*altfränkisch* in contemporary terms), structure of the *Reich* fell more and more out of synch with the post-baroque society of imperial princes, most of these minor potentates were still totally dependent on the archaic structure of the empire.

The cultural approach to the history of the Holy Roman Empire is not restricted to certain topics but can be used for the interpretation of all subjects. There can be cultural interpretations of an imperial economy (if there was ever such a thing) as well as cultural re-readings of religious violence and wars. Benjamin Marschke, for example, has demonstrated how to write a new form of biography using the eccentricity of a king such as Frederick William of Prussia as a starting point of analysis, not as something to censure in historiography. There are many of these figures in the history of the Holy Roman Empire waiting for such a biographical approach. My final suggestion is to use the voluminous editions of the *Reichstagsakten* in order to understand politics as rituals and rituals as politics, to read deliberations as discourses and discourses as deliberations, and to contribute to a deeper understanding of a phenomenon that, for more than 800 years, shaped the political landscape of pre-modern Europe. Leave the question of what has actually survived of the Holy Roman Empire in modern Germany to the students of contemporary history. They know it better.

Notes

1. Cf. the latest bibliography in Heinz Schilling et al., eds., *Heiliges Römisches Reich Deutscher Nation 962 bis 1806. Altes Reich und Neue Staaten 1495 bis 1806. Essays* (Dresden, 2006).
2. Cf. Georg Schmidt, *Geschichte des Alten Reiches. Staat und Nation in der Frühen Neuzeit 1495–1806* (Munich, 1999); G. Schmidt, "Das frühneuzeitliche Reich— komplementärer Staat und föderative Nation," in *Historische Zeitschrift* 273 (2001): 371–399.

3. Barbara Stollberg-Rilinger, *Des Kaisers alte Kleider. Verfassungsgeschichte und Symbolsprache des Alten Reiches* (Munich, 2008). For background on the concept *Anwesenheitsgesellschaft* of the Konstanz school, cf. the introduction to this volume by Jason Coy. For both major approaches, along with others, cf. Matthias Schnettger, eds., *Imperium Romanum—irregulare corpus—Teutscher Reichs-Staat* (Mainz, 2002). It must be stressed that other historians are also rejecting the *Reichs-Staat* approach, but without a culturalist interpretation of the Holy Roman Empire. See the contributions of Heinz Schilling and Ronald G. Asch, and furthermore Helmut Neuhaus, in *Das Reich in der Frühen Neuzeit* (Enzyklopädie Deutscher Geschichte 42) (Munich, 1997), 98. See for the cultural approach Barbara Stollberg-Rilinger, "Symbolische Kommunikation in der Vormoderne. Begriffe—Forschungsperspektiven—Thesen," in *Zeitschrift für Historische Forschung* 31 (2004): 489–527.
4. Stollberg-Rilinger, *Des Kaisers alte Kleider*, 15.
5. "Das liebe, heil'ge Röm'sche Reich, Wie hält's nur noch zusammen?" Cf. the introduction to this volume.
6. See Annette Baumann et al., eds., *Reichspersonal. Funktionsträger für Kaiser und Reich* (Cologne, Weimar, and Vienna, 2003), where this sort of skepticism was expressed by the contributors themselves.
7. Cf. the seminal study by Martin Fimpel, *Reichsjustiz und Territorialstaat. Württemberg als Kommissar von Kaiser und Reich im Schwäbischen Kreis (1648–1806)* (Tübingen, 2000).
8. In Münster, Maria von Loewenich works on the *Reichskammerrichter* office and concepts of prestige, and Thomas Dorfner studies the world of *Reichshofratsagenten*.
9. The works of Pierre Bourdieu can help to analyze such problems, see, for example, his, *Distinction: a Social Critique of the Judgment of Taste* (Cambridge, MA, 1984); Bourdieu, *Language and Symbolic Power* (Cambridge, MA, 1991).
10. Numerous helpful suggestions can still be found in Heinz Duchhardt, *Altes Reich und Europäische Staatenwelt 1648–1806* (Munich, 1990).
11. Cf. Martin Wrede, *Das Reich und seine Feinde. Politische Feindbilder in der reichspatriotischen Publizistik zwischen Westfälischem Frieden und Siebenjährigem Krieg* (Mainz, 2004); Alexander Schmidt, *Vaterlandsliebe und Religionskonflikt. Politische Diskurse im Alten Reich 1555–1648* (Leiden and Boston, 2007).
12. Cf. the forthcoming dissertation by Tilman Haug on the politics of the counts of Fürstenberg.
13. The seminal work is Nils Brunsson, *The Organization of Hypocrisy: Talk, Decisions and Actions in Organizations* (Chichester, 1991).

Glossary

Adelsprobe: proof of noble ancestry
Anwesenheitsgesellschaft: face to face society
Corpus Evangelicorum: Protestant group at the imperial diet
Fraisch (or *Hochgerichtsbarkeit*): high jurisdiction
Kirchengüter: chapters, churches, and even territories
Landesherr: territorial prince
Landschaft: territorial assembly
Landstände: provincial estates
Landtagen: territorial assemblies
Obrigkeit: magistrates or magistracy
Reichshofrat: Imperial Aulic Council
Reichskammergericht: Imperial Chamber Court
Reichskreis: imperial circle administration
Reichstag: imperial assembly
Reichsstände: imperial estates
Ritterschaften: noble corporations
Schwäbischer Bund: Swabian League

Bibliography

Ackermann, Jürgen. *Verschuldung, Reichsdebitverwaltung, Mediatisierung. Eine Studie zu den Finanzproblemen der mindermächtigen Stände im Alten Reich. Das Beispiel der Grafschaft Ysenburg-Büdingen 1687–1806.* Marburg: 2002.

Althoff, Gerd. *Spielregeln der Politik im Mittelalter. Kommunikation in Frieden und Fehde.* Darmstadt: 1997.

Am Ende, Bernhard. *Studien zur Verfassungsgeschichte Lübecks im 12. und 13. Jahrhundert.* Lübeck: 1975.

Annas, Gabrielle. *Hoftag—Gemeiner Tag—Reichstag: Studien zur strukturellen Entwicklung deutscher Reichsversammlungen des späten Mittelalters (1349–1471).* 2 vols. Göttingen: 2004.

Aretin, Karl Otmar Freiherr von. *Das Alte Reich, 1648–1806.* 4 vols. Stuttgart: 1993–2000.

———. *Föderalistische oder hierarchische Ordnung: 1648–1684*, vol. 1. In Aretin, *Das Alte Reich.*

———. *Heiliges Römisches Reich, 1776–1806: Reichsverfassung und Staatssouveränität.* 2 vols. Wiesbaden: 1967.

———. *Kaisertradition und österreichische Großmachtpolitik: 1684–1745*, vol. 2. In Aretin, *Das Alte Reich.*

Arlinghaus, Franz-Josef. *Inklusion/Exklusion. Funktion und Formen des Rechts in der spätmittelalterlichen Stadt. Das Beispiel Köln.* Konstanz: forthcoming.

Arndt, Johannes. *Das niederrheinisch-westfälische Reichsgrafenkollegium und seine Mitglieder (1653–1806).* Mainz: 1991.

———. "Kabale und Liebe in Detmold. Zur Geschichte einer Hofintrige und einer Fürstenabsetzung in Lippe während des ausgehenden 18. Jahrhunderts." In *Lippische Mitteilungen* 60 (1991): 27–74.

———. "Zwischen kollegialer Solidarität und persönlichem Aufstiegsstreben. Die Reichsgrafen im 17. und 18. Jahrhundert." In *Der europäische Adel im Ancien Régime*, edited by Ronald G. Asch, 105–128. Cologne, Weimar, and Vienna: 2001.

Arnim, Bernd Jacob von. *Von Thalern des Chürfürstlich-Brandenburgischen und Königlich-Preussischen regierenden Hauses*. Berlin: 1788.

Asch, Jürgen. *Rat und Bürgerschaft in Lübeck 1598–1669. Die verfassungsrechtlichen Auseinandersetzungen im 17. Jahrhundert und ihre sozialen Hintergründe*. Lübeck: 1961.

Asch, Ronald G. "Das monarchische Nobilitierungsrecht und die soziale Identität des Adels im 17. und 18. Jahrhundert." In *Die frühneuzeitliche Monarchie in Europa und ihr Erbe. Festschrift für Heinz Duchhardt zum 60. Geburtstag*, edited by Ronald G. Asch, Johannes Arndt, and Matthias Schnettger, 91–107. Münster: 2003.

———. "Estates and Princes after 1648: The Consequences of the Thirty Years' War." In *German History* 6 (1988): 113-132.

———. *Europäischer Adel in der Frühen Neuzeit*. Cologne, Weimar, and Vienna, 2008.

———. *Nobilities in Transition 1550–1700. Courtiers and Rebels in Britain and Europe*. London: 2003.

———. "Noble Corporations and Provincial Diets in Ecclesiastical Principalities of the Holy Roman Empire ca. 1648–1802." In *Realties of Representation: State Building in Early Modern Europe and European America*, edited by Maija Jansson, 93–111. New York: 2007.

———. *The Thirty Years War. The Holy Roman Empire and Europe, 1618–48*. London: 1997.

Asch, Ronald G. and Dagmar Freist, eds. *Staatsbildung als kultureller Prozess. Strukturwandel und Legitimation von Herrschaft in der Frühen Neuzeit*. Cologne, Weimar, and Vienna: 2005.

Assmann, Jan. *Das kulturelle Gedächtnis—Schrift, Erinnerung und politische Identität in frühen Hochkulturen*. Munich: 1997.

Bader, Karl Siegfried. "Die oberdeutsche Reichsstadt im alten Reich." In *Esslinger Studien* 11 (1965): 25.

Ballschmieter, Hans-Joachim. *Andreas Gottlieb von Bernstorff und der mecklenburgische Ständekampf (1680–1720)*. Cologne and Graz: 1962.

Barack, Karl, ed. *Zimmerische Chronik*. Vol. 1-4. Freiburg i. Br.: 1881–1882.

Barta-Fliedl, Ilsebill, Andreas Gugler, and Peter Parenzan, eds. *Tafeln bei Hofe. Zur Geschichte der fürstlichen Tafelkultur. Sammlungsband 4*. Hamburg: 1998.

Barthel, Johann Kaspar. *Tractatus Historico-Canonico-Pragmaticus Loco Dissertationis Tertiae de Concordatis Germaniae Specialis Exhibens Commentarium Hermeneuticum ad Eorundem Textum et Literam*. Würzburg: 1762.

Bauer, Richard. "München als Landeshauptstadt." *Zeitschrift für bayerische Landesgeschichte* 60 (1997): 115–121.

Bauer, Volker. *Hofökonomie: Der Diskurs über den Fürstenhof in Zeremonialwissenschaft, Hausväterliteratur und Kameralismus*. Vienna: 1997.

Baumann, Annette, et al., eds. *Reichspersonal. Funktionsträger für Kaiser und Reich*. Cologne, Weimar, and Vienna: 2003.

Baumgart, Peter. "Die Welt des Kronprinzen Friedrich und sein Konflikt mit dem Vater." In *Friedrich der Große. Herrscher zwischen Tradition und Fortschritt*, edited by Erhard Bethke, 46–58. Gütersloh: 1985. Reprinted, "Kronprintzenopposition: Zum Verhältnis Friedrichs zu seiner Vater Friedrich Wilhelm I." In *Friedrich der Große, Franken und das Reich*, edited by Heinz Duchhardt, 5–23. Cologne and Viena: 1986. Also reprinted, "Kronprinzenopposition: Friedrich und Friedrich Wilhelm I." In *Friedrich der Große in seiner Zeit (Neue Forschungen zur Brandenburgisch-Preussischen Geschichte 8)*, edited by Oswald Hauser, 1–16. Cologne and Vienna: 1987.

———. "Friedrich Wilhelm I. (1713–1740)." In *Preussens Herrscher: Von den ersten Hohenzollern bis Wilhelm II*, edited by Frank-Lothar Kroll, 134–159. Munich: 2000.

Beales, Derek. *Joseph II: In the Shadow of Maria Theresa, 1741–1780*. Cambridge and New York: 1987.

Beaune, Colette. *The Birth of an Ideology: Myths and Symbols of Nation in Late-Medieval France*. Translated by Susan Ross Huston and edited by Frederic L. Cheyette. Berkeley, CA: 1991.

Becker, Johann Nicolaus. *Beschreibung meiner Reise in den Departementern vom Donnersberge, vom Rhein und von der Mosel im sechsten Jahr der Französischen Republik in Briefen an einen Freund in Paris*. Berlin: 1799.

Behr, Hans-Joachim. "'Zu rettung deren hart getruckten Nassaw-Siegischen Unterthanen.' Der Niederrheinisch-Westfälische Kreis und Siegen im 18. Jahrhundert." In *Jahrbuch für westfälische Kirchengeschichte* 85 (1991): 159–184.

Bell, David A. "The Unrepresentable French?" In *Realities of Representation: State-Building in Early Modern Europe and European America*, edited by Maija Jansson, 75–92. New York: 2007.

———. *The Cult of the Nation in France: Inventing Nationalism, 1680–1800*. Cambridge, MA: 2001.

Bellabarba, Marco. "Zeugen der Macht: Adelige und tridentinische Bauerngemeinden vor den Richtern (16.–18. Jahrhundert)." In *Wahrheit, Wissen, Erinnerung. Zeugenverhörprotokolle als Quelle für soziale Wissensbestände der Frühen Neuzeit*, edited by Ralf-Peter Fuchs and Winfried Schulze, 201–224. Münster: 2002.

Belstler, Ulrich. *Die Stellung des Corpus Evangelicorum in der Reichsverfassung*. Bamberg: 1968.

Berger, Peter L. and Thomas Luckmann. *The Social Construction of Reality. A Treatise in the Sociology of Knowledge*. Garden City, NY: 1967.

Berns, Jörg J. and Thomas Rahn, eds. *Zeremoniell als höfische Ästhetik in Spätmittelalter und früher Neuzeit*. Tübingen: 1995.

Besold, Christoph. *De Jure Universitatum*. In *Iuridico-Politicae Dissertationes. De Iure Rerum, (2) Familiarum, (3) Collegiorum, (4) Academiarum (5) aliarumque Universitatum, (6) ac item Territoriorum*. 224–264. Strasbourg: 1624.

Binn, Heinrich and Ludolf Hugo. *De Statu Regionum Germaniae, Et Regimine Principum Summae Imperii Reip. Aemulo, Nec Non De Usu Autoritate Iuris Civilis Privati, Quam In Hac Parte Iuris Publici Obtinet, Disputatio Inauguralis*. Helmstedt: 1661.

Bireley, Robert. *Religion and Politics in the Age of the Counterreformation. Emperor Ferdinand II., William Lamormaini, S.J., and the Formation of Imperial Policy.* Chapel Hill, NC: 1981.

———. *The Jesuits and the Thirty Years War. Kings, Courts and Confessors.* Cambridge: 2003.

———. "The Thirty Years' War as Germany's Religious War." In *Krieg und Politik 1618–1648. Europäische Probleme und Perspektiven*, edited by Konrad Repgen, 85–106. Munich: 1988.

Bisson, Thomas N. "Celebration and Persuasion: Reflections on the Cultural Evolution of Medieval Consultation." In *Legislative Studies Quarterly* 7 (1982): 181–204.

Blanning, T.C.W. "Empire and State in Germany, 1648–1848." In *German History* 12:2 (1994): 220–236.

Bleckmann, Maren. "Suppliken zu Rangkonflikten an den Herzog von Braunschweig-Wolfenbüttel im 17. und 18. Jahrhundert." In *Formen der politischen Kommunikation in Europa vom 15. bis 18. Jahrhundert. Bitten, Beschwerden, Briefe*, edited by Cecilia Nubola and Andreas Würgler, 95–115. Berlin: 2004.

Bleisteiner, Claus D. "Der Doppeladler von Kaiser und Reich im Mittelalter: Imagination und Realität." In *Mitteilungen des Instituts für österreichischen Geschichtsforschung* 109 (2001): 4–52.

Blickle, Peter. *Das Alte Europa. Vom Hochmittelalter bis zur Moderne.* 2 vols. Munich: 2008.

———. *Kommunalismus. Skizzen einer gesellschaftlichen Organisationsform.* 2 vols. Munich: 2000.

———. "Politische Landschaften in Oberschwaben: Bäuerliche und bürgerliche Repräsentation im Rahmen des frühen europäischen Parlamentarismus." In *Landschaften und Landstände in Oberschwaben. Bäuerliche und bürgerliche Repräsentation im Rahmen des frühen europäischen Parlamentarismus*, edited by Peter Blickle, 11–32. Tübingen: 2000.

———. *The Communal Reformation: The People's Quest for Salvation in the Sixteenth Century.* Leiden: 1985. Originally published in German as *Gemeindereformation: die Menschen des 16. Jahrhunderts auf dem Weg zum Heil* (Munich, 1985).

———. *Unruhen in der ständischen Gesellschaft 1300–1800.* Munich: 1988.

Blickle, Peter, ed. *Gemeinde und Staat im Alten Europa.* Munich: 1998.

Blickle, Renate. "Laufen gen Hof. Die Beschwerden der Untertanen und die Entstehung des Hofrats in Bayern. Ein Beitrag zu den Varianten rechtlicher Verfahren im späten Mittelalter und in der frühen Neuzeit." In *Gemeinde und Staat im Alten Europa*, edited by Peter Blickle, 241–266. Munich: 1998.

Blitz, Hans-Martin. *Aus Liebe zum Vaterland. Die deutsche Nation im 18. Jahrhundert.* Hamburg: 2000.

Blockmans, Wim. "Limitations to Monarchial Power." In *Murder and Monarchy. Regicide in European History, 1300–1800*, edited by Robert von Friedeburg, 136–145. Basingstoke: 2004.

Boehm, Barbara Drake and Jiří Fajt, eds. *Prague: The Crown of Bohemia 1347–1437*. New Haven and London: 2005.
Boeselager, Johannes Freiherr von. *Die Osnabrücker Domherren des 18. Jahrhunderts*. Osnabrück: 1990.
Bohn, Cornelia. *Schriftlichkeit und Gesellschaft. Kommunikation und Sozialität der Neuzeit*. Opladen: 1999.
Bojcov, Michail A. "Ephemerität und Permanenz bei Herrschereinzügen im spätmittelalterlichen Deutschland." In *Marburger Jahrbuch für Kunstwissenschaft* 24 (1997): 87–107.
Boldt, Hans. "Parlament, parlamentarische Regierung, Parlamentarismus." In *Geschichtliche Grundbegriffe. Historisches Lexikon zur politisch-sozialen Sprache in Deutschland*, edited by Otto Brunner, Werner Conze, and Reinhart Koselleck. Vol. 4, 649–676. Stuttgart: 1978.
Bolland, Jürgen. "Zur städtischen Bursprake im hansischen Raum." In *Zeitschrift des Vereins für Lübeckische Geschichte und Altertumskunde* 36 (1956): 96–118.
Borchardt, Frank L. *German Antiquity in Renaissance Myth*. Baltimore, 1971.
Borgolte, Michael. *Sozialgeschichte des Mittelalters. Eine Forschungsbilanz nach der deutschen Einheit*. Munich: 1996.
Borst, Otto. *Geschichte der Stadt Esslingen am Neckar*. Esslingen: 1977.
Böttger, Hermann. *Friedrich Flender vor der Hardt. Ein Kämpfer für Recht und Freiheit des Siegerländer Volkes*. Siegen: 1957.
Bourdieu, Pierre. *Distinction: a Social Critique of the Judgment of Taste*. Cambridge, MA: 1984.
———. "Initiationsriten." In *Was heißt sprechen? Die Ökonomie des sprachlichen Tauschs*, edited by Pierre Bourdieu, 84–93. Vienna: 1990.
———. *Language and Symbolic Power*. Cambridge, MA: 1991.
———. "Marriage Strategies as Strategies of Social Reproduction." In *Family and Society. Selections from the Annales*, edited by Robert Forster and Orest Ranum, 117–144. London: 1976.
Brabant, Arthur. *Das Heilige Römische Reich teutscher Nation im Kampf mit Friedrich dem Großen*. Vol. 2, *Die Reichspolitik und der Feldzug in Kursachsen*. Berlin: 1911.
Brady, Thomas A. *Turning Swiss: Cities and Empire, 1450–1550*. Cambridge and New York: 1985.
Brandi, Karl. *Der Augsburger Religionsfriede vom 25. September 1555: Kritische Ausgabe des Textes mit den Entwürfen und der königlichen Deklaration*. Göttingen: 1927.
Brendle, Franz. *Dynastie, Reich und Reformation. Die württembergischen Herzöge Ulrich und Christoph, die Habsburger und Frankreich*. Stuttgart: 1998.
Brundage, James A. *Medieval Canon Law*. New York: 1995.
Brüning, Ulf. "Wege landständischer Entscheidungsfindung. Das Verfahren auf den Landtagen des rheinischen Erzstifts zur Zeit Clemens Augusts." In *Im Wechselspiel der Kräfte. Politische Entwicklungen des 17. und 18. Jahrhunderts in Kurköln*, edited by Frank Günter Zehnder, 161–184. Cologne: 1999.

———. "Wege landständischer Entscheidungsfindung: Das Verfahren auf den Landtagen des rheinischen Erzstifts zur Zeit Clemens Augusts." In *Der Riß im Himmel: Clemens August und seine Epoche*, edited by Frank Günter Zehnder, 161–184. Cologne: 1999.

Brunner, Otto. *Land and Lordship. Structures of Governance in Medieval Austria*. Translated and introduced by H. Kaminsky and J. Van Horn Melton. Philadelphia: 1992.

———. "Souveränitätsproblem und Sozialstruktur in den deutschen Reichsstädten der frühen Neuzeit." In *Neue Wege der Verfassungs- und Sozialgeschichte*. 2nd ed., 294–321. Göttingen: 1968.

Brunsson, Nils. *The Organization of Hypocrisy. Talk, Decisions and Actions in Organizations*. Chichester: 1989, 1991.

Buchholz, Stephan. "Rechtsgeschichte und Literatur: Die Doppelehe Philipps des Großmütigen." In *Landgraf Philipp der Großmütige von Hessen und seine Residenz Kassel*, edited by Heide Wunder, Christina Vanja, and Berthold Hinz, 57–73. Marburg: 2004.

Burkhardt, Johannes and Christine Werkstetter, eds. *Kommunikation und Medien in der Frühen Neuzeit*. Munich: 2005.

Bütikofer, Niklaus. "Konfliktregulierung auf den Eidgenössischen Tagsatzungen des 15. und 16. Jahrhunderts." In *Parliaments, Estates and Representation* 11 (1991): 103–115.

Bynum, Caroline Walker. *Wonderful Blood: Theology and Practice in Late Medieval Northern Germany and Beyond*. Philadelphia: 2007.

Camille, Michael. *Gothic Art*. London: 1996.

Cappellari, Mauro [Pope Gregory XVI]. *Il trionfo della santa sede e della chiesa contro gli assalti dei novatori combattuti e respinti colle stesse loro armi*. Venice: 1799.

Caroc, Georg Adolf. *Begründete Deduction von Land-Ständen, derselben Befugnissen, Pflichten und Nutzen, absonderlich in denen Landen des Reichs Teutscher Nation*. N.p.: 1718.

Carsten, Francis L. *Princes and Parliaments in Germany. From the 15th to the 18th Century*. Oxford and London: 1959. Reprinted, Oxford: 1963.

"Cérémonies." In *Encyclopédie ou Dictionnaire raisonné des sciences, des arts et des métiers*. Vol. 2, 838–839. Paris, 1752.

Chadraba, Rudolf. "'Der zweite Konstantin': Zum Verhältnis von Staat und Kirche in der karolinischen Kunst Böhmens." In *Umeni* 26 (1978): 505–520.

Chamberlain, Houston Stewart. *Demokratie und Freiheit*. Munich: 1917.

Châtellier, Louis. *The Europe of the Devout: The Catholic Reformation and the Formation of a New Society*. Translated by Jean Birrell. New York: 1989.

Christ, Günter. "Selbstverständnis und Rolle der Domkapitel in den geistlichen Territorien des alten deutschen Reiches in der Frühneuzeit." In *Zeitschrift für Historische Forschung* 16 (1989): 257–328.

Clanchy, M.T. *From Memory to Written Record: England 1066–1307*. London: 1979.

Clark, J.C.D. *English Society, 1660–1832. Religion, Ideology, and Politics during the Ancien Regime*. 2nd ed. Cambridge: 2000.

———. "Protestantism, Nationalism, and National Identity, 1660–1832." In *The Historical Journal* 43:1 (2000): 249–276.

Cohn, Henry J. "The electors and imperial rule at the end of the fifteenth century." In *Representations of Power in Medieval Germany 800–1500*, edited by Björn Weiler and Simon MacLean, 295–318. Turnhout: 2006.

Coleman, James S. *Foundations of Social Theory*. Cambridge, MA: 1990.

Colley, Linda. *Britons. Forging the Nation 1707–1837*. New Haven: 1992.

Coppenrath, Friedrich Wilhelm, ed. *Hof- und Adreß-Calender des Hochstifts Münster*. Münster: 1785. Reprinted, Vreden: 1988.

Cowan, Alexander. *Urban Europe 1500-1700*. London and New York: 1998.

Crivellari, Fabio and Marcus Sandl. "Die Medialität der Geschichte. Forschungsstand und Perspektiven einer interdisziplinären Zusammenarbeit von Geschichts- und Medienwissenschaften." In *Historische Zeitschrift* 277 (2003): 619–654.

Crivellari, Fabio, Kay Kirchmann, Marcus Sandl, and Rudolf Schlögl, eds. *Die Medien der Geschichte. Historizität und Medialität in interdisziplinärer Perspektive*. Konstanz: 2004.

Crossley, Paul. "The politics of presentation: the architecture of Charles IV of Bohemia." In *Courts and Regions in Medieval Europe*, edited by Sarah Rees Jones, Richard Marks, and A.J. Minnis, 99–172. Woodbridge: 2000.

Czech, Vinzenz. *Legitimation und Repräsentation. Zum Selbstverständnis thüringisch-sächsischer Reichsgrafen in der frühen Neuzeit*. Berlin: 2003.

Daniel, Ute. "Zwischen Zentrum und Peripherie der Hofgesellschaft: Zur biographischen Struktur eines Fürstenlebens der Frühen Neuzeit am Beispiel der Kurfürstin Sophie von Hannover." In *L´Homme. Zeitschrift für feministische Geschichtswissenschaft* 8:2 (1997): 208–217.

Darnton, Robert. "A Bourgeois Puts His World in Order: The City as a Text." In *The Great Cat-Massacre and Other Episodes in French Cultural History*, 107–143. New York: 1984.

Dartmann, Christoph and Carla Meyer, eds. *Identität und Krise. Zur Deutung vormoderner Selbst-, Welt- und Fremderfahrungen*. Münster: 2007.

Das fröliche Dretzden, als daselbst zu Ehren Sr. Königl. Majestät in Preußen 2c.2c. und Dero Kron-Printzen Königl. Hoheit, bey Dero selben hohen Anwesenheit täglich Lustbarkeiten angestellet und vergnüglich vollbracht worden. Mit allen merckwürdigen Umständen ausführlich beschrieben. Dresden: 1728.

Das frolockende Berlin, Oder Historische Nachricht Dererjenigen öffentlichen Freudens-Bezeigungen und sinnreichen Illuminationen, Die bey hoher Anwesenheit Jhro Königl. Majestät in Pohlen, Und Dero Königl. Printzens Hoheit Daselbst angestellet worden, nebst einem Anhange aller auf diese fröhliche Begebenheit verfertigter Gedichte. Berlin: 1728.

De Clerq, Carlo. "Die katholischen Fürsten von Nassau-Siegen." In *Nassauische Annalen* 73 (1962): 129–152.

Demandt, Karl E. "Die Hessischen Landstände nach dem 30jährigen Krieg." In *Ständische Vertretungen in Europa im 17. und 18. Jahrhundert*, edited by Dietrich Gerhard, 162–182. Göttingen: 1974.

———. *Geschichte des Landes Hessen*. Wiesbaden: 1972.

De Mauvillon, Éléazar. *The Life of Frederick-William I: Late King of Prussia. Containing Many Authentick Letters and Pieces, very necessary for understanding the Affairs of Germany and the Northern Kingdoms*. Translated by William Phelips. London: 1750.

De Pepliers, Robert Jean. *Verbesserter und viel vermehrter, Nöthiger Unterricht, Von denen Französischen Tituln*. Berlin: various editions.

Desing, Anselm. *Staatsfrage: Sind die Güter und Einkünfte der Geistlichkeit dem Staate schädlich oder nicht? Beantwortet und Lochstein und Neubergern entgegen gesetzt*. Munich: 1768.

Die europäische Fama welche den gegenwärtige Zustand der vornehmsten Höfe entdecket. 1702–1733.

Die neue Europäische Fama, welche den gegenwärtigen Zustand der vornehmsten Höfe entdecket. 1735–1756.

Dilcher, Gerhard. "Die Rechtsgeschichte der Stadt." In *Deutsche Rechtsgeschichte. Land und Stadt—Bürger und Bauer im alten Europa*, edited by Karl S. Bader and Gerhard Dilcher, 251–827. Berlin: 1999.

Dingel, Irene. "Augsburger Religionsfrieden und 'Augsburger Konfessionsverwandtschaft'—konfessionelle Lesearten." In *Der Augsburger Religionsfrieden 1555*, edited by Heinz Schilling and Heribert Smolinsky, 157–176. Münster: 2007.

Dinges, Martin. "Der 'feine Unterschied'. Die soziale Funktion der Kleidung in der höfischen Gesellschaft." In *Zeitschrift für Historische Forschung* 19 (1992): 49–76.

Doller, Carolin. "Bürgerliche Gattinnen. Standesungleiche Verbindungen im Hause Anhalt-Bernburg." In *Adel in Sachsen-Anhalt*, edited by Eva Labouvie, 17–48. Cologne: 2007.

Drabek, Anna M. *Reisen und Reisezeremoniell der römisch-deutschen Herrscher im Spätmittelalter*. Vienna: 1964.

Duchhardt, Heinz. *Altes Reich und Europäische Staatenwelt 1648–1806*. Munich: 1990.

Duchhardt, Heinz and Gert Melville, eds. *Im Spannungsfeld von Recht und Ritual: Soziale Kommunikation in Mittelalter und Früher Neuzeit*. Cologne: 1997.

Duhamelle, Christophe. *L'Héritage collectif: La noblesse d'Église rhénane, 17e 18e siècles*. Paris: 1998.

———. "The Making of Stability: Kinship, Church and Power among the Rhenish Imperial Knighthood." In *Kinship in Europe: Approaches to Long-Term Developments*, edited by David Warren Sabean, Simon Teuscher, and Jon Mathieu, 125–144. New York: 2007.

Duhr, Bernhard. *Geschichte der Jesuiten in den Ländern deutscher Zunge*. Freiburg: 1907.

Dülmen, Richard van. *Propst Franziskus Töpsl (1711–1796) und das Augustiner-Chorherrenstift Polling*. Kallmünz: 1967.
Dunk, Thomas H. von der. *Das Deutsche Denkmal: Eine Geschichte in Bronze und Stein vom Hochmittelalter bis zum Barock*. Cologne, Weimar, and Vienna: 1999.
Dünnebeil, Sonja. "Die drei großen Kompanien als genossenschaftliche Verbindungen der Lübecker Oberschicht." In *Genossenschaftliche Strukturen in der Hanse*, edited by Nils Jörn et. al., 205–222. Cologne: 1998.
Ebel, Wilhelm. "Bursprake, Echteding und Eddach in den niederdeutschen Stadtrechten." In *Festschrift für Hans Niedermeyer zum 70. Geburtstag*, 53–76. Göttingen: 1953.
———. *Lübisches Recht*. Vol. 1. Lübeck: 1971.
Eberlein, Ulrich. "Die Esslinger Bürgerprozesse. Eine Untersuchung der innerstädtischen Auseinandersetzungen in den letzten Jahren der Reichsunmittelbarkeit unter besonderer Berücksichtigung rechtlicher, wirtschaftlicher und sozialer Hintergründe. Zugleich ein Beitrag zur Rechtsgeschichte der schwäbischen Reichsstädte im 18. Jahrhundert." Ph.D. dissertation, University of Tübingen, 1987.
Eckhardt, Albrecht. "Die Burgmannenaufschwörungen und Ahnenproben der Reichsburg Friedberg in der Wetterau 1473–1805." In *Wetterauer Geschichtsblätter* 19 (1970): 133–167.
Edwards, Mark U. *Printing, Propaganda and Martin Luther*. Berkeley: 1994.
Ehbrecht, Wilfried. *Konsens und Konflikt. Skizzen und Überlegungen zur älteren Verfassungsgeschichte deutscher Städte*. Edited by Peter Johanek. Cologne: 2001.
Elkar, Rainer S. "Kommunikative Distanz: Überlegungen zum Verhältnis zwischen Handwerk und Obrigkeit in Süddeutschland während der frühen Neuzeit." In *Geschlechtergesellschaften, Zunft-Trinkstuben und Bruderschaften in spätmittelalterlichen und frühneuzeitlichen Städten*, edited by Gerhard Fouquet et. al., 163–179. Ostfildern: 2003.
Elton, G.R. "Parliament in the Sixteenth Century: Functions and Fortunes." *English Historical Review* 22 (1979): 255–278.
Enders, Lieselott. "Standeswechsel in der Stille. Vom Lehnbürger zum Landadligen, untersucht am Beispiel der Altmark." In *Jahrbuch für Brandenburgische Landesgeschichte* 57 (2006): 9–31.
Endres, Rudolf. *Adel in der frühen Neuzeit*. Munich: 1993.
Engels, Hans-Werner. "Friedrich Christian Laukhards Rechtfertigung der revolutionären Jakobinerdiktatur." In *Die demokratische Bewegung in Mitteleuropa im ausgehenden 18. und frühen 19. Jahrhundert*, edited by Otto Büsch and Walter Grab, 56–72. Berlin: 1980.
Enzel, Kathrin. "'Eins Raths Kirmiß...' Die 'Große Kölner Gottestracht' als Rahmen der politischen Selbstdarstellung städtischer Obrigkeiten." In *Interaktion und Herrschaft. Die Politik der frühneuzeitlichen Stadt*, edited by Rudolf Schlögl, 471–497. Konstanz: 2004.

Epple, Angelika. *Empfindsame Geschichtsschreibung. Eine Geschlechtergeschichte der Historiographie zwischen Aufklärung und Historismus*. Bielefeld: 2003.

Eßer, Raingard. "Landstände im Alten Reich. Ein Forschungsüberblick." In *Zeitschrift für Neuere Rechtsgeschichte* 25 (2005): 254–271.

Estor, Johann Georg and Johann Wilhelm Fech. *De Comitiis et Ordinibus Hassiae praesertim Cassellanae provincialibus opusculum*. Frankfurt: 1752.

Fackler, Claus. *Stiftsadel und geistliche Territorien 1670–1803. Untersuchungen zur Amtstätigkeit und Entwicklung des Stiftsadels, besonders in den Territorien Salzburg, Bamberg und Ellwangen*. St. Ottilien: 2006.

Fann, Willard R. "Foreigners in the Prussian Army, 1713–1756: Some Statistical and Interpretive Problems." In *Central European History* 123:1 (March 1990): 76–84.

Faßmann, David. *Das Glorwürdigste Leben und Thaten Friedrich Augusti, des Großen, Königs in Pohlen und Chur-Fürstens zu Sachsen....* Hamburg und Frankfurt: 1733.

———. *Der gelehrte Narr, Oder, Ganz natürliche Abbildung Solcher Gelehrten, Die da vermeynen all Gelehrsamkeit und Wissenschafften verschlucket zu haben, auch in dem Wahn stehen, daß ihres gleichen nicht auf Erden zu finden, wannenhero sie alle andere Menschen gegen sich verachten, einen unerträglichen Stoltz und Hochmuth von sich spüren lassen; in der That aber doch selber so, wie sie in ihrer Haut stecken, Ignoranten, Pedanten, ja Ertz-Fantasten und dumme Sympel sind, die von der wahren Gelehrsamkeit, womit die Weisheit verknüpffet seyn muß, weit entfernet....* Freiburg: 1729.

Feltmann, Gerhard Feltmann. *De impari matrimonio*. Bremen: 1691.

Feuchter, Jörg and Johannes Helmrath, eds. *Politische Redekultur in der Vormoderne. Die Oratorik europäischer Parlamente in Spätmittelalter und Früher Neuzeit*. Frankfurt a.M.: 2008.

Field, Geoffrey G. *Evangelist of Race. The Germanic Vision of Houston Stewart Chamberlain*. New York: 1981.

Fillitz, Hermann. "Die Reichskleinodien: Entstehung und Geschichte." In *Heiliges Römisches Reich Deutscher Nation 962 bis 1806: Von Otto dem Großen bis zum Ausgang des Mittelalters: Essays*, edited by Matthias Puhle and Claus-Peter Hasse. Dresden: 2006.

Fimpel, Martin. *Reichsjustiz und Territorialstaat. Württemberg als Kommissar von Kaiser und Reich im Schwäbischen Kreis (1648–1806)*. Tübingen: 2000.

Flaskamp, Franz. "Das Wiedenbrücker Verhör. Ein Beitrag zur Geschichte der Gegenreformation." In *Jahrbuch für westfälische Kirchengeschichte* 45/46 (1952/53): 151–192.

Fliessenhaussen, Johann Theodoretus von. *De Comitiis Provincialibus. Das ist gründlicher Bericht von Land-Tägen*. N.p.: 1692.

Folz, Robert. *Le Souvenir et la Légende de Charlemagne dans l'Empire germanique médiévale*. Paris: 1950.

Forster, Marc R. *The Counter-Reformation in the Villages: Religion and Reform in the Bishopric of Speyer, 1560–1720*. Ithaca: 1992.

Forster, Wilhelm. "Die kirchliche Aufklärung bei den Benediktinern der Abtei Banz." In *Studien und Mitteilungen zur Geschichte des Benediktinerordens und seiner Zweige* 63 (1951): 172–233, and 64 (1952): 110–233.

Frantz, Adolf. *Das Katholische Directorium des Corpus Evangelicorum. Nach handschriftlichen Quellen dargestellt.* Marburg: 1880.

Freist, Dagmar. "Einleitung: Staatsbildung, lokale Herrschaftsprozesse und kultureller Wandel in der Frühen Neuzeit." In *Staatsbildung als kultureller Prozess. Strukturwandel und Legitimation von Herrschaft in der Frühen Neuzeit*, edited by Ronald G. Asch and Dagmar Freist, 1–47. Cologne: 2005.

Frensdorff, F., ed. *Chronik von 1368 bis 1406 mit Fortsetzung bis 1447. Chroniken der deutschen Städte.* Vol. 4. Leipzig: 1865.

Friedeburg, Robert von. "Widerstandsrecht und Landespatriotismus: Territorialstaatsbildung und Patriotenpflichten in den Auseinandersetzungen der niederhessischen Stände mit Landgräfin Amelie Elisabeth und Landgraf Wilhelm VI. von Hessen-Kassel 1647–1653." In *Wissen, Gewissen und Wissenschaft im Widerstandsrecht (16.–18. Jh.)*, edited by Angela De Benedictis and Karl-Heinz Lingens, 267–327. Frankfurt a.M.: 2003.

Friedland, Paul. *Political Actors: Representative Bodies and Theatricality in the Age of the French Revolution.* Ithaca: 2002.

Friedrichs, Christopher R. *The Early Modern City, 1450–1750.* London and New York: 1995.

———. *Urban politics in Early Modern Europe.* London and New York: 2000.

Fritz, Wolfgang D., ed. *Fontes iuris Germanici antiqui in usum scholarum.* Vol. 11, *Die goldene Bulle Kaiser Karls IV. vom Jahre 1356. Monumenta Germaniae Historica.* Weimar: 1972.

Fuchs, Ralf-Peter. "Die Autorität von 'Normaljahren' bei der kirchlichen Neuordnung nach dem Dreißigjährigen Krieg—Das Fürstbistum Osnabrück und die Grafschaft Mark im Vergleich." In *Die Autorität der Zeit in der Frühen Neuzeit*, edited by Arndt Brendecke, Ralf-Peter Fuchs, and Edith Koller, 353–374. Berlin: 2007.

———. *Ein 'Medium zum Frieden'. Die Normaljahrsregel und die Beendigung des Dreißigjährigen Krieges.* Munich: 2010.

———. "Erinnerungsschichten: Zur Bedeutung der Vergangenheit für den 'Gemeinen Mann,'" In *Wahrheit, Wissen, Erinnerung. Zeugenverhörprotokolle als Quelle für soziale Wissensbestände der Frühen Neuzeit*, edited by Fuchs and Winfried Schulze, 89–154. Münster: 2002.

———. "'Gott läßt sich nicht verspotten.' Zeugen im Parteienkampf vor frühneuzeitlichen Gerichten." In *Kriminalitätsgeschichte. Beiträge zur Sozial- und Kulturgeschichte der Vormoderne*, edited by Andreas Blauert and Gerd Schwerhoff, 315–335. Konstanz: 2000.

———. "Soziales Wissen nach Reichskammergerichts-Zeugenverhören." In *Zeitenblicke* 1 (2002). http://www.zeitenblicke.de/2002/02/fuchs/index.html (accessed June 12, 2008).

Fuchs, Ralf-Peter and Winfried Schulze. *Wahrheit, Wissen, Erinnerung. Zeugenverhörprotokolle als Quelle für soziale Wissensbestände der Frühen Neuzeit.* Münster: 2002.

———. "Zeugenverhöre als historische Quellen—einige Vorüberlegungen." In Fuchs and Schulze, *Wahrheit, Wissen, Erinnerung.*

Füssel, Marian and Thomas Weller. "Einleitung." In *Ordnung und Distinktion. Praktiken sozialer Repräsentation in der ständischen Gesellschaft,* edited by Marian Füssel and Thomas Weller, 9–22. Münster: 2005.

Gall, Lothar, ed. *Vom alten zum neuen Bürgertum. Die mitteleuropäische Stadt im Umbruch; 1780–1820.* Munich: 1991.

Geary, Patrick J. *Phantoms of Remembrance: Memory and Oblivion at the end of the First Millennium.* Princeton, NJ: 1994.

Gehlen, Arnold. *Urmensch und Spätkultur. Philosophische Ergebnisse und Aussagen.* 6th ed. Frankfurt a.M.: 2004.

Geisberg, Max. *Die Stadt Münster.* Vol. 1. Münster: 1932.

Gerbert, Martin. *De communione potestatis ecclesiasticae inter summos ecclesiae principes pontificem, & episcopos.* 1761

———. *Historia Nigrae Silvae Ordinis Sancti Benedicti Coloniae.* St. Blasien: 1783. Reprinted in *Geschichte des Schwarzwaldes.* 2 vols., translated into German by Adalbert Weh. (Freiburg: 1993, 1996).

Gerteis, Klaus. *Die deutschen Städte in der Frühen Neuzeit. Zur Vorgeschichte der "bürgerlichen Welt."* Darmstadt: 1986.

Gestrich, Andreas. *Absolutismus und Öffentlichkeit. Politische Kommunikation in Deutschland zu Beginn des 18. Jahrhunderts.* Göttingen: 1994.

———. "Politik im Alltag: Zur Funktion politischer Information im deutschen Absolutismus des frühen 18. Jahrhunderts." In *Aufklärung* 5 (1990): 9–27.

Giel, Robert. *Politische Öffentlichkeit im spätmittelalterlich-frühneuzeitlichem Köln (1450–1550).* Berlin: 1998.

Gierke, Otto Friedrich von. *Das deutsche Genossenschaftsrecht.* Vol. 1, *Rechtsgeschichte der deutschen Genossenschaft.* Berlin: 1868.

———. "Über die Geschichte des Majoritätsprinzipes." In *Schmollers Jahrbuch für Gesetzgebung, Verwaltung und Volkswirtschaft im Deutschen Reiche* 39 (1915): 7–29.

Gierl, Martin. "Zeitschriften—Stadt—Information—London—Göttingen—Aufklärung." In *Jenseits der Diskurse. Aufklärungspraxis und Institutionenwelt in europäisch komparatistischer Perspektive,* edited by Martin Gierl et al., 243–264. Göttingen: 2007.

Gleba, Gudrun. *Die Gemeinde als alternatives Ordnungsmodell. Zur sozialen und politischen Differenzierung des Gemeindebegriffs in den innerstädtischen Auseinandersetzungen des 14. und 15. Jahrhunderts. Mainz, Magdeburg, München, Lübeck.* Cologne and Vienna: 1989.

Godsey, William D. *Nobles and Nation in Central Europe: Free Imperial Knights in the Age of Revolution, 1750–1850.* Cambridge: 2004.

Goody, Jack and Ian Watt. "Konsequenzen der Literalität." In *Entstehung und Folgen der Schriftkultur*, edited by Jack Goody, Ian Watt and Kathleen Gough, 63–122. Frankfurt a. M.: 1986.

Goppold, Uwe. *Politische Kommunikation in den Städten der Vormoderne. Zürich und Münster im Vergleich.* Cologne: 2007.

———. "Stadtrichter, Rat und Landesherr. Die Ratskur in Münster während des 17. Jahrhunderts." In *Interaktion und Herrschaft. Die Politik der frühneuzeitlichen Stadt*, edited by Rudolf Schlögl, 93–112. Konstanz: 2004.

Gorski, Philip. "The Mosaic Moment: An Early Modernist Critique of Modernist Theories of Nationalism." In *American Journal of Sociology* 105, no. 5 (2000): 1428–1468.

Gothelf, Rodney. "Frederick William I and the Beginnings of Prussian Absolutism, 1713–1740." In *The Rise of Prussia, 1700–1830*, edited by Philip G. Dwyer, 47–67. Harlow, UK: 2000.

Gotthard, Axel. *Das Alte Reich. 1495–1806.* Darmstadt: 2003.

———. *Der Augsburger Religionsfrieden.* Münster: 2004.

Graf, Klaus. "Eberhard im Bart und die Herzogserhebung, 1495." In *Württemberg wird Herzogtum. Dokumente aus dem Hauptstaatsarchiv Stuttgart zu einem epochalen Ereignis*, 9–43. Stuttgart:1995.

Granier, Gerhard. "Der deutsche Reichstag während des Spanischen Erbfolgekriegs (1700–1714)." Ph.D. dissertation, Bonn, 1954.

Graßmann, Antjekathrin. "Lübeck im 17. Jahrhundert: Wahrung des Erreichten." In *Lübeckische Geschichte*, edited by Antjekathrin Graßmann. 3rd ed., 435–488. Lübeck: 1997.

Graus, František. *Lebendige Vergangenheit: Überlieferung im Mittelalter und in den Vorstellungen vom Mittelalter.* Cologne and Vienna: 1975.

Graves, Michael A.R. *The Parliaments of Early Modern Europe.* Harlow: 2001.

Grimme, Ernst Günther. "Das gotische Rathaus der Stadt Aachen." In *Krönungen: Könige in Aachen—Geschichte und Mythos*, 2 vols., edited by Mario Kramp. Vol. 2, 509–515. Mainz: 1999.

Groebner, Valentin. *Defaced: The Visual Culture of Violence in the Late Middle Ages.* Translated by Pamela Selwyn. New York: 2004.

Großmann, Ulrich. "Burgen und Pfalzen des Reiches." In *Heiliges Römisches Reich Deutscher Nation 962 bis 1806: Von Otto dem Großen bis zum Ausgang des Mittelalters: Essays*, edited by Matthias Puhle and Claus-Peter Hasse, 222–235. Dresden: 2006.

Grundmann, Herbert and Hermann Heimpel, eds. *Staatsschriften des späteren Mittelalters.* Vol 1.1, *Alexander von Roes: Schriften*. Monumenta Germaniae Historica. Stuttgart: 1958.

Guenée, Bernard. *States and Rulers in Later Medieval Europe.* Translated by Juliet Vale. Oxford: 1985.

Gumbrecht, Hans Ulrich. *Production of Presence: What Meaning Cannot Convey.* Stanford: 2004. Translated as *Diesseits der Hermeneutik. Die Produktion von Präsenz.* Frankfurt a.M., 2004.

Häberlin, Carl Friedrich. *Pragmatische Geschichte der neuesten kaiserlichen Wahlcapitulation und der an kaiserliche Majestät erlassenen kurfürstlichen Collegialschreiben.* Leipzig: 1792.

Habermas, Jürgen. *The Structural Transformation of the Public Sphere: An Inquiry into a Category of Bourgeois Society.* Translated by Thomas Burger. Cambridge, MA: 1989.

Hackspiel-Mikosch, Elisabeth and Stefan Haas, eds. *Die zivile Uniform als symbolische Kommunikation: Kleidung zwischen Repräsentation, Imagination und Konsumption vom 18. bis zum 21. Jahrhundert.* Munich: 2006.

Hafner, Urs. *Republik im Konflikt. Schwäbische Reichsstädte und bürgerliche Politik in der frühen Neuzeit.* Tübingen: 2001.

Hagen, William W. "Descent of the *Sonderweg*: Hans Rosenberg's History of Old-Regime Prussia." In *Central European History* 24:1 (1991): 24-50.

Hahn, Peter-Michael. "Pracht und Selbstinszenierung. Die Hofhaltung Friedrich Wilhelms I. von Preußen." In *Der Soldatenkönig: Friedrich Wilhelm I. in seiner Zeit,* edited by Friedrich Beck and Julius H. Schoeps, 69–98. Potsdam: 2003.

Hammel-Kiesow, Rolf. "Neue Aspekte zur Geschichte Lübecks: von der Jahrtausendwende bis zum Ende der Hansezeit. Die Lübecker Stadtgeschichtsforschung der letzten zehn Jahre (1988–1997), Teil 2: Verfassungsgeschichte, Bürger, Rat und Kirche, Außenvertretungen und Weltwirtschaftspläne." In *Zeitschrift des Vereins für Lübeckische Geschichte und Altertumskunde* 80 (2000): 9–61.

———. "Stadtherrschaft und Herrschaft in der Stadt." In *Die Hanse. Lebenswirklichkeit und Mythos,* edited by Jörgen Bracker et. al. 3rd ed., 446–479. Lübeck: 1998.

Hanson, Michelle Zelinsky. *Religious Identity in an Early Reformation Community: Augsburg, 1517 to 1555.* Leiden, Boson: 2009.

Harding, Elizabeth. "'concludiret per majora' oder 'ausgemachet durch das los'—Entscheidungsverfahren landsässiger Ritterschaftskurien im 17. und 18. Jahrhundert." In *Zelebrieren und Verhandeln. Zur Praxis ständischer Institutionen im frühneuzeitlichen Europa,* edited by Tim Neu, Michael Sikora, and Thomas Weller, 195–211. Münster: 2008.

———. "Zeremoniell im Nebenland. Frühneuzeitliche Bischofseinsetzungen in Münster." In *Westfälische Forschungen* 57 (2007): 229–256.

Härter, Karl. "Der Rekurs des Fürsten Friedrich Karl von Wied-Neuwied. Zum Verhältnis von Reichskammergericht und Reichstag am Ende des Alten Reiches." In *Vorträge zur Justizforschung* 2 (1993): 245–284.

Hartmann, Peter-Claus. *Kulturgeschichte des Heiligen Römischen Reiches 1648 bis 1806.* Vienna: 2001.

Hartung, Fritz. "Die politischen Testamente der Hohenzollern." In *Forschungen zur brandenburgischen und preussischen Geschichte* 25 (1913): 333–363.

———. "König Friedrich Wilhelm I. Der Begründer des preussischen Staates." In *Preussischen Akademie der Wissenschaften Vorträge und Schriften* 11 (Berlin, 1942): 6, 10.
Harvey, P.D.A. *Medieval Maps*. London: 1991.
Haude, Sigrun. *In the Shadow of 'Savage Wolves': Anabaptist Münster and the German Reformation during the 1530s*. Atlantic Highlands: 2000.
Haug-Moritz, Gabriele. "Corpus Evangelicorum und deutscher Dualismus." In *Alternativen zur Reichsverfassung in der Frühen Neuzeit?* Schriftenreihe des Historischen Kollegs, Kolloquien 23, edited by Volker Press, 189–207. Munich: 1995.
———. "'Des'Kaysers rechter Arm': Der Reichshofrat und die Reichspolitik des Kaisers." In *Das Reich und seine Territorialstaaten im 17. und 18. Jahrhundert. Aspekte des Mit-, Neben- und Gegeneinander*. Historia profana et ecclesiastica 10, edited by Harm Klueting and Wolfgang Schmale, 23–42. Münster: 2004.
———. "Die Behandlung des württembergischen Ständekonflikts unter Herzog Carl Eugen durch den Reichshofrat (1763/64–1768/70)." In *Die politische Funktion des Reichskammergerichts*, edited by Bernhard Diestelkamp, 105–133. Cologne: 1993.
———. "Kaisertum und Parität. Reichspolitik und Konfessionen nach dem Westfälischen Frieden." In *Zeitschrift für historische Forschung* 19 (1992): 445–482.
———. "Reichstag, schmalkaldische Bundestage, ernestinische Land- und Ausschußtage der 1530er Jahre als ständische Institutionen – eine vergleichende Betrachtung." In *Zelebrieren und Verhandeln. Zur Praxis ständischer Institutionen im frühneuzeitlichen Europa*, edited by Tim Neu, Michael Sikora and Thomas Weller. Münster: forthcoming 2009.
———. *Württembergischer Ständekonflikt und deutscher Dualismus. Ein Beitrag zur Geschichte des Reichsverbands in der Mitte des 18. Jahrhunderts*. Veröffentlichungen der Kommission für geschichtliche Landeskunde in Baden-Württemberg, Reihe B, Forschungen, vol. 122. Stuttgart: 1992.
Hauptstaatsarchiv Dresden, Geheimes Konsilium, Loc. 5141.
Hauptstaatsarchiv Dresden, Geheimes Konsilium, Loc. 5143.
Hauptstaatsarchiv Dresden, Geheimes Konsilium, Loc. 5144.
Hauschild, Wolf-Dieter. "Frühe Neuzeit und Reformation: Das Ende der Großmachtstellung und die Neuorientierung der Stadtgemeinschaft." In *Lübeckische Geschichte*, edited by Antjekathrin Graßmann. 3rd ed., 341–432. Lübeck: 1997.
———. *Kirchengeschichte Lübecks. Christentum und Bürgertum in neun Jahrhunderten*. Lübeck: 1981.
Hausen, Karin. "Die Nicht-Einheit der Geschichte als historiographische Herausforderung. Zur historischen Relevanz und Anstößigkeit der Geschlechtergeschichte." In *Geschlechtergeschichte als Allgemeine Geschichte. Herausforderungen und Perspektiven*, edited by Hans Medick and Anne Charlott Trepp, 15–55. Göttingen: 1998.
Heckel, Martin. "Itio in partes. Zur Religionsverfassung des Heiligen Römischen Reichs Deutscher Nation." In *Zeitschrift der Savigny-Stiftung für Rechtsgeschichte, Kanonistische Abteilung* 64 (1978): 180–308.

Heerma van Voss, Lex. "Introduction." In *Petitions in Social History*, edited by Lex Heerma van Voss, 1–10. Cambridge: 2001.
Hegel, Carl, ed. *Chronik des Jacob Twinger von Königshofen. Chroniken der deutschen Städte*. Vols. 9 and 11. Leipzig: 1870.
Hehl, Ernst-Dieter. "Die Erzbischöfe von Mainz bei Erhebung, Salbung und Krönung des Königs (10. bis 14. Jahrhundert)." In *Krönungen: Könige in Aachen – Geschichte und Mythos*, 2 vols., edited by Mario Kramp. Vol. 1, 97–104. Mainz: 1999.
Heimpel, Hermann. *Dietrich von Niem (c.1340–1418)*. Münster: 1932.
Heinig, Paul-Joachim. "Der Wormser Reichstag von 1495 als Hoftag." In *Zeitschrift für historische Forschung* 33 (2006): 337–357.
———. "'Omnia vincit amor'—Das fürstliche Konkubinat im 15./16. Jahrhundert." In *Principes. Dynastien und Höfe im späten Mittelalter*, edited by Cordula Nolte, Karl-Heinz Spiess, and Ralf-Gunnar Werlich, 277–314. Stuttgart: 2002.
Helmrath, Johannes. "Rangstreite auf Generalkonzilien des 15. Jahrhunderts als Verfahren." In *Vormoderne politische Verfahren*, edited by Barbara Stollberg-Rilinger, 139–173. Berlin: 2001.
Hengerer, Mark. *Kaiserhof und Adel in der Mitte des 17. Jahrhunderts. Eine Kommunikationsgeschichte der Macht in der Vormoderne*. Konstanz, 2004.
Herre, Paul. *Die geheime Ehe des Erbprinzen Wilhelm Gustav von Anhalt-Dessau und die Reichsgrafen von Anhalt*. Zerbst: 1933. Reprinted, Dessau: 2006.
Herrich, Nikolaus August, ed. *Sammlung aller Conclusorum, Schreiben und anderer Verhandlungen des hochpreißlichen Corporis Evangelicorum vom Jahre 1753 bis 1786. Als eine Fortsetzung des Schaurothischen Werks, nach Ordnung der Materien zusammengetragen*. Regensburg: 1786.
Herrmann, Susanne. "Die Durchführung von Schuldenverfahren im Rahmen kaiserlicher Debitkommissionen im 18. Jahrhundert am Beispiel des Debitwesens der Grafen Montfort." In *Reichshofrat und Reichskammergericht—ein Konkurrenzverhältnis*, edited by Wolfgang Sellert, 111–128. Cologne: 1999.
Hersche, Peter. *Die deutschen Domkapitel im 17. und 18. Jahrhundert*. Bern: 1984.
———. *Muße und Verschwendung. Europäische Gesellschaft und Kultur im Barockzeitalter*. 2 vols. Freiburg: 2006.
Herzig, Arno. "Die Rekatholisierung in deutschen Territorien im 16. und 17. Jahrhundert." In *Geschichte und Gesellschaft* 26 (2000): 76–104.
Herzogenberg, Johanna von. "Die Bildnisse Kaiser Karls IV." In *Kaiser Karl IV.: Staatsmann und Mäzen*, edited by Ferdinand Seibt, 324–334. Munich: 1978.
Hessen, Rainer von, ed. *"Wir Wilhelm von Gottes Gnaden." Die Lebenserinnerungen Kurfürst Wilhelms I. von Hessen. 1743–1821*. Frankfurt: 1996.
Hinrichs, Carl. "Der Konflict zwischen Friedrich Wilhelm I. und Kronprinz Friedrich." In *Der Kronprinzenprozeß. Friedrich und Katte*, 5–20. Hamburg, 1936. Reprinted, *Preussen als historisches Problem, Gesammelte Abhandlungen*, edited by Gerhard Oestreich, 185–202. Berlin: 1964.

———. *Der Kronprinzen Prozeß: Friedrich und Katte*. Hamburg, 1936. Reprinted, "Friedrich Wilhelm I. und Kronprinz Friedrich," in *Preussen als historisches Problem: Gesammelte Abandlungen*, 185–202. Berlin: 1964.

———. "Der Regierungsantritt Friedrich Wilhelms I." *Jahrbuch für die Geschichte Mittel- und Ostdeutschlands* 5 (1956): 183–225. Reprinted, *Preussen als historisches Problem, Gesammelte Abhandlungen*, edited by Gerhard Oestreich, 91–137. Berlin: 1964.

Hintze, Otto. *The Historical Essays of Otto Hintze*. New York: 1975.

Hitler, Adolf. *Mein Kampf: Zwei Bände in einem Band*. Munich: 1934.

Hochmuth, Christian and Susanne Rau, eds. *Machträume der frühneuzeitlichen Stadt*. Konstanz: 2006.

Hoffmann, Christian. "Das Archiv der Osnabrücker Ritterschaft. Zur Geschichte eines ständischen Verwaltungsinstrumentes im 17. und 18. Jahrhundert." In *Osnabrücker Mitteilungen* 102 (1997): 195-208.

Hoffmann, Erich. "Lübeck im Hoch- und Spätmittelalter." In *Lübeckische Geschichte*, edited by Antjekathrin Graßmann. 3rd ed., 79–339. Lübeck: 1997.

Hoffmann, Philip R. "Soziale Differenzierung und politische Integration. Zum Strukturwandel der politischen Ordnung in Lübeck (15.–17. Jahrhundert)." In *Stadtgemeinde und Ständegesellschaft. Formen der Integration und Distinktion in der frühneuzeitlichen Stadt*, edited by Patrick Schmidt and Horst Carl, 166–197. Berlin: 2007.

Höfing. *Nutzung eines Versammlungslokals im Domportikus seitens der Osnabrückischen adeligen Ritterschaft*. Osnabrück: 1897.

Hofmann, Hanns Hubert. *Adelige Herrschaft und souveräner Staat. Studien über Staat und Gesellschaft in Franken und Bayern im 18. und 19. Jahrhundert*. Munich: 1962.

Hofmann, Hasso. "Der spätmittelalterliche Rechtsbegriff der Repräsentation in Reich und Kirche." In *Höfische Repräsentation. Das Zeremoniell und die Zeichen*, edited by Hedda Ragotzky and Horst Wenzel, 17–42. Tübingen: 1990.

———. *Repräsentation. Studien zur Wort- und Begriffsgeschichte von der Antike bis ins 19. Jahrhundert*. 4th ed. Berlin: 2003.

Hofmeister, Adolf. *Die Chronik des Mathias von Neuenburg*. Monumenta Germaniae Historica, Scriptores rerum Germanicarum in usum scholarum. Nova series, vol. 4. Berlin: 1924.

Hohkamp, Michaela. "Do Sisters have Brothers? – Or the Search for the 'rechte Schwester.' Brothers and Sisters in Aristocratic Society at the Turn of the Sixteenth Century." In *Sibling Relations and the Transformations of European Kinship, 1300-1900*, edited by Christopher H Johnson and David Warren Sabean (forthcoming).

———. "Eine Tante für alle Fälle: Tanten-Nichten-Beziehungen und ihre politische Bedeutung für die reichsfürstliche Gesellschaft der Frühen Neuzeit (16. bis 18. Jahrhundert)." In *Politiken der Verwandtschaft*, edited by Margareth Lanzinger and Edith Saurer, 149–171. Vienna: 2007.

———. "Sisters, Aunts and Cousins: Familial Architectures and the Political Field in Early Modern Europe." In *Kinship in Europe: Approaches to Long-Term Developments (1300–1900)*, edited by David Warren Sabean, Simon Teuscher, and Jon Mathieu, 128–145. Oxford and New York: 2007.
Holenstein, André. *Die Huldigung der Untertanen: Rechtskultur und Herrschaftshordnung (800–1800)*. Stuttgart: 1991.
———. "Empowering Interactions: Looking at Statebuilding from Below." In *Empowering Interactions. Political Cultures and the Emergence of the State in Europe, 1300-1900*, edited by Wim Blockmans, Andre Holenstein, Jon Mathieu and Daniel Schlappi, 1–31. Farnham and Burlington, VT: 2009.
———. *"Gute Policey" und lokale Gesellschaft im Staat des Ancien Régime. Das Fallbeispiel der Markgrafschaft Baden(-Durlach)*. Tübingen: 2003.
———, ed. *Statebuilding from Below*. Forthcoming.
Hollenberg, Günter. "Die hessen-kasselischen Landstände im 18. Jahrhundert." In *Hessisches Jahrbuch für Landesgeschichte* 38 (1988): 1–22.
———. "Die Repräsentation von Land und Leuten in Hessen." In *Reformation und Landesherrschaft*, edited by Inge Auerbach, 31–38. Marburg: 2005.
Hollenberg, Günter, ed. *Hessen-Kasselische Landtagsabschiede 1649–1798*. Marburg: 1989.
———. *Hessische Landtagsabschiede 1526–1603*. Marburg: 1994.
Holzem, Andreas. *Der Konfessionsstaat, 1555–1802*. Münster: 1998.
Hontheim, Niklaus. *Buch von dem Zustand der Kirche und der rechtmäßigen Gewalt des römischen Papsts die in der Religion widriggesinnten Christen zu vereinigen*. Wardigen: 1764.
———. *Commentarius in suam retractationem*. 1781. Reprinted and edited by Ulrich L. Lehner. Nordhausen: 2008.
———. *Febronius abbreviatus et emendatus*. 1777. Reprinted and edited by Ulrich L. Lehner. Nordhausen: 2008.
———. *Justini Febronii JCti de Statu Ecclesiae et Legitima Potestate Romani Pontificis Liber Singularis, ad Reuniendos Dissidentes in Religione Christianos Compositus*. 1763.
Hortleder, Friedrich, ed. *Von den Ursachen des Teutschen Krieges*. Frankfurt a.M.: 1617.
Hsia, R. Po-Chia. *Society and Religion in Münster, 1535–1618*. New Haven: 1984.
Hubensteiner, Benno. *Vom Geist des Barock. Kultur und Frömmigkeit im alten Bayern*. Munich: 1967.
Huber, Alfons. *Agnes Bernauer. Ein Quellen- und Lesebuch*. Straubing: 1999.
Hughes, Michael. *Early Modern Germany, 1477–1806*. Philadelphia: 1992.
———. *Law and Politics in Eighteenth Century Germany. The Imperial Aulic Council in the Reign of Charles VI*. Woodbridge: 1988.
Hülle, Werner. "Das Supplikenwesen in Rechtssachen. Anlageplan für eine Dissertation." In *Zeitschrift für Rechtsgeschichte, Germanistische Abteilung* 90 (1973): 194–212.

Iggers, Georg. *The German Conception of History: The National Tradition of Historical Thought from Herder to the Present*. Revised edition. Middletown: 1983.

Immenkötter, Herbert. "Die Auseinandersetzung des Domkapitels in Münster mit dem Geistlichen Rat." In *Von Konstanz nach Trient: Beiträge zur Geschichte der Kirche von den Reformkonzilien bis zum Tridentinum*, edited by in Remigius Bäumer, 713–727. Munich: 1972.

Ingrao, Charles W. *The Hessian Mercenary State. Ideas, Institutions, and Reform under Frederick II. 1760–1785*. Cambridge: 1987.

Isenmann, Eberhard. *Die deutsche Stadt im Spätmittelalter 1250–1500. Stadtgestalt, Recht, Stadtregiment, Kirche, Gesellschaft, Wirtschaft*. Stuttgart: 1988.

———. "Obrigkeit und Stadtgemeinde in der frühen Neuzeit." In *Einwohner und Bürger auf dem Weg zur Demokratie: Von den antiken Stadtrepubliken zur modernen Kommunalverfassung*, edited by Hans Eugen Specker, 74–126. Stuttgart: 1997.

———. "Ratsliteratur und städtische Ratsordnungen des späten Mittelalters und der frühen Neuzeit. Soziologie des Rats—Amt und Willensbildung—politische Kultur." In *Stadt und Recht im Mittelalter / La ville et le droit au Moyen Age*, edited by Pierre Monnet and Otto G. Oexle, 215–479. Göttingen: 2003.

Iwand, Fritz Georg. *Die Wahlkapitulationen des 17. und 18. Jahrhunderts und ihr Einfluß auf die Entwicklung des Ebenbürtigkeits- und Prädikatsrechts des deutschen hohen Adels*. Biberach: 1919.

Jahns, Sigrid. *Das Reichskammergericht und seine Richter: Verfassung und Sozialstruktur eines höchsten Gerichts im Alten Reich*. Part 2, vol. 2, Biographies. Cologne: 2003.

Jaitner, Klaus. *Die Konfessionspolitik des Pfalzgrafen Philipp Wilhelm von Neuburg in Jülich-Berg von 1647–1679*. Münster: 1973.

Jannasch, Wilhelm. *Reformationsgeschichte Lübecks von Petersablaß bis zum Augsburger Reichstag 1515–1530*. Lübeck: 1958.

Johanek, Peter. "Bürgerkämpfe und Verfassung in den mittelalterlichen deutschen Städten." In *Einwohner und Bürger auf dem Weg zur Demokratie: Von den antiken Stadtrepubliken zur modernen Kommunalverfassung*, edited by Hans Eugen Specker, 45–73. Stuttgart: 1997.

Jooß, Rainer. "Schwörtage in Esslingen vor 1802." In *Esslinger Studien* 31 (1992): 1–14.

Jüngling, Hans Jürgen. "Die Heiraten des Hauses Liechtenstein im 17. und 18. Jahrhundert." In *Liechtenstein—Fürstliches Haus und staatliche Ordnung*, edited by Volker Press and Dietmar Willoweit, 329–345. Munich and Vienna: 1987.

Kaiser, Peter. *Geschichte des Fürstenthums Liechtenstein*. Vol. 1. Chur: 1847. Reprinted, Vaduz: 1989.

Kalipke, Andreas. "'Weitläufftigkeiten' und 'Bedencklichkeiten'—die Behandlung konfessioneller Konflikte am Corpus Evangelicorum." In *Zeitschrift für historische Forschung* 35 (2008): 405–447.

———. "Verfahren—Macht—Entscheidung. Die Behandlung konfessioneller Streitigkeiten durch das *Corpus* Evangelicorum im 18. Jahrhundert aus verfahrensgeschichtlicher Perspektive." In *Herstellung und Darstellung verbindlicher Entscheidungen*.

Legitimation in vormodernen und modernen Gesellschaften, edited by Barbara Stollberg-Rilinger and André Krischer. Forthcoming.

Kalkoff, Paul. *Huttens Vagantenzeit und Untergang. Der geschichtliche Ulrich von Hutten und seine Umwelt*. Weimar: 1925.

Kaplan, Benjamin J. *Divided by Faith: Religious Conflict and the Practice of Toleration in Early Modern Europe*. Cambridge, MA: 2007.

——. "Fictions of Privacy: House Chapels and the Spatial Accommodation of Religious Dissent in Early Modern Europe." In *American Historical Review* 107 (2002): 1030–1064.

Kasten, Ingrid. "Einleitung: Lucien Febvre und die Folgen: zu einer Geschichte der Gefühle und ihrer Erforschung." In *Kulturen der Gefühle im Mittelalter und Früher Neuzeit*, edited by Ingrid Kasten et al., 9–21. Stuttgart: 2002.

Kaufmann, Thomas. "Apokalyptische Deutung und politisches Denken im lutherischen Protestantismus in der Mitte des 16. Jahrhunderts." In *Die Autorität der Zeit in der Frühen Neuzeit*, edited by Arndt Brendecke, Ralf-Peter Fuchs, and Edith Koller, 411–453. Berlin: 2007.

Kavka, František. "Karl IV. (1349–1378) und Aachen." In *Krönungen: Könige in Aachen–Geschichte und Mythos*, 2 vols., edited by Mario Kramp. Vol. 2, 477–484. Mainz: 1999.

Kazner, Johann Friedrich August. *Louise, Raugräfin zu Pfalz: eine wahre Geschichte von dem Verfasser des Lebens Friedrichs von Schomberg*. Vol. 1. Leipzig: 1798.

Keinemann, Friedrich. *Das Domkapitel zu Münster im 18. Jahrhundert: Verfassung, persönliche Zusammensetzung, Parteiverhältnisse*. Münster: 1967.

Kell, Eva. *Das Fürstentum Leiningen. Umbruchserfahrungen einer Adelsherrschaft zur Zeit der Französischen Revolution*. Kaiserslautern: 1993.

Keller, Hagen and Christel Meier, eds. *Schriftlichkeit und Lebenspraxis im Mittelalter. Erfassen, Bewahren, Verändern*. Munich: 1999.

Keller, Ludwig. *Die Gegenreformation in Westfalen und am Niederrhein: Actenstücke und Erläuterungen*. Leipzig: 1881–1895.

Kendall, Paul M. and Vincent Ilardi, eds. *Dispatches with Related Documents of Milanese Ambassadors in France and Burgundy, 1450–1483*. 3 vols. Athens, OH: 1971–1981.

Kieserling, André. *Kommunikation unter Anwesenden. Studien über Interaktionssysteme*. Frankfurt a.M.: 1999.

Kintzinger, Martin. "Die zwei Frauen des Königs, Zum politischen Handlungsspielraum von Fürstinnen im europäischen Spätmittelalter." In *Das Frauenzimmer. Die Frau bei Hofe in Spätmittelalter und früher Neuzeit. 6. Symposium der Residenzen-Kommission der Akademie der Wissenschaften in Göttingen*, edited by Jan Hirschbiegel and Werner Paravicini, 377–398. Stuttgart: 2000.

——. "Zeichen und Imaginationen des Reichs." In *Heilig—Römisch—Deutsch: Das Reich im mittelalterlichen Europa*, edited by Bernd Schneidmüller and Stefan Weinfurter, 345–371. Dresden: 2006.

Kirchhoff, Karl-Heinz. "Ständeversammlungen und erste Landtage im Stift Münster, 1212–1278, und der Landtagsplatz auf dem Laerbrock." In *Westfälische Forschungen* 30 (1988): 207–234.

———. *Die Täufer in Münster 1534/35: Untersuchungen zum Umfang und zur Sozialstruktur der Bewegung*. Münster: 1973.

Kirchner, Joachim. *Das Deutsche Zeitschriftenwesen. Seine Geschichte und seine Probleme. Part 1. Von den Anfängen bis zum Zeitalter der Romantik, and Part 2. neubearbeitete und erweiterte Auflage*. 2nd ed. Wiesbaden: 1958.

Kleinehagenbrock, Frank. "Die Erhaltung des Religionsfriedens. Konfessionelle Konflikte und ihre Beilegung im Alten Reich nach 1648." In *Historisches Jahrbuch* 126 (2006): 135–156.

Klein, Thomas. "Die Erhebungen in den weltlichen Reichsfürstenstand 1550–1806." In *Blätter für deutsche Landesgeschichte* 122 (1986): 137–192.

Klötzer, Ralf. *Die Täuferherrschaft von Münster: Stadtreformation und Welterneuerung*. Münster: 1992.

Kluge, Bernd. "Das Münzwesen des Mittelalters im Römisch-deutschen Reich." In *Heiliges Römisches Reich Deutscher Nation 962 bis 1806: Von Otto dem Großen bis zum Ausgang des Mittelalters: Essays*, edited by Matthias Puhle and Claus-Peter Hasse, 373–382. Dresden: 2006.

Klug, Ernst. "Friedrich Christian Laukhard und das Finanzwesen der Rheingrafen zu Gaugrehweiler." In *Mitteilungsblatt zur rheinhessischen Landeskunde* 17 (1968): 405–412.

Koch, Elisabeth. "Die Frau im Recht der Frühen Neuzeit. Juristische Lehren und Begründungen." In *Frauen in der Geschichte des Rechts. Von der Frühen Neuzeit bis zur Gegenwart*, edited by Ute Gerhard, 73–93. Munich: 1997.

Köcher, Adolf. *Memoiren der Herzogin Sophie nachmals Kurfürstin von Hannover*. Leipzig: 1879.

Kocka, Jürgen. "German History before Hitler: The Debate about the German Sonderweg." In *Journal of Contemporary History* 23 (1988): 3–16.

Kohl, Wilhelm. *Das Bistum Münster*. Berlin: 1999-2004.

———. *Das Domstift St. Paulus zu Münster*. Berlin and New York: 1982, 1987.

Köhler, Matthias. "Formalität—Repräsentation—Kalkül. Verhandlungen auf dem Kongress von Nimwegen, 1676–1679." In *Herstellung und Darstellung verbindlicher Entscheidungen. Legitimation in vormodernen und modernen Gesellschaften*, edited by Barbara Stollberg-Rilinger and André Krischer. Berlin: 2010.

Koller, Heinrich. *Kaiser Friedrich III*. Darmstadt: 2005.

Körber, Esther-Beate. *Öffentlichkeiten der frühen Neuzeit. Teilnehmer, Formen, Institutionen und Entscheidungen öffentlicher Kommunikation im Herzogtum Preußen von 1525 bis 1618*. Berlin and New York: 1998.

Korell, Günther. *Jürgen Wullenwever. Sein sozial-politisches Wirken in Lübeck und der Kampf mit den erstarkenden Mächten Nordeuropas*. Weimar: 1980.

Koselleck, Reinhart. *Critique and Crisis: Enlightenment and the Parthogenesis of Modern Society*. Cambridge, MA: 1988.

Köster, Gabriele. "Zwischen Grabmal und Denkmal: Das Kaiserdenkmal für Speyer und andere Grabmonumente für mittelalterliche Könige und Kaiser im 15. und 16. Jahrhundert." In *Heiliges Römisches Reich Deutscher Nation 962 bis 1806: Von Otto dem Großen bis zum Ausgang des Mittelalters: Essays*, edited by Matthias Puhle and Claus-Peter Hasse, 398–409. Dresden: 2006.

Kramp, Mario, ed. *Krönungen: Könige in Aachen—Geschichte und Mythos*. 2 vols. Mainz: 1999.

Krause, Hermann. "Gewohnheitsrecht." In *Handwörterbuch zur deutschen Rechtsgeschichte*, edited by Adalbert Erler and Ekkehard Kaufmann, vol. 1, 1675–1684. Berlin: 1971.

Krieger, Karl-Friedrich. *König, Reich und Reichsreform im Spätmittelalter*. Munich: 1992.

Krischer, André. "Grenzen Setzen. Macht, Raum und Ehre der Reichsstädte." In *Machträume der frühneuzeitlichen Stadt*, edited by Christian Hochmuth and Susanne Rau, 135–154. Konstanz: 2006.

———. "Inszenierung und Verfahren auf den Reichstagen der Frühen Neuzeit. Das Beispiel der Städtekurie und ihres politischen Verfahrens." In *Versammlungen. Ritualisierungen politischer Willensbildung im Vergleich*, edited by Gerald Schwedler, Jörg Peltzer, and Paul Töbelmann. Forthcoming.

———. *Reichsstädte in der Fürstengesellschaft. Politischer Zeichengebrauch in der Frühen Neuzeit*. Darmstadt: 2006.13

Krüger, Kersten. *Die landständische Verfassung*. Munich: 2003.

Kühn, Helga-Maria. "'… es gefellet mir reychtt woll hyr …' Die letzten Lebensjahre der Herzogin Sidonie 1573–1575 in Weißenfels." In *Das Weißenfelser St. Klaren-Kloster. Zum 700-jährigen Bestehen*, edited by Astrid Fick, 39–41. Weißenfels: 2001.

Kunisch, Johannes. "Funktion und Ausbau der kurfürstlich-königlichen Residenzen in Brandenburg-Preußen im Zeitalter des Absolutismus." In *Forschungen zur brandenburgischen und preußischen Geschichte*, Neue Folge 3 (1993): 167–192. Reprinted, *Potsdam, Märkische Kleinstadt, europäische Residenz: Reminiszenzen einer eintausenjährigen Geschichte*, edited by Peter-Michael Hahn, 61–83. Berlin: 1995.

———, ed. *Neue Studien zur frühneuzeitlichen Reichsgeschichte*. Berlin: 1987.

Küppers-Braun, Ute. *Frauen des hohen Adels im kaiserlich-freiweltlichen Damenstift Essen (1605–1803)*. Münster: 1997.

Langer, Herbert. "Innere Kämpfe und Bündnis mit Schweden. Ende des 16. Jahrhunderts bis 1630." In *Geschichte der Stadt Stralsund*, edited by Herbert Ewe, 137–167. Weimar: 1984.

Laslett, Peter. "The Face to Face Society." In *Philosophy, Politics and Society*, edited by Peter Laslett. Oxford: 1956.

Laukhard, Friedrich Christian. *Leben und Thaten des Rheingrafen Carl Magnus … zur Warnung für alle winzige Despoten, Leichtgläubige und Geschäftsmänner*. Leipzig: 1798.

La Vopa, Anthony. "Conceiving a Public: Ideas and Society in Eighteenth-Century Europe." In *Journal of Modern History* 64 (1992): 79–116.
Ledderhose, Conrad Wilhelm. *Von der landschaftlichen Verfassung der Hessen-Casselischen Lande*. In *Kleine Schriften*, vol. 1, 1–176. Marburg: 1787.
Leidinger, Georg, ed. *Chronica de gestis principum*. In *Bayerische Chroniken des XIV. Jahrhunderts*. Monumenta Germaniae Historica, Scriptores rerum Germanicarum in usum scholarum, vol. 19. Hannover and Leipzig: 1918.
Leistikow, Dankwart. "Die Aufbewahrungsorte der Reichskleinodien—vom Trifels bis Nürnberg." In *Die Reichskleinodien: Herrschaftszeichen des Heiligen Römischen Reiches*, edited by Die Gesellschaft für Staufische Geschichte, 184–213. Göppingen: 1997.
Lenin, Vladimir I. *Staat und Revolution. Die Lehre des Marxismus vom Staat und die Aufgaben des Proletariats in der Revolution*. In *Ausgewählte Werke*, vol. 2, 158–253. Berlin: 1951.
Leyers, Peter. "Reichshofratsgutachten an Kaiser Joseph II." PhD dissertation, University of Bonn: 1976.
Lilienthal, Andrea. *Die Fürstin und die Macht. Welfische Herzoginnen im 16. Jahrhundert: Elisabeth, Sidonia, Sophia*. Hannover: 2007.
Lindner, Michael. "Kaiser Karl IV. und Mitteldeutschland." In *Kaiser, Reich und Region: Studien und Texte aus der Arbeit an den Constitutiones des 14. Jahrhunderts und zur Geschichte der Monumenta Germaniae Historica*, edited by Michael Lindner, Eckhard Müller-Mertens, and Olaf B. Rader, 83–180. Berlin: 1997.
Litteratur des katholischen Deutschlands, zu dessen Ehre und Nutzen, herausgegeben von katholischen Patrioten. Coburg, 1775– .
Loen, Johann Michael von. "Der königlich Preußische Hof in Berlin, 1718." In *Des Herrn von Loen gesammelte Kleine Schrifften, Dritter Abschnitt*, edited by J.C. Schneider, 22–39. Frankfurt and Leipzig: 1750. Reprinted, Frankfurt a.M.: 1972.
———. "Der unglückliche Gelehrte am Hof. Oder: Einige Nachrichten von dem geheimen Rath und Ober-Ceremonienmeister, Freyherrn von Gundling," and "Abbildung des Professor G**." In *Des Herrn von Loen gesammelte [sic] Kleine Schrifften: Besorgt und herausgegeben von J.C. Schneider*, 198–218 and 218–221. Frankfurt and Leipzig: 1749. Reprinted, Frankfurt a.M.: 1972.
Löther, Andrea. *Prozessionen in spätmittelalterlichen Städten. Politische Partizipation, obrigkeitliche Inszenierung, städtische Einheit*. Cologne: 1999.
Löwenstein, Uta. "Voraussetzungen und Grundlagen von Tafelzeremoniell und Zeremonientafel." In *Zeremoniell als höfische Ästhetik in Spätmittelalter und Früher Neuzeit*, edited by Jörg Jochen Berns and Thomas Rahn, 266–279. Tübingen: 1995.
Lück, Alfred. *Siegerland und Nederland*. Siegen: 1981.
Luebke, David M. "Churchyard and Confession: Grave Desecration, Burial Practices, and Social Order during the Confessional Age—The Case of Warendorf." In *Leben bei den Toten: Kirchhöfe in der ländlichen Gesellschaft der Vormoderne*, edited by Jan Brademann and Werner Freitag, 193–213. Münster: 2007.

———. "Customs of Confession: Managing Religious Diversity in Late Sixteenth- and Early Seventeenth-Century Westphalia." In *Religion and Authority in Central Europe from the Reformation to the Enlightenment*, edited by Howard Louthan. Forthcoming.

———. "Signatures and Political Culture in Eighteenth-Century Germany." In *Journal of Modern History* 76 (2004): 497–530.

Luh, Jürgen. *Unheiliges Römisches Reich. Der konfessionelle Gegensatz 1648 bis 1806.* Quellen und Studien zur Geschichte und Kultur Brandenburg-Preußens, vol. 1. Potsdam: 1995.

Luhmann, Niklas. *Das Recht der Gesellschaft.* Frankfurt a.M.: 1995.

———. *Legitimation durch Verfahren.* Neuwied am Rhein and Berlin: 1969.

———. *Rechtssoziologie.* 2 vols. Hamburg: 1972.

———. *Soziale Systeme. Grundriß einer allgemeinen Theorie.* 7th ed. Frankfurt a.M.: 1999. In English as *Social Systems*, translated by John Bednarz, Jr. with Dirk Baecker (Stanford: 1995).

———. "The Evolutionary Differentiation between Society and Interaction." In *The Micro-Macro Link*, edited by Jeffrey C. Alexander et. al., 112–131. Berkeley: 1987.

Lünig, Johann Christian. *Teutsches Reichs-Archiv.* Vol. 2: Partis specialis Continuatio II, 3, Supplementa Ulteriora 11. Leipzig: 1712.

Luttenberger, Albrecht P. "Pracht und Ehre. Gesellschaftliche Repräsentation und Zeremoniell auf dem Reichstag." In *Alltag im 16. Jahrhundert. Studien zu Lebensformen in mitteleuropäischen Städten*, edited by Alfred Kohler, 290–326. Munich: 1987.

Lutz, Heinrich and Walter Ziegler. "Das konfessionelle Zeitalter. First part: Die Herzöge Wilhelm IV. und Albrecht V." In *Handbuch der bayerischen Geschichte, vol. 2: Das alte Bayern. Der Territorialstaat vom Ausgang des 12. Jahrhunderts bis zum Ausgang des 18. Jahrhunderts*, edited by Andreas Kraus, 324–392. Munich: 1988.

Machilek, Franz. "Privatfrömmigkeit und Staatsfrömmigkeit." In *Kaiser Karl IV.: Staatsmann und Mäzen*, edited by Ferdinand Seibt, 87–101. Munich: 1978.

Mack, Peter. *Elizabethan Rhetoric. Theory and Practice.* Cambridge: 2002.

Malettke, Klaus. "Die französisch-preußischen Beziehung unter Friedrich Wilhelm I. bis zum Frieden von Stockholm (1. Februar 1720)." In *Preußen, Europa, und das Reich*, edited by Oswald Hauser, 123–150. Cologne: 1987.

"Manifest, Oder Umständliche Nachricht Von der in Moscau Den 3,14. Februar. 1718 geschehenen *Renunciation* und *Degradirung* Ihrer Hoheit Des *Czarowitzen Alexii Petrowitz*, Und Ihro Hoheit dem Jüngeren *Czarowitzen Peter Petrowitzen*, inwiedrum conferirten *Succession* Auf die *Monarchie* Von Groß-Rußland. Samt Der Endes-Leistung, Welche die Stände deßfals ablegen müssen." 1718.

"Manifest Wegen der Gerichtlichen *Inquisition* und Urtheils, so auf hohe *Ordre* Sr. Zarischen Majestät Uber den Zarewitsch Alexium Petrowitsch Zu St. Petersburg gehalten, auch daselbst dem Publico zur Nachricht in Druck herausgegeben worden, den 25ten Junii st. v. 1718. Nach den Rußischen *Original* übersetzet." Frankfurt and Leipzig and Berlin: 1719.

Markschies, Alexander. "Ludwig IV., der Bayer (1314–1347): Krone und Krönungen." In *Krönungen: Könige in Aachen—Geschichte und Mythos*. Vol. 2, edited by Mario Kramp, pp. 469-476. Mainz: 1999.

Marquardt, Bernd. "Über jedem Fürsten und Grafen ein höherer Richter: Frühneuzeitliche Reichsexekutionen am Alpenrhein." In *Montfort* 54 (2002): 216–235.

———. "Zur reichsgerichtlichen Aberkennung der Herrschergewalt wegen Missbrauchs: Tyrannenprozesse vor dem Reichshofrat am Beispiel des südöstlichen schwäbischen Reichskreises." In *Prozesspraxis im Alten Reich*, edited by Anette Baumann et al., 53–89. Cologne: 2005.

Marra, Stephanie. *Allianzen des Adels. Dynastisches Handeln im Grafenhaus Bentheim im 16. und 17. Jahrhundert*. Cologne, Weimar, and Vienna: 2007.

Marschke, Benjamin. "The Crown Prince's Brothers and Sisters: Succession and Inheritance Problems and Solutions among the Hohenzollerns, From the Great Elector to Frederick the Great." In *Sibling Relationships and the Transformations of European Kinship, 1300-1900*, edited by Christopher H. Johnson and David Warren Sabean (in preparation).

———. "Experiencing King Frederick William I. Pietist Experiences, Understandings, and Explanations of the Prussian Court, 1713–1740." In *Pietismus un Erfuhrung: Beiträge zum III. Internationalen Kongress für Pietismusforschung 2009*, edited by Christian Soboth (forthcoming).

———. "'Von dem am Königl. Preußischen Hofe abgeschafften *Ceremoniel*:' Monarchical Representation and Court Ceremony in Frederick William I's Prussia." In *Orthodoxies and Diversity in Early Modern Germany*, edited by Randolph C. Head and Daniel Christensen, 227–252. Boston: 2007.

Maruhn, Armand. "Duale Staatsbildung contra ständisches Landesbewusstsein: 1655 als Epochenjahr der hessischen Landesgeschichte." In *Zeitschrift des Vereins für Hessische Geschichte und Landeskunde* 109 (2004): 71–94.

———. *Necessitäres Regiment und fundamentalgesetzlicher Ausgleich. Der hessische Ständekonflikt 1646–1655*. Darmstadt: 2004.

Maschke, Erich. "Die Stadt am Ausgang des Mittelalters." In *Städte und Menschen. Beiträge zur Geschichte der Stadt, der Wirtschaft und Gesellschaft 1959–1977*, 56–99. Wiesbaden: 1980.

———. "'Obrigkeit' im spätmittelalterlichen Speyer und in anderen Städten." In Maschke, *Städte und Menschen*, 121–137. Wiesbaden: 1980.

Maurer, Georg Ludwig von. *Geschichte der Städteverfassung in Deutschland*. 4 vols. Erlangen: 1869–71. Reprinted, Aalen: 1962.

Mazerath, Josef. *Adelsprobe an der Moderne. Sächsischer Adel 1763 bis 1866. Entkonkretisierung einer Sozialformation*. Stuttgart: 2006.

McManners, John. *Church and Society in Eighteenth-Century France*. 2 vols. Oxford: 1998.

Medick, Hans and David Warren Sabean, eds. *Emotionen und materielle Interessen. Sozialanthropologische und historische Beiträge zur Familienforschung*. Göttingen: 1984.

Mediger, Walther. *Mecklenburg, Rußland und England-Hannover 1706-1721*. Vol. 1. Hildesheim: 1967.
Meier, Christel, ed. *Pragmatische Dimensionen mittelalterlicher Schriftkultur*. Munich: 2002.
Meier, Ulrich and Klaus Schreiner. "Regimen civitatis. Zum Spannungsverhältnis von Freiheit und Ordnung in alteuropäischen Stadtgesellschaften." In *Stadtregiment und Bürgerfreiheit. Handlungsspielräume in deutschen und italienischen Städten des Späten Mittelalters und der Frühen Neuzeit*, edited by Klaus Schreiner and Ulrich Meier, 11–34. Göttingen: 1994.
Melanchthon, Philipp. *Philippi Melanthonis Opera quae supersunt omnia*. Vol. 3, edited by Karl Gottlieb Bretschneider. Halle: 1836. Reprinted, New York and London: 1963.
Melton, James Van Horn. *The Rise of the Public in Enlightenment Europe*. Cambridge: 2001.
Melville, Gert, ed. *Institutionalität und Symbolisierung: Verstetigung kultureller Ordnungsmuster in Vergangenheit und Gegenwart*. Cologne: 2001.
Merkel, Johannes. "Die Irrungen zwischen Herzog Erich II. und seiner Gemahlin Sidonie (1545–1575)." In *Zeitschrift des Historischen Vereins für Niedersachsen* (1899): 11–101.
Merten, Detlef. *Der Katte-Prozeß. Vortrag gehalten vor der Berliner Juristischen Gesellschaft am 14. Febrary 1979*. Berlin/New York, 1980.
Mertens, Dieter. "Württemberg." In *Handbuch der baden-württembergischen Geschichte*. Vol. 2, *Die Territorien im Alten Reich*, edited by Meinrad Schaab and Hansmartin Schwarzmaier, 1–163. Stuttgart: 1995.
Mesenhöller, Mathias. "Entwicklungspotentiale und –grenzen des Adelsparlamentarismus am Beispiel des polnischen Lehnsherzogtums / russischen Gouvernements Kurland." In *Aufbrüche in die Moderne. Frühparlamentarismus zwischen altständischer Ordnung und monarchischem Konstitutionalismus 1750–1850. Schlesien—Deutschland—Mitteleuropa*, edited by Roland Gehrke, 317–332. Cologne: 2005.
Meyer, Rudolf J. *Königs- und Kaiserbegräbnisse im Spätmittelalter: Von Rudolf von Habsburg bis zu Friedrich III*. Cologne, Weimar and Vienna: 2000.
Midelfort, H.C. Erik. *Mad Princes of Renaissance Germany*. Charlottesville, VA: 1994.
Militzer, Klaus. "Der Erzbischof von Köln und die Krönungen der deutschen Könige (936-1531)." In *Krönungen: Könige in Aachen—Geschichte und Mythos*, 2 vols., edited by Mario Kramp. Vol. 1, 105–111. Mainz: 1999.
Mitteis, Heinrich. *Die deutsche Königswahl. Ihre Rechtsgrundlagen bis zur Goldenen Bulle*. 2nd ed. Vienna: 1944. Reprinted, Darmstadt: 1987.
Mitterbauer, Helga and Katharina Scherke, eds. *Themenschwerpunkt: Gefühle*. Innsbruck: 2007.
Möller, Bernd. *Reichsstadt und Reformation*. Gütersloh: 1962.
Möller, Horst. *Aufklärung in Preussen: der Verleger, Publizist und Geschichtsschreiber Friedrich Nicolai*. Berlin: 1974.

Moraw, Peter. "Die Reichsregierung reist: die deutschen Kaiser von den Ottonen bis zu den Staufern ohne festen Regierungssitz." In *Die Hauptstädte der Deutschen: Von der Kaiserpfalz in Aachen zum Regierungssitz Berlin*, edited by Uwe Schultz, 22–32. Munich: 1993.

———. "Versuch über die Entstehung des Reichstags." In *Politische Ordnungen und soziale Kräfte im Alten Reich*, edited by Hermann Weber, 1–36. Wiesbaden: 1980.

———. "Vom Raumgefüge einer spätmittelalterlichen Königsherrschaft: Karl IV. im nordalpinen Reich." In *Kaiser, Reich und Region: Studien und Texte aus der Arbeit an den Constitutiones des 14. Jahrhunderts und zur Geschichte der Monumenta Germaniae Historica*, edited by Michael Lindner, Eckhard Müller-Mertens, and Olaf B. Rader, 61–81. Berlin: 1997.

———. *Von offener Verfassung zu gestalteter Verdichtung: Das Reich im späten Mittelalter*. Berlin: 1985.

Morgan, Edmund S. "Gouvernment by Fiction: The Idea of Representation." In *The Yale Review* 72 (1983): 321–339.

Morgenstern, Samuel. *Über Friedrich Wilhelm I. Ein nachgelassenes Werk vom Hofrath und Professor Morgenstern, Mitglied des Tobaks-Kollegii Friedrich Wilhelm I.* 1793. Reprinted, Osnabrück: 1978.

Moser, Carl Friedrich von. *Von dem Deutschen Nationalgeist.* 1766. Reprinted, Selb: 1976.

Moser, Johann Jacob. *Ihro Römisch-Kayserlichen Majestät Carls des Siebenden Wahl-Capitulation.* Part 1. Frankfurt a.M.: 1742.

———. *Neues Teutsches Staatsrecht.* Frankfurt a.M. and Leipzig: 1768–1774. Reprinted, Osnabrück: 1967–1968.

———. *Teutsches Nachbarliches Staatsrecht.* Vol. 19. In Moser, *Neues Teutsches Staatsrecht*.

———. *Teutsches Staatsrecht.* Part 24. Nürnberg: 1746. Reprinted, Osnabrück: 1968.

———. *Von denen Teutschen Reichstagsgeschäfften.* Vol. 4.1. In Moser, *Neues Teutsches Staatsrecht*.

———. *Von der Evangelischen Reichsstände Collegial-Rechten, Besonders in Ansehung ihrer inneren Verfaßung. Zur Prüfung derer Riefelischen Betrachtungen darüber.* Regensburg: 1772.

———. *Von der Reichs-Stättischen Regiments-Verfassung.* Vol. 18. In Moser, *Neues Teutsches Staatsrecht*.

———. *Von der Teutschen Reichs-Stände Landen, deren Landständen, Unterthanen, Landes-Freyheiten, Beschwerden, Schulden und Zusammenkünfften.* Frankfurt a.M. and Leipzig: 1769.

———. *Von der Teutschen Religionsverfassung.* Vol. 7. In Moser, *Neues Teutsches Staatsrecht*.

———. *Von Teutschen Reichs-Tägen.* Vol. 6.2. In Moser, *Neues Teutsches Staatsrecht*.

———. *Zusätze.* Vol. 2.1. In Moser, *Neues Teutsches Staatsrecht*.

Muir, Edward. *Ritual in Early Modern Europe.* 2nd ed. Cambridge: 1997.

Müller, Jan-Dirk. *Gedechtnus. Literatur und Hofgesellschaft um Maximilian I*. Munich: 1982.
Müller, Konrad, ed. *Instrumenta Pacis Westphalicae. Die Westfälischen Friedensverträge 1648*. Bern: 1949.
Müller, Regina. *Das Berliner Zeughaus: Die Baugeschichte*. Berlin: 1994.
Müller, Ulrich, ed. *Politische Lyrik des deutschen Mittelalters: Texte I—Von Friedrich II. bis Ludwig dem Bayern*. Göppingen: 1972.
Mutschler, Thomas. *Haus, Ordnung, Familie. Wetterauer Hochadel im 17. Jahrhundert am Beispiel des Hauses Ysenburg-Büdingen*. Darmstadt and Marburg: 2004.
Naujoks, Eberhard. *Obrigkeitsgedanke, Zunftverfassung und Reformation. Studien zur Verfassungsgeschichte von Ulm, Eßlingen und Schwäbisch Gmünd*. Stuttgart: 1958.
Nehlsen-von Stryk, Karin. "Andreas Gail." In *Rheinische Justiz: Geschichte und Gegenwart, 175 Jahre Oberlandesgericht Köln*, edited by Dieter Laum, 701–715. Cologne: 1994.
Neugebauer-Wölk, Monika. "Reichskammergericht, Reichsstadt und Aufklärung. Wetzlar im späten 18. Jahrhundert." In *Recht—Idee—Geschichte. Beiträge zur Rechts- und Ideengeschichte für Rolf Lieberwirth*, edited by Heiner Lück and Bernd Schildt, 89–114. Cologne, Weimar, and Vienna: 2000.
Neuhaus, Helmut. *Das Reich in der Frühen Neuzeit (Enzyklopädie Deutscher Geschichte 42)*. Munich: 1997.
———. "Der Streit um den richtigen Platz: Ein Beitrag zu reichsständischen Verfahrensformen in der Frühen Neuzeit." In *Vormoderne politische Verfahren*, edited by Barbara Stollberg-Rilinger, 281–302. Berlin: 2001.
Neu, Tim. "Inszenieren und Beschließen. Symbolisierungs- und Entscheidungsleistungen der Landtage im Fürstbistum Münster." In *Westfälische Forschungen* 57 (2007): 257–284.
———. "Landtag." In *Enzyklopädie der Neuzeit*, edited by Friedrich Jaeger, vol. 7, 564–566. Stuttgart and Weimar: 2008.
———. "Zeremonielle Verfahren: Zur Funktionalität vormoderner politisch-administrativer Prozesse am Beispiel des Landtags im Fürstbistum Münster." In *Im Schatten der Macht. Kommunikationskulturen in Politik und Verwaltung 1600–1950*, edited by Stefan Haas and Mark Hengerer, 23–50. Frankfurt a.M.: 2008.
Nieheim, Dietrich von. *Dietrich von Nieheim: Viridarium Imperatorum et Regum Romanorum*. Edited by Alphons Lhotsky and Karl Pivec. Vol. 5, *Staatsschriften des späteren Mittelalters*. Monumenta Germaniae Historica. Stuttgart: 1956.
Niehr, Klaus. "Herrscherliche Architektur." In *Heiliges Römisches Reich Deutscher Nation 962 bis 1806: Von Otto dem Großen bis zum Ausgang des Mittelalters: Essays*, edited by Mattias Puhle and Claus-Peter Hasse, 159–171. Dresden: 2006.
———. "Zeichen des mittelalterlichen Reichs? Speyer—Königslutter—Prag." In *Heilig—Römisch—Deutsch: Das Reich im mittelalterlichen Europa*, edited by Bernd Schneidmüller and Stefan Weinfurter, 372–398. Dresden: 2006.
Nijsten, Gerard. *In the Shadow of Burgundy: The Court of Guelders in the Late Middle Ages*. Translated by Tanis Guest. Cambridge: 2004.

Nordrhein-Westfälisches Landesarchiv—Staatsarchiv Münster, ed. *Ludwig Freiherr Vincke (1774–1844)*. Münster: 1994.
Nubola, Cecilia and Andreas Würgler, eds. *Forme della communicazione politica in europa nei secoli XV-XVIII. Suppliche, gravamina, lettere / Formen der politischen Kommunikation in Europa vom 15. bis 18. Jahrhundert. Bitten, Beschwerden, Briefe*. Bologna and Berlin: 2004.
Oberhammer, Evelin. "Gesegnet sei dies Band. Eheprojekte, Heiratspakten und Hochzeit im fürstlichen Haus." In *Der ganzen Welt ein Lob und Spiegel. Das Fürstenhaus Liechtenstein in der frühen Neuzeit*, edited by Evelin Oberhammer, 182–203. Vienna and Munich: 1990.
Obersteiner, Gernot Peter. "Das Reichshoffiskalat 1596 bis 1806. Bausteine zu seiner Geschichte aus Wiener Archiven." In *Reichspersonal. Funktionsträger für Kaiser und Reich*, edited by Anette Baumann, Peter Oestmann, Stephan Wendehorst, and Siegrid Westphal, 89–164. Cologne, Weimar, and Vienna: 2003.
Ocker, Christopher. *Church Robbers and Reformers in Germany, 1525–1547: Confiscation and Religious Purpose in the Holy Roman Empire*. Leiden: 2006.
Oelze, Patrick. "Am Rande der Stadt—Grenzkonflikte und herrschaftliche Integration im Umland von Schwäbisch Hall." In *Stadtgemeinde und Städtegesellschaft. Formen der Integration und Distinktion in der frühneuzeitlichen Stadt*, edited by Patrick Schmidt and Carl Horst, 140–165. Berlin: 2007.
———. "Die Austreibung der Geselligkeit. Der Wandel städtischer Politik im spätmittelalterlichen Konstanz." In *Kommunikation im Spätmittelalter. Spielarten—Wahrnehmungen—Deutungen*, edited by Romy Günthart and Michael Jucker, 27–39. Zürich: 2005.
———. "Die Gemeinde als strukturierendes Leitsymbol: Konstanz im Konflikt mit dem Kaiser (1510/11)." In *Interaktion und Herrschaft. Die Politik der frühneuzeitlichen Stadt*, edited by Rudolf Schlögl, 217–236. Konstanz: 2004.
———. "Fraischpfänder—Ein frühneuzeitlicher Rechtsbrauch im Südwesten des Alten Reichs." In *Zeitschrift für Württembergische Landesgeschichte* 69 (forthcoming, 2010).
———. "Decision-Making and Civic Participation in the Imperial City (Fifteenth and Sixteeth Century): Guild Conventions and Open Councils in Constance." In *Urban Elections and Decision-Making in Early Modern Europe, 1500–1800*, edited by Rudolf Schlögl, 147-178. Newcastle upon Tyne: 2009.
———. "Politische Kultur und soziale Ordnung in der frühneuzeitlichen Stadt. Das Projekt B4 im Kulturwissenschaftlichen Forschungskolleg/SFB 485 an der Universität Konstanz." In *Jahrbuch der historischen Forschung 2004*, 77–87. Munich, 2005.
———. "Recht haben und Recht behalten. Konflikte um die städtische Gerichtsbarkeit im Umland von Schwäbisch Hall (1500–1800)." Ph.D. dissertation, Konstanz, 2008.
Oer, Rudolfine Freiin von. "Landständische Verfassungen in den geistlichen Fürstentümern Nordwestdeutschlands." In *Ständische Vertretungen in Europa im 17. und 18. Jahrhundert*, edited by Dietrich Gerhard, 94–119. Göttingen: 1969.

———. "Münster." In *Die Territorien des Reichs im Zeitalter der Reformation und Konfessionalisierung: Land und Konfession 1500–1650*, edited by Anton Schindling and Walter Ziegler. Vol. 3, *Der Nordwesten*, 108–129. Münster: 1995.

Oertel, Christian Gottfried. *Repertorium der gesammten Evangelischen Religions-Beschwerden, welche bey dem Hochpreißlichen Corpore Evangelicorum von 1720. bis 1770. theils fortgesetzt theils neuerlich angebracht worden sind, aus Archival-Acten gefertiget*. Regensburg: 1770.

———. *Vollständiges Corpus Gravaminum Evangelicorum*. 8 parts. Regensburg: 1771–1775.

Oestreich, Gerhard. *Friedrich Wilhelm I.: Preußischer Absolutismus, Merkantilismus, Militarismus*. Göttingen: 1977.

Ogilvie, Sheilagh. "The State in Germany: A Non-Prussian View." In *Rethinking Leviathan. The Eighteenth-Century State in Britain and Germany*, edited by John Brewer and Eckhart Hellmuth, 167–202. Oxford: 1999.

O'Malley, John. *The First Jesuits*. Cambridge, MA: 1993.

Ortlieb, Eva. *Im Auftrag des Kaisers. Die kaiserlichen Kommissionen des Reichshofrats und die Regelung von Konflikten im Alten Reich (1637–1657)*. Cologne, Weimar, and Vienna: 2001.

Ortmann, Günther. "Katzensilber. Organisationsrituale und nachträgliche Sinnstiftung." In *Paragrana* 12 (2003): 539–556.

Oschmann, Antje, ed. *Die Friedensverträge mit Frankreich und Schweden*. Vol. 1., *Urkunden*. Acta Pacis Westphalicae. Serie III. Abt. B. Münster 1998.

Oßwald-Bargende, Sybille. *Die Mätresse, der Fürst und die Macht. Christina Wilhelmina von Grävenitz und die höfische Gesellschaft*. Frankfurt a.M. and New York: 2000.

Ottomeyer, Hans and Michaela Völkel, eds. *Die öffentliche Tafel: Tafelzeremoniell in Europa 1300–1900*. Wolfratshausen: 2002.

Paravicini, Werner. "Schuld und Sühne: Der Hansenmord zu Sluis in Flandern, anno 1436." In *Wirtschaft, Gesellschaft, Mentalitäten im Mittelalter: Festschrift zum 75. Geburtstag von Rolf Sprandel*, edited by Hans-Peter Baum, Rainer Leng, and Joachim Schneider, 401–451. Stuttgart: 2006.

Pehem, Josef Johann Nepomuk. *Praelectionum in Jus Ecclesiasticum*. 3 vols. Vienna: 1789-1791.

Pelizaeus, Ludolf. *Der Aufstieg Württembergs und Hessens zur Kurwürde 1692–1803*. Frankfurt: 2000.

Pelus, Marie-Louise. "Lübeck au milieu du XVIIe siècle: conflits politiques et sociaux, conjoncture économique." In *Revue d' Histoire diplomatique* 92 (1978): 189–209.

Pferschy-Maleczek, Bettina. "Der Nimbus des Doppeladlers: Mystik und Allegorie im Siegelbild Kaiser Sigmunds." In *Zeitschrift für historische Forschung* 28 (1996): 433–471.

Philippi, Hans. *Die Landgrafschaft Hessen-Kassel 1648–1806*. Marburg: 2007.

Pierach, Claus A. and Erich Jennewein. "Friedrich Wilhelm I. und Porphyrie." In *Sudhoffs Archiv* 83:1 (1999): 50–66.

Pinkard, Terry. *German Philosophy 1760–1860. The Legacy of Idealism*. New York: 2002.
Pitz, Ernst. *Bürgereinung und Städteeinung. Studien zur Verfassungsgeschichte der Hansestädte und der deutschen Hanse*. Cologne and Weimar: 2001.
Pitzer, Volker, "Febronius/Febronianismus." In *Theologische Realenzyklopädie* 11 (1983): 67-69.
———. *Justinus Febronius. Das Ringen eines katholichen Irenikers um die Einheit der Kirche im Zeitalter der Aufklärung*. Göttingen: 1976.
Poeck, Dietrich W. *Rituale der Ratswahl. Zeichen und Zeremoniell der Ratssetzung in Europa (12.–18. Jahrhundert)*. Cologne: 2003.
Postel, Rainer. "Bürgerausschüsse und Reformation in Hamburg." In *Städtische Führungsgruppen und Gemeinde in der werdenden Neuzeit*, edited by Wilfried Ehbrecht, 369–383. Cologne and Vienna: 1980.
———. "'Van gehorsame der overicheyt.' Obrigkeitsdenken in Hamburg zur Zeit der Reformation." In *Studien zur Sozialgeschichte des Mittelalters und der Frühen Neuzeit*, edited by Franklin Kopitzsch et al., 155–185. Hamburg: 1977.
Potthast, Augustus. *Liber de rebus memorabilioribus sive Chronicon Henrici de Hervordia*. Göttingen: 1859.
Prescher, Heinrich. *Geschichte und Beschreibung der zum fränkischen Kreise gehörigen Reichsgraffschaft Limpurg [...]*. Part 2. Stuttgart: 1790.
Press, Volker. "Der Merkantilismus und die Städte. Eine Einleitung." In *Städtewesen und Merksantismus in Mitteleuropa*, edited by Volker Press, 1–14. Cologne and Vienna: 1983.
———. "Die Entstehung des Fürstentums Liechtenstein." In *Das Fürstentum Liechtenstein. Ein landeskundliches Porträt*, edited by Wolfgang Müller, 63–91. Bühl: 1981.
———. "Die Reichsstadt in der altständischen Gesellschaft." In *Neue Studien zur frühneuzeitlichen Reichsgeschichte*, edited by Johannes Kunisch, 9–42. Berlin: 1987.
———. "Formen des Ständewesens in den deutschen Territorialstaaten des 16. und 17. Jahrhunderts." In *Ständetum und Staatsbildung in Brandenburg-Preussen. Ergebnisse einer internationalen Fachtagung*, edited by Peter Baumgart, 280–318. Berlin and New York: 1983.
———. *Kriege und Krisen: Deutschland, 1600–1715*. Munich: 1991.
Press, Volker and Dieter Stievermann, eds. *Alternativen zur Reichsverfassung in der Frühen Neuzeit?* Munich: 1995.
Printy, Michael. *Enlightenment and the Creation of German Catholicism*. New York: 2009.
———. "The Reformation of the Enlightenment: German Histories in the Eighteenth Century." In *Politics and Reformations: Histories and Reformations. Studies in Honor of Thomas A. Brady, Jr.*, edited by Christopher Ocker et al. Leiden: 2007.
Puhle, Matthias and Claus-Peter Hasse, eds. *Heiliges Römisches Reich Deutscher Nation 962 bis 1806: Von Otto dem Großen bis zum Ausgang des Mittelalters: Essays*. Dresden: 2006.

———. *Heiliges Römisches Reich Deutscher Nation 962 bis 1806: Von Otto dem Großen bis zum Ausgang des Mittelalters: Katalog.* Dresden: 2006.

Pütter, Johann Stephan. *Ueber Mißheirathen Teutscher Fürsten und Grafen.* Göttingen: 1796.

Raab, Herbert. *Die Concordata Nationis Germanicae in der kanonischen Diskussion des 17. bis 19. Jahrhunderts. Ein Beitrag zur Geschichte der episkopalischen Theorie in Deutschland.* Wiesbaden: 1956.

Rader, Olaf B. "Erinnern für die Ewigkeit: Die Grablegen der Herrscher des Heiligen Römischen Reiches." In *Heiliges Römisches Reich Deutscher Nation 962 bis 1806: Von Otto dem Großen bis zum Ausgang des Mittelalters: Essays,* edited by Matthias Puhle and Claus-Peter Hasse, 173–184. Dresden: 2006.

Raff, Gerhard. *Hie gut Wirtemberg allewege.* 3 vols. Vol. 1, *Das Haus Württemberg von Graf Ulrich dem Stifter bis Herzog Ludwig.* Stuttgart: 1988.

Ragotzky, Hedda and Horst Wenzel, eds. *Höfische Repräsentation. Das Zeremoniell und die Zeichen.* Tübingen: 1990.

Rau, Susanne and Gerd Schwerhoff, eds. *Zwischen Gotteshaus und Taverne. Öffentliche Räume in Spätmittelalter und Früher Neuzeit.* Cologne: 2004.

Rehberg, Karl-Siegbert. "Eine Grundlagentheorie der Institutionen: Arnold Gehlen: Mit systematischen Schlußfolgerungen für eine kritische Institutionentheorie." In *Die Rationalität politischer Institutionen. Interdisziplinäre Perspektiven,* edited by Gerhard Göhler, Kurt Lenk, and Rainer Schmalz-Bruns, 115–144. Baden-Baden: 1990.

———. "Institutionen als symbolische Ordnungen: Leitfragen und Grundkategorien zur Theorie und Analyse institutioneller Mechanismen." In *Die Eigenart der Institutionen. Zum Profil politischer Institutionentheorie,* edited by Gerhard Göhler, 47–84. Baden-Baden: 1994.

———. "Weltrepräsentanz und Verkörperung: Institutionelle Analyse und Symboltheorien. Eine Einführung in systematischer Absicht." In *Institutionalität und Symbolisierung: Verstetigung kultureller Ordnungsmuster in Vergangenheit und Gegenwart,* edited by Gert Melville, 3–49. Cologne: 2001.

Reichardt, Johann August and Michael de Huttern. *De statibus provincialibus eorumque variis iuribus.* Vol. 1. Jena: 1768.

Reif, Heinz. *Westfälischer Adel 1770–1860. Vom Herrschaftsstand zur regionalen Elite.* Göttingen: 1979.

Reinert, François. "Die Reichsprägung unter Sigismund von Luxemburg (1410–1437)," in *Sigismundus Rex et Imperator: Kunst und Kultur zur Zeit Sigismunds von Luxemburg 1387–1437: Ausstellungskatalog,* ed. Imre Takács, 173–179. Mainz, 2006.

Renger, Reinhard. *Landesherr und Landstände im Hochstift Osnabrück in der Mitte des 18. Jahrhunderts.* Göttingen: 1968.

Ritter, Gerhard. *Frederick the Great: A Historical Profile.* Translated by Peter Paret. Berkeley, 1974.

Roberts, Michael. "The Swedish Church." In *Sweden's Age of Greatness, 1632–1718,* edited by Michael Roberts. New York: 1973.

Rockwell, William Walker. *Die Doppelehe des Landgrafen Philipp von Hessen*. Marburg: 1904. Reprinted, Münster: 1985.
Rogge, Jörg. "Gefängnis, Flucht und Liebeszauber. Ursachen und Verlaufsformen von Geschlechterkonflikten im hohen Adel des deutschen Reiches im späten Mittelalter." In *Zeitschrift für Historische Forschung* 28 (2001): 487–511.
———. "Kommunikation, Herrschaft und politische Kultur. Zur Praxis der öffentlichen Inszenierung und Darstellung von Ratsherrschaft in Städten des deutschen Reiches um 1500." In *Interaktion und Herrschaft. Die Politik der frühneuzeitlichen Stadt*, edited by Rudolf Schlögl, 381–407. Konstanz: 2004.
———. "Stadtverfassung, städtische Gesetzgebung und ihre Darstellung in Zeremoniell und Ritual in deutschen Städten während des 14. bis 16. Jahrhunderts." In *Aspekte und Bestandteile der städtischen 'Identität' in Italien und Deutschland im 14.–16. Jahrhundert*, edited by Giorgio Chittolini and Peter Johanek, 193–226. Berlin and Bologna: 2003.
Rohr, Alheidis von. "Zur Wahrung des Standes - Die Uniformen der deutschen Ritterschaften." In *Nach Rang und Stand. Deutsche Ziviluniformen im 19. Jahrhundert*, edited by Elisabeth Hackspiel-Mikosch, 144–149. Krefeld: 2002.
Rommel, Christoph. *Geschichte von Hessen. Dritter Theil. Von der Theilung unter den Söhnen Ludwigs des Friedsamen bis zur Theilung unter den Söhnen Philipps des Großmüthigen oder bis zum Anfang der jetzigen Haupt-Linien, Erste Abteilung*. Kassel: 1827.
Roosen, William. "Early Modern Diplomatic Ceremonial: A Systems Approach." In *Journal of Modern History* 52 (1980): 452–476.
Rosario, Iva. *Art and Propaganda: Charles IV of Bohemia, 1346–1378*. Woodbridge: 2000.
Rosseaux, Ulrich. *Städte in der Frühen Neuzeit*. Darmstadt: 2006.
Rothert, Hugo, ed. "Die amtlichen Erkundigungen aus den Jahren 1664–1667." Part 4. In *Jahrbuch für westfälische Kirchengeschichte* 11/12 (1909/10): 183–303.
Roth, Felix. "Das 'Fürststift Kempten Archiv' im Staatsarchiv Augsburg." In *Veröffentlichungen des Liechtensteinischen Landesarchivs* 2 (2003): 21–40.
Rubin, Miri. *Corpus Christi: The Eucharist in Late Medieval Culture*. Cambridge: 1991.
Ruppel, Sophie. "Geschwisterbeziehungen im Adel und Norbert Elias' Figurationssoziologie." In *Höfische Gesellschaft und Zivilisationsprozeß. Norbert Elias' Werk in kulturwissenschaftlicher Perspektive*, edited by Claudia Opitz, pp. 207-224. Cologne: 2005.
———. *Verbündete Rivalen. Geschwisterbeziehungen im Hochadel des 17. Jahrhunderts*. Cologne, Weimar, and Vienna: 2006.
Rüther, Stefanie. *Prestige und Herrschaft. Zur Repräsentation der Lübecker Ratsherren in Mittelalter und Früher Neuzeit*. Cologne: 2003.
Sabean, David Warren. "Gute Haushaltung und schlechtes Gewissen." In Sabean, *Das zweischneidige Schwert. Herrschaft und Widerspruch im Württemberg der frühen Neuzeit*, 169–202. Berlin: 1986.

———. *Property, Production, and Family in Neckarshausen, 1700–1870*. Cambridge: 1990.

———. "Social Background to Vetterleswirtschaft: Kinship in Neckarshausen." In *Frühe Neuzeit—Frühe Moderne? Forschungen zur Vielschichtigkeit von Übergangsprozessen*, edited by Rudolf Vierhaus, 113–132. Göttingen: 1992.

Sabean, David Warren, Simon Teuscher and Jon Mathieu, eds. *Kinship in Europe: Approaches to Long-Term Developments (1300–1900)*. Oxford and New York: 2007.

Sabrow, Martin. *Herr und Hanswurst: Das tragische Schicksal des Hofgelehrten Jacob Paul von Gundling*. Stuttgart: 2001.

Sandl, Marcus. "Die Medialität der Geschichte. Forschungsstand und Perspektiven einer interdisziplinären Zusammenarbeit von Geschichts- und Medienwissenschaften." In *Historische Zeitschrift* 277 (2003): 619–654.

Sattler, Christoph Friderich. *Geschichte des Herzogthums Würtenberg unter der Regierung der Herzogen, mit 86 Urkunden und einigen Kupfern bestärket*. Vol. 3. Ulm: 1771.

Sauerländer, Willibald. "Two glances from the north: the presence and absence of Frederick II in the art of the Empire; the court art of Frederick II and the opus francigenum." In *Intellectual Life at the Court of Frederick II Hohenstaufen*, edited by William Tronzo, 188–209. Washington: 1994.

Saurma-Jeltsch, Lieselotte E. "Das mittelalterliche Reich in der Reichsstadt." In *Heilig—Römisch—Deutsch: Das Reich im mittelalterlichen Europa*, edited by Bernd Schneidmüller and Stefan Weinfurter, 403–411. Dresden: 2006.

———. "Zeichen des Reiches im 14. und frühen 15. Jahrhundert." In *Heiliges Römisches Reich Deutscher Nation 962 bis 1806: Von Otto dem Großen bis zum Ausgang des Mittelalters: Essays*, edited by Matthias Puhle and Claus-Peter Hasse, 337–347. Dresden: 2006.

Sauter, Frida. "Herzogin Sabine von Wirtenberg." In *Zeitschrift für württembergische Landesgeschichte (ZWLG)* 8 (1944–1948): 298–355.

Scales, Len and Oliver Zimmer, eds. *Power and the Nation in European History*. Cambridge: 2005.

Schaab, Meinrad. "Geleit und Territorium in Südwestdeutschland." In *Zeitschrift für Württembergische Landesgeschichte* 40 (1981): 398–417.

Schädler, Albert. "Regesten zu den Urkunden der liechtensteinschen Gemeindearchive und Alpgenossenschaften." In *Jahrbuch des Historischen Vereins für das Fürstentum Liechtenstein* 8 (1908): 105–170.

Schauroth, Eberhard Christian Wilhelm von, ed. *Vollständige Sammlung aller Conclusorum, Schreiben und anderer übrigen Verhandlungen des hochpreißlichen Corporis Evangelicorum von Anfang des jetzt fürwährenden hochansehnlichen Reichs-Convents bis auf die gegenwärtigen Zeiten*. 3 vols. Regensburg: 1751–1752.

Schenk, Gerrit Jasper. *Zeremoniell und Politik: Herrschereinzüge im spätmittelalterlichen Reich*. Cologne, Weimar, and Vienna: 2003.

Schenkluhn, Wolfgang. "Monumentale Repräsentation des Königtums in Frankreich und Deutschland." In *Krönungen: Könige in Aachen—Geschichte und Mythos*, 2 vols., edited by Mario Kramp. Vol. 1, 369–378. Mainz: 1999.
Scheper, Burchard. *Frühe bürgerliche Institutionen norddeutscher Hansestädte. Beiträge zu einer vergleichenden Verfassungsgeschichte Lübecks, Bremens, Lüneburgs und Hamburgs im Mittelalter*. Cologne and Vienna: 1975.
Schildhauer, Johannes. *Soziale, politische und religiöse Auseinandersetzungen in den Hansestädten Stralsund, Rostock und Wismar im ersten Drittel des 16. Jahrhunderts*. Weimar: 1959.
Schilling, Heinz. *Die Stadt in der frühen Neuzeit*. 2nd ed. Munich: 2004.
———. "Gab es im späten Mittelalter und zu Beginn der Neuzeit in Deutschland einen städtischen 'Republikanismus'? Zur politischen Kultur des alteuropäischen Stadtbürgertums." In *Republiken und Republikanismus im Europa der Frühen Neuzeit*, edited by Helmut G. Koenigsberger et al., 101–143. Munich: 1988.
———. *Konfessionskonflikt und Staatsbildung. Eine Fallstudie über das Verhältnis von religiösem und sozialem Wandel in der Frühneuzeit am Beispiel der Grafschaft Lippe*. Gütersloh: 1981.
———. "Stadt und frühmoderner Territorialstaat: Stadtrepublikanismus versus Fürstensouveränität. Die politische Kultur des deutschen Stadtbürgertums in der Konfrontation mit dem frühmodernen Staatsprinzip." In *Recht, Verfassung und Verwaltung in der frühneuzeitlichen Stadt*, edited by Michael Stolleis, 19–39. Cologne and Vienna: 1991.
Schilling, Heinz, Werner Heun, and Jutta Götzmann, eds. *Heiliges Römisches Reich Deutscher Nation 962 bis 1806. Altes Reich und Neue Staaten 1495 bis 1806. Essays*. Dresden: 2006.
Schipmann, Johannes Ludwig. *Politische Kommunikation in der Hanse (1550–1621). Hansetage und westfälische Städte*. Quellen and Darstellungen zur hansischen Geschichte, N.F., vol. 55. Cologne: 2004.
Schlaak, Alexander. "An den Grenzen des Machbaren. Zur Entwicklung von Schriftlichkeit in frühneuzeitlichen Reichsstädten am Beispiel des Esslinger Supplikenwesens." In *Esslinger Studien* 44 (2005): 63–83.
———. "Social Space and Urban Conflict: Unrest in the German Imperial City of Esslingen am Neckar 1729–1732." In *Political Space in Preindustrial Europe*, edited by Beat Kümin, 135–150. Aldershot: 2009.
Schlaich, Klaus. "Maioritas—protestatio—itio in partes—corpus Evangelicorum. Das Verfahren im Reichstag des Hl. Römischen Reiches Deutscher Nation nach der Reformation." In *Zeitschrift der Savigny-Stiftung für Rechtsgeschichte, Kanonistische Abteilung* 63 (1977): 264–299, and 64 (1978): 139–179.
Schlip, Harry. "Die neuen Fürsten." In *Liechtenstein—Fürstliches Haus und staatliche Ordnung*, edited by Volker Press and Dietmar Willoweit, 329–345. Munich and Vienna, 1987.

Schlögl, Rudolf. "Der frühneuzeitliche Hof als Kommunikationsraum. Interaktionstheoretische Perspektiven auf die Forschung." In *Geschichte und Systemtheorie. Exemplarische Fallstudien*, edited by Frank Becker, 185–225. Frankfurt a.M., 2004.

———. "Interaktion und Herrschaft. Probleme der politischen Kommunikation in der Stadt." In *Was heißt Kulturgeschichte des Politischen?*, edited by Barbara Stollberg-Rilinger, 115–128. Berlin: 2005.

———. "Kommunikation und Vergesellschaftung unter Anwesenden. Formen des Sozialen und ihre Transformation in der Frühen Neuzeit." In *Geschichte und Gesellschaft* 34 (2008): 155–224.

———. "Politik beobachten. Öffentlichkeit und Medien in der Frühen Neuzeit." In *Zeitschrift für historische Forschung* 25 (2008): 581–616.

———. "Politik- und Verfassungsgeschichte." In *Kompass der Geschichtswissenschaft. Ein Handbuch*, edited by Joachim Eibach and Günther Lottes, 95–111. Göttingen: 2002.

———. "Symbole in der Kommunikation. Zur Einführung." In *Die Wirklichkeit der Symbole. Grundlagen der Kommunikation in historischen und gegenwärtigen Gesellschaften*, edited by Rudolf Schlögl, Bernhard Giesen, and Jürgen Osterhammel, 9–38. Historische Kulturwissenschaft, vol. 1. Konstanz: 2004.

———. "Vergesellschaftung unter Anwesenden. Zur kommunikativen Form des Politischen in der vormodernen Stadt." In *Interaktion und Herrschaft. Die Politik der frühneuzeitlichen Stadt*, edited by Rudolf Schlögl, 9–60. Konstanz: 2004.

Schlumbohm, Jürgen. "Gesetze, die nicht durchgesetzt werden - ein Strukturmerkmal des frühneuzeitlichen Staates?" In *Geschichte und Gesellschaft* 23 (1997): 647–663.

Schmidt, Alexander. *Vaterlandsliebe und Religionskonflikt. Politische Diskurse im Alten Reich 1555-1648*. Leiden and Boston: 2007.

Schmidt, Georg. "Das frühneuzeitliche Reich—komplementärer Staat und föderative Nation." In *Historische Zeitschrift* 273 (2001): 371–399.

———. *Der Städtetag in der Reichsverfassung. Eine Untersuchung zur korporativen Politik der freien und Reichsstädte in der ersten Hälfte des 16. Jahrhunderts*. Beiträge zur Sozial- und Verfassungsgeschichte des Alten Reiches, no. 5; Veröffentlichungen des Instituts für europäische Geschichte Mainz, Abt. Universalgeschichte, vol. 113. Stuttgart: 1984.

———. *Geschichte des Alten Reiches. Staat und Nation in der Frühen Neuzeit 1495–1806*. Munich: 1999.

Schmidt, Patrick and Horst Carl, eds. Stadtgemeinde und Ständegesellschaft. Formen der Integration und Distinktion in der frühneuzeitlichen Stadt. Berlin: 2007.

Schmidt, Peter. *Das Collegium Germanicum in Rom und die Germaniker. Zur Funktion eines römischen Ausländerseminars (1552–1914)*. Tübingen: 1984.

Schmidt, Uwe. *Südwestdeutschland im Zeichen der Französischen Revolution. Bürgeropposition in Ulm, Reutlingen und Esslingen*. Ulm: 1993.

Schmieder, Felicitas. *Die mittelalterliche Stadt*. Darmstadt: 2005.

Schmitz-Kallenberg, Ludwig. "Die Landstände des Fürstbistums Münster bis zum 16. Jahrhundert." In *Westfälische Forschungen* 92 (1936): 1–88.

Schneidmüller, Bernd. "Reichsnähe—Königsferne: Goslar, Braunschweig und das Reich im späten Mittelalter." In *Niedersächsisches Jahrbuch für Landesgeschichte* 64 (1992): 1–52.

Schnettger, Matthias. *Imperium Romanum—irregulare corpus—Teutscher Reichs-Staat*. Mainz: 2002.

Schraut, Sylvia. "'Die Ehen werden in dem Himmel gemacht'. Ehe- und Liebeskonzepte der katholischen Reichsritterschaft im 17. und 18. Jahrhundert." In *Tugend, Vernunft und Gefühl. Geschlechterdiskurse der Aufklärung und weibliche Lebenswelten*, edited by Claudia Opitz, 15–32. Münster: 2000.

Schreiner, Klaus. "'Kommunebewegung' und 'Zunftrevolution.' Zur Gegenwart der mittelalterlichen Stadt im historisch-politischen Denken des 19. Jahrhunderts." In *Stadtverfassung, Verfassungsstaat, Pressepolitik. FS für Eberhard Naujoks zum 65. Geburtstag*, edited by Franz Quarthal and Wilfried Setzler, 139–168. Sigmaringen: 1980.

———. "Teilhabe, Konsens und Autonomie. Leitbegriffe kommunaler Ordnung in der politischen Theorie des späten Mittelalters und der frühen Neuzeit." In *Theorien kommunaler Ordnung in Europa*, edited by Peter Blickle, 35–61. Munich: 1996.

Schröder, Edward, ed. *Deutsche Chroniken*. Vol. 1, *Kaiserchronik eines Regensburger Geistlichen*. Monumenta Germaniae Historica. Berlin: 1892.

Schröer, Alois. *Die Kirche in Westfalen im Zeichen der Erneuerung (1555–1648)*. Münster: 1986–1987.

———. *Die Reformation in Westfalen*. Münster: 1979.

———. *Vatikanische Dokumente zur Geschichte der Reformation und der Katholischen Erneuerung in Westfalen*. Münster: 1993.

Schubert, Ernst. *Königsabsetzung im deutschen Mittelalter*. Göttingen: 2005.

———. "Königswahl und Königtum im spätmittelalterlichen Reich." *Zeitschrift für historische Forschung* 4 (1977): 257–338.

———. *König und Reich: Studien zur spätmittelalterlichen deutschen Verfassungsgeschichte*. Göttingen: 1979.

———. "Probleme der Königsherrschaft im spätmittelalterlichen Reich: Das Beispiel Ruprechts von der Pfalz (1400–10)." In *Das spätmittelalterliche Königtum im europäischen Vergleich*, edited by Reinhard Schneider, 135–184. Sigmaringen: 1987.

Schubert, Friedrich Hermann. *Die deutschen Reichstage in der Staatslehre der frühen Neuzeit*. Göttingen: 1960.

Schuhmann, Günther. *Die Markgrafen von Brandenburg-Ansbach. Eine Bilddokumentation zur Geschichte der Hohenzollern in Franken*. Ansbach: 1980.

Schuh, Robert. "Anspruch und Inhalt des Prädikats 'hoch' in der politischen und Verwaltungssprache des Absolutismus." In *Landeshoheit. Beiträge zur Entstehung, Ausformung und Typologie des römisch-deutschen Reiches*, edited by Erwin Riedenauer, 11–38. Stuttgart: 1994.

———. "Das vertraglich geregelte Herrschaftsgemenge. Die territorialstaatlichen Verhältnisse in Franken im 18. Jahrhundert im Lichte von Verträgen des Fürstentums Brandenburg-Ansbach mit Benachbarten." In *Jahrbuch für Fränkische Landesforschung* 55 (1995): 137–170.

Schulz, Günther, ed. *Sozialer Aufstieg. Funktionseliten im Spätmittelalter und in der frühen Neuzeit*. Munich: 2002.

Schulz, Knut. *"Denn sie lieben die Freiheit so sehr ..." Kommunale Aufstände und Entstehung des europäischen Bürgertums im Hochmittelalter*. Darmstadt: 1992.

Schulze, Winfried. *Bäuerlicher Widerstand und feudale Herrschaft in der frühen Neuzeit*. Stuttgart-Bad Canstatt: 1980. Reprinted, Stuttgart: 1998.

———. "Majority Decision in the Imperial Diets of the Sixteenth and Seventeenth Centuries." In *Journal of Modern History* 58 (1986): S46–S63.

———. "Zur Ergiebigkeit von Zeugenbefragungen und Verhören." In *Ego-Dokumente. Annäherung an den Menschen in der Geschichte*, edited by Winfried Schulze, 319–325. Berlin: 1996.

Schütz, Alfred and Thomas Luckmann. *Strukturen der Lebenswelt*. Vol. 1. Frankfurt a.M.: 1994.

Schwarzmaier, Hansmartin. "Von der fürsten tailung." In *Blätter für deutsche Landesgeschichte* 126 (1990): 161–183.

Schwerhoff, Gerd. "Apud populum potestas? Ratsherrschaft und korporative Partizipation im spätmittelalterlichen und frühneuzeitlichen Köln." In *Stadtregiment und Bürgerfreiheit. Handlungsspielräume in deutschen und italienischen Städten des Späten Mittelalters und der Frühen Neuzeit*, edited by Klaus Schreiner and Ulrich Meier, 188–243. Göttingen: 1994.

———. "Das Kölner Supplikenwesen in der Frühen Neuzeit. Annäherungen an ein Kommunikationsmedium zwischen Untertanen und Obrigkeit." In *Köln als Kommunikationszentrum. Studien zur frühneuzeitlichen Stadtgeschichte*, edited by Georg Mölich and Gerd Schwerhoff, 473–496. Cologne: 2000.

———. "Kommunikationsraum Dorf und Stadt. Einleitung." In *Kommunikation und Medien in der Frühen Neuzeit*, edited by Johannes Burkhardt and Christine Werkstetter, 137–146. Munich: 2005.

———. "Öffentliche Räume und politische Kultur in der frühneuzeitlichen Stadt: Eine Skizze am Beispiel der Reichsstadt Köln." In *Interaktion und Herrschaft. Die Politik der frühneuzeitlichen Stadt*, edited by Rudolf Schlögl, 113–136. Konstanz: 2004.

———. *Zungen wie Schwerter. Blasphemie in alteuropäischen Gesellschaften, 1200–1650*. Konstanz: 2005.

Schwinges, Rainer Christoph. "Verfassung und kollektives Verhalten: Zur Mentalität des Erfolges falscher Herrscher im Reich des 13. und 14. Jahrhunderts." In *Mentalitäten im Mittelalter: Methodische und inhaltliche Probleme. Vorträge und Forschungen*. Vol. 35, edited by František Graus, 177–202. Sigmaringen: 1987.

Scotti, Johann Josef. *Sammlung der Gesetze und Ordnungen, welche in dem Königlich Preußischen Erbfürstenthume Münster...über Gegenstände der Landeshoheit, Verfassung, Verwaltung und Rechtspflege...ergangen sind*. Münster: 1849.

Scribner, Bob. "Mündliche Kommunikation und Strategien der Macht in Deutschland im 16. Jahrhundert." In *Kommunikation und Alltag im Spätmittelalter und Früher Neuzeit*, 183–197. Vienna: 1992.

Seckendorff, Theresius von. *Versuch einer Lebensbeschreibung des Feldmarschalls Grafen von Seckendorf, meist aus ungedruckten Nachrichten bearbeitet*. 4 vols. Leipzig: 1792–1794.

Seemüller, Joseph, ed. *Deutsche Chroniken*. Vol. 5.1, *Ottokars österreichische Reimchronik*. Monumenta Germaniae Historica. Hannover: 1890.

Seibt, Ferdinand, ed. *Kaiser Karl IV.: Staatsmann und Mäzen*. Munich: 1978.

Sellert, Wolfgang. *Über die Zuständigkeitsabgrenzung von Reichshofrat und Reichskammergericht insbesondere in Strafsachen und Angelegenheiten der freiwilligen Gerichtsbarkeit*. Aalen: 1965.

Selwyn, Pamela Eve. *Everyday life in the German Book Trade: Friedrich Nicolai as Bookseller and Publisher in the Age of Enlightenment, 1750–1810*. University Park, PA: 2000.

Severidt, Ebba. *Familie, Verwandtschaft und Karriere bei den Gonzaga. Struktur und Funktion von Familie und Verwandtschaft bei den Gonzaga und ihren deutschen Verwandten (1444–1519)*. Leinfelden-Echterdingen: 2002.

Sherman, Claire Richter. *The Portraits of Charles V of France (1338–1380)*. New York: 1969.

Siebeck, Hans. *Die landständische Verfassung Hessens im sechzehnten Jahrhundert*. Kassel: 1914.

Sikora, Michael. *Der Adel in der frühen Neuzeit*. Darmstadt: 2009.

———. "Der Sinn des Verfahrens: Soziologische Deutungsangebote." In *Vormoderne politische Verfahren*, edited by Barbara Stollberg-Rilinger, 25–52. Berlin: 2001.

———. "Eine Missheirat im Hause Anhalt. Zur sozialen Praxis der ständischen Gesellschaft in der ersten Hälfte des 18. Jahrhundert." In *Die Fürsten von Anhalt. Herrschaftssymbolik, dynastische Vernunft und politische Konzepte in Spätmittelalter und Früher Neuzeit*, edited by Werner Freitag and Michael Hecht, 248–265. Halle: 2003.

———. "Ein kleiner Erbfolgekrieg. Die sachsen-meiningische Sukzessionskrise 1763 und das Problem der Ebenbürtigkeit." In *Menschen und Strukturen in der Geschichte Alteuropas. Festschrift für Johannes Kunisch zur Vollendung seines 65. Lebensjahres*, edited by Helmut Neuhaus and Barbara Stollberg-Rilinger, 319–339. Berlin: 2002.

———. "Über den Umgang mit Ungleichheit. Bewältigungsstrategien für Mesalliancen im deutschen Hochadel der Frühen Neuzeit—das Haus Anhalt als Beispiel." In *Zwischen Schande und Ehre. Erinnerungsbrüche und die Kontinuität des Hauses. Legitimationsmuster und Traditionsverständnis des frühneuzeitlichen Adels in Umbruch und Krise*, edited by Martin Wrede and Horst Carl, 97–124. Mainz: 2007.

———. "Ungleiche Verbindlichkeiten. Gestaltungsspielräume standesverschiedener Partnerschaften im deutschen Hochadel der Frühen Neuzeit." In *Zeitenblicke* 4, no. 3 (2005). http://www.zeitenblicke.de/2005/3/Sikora/index_html (accessed 12 December 2005).

Simmel, Georg. "Exkurs über die Überstimmung." In *Soziologie. Untersuchngen über die Formen der Vergesellschaftung*, edited by Otthein Rammstedt, 218–228. Berlin: 1992.

Simon, Gerhard. "Der Prozeß gegen den Thronfolger in Rußland (1718) und in Preußen (1730): Caravic Aleksej and Kronprinz Friedrich: Ein Vergleich." In *Jahrbücher für Geschichte Osteuropas* 36:2 (1988): 218–247.

Simon, Thomas. "Geltung: Der Weg von der Gewohnheit zur Positivität des Rechts." In *Rechtsgeschichte* 7 (2005): 100–137.

Smith, Helmut Walser. *The Continuities of German History: Nation, Religion and Race across the long Nineteenth Century*. New York: 2008.

Smith, Jeffrey Chipps. *Sensuous worship: Jesuits and the art of the early Catholic Reformation in Germany*. Princeton: 2002.

Southern, R.W. *Western Society and the Church in the Middle Ages*. Harmondsworth: 1970.

Speer, Heino, ed. *Deutsches Rechtswörterbuch. Wörterbuch der älteren deutschen Rechtssprache*. Vol. 10, *Notsache–Ræswa*. Weimar: 2001.

Spiess, Karl-Heinz. "Erbteilung, dynastische Räson und transpersonale Herrschaftsvorstellungen. Die Pfalzgrafen bei Rhein und die Pfalz im späten Mittelalter." In *Die Pfalz. Probleme einer Begriffsgeschichte vom Kaiserpalast auf dem Palatin bis zum heutigen Regierungsbezirk*, edited by Franz Staab, 159–181. Speyer: 1990.

———. *Familie und Verwandtschaft im deutschen Hochadel des Spätmittelalters. 13. bis Anfang des 16. Jahrhunderts*. Stuttgart: 1993.

Spillmann, Kurt R. and Kati Spillmann. "Friedrich Wilhelm I. und die preußische Armee: Versuch einer psychohistorischen Deutung." In *Historische Zeitschrift* 246 (1988): 549–589.

Spittler, Ludwig Timotheus. *Geschichte Wirtembergs unter der Regierung der Grafen und Herzoge*. Göttingen: 1783.Stachel, Peter. "Identität. Genese, Inflation und Probleme eines für die zeitgenössischen Sozial- und Kulturwissenschaften zentralen Begriffs." In *Archiv für Kulturgeschichte* 87 (2005): 395–425.

Stockert, Harald. *Adel im Übergang. Die Fürsten und Grafen von Löwenstein-Wertheim zwischen Landesherrschaft und Standesherrschaft 1780–1850*. Stuttgart: 2000.

Stollberg-Rilinger, Barbara. "Der Grafenstand in der Reichspublizistik." In *Dynastie und Herrschaftssicherung in der Frühen Neuzeit*, edited by Heide Wunder, 29–53. Berlin: 2002.

———. *Der Staat als Maschine: Zur politischen Metaphorik des absoluten Fürstenstaats*. Berlin: 1986.

———. *Des Kaisers alte Kleider. Verfassungsgeschichte und Symbolsprache des Alten Reiches*. Munich: 2008.

———. "Die Symbolik der Reichstage: Überlegungen zu einer Perspektivenumkehr." In *Der Reichstag 1486–1613: Kommunikation—Wahrnehmung—Öffentlichkeit*, edited by Maximilian Lanzinner and Arno Strohmeyer, 77–93. Göttingen: 2006.

———. "Die zeremonielle Inszenierung des Reiches, oder: Was leistet der kulturalistische Ansatz für die Reichsverfassungsgeschichte?" In *Imperium Romanum—irregulare corpus—Teutscher Reichs-Staat. Das Alte Reich im Verständnis seiner Zeitgenossen und der Historiographie*, edited by Matthias Schnettger, 233–246. Veröffentlichungen des Instituts für europäische Geschichte Mainz, Abt. Universalgeschichte, Beiheft, 57. Mainz: 2002.

———. "Herstellung und Darstellung politischer Einheit: Instrumentelle und symbolische Dimensionen politischer Repräsentation im 18. Jahrhundert." In *Die Sinnlichkeit der Macht. Herrschaft und Repräsentation seit der Frühen Neuzeit*, edited by Jan Andres, Alexa Geisthövel, and Matthias Schwengelbeck, 73–92. Frankfurt: 2005.

———. "Höfische Öffentlichkeit: Zur zeremoniellen Selbstdarstellung des brandenburgischen Hofes vor dem europäischen Publikum." In *Forschungen zur Brandenburgischen und Preußischen Geschichte*, Neue Folge 7:2 (1997): 145–176.

———. "Ordnungsleistung und Konfliktträchtigkeit der höfische Tafel." In *Zeichen und Raum. Ausstattung höfisches Zeremoniell in den deutschen Schlössern der Frühen Neuzeit*, edited by Peter-Michael Hahn and Ulrich Schütte, 103–122. Munich: 2006.

———. "Rang vor Gericht: Zur Verrechtlichung sozialer Rangkonflikte in der Frühen Neuzeit." In *Zeitschrift für historische Forschung* 28 (2001): 385–418.

———. "Ständische Repräsentation—Kontinuität oder Kontinuitätsfiktion?" In *Zeitschrift für Neuere Rechtsgeschichte* 28 (2006): 279–298.

———. "Symbolische Kommunikation in der Vormoderne. Begriffe—Forschungsperspektiven—Thesen." In *Zeitschrift für historische Forschung* 31 (2004): 489–527.

———. "Symbol und Diskurs: Das Beispiel des Reichstags in Augsburg 1530." In *Vormoderne Parlamentsoratorik*, edited by Johannes Helmrath. Berlin: forthcoming.

———. *Vormünder des Volkes? Konzepte landständischer Repräsentation in der Spätphase des Alten Reiches*. Berlin: 1999.

———. "Was heißt Kulturgeschichte des Politischen? Einleitung." In *Was heißt Kulturgeschichte des Politischen?*, edited by Stollberg-Rilinger, 9–24. Berlin: 2004.

———. "Zeremoniell als politisches Verfahren. Ranordnung und Rangstreit als Strukturmerkmale des frühneuzeitlichen Reichstages." In *Neue Studien zur frühneuzeitlichen Reichsgeschichte*, edited by Johannes Kunisch, 91–132. Berlin: 1997.

Stollberg-Rilinger, Barbara, ed. *Politisch-soziale Praxis und symbolische Kultur der landständischen Verfassungen im westfälischen Raum*. In *Westfälische Forschungen* 53 (2003): 1–240.

———. *Vormoderne politische Verfahren*. Berlin: 2001.

———. *Was heißt Kulturgeschichte des Politischen?* Berlin: 2005.

Stolleis, Michael. "Johann Jacob Moser oder: Der Erzpublizist des Alten Reiches." In *Johann Jacob Moser. Politiker—Pietist—Publizist*, edited by Andreas Gestrich and Rainer Lächele, 57–70. Karlsruhe: 2002.

Stoob, Heinz. *Die Hanse*. Graz: 1995.

Storz, Gerhard. "Herzog Carl Eugen (1737–1793)." In *900 Jahre Haus Württemberg*, edited by Robert Uhland, 237–266. Stuttgart: 1984.
Strauss, Gerald. "The Holy Roman Empire Revisited." In *Central European History* 11:3 (September 1978): 290–301.
Strayer, J.R. "France: the Holy Land, the Chosen People, and the Most Christian King." In *Action and Conviction in Early Modern Europe: Essays in Memory of E. H. Harbison*, edited by Theodore K. Rabb and Jerrold E. Seigel, 3–16. Princeton, NJ: 1969.
Streber, Ignaz von. *Andenken an Herzog Ludwig von Bayern, Wilhelm des IV. Bruder. Ein Beytrag zur vaterländischen Münzkunde*. Munich: 1819.
Strohm, Christoph. "Konfessionsspezifische Zugänge Zum Augsburger Religionsfrieden Bei Lutherischen, Reformierten Und Katholischen Juristen." In *Der Augsburger Religionsfrieden 1555*, edited by Heinz Schilling and Heribert Smolinsky, 127–156. Münster: 2007.
Struve, Tilman. "Die falschen Friedriche und die Friedenssehnsucht des Volkes im späten Mittelalter." In *Fälschungen im Mittelalter: Internationaler Kongress der Monumenta Germaniae Historica, München, 16.–19. September 1986*. Monumenta Germaniae Historica, Schriften. Vol. 33.1, 317–337. Hannover: 1988.
Suckale, Robert. "Die Hofkunst im 14. Jahrhundert." In *Heiliges Römisches Reich Deutscher Nation 962 bis 1806: Von Otto dem Großen bis zum Ausgang des Mittelalters: Essays*, edited by Matthias Puhle and Claus-Peter Hasse, 323–335. Dresden: 2006.
———. *Die Hofkunst Kaiser Ludwigs des Bayern*. Munich: 1993.
Tack, Wilhelm. "Aufnahme, Ahnenprobe und Kappengang der Paderborner Domherren im 17. und 18. Jahrhundert." In *Westfälische Zeitschrift. Zeitschrift für vaterländische Geschichte und Altertumskunde* 96 (1940): 3–51.
Tacke, Andreas, ed. *"... wir wollen der Liebe Raum geben." Konkubinate geistlicher und weltlicher Fürsten um 1500*. Göttingen: 2006.
Täubrich, Rainer. *Herzog Heinrich der Jüngere von Braunschweig-Wolfenbüttel (1489–1568). Leben und Politik bis zum Primogeniturvertrag von 1535*. Braunschweig: 1991.
Taylor, Charles. *Modern Social Imaginaries*. Durham, NC: 2004.
Teuscher, Simon. "Chains of Favor. Approaching the City Council in Late Medieval Bern." In *Forme delle comunicazione politica in Europa nei secoli XV-XVIII. Suppliche, gravamina, lettere / Formen der politischen Kommunikation in Europa vom 15. bis 18. Jahrhundert. Bitten, Beschwerden, Briefe*, edited by Cecilia Nubola and Andreas Würgler, 311–328. Bologna and Berlin: 2004.
Thies, Gunter. *Territorialstaat und Landesverteidigung. Das Landesdefensionswerk in Hessen-Kassel unter Landgraf Moritz (1592–1627)*. Darmstadt: 1973.
Thomas, Heinz. *Deutsche Geschichte des Spätmittelalters 1250–1500*. Stuttgart: 1983.
Thompson, Andrew C. *Britain, Hanover and the Protestant Interest, 1688–1756*. Studies in Early Modern Cultural, Political and Social History, vol. 3. Woodbridge: 2006.

Topalović, Elvira. *Sprachwahl—Textsorte—Dialogstruktur. Zu Verhörprotokollen aus Hexenprozessen des 17. Jahrhunderts.* Trier: 2003.
Trossbach, Werner. *Der Schatten der Aufklärung. Bauern, Bürger und Illuminaten in der Grafschaft Wied-Neuwied.* Fulda: 1991.
———. "'Mercks Baur.' Annäherung an die Struktur von Erinnerung und Überlieferung in den ländlichen Gesellschaften (vorwiegend zweite Hälfte des 16. Jahrhunderts)." In *Kommunikation in der ländlichen Gesellschaft*, edited by Werner Rösener, 209–240. Göttingen: 2000.
Trusen, W. "Rolandsäulen." In *Handwörterbuch zur deutschen Rechtsgeschichte*, vol. 4, edited by A. Erler and E. Kaufmann, cols. 1102–1106. Berlin: 1990.
Tschaikner, Manfred. "'Der Teufel und die Hexen müssen aus dem Land.' Frühneuzeitliche Hexenverfolgungen in Liechtenstein." In *Jahrbuch des Historischen Vereins für das Fürstentum Liechtenstein* 96 (1998): 1–197.
Umbach, Maiken, ed. *German Federalism: Past, Present, Future.* Houndmills and Basingstoke: 2002.
Van den Heuvel, Christine. *Beamtenschaft und Territorialstaat. Behördenentwicklung und Sozialstruktur der Beamtenschaft im Hochstift Osnabrück 1550–1800.* Osnabrück: 1984.
———. "Osnabrück am Ende des Alten Reichs und in hannoverscher Zeit." In *Geschichte der Stadt Osnabrück*, edited by Gerd Steinwascher, 313–444 and 913–923. Osnabrück: 2006.
Van Kley, Dale K. *The Religious Origins of the French Revolution: from Calvin to the Civil Constitution, 1560–1791.* New Haven: 1996.
Vann, James A. "New Directions for Study of the Old Reich." In *The Journal of Modern History* 58, Supplement: Politics and Society in the Holy Roman Empire (1986): 3–22.
Vazsonyi, Nicholas. "Montesquieu, Friedrich Carl von Moser, and the 'National Spirit Debate' in Germany, 1765–67." In *German Studies Review* 22:2 (1999): 225–246.
Vec, Milos. "Juristische Normen des Anstands: Zur Ausdifferenzierung und Konvergenz von Recht und Sitte bei Christian Thomasius." In *Rechtssymbolik und Wertevermittlung*, edited by Reiner Schulze, 69–100. Berlin: 2004.
Végh, János. "Die Bildnisse Kaiser Sigismunds von Luxemburg: Typus und Individuum in den Herrscherdarstellungen am Ende des Mittelalters." In *Künstlerischer Austausch / Artistic Exchange: Akten des XXVIII. Internationalen Kongresses für Kunstgeschichte, Berlin, 15–20 July 1992*, edited by Thomas W. Gaehtgens. Berlin, 1993.
Vick, Brian E. *Defining Germany. The 1848 Frankfurt Parliamentarians and National Identity.* Cambridge, MA: 2002.
Volk, Otto. "Von Grenzen ungestört—auf dem Weg nach Aachen: Die Krönungsfahrten der deutschen Könige im späten Mittelalter." In *Grenzen erkennen—Begrenzungen überwinden: Festschrift für Reinhard Schneider zur Vollendung seines 65. Lebensjahres*, edited by Wolfgang Haubrichs, Kurt-Ulrich Jäschke, and Michael Oberweis, 263–297. Sigmaringen: 1999.

Vötsch, Jochen. "Die Hohenloher Religionsstreitigkeiten in der Mitte des 18. Jahrhunderts." In *Württembergisch Franken* 77 (1993): 361–399.

———. *Kursachsen, das Reich und der mitteldeutsche Raum zu Beginn des 18. Jahrhunderts*. Frankfurt a.M.: 2003.

Wahrhafte Nachricht, von demjenigen, Was sich bey Ihro Königlichen Majestät in Preussen im Monat Julio und Augusto nach Böhmen unternommenen Reise Und daselbst mit beyderseits Kayserlichen Majest. Majestäten gehabten Zusammenkunfft zugetragen. 1732.

Waitz, Georg. *Lübeck unter Jürgen Wullenwever und die europäische Politik*. 3 vols. Berlin: 1855–1856.

Walker, Mack. *German Home Towns. Community, State and General Estate 1648–1871*. Ithaca, NY: 1971.

Walther, Stefanie. "Zwischen Emotionen und Interessen—Elisabeth Ernestine Antonie von Sachsen-Meiningen als Schwester, Schwägerin und Tante." In *Werkstatt Geschichte* 46 (2007): 25–40.

Wammetsberger, Helga. "Individuum und Typ in den Porträts Kaiser Karls IV.," *Wissenschaftliche Zeitschrift der Friedrich-Schiller-Universität Jena, Gesellschafts- und Sprachwissenschaftliche Reihe* 16 (1967): 79–93.

Watts, John L. "Looking for the state in later medieval England." In *Heraldry, Pageantry and Social Display*, edited by Peter Coss and Maurice Keen, 243–267. Woodbridge: 2002.

Weber, Lothar. *Die Parität der Konfessionen in der Reichsverfassung von den Anfängen der Reformation bis zum Untergang des alten Reiches im Jahre 1806*. Bonn: 1961.

Weber, Max. *Die Stadt*. Tübingen: 2000.

Weber, Raimund J. "Die Vellberger Handlungen der Reichsstadt Schwäbisch Hall. Der Übergang einer fränkischen reichsritterschaftlichen Herrschaft an eine Reichsstadt des Schwäbischen Kreises zwischen 1592 und 1611, seine Vorgeschichte und seiner verfassungsrechtlichen Probleme." In *Vellberg in Geschichte und Gegenwart*, edited by Hansmartin Decker-Hauff. Vol. 1: *Darstellungen*, 225–271. Sigmaringen: 1984.

———. *Reichspolitik und reichsgerichtliche Exekution. Vom Markgrafenkrieg (1552–1554) bis zum Lütticher Fall*. Wetzlar: 2000.

Weddigen, Peter Florens, ed. *Westphälisches Magazin zur Geographie, Historie und Statistik*. Vol. 9. Minden: 1787.

Wehrmann, Karl Friedrich. "Die obrigkeitliche Stellung des Raths in Lübeck." In *Hansische Geschichtsblätter* (1884): 53–73.

Weidner, Marcus. *Landadel in Münster 1600–1760: Stadtverfassung, Standesbehauptung und Fürstenhof*. 2 vols. Münster: 2000.

Weiland, Ludwig, ed. *Deutsche Chroniken*. Vol. 2, *Sächsische Weltchronik: Sächsische Fortsetzung*. Monumenta Germaniae Historica. Hannover: 1877.

Weisbrod, Andrea. *Von Macht und Mythos der Pompadour. Die Mätressen im politischen gefüge des französischen Absolutismus*. Königstein: 2000.

Weller, Thomas. *Theatrum Praecedentiae. Zeremonieller Rang und gesellschaftliche Ordnung in der frühneuzeitlichen Stadt: Leipzig 1500–1800*. Darmstadt: 2006.

Wesemann, H. *Die Cäsarfabeln des Mittelalters*. Löwenberg: 1879.

Westfälisches Landesarchiv—Staatsarchiv Münster, ed. *Ludwig Freiherr Vincke (1774–1844)*. Münster: 1994.

Westhoff-Krummacher, Hildegard, ed. *Johann Christoph Rincklake. Ein westfälischer Bildnismaler um 1800*. Munich, 1984.

Westphal, Siegrid. *Kaiserliche Rechtsprechung und herrschaftliche Stabilisierung. Reichsgerichtsbarkeit in den thüringischen Territorialstaaten 1648–1806*. Cologne, Weimar, and Vienna: 2002.

———. "Der Kaiserliche Reichshofrat als protestantisches 'scheidungsgericht.'" In *Österreichische Zeitschrift für Geschichte* 20:3 (2009): 31–58.

Weyer, Wilhelm. *Geschichte der Familie Flender*. Vol. 2. Bocholt: 1961.

Wick, Peter. *Versuche zur Errichtung des Absolutismus in Mecklenburg in der ersten Hälfte des 18. Jahrhunderts*. Berlin: 1964.

Wiesflecker, Hermann. *Kaiser Maximilian I. Das Reich, Österreich und Europa an der Wende zur Neuzeit*. Vol. V, *Der Kaiser und seine Umwelt. Hof, Staat, Wirtschaft, Gesellschaft und Kultur*. Munich: 1986.

Williamson, Paul. *Gothic Sculpture 1140–1300*. New Haven and London: 1995.

Willoweit, Dietmar. *Rechtsgrundlagen der Territorialgewalt. Landesobrigkeit, Herrschaftsrechte und Territorium in der Rechtswissenschaft der Neuzeit*. Cologne and Vienna: 1975.

———. *Standesungleiche Ehen des regierenden hohen Adels in der neuzeitlichen deutschen Rechtsgeschichte*. Munich: 2004.

Wilson, Peter H. "Still a Monstrosity? Some Reflections on Early Modern German Statehood." In *The Historical Journal* 49:2 (2006): 565–576.

———. *The Holy Roman Empire, 1495–1806*. New York: 1999.

Wittekind, Susanne. "Heiligen- und Reliquienverehrung in staufische Zeit." In *Heiliges Römisches Reich Deutscher Nation 962 bis 1806: Von Otto dem Großen bis zum Ausgang des Mittelalters: Essays*, edited by Matthias Puhle and Claus-Peter Hasse, 211-221. Dresden: 2006.

Wolf, Armin. *Die Entstehung des Kurfürstenkollegs 1198–1298: Zur 700-jährigen Wiederkehr der ersten Vereinigung der sieben Kurfürsten*. Idstein: 1998.

———. "Von den Königswählern zum Kurfürstenkolleg: Bilddenkmale als unerkannte Dokumente der Verfassungsgeschichte." In *Wahlen und Wählen im Mittelalter. Vorträge und Forschungen*. Vol. 37, edited by Reinhard Schneider and Harald Zimmermann, 15–78. Sigmaringen: 1990.

Wolf, Manfred. "Das 17. Jahrhundert." In *Westfälische Geschichte*. Vol. 1, *Von den Anfängen bis zum Ende des Alten Reiches*, edited by Wilhem Kohl, 537–604. Düsseldorf: 1983.

Wolf, Peter Philip. *Allgemeine Geschichte der Jesuiten. Von dem Ursprung ihres Ordens bis auf gegenwärtige Zeiten*. 4 vols. Zürich: 1789.

Wolff, Fritz. Corpus Evangelicorum und Corpus Catholicorum auf dem Westfälischen Friedenskongreß. Die Einfügung der konfessionellen Ständeverbindungen in die Reichsverfassung. Schriftenreihe der Vereinigung zur Erforschung der neueren Geschichte e.V., vol. 2. Münster: 1966.

Wrede, Martin. Das Reich und seine Feinde. Politische Feindbilder in der reichspatriotischen Publizistik zwischen Westfälischem Frieden und Siebenjährigem Krieg. Mainz: 2004.

Wunder, Gerd. "Reichsstädte als Landesherren (Nürnberg, Ulm, Rothenburg und Hall)." In Bauer, Bürger, Edelmann. Ausgewählte Aufsätze zur Sozialgeschichte von Gerd Wunder. Festgabe zu seinem 75. Geburtstag, edited by Kuno Ulshöfer, 231–234. Sigmaringen: 1984.

Wunder, Gerd, Max Schefold and Herta Beutter. Die Schenken von Limpurg und ihr Land. Sigmaringen: 1982.

Wunder, Heide. "Dynastie, Geschlecht, Herrschaft. Frauen des hohen Adels in der Frühen Neuzeit." In Frau und Bildnis 1600–1750. Barocke Repräsentationsfigur an europäischen Fürstenhöfen, edited by Gabriele Baumbach and Cordula Bischoff, 15–37. Kassel: 2001.

Würgler, Andreas. "Bitten und Begehren. Suppliken und Gravamina in der deutschsprachigen Frühneuzeitforschung." In Bittschriften und Gravamina. Politik, Verwaltung und Justiz in Europa (14.–18. Jahrhundert), edited by Cecilia Nubola and Andreas Würgler, 17–52. Berlin: 2005.

———. "Desideria und Landesordnungen: Kommunaler und landständischer Einfluß auf die fürstliche Gesetzgebung in Hessen-Kassel 1650–1800." In Gemeinde und Staat im alten Europa, edited by Peter Blickle, 149–207. Munich: 1998.

———. "Voices From Among the 'Silent Masses': Humble Petitions and Social Conflicts in Early Modern Central Europe." In International Review of Social History 46, Supplement 9 (2001): 11–34.

———. Unruhen und Öffentlichkeit. Städtische und ländliche Protestbewegungen im 18. Jahrhundert. Tübingen: 1995.

Zallwein, Gregor. Principia juris ecclesiastici universalis, et particularis Germaniae. 1763.

Zaret, David. "Petitions and the 'Invention' of Public Opinion in the English Revolution." In American Journal of Sociology 101 (1996): 1513.

———. Origins of Democratic Culture. Printing, Petitions and the Public Sphere in Early-Modern England. Princeton: 2000.

Zedler, Johann Heinrich. Grosses vollständiges Universal-Lexicon Aller Wissenschafften und Künste. Vol. 29. Leipzig and Halle: 1741.

Zeeden, Ernst Walter. Die Entstehung der Konfessionen. Grundlagen und Formen der Konfessionsbildung im Zeitalter der Glaubenskämpfe. Munich: 1965.

Zeumer, Karl, ed. Quellensammlung zur Geschichte der deutschen Reichsverfassung in Mittelalter und Neuzeit. Part 2, Von Maximilian I. bis 1806. 2nd ed. Tübingen: 1913.

INDEX

A
Aachen, 75–77, 79, 81
accords *(Rezess)*, 20
affection, 57, 180, 213, 269. See also emotion; marriage
agnate, 182–3, 185–87, 208n86, 214
Albrecht IV, Duke of Bavaria, 214
alliance, 59, 180, 255
Alps, 81, 267
Amort, Eusebius, 255
Anhalt-Bernburg, Prince Karl Friedrich of, 181, 190n22
Anhalt-Dessau, Prince Leopold of, 62n13, 67n64, 186
annus normalis, 232, 238
Anton Ulrich, Duke of Sachsen-Meiningen, 181, 183, 186–87
Apocalypse, 146
Aretin, Karl Otmar von, 2
Asch, Ronald G., 131
assembly
    civic, 14, 16, 18–22, 23, 32n57, 33n65
    territorial, *Landtagen*, 125, 145, 146, 154, 126
    See also diet
Assman, Jan, 96
audience, 80, 86, 113, 147, 154–55, 217
Augsburg, 75, 80
    Confession, 148, 154, 160n41
    Peace of, 3, 148, 151, 153, 155, 157
    Treaty of, 94
August II, King of Poland, 52, 56. See also Frederick Augustus I, Elector of Saxony
aunt, 215–16
Austria, 185, 196
    and Catholic church, 98, 263n21, 264n43
authorities, 13–15, 18–21, 23, 39–40, 44, 110, 166–67, 171, 178, 202–203, 216, 231–32, 251, 254
authority *(Obrigkeit)*, 21, 163, 238
autocratic, 13–14, 17
autonomous cities, 35–37, 43

B
Balthazar, 78
Baltic, 17
Bamberg, 77–78
Barthel, Johann Kaspar, 254
Basel, 82
Bavaria, duchy of, 40, 74, 77, 80, 82, 115, 148, 184, 187, 197, 214, 216–17, 258
Bellabarba, Marco, 100
Benedict XIV, Pope, 255
Berlin, 2, 50–53, 59, 63n22, 63n23, 64n33, 259
Bern, 44, 80
bishop, 100, 111, 147–57, 165, 192, 195, 249. See also prince-bishop; Münster; Osnabrück
Blaubeuren, Treaty of, 218
Blickle, Peter, 2, 14, 35,
body politic, 145–46, 155
Bogislav XIII, Duke of Pomerania, 172
Bohemia, 56–57, 59, 185
Bonnemann, Heinrich, 94
books, 38, 51, 100, 234, 249, 255, 259, 266
Borst, Otto, 215
bourgeois, 113, 213, 221
Brady, Thomas A., 2
Brandenburg-Ansbach, 5, 163–68, 170, 172–73, 181, 214, 216
Braunschweig-Bevern, 58–59
brother, 182–83, 192, 196–97, 215–21
    brother-in-law, 217
    half-brother, 206n46, 223

stepbrother, 183
Bühler, 167–68, 170

C

Caesar, 75–76
Calvinist, 193–95
canon law, 250–56, 263n21. *See also* law
catechism, 93, 253. *See also* Petrus Canisius, catechism of
Catholic Church, 93, 250, 255–56
Catholic Enlightenment, 253–54, 257–58. *See also* Enlightenment
Catholic League, 156
ceremony, 4, 50, 55–59, 67, 111, 114, 125, 127, 129–35, 143, 145–47, 156–57, 235, 238, 240
    and procedure, 4, 132, 135, 143, 146–47, 156–7, 235, 238, 240
    and rank, 129–131
    court ceremony, 50, 55, 56, 58, 59, 129, 238
    functions of, 131–134
    See also coronation; procession; ritual
Charlemagne, 76–78, 82, 88n31
Charles IV of Bohemia, 78–82, 84–85, 89n43
Charles V, Emperor, 217
Charles VI, Emperor, 56–57, 59, 187, 197, 201
Charles VII, Emperor, 187
Christendom, 93, 99
Christianity, 250
chroniclers, 73, 75, 80
chronicles, 4, 35, 171. *See also* commemorative publications
civic assembly. *See* assembly; diet
civic conventions, 17
civic participation, 13, 17–22, 24, 31n50
civic opposition, 19–20
civil law, 179, 185, 251–52. *See also* law
Clark, J.C.D., 252, 261
clergy, 54, 108, 114–15, 145, 148, 152, 192, 251, 255. *See also* bishop; priest; prince-bishop
Cleve, Duke of, 94, 103n12, 195–96
clothing, 52, 54, 79, 111, 116–17, 165. *See also* corporate symbols, uniform

Cologne
    cathedral, 194–5
    city, 12–13, 17, 22–23, 36, 40, 43, 75, 84, 148, 151
    civic assembly (Morgensprache), 22–23
    king-making, 83
commemorative publications, 58. *See also* chronicles
"communalism," 2, 35
communalistic order (*verfasste Gemeinde*), 14
communication
    face-to-face, 15–16, 21, 23–24, 36, 42, 44, 114, 130, 155, 266
    formal, 21, 24, 43, 152, 233, 239, 266
    informal, 21, 37, 43–44, 239
    legal, 15, 34n75, 39
    political, 12, 15–16, 18–19, 21, 24, 28, 33n60, 36–37, 39, 266
    public, 14, 16, 21–24,
    written, 3–4, 15–16, 23–24, 29, 34, 38–39, 41–44
community, 4, 17, 18, 26–27, 34–35, 40, 84, 97, 99–100, 108, 114, 151, 193, 200, 260,
    "community of presence," 3, 14
    Jewish, 198
    peasant, 193, 200, 209n108
    and religion, 100, 151
"composite state" (*komplementärer Staat*), 265
concubine, 99, 185
confession, 93–102, 110, 146–48, 154, 183, 194, 211, 231
    building (*Konfessionsbildung*), 99–101
confessional
    groups, 94, 95, 98, 230
    identity, 4, 97–99, 102, 253, 261
conflict
    and resolution, 44, 130, 154, 156, 170, 231
    micro-conflict, 171–73
    political conflict (*Wullenweversche Unruhen*), 18
    See also procedures; violence

coniuratio, 11, 13
consensus, 2–3, 18, 23, 26, 140, 145–57, 177, 233, 236–37, 239, 245, 267. See also unanimity
Constantine, 78
Constantinople, 78
contract, 77, 165, 167, 185
   of marriage, 179
coronation, 50, 62, 73, 81, 83, 154, 198. See also ceremony
corpora, 152–54, 156
corporate identity, 4, 107–111, 114, 116, 119, 138, 268
corporate symbols, 4, 108, 110–120, 268. See also seal clothing; seal; uniform
corporations (*Ritterschaften*), 14, 17–23, 107–111, 113–15, 119–21, 126–27, 133, 135, 145–46, 151, 153, 235
   civic corporations, 17–21, 23, 145, 153
corpus, 5, 128, 133, 145, 195, 229–40
   Evangelicorum, 5, 229–40
   mysticum, 147
correspondence, 110, 232–33. See also communication
council, 13–24, 32, 36–38, 40–44, 73, 130, 132, 148, 150–51, 155, 153, 164, 168, 170, 172–73, 178, 195, 209
   city council, 36–44
   See also Ecclesiastical Council; Privy Council; Small Council; Lyon, Council of; Trent, Council of
Counter-Reformation, 100, 259
court. See ceremony; culture
cousin, 79, 183, 193
culture
   court, 51
   moral, 178
   oral culture, 109
   political, 11, 14, 16, 19, 36, 40–44, 53, 126, 171–73
   significance (*Kulturbedeutung*), 13
   visual, 77–79, 81
curia, 108, 110, 127–28, 133, 147, 150, 249, 255–56

D
Dagsburg, territory of, 199

Darmstadt, 128
daughter, 54, 181–82, 186, 214–16
   daughter-in-law, 182
David, 78
decision-making, 4–5, 16, 22–23, 36–43, 107–108, 127, 131–32, 135, 146–47, 150, 156, 235, 237, 266–67
Declaratio Ferdinandea, 148
depositions, 82, 95–97, 102, 104, 198, 201
Der Gelehrte Narr, 54
De Statu, 254–55
Diderot, Denis, 146
diet, 4–5, 107, 109–11, 113, 115, 116, 119–20, 126–35, 145–46, 150–57, 184–85, 192, 194–95, 197–98, 201, 202, 215, 217–18, 229–32, 236, 267–68
Dortmund, 85

E
East Frisia, 235
Eastern Pomerania, 235
Ebel, Wilhelm, 17–18, 32n51
Ebersheimmünster, 75
Ebstorf, 75
Ecclesiastical Council, 148, 151
ecclesiastical law, 179. See also law
Elton, G.R., 147
Elisabeth Christine, Empress, 57
emotion, 108, 178, 213, 218, 221. See also affection; love
Encyclopédie, 146
endogamy, 54
England, 81, 196, 236, 252, 261
Enlightenment, 1, 5, 65, 249, 250–54, 257–59, 261–62. See also Catholic Enlightenment
Ernst, Duke of Bavaria, 148, 184
Esslingen, 36–37, 40–44
Estor, Johann Georg, 127
Eugene of Savoy, 58, 63n23
Europe, 1–3, 53, 55, 79, 84–6, 146–47, 196, 250–54, 256–57, 259, 265–66
   Latin Europe, 73, 78
evangelical, 94, 97, 99
eyewitness, 80, 130, 168. See also witness

F
Faßmann, David, 54
face-to-face (*Vergesellschaftung unter Anwesenden*). *See* communication
family, 5, 13, 41, 107, 109–110, 115–16, 119, 147–48, 151, 177–86, 194, 209, 213–15
father, 50, 55, 180, 182, 193, 200, 221, 258
    father-in-law, 184
Faust, 1, 268
Fech, Johann Wilhelm, 127
Feldkirch, county of, 191, 202
Ferdinand I, Duke of Bavaria, 148, 217
Ferdinand II, Emperor, 185
Ferdinand IV, Emperor, 192
feudal law, 179, 192. *See also* law
feudal lordship, 200–202
Flanders, 83
France, 74, 193, 250, 254–55, 261, 269
    and church, 250, 255, 261
    and language, 126, 255
    and politics, 2, 52–53, 126, 199, 232
    Franks, 76
    French Revolution, 146, 200, 202
Franz, Count Ferdinand Carl, 191–92
Frederick II, King of Prussia, 73, 82, 88n38
Frederick of Habsburg, 82
Frederick Augustus I, Elector of Saxony, 232. *See also* August II, King of Poland
Frederick William I, King of Prussia, 4, 49–60, 231, 269
French Revolution, 146, 200, 202
Fuchs, Ralf-Peter, 4, 267
Fürsten-Staat, 146

G
Galen, Christoph Bernhard von, 148
Gehlen, Arnold, 134
Gemeinde, 13–14, 16, 20–21
gender, 178, 213–14, 222–223
gendered formation (*Geschlechterverband*), 214
genealogical, 114, 119, 223
General History of the Jesuits, 257. *See also* Jesuits; Society of Jesus

genossenschaftlich, 13, 33
Gerbert, Martin, 255
Germania Sacra, 259
"German National Spirit," 260
Germany, 2–3, 39, 73–86, 146, 197, 200–202, 253, 269
    German Catholic, 249–61
    Lower, 14
    nationalism in, 2, 252–53
    Northern, 11, 17,
    northwestern, 101
    Protestant Germany, 250, 259
    Southern, 13
    southwestern, 193
    Upper, 14
    Western, 13
    writing in, 38–44
gestures, 152, 155, 234. *See also* communication
Giel, Robert, 14, 22, 52, 62n19, 63n28, 219
God, 98, 233
Goethe, 1, 268
Golden Bull of 1356, 83
Goody, Jack, 101
Goppold, Uwe, 37
Gorski, Philip, 252
gothic, 78, 80, 85–86,
Gregory XVI, Pope, 254
Greifswald, 172
Gundling, Paul Jacob von, 53–54, 60
Gründelhart, parish of, 163–65,
    Treaty of, 166–67, 170, 173

H
Habermas, Jürgen, 14
Habsburgs, 74, 215, 217
Halberstadt, 235
Hamburg, 56
Hanover, 115, 196–97, 232, 236
Hanseatic cities, 4, 12, 14, 17, 18, 22, 32n57, 34n73
Haseatic League, 16, 17, 19, 34n73
Harding, Elizabeth, 4, 107, 267
Hartung, Fritz, 49
Hausmacht, 82
Hauspriester, 150–151
Heidelberg, 81
Hell, 95

Hellmannshofen, 163–64
Henry II, Emperor, 77
Henry III, Emperor, 76
Herder, Johann Gottfried, 252
Herford, Heinrich von, 76, 81
Hessen-Kassel, 4, 125–35
Hessian, 127–28, 131, 133–34,
hierarchy, 119, 127, 131–32, 152–53, 155–57, 236, 240. *See also* order
Hitler, Adolf, 126
Hintze, Otto, 2
historiography, 1–5, 11–19, 107, 113, 119, 222, 224, 229, 269
Hoffman-Rehnitz, Philip, 4, 267
Hohenlohe, 237
Hohenlohe (family), 165–66, 231
Hohkamp, Michaela, 5, 213, 267
Holy Communion, 93–94, 97–101, 260
Holy Scripture, 93, 101
Hontheim, Niklaus, 249
    De Statu, 254–55
Hungary, 74
husband, 179–81, 186, 215–23
hypergamy, 180

I
iconoclasm, 50, 51, 77
iconography, 80–81, 85, 110, 267
identity
    confessional, 4, 97–99, 102, 253, 261
    national, 250, 252–53, 261
interaction. *See* communication
interrogator, 93–102
Italy, 180, 257
    envoys of, 74–75
    expeditions of, 74
    Italian language, 74, 255
    law, 179, 192
itio in partes, 230, 232, 235, 240
ius intercedendi, 230–31

J
Jerusalem, 78
Jesuits, 94, 256–59. *See also* the Society of Jesus
Jewish community, 198
Joseph I, Elector of the Palatine, 195

Joseph II, Emperor, 198–99, 201, 260, 263n21

K
Kalipke, Andreas, 5, 229, 267
Kammin, 235
Katzenelnbogen, Duke Philipp of, 222
Kempten, abbey, 191–93
kin, 44, 79, 200, 214, 223
Kirchengüter, 94
knight, 108–16, 119, 128–36, 179, 217
Kunisch, Johannes, 49

L
landgrave, 127–35
language, 94, 125, 255
    and nationalism, 253
    visual language, 79, 83, 85
    See also France; Italy; Latin
Latin, 97, 99, 251
Laukhard, Friedrich Christian, 202
law
    canon law, 250–56, 263n21
    civil law, 179, 185, 251–52
    ecclesiastical law, 179
    feudal law, 179, 192
    in Italy, 179, 192
    New Law, 78
    Old Law, 78
    Roman law, 185, 192, 201
lawyer, 38, 39, 126, 192, 238, 252. *See also* syndic
lawsuit, 154–56, 184
Leiningen-Guntersblum, Count Friedrich Ludwig of, 198–99
Lenin, Vladimir, 125
Leopold I, Emperor, 192, 201
letters, 38, 44, 64n33, 132, 165, 170–71, 194, 197, 215–18, 220–21
    newsletter, 80
    See also communication; correspondence
lineage, 76, 110, 113, 182
Loen, Johann Michael von, 54, 66n36
love, 180, 213, 215–16, 218–19, 221. *See also* affection; emotion
London, 196–97

Louis V, Prince-Elector and Regent of the Palatinate, 217
Louis XIV, King of France, 268
Lübeck, 12, 16–23, 84
Ludwig the Bavarian, 77, 80, 82
Luebke, David M., 145, 267
Luhmann, Niklas, 3, 24, 233, 235n28
Luther, Martin, 179
Lutheran, 93, 95, 97–101, 105n28, 148, 160n41, 250,
Luxemburg, 74, 82–84
Lyon, Council of, 73

M
Madrid, 195
Magdeburg, 77–78, 85, 235
Mainz, 75–76, 83, 198–99, 255
Mark, county of, 94–102
marriage, 5, 58, 131, 177–187, 203, 213–15, 219–21, 223
Marschke, Benjamin, 4, 49
Maximilian I, Emperor, 214, 217, 258
Mecklenburg, 196–202
Mecklenburg-Schwerin, Carl Leopold, 196
media, 3, 11–12, 15–16, 22–24, 29n29, 30, 34n76, 36, 39–40, 42, 66n59, 77, 79, 113
    written media, 15, 16, 23, 24, 29n29
Melchiorite Anabaptist, 146
Melchizedek, 78
memory, 4, 36–37, 72–86, 95–96, 101, 105n28, 171
mental illness, 199–200
    bizarre character, 49–60
    eccentric character, 49–60, 180, 269
    psychopath, 49
Minden, 235
Moraw, Peter, 74, 147, 214
Moser, Johann Jakob, 43, 166, 202
Moser, Friedrich Carl von, 260
mother, 180, 182, 214, 219–21
Munich, 81–82, 214, 216–17
Münster, 108–110, 114, 152
    prince-bishops of, 5, 147, 151, 153, 195
    university, 3

N
Napoleon I, Bonaparte, Emperor of France, 1, 254, 260
Nassau (family), 193, 196, 199
Nassau, Count Adolf of, 74, 76
Nassau-Siegen, territory of, 193
Nassau-Siegen, Prince Wilhelm Hyacinth of, 193, 195, 202
nation, 5, 240, 249–261, 265–66, 269. See also Germany
national identity. See identity
nationalism, 2, 252–53,
Nazism, 2
Netherlands, 53
    Dutch troops, 100
networks, 3, 43, 114, 203, 215, 223,
Neu, Tim, 4, 125, 156, 267
Nijmegen, 76
notaries, 96–97, 106n56

O
Ocker, Christopher, 250
Oelze, Patrick, 5, 164, 267
Oestreich, Gerhard, 49
oral communication, 16, 24, 36, 37–38, 41. See also communication
oral culture, 109. See also culture
Orange, prince of, 131, 193
order
    political, 13–24
    and rank, 11, 51, 59, 107–120, 127–32, 135, 145, 147, 151–53, 157, 177–78, 182–87, 234–40
    social, 13, 95, 107, 114, 145, 152, 185–86
    See also hierarchy
Order of Saint Benedict, 258
    Benedictine, 258–59
Order of Saint John, 113, 115
Order of Saint Joseph, 115
Order of Saint Michael, 155
Osnabrück, 93–100, 108, 110, 113–116
    Bishopric of, 95, 98, 101–102
    Treaty of, 192
Otto the Great, 77

P

Palatinate, 74, 195, 199, 217, 222, 231, 237, 241n15
Paris, 74, 195
parliament, 125–26, 134–36, 146, 236
Passau, 80
peasant, 94, 98
    community, 193, 200, 209n108
    movements, 29n29, 194,
pedigree, 109, 110, 113, 115, 183
personality, 8n8, 180–81, 222
personification, 82, 84
petitions, 39–43, 130, 132, 191, 194, 198, 200
Petrus Canisius, catechism of, 93. *See also* catechism
Pfalz-Neuburg, Duke of, 99
Philip II, King of Spain, 148
philosophe, 1
Pisa, 74
Pitz, Ernst, 14, 18
Pius VI, Pope, 254
Pius VII, Pope, 254
Poland, 236
    King of, 52, 56, 59, 232, 237
    Polish Succession, War of, 53
policy, 14, 148, 165, 172–73, 183, 186, 268
political culture, 11, 14, 16, 19, 36, 40, 42–44, 53, 84, 126, 171–73. *See also* culture
pope, 93, 98–99, 249, 256. *See also* Benedict XIV; Gregory XVI; Pius VI; Pius VII
Potsdam, 50–51, 54
power
    illegitimate, 220, 249
    legitimate, 100, 182, 214, 216, 220, 249
Prague, 58–59, 74, 78, 80–82
precedence, 5, 51, 52, 55, 57–59, 115, 119, 128, 145–46, 152, 157, 179
predetermination, 167, 170, 173
presence
    and society, 15, 100, 173
    community of, 3, 14
    media of, 15, 24
    principle of, 36,
    problem of, 24, 73–74
    production of, 15
    See also communication
Press, Volker, 14, 216
priest, 99–101, 198, 257. *See also* clergy
prince-bishop, 5, 114, 146–47, 150–53. *See also* bishop; Münster; Osnabrück
Principia Evangelicorum, 230, 235
printing press, 38
Privy Council, 41, 132. *See also* council
procedures
    and conflict, 4–5, 44, 95, 108, 113, 133–35, 145–47, 151, 154–57, 165, 170, 184, 229, 231, 233, 237–38
    See also ceremony; conflict; protocol
processions, 78, 98, 100–101, 195, 231. *See also* ceremony
Protestantism, 5, 94, 146, 148, 150–56, 159, 194, 203, 229–32, 235–37, 239–240, 250, 256–57, 260
protocol, 50–51, 55–59, 67n61, 129, 131, 145, 150, 153, 268
propaganda, 85, 218
Proposition, 129, 131–32, 145, 150, 152
Prussia, 49–60, 193, 195, 197, 206n46, 231–32, 235, 236, 239, 256, 260
    King of, 49–60, 64n30, 64n36, 193, 195, 231, 269
public
    display, 80–82, 108, 114, 119, 111, 113
    visibility, 74, 78, 81–82
purgatory, 93

Q

Quaternionen, heraldic assemblage, 84

R

Rangliste, 51
Raspe, Heinrich, 78, 94, 98
Ratsverfassung, 13, 19
Recess, 145
"Republicanism," 35
representation, 4, 15, 116, 133
    political, 13, 125, 128, 146–47, 155, 239, 267
    visual, 77, 82–86

Reformation, 11, 13–20, 33n60, 38, 250, 253, 259–60
    Pre–Reformation, 258
    See also Counter–Reformation
Reichshofrat, 184, 186, 191–203, 230, 268
Reichskreis, 194–95, 231
Reichsverfassung, 230
Reichsvikar, 195
Reichsstände, 229–30, 235–37, 239
Reichs-Staat, 3, 265
Reisersche Unruhen, 19–20, 33
religion
    and community, 100, 151
    and freedom, 148, 151, 253
    and practice, 96, 100, 151, 154, 235, 237, 252, 254, 256–58
    and toleration, 148, 146, 154
res publica, 16, 18, 21
Reutlingen, 216
revolt, 41
revolution, 1, 19, 182, 200, 254. See also French Revolution
Rheingrafenstein, Rhinegrave Carl Magnus of, 198
Rhine, 73, 75–76, 82–84, 201
Richard, King of Cornwall, 73
Ritter, Gerhard, 49
ritual, 14, 22, 36–37, 50, 97, 110, 113, 114, 127, 147, 234, 266–267, 269
Roes, Alexander von, 73
Roman law, 185, 192, 201. See also law
Rome, 5, 78, 250–51, 253–255, 257, 260
Rupert of the Palatinate, 74
Ryswick, Peace of, 231

S
Sabean, David Warren, 44
Sachsen-Meiningen, 181
Saint-Denis, 74
Salzburg, 191, 255, 257
Saxon World Chronicle, 75
Saxony, 36, 197, 232, 236, 239
Saxony-Poland, 52, 56
self-perception, 110, 116, 268
Seven Years' War, 231, 239, 260
Scales, Len, 4, 73, 267
scandal, 5, 60, 178, 201–202, 214–15
Schellenberg, 191

Schilling, Heinz, 35
Schlaak, Alexander, 4, 35, 267
Schlögl, Rudolf, 3, 15, 100
Schmidt, Georg, 265
Schwäbisch Hall, 163–68, 170–71, 173
Schwerhoff, Gerd, 23, 34n67, 40, 43
Schulz, Winfried, 41, 203
seal, 62n17, 79, 82, 110, 111, 113, 114, 119, 133. See also corporate symbols
self-authorization (Selbsthilfe), 231–32
Sigismund, Archduke of Austria, 222
Sikora, Michael, 5, 177, 267
Sluis, 83
Small Council, 41, 47n39. See also council
Smith, Helmut Walser, 252
Society of Jesus, 257–58. See also Jesuits
son, 54–55, 82, 93, 115, 181–82, 191, 217–18, 220–21, 223, 232
    son-in-law, 39, 58
Sonderweg, 2
Sophie, Queen of Prussia, 54
sovereign, 16, 39, 42, 45, 55, 59, 172, 193, 236, 256
    "quasi," 182
    rights, 167
    "sovereign," 13, 15, 22–23
    sovereignty, 1, 52, 146, 182, 199
    states, 268
Spain, 148, 254
    Spanish rule, 98, 100
    Spanish troops, 99
    Spanish Succession, War of, 196
spectacle, 51–52, 81, 154, 214
spectator, 84, 155, 233
Speyer, 74, 77
Spiess, Karl-Heinz, 214
Spittler, Timotheus, 217
Sprenger, Placidius, Benedictine monk, 259
Saint Wenceslas, 78
state
    and nation, 249–50, 252, 256, 259–60, 262, 265–69
    state-building, 187, 252
    statehood, Staatlichkeit, 2
Staufer (family), 4, 74, 77–78, 80, 82
Stollberg-Rilinger, Barbara, 3, 132, 147, 265–66

Stoob, Heinz, 17
Stralsund, 172
Strasbourg, 75, 79
Swabia, 36, 38, 42–43, 202
Swabian League, 217–18
Swedish troops, 101
syndic, 42, 44, 116. See also lawyer
symbolic capital, 42, 44, 182
symbolic communication, 3–5, 14, 55, 116, 119, 131, 233–35, 240. See also communication
symbolism, 75, 80, 82, 234, 267

T
Tack, Arnold, 94
Taylor, Charles, 252
territory
    provincial estates (Landstände), 126
    territorial assembly (Landtagen), 125, 126, 145, 146, 154
    territorial prince (Landesherr), 126
    territorial rule (Landesherrschaft), 163, 165–66, 183
testimony, 4, 93–94, 97, 99, 130
Teuscher, Simon, 44
Thirty Years' War, 4, 93–94, 102, 185, 192–96
Thumb, Ursula, mistress of Duke Ulrich of Württemberg, 215–16
travel, 50–51, 55–57, 59, 62, 75, 151
    "traveling tricksters," 74, 86
    travelogue, 35
Trent, Council of, 148, 153. See also council
Trier, 76–77, 249, 255
Trossbach, Werner, 5, 191
Twinger, Jakob, chronicler, 75–76

U
Ulm, 17, 36, 38, 43, 235
Ulrich, Duke of Württemberg, 213–223
unanimity, 156, 235, 237. See also consensus
uncle, 168, 173, 183, 214, 216, 221
uniform, 52, 111, 113–19, 134. See also corporate symbols
university, 191, 128, 257, 259
    University of Konstanz, 3

University of Marburg, 127–28
University of Salzburg, 191
University of Münster, 3
universal church, 254, 260

V
Vaduz, 191–94, 198–99, 201–202
Vellberg, 164–66, 168
Verobrigkeitlichung, 13
Vespasian, 78
Vienna, 81, 115, 195–97, 202, 218, 230, 237
violence, 41, 53, 60, 101, 153, 157, 175n30, 218, 221, 269. See also conflict
visual culture, 77–79, 81
Voltaire, 1
vota communia, 236
voting procedure (Umfrage), 236–37, 240
votum, 132, 135, 230
    votum commune, 237
    See also decision-making

W
Wahlkapitulation, 187, 192
Walber, Daniel, 39
Welck, Hans Ulrich, subject of Schwäbisch Hall, 163–67
Wenceslas of Luxemburg, 74
Westphalia, 2, 4, 93, 107–108, 238
    nobility of, 148
    Peace of, 1, 3, 93, 134, 165, 230, 238
Wied-Neuwied, Prince Friedrich Carl of, 200–201
Wiener Neustadt, 81
wife, 5, 179, 181–82, 186–87, 200, 214–16, 220–21, 223
Wilhelm I, Elector, former Landgrave Wilhelm IX, 135
William of Orange, King of England, 193. See also Orange, prince of
Wippermann, Christoph, witness, 93
witchcraft, 191, 222
witches, 202
witch trials, 191–92
witness, 4, 93–102, 171
Wittelsbach (family), 80, 82, 148, 197, 214, 218, 221

Wolf, Peter Philip, 257
    General History of the Jesuits, 257
Wolfegg-Waldsee, Xavier Gebhard of, 198–99
Wolfenbüttel, 58, 217
women, 5, 40, 99, 178–81, 185, 198, 214–16, 218, 221–22
Worms, 202

Wullenwever, Jürgen, 19–20
Württemberg, Anna von, 222
Württemberg, Duchess Sabine, 213–223
Württemberg, duchy of, 215–21

Z

Zaret, David, 39
Zurich, 36–37, 43

www.ingramcontent.com/pod-product-compliance
Lightning Source LLC
Chambersburg PA
CBHW072143100526
44589CB00015B/2068